T0293578

UNITED STATES
DEPARTMENT OF AGRICULTURE

NATIONAL AGRICULTURAL STATISTICS SERVICE

AGRICULTURAL
STATISTICS
2021

ISBN: 978-1-63671-096-9

Agricultural Statistics 2021

Agricultural Statistics, 2021 was prepared under the direction of Jackie Ross, Secretatary of the Agricultural Statistics Board, National Agricultural Statistics Service. Vincent Davis, Tina Hall, and Tanya Ray were responsible for coordination and technical editorial work.

The USDA and NASS invite you to explore their information via their respective web sites: **http://www.usda.gov/** and **http://www.nass.usda.gov/.**

For information on NASS products you may call the **Agricultural Statistics Hotline, 1–800–727–9540 or send e-mail to nass@nass.usda.gov.**

We gratefully acknowledge the cooperation of the contributors to this publication. Source notes below each table credit the various Government agencies which collaborated in providing information.

CONTENTS

Introduction

Agricultural Statistics is published each year to meet the diverse need for a reliable reference book on agricultural production, supplies, consumption, facilities, costs, and returns. Its tables of annual data cover a wide variety of facts in forms suited to most common use. The historical series in this volume are generally of data from 2011 and later.

Inquiries concerning more current or more detailed data, past and prospective revisions, or the statistical methodology used should be addressed directly to the agency credited with preparing the table. Most of the data were prepared or compiled in the U.S. Department of Agriculture.

Foreign agricultural trade statistics include Government as well as non-Government shipments of merchandise from the United States and Territories to foreign countries. They do not include U.S. shipments to the U.S. Armed Forces abroad for their own use or shipments between the States and U.S. Territories. The world summaries of production and trade of major farm products are prepared by the U.S. Department of Agriculture from reports of the U.S. Department of Commerce, official statistics of foreign governments, other foreign source materials, reports of U.S. Agricultural Attache and Foreign Service Officers, and the result of office research.

Statistics presented in many of the tables represent actual counts of the items covered. Most of the statistics relating to foreign trade and to Government programs, such as numbers and amounts of loans made to farmers, and amounts of loans made by the Commodity Credit Corporation, etc., are data of this type. A large number of other tables, however, contain data that are estimates made by the Department of Agriculture.

The estimates for crops, livestock, and poultry made by the U.S. Department of Agriculture are prepared mainly to give timely current State and national totals and averages. They are based on data obtained by sample surveys of farmers and of people who do business with farmers. The survey data are supplemented by information from the Censuses of Agriculture taken every five years and check data from various sources. Being estimates, they are subject to revision as more data become available from commercial or Government sources. Unless otherwise indicated, the totals for the United States shown in the various tables on area, production, numbers, price, value, supplies, and disposition are based on official Department estimates. They exclude States for which no official estimates are compiled.

DEFINITIONS

"Value of production" as applied to crops in the various tables, is derived by multiplying production by the estimated season average price received by farmers for that portion of the commodity actually sold. In the case of fruits and vegetables, quantities not harvested because of low prices or other economic factors are not included in value of production. The word "Value" is used in the inventory tables on livestock and poultry to mean value of the number of head on the inventory date. It is derived by multiplying the number of head by an estimated value per head as of the date.

The word "Year" (alone) in a column heading means calendar year unless otherwise indicated. "Ton" when used in this book without qualifications means a short ton of 2,000 pounds.

WEIGHTS, MEASURES, AND CONVERSION FACTORS

The following table on weights, measures, and conversion factors covers the most important agricultural products, or the products for which such information is most frequently asked of the U.S. Department of Agriculture. It does not cover all farm products nor all containers for any one product.

The information has been assembled from State schedules of legal weights, various sources within the U.S. Department of Agriculture, and other Government agencies. For most products, particularly fruits and vegetables, there is a considerable variation in weight per unit of volume due to differences in variety or size of commodity, condition and tightness of pack, degree to which the container is heaped, etc. Effort has been made to select the most representative and fairest average for each product. For those commodities which develop considerable shrinkage, the point of origin weight or weight at harvest has been used.

The approximate or average weights as given in this table do not necessarily have official standing as a basis for packing or as grounds for settling disputes. Not all of them are recognized as legal weight. The table was prepared chiefly for use of workers in the U.S. Department of Agriculture who have need of conversion factors in statistical computations.

WEIGHTS, MEASURES, AND CONVERSION FACTORS

Commodity	Unit[1]	Approximate net weight U.S. (Pounds)	Approximate net weight Metric (Kilograms)	Commodity	Unit[1]	Approximate net weight U.S. (Pounds)	Approximate net weight Metric (Kilograms)
Alfalfa seed	Bushel	60	27.2	Without tops	Burlap sack	74–80	33.6–36.3
Apples	....do	48	21.8	Castor beans	Bushel	41	18.6
Do	Loose pack	38–42	17.2–19.1	Castor oil	Gallon[7]	8	3.6
Do	Tray pack	40–45	18.1–20.4	Cauliflower	W.G.A. crate	50–60	22.7–27.2
Do	Cell pack	37–41	16.8–18.6	Do	Fiberboard box wrapper leaves removed film-wrapped, 2 layers	23–35	10.4–15.9
Apricots	Lug (brentwood)[2]	24	10.9	Celery	Crate[8]	60	27.2
Western	4–basket crate[3]	26	11.8	Cherries	Lug (Campbell)[9]	16	7.3
Artichokes:				Do	Lug	20	9.1
Globe	Ctn, by count and loose pack	20–25	9.1–11.3	Clover seed	Bushel	60	27.2
Jerusalem	Bushel	50	22.7	Coffee	Bag	132.3	60
Asparagus	Crate (NJ)	30	13.6	Corn:			
Avocados	Lug[4]	12–15	5.4–6.8	Ear, husked	Bushel[10]	70	31.8
Bananas	Fiber folding box[5].	40	18.1	Shelled	....do	56	25.4
Barley	Bushel	48	21.8	Meal	....do	50	22.7
Beans:				Oil	Gallon[7]	7.7	3.5
Lima, dry	....do	56	25.4	Syrup	....do	11.72	5.3
Other, dry	....do	60	27.2	Sweet	Wirebound crate	50	22.7
	Sack	100	45.4	Do	Ctn, packed 5 oz. ears	50	22.7
Lima unshelled	Bushel	28–32	12.7–14.5	Do	WDB crate, 4½–5 oz. (from FL & NJ)	42	19.1
Snap	....do	28–32	12.7–14.5	Cotton	Bale[11], gross	500	227
Beets:				Do	Bale[11], net	480	218
Topped	Sack	25	11.3	Cottonseed	Bushel[12]	32	14.5
Bunched	½ crate 2 dz-bchs	36–40	16.3–18.1	Cottonseed oil	Gallon[7]	7.7	3.5
Berries frozen pack:				Cowpeas	Bushel	60	27.2
Without sugar	50–gal. barrel	380	172	Cranberries	Barrel	100	45.4
3 + 1 pack	....do	425	193	Do	¼–bbl. box[13]	25	11.3
2 + 1 pack	....do	450	204	Cream, 40-percent butterfat.	Gallon	8.38	3.80
Blackberries	12, ½-pint basket.	6	2.7	Cucumbers	Bushel	48	21.8
Bluegrass seed	Bushel	14–30	6.4–13.6	Dewberries	24–qt. crate	36	16.3
Broccoli	Wirebound crate.	20–25	9.1–11.3	Eggplant	Bushel	33	15.0
Broomcorn (6 bales per ton)	Bale	333	151	Eggs, average size	Case, 30 dozen	47.0	21.3
Broomcorn seed	Bushel	44–50	20.0–22.7	Escarole	Bushel	25	11.3
Brussels sprouts	Ctn, loose pack	25	11.3	Figs, fresh	Box single layer[14]	6	2.7
Buckwheat	Bushel	48	21.8	Flaxseed	Bushel	56	25.4
Butter	Block	55,68	25,30.9	Flour, various	Bag	100	45.4
Cabbage	Open mesh bag	50	22.7	Do	Ctn or Crate, Bulk	30	13.6
Do	Flat crate (1¾ bu)	50–60	22.7–27.2	Garlic	Ctn of 12 tubes or 12 film bag pkgs 12 cloves each	10	4.5
Do	Ctn, place pack	53	24.0				
Cantaloups	Crate[6]	40	18.1				
Carrots	Film plastic Bags, mesh sacks & cartons holding 48 1 lb. film bags	55	24.9				

See footnotes on page viii.

WEIGHTS AND MEASURES—Continued

Commodity	Unit[1]	Approximate net weight U.S. (Pounds)	Approximate net weight Metric (Kilograms)	Commodity	Unit[1]	Approximate net weight U.S. (Pounds)	Approximate net weight Metric (Kilograms)
Grapefruit:				Spanish:			
Florida and Texas	½–box mesh bag	40	18.1	South-eastern ...	......do	25	11.3
Florida	1⅖ bu. box	85	38.6	South-western ..	......do	25	11.3
Texas	1⅖ bu. box	80	36.3	Pears:			
California and Arizona	Box[15,16]	67	30.4	California	Bushel	48	21.8
Grapes:				Other	......do	50	22.7
Eastern	12-qt. basket ...	20	9.1	Do	Std box, 4/5 bu	45–48	20.4–21.8
Western	Lug	28	12.7	Do	Ctn, Tight-fill pack	36–37	16.3–16.7
Do	4–basket crate[17]	20	9.1	Peas:			
Hempseed	Bushel	44	20.0	Green, unshelled ...	Bushel	28–30	12.7–13.6
Hickory nuts	.....do	50	22.7	Dry	.....do	60	27.2
Honey	Gallon	11.84	5.4	Peppers, green	......do	25–30	11.3–13.6
Honeydew melons	⅔ Ctn	28–32	12.7–14.5	Do	1½ bu carton ...	28	12.7
Hops	Bale, gross	200	90.7	Perilla seed	Bushel	37–40	16.8–18.1
Horseradish roots	Bushel	35	15.9	Pineapples	Carton	40	18.1
Do	Sack	50	22.7	Plums and prunes:			
Hungarian millet seed	Bushel	48–50	21.8–22.7	Do	Ctn & lugs	28	12.7
Kale	Ctn or crate	25	11.3	Do	½-bu. basket ...	30	13.6
Kapok seed	.....do	35–40	15.9–18.1	Popcorn:			
Lard	Tierce	375	170	On ear	Bushel[10]	70	31.8
Lemons:				Shelled	......do	56	25.4
California and Arizona	Box[18]	76	34.5	Poppy seed	......do	46	20.9
Do	Carton	38	17.2	Potatoes	Bushel	60	27.2
Lentils	Bushel	60	27.2	Do	Barrel	165	74.8
Lettuce, iceberg	carton packed 24.	43–52	19.5–23.6	Do	Box	50	22.7
Lettuce, hot-house	24-qt. basket	10	4.5	Do	...do	100	45.4
Limes (Florida) ...	Box	88	39.9	Quinces	Bushel	48	21.8
Linseed oil	Gallon[7]	7.7	3.5	Rapeseed	......do	50–60	22.7–27.2
Malt	Bushel	34	15.4	Raspberries	½-pint baskets	6	2.7
Maple syrup	Gallon	11.02	5.0	Redtop seed	Bushel	50–60	22.7–27.2
Meadow fescue seed	Bushel	24	10.9	Refiners' syrup ...	Gallon	11.45	5.2
Milk	Gallon	8.6	3.9	Rice:			
Millet	Bushel	48–60	21.8–27.2	Rough	Bushel	45	20.4
Molasses:				Do	Bag	100	45.4
edible	Gallon	11.74	5.3	Do	Barrel	162	73.5
inedible	...do	11.74	5.3	Milled	Pocket or bag ...	100	45.4
Mustard seed ...	Bushel	58–60	26.3–27.2	Rosin	Drum, net	520	236
Oats	...do	32	14.5	Rutabagas	Bushel	56	25.4
Olives	Lug	25–30	11.3–13.6	Rye	......do	56	25.4
Olive oil	Gallon	[7]7.6	3.4	Sesame seed ...	......do	46	20.9
Onions, dry	Sack	50	22.7	Shallots	Crate (4–7 doz. bunches)	20–35	9.1–15.9
Onions, green bunched	Ctn, 24-dz bchs	10–16	4.5–7.3	Sorgo:			
Oranges:				Seed	Bushel	50	22.7
Florida	Box	90	40.8	Syrup	Gallon	11.55	5.2
Texas	Box	85	38.5	Sorghum grain[19]	Bushel	56	25.4
California and Arizona	Box[15]	75	34.0	Soybeans	......do	60	27.2
Do	Carton	38	17.2	Soybean oil	Gallon[7]	7.7	3.5
Orchardgrass seed	Bushel	14	6.4	Spelt	Bushel	40	18.1
Palm oil	Gallon[7]	7.7	3.5	Spinach	...do	18–20	8.2–9.1
Parsnips	Bushel	50	22.7	Strawberries	24-qt. crate	36	16.3
Peaches	.....do	48	21.8	Do	12-pt. crate	9–11	4.1–5.0
Do	2 layer ctn or lug	22	10.0	Sudangrass seed	Bushel	40	18.1
Do	¾-Bu, Ctn/crate	38	17.2	Sugarcane:			
Peanut oil	Gallon[7]	7.7	3.5	Syrup (sulfured or un-sulfured)	Gallon	11.45	5.2
Peanuts, unshelled:				Sunflower seed	Bushel	24–32	10.9–14.5
Virginia type ..	Bushel	17	7.7	Sweet potatoes	Bushel[20]	55	24.9
Runners, South-eastern	...do	21	9.5	Do	Crate	50	22.7
				Tangerines:			
				Florida	Box	95	43.1
				Arizona	Box	75	34.0
				California	Box	75	34.0

See footnotes on page viii.

WEIGHTS AND MEASURES—Continued

Commodity	Unit [1]	Approximate net weight		Commodity	Unit [1]	Approximate net weight	
		U.S.	Metric			U.S.	Metric
		Pounds	*Kilograms*			*Pounds*	*Kilograms*
Timothy seed	Bushel	45	20.4	Turnips:			
Tobacco:				Without tops ..	Mesh sack	50	22.7
Maryland	Hogshead	775	352	Bunched	Crate [6]	70–80	31.8–36.3
Flue-cured	.....do	950	431	Turpentine	Gallon	7.23	3.3
Burley	.....do	975	442	Velvetbeans			
Dark air-cured	.....do	1,150	522	(hulled)	Bushel	60	27.2
Virginia fire-				Vetch seed	.....do	60	27.2
cured	.....do	1,350	612	Walnuts	Sacks	50	22.7
Kentucky and				Water 60° F	Gallon	8.33	3.8
Tennessee				Watermelons	Melons of aver-		
fire-cured	.....do	1,500	680		age or me-		
Cigar-leaf	Case	250–365	113–166		dium size	25	11.3
Do	Bale	150–175	68.0–79.4	Wheat	Bushel	60	27.2
Tomatoes	Crate	60	27.2	Various com-			
Do	Lug box	32	14.5	modities	Short ton	2,000	907
Do	2-layer flat	21	9.5	Do	Long ton	2,240	1,016
Tomatoes, hot-				Do	Metric ton	2,204.6	1,000
house	12-qt. basket	20	9.1				
Tung oil	Gallon [7]	7.8	3.5				

See footnotes on page viii.

To Convert From Avoirdupois Pounds

To	Multiply by
Kilograms	0.45359237
Metric tons	0.00045359237

Conversion Factors

1 Metric ton=2,204.622 pounds
1 Kilogram=2.2046 pounds
1 Acre=0.4047 hectares
1 Hectare=2.47 acres
1 Square mile=640 acres=259 hectares
1 Gallon=3.7853 liters

CONVERSION FACTORS

Commodity	Unit	Approximate equivalent
Apples	1 pound dried	7 pounds fresh; beginning 1943, 8 pounds fresh
Do	1 pound chops	5 pounds fresh
Do	1 case canned [21]	1.4 bushels fresh
Applesauce	....do [21]	1.2 bushels fresh
Apricots	1 pound dried	6 pounds fresh
Barley flour	100 pounds	4.59 bushels barley
Beans, lima	1 pound shelled	2 pounds unshelled
Beans, snap or wax	1 case canned [22]	0.008 ton fresh
Buckwheat flour	100 pounds	3.47 bushels buckwheat
Calves	1 pound live weight	0.611 pound dressed weight (1999 average)
Cattle	....do	0.607 pound dressed weight (1999 average)
Cane syrup	1 gallon	5 pounds sugar
Cherries, tart	1 case canned [21]	0.023 ton fresh
Chickens	1 pound live weight	0.72 pound ready-to-cook weight
Corn, shelled	1 bushel (56 lbs.)	2 bushels (70 pounds) of husked ear corn
Corn, sweet	1 case canned [22]	0.030 ton fresh
Cornmeal:		
Degermed	100 pounds	3.16 bushels corn, beginning 1946
Nondegermed	....do	2 bushels corn, beginning 1946
Cotton	1 pound ginned	3.26 pounds seed cotton, including trash [23]
Cottonseed meal	1 pound	2.10 pounds cottonseed
Cottonseed oil	....do	5.88 pounds cottonseed
Dairy products:		
Butter	....do	21.1 pounds milk
Cheese	....do	10 pounds milk
Condensed milk, whole	....do	2.3 pounds milk
Dry cream	....do	19 pounds milk
Dry milk, whole	....do	7.6 pounds milk
Evaporated milk, whole	....do	2.14 pounds milk
Malted milk	....do	2.6 pounds milk
Nonfat dry milk	....do	11 pounds liquid skim milk
Ice cream [24]	1 gallon	15 pounds milk
Ice cream [24] (eliminating fat from butter and concentrated milk).	....do	12 pounds milk
Eggs	1 case	47 pounds
Eggs, shell	....do	41.2 pounds frozen or liquid whole eggs
Do	....do	10.3 pounds dried whole eggs
Figs	1 pound dried	3 pounds fresh in California; 4 pounds fresh elsewhere
Flaxseed	1 bushel	About 2½ gallons oil
Grapefruit, Florida	1 case canned juice [22]	0.64 box fresh fruit
Hogs	1 pound live weight	0.737 pound dressed weight, excluding lard (1999 average)
Linseed meal	1 pound	1.51 pounds flaxseed
Linseed oil	....do	2.77 pounds flaxseed
Malt	1 bushel (34 lbs.)	1 bushel barley (48 lbs.)
Maple syrup	1 gallon	8 pounds maple sugar
Nuts:		
Almonds, imported	1 pound shelled	3½ pounds unshelled
Almonds, California	....do	2.22 pounds unshelled through 1949; 2 pounds thereafter
Brazil	....do	2 pounds unshelled
Cashews	....do	4.55 pounds unshelled
Chestnuts	....do	1.19 pounds unshelled
Filberts	....do	2.22 pounds unshelled through 1949; 2.5 pounds thereafter
Pecans:		
Seedling	....do	2.78 pounds unshelled
Improved	....do	2.50 pounds unshelled
Pignolias	....do	1.3 pounds unshelled
Pistachios	....do	2 pounds unshelled
Walnuts:		
Black	....do	5.88 pounds unshelled
Persian (English)	....do	2.67 pounds unshelled
Oatmeal	100 pounds	7.6 bushels oats, beginning 1943
Oranges, Florida	1 case canned juice [22]	0.53 box fresh
Peaches, California, freestone	1 pound dried	5⅓ pounds fresh through 1918; 6 pounds fresh for 1919–28; and 6½ pounds fresh from 1929 to date
Peaches, California, clingstone	....do	7½ pounds fresh
Peaches, clingstone	1 case canned [21]	1 bushel fresh
Do	....do	0.0230 ton fresh
Peanuts	1 pound shelled	1½ pounds unshelled
Pears	1 pound dried	6½ pounds fresh
Pears, Bartlett	1 case canned [22]	1.1 bushels fresh
Do	....do	0.026 ton fresh

See footnotes on page viii.

CONVERSION FACTORS—Continued

Commodity	Unit	Approximate equivalent
Peas, green	1 pound shelled	2½ pounds unshelled
Do	1 case canned [22]	0.009 ton fresh (shelled)
Prunes	1 pound dried	2.7 pounds fresh in California; 3 to 4 pounds fresh elsewhere
Raisins	1 pound	4.3 pounds fresh grapes
Rice, milled (excluding brewers)	100 pounds	152 pounds rough or unhulled rice
Rye flour	....do	2.23 bushels rye, beginning 1947
Sheep and lambs	1 pound live weight	0.504 pound dressed weight (1999 average)
Soybean meal	1 pound	1.27 pounds soybeans
Soybean oil	....do	5.49 pounds soybeans
Sugar	1 ton raw	0.9346 ton refined
Tobacco	1 pound farm-sales weight	Various weights of stemmed and unstemmed, according to aging and the type of tobacco (See circular 435, U.S. Dept. of Agr.)
Tomatoes	1 case canned [22]	0.018 ton fresh
Turkeys	1 pound live weight	0.80 pound ready-to-cook weight
Wheat flour	100 pounds	2.30 bushels wheat [25]
Wool, domestic apparel shorn	1 pound greasy	0.48 pounds scoured
Wool, domestic apparel pulled	....do	0.73 pound scoured

[1] Standard bushel used in the United States contains 2,150.42 cubic inches; the gallon, 231 cubic inches; the cranberry barrel, 5,826 cubic inches; and the standard fruit and vegetable barrel, 7,056 cubic inches. Such large-sized products as apples and potatoes sometimes are sold on the basis of a heaped bushel, which would exceed somewhat the 2,150.42 cubic inches of a bushel basket level full. This also applies to such products as sweetpotatoes, peaches, green beans, green peas, spinach, etc.

[2] Approximate inside dimensions, 4⅝ by 12½ by 16⅛ inches.

[3] Approximate inside dimensions, 4½ by 16 by 16⅛ inches.

[4] Approximate dimensions, 4½ by 13½ by 16⅛ inches.

[5] Approximate inside dimensions, 13 by 12 by 32 inches.

[6] Approximate inside dimensions, 13 by 18 by 21⅝ inches.

[7] This is the weight commonly used in trade practices, the actual weight varying according to temperature conditions.

[8] Approximate inside dimensions, 9¾ by 16 by 20 inches.

[9] Approximate inside dimensions, 4⅛ by 11½ by 14 inches.

[10] The standard weight of 70 pounds is usually recognized as being about 2 measured bushels of corn, husked, on the ear, because it required 70 pounds to yield 1 bushel, or 56 pounds, of shelled corn.

[11] For statistical purposes the bale of cotton is 500 pounds or 480 pounds net weight. Prior to Aug. 1, 1946, the net weight was estimated at 478 pounds. Actual bale weights vary considerably, and the customary average weights of bales of foreign cotton differ from that of the American square bale.

[12] This is the average weight of cottonseed, although the legal weight in some States varies from this figure of 32 pounds.

[13] Approximate inside dimensions, 9¼ by 10½ by 15 inches.

[14] Approximate inside dimensions, 1¾ by 11 by 16⅛ inches.

[15] Approximate inside dimensions, 11½ by 11½ by 24 inches.

[16] Beginning with the 1993-94 season, net weights for California Desert Valley and Arizona grapefruit were increased from 64 to 67 pounds, equal to the California other area net weight, making a 67 pound net weight apply to all of California.

[17] Approximate inside dimensions, 4¾ by 16 by 16⅛ inches.

[18] Approximate inside dimensions, 9⅞ by 13 by 25 inches.6 by 16 by 16⅛ inches.

[19] Includes both sorghum grain (kafir, milo, hegari, etc.) and sweet sorghum varieties.

[20] This average of 55 pounds indicates the usual weight of sweetpotatoes when harvested. Much weight is lost in curing or drying and the net weight when sold in terminal markets may be below 55 pounds.

[21] Case of 24 No. 2½ cans.

[22] Case of 24 No. 303 cans.

[23] Varies widely by method of harvesting.

[24] The milk equivalent of ice cream per gallon is 15 pounds. Reports from plants indicate about 81 percent of the butterfat in ice cream is from milk and cream, the remainder being from butter and concentrated milk. Thus the milk equivalent of the milk and cream in a gallon of ice cream is about 12 pounds.

[25] This is equivalent to 4.51 bushels of wheat per barrel (196 pounds) of flour and has been used in conversions, beginning July 1, 1957. Because of changes in milling processes, the following factors per barrel of flour have been used for earlier periods: 1790–1879, 5 bushels; 1880–1908, 4.75 bushels, 1909–17, 4.7 bushels; 1918 and 1919, 4.5 bushels; 1920, 4.6 bushels; 1921–44, 4.7 bushels; July 1944–Feb. 1946, 4.57 bushels; March 1946–Oct. 1946, average was about 4.31 bushels; and Nov. 1946–June 1957, 4.57 bushels.

CHAPTER I

STATISTICS OF GRAIN AND FEED

This chapter contains tables for wheat, rye, rice, corn, oats, barley, sorghum grain, and feedstuffs. Estimates are given of area, production, disposition, supply and disappearance, prices, value of production, stocks, foreign production and trade, price-support operations, animal units fed, and feed consumed by livestock and poultry.

Table 1-1.—Total grain: Supply and disappearance, United States, 2011–2019[1]

Year[2]	Supply				Disappearance			Ending stocks
	Beginning stocks	Production	Imports	Total	Domestic use	Exports	Total disappear-ance	
	Million metric tons	*Million metric tons*	*Million metric tons*	*Million metric tons*	*Million metric tons*	*Million metric tons*	*Million metric tons*	*Million metric tons*
2011	58.0	385.1	6.8	449.9	326.3	74.2	400.0	49.9
2012	49.9	355.7	11.0	416.6	318.7	53.1	371.8	44.7
2013	44.7	433.9	9.0	487.1	345.3	90.2	435.6	51.8
2014	51.5	442.4	8.5	503.4	348.8	84.6	433.3	69.7
2015	69.6	432.2	8.4	509.3	349.7	83.1	432.8	76.8
2016	76.8	475.6	7.4	560.1	365.4	98.3	463.7	96.4
2017	96.4	439.9	8.8	544.7	359.8	95.8	455.6	89.2
2018	89.2	439.4	7.3	536.1	359.5	84.7	444.2	91.9
2019	91.9	420.4	7.9	520.0	357.8	81.1	438.8	81.1

[1] Aggregate data on corn, sorghum, barley, oats, wheat, rye, and rice. [2] The marketing year for corn and sorghum begins September 1; for oats, barley, wheat, and rye, June 1; and for rice, August 1.
ERS, Market and Trade Economics Division, (202) 694–5313.

Table 1-2.—Wheat: Area, yield, production, and value, United States, 2011–2020

Year	Area		Yield per harvested acre	Production	Marketing year average price per bushel received by farmers[2]	Value of production[2]
	Planted[1]	Harvested				
	1,000 acres	*1,000 acres*	*Bushels*	*1,000 bushels*	*Dollars*	*1,000 dollars*
2011	54,277	45,687	43.6	1,993,111	7.24	14,269,225
2012	55,294	48,758	46.2	2,252,307	7.77	17,383,149
2013	56,236	45,332	47.1	2,134,979	6.87	14,604,442
2014	56,841	46,385	43.7	2,026,310	5.99	11,914,954
2015	54,999	47,318	43.6	2,061,939	4.89	10,018,323
2016	50,116	43,848	52.7	2,308,663	3.89	9,179,190
2017	46,052	37,555	46.4	1,740,910	4.72	8,255,119
2018	47,815	39,612	47.6	1,885,156	5.16	9,661,916
2019	45,485	37,394	51.7	1,932,017	4.58	8,919,117
2020	44,450	36,789	49.7	1,828,043	5.05	9,389,104

[1] Includes area seeded in preceding fall for winter wheat. [2] Includes allowance for loans outstanding and purchases by the Government valued at the average loan and purchase rate, by States, where applicable.
NASS, Crops Branch, (202) 720–2127.

Table 1-3.—Wheat, by type: Area, yield, production, and value, United States, 2011–2020

Year	Area		Yield per harvested acre	Production	Marketing year average price per bushel received by farmers [2]	Value of production [2]
	Planted [1]	Harvested				
	1,000 acres	*1,000 acres*	*Bushels*	*1,000 bushels*	*Dollars*	*1,000 dollars*

Winter wheat

Year	Planted	Harvested	Yield	Production	Price	Value
2011	40,596	32,378	46.1	1,493,130	6.81	10,154,257
2012	40,897	34,609	47.1	1,630,387	7.55	12,245,482
2013	43,230	32,650	47.3	1,542,902	6.89	10,590,949
2014	42,409	32,299	42.6	1,377,216	5.92	8,036,108
2015	39,681	32,346	42.5	1,374,690	4.80	6,555,216
2016	36,149	30,235	55.3	1,672,522	3.57	6,114,353
2017	32,726	25,301	50.2	1,270,282	4.32	5,522,949
2018	32,542	24,742	47.9	1,183,939	5.08	5,985,308
2019	31,474	24,592	53.6	1,316,963	4.53	6,048,221
2020	30,450	23,029	50.9	1,171,397	4.98	5,908,582

Durum wheat

Year	Planted	Harvested	Yield	Production	Price	Value
2011	1,337	1,280	36.8	47,043	9.68	445,186
2012	2,138	2,122	38.4	81,501	8.18	682,317
2013	1,400	1,338	43.3	57,976	7.46	432,733
2014	1,407	1,346	40.2	54,056	8.81	482,417
2015	1,951	1,911	44.0	84,009	7.36	615,160
2016	2,412	2,360	44.0	103,914	6.01	608,093
2017	2,307	2,106	26.0	54,777	6.35	344,791
2018	2,073	1,974	39.5	77,985	5.33	412,749
2019	1,341	1,177	45.8	53,959	4.90	267,055
2020	1,690	1,665	41.5	69,141	6.02	417,038

Other spring wheat [3]

Year	Planted	Harvested	Yield	Production	Price	Value
2011	12,344	12,029	37.7	452,938	8.24	3,669,782
2012	12,259	12,027	44.9	540,419	8.24	4,455,350
2013	11,606	11,344	47.1	534,101	6.73	3,580,760
2014	13,025	12,740	46.7	595,038	5.75	3,396,429
2015	13,367	13,061	46.2	603,240	4.78	2,847,947
2016	11,555	11,253	47.3	532,227	4.56	2,456,744
2017	11,019	10,148	41.0	415,851	5.71	2,387,379
2018	13,200	12,896	48.3	623,232	5.31	3,263,859
2019	12,670	11,625	48.3	561,095	4.66	2,603,841
2020	12,310	12,095	48.6	587,505	5.09	3,063,484

[1] Seeded in preceding fall for winter wheat. [2] Obtained by weighting State prices by quantity sold. [3] Includes small quantities of Durum wheat grown in other States.
NASS, Crops Branch, (202) 720–2127.

Table 1-4.—Wheat: Stocks on and off farms, United States, 2012–2020

Year beginning September	All wheat							
	On farms				Off farms [1]			
	Sept. 1	Dec. 1	Mar. 1	Jun. 1	Sept. 1	Dec. 1	Mar. 1	Jun. 1
	1,000 bushels							
2012	572,900	399,500	217,100	112,030	1,542,209	1,271,079	982,245	630,590
2013	555,000	398,400	236,970	120,150	1,314,637	1,076,451	997,860	597,739
2014	713,450	472,800	237,530	96,995	1,193,770	1,056,830	819,435	493,288
2015	650,200	503,450	278,710	155,170	1,446,889	1,242,457	861,697	597,224
2016	728,200	571,280	319,800	197,210	1,816,830	1,508,080	1,051,862	778,393
2017	492,500	394,180	349,500	191,755	1,774,275	1,479,335	1,309,175	988,847
2018	632,700	504,280	250,310	130,475	1,757,071	1,505,205	1,236,131	968,414
2019	734,500	519,470	367,870	206,545	1,611,025	1,321,305	1,225,201	873,216
2020	705,050	483,470	338,690	228,585	1,452,775	1,219,220	1,076,724	799,699

Year beginning September	Durum wheat [2]							
	On farms				Off farms [1]			
	Sept. 1	Dec. 1	Mar. 1	Jun. 1	Sept. 1	Dec. 1	Mar. 1	Jun. 1
	1,000 bushels							
2012	43,600	36,700	17,900	15,200	24,842	24,306	17,899	10,270
2013	42,900	32,800	21,400	13,600	23,465	21,175	21,088	9,450
2014	38,700	23,900	20,700	12,800	19,121	20,147	17,430	8,724
2015	44,900	35,700	16,200	10,250	29,146	24,787	21,454	15,406
2016	65,500	49,200	17,700	12,190	26,386	23,719	24,785	15,609
2017	33,400	30,700	32,400	18,350	32,756	25,351	20,584	17,953
2018	51,800	46,700	25,800	14,950	38,260	36,830	23,740	19,996
2019	49,600	33,200	40,600	26,050	38,773	31,187	33,789	28,920
2020	43,500	39,000	23,500	17,700	27,517	22,639	27,898	24,230

[1] Includes stocks at mills, elevators, warehouses, terminals, and processors. [2] Included in all wheat.
NASS, Crops Branch, (202) 720–2127.

GRAIN AND FEED

Table 1-5.—Wheat: Supply and disappearance, by class, United States, 2015–2019 [1]

Item	Year beginning June				
	2015	2016	2017	2018	2019
	Million bushels				
All wheat:					
Stocks, June 1	752	976	1,181	1,099	1,080
Production	2,062	2,309	1,741	1,885	1,920
Supply [2]	2,927	3,402	3,079	3,119	3,105
Exports [3]	778	1,051	906	937	965
Domestic disappearance	1,174	1,171	1,075	1,102	1,096
Stocks, May 31	976	1,181	1,099	1,080	1,044
Hard red winter:					
Stocks, June 1	294	446	589	581	516
Production	830	1,082	750	662	833
Supply [2]	1,130	1,533	1,346	1,248	1,351
Exports [3]	227	453	373	332	376
Domestic disappearance	458	490	392	400	454
Stocks, May 31	446	589	581	516	521
Soft red winter:					
Stocks, June 1	154	157	215	205	158
Production	359	345	293	286	239
Supply [2]	518	510	512	495	401
Exports [3]	120	91	91	128	92
Domestic disappearance	241	204	216	209	204
Stocks, May 31	157	215	205	158	105
Hard red spring:					
Stocks, June 1	212	272	235	191	263
Production	568	491	384	587	522
Supply [2]	842	830	707	845	838
Exports [3]	254	319	229	259	268
Domestic disappearance	316	276	287	324	289
Stocks, May 31	272	235	191	263	280
Durum:					
Stocks, June 1	26	28	36	35	55
Production	84	104	55	78	54
Supply [2]	143	162	143	165	150
Exports [3]	29	25	18	22	42
Domestic disappearance	86	101	90	88	65
Stocks, May 31	28	36	35	55	43
White:					
Stocks, June 1	67	74	105	87	88
Production	221	286	259	272	272
Supply [2]	294	368	371	365	366
Exports [3]	147	163	195	197	187
Domestic disappearance	73	100	90	81	84
Stocks, May 31	74	105	87	88	95

[1] Data except production are approximations. [2] Total supply includes imports. [3] Import and exports include flour and products in wheat equivalent.
ERS, Market and Trade Economics Division, (202) 694–5285.

Table 1-6.—Wheat: Supply and disappearance, United States, 2010–2019

Year be-ginning June	Supply				Disappearance						Ending stocks May 31
	Beginning stocks	Production	Imports [1]	Total	Domestic use				Exports [1]	Total disappearance	
					Food	Seed	Feed [2]	Total			
	Million bushels										
2010	976	2,207	97	3,236	926	71	85	1,081	1,291	2,373	863
2011	863	1,993	112	2,969	941	76	159	1,176	1,051	2,227	743
2012	743	2,252	124	3,119	951	73	365	1,389	1,012	2,401	718
2013	718	2,135	172	3,025	955	76	228	1,259	1,176	2,435	590
2014	590	2,026	151	2,768	958	79	113	1,151	864	2,015	752
2015	752	2,062	113	2,927	957	67	149	1,174	778	1,951	976
2016	976	2,309	118	3,402	949	61	161	1,171	1,051	2,222	1,181
2017	1,181	1,741	158	3,079	964	63	47	1,075	906	1,981	1,099
2018	1,099	1,885	135	3,119	955	59	88	1,102	937	2,039	1,080
2019	1,080	1,920	105	3,105	962	61	73	1,096	965	2,061	1,044

[1] Imports and exports include flour and other products expressed in wheat equivalent.　[2] Approximates feed and residual use and includes negligible quantities used for distilled spirits.
Totals may not add due to independent rounding.
ERS, Market and Trade Economics Division, (202) 694–5296. Data as of September 21, 2020.

Table 1-7.—All Wheat: Area, yield, and production, by State and United States, 2018–2020

State	Area planted [1]			Area harvested		
	2018	2019	2020	2018	2019	2020
	1,000 acres					
Alabama	160	130	135	110	85	70
Arizona	96	36	050	77	35	49
Arkansas	175	110	145	95	50	75
California	425	420	410	147	122	102
Colorado	2,260	2,150	1,900	1,954	2,000	1,520
Delaware	75	60	75	45	50	55
Florida [2]	15	15	(NA)	10	10	(NA)
Georgia	200	150	190	70	50	85
Idaho	1,191	1,195	1,240	1,136	1,125	1,164
Illinois	600	650	750	560	565	520
Indiana	310	330	300	260	260	250
Iowa [2]	16	16	(NA)	6	6	(NA)
Kansas	7,700	7,100	6,600	7,300	6,700	6,250
Kentucky	450	460	490	300	330	340
Louisiana [2]	15	15	(NA)	10	10	(NA)
Maryland	360	345	355	200	165	150
Michigan	510	550	490	470	490	450
Minnesota	1,621	1,450	1,430	1,575	1,400	1,360
Mississippi	55	45	40	30	21	20
Missouri	740	550	480	520	390	370
Montana	5,390	5,450	5,595	5,165	5,135	5,490
Nebraska	1,100	1,070	900	1,010	970	830
Nevada [2]	23	19	(NA)	8	8	(NA)
New Jersey	18	18	25	15	14	18
New Mexico	320	365	335	105	110	115
New York	110	90	150	95	66	120
North Carolina	460	290	450	370	225	350
North Dakota	7,735	7,505	6,650	7,635	6,630	6,563
Ohio	490	500	530	450	385	490
Oklahoma	4,400	4,200	4,250	2,500	2,750	2,600
Oregon	800	740	740	770	730	725
Pennsylvania	195	180	235	145	140	190
South Carolina	80	70	110	65	45	95
South Dakota	1,883	1,500	1,400	1,628	1,360	1,355
Tennessee	380	280	300	285	215	230
Texas	4,500	4,600	4,900	1,750	2,100	2,050
Utah	130	125	110	103	116	98
Virginia	230	180	220	155	105	130
Washington	2,220	2,270	2,350	2,165	2,215	2,295
West Virginia [2]	7	7	(NA)	3	3	(NA)
Wisconsin	240	195	160	200	150	125
Wyoming	130	125	120	115	110	90
United States	47,815	45,485	44,450	39,612	37,394	36,789

See footnote(s) at end of table.

GRAIN AND FEED

Table 1-7.—All Wheat: Area, yield, and production, by State and United States, 2018–2020—Continued

State	Yield per harvested acre			Production		
	2018	2019	2020	2018	2019	2020
	Bushels			1,000 bushels		
Alabama	72.0	72.0	72.0	7,920	6,120	5,040
Arizona	102.6	104.0	99.0	7,898	3,640	4,851
Arkansas	55.0	52.0	55.0	5,225	2,600	4,125
California	81.5	59.4	77.0	11,985	7,244	7,854
Colorado	36.1	49.0	27.0	70,504	98,000	41,040
Delaware	71.0	72.0	73.0	3,195	3,600	4,015
Florida [2]	36.0	(NA)	(NA)	360	(NA)	(NA)
Georgia	54.0	56.0	55.0	3,780	2,800	4,675
Idaho	91.9	87.8	96.7	104,410	98,755	112,506
Illinois	66.0	67.0	68.0	36,960	36,850	35,360
Indiana	71.0	62.0	70.0	18,460	16,120	17,500
Iowa [2]	58.0	(NA)	(NA)	348	(NA)	(NA)
Kansas	38.0	52.0	45.0	277,400	348,400	281,250
Kentucky	66.0	76.0	63.0	19,800	25,080	21,420
Louisiana [2]	65.0	(NA)	(NA)	650	(NA)	(NA)
Maryland	63.0	75.0	73.0	12,600	12,375	10,950
Michigan	76.0	71.0	75.0	35,720	34,790	33,750
Minnesota	59.0	57.0	53.0	92,930	79,800	72,080
Mississippi	49.0	47.0	48.0	1,470	987	960
Missouri	59.0	63.0	62.0	30,680	24,570	22,940
Montana	38.3	42.4	41.7	197,630	217,725	228,680
Nebraska	49.0	57.0	41.0	49,490	55,290	34,030
Nevada [2]	112.5	(NA)	(NA)	900	(NA)	(NA)
New Jersey	62.0	66.0	67.0	930	924	1,206
New Mexico	15.0	30.0	28.0	1,575	3,300	3,220
New York	69.0	63.0	66.0	6,555	4,158	7,920
North Carolina	57.0	56.0	60.0	21,090	12,600	21,000
North Dakota	47.6	48.4	47.6	363,483	321,185	312,587
Ohio	75.0	56.0	71.0	33,750	21,560	34,790
Oklahoma	28.0	40.0	40.0	70,000	110,000	104,000
Oregon	67.0	68.0	64.0	51,590	49,640	46,400
Pennsylvania	65.0	73.0	71.0	9,425	10,220	13,490
South Carolina	54.0	48.0	51.0	3,510	2,160	4,845
South Dakota	44.4	48.1	51.9	72,294	65,410	70,285
Tennessee	65.0	67.0	59.0	18,525	14,405	13,490
Texas	32.0	34.0	30.0	56,000	71,400	61,500
Utah	52.0	54.0	53.0	5,356	6,264	5,194
Virginia	60.0	62.0	60.0	9,300	6,510	7,800
Washington	70.8	64.7	72.4	153,210	143,205	166,245
West Virginia [2]	46.0	(NA)	(NA)	138	(NA)	(NA)
Wisconsin	71.0	64.0	69.0	14,200	9,600	8,625
Wyoming	34.0	43.0	26.0	3,910	4,730	2,340
United States	47.6	51.7	49.7	1,885,156	1,932,017	1,828,043

(NA) Not available. [1] Includes area planted preceding fall. [2] Estimates discontinued in 2020.
NASS, Crops Branch, (202) 720–2127.

Table 1-8.—Wheat, by type: Area, yield, and production, by State and United States, 2018–2020

State	Area planted [1]			Area harvested		
	2018	2019	2020	2018	2019	2020
	1,000 acres					
	Winter wheat					
Alabama	160	130	135	110	85	70
Arizona [2]	22	(NA)	(NA)	4	(NA)	(NA)
Arkansas	175	110	145	95	50	75
California	380	390	385	110	100	85
Colorado	2,250	2,150	1,900	1,950	2,000	1,520
Delaware	75	60	75	45	50	55
Florida [2]	15	(NA)	(NA)	10	(NA)	(NA)
Georgia	200	150	190	70	50	85
Idaho	720	730	720	680	680	660
Illinois	600	650	570	560	550	520
Indiana	310	330	300	260	260	250
Iowa [2]	16	(NA)	(NA)	6	(NA)	(NA)
Kansas	7,700	7,100	6,600	7,300	6,700	6,250
Kentucky	450	460	510	300	330	340
Louisiana [2]	15	(NA)	(NA)	10	(NA)	(NA)
Maryland	360	345	355	200	165	150
Michigan	510	550	490	470	490	450
Minnesota [2]	11	(NA)	(NA)	5	(NA)	(NA)
Mississippi	55	45	40	30	21	20
Missouri	740	550	480	520	390	370
Montana	1,650	2,000	1,550	1,570	1,900	1,490
Nebraska	1,100	1,070	900	1,010	970	830
Nevada [2]	13	(NA)	(NA)	5	(NA)	(NA)
New Jersey	18	19	25	15	14	18
New Mexico	320	365	335	105	110	115
New York	110	90	150	95	66	120
North Carolina	460	290	450	370	225	350
North Dakota	85	85	40	70	70	33
Ohio	490	500	530	450	385	490
Oklahoma	4,400	4,200	4,250	2,500	2,750	2,600
Oregon	720	740	740	695	730	725
Pennsylvania	195	180	235	145	140	190
South Carolina	80	70	110	65	45	95
South Dakota	830	860	630	660	770	600
Tennessee	380	280	300	285	215	230
Texas	4,500	4,600	4,900	1,750	2,100	2,050
Utah	120	125	110	94	116	98
Virginia	230	180	220	155	105	130
Washington	1,700	1,750	1,800	1,650	1,700	1,750
West Virginia [2]	7	(NA)	(NA)	3	(NA)	(NA)
Wisconsin	240	195	160	200	150	125
Wyoming	130	125	120	115	110	90
United States	32,542	31,474	30,450	24,742	24,592	23,029
	Other spring wheat					
Colorado [2]	10	(NA)	(NA)	4	(NA)	(NA)
Idaho	460	460	510	445	440	495
Minnesota	1,610	1,450	1,430	1,570	1,400	1,360
Montana	2,900	2,900	3,350	2,820	2,730	3,310
Nevada [2]	10	(NA)	(NA)	3	(NA)	(NA)
North Dakota	6,550	6,700	5,700	6,490	5,950	5,630
Oregon [2]	80	(NA)	(NA)	75	(NA)	(NA)
South Dakota	1,050	640	770	965	590	755
Utah [2]	10	(NA)	(NA)	9	(NA)	(NA)
Washington	520	520	550	515	515	545
United States	13,200	12,670	12,310	12,896	11,625	12,095
	Durum wheat					
Arizona	74	36	50	73	35	49
California	45	30	25	37	22	17
Idaho	11	5	10	11	5	9
Montana	840	550	695	775	505	690
North Dakota	1,100	720	910	1,075	610	900
South Dakota [2]	3	(NA)	(NA)	3	(NA)	(NA)
United States	2,073	1,341	1,690	1,974	1,177	1,665

See footnote(s) at end of table.

Table 1-8.—Wheat, by type: Area, yield, and production, by State and United States, 2018–2020—Continued

State	Yield per harvested acre			Production		
	2018	2019	2020	2018	2019	2020
	Bushels			1,000 bushels		
Winter wheat						
Alabama	72.0	72.0	72.0	7,920	6,120	5,040
Arizona [2]	40.0	(NA)	(NA)	160	(NA)	(NA)
Arkansas	55.0	52.0	55.0	5,225	2,600	4,125
California	77.0	50.0	75.0	8,470	5,000	6,375
Colorado	36.0	49.0	27.0	70,200	98,000	41,040
Delaware	71.0	72.0	73.0	3,195	3,600	4,015
Florida [2]	36.0	(NA)	(NA)	360	(NA)	(NA)
Georgia	54.0	56.0	55.0	3,780	2,800	4,675
Idaho	90.0	87.0	101.0	61,200	59,160	66,660
Illinois	66.0	67.0	68.0	36,960	36,850	35,360
Indiana	71.0	62.0	70.0	18,460	16,120	17,500
Iowa [2]	58.0	(NA)	(NA)	348	(NA)	(NA)
Kansas	38.0	52.0	45.0	277,400	348,400	281,250
Kentucky	66.0	76.0	63.0	19,800	25,080	21,420
Louisiana [2]	65.0	(NA)	(NA)	650	(NA)	(NA)
Maryland	63.0	75.0	73.0	12,600	12,375	10,950
Michigan	76.0	71.0	75.0	35,720	34,790	33,750
Minnesota [2]	60.0	(NA)	(NA)	300	(NA)	(NA)
Mississippi	49.0	47.0	48.0	1,470	987	960
Missouri	59.0	63.0	62.0	30,680	24,570	22,940
Montana	50.0	50.0	51.0	78,500	95,000	75,990
Nebraska	49.0	57.0	41.0	49,490	55,290	34,030
Nevada [2]	120.0	(NA)	(NA)	600	(NA)	(NA)
New Jersey	62.0	66.0	67.0	930	924	1,206
New Mexico	15.0	30.0	28.0	1,575	3,300	3,220
New York	69.0	63.0	66.0	6,555	4,158	7,920
North Carolina	57.0	56.0	60.0	21,090	12,600	21,000
North Dakota	43.0	53.0	49.0	3,010	3,710	1,617
Ohio	75.0	56.0	71.0	33,750	21,560	34,790
Oklahoma	28.0	40.0	40.0	70,000	110,000	104,000
Oregon	67.0	68.0	64.0	46,565	49,640	46,400
Pennsylvania	65.0	73.0	71.0	9,425	10,220	13,490
South Carolina	54.0	48.0	51.0	3,510	2,160	4,845
South Dakota	48.0	52.0	58.0	31,680	40,040	34,800
Tennessee	65.0	67.0	59.0	18,525	14,405	13,570
Texas	32.0	34.0	30.0	56,000	71,400	61,500
Utah	52.0	54.0	53.0	4,888	6,264	5,194
Virginia	60.0	62.0	60.0	9,300	6,510	7,800
Washington	76.0	70.0	76.0	125,400	119,000	133,000
West Virginia [2]	46.0	(NA)	(NA)	138	(NA)	(NA)
Wisconsin	71.0	64.0	69.0	14,200	9,600	8,625
Wyoming	34.0	43.0	26.0	3,910	4,730	2,340
United States	47.9	53.6	50.9	1,183,939	1,316,963	1,171,397
Other spring wheat						
Colorado [2]	76.0	(NA)	(NA)	304	(NA)	(NA)
Idaho	95.0	89.0	91.0	42,275	39,160	45,045
Minnesota	59.0	57.0	53.0	92,630	79,800	72,080
Montana	34.0	37.0	38.0	95,880	101,010	125,780
Nevada [2]	100.0	(NA)	(NA)	300	(NA)	(NA)
North Dakota	49.0	49.0	49.0	318,010	291,550	275,870
Oregon [2]	67.0	(NA)	(NA)	5,025	(NA)	(NA)
South Dakota	42.0	43.0	47.0	40,530	25,370	35,485
Utah [2]	52.0	(NA)	(NA)	468	(NA)	(NA)
Washington	54.0	47.0	61.0	27,810	24,205	32,245
United States	48.3	48.3	48.6	623,232	561,095	587,505
Durum wheat						
Arizona	106.0	104.0	99.0	7,738	3,640	4,851
California	95.0	102.0	87.0	3,515	2,244	1,479
Idaho	85.0	87.0	89.0	935	435	801
Montana	30.0	43.0	39.0	23,250	21,715	26,910
North Dakota	39.5	42.5	39.0	42,463	25,925	35,100
South Dakota [2]	28.0	(NA)	(NA)	84	(NA)	(NA)
United States	39.5	45.8	41.5	77,985	53,959	69,141

(NA) Not available. [1] Includes area planted preceding fall. [2] Estimates discontinued in 2020.
NASS, Crops Branch, (202) 720–2127.

Table 1-9.—Wheat: Support operations, United States, 2014–2021

Marketing year beginning June 1	Income support payment rates per bushel [1]	Program price levels per bushel		Put under loan		Acquired by CCC under loan program [3]	Owned by CCC at end of marketing year
		Loan	Reference	Quantity	Percentage of production [2]		
	Dollars	*Dollars*	*Dollars*	*Million bushels*	*Percent*	*Million bushels*	*Million bushels*
2014/2015 ...	0.00	2.94	5.50	43.1	2.1	0	0
2015/2016 ...	0.61	2.94	5.50	80.9	3.9	0	0
2016/2017 ...	1.61	2.94	5.50	150.7	6.5	0	0
2017/2018 ...	0.78	2.94	5.50	44.7	2.6	0.25	0
2018/2019 ...	0.34	2.94	5.50	65.1	3.5	0	0
2019/2020 ...	0.92	3.38	5.50	69.1	3.6	0	0
2020/2021 [4]	0.50	3.38	5.50	41.0	2.2	0	0

[1] The entry is the price loss coverage (PLC) payment rate. Agricultural Risk Coverage (ARC) is also available, but payment rates are established at the county or farm levels.   [2] Percent of production is on a grain basis.   [3] Acquisitions as of September 30, 2020.   [4] 2020/21 payment rate forecast as of March 2021.
FPAC-BC, Commodity Analysis Branch.

Table 1-10.—Wheat: Marketing year average price and value, by State and United States, 2018–2020

State	Marketing year average price per bushel			Value of production		
	2018	2019	2020 [1]	2018	2019	2020 [1]
	Dollars			*1,000 dollars*		
Alabama	4.60	4.95	5.05	35,420	39,204	30,906
Arizona	7.06	7.01	6.55	70,822	55,038	22,480
Arkansas	4.46	4.88	4.85	28,990	25,498	12,610
California	5.42	6.39	6.10	67,730	76,413	44,336
Colorado	3.88	4.61	3.95	339,873	324,789	387,100
Delaware	4.63	4.90	4.95	20,279	15,656	17,820
Florida [2]	4.00	4.40	(NA)	1,480	1,584	(NA)
Georgia	4.10	4.80	4.90	13,489	18,144	13,720
Idaho	4.64	5.15	5.05	426,305	539,010	500,954
Illinois	4.59	4.77	4.95	163,955	176,299	182,408
Indiana	4.78	4.90	4.95	84,893	90,454	79,794
Iowa [2]	3.90	4.75	(NA)	2,122	1,653	(NA)
Kansas	4.07	4.93	4.05	1,357,752	1,367,582	1,368,900
Kentucky	4.68	5.19	5.25	111,712	102,762	131,670
Louisiana [2]	4.20	5.10	(NA)	2,512	3,315	(NA)
Maryland	4.63	4.90	4.95	60,815	61,740	105,806
Michigan	4.54	5.08	5.20	152,431	181,458	177,216
Minnesota	5.76	5.25	4.70	438,062	487,796	375,060
Mississippi	4.30	4.88	5.10	6,235	7,174	5,034
Missouri	4.47	4.84	5.15	164,138	148,491	126,536
Montana	5.34	5.24	4.65	695,891	1,041,736	1,022,114
Nebraska	4.03	4.71	3.80	189,088	233,098	210,102
Nevada [2]	4.70	5.18	(NA)	7,233	4,749	(NA)
New Jersey	4.60	4.90	4.95	5,005	4,557	4,574
New Mexico	4.20	4.75	4.50	17,010	7,481	14,175
New York	4.88	5.31	5.50	40,870	34,807	22,869
North Carolina	4.70	4.80	5.30	96,938	101,232	66,780
North Dakota	5.74	5.09	4.45	1,362,415	1,848,508	1,424,229
Ohio	4.90	5.08	5.25	166,796	171,450	113,190
Oklahoma	3.98	5.10	4.30	392,428	357,000	473,000
Oregon	5.16	5.80	5.70	245,537	298,465	282,948
Pennsylvania	5.21	5.30	5.55	56,268	49,953	56,721
South Carolina	4.20	4.70	5.25	15,435	16,497	11,340
South Dakota	5.52	5.24	4.55	233,427	378,573	298,447
Tennessee	4.60	5.24	5.45	88,550	97,071	78,507
Texas	3.89	5.17	4.40	265,104	289,520	306,680
Utah	5.20	6.00	4.95	32,448	30,998	31,007
Virginia	4.60	4.70	5.00	44,022	43,710	32,550
Washington	4.85	5.51	5.55	690,902	844,592	790,976
West Virginia [2]	4.70	4.90	(NA)	1,297	676	(NA)
Wisconsin	4.15	4.55	4.35	47,974	64,610	41,760
Wyoming	3.90	4.75	3.90	11,466	18,573	18,447
United States	4.72	5.16	4.55	8,255,119	9,661,916	8,882,766

(NA) Not available. [1] Preliminary. [2] Estimates discontinued in 2020.
NASS, Crops Branch, (202) 720–2127.

GRAIN AND FEED

Table 1-11.—International Wheat: Area, yield, and production in specified countries, 2017/2018–2019/2020

Country	Area			Yield per hectare			Production		
	2017/ 2018	2018/ 2019	2019/ 2020	2017/ 2018	2018/ 2019	2019/ 2020	2017/ 2018	2018/ 2019	2019/ 2020
	1,000 hectares			Metric tons			1,000 metric tons		
European Union ...	26,160	25,581	26,065	5.78	5.35	5.91	151,125	136,863	154,000
China	24,508	24,268	23,730	5.48	5.42	5.63	134,334	131,430	133,590
India	30,785	29,651	29,319	3.20	3.37	3.53	98,510	99,870	103,600
Russia	27,370	26,344	27,312	3.11	2.72	2.70	85,167	71,685	73,610
United States	15,198	16,030	15,039	3.12	3.20	3.48	47,380	51,306	52,258
Canada	8,983	9,881	9,660	3.38	3.26	3.35	30,377	32,201	32,350
Ukraine	6,642	6,718	7,050	4.06	3.73	4.11	26,981	25,057	29,000
Pakistan	9,050	8,800	8,798	2.94	2.85	2.91	26,600	25,100	25,600
Argentina	5,800	6,050	6,500	3.19	3.22	3.00	18,500	19,500	19,500
Turkey	7,800	7,615	7,200	2.69	2.50	2.50	21,000	19,000	18,000
Iran	6,700	6,700	6,700	2.09	2.16	2.51	14,000	14,500	16,800
Australia	10,919	10,159	10,100	1.92	1.70	1.51	20,941	17,298	15,200
Kazakhstan	11,912	11,354	11,339	1.24	1.23	1.01	14,802	13,947	11,452
Egypt	1,320	1,320	1,370	6.40	6.40	6.40	8,450	8,450	8,770
Uzbekistan	1,446	1,400	1,400	4.80	4.29	4.86	6,941	6,000	6,800
Brazil	1,916	2,042	2,040	2.23	2.66	2.55	4,264	5,428	5,200
Afghanistan	2,104	2,000	2,300	2.04	1.80	2.17	4,281	3,600	5,000
Ethiopia	1,717	1,840	1,850	2.81	2.61	2.60	4,831	4,800	4,800
Iraq	2,200	1,700	2,400	1.82	1.77	2.00	4,000	3,000	4,800
Syria	1,100	1,100	1,600	2.00	1.82	3.00	2,200	2,000	4,800
Algeria	1,600	2,074	2,100	1.50	1.90	1.91	2,400	3,940	4,000
Morocco	3,321	2,850	2,750	2.14	2.58	1.46	7,091	7,340	4,000
Mexico	667	540	593	5.24	5.56	5.42	3,494	3,000	3,215
Belarus	718	660	750	3.65	2.75	3.83	2,620	1,815	2,875
Serbia	540	648	580	4.26	4.63	4.48	2,300	3,000	2,600
Azerbaijan	596	680	700	2.97	3.00	2.86	1,770	2,040	2,000
Nepal	770	760	760	2.31	2.35	2.35	1,780	1,786	1,786
South Africa	492	503	540	3.12	3.71	2.78	1,535	1,868	1,500
Tunisia	579	536	620	1.91	2.00	2.42	1,104	1,070	1,500
Turkmenistan	900	750	880	1.11	0.93	1.71	1,000	700	1,500
Chile	236	223	230	6.23	6.28	6.30	1,469	1,400	1,450
Bangladesh	370	320	340	3.12	3.44	3.53	1,153	1,100	1,200
Moldova	336	372	352	3.72	3.13	3.25	1,251	1,163	1,145
Paraguay	510	485	480	2.00	2.80	2.38	1,020	1,360	1,140
Japan	213	212	212	4.56	4.06	4.53	972	860	960
Tajikistan	286	300	300	3.15	2.33	2.77	900	700	830
Uruguay	186	198	230	2.37	3.68	3.30	440	728	760
Saudi Arabia	2	87	120	5.00	5.75	5.83	10	500	700
Sudan	168	200	200	2.76	2.98	3.00	463	595	600
Kyrgyzstan	250	300	280	2.40	2.05	2.11	601	616	590
Switzerland	90	90	90	6.00	6.00	6.00	540	540	540
Norway	76	58	80	5.28	2.19	5.25	401	127	420
New Zealand	41	42	45	9.88	8.81	9.11	405	370	410
Mongolia	366	342	327	0.63	1.28	1.10	231	436	360
Albania	68	75	72	4.04	4.13	4.17	275	310	300
Macedonia	73	71	80	2.74	3.39	3.75	200	241	300
Bosnia and Herzegovina	65	73	71	4.45	4.00	4.01	289	292	285
Bolivia	200	150	200	1.51	1.20	1.40	302	180	280
Peru	128	127	130	1.50	1.54	1.62	192	195	210
Kenya	86	170	125	1.92	2.12	1.60	165	360	200
Libya	165	165	165	1.21	1.21	1.21	200	200	200
Armenia	81	66	60	2.17	2.83	3.00	176	187	180
Zambia	27	22	24	7.19	5.18	6.33	194	114	152
Lebanon	39	40	41	3.33	3.25	3.42	130	130	140
Yemen	100	100	90	1.50	1.40	1.56	150	140	140
Burma	87	85	65	1.55	1.53	1.54	135	130	100
Georgia	44	43	40	2.23	2.49	2.50	98	107	100
Tanzania	102	100	100	1.00	1.00	1.00	102	100	100
Zimbabwe	44	56	25	3.59	3.57	4.00	158	200	100

FAS, Office of Global Analysis, (202) 720-6301. Prepared or estimated on the basis of official USDA production, supply, and distribution statistics from foreign governments.

Table 1-12.—Wheat and flour: United States imports, 2010–2019

Year beginning June	All wheat grain	All wheat flour [1]	All wheat products [2]	Total all wheat [3]
	1,000 bushels	*1,000 bushels [4]*	*1,000 bushels [4]*	*1,000 bushels*
2010	69,053	11,283	16,582	96,918
2011	84,382	10,666	18,068	113,116
2012	96,103	10,151	18,063	124,317
2013	141,665	11,535	19,267	172,467
2014	116,973	14,332	19,944	151,249
2015	76,433	15,822	20,470	112,725
2016	83,849	14,574	19,717	118,140
2017	120,746	16,814	20,424	157,984
2018	97,657	17,016	19,959	134,633
2019	65,345	17,095	22,569	105,009

[1] Includes meal, groats, and durum. [2] Includes bulgur, couscous, and selected categories of pasta. [3] Totals may not add due to rounding. [4] Expressed in grain-equivalent bushels.
ERS, Market and Trade Economics Division, (202) 694–5285. Data as of September 21, 2020.

Table 1-13.—Wheat: International trade, 2017/2018–2019/2020

Country	2017/2018	2018/2019	2019/2020
	1,000 metric tons	*1,000 metric tons*	*1,000 metric tons*
Principle importing countries:			
Egypt	12,407	12,347	12,500
Indonesia	10,763	10,934	11,000
Turkey	6,043	6,366	10,500
Brazil	7,021	7,020	7,500
Philippines	6,059	7,546	7,300
Algeria	8,172	7,515	6,500
Bangladesh	6,472	5,100	6,500
Japan	5,876	5,726	5,900
Mexico	5,245	4,861	5,200
Nigeria	5,162	4,585	5,100
European Union	5,824	5,762	4,800
Morocco	3,676	3,724	4,800
Korea, South	4,269	3,908	4,100
China	3,937	3,145	4,000
Yemen	3,010	3,675	3,800
Vietnam	4,709	3,149	3,500
Thailand	3,173	2,899	3,300
Saudi Arabia	3,449	2,898	3,200
Afghanistan	3,300	3,700	3,000
Uzbekistan	3,119	2,837	3,000
United States	4,301	3,674	2,858
Sudan	2,580	2,222	2,600
Iraq	4,158	3,915	2,500
Kenya	2,158	2,000	2,300
Peru	2,030	2,109	2,100
Principle exporting countries:			
Russia	41,431	35,838	35,000
United States	23,383	23,310	32,000
Canada	24,655	25,477	27,216
European Union	22,000	24,404	23,000
Ukraine	17,775	16,019	20,500
Argentina	12,730	12,188	13,500
Australia	13,849	9,006	8,000
Kazakhstan	6,194	6,350	6,800
Turkey	9,000	8,296	6,000
Pakistan	1,004	1,006	1,100
Serbia	1,147	526	1,100
China	781	1,090	900
Brazil	840	1,078	700
Moldova	230	602	600
Paraguay	650	410	600
Egypt	656	600	600
Mexico	230	538	550
India	569	496	500
Iran	1,206	1,965	500
Nigeria	400	400	400
Egypt	318	274	300
Mexico	292	293	300
India	44	325	300
Iran	277	286	280
Nigeria	257	275	275

FAS, Office of Global Analysis, (202) 720-6301. Prepared or estimated on the basis of official USDA production, supply, and distribution statistics from foreign governments.

GRAIN AND FEED

Table 1-14.—Wheat and flour: United States exports by country of destination, 2018–2020

Country of destination	Year		
	2018	2019	2020
	Metric tons	*Metric tons*	*Metric tons*
Wheat:			
Philippines	2,644,825	2,953,465	3,368,926
Mexico	2,802,765	3,547,273	3,147,942
Japan	2,860,604	2,577,495	2,629,020
China	396,987	236,062	2,252,242
Korea, South	1,533,432	1,289,354	1,447,110
Nigeria	814,014	2,114,197	1,339,484
Indonesia	779,435	1,229,624	1,200,907
Taiwan	983,300	1,249,857	1,171,937
Yemen(*)	480,382	739,849	865,118
Italy(*)	485,893	770,396	820,734
Brazil	266,462	416,427	765,147
Thailand	696,252	674,581	694,548
Guatemala	541,021	590,207	596,047
Colombia	407,750	646,350	570,550
Vietnam	277,097	304,290	533,363
Ecuador	266,703	428,658	440,790
Chile	297,856	374,240	423,417
Ethiopia(*)	218,500	288,038	320,530
Bangladesh	449,751	225,973	311,625
Malaysia	191,605	505,675	304,574
Venezuela	340,793	122,149	282,152
Honduras	326,588	298,535	277,035
Peru	241,716	466,879	217,900
Dominican Republic	291,581	308,326	195,697
Jamaica	194,670	208,377	176,999
El Salvador	278,781	267,962	147,528
Sri Lanka	107,643	135,440	138,896
Haiti	94,172	125,515	138,498
Panama	142,937	142,811	138,372
Canada	68,599	155,225	134,516
Rest of World	2,758,914	3,541,847	1,002,900
World Total	22,241,028	26,935,077	26,054,504
Wheat flour:			
Mexico	195,588	201,996	204,845
Canada	54,397	52,155	44,884
Bahamas, The	2,045	2,530	2,886
Dominican Republic	2,019	2,187	2,231
Netherlands Antilles(*)	2,159	2,185	2,129
Sweden	1,763	1,858	2,081
Malaysia	1,325	2,099	1,826
Leeward-Windward Islands(*)	1,015	1,144	1,597
Djibouti	1,071	2,388	1,403
Guatemala	585	367	1,287
China	571	593	958
Panama	503	892	876
Barbados	763	649	862
Brazil	472	371	716
Trinidad and Tobago	1,126	1,119	687
Japan	487	465	549
Colombia	340	390	470
Taiwan	182	380	459
Senegal	0	0	450
New Zealand(*)	405	406	417
Korea, South	276	531	348
Hong Kong	102	111	298
Turks and Caicos Islands	368	331	258
Cayman Islands	175	213	248
Haiti	0	423	241
Netherlands	219	268	241
Jamaica	280	200	239
Australia(*)	132	165	211
Saudi Arabia	146	180	208
Kuwait	77	134	186
Rest of World	8,605	2,566	2,836
World Total	277,197	279,295	276,925

(*) Denotes a country that is a summarization of its component countries.
FAS, Office of Global Analysis, (202) 720-6301.   Prepared or estimated on the basis of official USDA production, supply, and distribution, supply, and distribution statistics from foreign governments.

Table 1-15.—Rye: Area, yield, production, disposition, and value, United States, 2011–2020

Year	Area		Yield per harvested acre	Production	Marketing year average price per bushel received by farmers [2]	Value of production [2]
	Planted [1]	Harvested				
	1,000 acres	1,000 acres	Bushels	1,000 bushels	Dollars	1,000 dollars
2011	1,227	239	25.3	6,051	7.81	47,250
2012	1,271	250	26.2	6,542	7.69	50,304
2013	1,451	278	27.4	7,626	7.95	60,598
2014	1,434	258	27.9	7,189	7.74	55,639
2015	1,584	365	31.8	11,616	6.50	75,497
2016	1,891	411	32.5	13,337	5.12	68,343
2017	1,961	300	34.2	10,252	4.70	48,180
2018	2,011	273	30.9	8,432	6.27	52,870
2019	1,855	310	34.3	10,622	6.01	63,827
2020	1,955	330	34.9	11,532	5.35	61,786

[1] Area planted in preceding fall. [2] 2020 data is preliminary.
NASS, Crops Branch, (202) 720-2127.

Table 1-16.—Rye: Supply and disappearance, United States, 2011–2020

Year begin-ning June	Supply				Disappearance								Ending stocks May 31
	Begin-ning stocks	Produc-tion	Imports	Total	Domestic use					Exports	Total dis-appear-ance [2]	
					Food	Seed	Indus-try [1]	Residual use	Total			
					1,000 bushels							
2011 ..	801	6,051	5,994	12,846	3,310	3,000	3,010	2,917	12,237	157	12,394	452
2012 ..	452	6,542	8,966	15,960	3,400	3,000	3,020	5,829	15,249	310	15,559	401
2013 ..	401	7,626	9,213	17,240	3,430	3,000	3,030	7,227	16,687	268	16,955	285
2014 ..	285	7,189	9,320	16,794	3,460	3,000	3,040	6,465	15,965	240	16,205	589
2015 ..	589	11,616	8,757	20,962	3,630	3,000	3,050	10,646	20,326	181	20,507	455
2016 ..	455	13,337	6,586	20,378	3,500	6,168	4,110	5,727	19,505	175	19,680	698
2017 ..	698	10,252	8,825	19,775	3,530	5,445	4,250	5,800	19,025	157	19,182	593
2018 ..	593	8,432	11,964	20,989	3,550	6,982	3,890	6,000	20,422	148	20,570	419
2019 ..	419	10,622	11,899	22,940	3,570	7,285	4,680	6,100	21,635	205	21,840	1,100
2020 ..	932	7,480	5,552	13,964	3,300	3,000	3,000	3,714	13,014	149	13,163	801

[1] Includes commercial adhesives, packaging materials, thatching, mattresses, hats, and paper.   [2] Totals may not add due to independent rounding.
ERS, Market and Trade Economics Division, (202) 694-5302.

GRAIN AND FEED

Table 1-17.—Rye: Area, yield, and production, by State and United States, 2018–2020

State	Area planted [1]			Area harvested		
	2018	2019	2020	2018	2019	2020
	1,000 acres	*1,000 acres*	*1,000 acres*	*1,000 acres*	*1,000 acres*	*1,000 acres*
Georgia	190	(D)	(D)	15	(D)	(D)
Minnesota	(D)	50	45	(D)	18	15
North Dakota	(D)	85	75	(D)	57	50
Oklahoma	240	260	270	50	55	52
Pennsylvania	(D)	100	175	(D)	14	36
Wisconsin	(D)	220	215	(D)	20	20
Other States [2]	1,581	1,140	1,175	208	146	157
United States	2,011	1,855	1,955	273	310	330

State	Yield per harvested acre			Production		
	2018	2019	2020	2018	2019	2020
	Bushels	*Bushels*	*Bushels*	*1,000 bushels*	*1,000 bushels*	*1,000 bushels*
Georgia	26.0	(D)	(D)	390	(D)	(D)
Minnesota	(D)	39.0	38.0	(D)	702	570
North Dakota	(D)	45.0	44.0	(D)	2,565	2,200
Oklahoma	22.0	27.0	14.0	1,100	1,485	728
Pennsylvania	(D)	26.0	52.0	(D)	364	1,872
Wisconsin	(D)	34.0	40.0	(D)	680	800
Other States [2]	33.4	33.1	34.2	6,942	4,826	5,362
United States	30.9	34.3	34.9	8,432	10,622	11,532

(D) Withheld to avoid disclosing data for individual operations. [1] Includes area planted preceding fall. [2] In 2019 and 2020, Other States include Illinois, Kansas, Maine, Maryland, Michigan, Minnesota, Nebraska, New Jersey, New York, North Carolina, North Dakota, Pennsylvania, South Carolina, South Dakota, Texas, Virginia, and Wisconsin. Beginning in 2020, Other States include Georgia, Illinois, Kansas, Michigan, Nebraska, New York, North Carolina, South Dakota, and Texas.
NASS, Crops Branch, (202) 720–2127.

Table 1-18.—Rye: Marketing year average price and value, by State and United States, 2018–2020

State	Marketing year average price per bushel			Value of production		
	2018	2019	2020 [1]	2018	2019	2020 [1]
	Dollars	*Dollars*	*Dollars*	*1,000 dollars*	*1,000 dollars*	*1,000 dollars*
Georgia	7.05	(D)	(D)	2,750	(D)	(D)
Minnesota	(D)	4.60	4.20	(D)	3,229	2,394
North Dakota	(D)	4.56	4.11	(D)	11,696	9,042
Oklahoma	7.55	8.25	7.55	8,305	12,251	5,496
Pennsylvania	(D)	5.90	(D)	(D)	2,148	(D)
Wisconsin	(D)	7.00	(D)	(D)	4,760	(D)
Other States [2]	6.02	6.16	5.39	41,815	29,743	44,854
United States	6.27	6.01	5.35	52,870	63,827	61,786

(D) Withheld to avoid disclosing data for individual operations. [1] Preliminary. [2] In 2019 and 2020, Other States include Illinois, Kansas, Maine, Maryland, Michigan, Minnesota, Nebraska, New Jersey, New York, North Carolina, North Dakota, Pennsylvania, South Carolina, South Dakota, Texas, Virginia, and Wisconsin. Beginning in 2020, Other States include Georgia, Illinois, Kansas, Michigan, Nebraska, New York, North Carolina, South Dakota, and Texas.
NASS, Crops Branch, (202) 720-2127.

Table 1-19.—International Rye: Area, yield, and production in specified countries, 2017/2018–2019/2020

Country	Area			Yield			Production		
	2017/ 2018	2018/ 2019	2019/ 2020	2017/ 2018	2018/ 2019	2019/ 2020	2017/ 2018	2018/ 2019	2019/ 2020
	1,000 hectares			*Metric tons per hectare*			*1,000 metric tons*		
European Union ...	1,931	1,920	2,070	3.84	3.23	3.84	7,405	6,208	7,950
Russia	1,171	957	823	2.17	2.00	1.73	2,540	1,914	1,424
Belarus	256	252	200	2.62	2.00	3.25	670	503	650
Ukraine	172	149	110	2.97	2.66	3.09	510	396	340
Canada	101	79	100	3.39	2.99	3.30	342	236	330
Turkey	101	110	110	3.17	2.91	2.91	320	320	320
United States	121	110	125	2.15	1.95	2.16	260	214	270
Argentina	45	49	56	1.91	1.78	2.14	86	87	120
Norway	9	3	9	5.56	3.00	5.56	50	9	50
Australia	40	44	44	0.75	0.68	0.68	30	30	30
Kazakhstan	31	22	23	1.26	1.05	1.00	39	23	23
Bosnia and Herzegovina	3	4	4	3.67	2.75	3.50	11	11	14
Switzerland	2	2	2	5.50	5.50	5.50	11	11	11
Serbia	4	4	4	2.50	2.50	2.50	10	10	10
Macedonia	4	4	4	2.00	2.25	2.00	8	9	8
Brazil	4	4	4	1.50	2.00	1.75	6	8	7
Chile	1	1	1	5.00	5.00	5.00	5	5	5
Albania	1	1	1	3.00	3.00	3.00	3	3	3
South Africa	20	20	20	0.15	0.15	0.15	3	3	3

FAS, Office of Global Analysis, (202) 720-6301. Prepared or estimated on the basis of official USDA production, supply, and distribution, supply, and distribution statistics from foreign governments.

Table 1-20.—Rye:[1] International trade, 2017/2018–2019/2020[2]

Country	2017/2018	2018/2019	2019/2020
	1,000 metric tons	*1,000 metric tons*	*1,000 metric tons*
Principle exporting countries:			
European Union	81	195	200
Canada	193	144	150
Ukraine	38	88	30
Russia	71	283	25
United States	4	4	5
Principle importing countries:			
United States	224	304	305
European Union	61	298	25
Israel	21	15	20
Japan	21	23	20
Belarus	15	21	10
Korea, South	3	3	5
Norway	4	18	5
Canada	1	2	2
Switzerland	2	2	2
Bosnia and Herzegovina	1	1	1
Ukraine	0	2	1

[1] Flour and products reported in terms of grain equivalent.　[2] Year beginning July 1.
FAS, Office of Global Analysis, (202) 720-6301. Prepared or estimated on the basis of official USDA production, supply, and distribution statics from foreign governments.

GRAIN AND FEED

Table 1-21.—Rice, rough: Area, yield, production, and value, United States, 2011–2020

Year	Area planted	Area harvested	Yield per acre	Production	Marketing year average price per cwt. received by farmers	Value of production
	1,000 acres	*1,000 acres*	*Pounds*	*1,000 cwt*	*Dollars*	*1,000 dollars*
2011	2,689	2,617	7,067	184,941	14.50	2,737,423
2012	2,700	2,679	7,463	199,939	15.10	3,067,365
2013	2,490	2,463	7,694	189,500	16.30	3,175,107
2014	2,954	2,933	7,576	222,215	13.40	3,075,618
2015	2,625	2,584	7,472	193,080	12.20	2,421,111
2016	3,150	3,097	7,237	224,145	10.40	2,384,690
2017	2,463	2,374	7,507	178,228	12.90	2,360,439
2018	2,946	2,910	7,692	223,833	12.60	2,903,041
2019	2,550	2,477	7,473	185,104	13.60	2,631,955
2020	3,036	2,986	7,619	227,514	14.40	3,314,161

NASS, Crops Branch, (202) 720–2127.

Table 1-22.—Rice, rough: Stocks on and off farms, United States, 2011–2020

Year beginning previous December	On farms			Off farms [1]		
	Dec. 1	Mar. 1	Aug. 1	Dec. 1	Mar. 1	Aug. 1
	1,000 cwt					
2011	41,180	33,895	3,772	105,689	86,720	37,917
2012	39,385	23,825	910	108,650	82,666	35,052
2013	36,935	18,430	640	96,636	85,839	29,880
2014	47,865	14,995	305	110,061	73,959	26,299
2015	43,245	25,810	1,480	101,804	86,658	41,293
2016	48,595	18,255	3,762	111,734	90,507	34,983
2017	31,570	21,600	4,693	88,104	85,969	34,077
2018	40,115	12,565	1,902	98,602	70,831	21,962
2019	33,625	23,305	6,663	90,120	80,515	31,927
2020	41,370	14,370	2,828	94,704	71,775	21,567

[1] Stocks at mills and in attached warehouses, in warehouses not attached to mills, and in ports or in transit.
NASS, Crops Branch, (202) 720–2127.

Table 1-23.—Rice, by length of grain: Harvest, yield, and production, United States, 2011–2020

Year	Area harvested			Yield per acre			Production		
	Long grain	Medium grain	Short grain	Long grain	Medium grain	Short grain	Long grain	Medium grain	Short grain
	1,000 acres	*1,000 acres*	*1,000 acres*	*Pounds*	*Pounds*	*Pounds*	*1,000 cwt*	*1,000 cwt*	*1,000 cwt*
2011	1,739	834	44	6,691	7,861	6,880	116,352	65,562	3,027
2012	1,979	643	57	7,291	8,059	6,737	144,280	51,819	3,840
2013	1,762	654	47	7,464	8,385	6,685	131,518	54,840	3,142
2014	2,196	700	37	7,407	8,175	6,292	162,665	57,222	2,328
2015	1,848	698	38	7,219	8,162	7,121	133,401	56,973	2,706
2016	2,403	651	43	6,927	8,377	7,319	166,465	54,533	3,147
2017	1,748	587	39	7,314	8,155	6,438	127,850	47,867	2,511
2018	2,176	693	41	7,517	8,274	7,112	163,578	57,339	2,916
2019	1,730	713	34	7,261	8,008	7,047	125,610	57,098	2,396
2020	2,301	644	41	7,422	8,373	6,854	170,784	53,920	2,810

NASS, Crops Branch, (202) 720-2127.

Table 1-28.—Rice: Marketing year average price and value, by State and United States, 2018–2020

State	Marketing year average price per cwt.			Value of production		
	2018	2019	2020[1]	2018	2019	2020[1]
	Dollars	Dollars	Dollars	1,000 dollars	1,000 dollars	1,000 dollars
Arkansas	10.70	11.90	12.50	1,148,378	1,002,658	1,351,338
California	21.30	21.80	22.80	924,953	923,492	846,909
Louisiana	11.20	11.80	12.60	348,253	311,614	406,186
Mississippi	10.80	11.90	12.50	110,344	98,794	153,013
Missouri	10.70	12.10	12.10	182,863	154,239	187,816
Texas	12.50	12.80	13.30	188,250	141,158	194,140
United States	12.60	13.60	14.40	2,903,041	2,631,955	3,069,000

[1] Preliminary.
NASS, Crops Branch, (202) 720–2127.

Table 1-29.—Rice, milled, by length of grain: Stocks in all positions, United States, 2011–2020

Year beginning previous December	Whole kernels (head rice)				
	Dec. 1	Mar. 1	Jun. 1	Aug. 1	Oct.. 1[1]
	Long grain				
	1,000 cwt	1,000 cwt	1,000 cwt	1,000 cwt	1,000 cwt
2011	2,665	3,038	3,291	1,924	[2]
2012	2,699	1,856	1,906	1,550	1
2013	2,574	3,144	(NA)	1,704	[2]
2014	3,348	2,379	[3]	1,556	[2]
2015	2,308	1,952	2,523	1,792	[2]
2016	2,716	2,616	3,463	2,022	[2]
2017	2,453	2,659	2,056	1,969	[2]
2018	2,037	1,717	2,633	2,026	[2]
2019	2,516	1,657	2,451	2,422	[2]
2020	2,271	2,727	1,805	1,454	[2]
	Medium grain				
	1,000 cwt	1,000 cwt	1,000 cwt	1,000 cwt	1,000 cwt
2011	1,743	1,803	981	845	399
2012	1,406	935	1,041	496	281
2013	1,638	772	(NA)	726	[2]
2014	1,285	1,584	1,601	472	603
2015	1,694	1,139	1,662	878	1,430
2016	1,279	1,459	1,030	1,324	389
2017	1,017	971	1,292	609	388
2018	988	1,317	909	804	[2]
2019	1,816	1,057	748	466	281
2020	1,275	542	1,467	770	437
	Short grain				
	1,000 cwt	1,000 cwt	1,000 cwt	1,000 cwt	1,000 cwt
2011	97	62	53	45	[2]
2012	199	49	60	38	69
2013	99	64	(NA)	61	28
2014	58	48	[2]	47	[2]
2015	51	59	54	37	[2]
2016	75	62	41	40	[2]
2017	65	75	101	45	[2]
2018	78	62	56	43	[2]
2019	48	48	42	52	[2]
2020	38	61	44	44	[2]

See footnote(s) at end of table.

Table 1-29.—Rice, milled, by length of grain: Stocks in all positions, United States, 2011–2020—Continued

Year beginning previous December	Broken kernels				
	Dec. 1	Mar. 1	Jun. 1	Aug. 1	Oct. 1[1]
	Second heads				
	1,000 cwt	1,000 cwt	1,000 cwt	1,000 cwt	1,000 cwt
2011	888	634	817	992	(2)
2012	1,037	1,021	778	870	(2)
2013	1,231	1,225	(NA)	1,104	(2)
2014	1,243	1,064	1,159	797	(2)
2015	727	1,663	1,227	1,120	(2)
2016	1,385	1,550	1,634	1,436	(2)
2017	1,777	1,924	1,222	1,588	(2)
2018	676	1,559	887	566	(2)
2019	707	1,046	665	701	(2)
2020	730	1,006	642	418	205
	Screenings[3]				
	1,000 cwt	1,000 cwt	1,000 cwt	1,000 cwt	1,000 cwt
2011	110	91	153	75	
2012	192	82	145	51	
2013	136	271	(NA)	153	
2014	96	118	72	92	
2015	118	115	153	88	
2016	56	61	70	33	
2017	82	81	76	84	
2018	12	118	205	138	
2019	101	136	123	217	
2020	161	107	68	115	
	Brewers				
	1,000 cwt	1,000 cwt	1,000 cwt	1,000 cwt	1,000 cwt
2011	799	647	673	786	(2)
2012	710	551	532	573	(2)
2013	1,241	1,189	(NA)	384	(2)
2014	575	651	589	747	(2)
2015	748	941	1,153	141	(2)
2016	734	387	678	551	(2)
2017	401	510	650	798	(2)
2018	170	687	364	285	(2)
2019	368	223	707	525	(2)
2020	203	796	281	186	41

(NA) Not available. [1] California only; included in Second heads. [2] Not published to avoid disclosing individual operations. [3] Screenings included in Second heads in California.
NASS, Crops Branch, (202) 720–2127.

Table 1-30.—Rice, rough: Support operations, United States, 2017–2020

Marketing year beginning August 1	Price loss coverage payment rates per cwt	Program price levels per cwt		Put under loan		Acquired by CCC under loan program [1]	Owned by CCC at end of marketing year
		Loan	Reference	Quantity	Percentage of production		
	Dollars	Dollars	Dollars	Million cwt	Percent	1,000 cwt	1,000 cwt
Long grain							
2017/2018	2.50	6.50	14.00	17.07	13.35	0	0
2018/2019	3.20	6.50	14.00	21.11	12.88	0	0
2019/2020	2.00	7.00	14.00	16.53	13.16	0	0
2020/2021 [2]	1.80	7.00	14.00	23.61	13.82	0	0
Medium grain [3]							
2017/2018	2.30	6.50	14.00	12.19	24.20	0	0
2018/2019	1.70	6.50	14.00	15.19	25.21	0	0
2019/2020	2.40	7.00	14.00	18.02	30.49	0	0
2020/2021 [2]	1.50	7.00	14.00	14.29	25.18	0	0
Temperate Japonica [4]							
2017/2018	0.00	6.50	16.10	10.98	29.86	0	0
2018/2019	0.00	6.50	16.10	12.95	30.29	0	0
2019/2020	0.00	7.00	17.30	14.38	34.91	0	0
2020/2021 [2]	0.00	7.00	17.30	12.44	29.88	0	0

[1] Projected acquisitions as of March 9, 2021. [2] Payment rate as of the February 26, 2021 NASS Agricultural Prices Report. [3] Medium Grain includes all short grain rice and medium grain rice for the marketing assistance loan program. The quantity under loan for 2014/2015 includes the medium and short grain rice in California. The medium and short grain rice in California is also shown in the Temperate Japonica section below. [4] Temperate Japonica Rice is medium and short grain rice in California starting with the 2014/2015 crop. Prior to the 2014/2015 crop, temperate japonica rice was classified as medium grain rice for program purposes.
FPAC, (202) 690-0734.

Table 1-31.—Rice: United States exports (milled basis), by country of destination, 2018–2020 [1]

Country of destination	Year		
	2018	2019	2020
	Metric tons	Metric tons	Metric tons
Mexico	756,638	862,395	616,179
Haiti	412,253	449,841	461,290
Japan	274,058	339,469	317,429
Canada	236,604	250,490	249,005
Korea, South	111,325	149,163	200,842
Colombia	147,059	147,358	187,513
Honduras	196,139	160,813	122,753
Brazil	595	146	119,707
Saudi Arabia	94,335	119,420	116,008
Nicaragua	10,675	131,920	92,390
Venezuela	42,218	53,776	91,896
Jordan	80,921	89,991	89,059
Guatemala	121,320	114,794	83,779
El Salvador	78,712	78,478	75,285
Taiwan	46,887	64,470	62,035
Costa Rica	73,582	76,054	53,867
Dominican Republic	20,176	22,838	37,364
Israel(*)	10,336	19,905	36,088
United Kingdom	25,341	10,086	28,077
Cote d'Ivoire	19,003	11,875	27,509
Turkey	1,057	2,667	27,251
Cameroon	1,933	5,731	26,596
Panama	24,015	51,275	24,138
Togo	625	9,444	10,954
Australia(*)	10,020	9,969	10,669
United Arab Emirates	3,867	7,503	9,381
Bahamas, The	7,362	7,631	7,559
Hong Kong	6,212	7,985	7,558
Portugal	351	6,252	6,410
Jamaica	4,156	3,743	6,078
Rest of World	382,917	378,278	105,148
World Total	3,200,692	3,643,758	3,309,813

(*) Denotes a country that is a summarization of its component countries. [1] Year beginning Jan 1.
FAS, Grain and Feed Division, (202) 720–6219. www.fas.usda.gov/grain/default.html.

Table 1-32.—International Rice, milled: Area, yield, and production in specified countries, 2017/2018–2019/2020

Country	Area			Yield per hectare			Production		
	2017/ 2018	2018/ 2019	2019/ 2020	2017/ 2018	2018/ 2019	2019/ 2020	2017/2018	2018/2019	2019/2020
	1,000 hectares			Metric tons			1,000 metric tons		
China	30,747	30,189	29,690	6.92	7.03	7.06	148,873	148,490	146,730
India	43,774	43,800	44,000	3.86	3.99	4.02	112,760	116,480	118,000
Indonesia	12,250	12,100	12,000	4.76	4.78	4.79	37,000	36,700	36,500
Bangladesh	11,272	11,770	11,830	4.35	4.45	4.55	32,650	34,909	35,850
Vietnam	7,645	7,615	7,665	5.79	5.83	5.91	27,657	27,767	28,300
Thailand	10,756	10,830	10,000	2.90	2.85	2.80	20,577	20,340	18,500
Burma	7,100	7,100	7,100	2.91	2.90	2.93	13,200	13,175	13,300
Philippines	4,844	4,741	4,700	4.01	3.93	4.05	12,235	11,732	12,000
Japan	1,557	1,550	1,545	6.87	6.79	6.94	7,787	7,657	7,800
Pakistan	2,800	2,880	2,900	4.02	3.80	3.88	7,500	7,300	7,500
Brazil	1,973	1,700	1,680	6.12	6.18	6.25	8,204	7,140	7,140
United States	961	1,178	1,000	8.41	8.62	8.38	5,659	7,107	5,864
Cambodia	3,184	3,240	3,190	2.86	2.91	2.92	5,554	5,742	5,688
Nigeria	3,600	3,600	3,600	2.08	2.11	2.16	4,725	4,788	4,900
Egypt	762	462	760	8.18	8.78	8.20	4,300	2,800	4,300
Korea, South ..	755	738	730	7.02	6.99	6.84	3,972	3,868	3,744
Nepal	1,490	1,500	1,500	3.34	3.73	3.53	3,310	3,730	3,530
Sri Lanka	769	975	900	4.30	4.72	4.44	2,248	3,131	2,720
Madagascar ...	1,425	1,500	1,500	2.18	2.67	2.80	1,984	2,560	2,688
Peru	422	438	425	7.20	7.99	7.53	2,097	2,415	2,208
Laos	964	856	985	3.29	3.12	3.30	2,000	1,680	2,050
Tanzania	1,170	1,200	1,200	2.46	2.58	2.58	1,896	2,046	2,046

FAS, Office of Global Analysis, (202) 720-6301. Prepared or estimated on the basis of official USDA production, supply, and distribution, supply, and and distribution statistics from foreign governments.

Table 1-33.—Rice, milled equivalent: International trade, 2017/2018–2019/2020

Country	2017/2018	2018/2019	2019/2020
	1,000 metric tons		
Principle exporting countries:			
India	12,041	10,420	12,500
Thailand	11,056	7,562	9,800
Vietnam	6,590	6,581	6,500
Pakistan	4,011	4,500	4,000
China	1,364	2,770	2,858
United States	2,764	2,971	2,800
Burma	2,750	2,500	2,600
Cambodia	1,300	1,350	1,300
Uruguay	756	800	785
Brazil	1,152	830	650
Paraguay	653	689	650
Guyana	455	414	414
Argentina	426	370	330
European Union	349	302	300
Russia	139	153	150
South Africa	112	112	125
Kazakhstan	95	88	100
Cote d'Ivoire	80	100	100
Egypt	50	20	95
Guinea	80	100	90
Principle importing countries:			
Philippines	1,300	3,600	2,600
China	5,500	3,000	2,400
European Union	2,007	2,150	2,200
Nigeria	2,000	1,900	1,500
Saudi Arabia	1,290	1,425	1,450
Cote d'Ivoire	1,370	1,350	1,350
Iraq	1,130	1,200	1,200
Brazil	562	900	1,100
Iran	1,200	1,200	1,100
Senegal	1,100	1,100	1,050
South Africa	1,074	1,010	1,050
United States	874	920	1,032
Indonesia	2,350	600	1,000
Malaysia	800	1,000	1,000
Ghana	780	900	950
United Arab Emirates	775	850	925
Mexico	813	744	785
Nepal	670	630	750
Japan	686	631	685
Kenya	575	625	675

FAS, Office of Global Analysis, (202) 720-6301. Prepared or estimated on the basis of official USDA production, supply, and distribution statistics from foreign governments.

AGRICULTURAL STATISTICS 2021

I–21

Table 1-34.—Food grains: Average price, selected markets and grades, 2010–2019[1]

Calendar year[2]	Kansas City Wheat, No. 1 Hard Winter, Ordinary Protein (rail)	Kansas City Wheat, No. 1 Hard Winter, 13% protein (rail)	Kansas City Wheat, No. 2 Soft Red Winter (rail)	Minneapolis (rail) Wheat, No. 1 Hard Amber Durum (milling) (rail)	Minneapolis (rail) Wheat, No. 1 Dark Northern Spring (rail), 14% protein	Minneapolis (rail) Rye, No. 2, 20 day delivery (truck)	Portland Wheat No. 1 Soft White	St. Louis Wheat, No. 2 Soft Red Winter (truck)
				Dollars per bushel				
2010	5.90	6.58	6.03	8.75	7.79	4.58	5.45	5.36
2011	8.44	9.17	7.87	....	11.36	....	7.08	7.49
2012	8.47	8.96	7.25	....	9.69	....	7.74	7.56
2013	7.22	8.60	6.67	(NA)	8.08	(NA)	7.67	6.97
2014	7.89	7.95	5.72	(NA)	8.73	5.75	7.09	6.45
2015	6.05	6.16	4.43	(NA)	7.00	5.75	5.88	4.81
2016	4.80	5.50	3.35	(NA)	6.60	4.48	4.95	4.32
2017	5.03	6.25	3.98	(NA)	7.18	4.07	4.99	4.36
2018	6.22	6.67	6.19	(NA)	7.12	5.38	5.88	(NA)
2019	5.62	6.10	4.79	(NA)	6.56	7.12	5.91	5.14

Calendar year[2]	Chicago Wheat, No. 2 Soft Red Winter (rail)	Denver Wheat, No. 1 Hard Winter (truck red)	S.W. Louisiana Milled Rice Medium	S.W. Louisiana Milled Rice Long	Arkansas Milled Rice Medium	Arkansas Milled Rice Long	Texas Milled Rice Long
	Dollars per bushel		*Dollars per cwt*				
2010	5.36	5.00	30.80	23.12	29.68	23.91	26.46
2011	6.83	7.36	33.47	26.20	34.99	27.10	29.25
2012	7.44	7.44	28.89	25.77	27.91	26.18	27.18
2013	6.84	7.27	30.56	28.48	28.68	28.52	29.61
2014	5.89	6.38	30.76	27.04	31.30	27.62	29.15
2015	5.08	4.77	27.88	23.30	27.41	23.35	25.31
2016	4.31	3.35	27.39	22.65	22.92	23.01	23.92
2017	4.22	3.45	22.88	22.88	23.75	22.52	23.07
2018	4.88	4.52	29.43	22.54	27.41	27.41	26.37
2019	4.91	4.21	31.50	22.84	30.93	24.52	26.34

(NA) Not available. [1] Simple average of daily prices. [2] For wheat and rye, crop year begins in June. For rice, crop year begins in August.
AMS, Livestock and Grain Market News branch, (202) 720–6231.

Table 1-35.—Corn: Area, yield, production, and value, United States, 2011–2020

Year	Area planted, all purposes	Corn for grain Area harvested	Corn for grain Yield per harvested acre	Corn for grain Production	Corn for grain Marketing year average price per bushel	Corn for grain Value of production	Corn for silage Area harvested	Corn for silage Yield per harvested acre	Corn for silage Production
	1,000 acres	*1,000 acres*	*Bushels*	*1,000 bushels*	*Dollars*	*1,000 dollars*	*1,000 acres*	*Tons*	*1,000 tons*
2011	91,936	83,879	146.8	12,313,956	6.22	76,651,242	5,935	18.4	109,091
2012	97,291	87,365	123.1	10,755,111	6.89	74,155,299	7,419	15.7	116,148
2013	95,365	87,451	158.1	13,828,964	4.46	61,927,548	6,281	18.8	118,296
2014	90,597	83,136	171.0	14,215,532	3.70	52,951,760	6,371	20.1	128,048
2015	88,019	80,753	168.4	13,601,964	3.61	49,339,261	6,237	20.4	127,311
2016	94,004	86,748	174.6	15,148,038	3.36	51,304,297	6,206	20.3	126,020
2017	90,167	82,733	176.6	14,609,407	3.36	49,567,854	6,385	20.0	127,434
2018	88,871	81,276	176.4	14,340,369	3.61	52,102,404	6,120	19.9	121,564
2019	89,745	81,337	167.5	13,619,928	3.56	48,940,622	6,615	20.2	133,522
2020	90,652	82,313	171.4	14,111,449	4.53	64,313,524	6,711	20.5	137,675

NASS, Crops Branch, (202) 720–2127.

GRAIN AND FEED

Table 1-36.—Corn: Area, yield, and production, by State and United States, 2018–2020

State	Area planted for all purposes			Area harvested for grain		
	2018	2019	2020	2018	2019	2020
	1,000 acres					
Alabama	255	320	330	245	305	320
Arizona	80	90	75	20	37	29
Arkansas	660	770	620	645	735	605
California	430	480	440	65	60	60
Colorado	1,460	1,550	1,420	1,190	1,300	1,060
Connecticut	23	23	24	(NA)	(NA)	(NA)
Delaware	170	185	180	166	180	176
Florida	95	95	100	62	54	61
Georgia	325	395	420	285	350	390
Idaho	350	390	390	125	150	130
Illinois	11,000	10,500	11,300	10,800	10,200	11,100
Indiana	5,300	5,000	5,400	5,120	4,820	5,250
Iowa	13,200	13,500	13,600	12,750	13,050	12,900
Kansas	5,450	6,400	6,100	4,980	6,020	5,720
Kentucky	1,330	1,550	1,470	1,220	1,450	1,360
Louisiana	460	570	500	450	545	485
Maine	30	29	30	(NA)	(NA)	(NA)
Maryland	440	510	480	380	460	430
Massachusetts	14	14	14	(NA)	(NA)	(NA)
Michigan	2,250	2,000	2,350	1,890	1,610	1,990
Minnesota	7,900	7,800	8,000	7,460	7,250	7,510
Mississippi	480	660	510	460	620	490
Missouri	3,500	3,200	3,450	3,330	2,990	3,280
Montana	115	115	115	68	60	61
Nebraska	9,600	10,100	10,200	9,300	9,810	9,890
Nevada	13	15	13	(NA)	(NA)	(NA)
New Hampshire	13	12	13	(NA)	(NA)	(NA)
New Jersey	70	77	80	60	68	73
New Mexico	135	150	125	35	48	37
New York	1,070	1,020	1,030	615	545	500
North Carolina	910	990	990	830	930	940
North Dakota	3,150	3,500	1,950	2,930	3,130	1,780
Ohio	3,500	2,800	3,550	3,300	2,570	3,300
Oklahoma	310	370	360	270	330	320
Oregon	75	85	100	40	49	65
Pennsylvania	1,300	1,450	1,500	890	1,060	1,000
Rhode Island	2	2	2	(NA)	(NA)	(NA)
South Carolina	340	380	390	310	350	370
South Dakota	5,300	4,350	4,900	4,860	3,870	4,450
Tennessee	720	970	860	670	910	815
Texas	2,200	2,500	2,250	1,750	2,150	1,810
Utah	70	85	85	22	26	29
Vermont	85	81	85	(NA)	(NA)	(NA)
Virginia	485	540	560	325	380	420
Washington	165	175	195	85	90	85
West Virginia	46	52	51	33	38	38
Wisconsin	3,900	3,800	3,950	3,170	2,670	2,930
Wyoming	95	95	95	70	67	54
United States	88,871	89,745	90,652	81,276	81,337	82,313

See footnote(s) at end of table.

Table 1-36.—Corn: Area, yield, and production, by State and United States, 2018–2020—Continued

State	Corn for grain					
	Yield per harvested acre			Production		
	2018	2019	2020	2018	2019	2020
	1,000 acres					
Alabama	156.0	147.0	158.0	38,220	44,835	50,560
Arizona	220.0	231.0	202.0	4,400	8,547	5,858
Arkansas	181.0	175.0	184.0	116,745	128,625	111,320
California	173.0	168.0	187.0	11,245	10,080	11,220
Colorado	130.0	123.0	116.0	154,700	159,900	122,960
Connecticut	(NA)	(NA)	(NA)	(NA)	(NA)	(NA)
Delaware	145.0	161.0	160.0	24,070	28,980	28,160
Florida	157.0	161.0	138.0	9,734	8,694	8,418
Georgia	176.0	160.0	180.0	50,160	56,000	70,200
Idaho	213.0	205.0	199.0	26,625	30,750	25,870
Illinois	210.0	181.0	191.0	2,268,000	1,846,200	2,120,100
Indiana	189.0	169.0	187.0	967,680	814,580	981,750
Iowa	196.0	198.0	177.0	2,499,000	2,583,900	2,283,300
Kansas	129.0	133.0	134.0	642,420	800,660	766,480
Kentucky	175.0	169.0	184.0	213,500	245,050	250,240
Louisiana	173.0	165.0	181.0	77,850	89,925	87,785
Maine	(NA)	(NA)	(NA)	(NA)	(NA)	(NA)
Maryland	146.0	161.0	155.0	55,480	74,060	66,650
Massachusetts	(NA)	(NA)	(NA)	(NA)	(NA)	(NA)
Michigan	153.0	147.0	153.0	289,170	236,670	304,470
Minnesota	182.0	173.0	191.0	1,357,720	1,254,250	1,434,410
Mississippi	185.0	174.0	180.0	85,100	107,880	88,200
Missouri	140.0	155.0	171.0	466,200	463,450	560,880
Montana	85.0	95.0	109.0	5,780	5,700	6,649
Nebraska	192.0	182.0	180.0	1,785,600	1,785,420	1,780,200
Nevada	(NA)	(NA)	(NA)	(NA)	(NA)	(NA)
New Hampshire	(NA)	(NA)	(NA)	(NA)	(NA)	(NA)
New Jersey	141.0	155.0	156.0	8,460	10,540	11,388
New Mexico	187.0	135.0	195.0	6,545	6,480	7,215
New York	159.0	158.0	157.0	97,785	86,110	78,500
North Carolina	113.0	111.0	113.0	93,790	103,230	106,220
North Dakota	153.0	131.0	139.0	448,290	410,030	247,420
Ohio	187.0	164.0	171.0	617,100	421,480	564,300
Oklahoma	134.0	137.0	135.0	36,180	45,210	43,200
Oregon	195.0	237.0	241.0	7,800	11,613	15,665
Pennsylvania	140.0	153.0	138.0	124,600	162,180	138,000
Rhode Island	(NA)	(NA)	(NA)	(NA)	(NA)	(NA)
South Carolina	127.0	106.0	132.0	39,370	37,100	48,840
South Dakota	160.0	144.0	162.0	777,600	557,280	720,900
Tennessee	168.0	177.0	170.0	112,560	161,070	138,550
Texas	108.0	133.0	128.0	189,000	285,950	231,680
Utah	182.0	143.0	149.0	4,004	3,718	4,321
Vermont	(NA)	(NA)	(NA)	(NA)	(NA)	(NA)
Virginia	146.0	144.0	122.0	47,450	54,720	51,240
Washington	220.0	237.0	228.0	18,700	21,330	19,380
West Virginia	152.0	165.0	144.0	5,016	6,270	5,472
Wisconsin	172.0	166.0	173.0	545,240	443,220	506,890
Wyoming	164.0	123.0	122.0	11,480	8,241	6,588
United States	176.4	167.5	171.4	14,340,369	13,619,928	14,111,449

(NA) Not available.
NASS, Crops Branch, (202) 720–2127.

GRAIN AND FEED

Table 1-37.—Corn: Supply and disappearance, United States, 2011–2020

Year beginning September 1	Supply				Disappearance					Ending stocks Aug. 31
	Beginning stocks	Production	Imports	Total[1]	Domestic use			Exports	Total disappearance	
					Feed and residual	Food, seed, and industrial	Total			
					Million bushels					
2011	1,128	12,314	29	13,471	4,519	6,424	10,943	1,539	12,482	989
2012	989	10,755	160	11,904	4,315	6,038	10,353	730	11,083	821
2013	821	13,831	36	14,686	5,040	6,493	11,534	1,920	13,454	1,232
2014	1,232	14,217	32	15,481	5,287	6,595	11,883	1,867	13,750	1,731
2015	1,731	13,602	68	15,401	5,118	6,647	11,765	1,899	13,664	1,737
2016	1,737	15,148	57	16,942	5,468	6,885	12,353	2,296	14,649	2,293
2017	2,293	14,609	36	16,938	5,304	7,057	12,361	2,438	14,798	2,140
2018	2,140	14,340	28	16,508	5,429	6,793	12,222	2,066	14,288	2,221
2019	2,221	13,620	42	15,883	5,903	6,282	12,185	1,778	13,963	1,919
2020	1,919	14,111	24	16,054	4,777	6,426	11,202	1,831	13,033	1,235

Latest data may be preliminary or projected. [1] Total may not add due to rounding.
ERS, Market and Trade Economics Division, (202) 694–5313. Source: USDA, World Agricultural Outlook Board, World Agricultural Supply and Demand Estimates and supporting materials.

Table 1-38.—Corn: Stocks on and off farms, United States, 2011–2020

Year beginning previous December	On farms				Off farms[1]			
	Dec. 1	Mar. 1	Jun. 1	Sep. 1[2]	Dec. 1	Mar. 1	Jun. 1	Sep. 1[2]
	1,000 bushels							
2011	6,302,000	3,384,000	1,681,500	314,950	3,754,769	3,139,228	1,988,832	812,695
2012	6,175,000	3,192,000	1,482,000	313,700	3,471,823	2,831,356	1,666,204	675,327
2013	4,586,000	2,669,200	1,260,100	275,000	3,446,732	2,730,726	1,506,144	546,185
2014	6,380,000	3,860,500	1,863,200	462,000	4,072,532	3,147,623	1,988,516	769,904
2015	7,087,000	4,380,000	2,275,000	593,000	4,124,380	3,369,806	2,177,988	1,138,164
2016	6,829,000	4,335,000	2,471,400	627,400	4,406,178	3,487,233	2,239,679	1,109,658
2017	7,611,000	4,908,000	2,841,400	787,000	4,772,471	3,713,992	2,387,682	1,506,303
2018	7,451,000	5,002,000	2,750,100	620,000	4,485,798	3,890,126	2,554,704	1,520,335
2019	7,103,000	5,131,000	2,949,600	814,100	4,224,338	3,482,206	2,252,636	1,406,649
2020	7,046,000	4,454,000	2,867,000	750,800	4,247,750	3,497,576	2,135,987	1,168,662

[1] Includes stocks at mills, elevators, warehouses, terminals, and processors.   [2] Old crop only.
NASS, Crops Branch, (202) 720–2127.

Table 1-39.—Corn: Utilization for silage, by State and United States, 2018–2020

State	Silage								
	Area harvested			Yield per acre			Production		
	2018	2019	2020	2018	2019	2020	2018	2019	2020
	1,000 acres	*1,000 acres*	*1,000 acres*	*Tons*	*Tons*	*Tons*	*1,000 tons*	*1,000 tons*	*1,000 tons*
Alabama	5	7	5	16.0	13.0	16.0	80	91	80
Arizona	58	50	45	29.0	29.0	29.0	1,682	1,450	1,305
Arkansas	3	7	6	21.0	16.0	15.0	63	112	90
California	360	415	375	27.5	27.0	27.0	9,900	11,205	10,125
Colorado	190	175	230	22.0	24.0	23.0	4,180	4,200	5,290
Connecticut	20	21	22	19.0	21.0	16.0	380	441	352
Delaware	3	4	4	24.0	23.0	19.0	72	92	76
Florida	30	35	35	21.0	20.0	19.0	630	700	665
Georgia	30	25	25	21.0	22.0	18.0	630	550	450
Idaho	220	235	260	30.0	28.0	29.0	6,600	6,580	7,540
Illinois	100	170	110	20.0	20.0	20.0	2,000	3,400	2,200
Indiana	100	110	130	21.0	20.0	21.0	2,100	2,200	2,730
Iowa	270	360	260	20.5	22.0	20.5	5,535	7,920	5,330
Kansas	390	250	250	13.5	17.5	19.5	5,265	4,375	4,875
Kentucky	90	80	95	21.0	21.0	20.0	1,890	1,680	1,900
Louisiana	2	3	3	20.0	19.0	17.0	40	57	51
Maine	27	26	27	20.0	19.0	19.0	540	494	513
Maryland	45	40	40	19.0	22.0	17.0	855	880	680
Massachusetts ...	12	11	12	20.0	20.0	16.0	240	220	192
Michigan	340	340	350	17.5	18.5	17.5	5,950	6,290	6,125
Minnesota	340	460	420	22.0	19.0	23.0	7,480	8,740	9,660
Mississippi	7	7	7	15.0	15.0	14.0	105	105	98
Missouri	100	70	100	13.0	16.0	17.0	1,300	1,120	1,700
Montana	37	50	51	20.0	23.0	21.0	740	1,150	1,071
Nebraska	220	200	260	21.0	23.0	19.0	4,620	4,600	4,940
Nevada	7	12	13	26.0	25.0	26.0	182	300	338
New Hampshire ..	12	11	12	21.0	20.0	20.0	252	220	240
New Jersey	6	7	6	19.0	22.0	20.0	114	154	120
New Mexico	95	93	79	22.0	20.0	21.0	2,090	1,860	1,659
New York	445	445	520	19.0	18.0	18.0	8,455	8,010	9,360
North Carolina	50	50	40	16.0	18.0	14.0	800	900	560
North Dakota	170	140	145	15.0	19.5	15.5	2,550	2,730	2,248
Ohio	160	170	200	20.0	19.0	21.0	3,200	3,230	4,200
Oklahoma	20	20	20	11.0	13.0	14.0	220	260	280
Oregon	34	35	34	23.0	24.0	23.0	782	840	782
Pennsylvania	390	380	485	19.0	20.0	19.0	7,410	7,600	9,215
Rhode Island	2	2	2	21.0	20.0	13.0	42	40	26
South Carolina ...	19	13	9	14.0	14.0	15.0	266	182	135
South Dakota	360	340	360	16.5	17.5	18.0	5,940	5,950	6,480
Tennessee	38	40	35	19.0	20.0	18.0	722	800	630
Texas	270	280	270	16.0	20.0	18.0	4,320	5,600	4,860
Utah	45	55	52	23.0	24.0	23.0	1,035	1,320	1,196
Vermont	79	77	80	19.0	18.0	19.0	1,501	1,386	1,520
Virginia	135	135	120	19.0	19.0	17.0	2,565	2,565	2,040
Washington	80	85	110	26.0	23.0	26.0	2,080	1,955	2,860
West Virginia	11	12	12	19.0	20.0	19.0	209	240	228
Wisconsin	670	1,040	960	20.0	17.5	21.0	13,400	18,200	20,160
Wyoming	23	22	25	24.0	24.0	20.0	552	528	500
United States	6,120	6,615	6,711	19.9	20.2	20.5	121,564	133,522	137,675

NASS, Crops Branch, (202) 720–2127.

Table 1-40.—Corn for grain: Marketing year average price and value, by State and United States, 2018–2020

State	Marketing year average price per bushel			Value of production		
	2018	2019	2020 [1]	2018	2019	2020 [1]
	Dollars	Dollars	Dollars	1,000 dollars	1,000 dollars	1,000 dollars
Alabama	4.11	3.99	5.14	157,084	178,892	259,878
Arizona	4.96	5.40	5.40	21,824	46,154	31,633
Arkansas	3.80	3.86	4.49	443,631	496,493	499,827
California	4.40	4.60	4.75	49,478	46,368	53,295
Colorado	3.70	3.68	4.62	572,390	588,432	568,075
Delaware	4.11	4.30	5.60	98,928	124,614	157,696
Florida	4.47	4.39	5.67	43,511	38,167	47,730
Georgia	4.35	4.53	5.08	218,196	253,680	356,616
Idaho	4.42	4.47	4.80	117,683	137,453	124,176
Illinois	3.62	3.55	4.46	8,210,160	6,554,010	9,455,646
Indiana	3.78	3.84	4.65	3,657,830	3,127,987	4,565,138
Iowa	3.59	3.50	4.64	8,971,410	9,043,650	10,594,512
Kansas	3.58	3.56	4.35	2,299,864	2,850,350	3,334,188
Kentucky	3.84	3.92	4.52	819,840	960,596	1,131,085
Louisiana	3.86	3.86	3.74	300,501	347,111	328,316
Maryland	4.11	4.30	5.60	228,023	318,458	373,240
Michigan	3.72	3.73	4.72	1,075,712	882,779	1,437,098
Minnesota	3.47	3.26	4.52	4,711,288	4,088,855	6,483,533
Mississippi	3.80	3.86	4.03	323,380	416,417	355,446
Missouri	3.68	3.67	4.59	1,715,616	1,700,862	2,574,439
Montana	3.79	3.70	4.40	21,906	21,090	29,256
Nebraska	3.58	3.52	4.47	6,392,448	6,284,678	7,957,494
New Jersey	3.90	4.30	5.70	32,994	45,322	64,912
New Mexico	4.30	4.40	4.70	28,144	28,512	33,911
New York	4.16	4.20	6.10	406,786	361,662	478,850
North Carolina	4.39	4.41	4.70	411,738	455,244	499,234
North Dakota	3.32	3.07	4.44	1,488,323	1,258,792	1,098,545
Ohio	3.74	3.91	4.69	2,307,954	1,647,987	2,646,567
Oklahoma	3.86	4.00	4.35	139,655	180,840	187,920
Oregon	4.13	4.34	5.45	32,214	50,400	85,374
Pennsylvania	4.22	4.13	5.51	525,812	669,803	760,380
South Carolina	4.50	4.64	4.36	177,165	172,144	212,942
South Dakota	3.38	3.32	4.37	2,628,288	1,850,170	3,150,333
Tennessee	3.76	3.78	4.70	423,226	608,845	651,185
Texas	4.13	4.20	4.52	780,570	1,200,990	1,047,194
Utah	4.31	4.30	5.35	17,257	15,987	23,117
Virginia	4.06	4.10	5.10	192,647	224,352	261,324
Washington	4.11	4.13	4.70	76,857	88,093	91,086
West Virginia	4.08	4.10	4.70	20,465	25,707	25,718
Wisconsin	3.52	3.43	4.44	1,919,245	1,520,245	2,250,592
Wyoming	3.69	3.45	3.95	42,361	28,431	26,023
United States	3.61	3.56	4.53	52,102,404	48,940,622	64,313,524

[1] Preliminary.
NASS, Crops Branch, (202) 720–2127.

Table 1-41.—International Corn: Area, yield, and production in specified countries, 2017/2018–2019/2020

Country	Area			Yield per hectare			Production		
	2017/ 2018	2018/ 2019	2019/ 2020	2017/ 2018	2018/ 2019	2016/ 2017	2017/ 2018	2018/ 2019	2019/ 2020
	1,000 hectares			Metric tons			1,000 metric tons		
United States	33,481	32,891	32,975	11.08	11.08	10.55	371,096	364,262	347,782
China	42,399	42,129	41,280	6.11	6.11	6.32	259,071	257,330	260,770
Brazil	16,600	17,500	18,100	4.94	5.77	5.58	82,000	101,000	101,000
European Union	8,258	8,241	8,700	7.51	7.82	7.47	62,007	64,440	65,000
Argentina	5,200	6,100	6,200	6.15	8.36	8.07	32,000	51,000	50,000
Ukraine	4,433	4,567	5,000	5.44	7.84	7.16	24,115	35,805	35,800
India	9,380	9,275	9,300	3.07	2.99	3.07	28,753	27,715	28,500
Mexico	7,322	7,200	6,800	3.77	3.83	3.68	27,569	27,600	25,000
South Africa	2,634	2,597	3,000	4.98	4.55	5.33	13,104	11,824	16,000
Russia	2,694	2,373	2,504	4.90	4.81	5.70	13,201	11,415	14,275
Canada	1,406	1,431	1,450	10.03	9.70	9.24	14,095	13,885	13,400
Indonesia	3,650	3,700	3,900	3.26	3.24	3.26	11,900	12,000	12,700
Nigeria	6,540	6,500	6,500	1.59	1.69	1.69	10,420	11,000	11,000
Ethiopia	2,230	2,300	2,300	3.77	3.63	3.65	8,400	8,350	8,400
Philippines	2,604	2,480	2,550	3.11	3.07	3.18	8,084	7,608	8,100
Serbia	1,000	900	950	4.00	7.78	7.11	4,000	7,000	6,750
Egypt	800	850	800	8.00	8.00	8.00	6,400	6,800	6,400
Tanzania	4,200	4,200	4,200	1.59	1.49	1.48	6,681	6,273	6,200
Pakistan	1,230	1,320	1,330	4.64	4.62	4.59	5,701	6,100	6,100
Turkey	530	530	520	10.00	10.76	11.54	5,300	5,700	6,000

FAS, Office of Global Analysis, (202) 720-6301. Prepared or estimated on the basis of offical USDA production, supply, and distribution statistics from foreign governments.

Table 1-42.—Corn: International trade, 2017/2018–2019/2020

Country	2017/2018	2018/2019	2019/2020
	Metric tons		
Principle exporting countries:			
United States	61,916	52,457	43,817
Argentina	24,154	39,749	36,000
Brazil	22,473	37,000	33,500
Ukraine	18,036	30,321	32,000
Russia	5,532	2,770	4,700
Serbia	1,749	3,629	2,900
European Union	2,069	1,170	2,500
Paraguay	819	2,836	2,200
Canada	1,739	2,800	2,000
Burma	1,400	1,500	1,400
South Africa	1,936	1,797	900
Mexico	958	718	700
Cambodia	500	500	500
India	500	500	500
Moldova	1,089	419	400
Vietnam	460	581	400
Laos	200	200	200
Zambia	50	100	200
Indonesia	1,200	600	100
Thailand	400	100	100
Principle importing countries:			
European Union	18,465	25,209	21,000
Mexico	16,129	16,658	17,500
Japan	15,668	16,047	16,000
Vietnam	8,600	10,200	11,500
Korea, South	10,018	10,856	10,800
Iran	8,900	9,000	10,000
Egypt	9,464	9,367	9,900
China	3,456	4,483	7,000
Colombia	5,201	6,048	6,200
Algeria	4,184	4,521	4,500
Taiwan	4,410	4,508	4,300
Malaysia	3,645	3,674	4,000
Peru	3,402	3,694	4,000
Saudi Arabia	3,983	3,662	4,000
Morocco	2,558	2,341	3,000
Turkey	2,719	2,876	3,000
Chile	2,132	2,300	2,600
Israel	1,861	1,611	2,000
Canada	1,669	2,633	1,500
Dominican Republic	1,329	1,536	1,500

FAS, Office of Global Analysis, (202) 720-6301. Prepared or estimated on the basis of official USDA production, supply, and distribution statistics from foreign governments.

Table 1-43.—Corn: Support operations, United States, 2014–2020

Marketing year beginning September 1	Income support payment rates per bushel [1]	Program price levels per bushel		Put under loan		Acquired by CCC under loan program [3]	Owned by CCC at end of marketing year
		Loan	Reference	Quantity	Percentage of production [2]		
	Dollars	*Dollars*	*Dollars*	*Million bushels*	*Percent*	*Million bushels*	*Million bushels*
2014/2015	0.00	1.95	3.70	574	4.0	0	0
2015/2016	0.09	1.95	3.70	746	5.5	0	0
2016/2017	0.34	1.95	3.70	880	5.8	0	0
2017/2018	0.34	1.95	3.70	980	6.7	0	0
2018/2019	0.09	1.95	3.70	919	6.4	0	0
2019/2020	0.14	2.20	3.70	805	5.9	0	0
2020/2021 [4]	0.00	2020	2.63	460	3.3	0	0

[1] The entry is the price loss coverage (PLC) payment rate. For 2017/2018, projected PLC payment rate is based on March 2018 WASDE MY price. Agricultural Risk Coverage (ARC) is also available, but payment rates are established at the county or farm levels. [2] Percent of production is on a grain basis. [3] Acquisitions as of March 9, 2021. [4] Payment rate as of the February 26, 2021 NASS Agricultural Prices Report.
FPAC, (202) 690-0734.

Table 1-44.—Corn: United States exports, specified by country of destination, 2018–2020 [1]

Country of destination	2018	2019	2020
	Metric tons		
Mexico	16,698,898	14,488,584	14,573,004
Japan	15,266,691	10,553,055	10,327,415
China	290,173	312,473	6,933,312
Colombia	5,511,589	3,910,261	5,075,001
Korea, South	7,263,478	1,881,867	2,986,068
Canada	1,971,929	2,106,797	1,729,313
Guatemala	1,149,313	1,001,003	1,261,157
Taiwan	3,208,973	1,187,301	907,986
Costa Rica	850,465	835,592	869,188
Saudi Arabia	1,724,045	623,485	846,051
Peru	3,046,412	1,018,891	711,932
Honduras	617,583	674,365	711,554
Venezuela	509,994	34,898	560,146
El Salvador	601,587	584,865	550,118
Dominican Republic	939,054	368,859	537,935
Panama	507,012	503,289	494,438
Israel(*)	814,810	84,791	488,428
Nicaragua	338,400	287,332	388,426
Jamaica	277,224	260,366	271,324
Vietnam	1,908,658	65,266	221,560
Tunisia	452,874	0	175,615
Chile	21,325	7,555	153,727
Morocco	820,957	61,752	129,516
Trinidad and Tobago	91,781	80,079	91,698
Philippines	166,346	78,805	89,936
Algeria	47,627	0	63,163
Egypt	1,865,135	0	48,551
Guyana	44,549	41,076	46,405
Hong Kong	34,105	34,322	37,408
New Zealand(*)	46,531	125,596	36,599
Rest of World	2,633,034	236,893	311,913
World Total	69,720,552	41,449,418	51,628,887

[1] Data Source: U.S. Census Bureau trade data. Excludes seed, popcorn.
FAS, Office of Global Analysis, (202) 720-6301.

Table 1-45.—Oats: Area, yield, production, and value, United States, 2011–2020

Year	Area		Yield per harvested acre	Production	Marketing year average price per bushel received by farmers	Value of production
	Planted [1]	Harvested				
	1,000 acres	*1,000 acres*	*Bushels*	*1,000 bushels*	*Dollars*	*1,000 dollars*
2011	2,349	875	57.3	50,126	3.49	175,523
2012	2,700	1,005	61.2	61,486	3.89	243,018
2013	2,980	1,009	64.1	64,642	3.75	239,643
2014	2,753	1,035	67.9	70,232	3.21	241,472
2015	3,088	1,275	70.2	89,455	2.12	214,415
2016	2,829	979	66.0	64,628	2.06	153,824
2017	2,589	804	61.7	49,585	2.59	139,635
2018	2,746	865	64.9	56,130	2.66	167,640
2019	2.830	828	64.3	53,258	2.82	164,373
2020	3,009	1,009	65.1	65,594	2.77	196,245

[1] Relates to the total area of oats sown for all purposes, including oats sown in the preceding fall.
NASS, Crops Branch, (202) 720–2127.

Table 1-46.—Oats: Stocks on and off farms, United States, 2011–2020

Year beginning September	On farms				Off farms [1]			
	Sep. 1	Dec. 1	Mar. 1	Jun. 1	Sep. 1	Dec. 1	Mar. 1	Jun. 1
2011	30,300	24,600	19,550	11,070	47,391	54,244	55,044	43,869
2012	34,100	26,100	18,900	11,380	50,872	47,051	33,726	24,957
2013	37,150	25,650	19,800	9,710	26,339	22,394	15,323	15,029
2014	41,400	31,300	20,810	15,120	32,910	35,670	38,609	38,625
2015	47,800	36,750	26,800	18,350	46,066	45,981	48,429	38,452
2016	37,400	30,430	22,320	13,540	41,190	45,058	40,885	36,790
2017	33,950	23,300	17,240	11,410	38,039	43,166	37,699	29,606
2018	39,200	25,410	18,050	10,500	35,573	41,864	32,232	27,314
2019	37,900	24,770	16,970	10,070	22,153	29,139	30,722	26,693
2020	39,850	28,830	16,880	12,540	27,017	33,712	34,585	25,513

[1] Includes stocks at mills, elevators, warehouses, terminals, and processors.
NASS, Crops Branch, (202) 720–2127.

Table 1-47.—Oats: Supply and disappearance, United States, 2010–2019

Year beginning June 1	Supply				Disappearance					Ending stocks May 31 [1]
	Beginning stocks	Production	Imports	Total	Domestic use			Exports	Total disappearance	
					Feed and residual	Food, seed, and industrial	Total			
					Million bushels					
2010	80	82	85	247	103	74	177	3	180	68
2011	68	50	94	212	78	76	154	2	157	55
2012	55	61	93	209	96	76	172	1	173	36
2013	36	65	97	198	98	73	172	2	173	25
2014	25	70	109	204	71	77	148	2	150	54
2015	54	89	86	229	93	76	170	2	172	57
2016	57	65	90	212	82	76	158	3	161	50
2017	50	50	89	189	68	77	146	2	148	41
2018	41	56	86	184	66	78	144	2	146	38
2019	48	53	92	183	63	81	144	2	146	37

[1] Privately held: Includes quantity under loan and farmer-owned reserve.
Latest data may be preliminary or projected. Totals may not add due to rounding.
ERS, Market and Trade Economics Division, (202) 694–5313. Source: USDA, World Agricultural Outlook Board, World Agricultural Supply and Demand Estimates and supporting materials.

Table 1-49.—Oats: Support operations, United States, 2014–2020

Marketing Year beginning June 1	Income support payment rates per bushel [1]	Program price levels per bushel		Put under loan		Acquired by CCC under loan program [3]	Owned by CCC at end of marketing year
		Loan	Target/reference	Quantity	Percentage of production [2]		
	Dollars	*Dollars*	*Dollars*	*Million bushels*	*Percent*	*Million bushels*	*Million bushels*
2014/2015	0.00	1.39	2.40	0.5	0.7	0	0
2015/2016	0.28	1.39	2.40	1.1	1.3	0	0
2016/2017	0.34	1.39	2.40	0.8	1.2	0	0
2017/2018	0.00	1.39	2.40	0.4	0.8	0	0
2018/2019	0.00	1.39	2.40	0.4	0.7	0	0
2019/2020	0.00	2.00	2.40	1.1	2.1	0	0
2020/2021 [4]	0.00	1.39	1.79	0.3	0.5	0	0

[1] The entry is the price loss coverage (PLC) payment rate. Agricultural Risk Coverage (ARC) is also available, but payment rates are established at the county or farm levels. [2] Percent of production is on a grain basis. [3] Acquisitions as of March 9, 2021. [4] Payment rate as of the February 26, 2021 NASS Agricultural Prices Report.
FPAC, (202) 690-0734.

Table 1-50.—Oats: Marketing year average price and value of production, by State and United States, 2018–2020

State	Marketing year average price per bushel			Value of production		
	2018	2019	2020 [1]	2018	2019	2020 [1]
	Dollars	*Dollars*	*Dollars*	*1,000 dollars*	*1,000 dollars*	*1,000 dollars*
Alabama	4.50	(NA)	(NA)	4,253	(NA)	(NA)
Arkansas	2.75	2.80	3.00	1,444	588	960
California	(D)	(D)	3.00	(D)	(D)	900
Colorado	3.66	(NA)	(NA)	1,281	(NA)	(NA)
Georgia	4.15	4.10	4.35	4,420	3,383	4,698
Idaho	2.80	3.27	3.15	2,352	3,610	5,141
Illinois	3.12	4.10	4.35	6,474	2,665	3,785
Iowa	2.93	3.53	3.19	6,091	14,127	18,164
Kansas	3.32	3.40	3.05	2,928	3,917	2,538
Maine	2.80	2.95	3.00	3,564	4,260	4,158
Michigan	3.31	3.63	3.16	10,427	5,173	5,214
Minnesota	2.49	2.63	2.56	15,426	16,306	27,034
Missouri	3.00	3.90	4.15	2,160	1,100	1,785
Montana	2.71	3.14	3.12	2,680	4,490	5,756
Nebraska	2.85	3.09	2.85	4,326	3,504	5,207
New York	2.92	3.61	4.08	6,780	8,447	6,920
North Carolina	3.10	3.10	3.05	2,251	1,541	2,452
North Dakota	2.41	2.47	2.54	20,750	24,428	20,803
Ohio	3.76	3.75	3.96	7,332	4,313	3,564
Oklahoma	2.75	2.10	3.55	1,320	2,625	1,757
Oregon	(D)	(D)	2.62	(D)	(D)	1,834
Pennsylvania	4.02	4.18	4.04	6,472	11,077	11,110
South Carolina	3.95	(NA)	(NA)	1,714	(NA)	(NA)
South Dakota	2.67	2.81	2.66	20,799	17,282	28,675
Texas	4.82	4.26	4.17	12,050	8,520	11,259
Washington	2.18	(NA)	(NA)	401	(NA)	(NA)
Wisconsin	2.77	3.13	2.73	15,207	20,282	22,531
Wyoming	3.60	(NA)	(NA)	1,847	(NA)	(NA)
Other States	3.16	2.75	(X)	2,891	2,735	-
United States	2.66	2.82	2.77	167,640	164,373	196,245

(D) Withheld to avoid disclosing data for individual. (NA) Not available. (X) Not applicable. [1] Final.
NASS, Crops Branch, (202) 720–2127.

Table 1-51.—International Oats: Area, yield, and production in specified countries, 2017/2018–2019/2020

Country	Area			Yield per hectare			Production		
	2017/ 2018	2018/ 2019	2019/ 2020	2017/ 2018	2018/ 2019	2019/ 2020	2017/ 2018	2018/ 2019	2019/ 2020
	1,000 hectares			Metric tons			1,000 metric tons		
European Union	2,666	2,711	2,552	3.02	2.85	3.10	8,058	7,715	7,920
Russia	2,780	2,725	2,429	1.96	1.73	1.82	5,448	4,715	4,420
Canada	1,052	1,005	1,160	3.55	3.42	3.59	3,733	3,436	4,160
Australia	874	680	675	1.40	1.31	1.39	1,227	888	935
Brazil	340	376	381	1.87	2.11	2.17	634	795	825
United States	325	350	334	2.22	2.33	2.31	720	815	771
China	475	500	525	1.16	1.15	1.19	550	575	625
Belarus	150	151	150	3.33	2.27	3.00	500	342	450
Chile	108	75	80	5.31	5.13	5.50	573	385	440
Ukraine	208	198	180	2.31	2.14	2.39	481	423	430
Argentina	220	238	143	2.24	2.40	2.31	492	572	330
Norway	68	69	70	4.16	2.09	4.29	283	144	300
Kazakhstan	213	235	243	1.34	1.43	1.10	285	336	267
Turkey	113	100	100	2.21	2.30	2.30	250	230	230
Algeria	85	85	85	1.29	1.29	1.29	110	110	110
Mexico	44	50	50	1.64	2.06	1.80	72	103	90
Serbia	30	30	30	2.17	2.17	2.17	65	65	65
Bosnia and Herzegovina	11	14	14	2.73	2.79	3.00	30	39	42
Morocco	30	45	45	1.17	1.40	0.89	35	63	40
South Africa	15	20	25	1.53	1.65	1.60	23	33	40
New Zealand	6	5	6	5.83	5.00	5.50	35	25	33
Albania	15	13	14	2.27	2.08	2.14	34	27	30
Uruguay	19	26	14	1.68	2.04	1.86	32	53	26

FAS, Office of Global Analysis, (202) 720-6301. Prepared or estimated on the basis of official USDA production, supply, and distribution, supply, and and distribution statistics from foreign governments.

Table 1-52. Oats: International trade, 2017/2018–2019/2020

Country	2017/2018	2018/2019	2019/2020
	1,000 metric tons		
Principle exporting countries:			
Canada	1,631	1,734	1,800
Australia	550	240	250
European Union	186	106	125
Russia	28	122	110
Chile	38	38	40
United States	35	25	29
Kazakhstan	10	29	20
Ukraine	9	8	10
Argentina	0	0	5
Brazil	4	6	5
Serbia	1	1	2
Principle importing countries:			
United States	1,537	1,493	1,637
China	389	224	200
Mexico	129	151	100
Japan	44	46	50
Switzerland	51	54	50
South Africa	39	23	40
Ecuador	41	30	30
Norway	16	92	30
Korea, South	46	31	25
Algeria	7	1	20
India	19	21	20
Belarus	2	26	10
Canada	14	11	10
Bosnia and Herzegovina	6	3	5
Colombia	1	5	5
European Union	4	14	5
Turkey	0	0	5
Uruguay	6	5	5
Serbia	1	1	3
Morocco	2	2	2
Ukraine	0	3	1
Kazakhstan	0	1	0

FAS, Office of Global Analysis, (202) 720-6301. Prepared or estimated on the basis of official USDA production, supply, and distribution statistics from foreign governments.

GRAIN AND FEED

Table 1-53.—Barley: Area, yield, production, and value, United States, 2011–2020

Year	Area		Yield per harvested acre	Production	Marketing year average price per bushel received by farmers	Value of production
	Planted [1]	Harvested				
	1,000 acres	1,000 acres	Bushels	1,000 bushels	Dollars	1,000 dollars
2011	2,564	2,241	69.1	154,788	5.35	808,741
2012	3,660	3,274	66.9	218,990	6.43	1,371,381
2013	3,528	3,040	71.3	216,745	6.06	1,265,798
2014	3,031	2,497	72.7	181,542	5.30	914,955
2015	3,583	3,158	69.1	218,187	5.52	1,149,831
2016	3,059	2,565	77.9	199,914	4.96	949,876
2017	2,486	1,962	73.0	143,258	4.47	624,184
2018	2,548	1,982	77.5	153,527	4.62	697,598
2019	2,772	2,221	77.7	172,499	4.69	788,711
2020	2,726	2,214	77.2	170,813	4.75	788,036

[1] Barley sown for all purposes, including barley sown in the preceding fall.
NASS, Crops Branch, (202) 720–2127.

Table 1-54.—Barley: Stocks on and off farms, United States, 2011–2020

Year beginning September	On farms				Off farms [1]			
	Sep. 1	Dec. 1	Mar. 1	June 1	Sep. 1	Dec. 1	Mar. 1	June 1
	1,000 bushels							
2011	93,050	55,320	57,700	26,040	82,007	82,999	80,424	63,311
2012	112,550	72,580	26,480	9,670	85,226	85,473	67,248	50,317
2013	105,620	81,340	35,180	15,840	90,470	88,063	81,897	64,557
2014	97,820	74,510	43,830	19,110	81,997	81,625	77,734	63,145
2015	135,840	96,670	41,990	20,940	83,132	83,738	76,247	57,639
2016	130,600	99,100	57,910	27,740	99,737	93,429	79,832	74,370
2017	90,400	74,340	56,490	27,050	89,283	84,528	88,211	79,314
2018	91,350	72,070	48,540	26,420	83,456	80,561	81,491	68,061
2019	116,720	87,630	46,180	22,870	73,112	69,756	75,216	63,653
2020	108,980	85,190	51,580	25,100	70,484	63,437	63,760	55,153

[1] Includes stocks at mills, elevators, warehouses, terminals, and processors.
NASS, Crops Branch, (202) 720–2127.

Table 1-55.—Barley: Supply and disappearance, United States, 2011–2020

Year beginning June 1	Supply				Disappearance					Ending stocks May 31
	Beginning stocks	Production	Imports	Total	Domestic use			Exports	Total disappearance	Total [1]
					Feed and residual	Food, seed, and industrial	Total			
	Million bushels									
2011	89	155	16	260	37	155	192	9	200	60
2012	60	219	23	302	66	147	213	9	222	80
2013	80	217	19	316	66	153	219	14	234	82
2014	82	182	24	287	34	160	194	14	209	79
2015	79	218	19	315	44	158	202	11	213	102
2016	102	200	10	312	45	156	201	4	205	106
2017	106	143	9	259	7	152	159	5	164	94
2018	94	154	6	254	14	148	162	5	167	87
2019	87	172	7	266	39	142	180	6	186	80
2020	115	180	9	305	50	159	208	8	216	89

[1] Privately held: Includes quantity under loan and farmer-owned reserve.
Includes quantity under loan and farmer–owned reserve. Latest data may be preliminary or projected. Totals may not add due to independent rounding.
ERS, Market and Trade Economics Division, (202) 694–5313.

Table 1-57.—Barley: Marketing year average price and value, by State and United States, 2018–2020

State	Marketing year average price per bushel			Value of production		
	2018	2019	2020[1]	2018	2019	2020[1]
	Dollars	Dollars	Dollars	1,000 dollars	1,000 dollars	1,000 dollars
Alaska[2]	5.20	5.20	5.10	894	988	1,097
Arizona	3.84	4.15	4.55	4,224	7,844	4,441
California	4.84	4.61	4.64	8,683	14,300	7,197
Colorado	4.55	4.87	4.89	34,967	34,947	33,325
Delaware	2.60	3.35	3.45	2,839	3,752	4,347
Idaho	5.03	5.02	4.92	269,256	276,702	270,600
Kansas[3]	3.20	2.45	3.70	595	323	1,132
Maine[3]	2.90	3.20	3.50	3,387	3,674	2,646
Maryland	2.60	3.35	3.50	4,368	4,841	5,366
Michigan[3]	2.45	3.00	3.95	527	1,056	1,770
Minnesota	4.22	4.38	4.34	21,488	16,140	10,199
Montana	4.62	4.43	4.40	155,232	198,641	218,988
New York[3]	2.90	3.85	3.80	1,346	801	1,140
North Carolina[3]	2.70	3.25	3.00	1,728	1,287	1,848
North Dakota	4.24	4.16	4.56	120,798	133,286	132,149
Oregon	3.28	3.80	3.90	4,520	10,374	8,424
Pennsylvania	2.90	3.90	3.60	6,029	6,825	8,208
South Dakota[3]	3.65	3.55	4.74	2,610	1,374	2,920
Utah	3.69	3.70	4.00	5,077	3,785	4,080
Virginia	2.60	3.00	3.00	1,638	1,365	1,323
Washington	4.40	5.08	5.09	21,520	29,870	32,525
Wisconsin[3]	4.00	5.25	4.35	1,800	1,932	2,601
Wyoming	4.72	4.90	4.93	24,072	34,604	31,710
United States	4.62	4.69	4.75	697,598	788,711	788,036

(NA) Not available. (X) Not applicable. [1] Preliminary. [2] Alaska data previously included in a separate table for Alaska. [3] Estimates began in 2018. [4] Beginning in 2018, United States total includes data for Alaska.
NASS, Crops Branch, (202) 720–2127.

Table 1-58.—Barley: Support operations, United States, 2014–2020

Marketing year beginning June 1	Income support payment rates per bushel[1]	Program price levels per bushel		Put under loan		Acquired by CCC under loan program[3]	Owned by CCC at end of marketing year
		Loan	Reference	Quantity	Percentage of production[2]		
	Dollars	Dollars	Dollars	Million bushels	Percent	Million bushels	Million bushels
2014/2015	0.00	1.95	4.95	3.9	2.1	0	0
2015/2016	0.00	1.95	4.95	8.3	3.8	0	0
2016/2017	0.00	1.95	4.95	9.3	4.6	0	0
2017/2018	0.48	1.95	4.95	4.8	3.3	0	0
2018/2019	0.33	1.95	4.95	5.1	3.3	0	0
2019/2020	0.26	2.50	4.95	6.1	3.6	0	0
2020/2021[4]	0.25	2.50	4.95	5.6	3.4	0	0

[1] The entry is the price loss coverage payment rate. Agricultural Risk Coverage (ARC) is also available, but payment rates are established at the county or farm levels. [2] Percent of production is on a grain basis. [3] Acquisitions as of January 31, 2020. [4] Payment rate as of the February 26, 2021 NASS Agricultural Prices Report.
FPAC, (202) 690-0734.

Table 1-59.—International Barley: Area, yield, and production in specified countries, 2017/2018–2019/2020

Country	Area			Yield per hectare			Production		
	2017/ 2018	2018/ 2019	2019/ 2020	2017/ 2018	2018/ 2019	2019/ 2020	2017/ 2018	2018/ 2019	2019/ 2020
	1,000 hectares			*Metric tons*			*1,000 metric tons*		
European Union	12,095	12,278	12,380	4.85	4.56	5.07	58,654	55,947	62,750
Russia	7,714	7,784	8,403	2.62	2.15	2.37	20,211	16,737	19,939
Canada	2,114	2,395	2,700	3.73	3.50	3.85	7,891	8,380	10,400
Ukraine	2,652	2,569	2,700	3.28	2.96	3.52	8,695	7,604	9,500
Australia	4,124	3,719	3,950	2.24	2.24	2.23	9,254	8,310	8,800
Turkey	3,400	3,600	3,800	1.88	1.94	2.08	6,400	7,000	7,900
Kazakhstan	2,069	2,516	2,977	1.60	1.58	1.29	3,305	3,971	3,830
Argentina	935	1,200	1,000	4.00	4.22	3.80	3,740	5,060	3,800
United States	794	802	883	3.93	4.17	4.18	3,119	3,343	3,692
Iran	1,600	1,550	1,700	1.94	1.81	2.12	3,100	2,800	3,600
Ethiopia	955	1,000	1,000	2.13	2.20	2.30	2,032	2,200	2,300
Algeria	763	1,026	1,025	1.27	1.90	2.00	968	1,950	2,050
Syria	800	800	1,500	0.97	0.50	1.33	777	400	2,000
India	656	661	696	2.66	2.69	2.35	1,747	1,781	1,633
Iraq	775	600	1,200	1.26	1.30	1.33	975	780	1,600
Belarus	452	429	400	3.14	2.20	3.50	1,420	944	1,400
Morocco	1,893	1,597	1,450	1.30	1.82	0.83	2,466	2,910	1,200
Mexico	358	353	360	2.81	2.82	2.81	1,005	996	1,010
China	330	263	260	3.29	3.64	3.46	1,085	957	900
Azerbaijan	319	337	320	2.48	2.72	2.72	792	916	870

FAS, Office of Global Analysis, (202) 720-6301. Prepared or estimated on the basis of official USDA production, supply, and distribution statistics from foreign governments.

Table 1-60.—Barley: International trade, 2017/2018–2019/2020

Country	2017/2018	2018/2019	2019/2020
	1,000 metric tons		
Principle importing countries:			
Saudi Arabia	8,000	6,500	7,500
China	8,144	5,181	6,500
Iran	3,200	3,100	3,000
Japan	1,253	1,158	1,200
Morocco	429	204	1,000
Jordan	773	916	900
Brazil	547	656	700
Turkey	753	279	700
Libya	438	888	650
European Union	451	127	600
Tunisia	604	639	500
Kuwait	521	474	400
United Arab Emirates	263	476	400
Colombia	324	341	350
Israel	234	236	300
Thailand	147	206	300
India	211	135	250
Algeria	522	323	200
Egypt	21	78	200
Lebanon	197	191	200
Mexico	5	1	200
Belarus	49	197	175
United States	199	128	174
Principle exporting countries:			
European Union	5,667	5,899	5,000
Russia	2,951	5,884	4,800
Australia	9,190	5,725	4,600
Ukraine	5,354	4,289	3,800
Argentina	2,556	2,500	3,100
Canada	1,546	2,021	2,200
Kazakhstan	682	1,347	1,800
United States	95	111	109
Turkey	14	0	100
Uruguay	114	5	100
Serbia	26	53	85
Moldova	117	127	70
India	1	1	7
Belarus	16	0	0
Azerbaijan	7	0	0

FAS, Office of Global Analysis, (202) 720-6301. Prepared or estimated on the basis of official USDA production, supply, and distribution statistics from foreign governments.

Table 1-61.—Grains and grain products: Food availability, United States, 2010–2019

Year [1]	Wheat flour [2] Per capita availability	Rye Total [3]	Rye Per capita availability of rye flour	Oats Total [4]	Oats Per capita availability of food products
	Pounds	Million bushels	Pounds	Million Bushels	Pounds
2010	134.8	3.4	0.5	67.2	4.7
2011	132.5	3.4	0.5	68.8	4.8
2012	134.3	3.4	0.5	68.1	4.7
2013	135.0	3.4	0.5	66.2	4.5
2014	134.7	3.5	0.5	69.0	4.7
2015	133.0	3.5	0.5	69.4	4.7
2016	131.7	3.5	0.5	69.9	4.7
2017	131.8	3.5	0.5	70.6	4.7
2018	132.1	3.6	0.5	70.9	4.7
2019	131.1	3.6	0.5	74.0	4.9

Year [1]	Corn Per capita availability of food products Flour and meal	Corn Hominy and grits	Corn Food Starch	Corn Total	Barley Total [5]	Barley Per capita availability of food products [6]
	Pounds	Pounds	Pounds	Pounds	Million bushels	Pounds
2010	19.3	9.3	4.5	33.1	6.8	0.7
2011	19.9	9.6	4.6	34.1	6.8	0.7
2012	19.8	9.5	4.6	33.9	6.5	0.6
2013	19.8	9.5	4.6	33.9	7.5	0.7
2014	19.9	9.5	4.6	34.0	7.7	0.7
2015	19.9	9.5	4.6	34.0	8.0	0.8
2016	20.0	9.5	4.7	34.2	9.0	0.8
2017	20.2	9.6	4.8	34.6	9.5	0.9
2018	20.4	9.7	4.8	34.9	9.7	0.9
2019	21.4	10.1	5.0	36.5	8.0	0.7

[1] Data are in marketing year; for corn, September 1-August 31; for oats and barley, June 1-May 31. Wheat, rye, syrup, and sugar are in calendar year. [2] Includes white, whole wheat, and semolina flour. [3] Excludes quantities used in alcoholic beverages. [4] Oats used in oatmeal, prepared breakfast foods, infant foods, and food products. [5] Malt for food, breakfast food uses, pearl barley, and flour. [6] Malt equivalent of barley food products.

ERS, Market & Trade Economics Division, (202) 694-5290. All figures are estimates based on data from private industry sources, the U.S. Department of Commerce, the Internal Revenue Service, and other Government agencies.

Table 1-62.—Sorghum: Area, yield, production, and value, United States, 2011–2020

Year	Area planted for all purposes [1]	Sorghum for grain [2]					Sorghum for silage		
		Area harvested	Yield per harvested acre	Production	Marketing year average price per cwt [3]	Value of production [3]	Area harvested	Yield per harvested acre	Production
	1,000 acres	*1,000 acres*	*Bushels*	*1,000 bushels*	*Dollars*	*1,000 dollars*	*1,000 acres*	*Tons*	*1,000 tons*
2011 ..	5,451	3,945	54.0	212,993	10.70	1,259,635	226	10.4	2,353
2012 ..	6,259	4,995	49.6	247,742	11.30	1,606,237	353	11.9	4,196
2013 ..	8,076	6,585	59.6	392,331	7.64	1,716,927	380	14.3	5,420
2014 ..	7,138	6,401	67.6	432,575	7.20	1,721,330	315	13.1	4,123
2015 ..	8,459	7,851	76.0	596,751	5.91	2,064,638	306	14.6	4,475
2016 ..	6,690	6,163	77.9	480,261	4.98	1,352,438	298	14.0	4,171
2017 ..	5,629	5,044	71.7	361,871	5.75	1,168,526	282	13.4	3,772
2018 ..	5,690	5,061	72.1	364,986	5.82	1,180,847	264	12.6	3,326
2019 ..	5,265	4,675	73.0	341,460	5.96	1,125,759	339	11.9	4,019
2020 ..	5,880	5,095	73.2	372,960	9.00	1,767,884	239	13.1	3,125

[1] Grain and sweet sorghum for all uses, including syrup.　[2] Includes both grain sorghum for grain, and sweet sorghum for grain or seed.　[3] Based on the reported price of grain sorghum.
NASS, Crops Branch, (202) 720–2127.

Table 1-63.—Sorghum grain: Stocks on and off farms, United States, 2011–2020

Year beginning previous Dec.	On farms				Off farms [1]			
	Dec. 1	Mar. 1	Jun. 1	Sep. 1	Dec. 1	Mar. 1	Jun. 1	Sep. 1
	1,000 bushels	*1,000 bushels*	*1,000 bushels*	*1,000 bushels*	*1,000 bushels*	*1,000 bushels*	*1,000 bushels*	*1,000 bushels*
2011	27,850	13,020	3,140	2,030	123,101	158,027	76,894	25,420
2012	17,600	12,800	4,120	1,160	122,247	95,266	54,405	21,792
2013	32,950	10,850	2,710	602	198,466	80,685	38,398	14,551
2014	30,500	15,950	4,500	1,945	192,094	159,784	87,924	32,087
2015	51,500	9,000	2,960	1,895	271,035	110,856	31,329	16,514
2016	43,000	25,000	9,700	3,755	266,079	176,584	80,654	32,877
2017	33,800	21,250	8,620	4,280	193,692	159,495	76,088	29,179
2018	44,200	13,250	5,220	3,355	214,580	127,006	60,113	31,499
2019 [2]	30,200	24,990	9,470	3,210	220,161	167,736	107,962	60,451
2020	21,300	17,220	8,360	2,955	198,386	147,725	64,227	27,140

[1] Includes stocks at mills, elevators, warehouses, terminals, and processors.　[2] Preliminary.
NASS, Crops Branch, (202) 720–2127.

Table 1-64.—Sorghum: Supply and disappearance, United States, 2010–2019

Year beginning September 1	Supply			Disappearance					Ending stocks Aug. 31 [1]
				Domestic use					
	Beginning stocks	Production	Total	Feed and residual	Food, seed, and industrial	Total	Exports	Total disappearance	
	Million bushels								
2010	41	345	345	123	85	208	152	359	27
2011	27	213	213	69	85	154	63	218	23
2012	23	248	280	93	95	189	76	265	15
2013	15	392	408	93	70	162	211	374	34
2014	34	433	467	82	15	97	352	449	18
2015	18	597	620	104	137	241	342	583	37
2016	37	480	519	133	115	247	238	485	33
2017	33	362	397	102	60	162	200	362	35
2018	35	365	400	138	106	244	93	336	64
2019	64	341	405	97	75	171	204	375	30

[1] Includes quantity under loan and farmer–owned reserve.
Latest data may be preliminary or projected.　Totals may not add due to independent rounding.
ERS, Market and Trade Economics Division, (202) 694–5313. Source: USDA, World Agricultural Outlook Board, World Agricultural Supply and Demand Estimates and supporting materials.l

Table 1-65.—Sorghum: Area, yield, and production, by State and United States, 2018–2020

State	Area planted for all purposes			Sorghum for grain		
				Area harvested		
	2018	2019	2020	2018	2019	2020
	1,000 acres	1,000 acres	1,000 acres	1,000 acres	1,000 acres	1,000 acres
Arkansas	12	(NA)	(NA)	10	(NA)	(NA)
Colorado	355	365	370	325	310	255
Georgia	25	(NA)	(NA)	15	(NA)	(NA)
Illinois	18	(NA)	(NA)	16	(NA)	(NA)
Kansas	2,800	2,600	3,000	2,650	2,400	2,800
Louisiana	8	(NA)	(NA)	6	(NA)	(NA)
Mississippi	4	(NA)	(NA)	3	(NA)	(NA)
Missouri	30	(NA)	(NA)	21	(NA)	(NA)
Nebraska	230	200	195	170	130	150
New Mexico	80	(NA)	(NA)	47	(NA)	(NA)
North Carolina	18	(NA)	(NA)	8	(NA)	(NA)
Oklahoma	300	300	305	240	260	230
South Dakota	260	250	210	200	175	160
Texas	1,550	1,550	1,800	1,350	1,400	1,500
United States	5,690	5,265	5,880	5,061	4,675	5,095

State	Yield per harvested acre			Production		
	2018	2019	2020	2018	2019	2020
	Bushels	Bushels	Bushels	1,000 bushels	1,000 bushels	1,000 bushels
Arkansas	77.0	(NA)	(NA)	770	(NA)	(NA)
Colorado	53.0	41.0	20.0	17,225	12,710	5,100
Georgia	53.0	(NA)	(NA)	795	(NA)	(NA)
Illinois	111.0	(NA)	(NA)	1,776	(NA)	(NA)
Kansas	88.0	85.0	85.0	233,200	204,000	238,000
Louisiana	84.0	(NA)	(NA)	504	(NA)	(NA)
Mississippi	90.0	(NA)	(NA)	270	(NA)	(NA)
Missouri	100.0	(NA)	(NA)	2,100	(NA)	(NA)
Nebraska	94.0	93.0	91.0	15,980	12,090	13,650
New Mexico	38.0	(NA)	(NA)	1,786	(NA)	(NA)
North Carolina	60.0	(NA)	(NA)	480	(NA)	(NA)
Oklahoma	50.0	51.0	45.0	12,000	13,260	10,350
South Dakota	80.0	80.0	71.0	16,000	14,000	· 11,360
Texas	46.0	61.0	63.0	62,100	85,400	94,500
United States	72.1	73.0	73.2	364,986	341,460	372,960

(NA) Not available.
NASS, Crops Branch, (202) 720–2127.

Table 1-66.—Sorghum silage: Area harvested, yield, and production, by State and United States, 2018–2020

State	Silage								
	Area harvested			Yield per acre			Production		
	2018	2019	2020	2018	2019	2020	2018	2019	2020
	1,000 acres	1,000 acres	1,000 acres	Tons	Tons	Tons	1,000 tons	1,000 tons	1,000 tons
Arkansas	1	(NA)	(NA)	18.0	(NA)	(NA)	18	(NA)	(NA)
Colorado	8	18	23	14.0	17.0	11.0	112	306	253
Georgia	8	(NA)	(NA)	11.0	(NA)	(NA)	88	(NA)	(NA)
Illinois	1	(NA)	(NA)	14.0	(NA)	(NA)	14	(NA)	(NA)
Kansas	60	95	60	15.0	11.0	15.0	900	1,045	900
Louisiana	1	(NA)	(NA)	12.0	(NA)	(NA)	12	(NA)	(NA)
Mississippi	1	(NA)	(NA)	10.0	(NA)	(NA)	10	(NA)	(NA)
Missouri	7	(NA)	(NA)	12.0	(NA)	(NA)	84	(NA)	(NA)
Nebraska	20	60	15	11.0	10.0	12.0	220	600	180
New Mexico	18	(NA)	(NA)	11.0	(NA)	(NA)	198	(NA)	(NA)
North Carolina	7	(NA)	(NA)	10.0	(NA)	(NA)	70	(NA)	(NA)
Oklahoma	12	16	16	5.0	10.0	12.0	60	160	192
South Dakota	40	65	25	12.5	13.0	14.0	500	845	350
Texas	80	85	100	13.0	12.5	12.5	1,040	1,063	1,250
United States	264	339	239	12.6	11.9	13.1	3,326	4,019	3,125

(NA) Not available.
NASS, Crops Branch, (202) 720–2127.

Table 1-67.—Sorghum grain: Marketing year average price and value of production, by State and United States, 2018–2020

State	Marketing year average price per cwt			Value of production		
	2018	2019	2020[1]	2018	2019	2020[1]
	Dollars	Dollars	Dollars	1,000 dollars	1,000 dollars	1,000 dollars
Arkansas	(D)	(NA)	(NA)	(D)	(NA)	(NA)
Colorado	4.93	4.95	7.00	47,555	35,232	19,992
Georgia	7.40	(NA)	(NA)	3,294	(NA)	(NA)
Illinois	6.14	(NA)	(NA)	6,107	(NA)	(NA)
Kansas	5.59	5.70	8.85	730,009	651,168	1,179,528
Louisiana	6.10	(NA)	(NA)	1,722	(NA)	(NA)
Mississippi	(D)	(NA)	(NA)	(D)	(NA)	(NA)
Missouri	6.40	(NA)	(NA)	7,526	(NA)	(NA)
Nebraska	5.45	5.58	8.23	48,771	37,779	62,910
New Mexico	6.98	(NA)	(NA)	6,981	(NA)	(NA)
North Carolina	6.60	(NA)	(NA)	1,774	(NA)	(NA)
Oklahoma	5.95	6.00	9.05	39,984	44,554	52,454
South Dakota	5.86	5.95	8.23	52,506	46,648	52,356
Texas	6.64	6.49	7.57	203,913	310,378	400,604
Other States [2]	6.36	(X)	(X)	3.705 -	3,705	-
United States	5.82	5.96	9.00	1,180,847	1,125,759	1,767,844

(D) Withheld to avoid disclosing data for individual operations. (NA) Not available. (X) Not applicable. [1] Final. [2] Includes data withheld above.
NASS, Crops Branch, (202) 720–2127.

Table 1-68.—Sorghum grain: Support operations, United States, 2014–2020

Marketing year beginning September 1	Income support payment rates per cwt [1]	Program price levels per cwt		Put under support		Acquired by CCC under loan program [3]	Owned by CCC at end of marketing year
		Loan	Reference	Quantity	Percentage of production [2]		
	Dollars	Dollars	Dollars	Million cwt	Percent	Millions cwt	Million cwt
2014/2015	0.00	3.48	7.05	0.4	0.2	0	0
2015/2016	0.64	3.48	7.05	1.4	0.4	0	0
2016/2017	1.16	3.48	7.05	1.9	0.7	0	0
2017/2018	0.73	3.48	7.05	1.3	0.6	0	0
2018/2019	0.69	3.48	7.05	1.2	0.6	0	0
2019/2020	0.61	3.93	7.05	1.6	0.8	0	0
2020/2021 [4]	0.00	3.93	7.05	1.7	0.8	0	0

[1] The entry is the price loss coverage (PLC) payment rate. For 2017/2018, projected PLC payment rate is based on March 2018 WASDE MY price. Agricultural Risk Coverage (ARC) is also available, but payment rates are established at the county or farm levels. [2] Percent of production is on a grain basis. [3] Acquisitions as of January 31, 2020. [4] Payment rate as of the February 26, 2021 NASS Agricultural Prices Report.
FPAC, (202) 690-0734.

Table 1-69.—International Sorghum: Area, yield, and production in specified countries, 2017/2018–2019/2020

Country	Area			Yield per hectare			Production		
	2017/ 2018	2018/ 2019	2019/ 2020	2017/ 2018	2018/ 2019	2019/ 2020	2017/ 2018	2018/ 2019	2019/ 2020
	1,000 hectares			Metric tons			1,000 metric tons		
United States	2,041	2,048	1,892	4.50	4.53	4.58	9,192	9,271	8,673
Nigeria	5,820	5,800	5,900	1.19	1.17	1.17	6,939	6,800	6,900
Ethiopia	1,900	1,900	1,900	2.72	2.71	2.74	5,170	5,150	5,200
Mexico	1,350	1,350	1,350	3.37	3.48	3.33	4,545	4,700	4,500
Sudan	5,024	3,919	4,600	0.96	0.89	0.96	4,803	3,475	4,400
India	5,412	7,000	7,000	0.69	0.71	0.57	3,743	4,953	4,000
China	506	720	750	4.87	4.79	4.80	2,465	3,450	3,600
Argentina	700	630	575	4.29	3.97	4.35	3,000	2,500	2,500
Brazil	782	732	730	2.73	2.97	2.88	2,136	2,177	2,100
Niger	3,821	3,700	3,700	0.51	0.57	0.51	1,945	2,100	1,900
Burkina	1,667	1,800	1,800	0.82	1.07	1.00	1,366	1,930	1,800
Mali	1,386	1,500	1,500	1.03	0.98	0.87	1,424	1,470	1,300
Cameroon	852	850	850	1.59	1.41	1.41	1,352	1,200	1,200
Australia	1,147	1,100	1,100	0.83	0.90	0.86	946	988	950
Chad	388	285	335	2.64	2.74	2.60	1,023	780	871
Tanzania	124	135	157	5.32	5.46	5.22	660	737	820
Bolivia	783	800	800	0.96	0.84	1.00	755	672	800
Egypt	140	140	140	5.36	5.36	5.36	750	750	750
European Union ...	600	600	600	1.11	1.08	1.17	667	650	700
South Sudan	462	496	250	2.72	2.58	1.60	1,257	1,278	400

FAS, Office of Global Analysis, (202) 720-6301. Prepared or estimated on the basis of official USDA production, supply, and distribution statistics from foreign governments.

Table 1-70.—Sorghum: International trade, 2017/2018–2019/2020

Country	2017/2018	2018/2019	2019/2020
	1,000 metric tons		
Principle exporting countries:			
United States	5,089	2,351	3,429
Argentina	36	196	200
Nigeria	100	100	100
Ukraine	123	93	100
Ethiopia	75	75	75
India	125	51	50
Australia	456	110	40
China	43	49	40
Kenya	129	41	30
Bolivia	21	18	20
Paraguay	4	15	15
Brazil	1	33	5
Burkina	5	5	5
South Africa	6	5	5
Sudan	100	50	5
Tanzania	5	5	5
Uganda	5	5	5
European Union ...	2	7	2
Thailand	5	1	2
Principle importing countries:			
China	4,436	652	1,300
Mexico	98	596	700
Japan	594	452	500
European Union ...	420	759	200
Sudan	150	160	200
Kenya	119	129	150
South Sudan	148	26	150
Chile	76	40	100
Colombia	56	0	50
Somalia	80	85	50
South Africa	48	60	50
Taiwan	64	70	50
Uganda	35	35	40
Eritrea	30	60	30
Botswana	4	1	25
Cameroon	15	25	25
Chad	25	25	25
Niger	25	25	25
Pakistan	63	27	25
Israel	29	36	20
Philippines	21	36	20
Rwanda	20	20	20

FAS, Office of Global Analysis, (202) 720-6301. Prepared or estimated on the basis of official USDA production, supply, and distribution statistics from foreign governments.

Table 1-71.—International Mixed grain: Area, yield, and production in specified countries, 2017/2018–2019/2020

Country	Area			Yield per hectare			Production		
	2017/ 2018	2018/ 2019	2019/ 2020	2017/ 2018	2018/ 2019	2019/ 2020	2017/ 2018	2018/ 2019	2019/ 2020
	1,000 hectares			Metric tons			1,000 metric tons		
Bangladesh	35	35	35	0.71	0.71	0.71	25	25	25
Canada	66	90	95	2.76	2.96	2.79	182	266	265
European Union ...	3,900	3,872	4,016	3.93	3.39	3.64	15,320	13,138	14,600
Switzerland	10	10	10	6.00	6.00	6.00	60	60	60
Turkey	1	1	1	1.00	1.00	1.00	1	1	1

FAS, Office of Global Analysis, (202) 720-6301. Prepared or estimated on the basis of official USDA production, supply, and distribution statistics from foreign governments.

Table 1-72.—Commercial feeds: Disappearance for feed, United States, 2010–2019

Year beginning October	Oilseed cake and meal						
	Soybean	Cottonseed	Linseed	Peanut [1]	Sunflower	Canola	Total
	1,000 Short tons						
2010	30,301	2,452	209	83	255	2,969	32,952
2011	31,541	2,406	194	102	179	3,754	34,655
2012	28,999	2,351	199	99	219	4,259	32,815
2013	29,515	1,797	152	112	243	4,751	33,213
2014	32,278	2,195	212	118	192	4,891	36,223
2015	33,118	1,774	196	128	261	4,980	36,731
2016	30,314	2,000	173	131	266	4,550	37,464
2017	32,237	2,328	150	161	237	4,192	39,273
2018	32,851	2,020	155	130	233	4,185	39,560
2019	34,222	2,258	189	116	181	4,535	41,517

Year beginning October	Animal protein				Mill products [3]					Total commercial feeds
	Tankage and meat meal	Fish meal	Dried milk [2]	Total	Wheat millfeeds	Gluten feed and meal [4]	Rice millfeeds	Alfalfa meal	Total	
	1,000 Short tons									
2010	2,027	298	436	2,762	6,204	4,567	608	225	11,603	47,318
2011	2,196	198	463	2,857	6,404	5,237	535	225	12,400	49,913
2012	2,161	198	368	2,728	6,345	5,178	531	225	12,279	47,821
2013	2,128	198	219	2,545	6,345	5,127	447	225	12,144	47,903
2014	2,162	198	248	2,608	6,603	5,295	845	225	12,968	51,800
2015	2,594	198	248	3,041	6,513	5,371	235	225	12,344	52,116
2016	2,092	180	225	2,497	5,741	5,362	674	225	12,002	51,963
2017	2,307	180	225	2,712	5,721	5,147	545	225	11,637	53,622
2018	2,307	180	225	2,712	5,677	5,030	566	225	11,497	53,770
2019	2,307	180	225	2,712	11,792	5,109	657	225	17,783	62,012

This data has not been updated, but contains the most recent data available. [1] Year beginning August 1. [2] Includes dried skim milk, and whey for feed, but does not include any milk products fed on farms. [3] Other mill products that are not listed include screenings, hominy, and oats feed etc., for which no statistics are available. [4] Adjusted for export data.
ERS, Market and Trade Economics Division, (202) 694–5313.

Table 1-73.—High-protein feeds: Quantity for feeding, high-protein animal units, quantity per animal unit, and prices, United States, 2007–2016

Year beginning October	Quantity for feeding [1]						High-protein animal units	Quantity per animal unit	High protein feed prices
	Oilseed meal			Animal protein	Grain protein [3]	Total			
	Soybean meal	Other oilseed meals [2]	Total						
	1,000 tons	*1,000 tons*	*1,000 tons*	*1,000 tons*	*1,000 tons*	*1,000 tons*	*Million units*	*Pounds*	*Index numbers 1992=100*
2007	36,555	2,945	39,500	3,207	2,715	45,422	71	1,271	173
2008	33,827	2,282	36,109	3,113	3,076	42,298	71	1,193	171
2009	33,703	2,262	35,965	3,049	3,098	42,112	70	1,195	153
2010	33,331	2,814	36,145	2,950	2,998	42,093	69	1,214	177
2011	34,695	2,721	37,416	3,037	3,437	43,890	68	1,290	203
2012	31,899	2,689	34,587	2,965	3,398	40,951	68	1,212	239
2013	32,466	2,166	34,632	2,879	3,365	40,877	67	1,225	250
2014	35,506	2,546	38,052	2,929	3,476	44,456	67	1,319	191
2015	36,430	2,211	38,641	3,450	3,526	45,616	69	1,313	166
2016	36,630	2,686	39,316	3,858	3,492	46,665	71	1,316	159

This data has not been updated, but contains the most recent data available.   [1] In terms of 44 percent protein soybean meal equivalent.   [2] Includes cottonseed, linseed, peanut meal, and sunflower meal.   [3] Beginning 1974, adjusted for exports of corn gluten feed and meal.
ERS, Market and Trade Economics Division, (202) 694–5313.

Table 1-74.—Feed concentrates: Fed to livestock and poultry, 2007–2016

Year beginning October	Feed grains				Wheat [2]	Rye [2]	By-product feeds [3]	Total con-centrates	Grain con-suming animal units	Concen-trates fed per grain-con-suming animal unit
	Corn [1]	Sor-ghum [1]	Oats [2] and barley [2]	Total						
	Million tons	*Million tons*	*Million tons*	*Million tons*	*Million tons*	*Million tons*	*Million tons*	*Million tons*	*Millions*	*Tons*
2007	163.9	4.6	3.2	171.7	4.9	0.1	62.0	238.8	92.7	2.58
2008	143.6	6.6	3.2	153.4	3.4	0.1	58.2	215.1	91.7	2.35
2009	142.7	3.9	3.0	149.6	3.2	0.1	57.3	210.1	92.4	2.27
2010	133.6	3.4	2.7	139.7	2.1	0.1	57.7	196.6	92.9	2.15
2011	126.3	1.9	3.0	131.3	10.8	0.1	57.7	202.9	93.1	2.18
2012	120.6	2.6	3.6	126.9	11.6	0.1	57.6	196.7	92.3	2.13
2013	140.1	2.6	3.1	145.7	1.8	0.1	57.7	206.3	90.5	2.28
2014	148.0	2.3	2.5	152.8	4.7	0.1	63.3	220.9	92.4	2.39
2015	143.2	3.0	2.7	148.9	3.5	0.1	63.6	216.1	94.2	2.29
2016	153.0	3.6	2.4	159.0	2.2	0.1	68.0	229.3	95.8	2.39

This data has not been updated, but contains the most recent data available. [1] Marketing year beginning September 1.
[2] Marketing year beginning June 1.   [3] Oilseed meals, animal protein feeds, mill byproducts, and mineral supplements.
ERS, Market and Trade Economics Division, (202) 694–5313.

Table 1-75.—Feed: Consumed per head and per unit of production, by class of livestock or poultry, with quantity expressed in equivalent feeding value of corn, 2007–2016

Year beginning October	Dairy cattle			Beef cattle				Sheep and lambs	
	Milk cows		Other dairy cattle per head	Cattle on feed per head Jan. 1 [1]	Other beef cattle per head	All beef cattle per head	Cattle and calves per 100 pounds produced [2]	Per head	Per 100 pounds produced [3]
	Per head	Per 100 pounds milk produced							
	Pounds	Pounds	Pounds	Pounds	Pounds	Pounds	Pounds	Pounds	Pounds
2007	12,949	65	6,526	9,114	5,307	5,993	1,261	1,271	1,718
2008	12,265	60	6,473	8,854	5,283	5,895	1,214	1,263	1,741
2009	12,303	59	6,425	8,942	5,269	5,896	1,227	1,260	1,680
2010	12,013	57	6,378	8,403	5,253	5,815	1,183	1,254	1,695
2011	12,030	57	6,369	8,056	5,263	5,782	1,145	1,261	1,669
2012	11,918	57	6,364	7,830	5,255	5,717	1,137	1,261	1,659
2013	12,143	56	6,434	8,677	5,314	5,891	1,143	1,269	1,631
2014	12,345	56	6,453	8,912	5,292	5,919	1,183	1,265	1,649
2015	12,224	55	6,399	8,577	5,280	5,838	1,173	1,260	1,649
2016	12,408	55	6,905	9,398	5,282	5,958	1,180	1,265	1,624

Year beginning October	Poultry								Hogs per 100 pounds produced	Horses and mules two years and over per head
	Hens and pullets		Chickens raised		Broilers produced		Turkeys raised			
	Per head Jan. 1	Per 100 eggs	Per head	Per 100 pounds live weight	Per head	Per 100 pounds produced	Per head	Per 100 pounds produced		
	Pounds	Pounds	Pounds	Pounds	Pounds	Pounds	Pounds	Pounds	Pounds	Pounds
2007	136	47	28	1,045	11	197	86	313	574	3,832
2008	126	44	27	1,017	10	175	84	270	496	3,735
2009	119	43	26	1,077	10	180	85	293	487	3,707
2010	113	40	24	1,037	9	162	82	285	487	3,650
2011	119	42	25	1,019	10	163	79	272	486	3,663
2012	117	41	25	1,049	9	160	78	252	447	3,641
2013	119	40	26	1,156	9	165	82	255	471	3,674
2014	115	41	30	1,321	10	173	89	287	516	3,723
2015	106	43	28	1,255	10	164	85	290	483	3,695
2016	115	43	28	1,316	10	170	87	284	498	3,728

This data has not been updated, but contains the most recent data available.   [1] Feed consumed by all cattle divided by the number on feed January 1.   [2] Feed for all cattle, except milk cows, divided by the net live-weight production of cattle and calves. It includes the growth on dairy heifers and calves as well as all beef cattle.   [3] Including wool produced.
ERS, Market and Trade Economics Division, (202) 694-5313.

Table 1-76.—Feed: Consumed by livestock and poultry, by type of feed, with quantity expressed in equivalent feeding value of corn, 2007–2016

Year beginning October	Concentrates	Harvested roughage	Pasture	Total
	Million tons	Million tons	Million tons	Million tons
2007	239	80	163	482
2008	215	83	158	456
2009	210	83	156	450
2010	200	81	155	435
2011	203	76	155	434
2012	197	75	155	427
2013	206	78	149	433
2014	221	82	148	450
2015	216	81	155	452
2016	229	81	160	470

This data has not been updated, but contains the most recent data available.
ERS, Market and Trade Economics Division, (202) 694-5313.

Table 1-77.—Animal units fed: Grain-consuming, roughage-consuming, and grain-and-roughage-consuming, United States, 2010–2019 [1]

Year beginning October	Grain-consuming [2]	Roughage-consuming [3]	Grain and roughage-consuming [4]
	1,000 units	1,000 units	1,000 units
2010	92,851	69,233	77,786
2011	93,104	68,023	77,192
2012	92,311	67,593	76,617
2013	90,502	66,758	75,347
2014	92,499	67,432	76,575
2015	94,299	69,490	78,532
2016	95,889	70,933	80,032
2017	98,812	70,940	81,152
2018	100,606	71,293	82,049
2019	102,250	70,502	82,170

[1] Index series based on average feeding rates for years 1969–71. In calculations for the feeding years 1969 to date, cattle numbers used are the new categories shown in the Livestock and Poultry Inventory, published by NASS, USDA. [2] Livestock and poultry numbers weighted by all concentrates consumed. [3] Livestock and poultry numbers weighted by all roughage (including pasture) consumed. [4] Livestock and poultry numbers weighted by all feed (including pasture) fed to livestock.
ERS, Market and Trade Economics Division, (202) 694–5313.

Table 1-78.—Feed grains: Average price, selected markets and grades, 2010–2019 [1]

Calendar year	Kansas City			Minneapolis		
	Corn, No. 2 Yellow (truck)	Corn, No. 2 White (rail)	Sorghum, No. 2 Yellow (truck)	Corn, No. 2 Yellow	Barley, No. 3 or Better malting	Oats, No. 2 White
	Dollars per bushel					
2010	4.08	4.27	6.94	3.65	4.70	2.74
2011	6.81	7.11	11.73	6.58	6.96	3.72
2012	7.17	7.29	11.81	6.87	7.06	3.67
2013	6.28	6.35	10.40	5.97	6.35	3.90
2014	4.07	4.30	7.30	3.83	6.23	4.02
2015	3.76	3.82	6.97	3.45	6.23	2.84
2016	3.49	3.93	5.59	3.18	(NA)	2.57
2017	3.43	3.62	5.61	3.19	4.70	3.43
2018	3.57	3.73	5.87	3.21	2.74	2.96
2019	3.85	4.00	6.28	3.55	2.79	3.17

Calendar year	Omaha: Corn, No. 2 Yellow (truck)	Chicago: Corn, No. 2 Yellow	Texas High Plains: Sorghum, No. 2 Yellow	Memphis Corn, No. 2 Yellow	St. Louis: Corn, No. 2 Yellow (truck)
	Dollars per bushel			Dollars per cwt	
2010	4.03	4.16	7.81	4.25	4.26
2011	6.72	6.78	12.64	6.85	7.08
2012	7.06	6.86	13.15	6.95	7.08
2013	6.23	5.81	10.51	6.07	6.25
2014	3.99	4.03	7.26	4.33	4.84
2015	3.66	3.68	6.72	3.87	3.87
2016	3.34	3.61	5.53	3.67	3.70
2017	3.29	3.44	5.85	(NA)	3.62
2018	3.49	3.50	5.85	(NA)	3.73

[1] Simple average of daily prices.
AMS, Livestock and Grain Market News Branch, (202) 720–6231.

Table 1-79.—Feedstuffs: Average price per ton bulk, in wholesale lots, at leading markets, 2010–2019

Year beginning October	Soybean meal 48% protein Decatur	Cottonseed meal 41% protein Kansas City	Cottonseed meal 41% protein Memphis	Linseed meal 34% protein Min- neapolis	Meat meal 50% protein Kansas City	Fish meal 60% protein Gulf Coast	Wheat bran Kansas City	Wheat middlings Minneapolis
	Dollars per ton							
2010	313.47	249.72	212.57	210.80	299.05	1,265.78	94.62	94.44
2011	333.73	310.43	275.43	242.60	342.84	1,198.89	176.20	172.74
2012	439.77	336.79	303.37	282.67	391.49	1,168.09	175.06	192.91
2013	464.61	430.80	333.42	(NA)	467.00	(NA)	129.57	182.40
2014	478.26	410.64	369.30	(NA)	456.61	1,466.28	119.45	117.43
2015	341.20	333.31	291.97	(NA)	328.33	1,531.77	98.42	93.66
2016	328.64	290.99	247.63	(NA)	275.20	1,386.72	75.10	73.51
2017	307.57	246.30	209.00	(NA)	254.17	1,291.67	75.47	69.59
2018	334.68	307.24	264.85	(NA)	270.39	(NA)	141.88	(NA)
2019	300.28	271.81	224.58	(NA)	233.60	(NA)	125.95	92.46

Year beginning October	Wheat shorts or middlings Kansas City	Wheat millrun Portland	Gluten feed 21% protein Illinois Points	Hominy feed Midwest	Distillers' dried grains Lawrenceburg	Alfalfa meal Dehydrated, 17% protein Kansas City	Alfalfa meal Sun-cured Kansas City
	Dollars per ton						
2010	94.62	124.06	....	115.61	122.77	210.36	178.16
2011	176.20	187.71	....	206.85	202.42	254.72	243.29
2012	174.78	219.71	....	....	200.00	347.23	....
2013	129.99	228.57	166.35	202.42	236.07	339.28	275.70
2014	119.41	191.60	165.00	124.84	172.22	324.74	267.10
2015	98.42	170.20	98.28	103.53	164.40	283.53	206.99
2016	75.10	144.76	90.72	92.12	148.60	253.90	185.82
2017	74.08	131.65	(NA)	95.20	(NA)	227.37	190.02
2018	102.72	143.33	(NA)	(NA)	80.00	247.07	231.43
2019	90.70	162.26	106.27	106.30	(NA)	306.44	(NA)

(NA) Not available.
AMS, Livestock and Grain Market News Branch, (202) 720–6231.

Table 1-80.—International Millet: Area, yield, and production in specified countries, 2017/2018–2019/2020

Country	Area 2017/ 2018	Area 2018/ 2019	Area 2019/ 2020	Yield per hectare 2017/ 2018	Yield per hectare 2018/ 2019	Yield per hectare 2019/ 2020	Production 2017/ 2018	Production 2018/ 2019	Production 2019/ 2020
	1,000 hectares			*Metric tons*			*1,000 metric tons*		
India	9,221	8,146	8,000	1.26	1.26	1.36	11,640	10,236	10,900
Niger	6,999	7,000	7,000	0.54	0.55	0.54	3,790	3,847	3,800
China	861	870	900	2.96	2.53	2.56	2,548	2,200	2,300
Nigeria	2,212	2,000	2,000	0.68	1.06	1.00	1,500	2,119	2,000
Mali	2,156	2,000	2,000	0.69	0.92	0.73	1,493	1,840	1,450
Burkina	1,223	1,200	1,200	0.68	0.99	0.92	828	1,189	1,100
Ethiopia	464	450	450	2.32	2.22	2.44	1,078	1,000	1,100
Sudan	2,142	3,000	2,500	0.45	0.67	0.40	954	2,000	1,000
Senegal	850	850	850	1.03	1.06	1.00	875	897	850
Chad	1,165	1,100	1,100	0.57	0.69	0.64	660	756	700
Russia	235	187	350	1.34	1.16	1.25	315	217	437
Tanzania	333	350	350	1.17	0.90	1.00	389	316	350
Pakistan	489	476	470	0.69	0.65	0.64	335	307	300
Nepal	260	260	260	0.96	0.96	0.96	250	250	250
Burma	240	240	240	1.00	1.00	1.00	240	240	240
Uganda	151	175	175	1.42	1.45	1.37	214	253	240
Guinea	194	200	200	1.09	1.07	1.00	211	214	200
Ghana	167	160	160	1.00	1.09	1.09	167	175	175
Ukraine	58	55	90	1.50	1.47	1.89	87	81	170
Cameroon ..	72	72	72	1.39	1.39	1.39	100	100	100

FAS, Office of Global Analysis, (202) 720-6301. Prepared or estimated on the basis of official USDA production, supply, and distribution statistics from foreign governments.

Table 1-81.—Proso millet: Area, yield, production, and value, United States, 2011–2020

Year	Area		Yield per harvested acre	Production	Marketing year average price per bushel received by farmers	Value of production
	Planted	Harvested				
	1,000 acres	1,000 acres	Bushels	1,000 dollars	Dollars	1,000 dollars
2011	370	338	27.1	9,149	6.01	54,974
2012	335	205	15.0	3,075	15.10	46,548
2013	720	638	28.9	18,436	4.61	84,915
2014	505	430	31.4	13,483	3.35	45,104
2015	445	418	33.9	14,159	2.93	41,547
2016	443	413	30.4	12,558	2.87	36,065
2017	478	403	36.9	14,889	3.32	49,444
2018	443	390	29.7	11,595	5.22	60,566
2019	506	465	35.7	16,608	5.54	92,032
2020	609	509	18.8	9,573	11.20	107,037

NASS, Crops Branch, (202) 720–2127.

Table 1-82.—Proso millet: Area, yield, and production, by State and United States, 2018–2020

State	Area planted			Area harvested		
	2018	2019	2020	2018	2019	2020
	1,000 acres	1,000 acres	1,000 acres	1,000 acres	1,000 acres	1,000 acres
Colorado	300	340	425	270	320	335
Nebraska	95	115	130	81	106	125
South Dakota	48	51	54	39	39	49
United States	443	506	609	390	465	509

State	Yield per acre			Production		
	2018	2019	2020	2018	2019	2020
	Bushels	Bushels	Bushels	1,000 bushels	1,000 bushels	1,000 bushels
Colorado	28.0	37.0	14.5	7,560	11,840	4,858
Nebraska	32.0	31.0	24.0	2,592	3,286	3,000
South Dakota	37.0	38.0	35.0	1,443	1,482	1,715
United States	29.7	35.7	18.8	11,595	16,608	9,573

NASS, Crops Branch, (202) 720–2127.

Table 1-83.—Proso millet: Marketing year average price and value, by State and United States, 2018–2020

State	Marketing year average price per bushel			Value of production		
	2018	2019	2020	2018	2019	2020
	Dollars	Dollars	Dollars	1,000 dollars	1,000 dollars	1,000 dollars
Colorado	5.42	5.67	12.60	40,975	67,133	61,211
Nebraska	5.07	5.25	9.33	13,141	17,252	27,990
South Dakota	4.47	5.16	10.40	6,450	7,647	17,836
United States	5.22	5.54	11.20	60,566	92,032	107,037

NASS, Crops Branch, (202) 720–2127.

CHAPTER II

STATISTICS OF COTTON, TOBACCO, SUGAR CROPS, AND HONEY

This chapter includes data on cotton, sugar, honey, caloric sweeteners, and tobacco.

Table 2-1.—Cotton: Area, yield, production, market year average price, and value, United States, 2011–2020

Year	Area		Yield per harvested acre	Production	Marketing year average price per pound received by farmers [2]	Value of production [2]
	Planted	Harvested				
	1,000 acres	*1,000 acres*	*Pounds*	*1,000 bales [1]*	*Dollars*	*1,000 dollars*
2011	14,735.4	9,460.9	790	15,573.2	0.935	6,985,976
2012	12,264.4	9,321.8	892	17,313.8	0.757	6,291,813
2013	10,407.0	7,359.4	822	12,909.2	0.838	5,191,505
2014	11,148.4	9,351.8	838	16,319.4	0.657	5,147,241
2015	8,580.5	8,074.9	766	12,888.0	0.645	3,988,978
2016	10,073.5	9,507.8	867	17,169.9	0.705	5,813,774
2017	12,717.5	11,100.4	905	20,922.5	0.719	7,222,535
2018	14,100.3	9,990.8	882	18,367.0	0.723	6,375,167
2019	13,735.7	11,497.4	831	19,912.5	0.623	5,865,099
2020	12,092.0	8,274.5	847	14,607.5	0.689	4,482,779

[1] Value based on 480-pound net weight bale. [2] Based on marketings and monthly prices received from August1, 2019 - December 31, 2019.
NASS, Crops Branch, (202) 720–2127.

Table 2-2.—Cotton: Marketing year average price per pound, and value, by State and United States, 2018–2020

State	Marketing year average price per pound			Value of production [1]		
	2018	2019 v	2020 [2]	20180	2019	2020 [2]
	Dollars	*Dollars*	*Dollars*	*1,000 dollars*	*1,000 dollars*	*1,000 dollars*
Upland:						
Alabama	0.730	0.624	0.684	311,155	297,544	240,987
Arizona	0.680	0.072	0.662	142,637	104,150	95,964
Arkansas	0.708	0.662	0.684	385,039	442,403	419,265
California	(D)	(D)	0.(D)	(D)	(D)	(D)
Florida	0.709	0.633	0.722	35,053	57,958	35,696
Georgia	0.741	0.682	0.782	695,354	806,218	761,779
Kansas	0.600	0.538	0.583	98,208	81,043	83,952
Louisiana	0.755	0.636	0.669	152,208	179,070	108,860
Mississippi	0.751	0.619	0.697	527,022	469,960	394,781
Missouri	0.712	0.636	0.672	314,761	262,642	220,631
New Mexico	(D)	(D)	0.(D)	(D)	(D)	(D)
North Carolina	0.748	0.661	0.695	252,046	302,016	174,139
Oklahoma	0.653	0.632	0.677	213,766	196,435	206,675
South Carolina	0.747	0.654	0.708	150,595	141,705	101,612
Tennessee	0.696	0.657	0.688	257,242	271,411	201,777
Texas	0.679	0.609	0.623	2,232,552	1,762,522	1,366,613
Virginia	0.718	0.627	0.658	62,380	70,684	40,112
Other States [3]	0.702	0.056	0.678	101,433	71,775	64,118
United States	0.703	0.596	0.663	5,931,451	5,517,536	4,516,961
American-Pima:						
Arizona	(D)	(D)	(D)	(D)	(D)	(D)
California	(D)	(D)	(D)	(D)	(D)	(D)
New Mexico	(D)	(D)	(D)	(D)	(D)	(D)
Texas	(D)	(D)	(D)	(D)	(D)	(D)
Other States [3]	1.150	1.060	1.190	443,716	347,563	311,818
United States	1.150	1.06	1.190	443,716	347,563	311,818
All:						
United States	0.723	0.614	0.689	6,375,167	5,865,099	4,828,779

(D) Withheld to avoid disclosing data for individual operations. [1] Value based on 480-pound net weight bale. [2] Based on marketings and monthly prices received from August 1, 2020-December 31, 2020. [3] Includes data withheld above.
NASS, Crops Branch, (202) 720–2127.

GRAIN AND FEED

Table 2-3.—Cotton: Area, yield, production, and type by State and United States, 2018–2020

State	Area planted			Area harvested		
	2018	2019	2020	2018	2019	2020
	1,000 acres	*1,000 acres*	*1,000 acres*	*1,000 acres*	*1,000 acres*	*1,000 acres*
Upland:						
Alabama	510.0	540.0	450.0	494.0	532.0	446.0
Arizona	160.0	160.0	125.0	159.0	158.0	123.0
Arkansas	485.0	620.0	525.0	480.0	610.0	520.0
California	48.0	54.0	34.0	47.0	53.0	33.5
Florida	117.0	112.0	98.0	93.0	110.0	93.0
Georgia	1,430.0	1,400.0	1,190.0	1,290.0	1,380.0	1,180.0
Kansas	165.0	175.0	195.0	151.0	149.0	181.0
Louisiana	195.0	280.0	170.0	189.0	268.0	165.0
Mississippi	620.0	710.0	530.0	615.0	700.0	525.0
Missouri	325.0	380.0	295.0	322.0	368.0	287.0
New Mexico	77.0	63.0	43.0	55.0	44.0	26.0
North Carolina	430.0	510.0	360.0	415.0	500.0	330.0
Oklahoma	780.0	640.0	525.0	510.0	450.0	430.0
South Carolina ...	300.0	300.0	190.0	270.0	295.0	179.0
Tennessee	360.0	410.0	280.0	355.0	405.0	275.0
Texas	7,750.0	7,050.0	6,800.0	4,200.0	5,150.0	3,150.0
Virginia	98.0	103.0	80.0	97.0	102.0	79.0
United States	13,850.0	13,507.0	11,890.0	9,742.0	11,274.0	8,022.5
American Pima:						
Arizona	14.5	7.5	6.5	14.5	7.5	6.5
California	211.0	204.0	147.0	210.0	201.0	146.0
New Mexico	6.8	5.2	10.5	6.8	4.9	10.5
Texas	18.0	12.0	38.0	17.5	10.0	31.0
United States	250.3	228.7	202.0	248.8	223.4	194.0
All:						
United States	14,100.3	13,735.7	13,737.8	9,990.8	11,497.4	8,216.5

State	Yield per harvested acre			Production [1]		
	2018	2019	2020	2018	2019	2020
	Pounds	*Pounds*	*Pounds*	*1,000 bales [2]*	*1,000 bales [2]*	*1,000 bales [2]*
Upland:						
Alabama	863	928	790	888.0	1,028.0	734.0
Arizona	1,319	1,154	1,179	437.0	380.0	302.0
Arkansas	1,133	1,185	1,179	1,133.0	1,506.0	1,277.0
California	1,910	1,576	2,006	187.0	174.0	140.0
Florida	532	895	532	103.0	205.0	103.0
Georgia	727	953	887	1,955.0	2,740.0	2,180.0
Kansas	1,084	902	796	341.0	280.0	300.0
Louisiana	1,067	1,042	986	420.0	582.0	339.0
Mississippi	1,141	1,112	1,079	1,462.0	1,621.0	1,180.0
Missouri	1,373	1,193	1,144	921.0	915.0	684.0
New Mexico	995	840	1,052	114.0	77.0	57.0
North Carolina	812	998	759	702.0	1,040.0	522.0
Oklahoma	642	703	710	682.0	659.0	636.0
South Carolina ...	747	809	802	420.0	497.0	299.0
Tennessee	1,041	1,138	1,066	770.0	960.0	611.0
Texas	783	589	696	6,850.0	6,320.0	4,570.0
Virginia	896	1,144	772	181.0	243.0	127.0
United States	865	819	841	17,566.0	19,227.0	14,061.0
American Pima:						
Arizona	943	800	1,034	28.5	12.5	14.0
California	1,662	1,545	1,562	727.0	647.0	475.0
New Mexico	812	882	663	11.5	9.0	14.5
Texas	933	816	666	34.0	17.0	43.0
United States	1,545	1,473	1,352	801.0	685.5	546.5
All:						
United States	882	831	853	18,367.0	19,912.5	14,607.5

[1] Production ginned and to be ginned. [2] 480-pound net weight bales.
NASS, Crops Branch, (202) 720–2127.

Table 2-4.—Cotton, American Upland: Support operations, United States, 2014–2020

Marketing Year beginning August 1	Income support payment rates per pound [1]	Program price levels per pound		Put under Loan [3]		Acquired by CCC under loan program [4]	Owned by CCC at end of marketing year
		Loan	Reference [2]	Quantity	Percentage of production		
	Cents	*Cents*	*Cents*	*1,000 bales*	*Percent*	*1,000 bales*	*1,000 bales*
2014/2015	(NA)	52.00	(NA)	7,625	48.4	0	0
2015/2016	(NA)	52.00	(NA)	6,758	54.3	0	0
2016/2017	(NA)	52.00	(NA)	9,373	56.4	0	0
2017/2018	(NA)	49.49	(NA)	9,597	46.7	0.1	0
2018/2019	2.17	52.00	36.70	8,250	47.0	73	0
2019/2020	6.12	52.00	36.70	11,787	61.3	0	0
2020/2021 [5]	2.06	52.00	36.70	8,326	59.2	0	0

(NA) Not available. [1] The Agricultural Act of 2014 excludes upland cotton as a covered commodity for the Agricultural Risk Coverage and Price Loss Coverage Programs. The Bipartisan Budget Act of 2018 amended the Agricultural Act of 2014 to make seed cotton a covered commodity for the Agriculture Risk Coverage and Price Loss Coverage Programs effective with the 2018 crop year. The Agriculture Improvement Act of 2018 continued seed cotton as a covered commodity for the Agriculture Risk Coverage and Price Loss Coverage Programs. Beginning with 2018, the income support payment rate is the Price Loss Coverage payment rate for seed cotton. [2] Beginning with 2018, Reference Price is for seed cotton. Beginning with 2019, value represents Effective Reference Price for seed cotton. [3] Upland cotton put under loan as of February 18, 2021. [4] Aquisitions as of February 18, 2021. [5] Payment rate as of February 2021.
FPAC, (202) 690-0734.

Table 2-5.—International Cotton: Area, yield, and production in specified countries, 2017/2018–2019/2020

Country	Area			Yield			Production		
	2017/ 2018	2018/ 2019	2019/ 2020	2017/ 2018	2018/ 2019	2019/ 2020	2017/ 2018	2018/ 2019	2019/ 2020
	1,000 hectares			*Kilograms per hectare*			*1,000 480 lb. bales*		
India	12,600	12,600	13,000	501	446	494	29,000	25,800	29,500
China	3,400	3,500	3,450	1,761	1,726	1,720	27,500	27,750	27,250
United States	4,492	4,130	4,777	1,014	968	902	20,923	18,367	19,800
Brazil	1,175	1,640	1,700	1,708	1,726	1,665	9,220	13,000	13,000
Pakistan	2,700	2,300	2,500	661	719	575	8,200	7,600	6,600
Uzbekistan ...	1,250	1,100	1,010	672	648	754	3,860	3,275	3,500
Turkey	470	520	560	1,853	1,549	1,322	4,000	3,700	3,400
Greece	230	245	280	1,157	1,253	1,283	1,222	1,410	1,650
Mexico	210	243	225	1,617	1,555	1,519	1,560	1,735	1,570
Benin	530	650	675	468	469	468	1,140	1,400	1,450
Mali	705	725	735	432	381	400	1,400	1,270	1,350
Argentina	320	380	360	558	642	605	820	1,120	1,000
Burkina	850	630	575	307	294	379	1,200	850	1,000
Cote d'Ivoire	327	392	425	536	520	512	805	937	1,000
Turkmenistan	545	545	545	535	364	399	1,340	910	1,000
Burma	249	240	240	634	635	635	725	700	700
Australia	530	380	60	1,972	1,261	2,449	4,800	2,200	675
Cameroon	225	250	260	484	523	540	500	600	645
Sudan	180	180	200	575	605	653	475	500	600
Tajikistan	185	180	180	671	502	689	570	415	570
Tanzania	350	420	450	143	194	242	230	375	500
Azerbaijan	130	130	140	569	653	700	340	390	450
Kazakhstan ..	125	128	125	523	587	644	300	345	370
Egypt	91	141	100	718	772	762	300	500	350
Chad	120	60	250	181	145	283	100	40	325
Spain	63	65	65	1,016	1,005	1,005	294	300	300
Iran	85	80	80	640	748	748	250	275	275
Togo	160	180	185	299	308	312	220	255	265
Ethiopia	60	77	80	639	687	680	176	243	250
Nigeria	270	270	270	190	190	190	235	235	235

FAS, Office of Global Analysis, (202) 720–6301. Prepared or estimated on the basis of official USDA production, supply, and distribution statistics from foreign governments.

Table 2-6.—Cotton: United States exports by country of destination, 2018–2020

Country of destination	Year		
	2018	2019	2020
	Metric tons	*Metric tons*	*Metric tons*
Cotton linters:			
China	5,515	3,146	10,324
Japan	6,629	3,258	4,039
Spain	229	0	484
Germany(*)	980	662	477
Canada	71	31	102
United Kingdom	19	43	49
Guatemala	31	25	45
South Africa	12	17	34
Chile	19	29	21
Turkey	23	34	20
Sweden	27	24	12
Vietnam	134	773	10
Costa Rica	0	36	7
Qatar	0	0	1
Australia(!)	0	17	0
United Arab Emirates	11	0	0
Argentina	41	0	0
Australia(*)	0	17	0
Brazil	27	0	0
Colombia	0	21	0
Dominican Republic	0	1	0
France(!)	32	0	0
France(*)	32	0	0
Italy(!)	13	0	0
Israel(!)	3	0	0
Israel(*)	3	0	0
Italy(*)	13	0	0
Korea, South	18	0	0
Libya	6	0	0
Mexico	0	22	0
Other Partners	642	768	0
World Total	14,529	8,924	15,622
Cotton <1:			
Vietnam	31,740	79,716	63,708
China	26,059	10,937	19,470
Pakistan	5,948	13,134	18,324
Thailand	17,821	16,521	14,857
Indonesia	29,613	23,347	14,347
Taiwan	17,391	15,145	11,221
Turkey	19,355	13,257	7,017
Japan	6,637	8,222	6,997
Bangladesh	2,919	6,138	2,686
Korea, South	4,843	8,217	2,627
India	7,613	3,154	1,043
Malaysia	1,035	2,445	1,026
Oman	0	555	725
Venezuela	0	4	612
Egypt	0	0	505
Nicaragua	9	0	426
Mexico	1,139	1,204	410
Ecuador	0	647	303
Brazil	0	1	116
Italy(*)	327	23	33
Sri Lanka	0	0	21
France(*)	69	0	10
Portugal	31	6	4
Israel(*)	0	4	4
Colombia	1	901	1
United Arab Emirates	16	0	0
Australia(*)	0	0	0
Belgium-Luxembourg(*)	98	0	0
Dominican Republic	23	6	0
Germany(*)	12	0	0
Rest of World	1,354	1,571	0
World Total	174,053	205,154	166,494

See footnote(s) at end of table.

Table 2-6.—Cotton: United States exports by country of destination, 2018–2020—Continued

Partners of destination	Year		
	2018	2019	2020
	Metric tons		
Cotton >1 <1 1/8:			
Vietnam	348,245	319,357	321,272
China	88,241	55,229	261,069
Pakistan	99,618	70,305	159,784
Turkey	157,895	119,659	156,637
Bangladesh	65,779	98,478	108,134
Mexico	176,629	145,610	106,020
Indonesia	112,260	84,746	69,339
Thailand	48,507	37,962	25,644
El Salvador	13,809	14,668	21,813
Taiwan	32,660	35,537	15,992
Korea, South	20,335	10,170	14,735
India	19,633	49,202	12,621
Guatemala	38,031	29,106	12,504
Malaysia	26,394	25,692	10,996
Japan	10,117	9,965	10,672
Egypt	803	4,691	9,690
Peru	16,766	5,435	7,169
Honduras	319	2,029	4,944
Colombia	15,845	10,843	4,585
Hong Kong	2	1,051	4,031
Nicaragua	616	80	3,875
Ecuador	8,466	3,753	1,687
Oman	0	405	863
Austria	0	97	786
Italy(!)	1,906	1,081	722
Italy(*)	1,906	1,081	722
Spain	1	2	405
Philippines	6,097	3,425	335
Dominican Republic	46	70	121
Brazil	1,734	18	112
Other Partners	7,470	5,043	625
World Total	1,320,128	1,144,788	1,347,902
Pima >= 1 3/8:			
India	36,931	40,782	28,497
China	38,823	33,377	23,215
Pakistan	5,457	10,338	9,419
Bangladesh	1,972	2,724	7,018
Vietnam	7,378	12,178	5,213
Turkey	2,362	6,964	4,116
Peru	6,236	5,652	3,337
El Salvador	40	2,011	2,884
Egypt	3,282	1,738	2,216
Bahrain	178	850	1,742
Italy(!)	84	330	1,193
Italy(*)	84	330	1,193
Thailand	2,852	2,768	1,153
Austria	982	2,242	1,017
Indonesia	2,053	1,355	823
Greece	0	116	674
Honduras	0	139	597
Japan	1,417	791	467
Taiwan	1,383	744	435
Korea, South	0	196	425
Germany(*)	861	789	397
Brazil	271	104	120
Guatemala	0	99	69
Ethiopia(!)	0	294	59
Ethiopia(*)	0	294	59
Colombia	39	97	58
Portugal	1	40	40
Malaysia	137	1,051	38
Czech Republic	0	0	20
Oman	0	0	19
Other Partners	776	1,290	60
World Total	113,598	129,685	96,570

See footnote(s) at and of table.

Table 2-6.—Cotton: United States exports by country of destination, 2018–2020—Continued

Area/Partners of destination	Year		
	2018	2019	2020
	Metric tons	*Metric tons*	*Metric tons*
Cotton Other > 1 1/8:			
China	332,129	275,081	878,661
Vietnam	367,884	450,385	390,072
Pakistan	233,957	281,007	320,003
Turkey	210,493	252,281	198,900
Bangladesh	131,205	115,606	89,396
Indonesia	193,063	133,042	78,773
Korea, South	93,798	77,389	52,681
Malaysia	34,739	36,759	40,640
Thailand	76,714	65,262	33,087
India	91,222	235,395	27,177
Peru	30,962	35,469	23,725
Guatemala	15,412	20,598	15,301
Taiwan	54,689	35,859	13,259
Japan	6,312	7,083	5,886
Costa Rica	9,281	8,652	5,511
Honduras	4,199	5,066	5,240
Ecuador	7,376	7,232	4,915
Egypt	22,520	10,724	3,996
Mexico	13,964	12,988	3,962
Singapore	695	196	3,392
El Salvador	2,653	1,094	2,543
Portugal	122	957	2,121
Philippines	6,243	3,518	1,790
Brazil	13,353	439	1,258
Italy(*)	799	613	1,225
Colombia	6,390	2,017	1,125
Nicaragua	1,259	1,765	1,006
Netherlands	5	0	942
Ethiopia(*)	0	0	872
Germany(*)	1,237	412	844
Rest of World	8,052	6,693	3,241
World Total	1,970,721	2,083,583	2,211,542

(*) Denotes a country that is a summarization of its component countries.

Users should use cautious interpretation on quantity reports using mixed units of measure. Quantity line items will only include statistics on the units of measure that are equal to, or are able to be converted to, the assigned unit of measure of the grouped commodities.

FAS, Office of Global Analysis, (202) 720–6301.

Table 2-7.—Cotton, excluding linters: United States exports and imports, 2017–2019

Area/Partners of Destination	Year beginning August		
	2017	2018	2019
	Metric tons		
Exports:			
Vietnam	643,745	729,216	833,136
China	502,957	571,651	356,510
Pakistan	187,406	317,087	320,614
Turkey	423,336	412,162	360,243
Bangladesh	139,819	194,854	184,834
Indonesia	321,331	345,488	225,843
Mexico	219,210	206,572	172,874
India	240,827	160,850	291,289
Thailand	125,633	144,903	122,579
Korea, South	130,162	131,949	97,883
Taiwan	91,823	101,354	93,808
Malaysia	44,972	53,681	65,320
Peru	42,486	52,186	50,294
Guatemala	42,725	46,786	53,491
Japan	26,387	26,467	21,982
El Salvador	13,901	14,549	15,831
Egypt	20,919	24,647	18,686
Honduras	2,950	4,141	5,382
Colombia	17,878	24,895	15,798
Ecuador	14,076	15,829	13,199
Costa Rica	8,618	8,482	8,772
Italy(!)	1,894	3,096	2,054
Italy(*)	1,894	3,096	2,054
Hong Kong	123	494	1,484
Oman	0	1	0
Portugal	2,989	2,482	2,668
Bahrain	4,330	3,154	2,797
Philippines	14,126	12,418	10,054
Austria	785	1,736	2,334
Nicaragua	449	1,938	2,149
Other Partners	50,831	27,715	13,657
World Total	3,338,578	3,643,879	3,367,620

Country of origin	Year beginning August		
	2017	2018	2019
	Metric tons		
Imports:			
Turkey	6,141	5,106	4,984
Mexico	4,619	2,539	2,679
India	3,279	3,558	2,677
Pakistan	1,830	1,633	1,457
Indonesia	513	947	828
Egypt	537	695	726
Uzbekistan, Republic of	0	0	0
Canada	131	98	80
Bangladesh	119	177	44
Germany(*)	17	210	327
China	5	78	92
Costa Rica	0	0	19
Italy(!)	0	0	2
Italy(*)	0	0	2
Brazil	236	1,412	347
Vietnam	0	0	0
Spain	61	116	10
Dominican Republic	290	114	0
Belgium(!)	0	0	40
Belgium-Luxembourg(*)	0	0	40
Tajikistan	20	0	0
Ireland	0	0	0
Taiwan	1	0	-
Haiti	0	0	0
Peru	0	55	1
United Kingdom	0	0	29
Hungary	0	0	1
Thailand	0	0	1
Japan	0	1	1
Czech Republic	0	15	-
Other Partners	1,039	423	254
World Total	18,838	17,177	14,638

(*) Denotes a country that is a summarization of its component countries.
All zeroes for a data item may show that statistics exist in the other import type.
Users should use cautious interpretation on quantity reports using mixed units of measure.   Quantity line items will only
include statistics on the units of measure that are equal to, or are able to be converted to, the assigned unit of measure of
the grouped commodities.
FAS, Office of Global Analysis, (202) 720-6301. Product Group: FATUS.

Table 2-8.—Cotton: International trade, 2017/2018–2019/2020 [1]

Country	2017/2018	2018/2019	2019/2020
	1,000 480 lb. bales		
Principle exporting countries:			
United States	16,279	14,763	16,500
Brazil	4,174	6,018	8,800
India	5,182	3,511	3,600
Greece	1,076	1,355	1,500
Benin	1,000	1,400	1,400
Australia	3,915	3,632	1,300
Mali	1,300	1,350	1,300
Cote d'Ivoire	620	895	1,000
Burkina	1,225	940	900
Cameroon	400	575	600
Argentina	168	545	500
Sudan	350	425	500
Malaysia	152	313	450
Mexico	350	500	425
Tajikistan	505	350	425
Azerbaijan	162	384	350
Turkey	325	482	350
Kazakhstan	250	275	300
Spain	239	322	300
Uzbekistan	1,000	750	300
Egypt	220	350	250
Tanzania	90	200	250
Togo	200	225	250
Turkmenistan	625	150	250
Chad	250	100	200
Zambia	117	156	200
Principle importing countries:			
China	5,710	9,640	8,250
Bangladesh	7,600	7,200	7,300
Vietnam	7,000	6,900	6,800
Turkey	4,024	3,499	4,300
Pakistan	3,400	2,850	4,200
Indonesia	3,517	3,051	3,000
India	1,677	1,800	2,300
Malaysia	739	744	1,000
Thailand	1,149	1,075	950
Mexico	925	850	800
Korea, South	904	781	600
Taiwan	632	592	525
Egypt	550	520	500
Iran	325	300	300
Japan	262	230	250
Peru	242	214	250
El Salvador	156	177	180
Portugal	184	174	170
Italy	171	159	160
Guatemala	118	148	150
Mauritius	115	120	120
Russia	200	150	100

[1] Marketing year beginning August 1.

FAS, Office of Global Analysis, (202) 720–6301.   Prepared or estimated on the basis of official USDA production, supply, and distribution statistics from foreign governments.

Table 2-9.—Sugarbeets: Area, yield, production, and value, United States, 2011–2020 [1]

Year	Area		Yield per harvested acre	Production	Marketing year average price per ton received by farmers	Value of production
	Planted	Harvested				
	1,000 acres	*1,000 acres*	*tons*	*1,000 tons*		*1,000 dollars*
2011	1,232.8	1,213.2	23.8	28,896	69.40	2,004,116
2012	1,230.1	1,204.1	29.3	35,224	66.40	2,338,789
2013	1,198.0	1,154.0	28.4	32,789	46.60	1,526,821
2014	1,162.5	1,146.3	27.3	31,285	46.00	1,440,068
2015	1,159.8	1,145.4	30.9	35,371	47.20	1,669,310
2016	1,163.4	1,126.4	32.8	36,920	35.70	1,318,267
2017	1,131.4	1,113.8	31.7	35,317	41.20	1,456,165
2018	1,113.1	1,096.4	30.4	33,282	35.60	1,183,421
2019	1,133.0	980.1	29.2	28,650	38.30	1,098,421
2020	1,162.2	1,141.8	29.4	33,610	50.50	1,696,742

[1] Relates to year of intended harvest for fall planted beets in central California and to year of planting for overwintered beets in central and southern California.
NASS, Crops Branch, (202) 720–2127.

Table 2-10.—Sugarbeets: Area, yield, and production, by State and United States, 2018–2020

State	Area planted			Area harvested			Yield per harvested acre			Production		
	2018	2019	2020	2018	2019	2020	2018	2019	2020	2018	2019	2020
	1,000 acres	*1,000 acres*	*1,000 acres*	*1,000 acres*	*1,000 acres*	*1,000 acres*	*Tons*	*Tons*	*Tons*	*1,000 tons*	*1,000 tons*	*1,000 tons*
California [1] ...	24.6	24.5	24.1	24.6	24.4	23.4	48.8	45.4	46.6	1,200	1,108	1,090
Colorado	26.3	25.1	24.2	25.5	24.3	23.7	32.6	30.7	31.3	831	746	742
Idaho	163.0	171.0	171.0	163.0	165.0	168.0	40.5	39.0	40.5	6,602	6,435	6,804
Michigan	150.0	146.0	157.0	148.0	145.0	154.0	29.1	28.6	28.3	4,307	4,147	4,358
Minnesota	415.0	425.0	433.0	408.0	337.0	429.0	25.7	25.0	26.1	10,486	8,425	11,197
Montana	43.5	41.8	43.6	42.4	36.5	38.1	31.1	31.6	31.3	1,319	1,153	1,193
Nebraska	45.5	44.0	46.2	44.1	42.1	45.7	31.9	25.4	31.0	1,407	1,069	1,417
North Dakota	202.0	212.0	221.0	199.0	170.0	218.0	28.8	26.0	24.9	5,731	4,420	5,428
Oregon	9.3	10.0	9.5	9.3	9.8	9.4	39.4	38.5	40.9	366	377	384
Washington [2]	1.8	2.0	1.9	1.8	2.0	1.9	48.2	45.4	47.8	87	91	91
Wyoming	32.1	31.6	30.7	30.7	24.0	30.6	30.8	28.3	29.6	946	679	906
United States	1,113.1	1,133.0	1,162.2	1,096.4	980.1	1,141.8	30.4	29.2	29.4	33,282	28,650	33,610

[1] Relates to year of intended harvest for fall planted beets in central California and to year of planting for overwintered beets in central and southern California.
NASS, Crops Branch, (202) 720–2127.

Table 2-11.—Sugarbeets: Production and value, by State and United States, 2019–2020

State	Production		Marketing year average price per ton received by farmers		Value of production	
	2019	2020	2019	2020	2019	2020
	1,000 tons	*1,000 tons*	*Dollars*	*Dollars*	*1,000 dollars*	*1,000 dollars*
California [1]	1,108	1,090	48.60	46.60	53,849	53,230
Colorado	746	742	16.90	44.50	12,607	33,019
Idaho	6,435	6,804	50.90	53.50	327,542	364,014
Michigan	4,147	4,358	35.00	55.00	145,145	239,690
Minnesota	8,425	11,197	35.40	49.30	298,245	552,01
Montana	1,153	1,193	29.20	47.20	33,668	56,310
Nebraska	1,069	1,417	16.90	44.50	18,066	63,057
North Dakota ..	4,420	5,428	38.00	49.30	167,960	267,600
Oregon	377	384	50.90	53.50	19,189	20,544
Washington [2]	91	91	50.90	53.50	4,632	4,869
Wyoming	679	906	25.80	47.80	17,518	43,307
United States	28,650	33,610	38.30	50.50	1,098,421	1,696,742

[1] Relates to year of intended harvest for fall planted beets in central California and to year of planting for overwintered beets in central and southern California.
NASS, Crops Branch, (202) 720–2127.

Table 2-12.—Sugarcane for sugar and seed: Area, yield, production, and value, United States, 2011–2020

Year	Area harvested			Yield per acre[1]			Production[1]		
	For sugar	For seed	Total	For sugar	For seed	For sugar and seed	For sugar	For seed	Total
	1,000 acres	*1,000 acres*	*1,000 acres*	*Tons*	*Tons*	*Tons*	*1,000 tons*	*1,000 tons*	*1,000 tons*
2011	827.1	45.5	872.6	33.5	32.7	33.5	27,738	1,486	29,224
2012	854.9	47.5	902.4	35.7	36.4	35.7	30,500	1,727	32,227
2013	859.6	51.2	910.8	33.8	33.9	33.8	29,023	1,521	30,761
2014	823.7	44.8	868.5	35.1	34.1	35.0	28,895	1,529	30,424
2015	831.1	43.6	874.7	36.8	35.9	36.7	30,535	1,567	32,122
2016	853.2	49.9	903.1	35.6	35.0	35.6	30,371	1,747	32,118
2017	851.5	52.6	904.1	36.6	39.1	36.8	31,182	2,056	33,238
2018	859.6	40.1	899.7	38.3	40.1	38.4	32,934	1,608	34,542
2019	870.3	42.9	913.2	34.8	38.5	35.0	30,287	1,650	31,937
2020	896.5	44.0	940.5	37.6	39.5	37.7	33,718	1,739	35,457

Year	Marketing year average price per ton received by farmers	Value of production	
		Of cane used for sugar	Of cane used for sugar and seed[2]
	Dollars	*1,000 dollars*	*1,000 dollars*
2011	47.20	1,308,951	1,379,498
2012	41.90	1,276,631	1,348,361
2013	31.40	910,377	962,807
2014	34.70	1,002,138	1,054,657
2015	31.20	953,328	1,000,620
2016	32.60	990,209	966,757
2017	31.00	966,757	1,025,524
2018	33.40	1,100,218	1,154,907
2019	38.30	1,159,550	1,223,686
2020	40.90	1,403,937	1,476,508

[1] Net tons.   [2] Price per ton of cane for sugar used in evaluating value of production for seed.
NASS, Crops Branch, (202) 720–2127.

Table 2-13.—Sugarcane for sugar and seed: Production and value, by State and United States, 2019–2020

State	Sugarcane for sugar						Sugar and seed: Value of production[1]	
	Production[2]		Price per ton		Value of production		2019	2020
	2019	2020	2019	2020	2019	2020		
	1,000 tons	*1,000 tons*	*Dollars*	*Dollars*	*1,000 dollars*	*1,000 dollars*	*1,000 dollars*	*1,000 dollars*
Florida	16,992	17,564	36.70	39.30	623,606	712,077	647,534	738,644
Louisiana	12,243	15,015	42.10	44.00	515,430	667,348	554,078	711,348
Texas	1,052	1,139	19.50	23.30	20,514	24,512	22,074	26,516
United States	30,287	33,718	38.30	40.90	1,159,550	1,403,937	1,223,686	1,476,508

[1] Price per ton of cane for sugar used in evaluating value of production for seed.   [2] Net tons.
NASS, Crops Branch, (202) 720–2127.

Table 2-14.—Sugarcane for sugar and seed: Area, yield, and production, by State and United States, 2018–2020

State	Area harvested			Yield per acre [1]			Cane production [1]		
	2018	2019	2020	2018	2019	2020	2018	2019	2020
For sugar:	1,000 acres	1,000 acres	1,000 acres	Tons	Tons	Tons	1,000 tons	1,000 tons	1,000 tons
Florida	397	397	409	41.7	42.8	44.3	16,555	16,992	18,119
Louisiana	425	442	461	35.3	27.7	32.9	15,003	12,243	15,167
Texas	37.6	31.3	33.4	36.6	33.6	31.5	1,376	1,052	1,052
United States	859.6	870.3	903.4	38.3	34.8	38.0	32,934	30,287	34,338
For seed:									
Florida	15.3	13.7	14.3	45.8	47.6	47.3	701	652	676
Louisiana	23.5	27.0	27.4	36.5	34.0	36.5	858	918	1,000
Texas	1.3	2.2	2.5	37.9	36.5	34.3	49	80	86
United States	40.1	42.9	44.2	40.1	38.5	39.9	1,608	1,650	1,762
For sugar and seed:									
Florida	412.3	410.7	423.3	41.9	43.0	44.4	17,256	17,644	18,795
Louisiana	448.5	469.0	488.4	35.4	28.1	33.1	15,861	13,161	16,167
Texas	38.9	33.5	35.9	36.6	33.8	31.7	1,425	1,132	1,138
United States	899.7	913.2	947.6	38.4	35.0	38.1	34,542	31,937	36,100

[1] Net tons.
NASS, Crops Branch, (202) 720–2127.

Table 2-15.—Sugar, cane (raw value [1]): Refiners' raw stocks, receipts, meltings, continental United States, 2011–2020

Year	Jan. 1 stocks	Receipts [2]	Meltings
		1,000 tons	
2011	257	5,776	5,534
2012	498	5,880	5,805
2013	574	5,956	5,938
2014	592	6,099	6,135
2015	556	6,319	6,552
2016	322	6,473	6,434
2017	362	6,272	6,096
2018	538	6,328	6,339
2019	528	6,487	6,450
2020	565	6,506	6,511

[1] Raw value is the equivalent in terms of 96° sugar. [2] Receipts include refiners' total offshore raw sugar receipts in continental U.S. ports, whether entered through the customs or held pending availability of quota and raw cane sugar produced from sugarcane in the continental United States.
FPAC, (202) 690-0734.

Table 2-16.—Sugar, cane and beet: Domestic marketings, by source of supply, continental United States, 2018–2020

Area of supply	2018	2019	2020
	1,000 tons		
Domestic areas			
Mainland (beet)	5,096	5,045	4,658
Mainland and Hawaii (cane)	3,937	4,018	3,849
Total domestic areas	9,033	9,063	8,507

FPAC, (202) 690-0734.

GRAIN AND FEED

Table 2-17.—Sugar, cane and beet (refined): Stocks, production, and food use deliveries, continental United States, 2011–2020

Item and year	Cane refiners	Sugarbeet processors	Importers of direct consumption sugar	Mainland cane processors [1]	Total
	1,000 short tons, raw value				
Stocks as of Jan. 1 [2]					
2011	466	1,691	0	4	2,161
2012	315	1,597	0	6	1,918
2013	388	2,013	0	3	2,404
2014	572	1,603	0	5	2,180
2015	351	1,589	0	4	1,944
2016	413	1,889	0	4	2,307
2017	325	2,029	0	0	2,354
2018	316	1,716	0	0	2,032
2019	288	1,889	0	0	2,177
2020	326	1,454	0	8	1,779
Sugar Production					
2011	5,476	4,561	0	19	10,056
2012	5,841	5,070	0	16	10,927
2013	5,883	4,881	0	17	10,781
2014	6,106	4,895	0	10	11,012
2015	6,528	4,878	0	42	11,448
2016	6,419	4,990	0	82	11,491
2017	6,084	5,198	0	0	11,282
2018	6,303	5,322	0	0	11,625
2019	6,366	4,658	0	0	11,024
2020	6,460	4,686	0	0	11,146
Food and Beverage Deliveries [3]					
2011	5,554	4,552	995	17	11,118
2012	5,630	4,633	977	18	11,257
2013	5,834	4,777	949	15	11,575
2014	6,058	4,875	796	11	11,740
2015	6,274	4,614	1,034	11	11,933
2016	6,373	4,809	921	12	12,115
2017	5,976	5,425	682	0	12,083
2018	6,219	5,121	705	0	12,045
2019	6,317	5,099	645	0	12,062
2020	6,593	4,387	1,280	0	11,054

[1] Sugar for human consumption only. [2] Stocks include sugar in bond and in Customs custody and control. [3] Consists of all refined sugar.

FPAC-BC, Commodity Analysis Branch, (202) 690-0734.

Table 2-18.—Sugar (raw and refined): Average price per pound at specified markets, 2010–2019

Year	Cane sugar		Refined beet: Mid-west markets, U.S. wholesale	Retail price, granulated: United States
	Raw, 96 centrifugal			
	Intercontinental contract No. 11, nearby futures, world price	Duty fee paid, New York, U.S. price		
	Cents	Cents	Cents	Cents
2010	22.49	35.97	53.23	62.86
2011	27.22	38.12	56.22	68.30
2012	21.69	28.90	43.38	69.41
2013	17.46	20.46	27.22	64.32
2014	16.34	24.15	32.86	60.90
2015	13.14	24.88	33.88	65.36
2016	18.13	27.65	29.65	64.19
2017	15.81	27.92	31.33	64.76
2018	12.25	25.37	35.54	61.63
2019	12.36	26.16	36.14	59.01

ERS, Market and Trade Economics Division, (202) 694–5247. Compiled from the following sources: (New York) Coffee, Sugar & Cocoa Exchange; the U.S. Department of Labor, Bureau of Labor Statistics; Milling and Baking News, New York Board of Trade; Intercontinental Exchange,.

Table 2-19.—Sugar, centrifugal: International trade, 2017/2018–2019/2020

Country	2017/2018	2018/2019	2019/2020
	1,000 metric tons, raw value		
Principle exporting countries:			
Brazil	28,200	19,600	18,620
Thailand	10,907	9,300	10,500
India	2,236	4,700	5,000
Australia	3,600	3,800	3,500
Guatemala	1,881	1,999	2,019
Mexico	1,146	2,337	1,693
South Africa	768	1,041	1,600
European Union	3,920	1,800	1,500
Eswatini	519	680	760
Colombia	732	720	750
Algeria	610	651	671
Cuba	553	592	610
Russia	621	315	605
Pakistan	1,600	600	500
Morocco	380	450	470
El Salvador	449	451	465
United Arab Emirates	458	430	430
Belarus	393	400	420
Nicaragua	388	421	420
Mauritius	390	347	360
Principle importing countries:			
Indonesia	4,298	5,362	4,500
China	4,350	4,100	4,000
United States	2,972	2,816	2,866
Bangladesh	2,654	2,455	2,480
Algeria	2,349	2,217	2,170
Malaysia	2,002	2,125	2,050
European Union	1,341	1,900	2,000
Nigeria	1,870	1,870	1,890
Korea, South	1,864	1,996	1,860
Saudi Arabia	1,486	1,528	1,600
India	2,071	1,300	1,500
United Arab Emirates	2,804	1,573	1,330
Canada	1,243	1,285	1,325
Japan	1,240	1,187	1,196
Iraq	1,340	1,154	1,175
Morocco	1,128	1,058	1,142
Venezuela	1,030	1,000	1,000
Iran	237	851	851
Egypt	990	860	830
Sudan	827	805	825

FAS, Office of Global Analysis, (202) 720–6301.   Prepared or estimated on the basis of official USDA production, supply, and distribution statistics from foreign governments.

Table 2-20.—U.S. Sugar (raw value): Supply and use, includes Puerto Rico, 2009/10–2018/19

Fiscal Year	Beginning stocks	Production	Imports	Exports	Total deliveries, domestic use
	1,000 short tons				
2009/10	1,534	7,963	3,320	211	11,152
2010/11	1,498	7,831	3,738	248	11,422
2011/12	1,378	8,488	3,632	269	11,313
2012/13	1,979	8,981	3,224	274	11,776
2013/14	2,158	8,462	3,742	306	12,246
2014/15	1,810	8,656	3,553	185	12,019
2015/16	1,815	8,989	3,341	74	12,051
2016/17	2,054	8,970	3,244	95	12,258
2017/18	1,876	9,293	3,277	170	12,185
2018/19	2,008	8,948	2,875	35	12,270

ERS, Market and Trade Economics Division, (202) 694–5247. Source: ERS Sugar and Sweetener Outlook

Table 2-21.—Honey: United States exports for consumption, by country of destination, 2018–2020

Country	2018	2019	2020
	Metric tons	*Metric tons*	*Metric tons*
Philippines	507	773	1,275
Canada	734	628	1,230
Korea, South	812	672	729
Japan	538	571	359
Kuwait	150	407	347
Yemen(*)	59	130	177
China	72	180	161
United Arab Emirates	120	155	121
India	66	99	119
Panama	76	44	118
Trinidad and Tobago	48	64	89
Barbados	157	135	85
Vietnam	511	56	62
Hong Kong	20	70	58
Bahamas, The	41	45	49
Netherlands Antilles	31	42	44
Bahrain	53	0	43
Taiwan	0	11	40
Bermuda	37	24	32
Singapore	19	23	27
Nicaragua	51	40	25
Pakistan(*)	5	7	19
United Kingdom	6	34	15
Cambodia	1	0	13
Austria	11	11	8
Germany(*)	0	4	8
Costa Rica	0	0	5
Netherlands	0	0	5
Romania)	5	14	4
Cayman Islands	4	5	4
Rest of World	272	102	28
World Total	4,402	4,343	5,298

(*) Denotes a country that is a summarization of its component countries.
FAS, Office of Global Analysis, (202) 720-6301.   Data Source: U.S. Census Bureau Trade Data, as of March 2021.

Table 2-22.—Honey: Number of colonies, yield, production, stocks, price, and value, United States, 2011–2020 [1]

State	Honey producing colonies [2]	Yield per colony	Production [3]	Stocks Dec 15 [4]	Average price per pound [5]	Value of production
	1,000	Pounds	1,000 pounds	1,000 pounds	Cents	1,000 dollars
2011	2,491	59.6	148,357	36,761	176.5	261,850
2012	2,539	56.0	142,296	31,829	199.2	283,454
2013	2,641	56.6	149,550	38,175	214	320,037
2014	2,741	65.1	178,310	41,207	217	386,933
2015	2,661	58.9	156,705	42,205	208	325,946
2016	2,780	58.4	162,246	41,314	212	343,962
2017	2,684	55.5	149,025	30,671	220	327,855
2018	2,828	54.5	154,008	29,303	221	340,358
2019	2,812	55.8	156,922	40,861	199	312,275
2020	2,706	54.5	147,594	39,715	203.0	299,616

[1] For producers with 5 or more colonies that also qualify as a farm. Colonies which produced honey in more than one State were counted in each State. [2] Honey producing colonies are the maximum number of colonies from which honey was taken during the year. It is possible to take honey from colonies which did not survive the entire year. [3] Due to rounding, total colonies multiplied by total yield may not exactly equal production. [4] Stocks held by producers. [5] Average price per pound based on expanded sales.
NASS, Livestock Branch, (202) 720–3570.

Table 2-23.—Honey: Number of colonies, yield, production, stocks, price and value, by State and United States, 2019 [1]

State	Honey producing colonies [2]	Yield per colony	Production	Stocks Dec 15 [3]	Average price per pound [4]	Value of production [5]
	1,000	Pounds	1,000 pounds	1,000 pounds	Cents	1,000 dollars
Alabama	7	42	294	44	372	994
Arizona	23	46	1,058	201	301	2,158
Arkansas	20	55	1,100	176	188	1,815
California	335	48	16,080	3,216	211	25,728
Colorado	32	46	1,472	500	205	3,444
Florida	205	45	9,225	830	240	22,694
Georgia	102	33	3,366	370	276	8,987
Hawaii	16	80	1,280	51	192	1,664
Idaho	92	32	2,944	677	196	4,769
Illinois	11	39	429	116	483	1,767
Indiana	9	55	495	188	358	1,871
Iowa	38	55	2,090	1,170	240	4,912
Kansas	7	79	553	171	310	1,300
Kentucky	6	41	246	44	543	1,146
Louisiana	54	72	3,888	428	191	8,359
Maine	15	35	525	110	298	1,722
Michigan	94	50	4,700	1,363	249	12,032
Minnesota	118	59	6,962	3,063	194	12,740
Mississippi	22	80	1,760	141	207	3,291
Missouri	10	43	430	73	283	1,441
Montana	173	86	14,878	5,802	190	22,168
Nebraska	39	52	2,028	223	201	2,920
New Jersey	15	28	420	155	747	1,966
New York	59	58	3,422	1,027	324	13,688
North Carolina ...	14	42	588	118	576	2,417
North Dakota	520	65	33,800	6,422	187	48,334
Ohio	15	67	1,005	442	372	3,477
Oregon	87	32	2,784	1,141	236	6,960
Pennsylvania	19	50	950	409	389	4,190
South Carolina ...	16	47	752	45	317	3,783
South Dakota	270	72	19,440	7,582	191	30,326
Tennessee	8	57	456	91	411	2,152
Texas	126	60	7,560	1,663	212	17,539
Utah	22	29	638	89	210	1,257
Vermont	6	48	288	84	376	1,290
Virginia	5	39	195	49	724	1,402
Washington	81	35	2,835	1,191	215	6,180
West Virginia	6	37	222	47	433	946
Wisconsin	46	47	2,162	692	295	6,486
Wyoming	39	56	2,184	306	191	3,123
Other States [6][7]	30	47	1,418	351	602	6,594
United States [7][8]	2,812	55.8	156,922	40,861	221	312,275

[1] For producers with 5 or more colonies that also qualify as a farm. Colonies which produced honey in more than one State were counted in each State. [2] Honey producing colonies are the maximum number of colonies from which honey was taken during the year. It is possible to take honey from colonies which did not survive the entire year. [3] Stocks held by producers. [4] Average price per pound based on expanded sales. [5] Value of production is equal to production multiplied by average price per pound. [6] Alaska, Connecticut, Delaware, Maryland, Massachusetts, Nevada, New Hampshire, New Mexico, Oklahoma, and Rhode Island not published separately to avoid disclosing data for individual operations. [7] Due to rounding, total colonies multiplied by total yield may not exactly equal production. [8] United States value of production will not equal summation of States.
NASS, Livestock Branch, (202) 720–3570.

Table 2-24.—Honey: Number of colonies, yield, production, stocks, price and value, by State and United States, 2019 [1]

State	Honey producing colonies [2]	Yield per colony	Production	Stocks Dec 15 [3]	Average price per pound [4]	Value of production [5]
	1,000	Pounds	1,000 pounds	1,000 pounds	Cents	1,000 dollars
Alabama	7	42	294	44	320	941
Arizona	23	46	1,058	201	197	2,084
Arkansas	20	55	1,100	176	153	1,683
California	335	48	16,080	3,216	156	25,085
Colorado	33	46	1,472	500	214	3,150
Florida	205	45	9,225	830	248	22,878
Georgia	102	33	3,366	370	261	8,785
Hawaii	16	80	1,280	51	128	1,638
Idaho	92	32	2,944	677	167	4,916
Illinois	11	39	429	116	431	1,849
Indiana	9	55	495	198	395	1,955
Iowa	38	55	2,090	1,170	224	4,682
Kansas	7	79	553	171	295	1,631
Kentucky	6	41	246	44	450	1,107
Louisiana	54	72	3,888	428	204	7,932
Maine	15	35	525	110	292	1,533
Michigan	94	50	4,700	1,363	236	11,092
Minnesota	118	59	6,962	3,063	163	11,348
Mississippi	22	80	1,760	141	185	3,256
Missouri	10	43	430	73	332	1,428
Montana	173	86	14,878	5,802	148	22,019
Nebraska	39	52	2,028	223	146	2,961
New Jersey	15	28	420	155	333	1,399
New York	59	58	3,422	1,027	449	15,365
North Carolina	14	42	588	118	406	2,387
North Dakota	520	65	33,800	6,422	140	47,320
Ohio	15	67	1,005	442	342	3,437
Oregon	87	32	2,784	1,141	207	5,763
Pennsylvania	19	50	950	409	424	4,028
South Carolina	16	47	752	45	501	3,768
South Dakota	270	72	19,440	7,582	153	29,743
Tennessee	8	57	456	91	465	2,120
Texas	126	60	7,560	1,814	230	17,388
Utah	22	29	638	89	206	1,314
Vermont	6	48	288	84	434	1,250
Virginia	5	39	195	49	751	1,464
Washington	81	35	2,835	1,191	212	6,010
West Virginia	6	37	222	47	450	999
Wisconsin	46	47	2,162	692	299	6,464
Wyoming	39	56	2,184	306	135	2,948
Other States [6] [7]	30	47	1,418	351	591	8,380
United States [7] [8]	2,812	55.8	156,922	41,022	197	309,136

[1] For producers with 5 or more colonies that also qualify as a farm.   Colonies which produced honey in more than one State were counted in each State.   [2] Honey producing colonies are the maximum number of colonies from which honey was taken during the year.   It is possible to take honey from colonies which did not survive the entire year.   [3] Stocks held by producers.   [4] Average price per pound based on expanded sales.   [5] Value of production is equal to production multiplied by average price per pound.   [6] Alaska, Connecticut, Delaware, Maryland, Massachusetts, Nevada, New Hampshire, New Mexico, Oklahoma, and Rhode Island not published separately to avoid disclosing data for individual operations.   [7] Due to rounding, total colonies multiplied by total yield may not exactly equal production.   [8] United States value of production will not equal summation of States.
NASS, Livestock Branch, (202) 720–3570.

Table 2-25.—U.S. per capita caloric sweeteners estimated deliveries for domestic food and beverage use, by calendar year 2009–2018 [1][2]

Calendar year	U.S. population [3] (July 1)	Refined sugar [4]	HFCS	Corn Sweeteners			Pure honey	Edible syrups	Total caloric sweeteners
				Glucose syrup	Dextrose	Total			
	Millions	*Pounds, dry basis*							
2009	307.2	63.4	49.7	13.0	2.7	65.3	0.9	0.6	130.3
2010	309.3	66.0	48.4	12.6	2.9	64.0	1.0	0.7	131.7
2011	311.6	66.0	46.7	12.2	2.9	61.8	1.1	0.7	129.6
2012	313.9	66.7	45.8	12.5	2.7	61.0	1.1	0.7	129.5
2013	316.1	68.0	43.8	12.0	2.6	58.4	1.2	0.7	128.3
2014	318.4	68.2	43.4	12.2	3.0	58.6	1.3	0.8	128.9
2015	320.7	69.1	42.6	12.3	3.0	57.8	1.3	0.9	129.0
2016	323.1	69.5	41.4	12.4	2.7	56.5	1.3	0.7	128.0
2017	325.1	69.1	40.5	13.1	3.0	56.5	1.4	0.7	127.7
2018	327.2	68.5	37.6	13.1	3.0	53.7	1.4	0.7	124.4

[1] Per capita deliveries of sweeteners by U.S. processors and refiners and direct-consumption imports to food manufacturers, retailers, and other end users represent the per capita supply of caloric sweeteners. The data exclude deliveries to manufacturers of alcoholic beverages. Actual human intake of caloric sweeteners is lower because of uneaten food, spoilage, and other losses. See Table 51 of the Sugar and Sweeteners Yearbook series for estimated intake of sugar. [2] Totals may not add due to rounding. [3] Source: U.S. Census Bureau. [4] Based on U.S. sugar deliveries for domestic food and beverage use.
ERS, Market and Trade Economics Division (202) 694–5247. Source: ERS Sugars and Sweeteners Outlook.

Table 2-26.—Tobacco: Area, yield, production, price, and value, United States, 2011–2020

Year	Area harvested	Yield per acre	Production	Marketing year average price per pound received by farmers	Value of production
	Acres	*Pounds*	*1,000 pounds*	*Dollars*	*1,000 dollars*
2011	325,040	1,841	598,252	1.857	1,110,737
2012	336,245	2,268	762,709	2.027	1,557,604
2013	356,250	2,033	724,266	2.181	1,579,823
2014	378,480	2,316	876,689	2.094	1,835,663
2015	328,850	2,188	719,563	2.006	1,443,320
2016	319,660	1,967	628,720	2.007	1,262,087
2017	321,470	2,209	710,161	2.058	1,461,855
2018	291,430	1,830	533,241	2.051	1,093,418
2019	227,120	2,060	467,956	2.009	946,252
2020	191,110	1,951	372,877	2.102	819,102

Table 2-27.—Tobacco: Area, yield, and production, by State and United States, 2017–2019

State	Area harvested			Yield per harvested acre			Production		
	2017	2018	2019	2017	2018	2019	2017	2018	2019
	Acres	*Acres*	*Acres*	*Pounds*	*Pounds*	*Pounds*	*1,000 pounds*	*1,000 pounds*	*1,000 pounds*
Georgia	12,500	12,500	9,000	2,100	1,900	2,100	26,250	23,750	18,900
Kentucky	80,500	68,100	57,400	2,277	1,973	2,150	183,300	134,370	123,390
North Carolina ...	163,900	152,750	117,400	2,197	1,649	1,999	360,040	251,925	234,700
Pennsylvania ...	8,100	7,800	5,700	2,344	2,231	2,509	18,990	17,400	14,300
South Carolina ...	12,000	12,300	8,300	2,100	1,800	1,900	25,200	22,140	15,770
Tennessee	21,100	15,700	13,300	2,038	2,523	2,292	43,000	39,610	30,490
Virginia	23,370	22,280	16,020	2,284	1,977	1,898	53,381	44,046	30,406
United States ...	321,470	291,430	227,120	2,209	1,830	2,060	710,161	533,241	467,956

CHAPTER III

STATISTICS OF OILSEEDS, FATS, AND OILS

This chapter includes information on cottonseed, flaxseed, olive oil, peanuts, soybeans, and fats and oils. Most butter statistics are included in the chapter on dairy and poultry statistics. Lard data are mostly in the chapter on livestock.

Table 3-1.—Cottonseed: All cotton harvested area and cottonseed production, farm disposition, marketing year average price per ton received by farmers, and value, United States, 2011–2020

Year	Harvested area of all cotton	Cottonseed				
		Production	Farm disposition		Marketing year average price [2]	Value of production
			Sales to oil mills	Other [1]		
	1,000 acres	*1,000 tons*	*1,000 tons*	*1,000 tons*	*Dollars*	*1,000 dollars*
2011	9,460.9	5,370.0	2,695.0	2,675.0	260.00	1,413,343
2012	9,321.8	5,666.0	2,985.0	2,681.0	252.00	1,456,245
2013	7,539.4	4,203.0	2,070.0	2,133.0	246.00	1,054,003
2014	9,351.8	5,125.0	2,459.0	2,666.0	194.00	1,015,607
2015	8,074.9	4,043.0	1,916.0	2,127.0	227.00	932,894
2016	9,507.8	5,369.0	2,921.0	2,448.0	195.00	1,055,924
2017	11,100.4	6,422.0	3,059.0	3,363.0	142.00	911,925
2018	9,990.8	5,631.0	2,435.0	3,196.0	155.00	878,254
2019	11,497.4	5,945.0	2,575.0	3,370.0	161.00	968,027
2020	8,216.5	4,468.0	1,793.0	2,675.0	194.00	875,057

[1] Includes planting seed, feed, exports, inter-farm sales, shrinkage, losses, and other uses.   [2] 2018 based on monthly prices received from August 1, 2018 - December 31, 2018.
NASS, Crops Branch, (202) 720–2127.

Table 3-2.—Cottonseed: Production and farm disposition, by State and United States, 2019 and 2020

State	Production		Farm disposition				Seed for planting [1]	
	2019	2020	Sales to oil mills		Other [2]		2019	2020
			2019	2020	2019	2020		
	1,000 tons	*1,000 tons*	*1,000 tons*	*1,000 tons*	*1,000 tons*	*1,000 tons*	*1,000 tons*	*1,000 tons*
Alabama	267.0	205.0	46.0	20.0	221.0	185.0	3.0	2.6
Arizona	136.0	107.0	....	....	136.0	107.0	1.0	0.8
Arkansas	472.0	402.0	280.0	292.0	192.0	110.0	3.7	3.0
California	290.0	214.0	69.0	77.0	221.0	137.0	1.8	1.0
Florida	57.0	28.0	39.0	20.0	18.0	8.0	0.6	0.6
Georgia	778.0	613.0	296.0	253.0	482.0	360.0	6.2	5.7
Kansas	85.0	99.0	....	106.0	85.0	99.0	1.1	1.0
Louisiana	192.0	109.0	121.0	63.0	71.0	46.0	1.4	0.7
Mississippi	503.0	373.0	265.0	195.0	238.0	178.0	4.3	3.1
Missouri	253.0	210.0	117.0	52.0	136.0	158.0	2.2	2.1
New Mexico	26.0	22.0	....	....	26.0	22.0	0.5	0.3
North Carolina	308.0	146.0	4.0	....	304.0	146.0	3.3	2.6
Oklahoma	191.0	189.0	132.0	123.0	59.0	66.0	3.7	2.8
South Carolina	116.0	84.0	41.0	....	75.0	84.0	1.5	1.0
Tennessee	301.0	186.0	255.0	108.0	46.0	78.0	2.3	1.9
Texas	1,902.0	1,448.0	910.0	590.0	992.0	858.0	39.3	40.8
Virginia	68.0	33.0	....	....	68.0	33.0	0.6	0.5
United States	5,945.0	4,468.0	2,575.0	1,793.0	3,370.0	2,675.0	76.5	70.5

[1] Included in "other" farm disposition. Seed for planting is produced in crop year shown, but used in the following year.   [2] Includes planting seed, feed, exports, inter-farm sales, shrinkage, losses, and other uses.
NASS, Crops Branch, (202) 720–2127.

Table 3-3.—Cottonseed: Marketing year average price per ton and value of production, by State and United States, crop of 2018–2020

State	Marketing year average price per ton			Value of production		
	2018	2019	2020[1]	2018	2019	2020[1]
	Dollars	Dollars	Dollars	1,000 dollars	1,000 dollars	1,000 dollars
Alabama	118.00	120.00	139.00	29,972	32,040	28,495
Arizona	214.00	254.00	278.00	33,384	34,544	29,746
Arkansas	152.00	174.00	196.00	55,632	82,128	78,792
California	260.00	301.00	350.00	88,920	87,290	74,900
Florida	110.00	120.00	135.00	2,970	6,840	3,780
Georgia	113.00	115.00	152.00	61,698	89,470	93,176
Kansas	175.00	170.00	196.00	18,550	14,450	19,404
Louisiana	148.00	157.00	189.00	19,980	30,144	20,601
Mississippi	157.00	163.00	219.00	70,807	81,989	81,687
Missouri	153.00	169.00	223.00	47,430	42,757	46,830
New Mexico	200.00	210.00	291.00	8,400	5,460	4,074
North Carolina	127.00	141.00	192.00	28,448	43,428	23,232
Oklahoma	140.00	152.00	186.00	27,580	29,032	35,154
South Carolina	123.00	124.00	180.00	14,391	14,384	15,120
Tennessee	143.00	157.00	232.00	31,317	47,257	43,152
Texas	159.00	167.00	187.00	331,992	317,634	270,776
Virginia	133.00	135.00	186.00	6,783	9,180	6,138
United States	155.00	161.00	194.00	878,254	968,027	875,057

[1] Based on monthly prices received from August 1, 2020 - December 31, 2020.
NASS, Crops Branch, (202) 720–2127.

Table 3-4.—Cottonseed: Crushings, output of products and product prices, United States, 2010–2019

Year beginning August	Quantity crushed	Cottonseed products and prices			
		Oil		Cake and meal	
		Quantity	Price[1]	Quantity	Price[2]
	1,000 tons	Million pounds	Cents per pound	1,000 tons	Dollars per ton
2010	2,563	835	54.50	1,163	273.84
2011	2,400	755	53.20	1,090	275.13
2012	2,500	800	48.60	1,125	331.52
2013	2,000	630	60.66	900	377.51
2014	1,900	610	45.74	855	304.27
2015	1,500	465	45.90	705	261.19
2016	1,769	542	40.90	805	208.61
2017	1,854	561	31.87	845	260.88
2018	1,760	456	35.14	748	228.64
2019	1,712	481	40.18	780	247.04

[1] Tanks, f.o.b. Valley Points.   [2] 41 percent protein, solvent, Memphis.
ERS, Field Crops Branch, (202) 694–5300. Formerly compiled from annual reports of the U.S. Department of Commerce.

Table 3-5.—International meal, cottonseed: Production in specified countries, 2017/2018–2019/2020

Country	2017/2018	2018/2019	2019/2020
	1,000 metric tons		
India	4,301	3,975	4,535
China	4,116	4,093	4,038
Brazil	1,310	1,875	1,900
Pakistan	1,465	1,395	1,350
United States	766	678	726
Turkey	710	732	605
Uzbekistan	651	558	600
Benin	145	166	173
Mali	167	172	162
European Union	130	135	158
Turkmenistan	205	144	153
Australia	386	300	145
Burma	141	134	131
Burkina	116	97	104
Cameroon	84	88	95

FAS, Office of Global Analysis, (202) 720-6301.   Prepared or estimated on the basis of official USDA production, supply, and distribution statistics from foreign governments.

Table 3-6.—Cottonseed and Cottonseed oil: United States exports by country of destination, 2018–2020

Country of destination	2018	2019	2020
	Metric tons	*Metric tons*	*Metric tons*
Cottonseed:			
Korea, South	131,012	118,312	130,747
Japan	63,478	58,635	65,524
Saudi Arabia	82,694	65,726	52,845
Mexico	95,329	36,400	39,313
China	2,330	985	7,136
Morocco	6,194	6,077	3,976
Canada	3,366	2,865	2,141
Vietnam	50	0	605
Oman	1,145	2,865	460
Colombia	6	86	269
United Arab Emirates	11,270	3,068	201
Panama	1	0	2
Bangladesh	824	0	0
Ireland	0	7	0
Guatemala	1	1	0
Hong Kong	0	8	0
Indonesia	894	0	0
Italy(*)	745	0	0
Jordan	1,576	1,483	0
Lebanon	639	0	0
Malaysia	0	579	0
Qatar	4,872	1,991	0
Philippines	420	0	0
Trinidad and Tobago	5	0	0
Taiwan	325	1,675	0
United Kingdom	744	168	0
World Total	407,919	300,930	303,219
Cottonseed oil:			
Mexico	17,089	21,069	18,883
Australia(*)	7,782	7,924	5,640
Canada	6,304	3,990	5,097
Japan	1,101	1,242	1,800
Malaysia	8,080	1,304	1,221
Thailand	108	31	214
India	1,857	84	200
Spain	0	0	83
Korea, South	43	110	69
United Kingdom	9	5	51
Portugal	71	15	38
Brazil	65	28	23
Belgium-Luxembourg(*)	56	13	22
Hungary	26	0	15
China	0	5	14
Turkey	20	9	9
Germany(*)	1	6	6
Bermuda	0	0	5
Dominican Republic	0	0	2
Saudi Arabia	0	0	2
Chile	29	1	1
Singapore	326	0	1
Bahamas, The	5	0	1
Ecuador	0	0	1
Colombia	1	3	0
Argentina	38	0	0
Costa Rica	2	0	0
Egypt	3,150	0	0
El Salvador	0	2	0
Libya	0	1,805	0
Rest of World	1,159	101	0
World Total	47,319	37,748	33,398

(*) Denotes a country that is a summarization of its component countries.
FAS, Office of Global Analysis, (202) 720-6301. Data Source: U.S. Census Bureau Trade Data

Table 3-7.—International oilseed, cottonseed: Area and production in specified countries, 2017/2018–2019/2020

Country	Area			Production		
	2017/2018	2018/2019	2019/2020	2017/2018	2018/2019	2019/2020
	1,000 hectares			1,000 metric tons		
India	12,600	12,600	13,000	12,312	10,953	12,524
China	3,400	3,500	3,450	10,800	10,875	10,679
United States	4,492	4,130	4,777	5,826	5,108	5,654
Brazil	1,175	1,640	1,700	3,019	4,254	4,254
Pakistan	2,700	2,300	2,500	3,552	3,292	2,900
Uzbekistan	1,250	1,100	1,010	1,512	1,283	1,374
Turkey	470	520	560	1,300	1,350	1,110
European Union	295	312	347	487	550	627
Mexico	210	243	225	530	593	533
Benin	530	650	675	376	463	479
Turkmenistan	545	545	545	525	356	391
Mali	705	725	735	396	359	382
Argentina	320	380	360	277	414	370
Cameroon	225	250	260	250	300	322
Sudan	180	180	200	243	255	308
Burma	249	240	240	310	295	289
Burkina	850	630	575	331	235	276
Cote d'Ivoire	327	392	425	215	250	267
Tajikistan	185	180	180	180	162	223
Tanzania	350	420	450	101	163	219
Australia	530	380	60	1,442	661	202
Azerbaijan	130	130	140	133	152	176
Uganda	109	81	89	150	141	149
Kazakhstan	125	128	125	117	135	145
Chad	120	60	250	40	16	130
Togo	160	180	185	100	116	121
Egypt	91	141	100	91	152	106
Nigeria	270	270	270	102	102	102

FAS, Office of Global Analysis, (202) 720–6301.   Prepared or estimated on the basis of official USDA production, supply, and distribution statistics from foreign governments.

Table 3-8.—International oil, cottonseed: Production in specified countries, 2017/2018–2019/2020 [1]

Country	2017/2018	2018/2019	2019/2020
	1,000 metric tons		
India	1,325	1,225	1,400
China	1,382	1,374	1,356
Brazil	440	632	640
Pakistan	488	465	450
United States	255	207	234
Uzbekistan	230	197	212
Turkey	232	240	198
Benin	48	56	58
Turkmenistan	77	54	57
Mali	56	58	54
European Union	44	45	53
Australia	133	104	50
Burma	50	48	47
Burkina	36	30	32
Cameroon	28	30	32
Tanzania	13	21	26
Tajikistan	21	22	25
Kazakhstan	18	22	23
Sudan	18	21	23
Uganda	22	22	23
Chad	6	2	20
Korea, South	20	20	20
Egypt	14	23	16
Nigeria	16	16	16
Argentina	20	15	15

[1] Year beginning July 1.
FAS, Office of Global Analysis, (202) 720–6301.   Prepared or estimated on the basis of official USDA production, supply, and distribution statistics from foreign governments.

Table 3-9.—Flaxseed: Area, yield, production, disposition, and value, United States, 2011–2020

Year	Area planted	Area harvested	Yield per harvested acre	Production	Marketing year average price per bushel received by farmers	Value of production
	1,000 acres	*1,000 acres*	*Bushels*	*1,000 bushels*	*Dollars*	*1,000 dollars*
2011	178	173	16.1	2,791	13.90	38,570
2012	349	336	17.3	5,798	13.80	79,919
2013	181	172	19.5	3,356	13.80	46,325
2014	311	302	21.1	6,368	11.80	75,077
2015	463	456	22.1	10,095	8.95	90,561
2016	374	366	23.7	8,656	8.00	69,352
2017	303	272	14.1	3,842	9.53	36,340
2018	208	198	22.6	4,466	9.89	43,533
2019	374	284	19.8	5,625	9.15	49,734
2020	305	296	19.3	5,706	11.10	62,357

NASS, Crops Branch, (202) 720–2127.

Table 3-10.—Flaxseed: Area, yield, and production, by State and United States, 2018–2020

State	Area planted			Area harvested		
	2018	2019	2020	2018	2019	2020
	1,000 acres	*1,000 acres*	*1,000 acres*	*1,000 acres*	*1,000 acres*	*1,000 acres*
Montana	39	99	105	37	89	102
North Dakota	165	275	200	158	195	194
South Dakota [1] ...	4	(NA)	(NA)	....	....	(NA)
United States	208	374	305	198	284	296

State	Yield per harvested acre			Production		
	2018	2019	2020	2018	2019	2020
	Bushels	*Bushels*	*Bushels*	*1,000 bushels*	*1,000 bushels*	*1,000 bushels*
Montana	17.0	15.0	16.0	629	1,335	1,632
North Dakota	24.0	22.0	21.0	3,792	4,290	4,074
South Dakota [1] ...	15	(NA)	....	45	....	(NA)
United States	22.6	19.8	19.3	4,466	5,625	5,706

(NA) Not available. [1] Estimates discontinued in 2020.
NASS, Crops Branch, (202) 720–2127.

Table 3-11.—Flaxseed: Marketing year average price and value of production, by State and United States, 2018–2020

State	Marketing year average price per bushel			Value of production		
	2018	2019	2020	2018	2019	2020
	Dollars	*Dollars*	*Dollars*	*1,000 dollars*	*1,000 dollars*	*1,000 dollars*
Montana	8.89	7.85	10.5	5,592	10,480	17,136
North Dakota	9.89	9.15	11.10	37,503	39,254	45,221
South Dakota [1]	9.73	(NA)	(NA)	438	(NA)	(NA)
United States	9.89	9.15	11.10	43,533	49,734	62,357

(NA) Not available. [1] Estimates discontinued in 2020.
NASS, Crops Branch, (202) 720–2127.

Table 3-12.—Flaxseed: Support operations, United States, 2014–2020

Marketin year beginning June 1	Income support payment rates per bushels [1]	Program price levels per bushel		Put under loan		Acquired by CCC under loan program [2]	Owned by CCC at end of marketing year
		Loan	Target/ Reference	Quantity	Percentage of production		
	Dollars	*Dollars*	*Dollars*	*1,000 bushels*	*Percent*	*1,000 bushels*	*1,000 bushels*
2014/2015	0.00	5.65	11.28	37.5	0.6	0	0
2015/2016	2.33	5.65	11.28	269.6	2.7	0	0
2016/2017	3.28	5.65	11.28	236.1	2.7	0	0
2017/2018	1.75	5.65	11.28	76.8	1.1	0	0
2018/2019	1.39	5.65	11.28	81.4	1.0	0	0
2019/2020	2.13	5.65	11.28	78.4	0.8	0	0
2020/2021	0.98	5.65	11.28	59.5	0.6	0	0

[1] The entry is the price loss coverage payment rate. For 2020/2021, projected rates is based on March 2021 WASDE MY price. Agricultural Risk Coverage (ARC) is also available, but payment rates are established at the county or farm levels.   [2] Acquisitions as of March 11, 2021.
FPAC-BC, Commodity Analysis Branch.

Table 3-13.—Flaxseed: Supply and disappearance, United States, 2010–2019

Year beginning June	Supply				Disappearance			
	Stocks June 1	Production	Imports	Total	Total used for seed	Exports	Crushings [1]	Total domestic disappearance [2]
	1,000 bushels	*1,000 bushels*	*1,000 bushels*	*1,000 bushels*	*1,000 bushels*	*1,000 bushels*	*1,000 bushels*	*1,000 bushels*
2010	1,557	9,056	6,040	16,653	144	2,130	11,635	12,353
2011	2,170	2,791	8,286	13,247	279	654	10,500	11,473
2012	1,120	5,798	6,928	13,757	147	1,020	11,000	11,813
2013	924	3,356	6,759	11,039	252	599	8,700	9,677
2014	763	6,368	7,351	14,482	375	528	11,850	13,146
2015	808	10,095	4,481	15,339	303	870	10,700	11,556
2016	2,914	8,656	3,086	14,656	245	1,332	10,500	11,155
2017	2,170	3,842	5,451	11,463	168	480	9,000	9,354
2018	1,629	4,466	5,503	11,598	303	262	9,300	9,774
2019 [3]	1,562	5,625	4,381	11,568	247	855	8,950	9,450

[1] From domestic and imported seed.   [2] Total supply minus exports and stocks June 1 of following year.   [3] Preliminary.
ERS, Field Crops Branch, (202) 694–5300.

Table 3-14.—Flaxseed and linseed oil and meal: Average price Minneapolis, 2010–2019

Year	Average price received by farmers per bushel	Minneapolis	
		Oil, per pound [1]	Linseed meal, per ton [2]
	Dollars	Cents	Dollars
2010	12.20	67.49	223.23
2011	13.90	(NA)	238.35
2012	13.80	(NA)	320.13
2013	13.80	(NA)	359.42
2014	11.80	(NA)	263.90
2015	8.95	(NA)	234.78
2016	8.00	(NA)	313.17
2017	9.53	(NA)	236.92
2018	9.89	(NA)	236.37
2019 [3]	9.15	(NA)	241.57

(NA) Not available.　[1] Raw oil in tank cars.　[2] Bulk carlots, 34 percent protein.　[3] Preliminary.
ERS, Field Crops Branch, (202) 694–5300.

Table 3-15.—Flaxseed crushed; production, imports, and exports of linseed oil, cake, and meal; and June 1 stocks of oil, United States, 2010–2019

Year beginning June	Total flaxseed crushed	Linseed oil			Linseed cake and meal		
		Stocks June 1	Production	Exports	Production	Imports for consumption	Exports
	1,000 bushels	Million pounds	Million pounds	Million pounds	1,000 tons	1,000 tons	1,000 tons
2010	11,635	37	227	101	209	7	7
2011	10,500	38	205	89	189	8	3
2012	11,000	35	215	94	198	6	5
2013	8,700	35	170	58	157	1	6
2014	11,850	35	231	52	213	3	4
2015	10,700	35	209	17	193	7	4
2016	10,500	35	205	15	189	6	5
2017	9,000	35	176	14	162	7	3
2018	9,300	35	178	11	165	8	2
2019 [1]	8,950	35	175	5	161	4	1

[1] Preliminary.
ERS, Field Crops Branch, (202) 694–5300.

Table 3-16.—Peanuts: Area, yield, production, disposition, marketing year average price per pound received by farmers, and value, United States, 2011–2020

Year	Area planted	Peanuts for nuts				
		Area harvested	Yield per acre	Production [1]	Marketing year average price [2]	Value of production
	1,000 acres	*1,000 acres*	*Pounds*	*1,000 pounds*	*Cents*	*1,000 dollars*
2011	1,140.6	1,080.6	3,386	3,658,590	22.5	1,168,587
2012	1,638.0	1,604.0	4,211	6,753,880	30.1	2,026,326
2013	1,067.0	1,043.0	4,001	4,173,170	24.9	1,055,095
2014	1,353.5	1,322.5	3,923	5,188,665	22.0	1,158,251
2015	1,625.0	1,560.9	3,845	6,001,357	19.3	1,160,560
2016	1,671.0	1,536.0	3,634	5,581,570	19.7	1,088,165
2017	1,871.6	1,775.6	4,007	7,115,410	22.9	1,634,017
2018	1,425.5	1,373.5	4,001	5,495,935	21.5	1,169,953
2019	1,432.7	1,389.7	3,934	5,466,487	20.5	1,131,374
2020	1,662.5	1,615.0	3,813	6,158,350	21.0	1,294,488

[1] Estimates comprised of quota and non-quota peanuts. [2] Based on marketings and monthly prices received from August 1, 2019 - December 31, 2019.
NASS, Crops Branch, (202) 720–2127.

Table 3-17.—Peanuts, farmer stock: Stocks, production, and quantity milled, United States, 2011–2020

Year beginning August	Stocks Aug. 1 [1]	Production harvested for nuts [1]	Imports	Total supply	Milled [1][2]
			1,000 pounds		
2011	769,016	3,658,590	1,299	4,428,905	3,949,494
2012	272,838	6,753,880	3,117	7,029,835	4,979,182
2013	1,924,996	4,173,170	174	6,098,340	4,955,484
2014	1,059,524	5,188,665	11	6,248,200	4,775,454
2015	1,059,524	6,001,357	287	7,446,954	4,998,028
2016	1,051,096	5,581,570	574	6,633,240	4,998,028
2017	732,966	7,115,410	0	7,848,376	4,699,164
2018	1,916,798	5,495,935	4,232	7,416,965	4,448,304
2019	1,627,938	5,466,487	3	7,094,428	4,498,876
2020	1,363,368	6,158,350	163	5,148,397	4,472,126

[1] Net weight basis. [2] Includes peanuts milled for seed.
NASS, Crops Branch, (202) 720–2127, ERS, and Foreign trade from the Bureau of the Census.

Table 3-18.—Peanuts: Crushings, and oil and meal stocks, production, and foreign trade, United States, 2011–2020

Year beginning August	Peanuts crushed (shelled basis)	Peanut oil				Peanut cake and meal	
		Stocks Aug. 1 [1]	Production of crude	Imports	Exports [2]	Stocks Aug. 1 [3]	Production
				1,000 pounds			
2011	453,835	6,836	188,479	28,290	15,646	9,959	250,037
2012	493,835	2,478	210,702	10,359	12,598	10,446	270,328
2013	497,272	(NA)	209,808	55,265	8,940	(NA)	268,554
2014	506,677	(NA)	214,041	30,174	18,840	(NA)	278,380
2015	531,770	2,667	226,219	93,314	10,253	3,197	291,193
2016	531,770	4,868	226,219	40,445	11,908	5,460	291,193
2017	659,966	10,646	283,689	71,354	10,943	8,750	357,751
2018	528,750	9,250	231,748	58,844	9,399	4,552	282,346
2019	486,398	10,181	219,334	3,338	26,843	4,721	255,683
2020	580,628	8,215	254,109	60,012	15,933	11,244	304,718

(NA) Not available. [1] Crude plus refined. [2] Reported as edible peanut oil and crude peanut oil; in this tabulation added without converting. [3] Holding at producing mills only.
NASS, Crops Branch, (202) 720–2127, ERS, and Foreign trade from the Bureau of the Census.

Table 3-19.—Cleaned peanuts (roasting stock): Supply and disposition, United States, 2011–2020

Year beginning August	Supply				Disposition		
	Stocks Aug. 1	Production	Imports	Total	Exports	Domestic disappearance	
						Total	Per capita
	1,000 pounds	1,000 pounds	1,000 pounds	1,000 pounds	1,000 pounds	1,000 pounds	Pounds
2011	58,970	226,481	1,299	286,750	66,819	179,965	0.58
2012	39,966	323,731	3,117	366,814	194,821	100,098	0.32
2013	71,895	323,607	174	395,676	143,921	178,602	0.56
2014	73,153	248,170	11	321,334	168,504	112,495	0.35
2015	40,335	251,484	287	292,106	418,066	112,495	0.35
2016	31,599	251,484	574	262,710	183,379	46,853	0.14
2017	32,478	230,537	0	257,953	159,366	43,054	0.13
2018	55,533	225,475	4,232	247,988	140,540	64,814	0.20
2019	42,633	188,223	3	237,471	550,735	(350,601)	(1.06)
2020	37,337	194,835	163	322,048	78,693	184,385	0.60

NASS, Crops Branch, (202) 720–2127, ERS, and Foreign trade from the Bureau of the Census.

Table 3-20.—Shelled peanuts (all grades): Supply, exports, and quantity crushed, United States, 2011–2020

Year beginning August	Supply						Exports	Crushed
	Stocks Aug. 1		Production		Imports	Total		
	Edible	Oil stock	Edible	Oil stock				
	1,000 pounds	1,000 pounds	1,000 pounds	1,000 pounds	1,000 pounds	1,000 pounds	1,000 pounds	1,000 pounds
2011	473,878	43,380	2,399,094	345,565	203,836	3,465,753	352,994	453,835
2012	466,310	52,883	3,125,786	351,284	90,472	4,086,735	741,109	493,205
2013	547,965	33,883	3,098,392	373,008	65,709	4,118,957	708,391	497,272
2014	519,824	25,364	2,997,078	391,728	69,278	4,003,272	675,930	506,677
2015	431,674	31,012	3,141,099	442,650	66,951	4,113,386	839,203	531,770
2016	467,139	65,350	2,944,760	442,650	114,730	4,040,356	852,040	531,770
2017	482,010	26,372	2,853,147	448,377	127,903	3,847,714	810,578	659,966
2018	535,730	24,232	2,932,229	358,282	84,172	3,944,531	785,928	528,750
2019	540,802	23,498	2,908,778	368,168	79,280	3,957,980	786,790	486,398
2020	554,295	29,092	2,450,639	405,622	46,031	3,443,593	395,554	580,628

NASS, Crops Branch, (202) 720–2127, ERS, and Foreign trade from the U.S. Bureau of the Census.

Table 3-21.—Peanuts: Shelled (raw basis) by types, used in primary products and apparent disappearance of peanuts, United States, 2011–2020

Type and year beginning August	Edible grades used in products					Apparent disappearance [2]
	Peanut butter [1]	Peanut snack	Peanut candy	Other products	Total	
	1,000 pounds	*1,000 pounds*	*1,000 pounds*	*1,000 pounds*	*1,000 pounds*	*1,000 pounds*
Virginia and Valencia:						
2011	(D)	78,333	17,856	(D)	203,958	
2012	82,981	83,722	17,731	8,452	192,888	
2013	86,759	85,298	17,109	13,373	202,536	
2014	102,340	91,909	12,079	26,440	232,768	
2015	108,156	89,766	14,319	26,258	238,494	
2016	108,156	89,766	14,319	26,258	238,494	
2017	118,109	92,331	13,427	23,606	247,473	
2018	129,823	84,479	15,455	28,998	258,754	
2019	120,939	81,418	15,589	18,753	236,696	
2020	140,527	94,614	9,145	19,836	264,121	
Runner:						
2011	1,091,541	303,631	360,797	14,840	1,770,809	
2012	1,143,108	309,860	347,428	12,195	1,812,591	
2013	1,128,206	337,934	(D)	(D)	1,844,490	
2014	1,196,277	329,930	348,367	26,737	1,901,311	
2015	1,186,810	408,726	346,831	35,128	1,977,495	
2016	1,186,810	408,726	346,831	35,128	1,977,495	
2017	1,215,212	370,766	379,549	33,156	1,998,683	
2018	1,179,186	434,139	346,831	66,943	2,027,253	
2019	1,213,018	380,165	349,081	93,897	2,036,161	
2020	1,259,768	(D)	372,153	(D)	2,084,164	
Spanish:						
2011	(D)	8,104	16,025	(D)	27,390	
2012	(D)	6,847	16,755	(D)	25,389	
2013	(D)	6,564	15,996	(D)	(D)	
2014	(D)	6,638	15,410	(D)	27,188	
2015	(D)	7,200	16,355	(D)	28,225	
2016	(D)	7,200	16,355	(D)	28,225	
2017	(D)	7,195	14,725	(D)	26,801	
2018	8,480	6,227	17,064	(D)	28,851	
2019	8,480	(D)	16,266	(D)	30,840	
2020	9,969	(D)	14,349	(D)	30,622	
All types:						
2011	1,197,748	390,068	394,678	19,661	2,002,155	2,742,724
2012	1,227,859	400,429	381,914	20,664	2,030,866	3,417,047
2013	1,218,170	429,796	395,726	29,103	2,072,795	3,508,060
2014	1,303,755	428,477	375,856	53,179	2,161,267	3,471,308
2015	1,299,634	505,692	377,505	61,388	2,244,219	3,513,946
2016	1,229,634	505,692	377,505	61,388	2,244,219	3,417,244
2017	1,338,195	470,292	407,701	56,769	2,272,957	3,159,849
2018	1,314,567	524,845	379,504	95,943	2,314,859	3,296,059
2019	1,342,437	467,676	380,936	112,651	9,303,700	312,949
2020	1,410,264	481,430	395,647	91,567	2,378,908	192,162

(D) Data withheld to avoid disclosure of individual operations.　[1] Excludes peanut butter made by manufacturers for own use in candy. Includes peanut butter used in spreads, sandwiches, and cookies.　[2] Apparent disappearance represents stocks beginning of year plus production, minus stocks at end of year. Includes edible grades and oilstocks.
NASS, Crops Branch, (202) 720–2127, and ERS.

Table 3-22.—Peanuts: Area, yield, and production, by State and United States, 2018–2020

State	Area planted			Peanuts for nuts		
				Area harvested		
	2018	2019	2020	2018	2019	2020
	1,000 acres					
Alabama	165.0	160.0	185.0	161.0	156.0	183.0
Arkansas	26.0	34.0	39.0	23.0	33.0	38.0
Florida	155.0	165.0	175.0	143.0	155.0	166.0
Georgia	665.0	675.0	810.0	655.0	660.0	805.0
Mississippi	25.0	20.0	23.0	24.0	19.0	22.0
New Mexico	5.5	4.7	6.5	5.5	4.7	5.2
North Carolina	102.0	104.0	107.0	98.0	102.0	105.0
Oklahoma	16.0	15.0	15.0	15.0	14.0	14.0
South Carolina ...	87.0	65.0	84.0	80.0	62.0	80.0
Texas	155.0	165.0	190.0	145.0	160.0	170.0
Virginia	24.0	25.0	28.0	24.0	24.0	27.0
United States	1,425.5	1,432.7	1,662.5	1,373.5	1,389.7	1,615.2

State	Peanuts for nuts					
	Yield per harvested acre			Production		
	2018	2019	2020	2018	2019	2020
	Pounds			1,000 pounds		
Alabama	3,550	3,350	3,400	571,550	522,600	622,200
Arkansas	4,900	5,200	4,800	112,700	171,600	182,400
Florida	3,950	3,800	3,400	564,850	589,000	564,400
Georgia	4,390	4,170	4,120	2,875,450	2,752,200	3,316,600
Mississippi	3,900	4,000	4,400	93,600	76,000	96,800
New Mexico	2,850	3,210	2,850	15,675	15,087	14,820
North Carolina	3,870	4,400	3,900	379,260	448,800	409,500
Oklahoma	3,070	4,000	4,220	46,050	56,000	59,080
South Carolina ...	3,400	3,800	3,700	272,000	235,600	296,000
Texas	3,200	3,050	2,850	464,000	488,000	484,500
Virginia	4,200	4,650	4,150	100,800	111,600	112,050
United States	4,001	3,934	3,813	5,495,935	5,466,487	6,158,350

NASS, Crops Branch, (202) 720–2127.

Table 3-23.—Peanuts: Marketing year average price, and value of production, by State and United States, 2018–2020

State	Marketing year average price per pound			Value of production		
	2018	2019	2020 [1]	2018	2019	2020
	Dollars			1,000 dollars		
Alabama	0.208	0.194	0.211	114,566	101,384	131,284
Arkansas	0.190	0.198	0.193	21,850	33,977	35,203
Florida	0.207	0.201	0.204	104,328	118,389	115,138
Georgia	0.205	0.195	0.203	592,963	536,679	673,270
Mississippi	0.202	0.189	0.194	19,392	14,364	18,779
New Mexico	0.292	0.274	0.286	4,818	4,134	4,239
North Carolina	0.230	0.221	0.220	87,906	99,185	90,090
Oklahoma	0.234	0.235	0.222	10,881	13,160	13,116
South Carolina	0.213	0.206	0.214	59,384	48,534	63,344
Texas	0.275	0.281	0.259	131,588	137,128	125,486
Virginia	0.221	0.219	0.219	22,277	24,440	24,539
United States	0.215	0.205	0.210	1,169,953	1,131,374	1,294,488

[1] Based on monthly prices received from August 1, 2020 - December 31, 2020.
NASS, Crops Branch, (202) 720–2127.

Table 3-24.—Peanuts, farmer's stock: Support operations, United States, 2012–2018

Marketing year beginning August 1	Income support payment rates per short ton [1]	Program price levels per short ton		Put under support		Acquired by CCC under loan program	Owned by CCC at end of marketing year
		Loan [2]	Target/ Reference [3]	Quantity	Percentage of production		
	Dollars	Dollars	Dollars	1,000 short tons	Percent	1,000 short tons	1,000 short tons
2012/2013	36.00/0.00	355.00	495.00	2,640	78.2	55.9	0.0
2013/2014	36.00/0.00	355.00	495.00	1,452	69.6	6.1	2.5
2014/2015	95.00	355.00	535.00	2,123	81.8	173.2	6.8
2015/2016	149.00	355.00	535.00	2,233	74.4	0.0	0.0
2016/2017	141.00	355.00	535.00	2,270	79.9	39.1	0.0
2017/2018	77.00	355.00	535.00	2,735	75.6	121.7	0.0
2018/2019	105.00	355.00	535.00	2,340	85.7	42.0	0.0

[1] The first entry is the direct payment rate and the second entry is the counter-cyclical payment rate for 2004/2005-2013/2014. The 2014 Act eliminated direct payments and replaced the counter-cyclical rate with a new reference price. For 2009/2010-2013/2014, producers who participated in the Average Crop Revenue (ACRE) program got a 20 percent reduction in their direct payment, not calculated in this table. For 2014/2015 and after, the entry is the price loss coverage payment rate. For 2017/2018, projected PLC payment rate is based on March 2018 WASDE MY price. Agricultural Risk Coverage (ARC) is also available, but payment rates are established at the county or farm levels. [2] For 2009/2010-2013/2014, producers who participate in the ACRE program get a 30 percent reduction in their loan rate, not calculated in this table. [3] Target applies to 2003/2004-2013/2014 and Reference applies beginning with 2014/2015. [4] Acquisitions as of September 30, 2019.
FPAC-BC, Commodity Analysis Branch.

Table 3-25.—International oilseed, peanut: Area and production in specified countries, 2017/2018–2019/2020

Country	Area			Production		
	2017/2018	2018/2019	2019/2020	2017/2018	2018/2019	2019/2020
	1,000 hectares			1,000 metric tons		
China	4,608	4,620	4,600	17,092	17,333	17,500
India	4,888	4,990	4,700	6,650	4,720	6,200
Nigeria	2,820	2,820	2,800	4,248	4,422	3,500
United States	719	556	563	3,228	2,493	2,493
Sudan	2,215	3,065	2,300	1,648	2,884	1,800
Burma	989	1,034	885	1,572	1,583	1,375
Argentina	382	326	320	867	1,419	1,255
Senegal	1,254	1,250	1,200	1,412	1,450	1,100
Tanzania	1,000	1,000	1,000	1,100	1,100	1,100
Indonesia	580	570	550	1,075	1,025	990
Chad	768	770	770	870	890	850
Guinea	670	680	680	696	770	750
Cameroon	430	430	430	600	600	600
Brazil	139	147	155	516	435	550
Niger	922	925	900	462	592	500
Vietnam	190	190	190	450	458	469

FAS, Office of Global Analysis, (202) 720–6301.   Prepared or estimated on the basis of official USDA production, supply, and distribution statistics from foreign governments.

Table 3-26.—International meal, peanut: Production in specified countries, 2017/2018–2019/2020

Country	2017/2018	2018/2019	2019/2020
	1,000 metric tons		
China	3,580	3,660	3,680
India	1,555	1,385	1,510
Burma	325	325	325
Sudan	259	268	272
Nigeria	245	245	245
Tanzania	170	170	170
United States	128	116	132
Argentina	117	117	130
Senegal	76	90	108
Burkina	90	90	96
Chad	84	84	84
Brazil	73	62	70
Cameroon	57	57	57
Niger	54	54	54
Congo (Kinshasa)	50	50	50

FAS, Office of Global Analysis, (202) 720–6301.   Prepared or estimated on the basis of official USDA production, supply, and distribution statistics from foreign governments.

Table 3-27.—Soybeans: Area, yield, production, and value, United States, 2011–2020

| Year | Area planted | Soybeans for beans | | | | |
		Area harvested	Yield per acre	Production	Marketing year average price per bushel received by farmers [1]	Value of production [1]
	1,000 acres	*1,000 acres*	*Bushels*	*1,000 bushels*	*Dollars*	*1,000 dollars*
2011	75,046	73,776	42.0	3,097,179	12.50	38,542,177
2012	77,198	76,144	40.0	3,042,044	14.40	43,723,144
2013	76,820	76,233	44.0	3,357,004	13.00	43,570,161
2014	83,296	82,611	47.5	3,928,070	10.10	39,484,465
2015	82,660	81,742	48.0	3,926,779	8.95	35,195,882
2016	83,453	82,706	51.9	4,296,496	9.47	40,694,573
2017	90,162	89,542	49.3	4,411,633	9.33	41,308,740
2018	89,167	87,594	50.6	4,428,150	8.48	36,819,008
2019	76,100	74,939	47.4	3,551,908	8.57	30,525,122
2020	83,354	82,603	51.0	4,216,306	10.80	45,732,122

[1] Based on marketings and monthly prices received from August 1, 2020 - December 31, 2020.
NASS, Crops Branch, (202) 720–2127.

Table 3-28.—Soybeans: Stocks on and off farms, United States, 2010–2019

| Year beginning previous December | On farms | | | | Off farms [1] | | | |
	Dec. 1	Mar. 1	June 1	Sep. 1 [2]	Dec. 1	Mar. 1	June 1	Sep. 1 [2]
	1,000 bushels	*1,000 bushels*	*1,000 bushels*	*1,000 bushels*	*1,000 bushels*	*1,000 bushels*	*1,000 bushels*	*1,000 bushels*
2010	1,091,000	609,200	232,600	35,400	1,187,084	660,868	338,523	115,485
2011	1,139,000	505,000	217,700	48,500	1,230,885	743,800	401,583	166,513
2012	910,000	555,000	179,000	38,250	1,056,161	819,488	488,465	131,120
2013	955,000	456,700	171,100	39,550	1,198,621	541,320	263,564	101,007
2014	1,218,000	381,900	109,100	21,325	1,309,744	611,928	295,945	70,666
2015	1,308,500	609,200	246,300	49,700	1,405,577	717,399	380,768	140,910
2016	1,335,000	727,500	281,300	41,560	1,564,056	803,406	590,481	155,169
2017	1,485,000	668,500	332,500	87,900	1,675,679	1,070,433	633,356	213,695
2018	1,935,000	855,000	377,000	101,000	1,810,824	1,254,303	842,329	337,105
2019	1,519,500	1,270,000	730,000	265,000	1,732,988	1,457,069	1,053,080	644,052

[1] Includes stocks at mills, elevators, warehouses, terminals, and processors.　　[2] Old crop only.
NASS, Crops Branch, (202) 720–2127.

Table 3-29.—Soybeans, soybean meal, and oil: Average price at specified markets, 2011–2019

Year [1]	Soybeans per bushel: No. 1 Yellow Chicago	Soybean oil per pound crude, tanks, f.o.b. Decatur	Soybean meal per short ton: 48 percent protein Decatur
	Dollars	*Cents*	*Dollars*
2010	12.97	53.20	345.52
2011	13.49	51.90	393.53
2012	14.86	47.13	468.11
2013	13.51	38.23	489.94
2014	9.84	31.60	368.49
2015	9.45	29.86	324.56
2016	9.64	32.55	316.88
2017	9.43	30.04	345.02
2018	8.37	28.26	308.28
2019 [2]	8.73	29.67	299.50

[1] Year beginning September for soybeans and October for oil and meal.　[2] Forecast.
ERS, Field Crops Branch, (202) 694–5300. Formerly compiled from annual reports of the U.S. Department of Commerce.

Table 3-30.—Soybeans: Supply and disappearance, United States, 2010–2019

Year beginning September	Supply				
	Stocks by position			Production	Total [1]
	On-Farm, Sep 1	Terminal market, interior mill, elevator, and warehouse	Beginning, Sep-Nov		
	1,000 bushels	*1,000 bushels*	*1,000 bushels*	*1,000 bushels*	*1,000 bushels*
2010	35,400	115,485	150,885	3,331,306	3,496,640
2011	48,500	166,513	215,013	3,097,179	3,328,324
2012	38,250	131,120	169,370	3,042,044	3,251,930
2013	39,550	101,007	140,557	3,357,004	3,569,338
2014	21,325	70,666	91,991	3,928,070	4,053,306
2015	49,700	140,910	190,610	3,926,779	4,140,930
2016	41,560	155,169	196,729	4,296,496	4,515,506
2017	87,900	213,695	301,595	4,411,633	4,735,038
2018	101,000	337,105	438,105	4,428,150	4,880,312
2019	265,000	644,052	909,052	3,551,908	4,476,360

Year beginning September	Disappearance			
	Crushed [2]	Seed, feed and residual	Exports	Total
	1,000 bushels	*1,000 bushels*	*1,000 bushels*	*1,000 bushels*
2010	1,648,043	128,606	1,504,978	3,281,627
2011	1,703,019	89,600	1,366,335	3,158,954
2012	1,688,903	94,944	1,327,526	3,111,373
2013	1,733,888	104,900	1,638,559	3,477,347
2014	1,873,494	147,007	1,842,175	3,862,676
2015	1,886,237	115,358	1,942,606	3,944,201
2016	1,901,198	146,163	2,166,550	4,213,911
2017	2,054,932	108,271	2,133,730	4,296,933
2018	2,091,990	127,461	1,751,809	3,971,260
2019	2,164,554	105,242	1,682,023	3,951,819

[1] Includes imports.   [2] Reported by the U.S. Department of Commerce.
ERS, Field Crops Branch, (202) 694–5300.

Table 3-31.—Soybeans: Support operations, United States, 2014–2020

Marketing year beginning September 1	Income support payment rates per bushels [1]	Program price levels per bushel	Put under loan		Acquired by CCC under loan program [2]	Owned by CCC at end of marketing year
		Loan	Quantity	Percentage of production		
	Dollars	*Dollars*	*Dollars*	*Million bushels*	*Percent*	*Million bushels*	*Million bushels*
2014/2015	0.00	5.00	8.40	80	2.0	0	0
2015/2016	0.00	5.00	8.40	124	3.2	0	0
2016/2017	0.00	5.00	8.40	105	2.4	0	0
2017/2018	0.00	5.00	8.40	145	3.3	0	0
2018/2019	0.00	5.00	8.40	218	4.9	0	0
2019/2020	0.00	6.20	8.40	155	4.4	0	0
2020/2021	0.00	6.20	8.40	75	1.8	0	0

[1] The entry is the price loss coverage (PLC) payment rate. For 2017/2018, projected PLC payment rate is based on March 2018 WASDE MY price. Agricultural Risk Coverage (ARC) is also available, but payment rates are established at the county or farm levels.   [2] Acquisitions as of September 30, 2020.
FPAC-BC, Commodity Analysis Branch.

Table 3-32.—Soybeans for beans: Area, yield, and production, by State and United States, 2018–2020

State	Area planted			Area harvested		
	2018	2019	2020	2018	2019	2020
	1,000 acres	1,000 acres	1,000 acres	1,000 acres	1,000 acres	1,000 acres
Alabama	345	265	280	335	260	275
Arkansas	3,270	2,650	2,820	3,210	2,610	2,800
Delaware	170	155	150	168	153	148
Florida [1]	18	(NA)	(NA)	12	(NA)	(NA)
Georgia	145	100	100	130	86	95
Illinois	10,800	9,950	10,300	10,500	9,860	10,250
Indiana	6,000	5,400	5,750	5,960	5,360	5,730
Iowa	9,950	9,200	9,450	9,830	9,120	9,370
Kansas	4,750	4,550	4,800	4,690	4,490	4,750
Kentucky	1,950	1,700	1,850	1,930	1,690	1,840
Louisiana	1,340	890	1,050	1,190	860	1,020
Maryland	530	480	485	515	475	465
Michigan	2,330	1,760	2,200	2,310	1,720	2,190
Minnesota	7,750	6,850	7,450	7,650	6,770	7,380
Mississippi	2,230	1,660	2,090	2,190	1,630	2,060
Missouri	5,850	5,100	5,850	5,780	5,010	5,810
Nebraska	5,650	4,900	5,200	5,590	4,840	5,160
New Jersey	110	95	94	107	92	93
New York	335	235	315	325	225	312
North Carolina	1,650	1,540	1,600	1,570	1,520	1,570
North Dakota	6,900	5,600	5,750	6,840	5,400	5,700
Ohio	5,050	4,300	4,950	5,020	4,270	4,920
Oklahoma	640	465	560	600	440	540
Pennsylvania	640	620	640	630	610	630
South Carolina	390	335	310	330	315	295
South Dakota	5,650	3,500	4,950	5,580	3,440	4,920
Tennessee	1,700	1,400	1,650	1,670	1,370	1,620
Texas	175	80	120	135	73	110
Virginia	600	570	570	590	560	560
West Virginia [1]	29	(NA)	(NA)	27	(NA)	(NA)
Wisconsin	2,220	1,750	2,020	2,180	1,690	1,990
United States	89,167	76,100	83,354	87,594	74,939	82,603

State	Yield per harvested acre			Production		
	2018	2019	2020	2018	2019	2020
	Bushels	Bushels	Bushels	1,000 bushels	1,000 bushels	1,000 bushels
Alabama	40.0	36.0	41.0	13,400	9,360	11,275
Arkansas	50.5	49.0	51.5	162,105	127,890	144,200
Delaware	41.5	47.0	49.0	6,972	7,191	7,252
Florida [1]	37.0	(NA)	(NA)	444	(NA)	(NA)
Georgia	39.5	29.0	41.0	5,135	2,494	3,895
Illinois	63.5	54.0	60.0	666,750	532,440	615,000
Indiana	57.5	51.0	59.0	342,700	273,360	338,070
Iowa	56.0	55.0	54.0	550,480	501,600	505,980
Kansas	43.0	41.5	41.0	201,670	186,335	194,750
Kentucky	51.0	46.0	55.0	98,430	77,740	101,200
Louisiana	51.5	48.0	53.0	61,285	41,280	54,060
Maryland	47.5	44.0	47.0	24,463	20,900	21,855
Michigan	47.5	40.5	48.0	109,725	69,660	105,120
Minnesota	49.0	44.0	50.0	374,850	297,880	369,000
Mississippi	54.0	50.0	54.0	118,260	81,500	111,240
Missouri	44.5	46.0	51.0	257,210	230,460	296,310
Nebraska	58.0	58.5	58.0	324,220	283,140	299,280
New Jersey	39.5	37.0	46.0	4,227	3,404	4,278
New York	52.0	48.0	51.0	16,900	10,800	15,912
North Carolina	33.0	35.0	38.0	51,810	53,200	59,660
North Dakota	35.0	31.5	34.0	239,400	170,100	193,800
Ohio	56.0	49.0	55.0	281,120	209,230	270,600
Oklahoma	28.0	29.0	30.0	16,800	12,760	16,200
Pennsylvania	44.5	49.0	46.0	28,035	29,890	28,980
South Carolina	29.0	26.0	35.0	9,570	8,190	10,325
South Dakota	45.0	42.5	46.0	251,100	146,200	226,320
Tennessee	45.5	47.0	50.0	75,985	64,390	81,000
Texas	31.5	28.0	34.0	4,253	2,044	3,740
Virginia	42.0	34.0	42.0	24,780	19,040	23,520
West Virginia [1]	53.0	(NA)	(NA)	1,431	(NA)	(NA)
Wisconsin	48.0	47.0	52.0	104,640	79,430	103,480
United States	50.6	47.4	51.0	4,428,150	3,551,908	4,216,302

(NA) Not available. [1] Estimates discontinued in 2019.
NASS, Crops Branch, (202) 720–2127.

Table 3-33.—Soybeans: Crushings, and oil and meal stocks, production, and foreign trade, United States, 2010–2019

Year beginning October	Soybeans crushed	Soybean oil			Soybean cake and meal		
		Stocks Oct. 1	Production	Exports	Stocks Oct. 1	Production	Exports
	1,000 bushels	*Million pounds*	*Million pounds*	*Million pounds*	*1,000 tons*	*1,000 tons*	*1,000 tons*
2010	1,633,349	3,406	18,888	3,233	302	39,251	9,081
2011	1,712,895	2,675	19,740	1,464	350	41,036	9,750
2012	1,677,279	2,590	19,820	2,163	300	39,875	11,146
2013	1,724,791	1,655	20,130	1,877	275	40,684	11,578
2014	1,903,278	1,165	21,399	2,014	250	45,062	13,107
2015	1,889,941	1,855	21,950	2,243	260	44,672	11,953
2016	1,908,305	1,687	22,123	2,556	264	44,787	11,580
2017	2,079,208	1,711	23,772	2,443	401	49,226	14,019
2018	2,084,675	1,995	24,197	1,940	555	48,814	13,438
2019 [1]	2,173,275	1,775	24,912	2,839	402	51,100	14,077

[1] Forecast.
ERS, Field Crops Branch, (202) 694–5300. Data formerly from the U.S. Department of Commerce.

Table 3-34.—Soybeans for beans: Marketing year average price and value, by State and United States, 2018–2020

State	Marketing year average price per bushel			Value of production		
	2018	2019	2020 [1]	2018	2019	2020 [1]
	Dollars	*Dollars*	*Dollars*	*1,000 dollars*	*1,000 dollars*	*1,000 dollars*
Alabama	8.50	9.10	11.70	113,900	85,176	131,918
Arkansas	8.81	8.87	10.50	1,428,145	1,134,384	1,514,100
Delaware	8.25	8.35	11.60	57,519	60,045	84,123
Florida [2]	8.10	(NA)	(NA)	3,596	(NA)	(NA)
Georgia	7.90	8.95	13.00	40,567	22,321	50,635
Illinois	8.74	8.84	10.90	5,827,395	4,706,770	6,703,500
Indiana	8.73	8.92	11.10	2,991,771	2,438,371	3,752,577
Iowa	8.46	8.48	11.10	4,657,061	4,253,568	5,616,378
Kansas	7.93	8.28	10.70	1,599,243	1,542,854	2,083,825
Kentucky	8.79	8.98	10.80	865,200	698,105	1,092,960
Louisiana	8.95	8.70	10.00	548,501	359,136	540,600
Maryland	8.12	8.35	11.60	198,640	174,515	253,518
Michigan	8.53	8.81	11.70	935,954	613,705	1,229,904
Minnesota	8.40	8.29	11.00	3,148,740	2,469,425	4,059,000
Mississippi	8.85	8.80	10.20	1,046,601	717,200	1,134,648
Missouri	8.56	8.75	11.10	2,201,718	2,016,525	3,289,041
Nebraska	8.20	8.27	10.20	1,920,604	2,341,568	3,052,656
New Jersey	7.98	8.45	11.50	33,731	28,764	49,197
New York	8.20	8.50	11.30	137,760	91,800	179,806
North Carolina	8.66	8.71	11.20	448,675	463,372	668,192
North Dakota	7.98	7.93	10.20	1,910,412	1,348,893	1,976,760
Ohio	8.69	9.04	11.30	2,442,933	1,891,439	3,057,780
Oklahoma	7.89	8.45	10.10	132,552	107,822	163,620
Pennsylvania	8.42	8.50	11.30	236,055	254,065	327,474
South Carolina	9.10	9.20	12.00	87,087	75,348	123,900
South Dakota	7.97	8.22	10.30	2,001,267	1,201,764	2,331,096
Tennessee	8.75	8.96	10.80	664,869	576,934	874,800
Texas	7.59	7.70	9.10	32,280	15,739	34,034
Virginia	8.30	8.80	11.90	205,674	167,552	279,888
West Virginia [2]	8.50	(NA)	(NA)	12,164	(NA)	(NA)
Wisconsin	8.49	8.42	10.40	888,394	688,801	1,076,192
United States	8.48	8.57	10.80	36,819,008	30,525,961	45,732,122

(NA) Not available. [1] Final. [2] Estimates discontinued in 2019.
NASS, Crops Branch, (202) 720–2127.

Table 3-35.—International oilseed, soybean: Area and production in specified countries, 2017/2018–2019/2020

Country	Area			Production		
	2017/2018	2018/2019	2019/2020	2017/2018	2018/2019	2019/2020
	1,000 hectares			*1,000 Metric tons*		
Brazil	35,150	35,900	36,900	122,000	117,000	126,000
United States	36,236	35,448	30,360	120,065	120,515	96,841
Argentina	16,300	16,600	17,000	37,800	55,300	54,000
China	8,245	8,413	9,300	15,283	15,967	18,100
Paraguay	3,380	3,700	3,540	10,478	8,850	9,900
India	10,400	11,330	11,250	8,350	10,930	9,300
Canada	2,935	2,540	2,300	7,717	7,267	6,000
Russia	2,568	2,739	2,776	3,621	4,027	4,359
Ukraine	2,020	1,875	1,600	3,985	4,831	3,700
Bolivia	1,315	1,400	1,400	2,819	2,700	2,800
European Union	926	926	910	2,540	2,664	2,600
Uruguay	1,098	965	950	1,334	2,828	2,200
South Africa	787	730	800	1,540	1,170	1,450
Nigeria	1,000	1,000	1,000	994	1,054	1,100
Serbia	200	220	220	460	625	600
Indonesia	420	410	400	540	520	510
Zambia	225	192	196	351	303	281
Japan	150	147	150	249	213	253
Mexico	263	191	150	433	335	235
Korea, North	150	150	150	223	225	225
Iran	83	70	70	200	160	170
Burma	143	150	150	149	160	160
Bangladesh	82	82	82	156	156	156
Turkey	24	25	27	90	95	105
Ethiopia	39	42	40	84	120	100

FAS, Office of Global Analysis, (202) 720–6301.   Prepared or estimated on the basis of official USDA production, supply, and distribution statistics from foreign governments.

Table 3-36.—Soybeans: United States exports by country of destination, 2018–2020

Country of destination	2018	2019	2020
	Metric tons		
China	8,235,317	22,612,170	34,573,597
Mexico	4,802,990	5,175,412	4,964,851
Egypt	3,186,587	2,789,926	4,021,191
Netherlands	3,482,933	2,312,282	2,981,841
Japan	2,268,969	2,465,544	2,512,028
Indonesia	2,634,121	2,428,797	2,366,226
Taiwan	2,263,146	1,867,302	1,511,966
Thailand	1,600,145	1,426,267	1,347,320
Bangladesh	1,192,983	1,136,782	1,307,227
Vietnam	1,254,177	713,152	1,039,008
Pakistan	1,733,277	1,130,977	1,017,797
Spain	1,737,344	1,596,462	903,314
Korea, South	837,727	1,065,727	708,358
Malaysia	590,517	644,228	612,854
Colombia	708,737	639,501	507,388
Italy(*)	879,428	398,333	392,555
Tunisia	451,168	218,864	371,688
Portugal	538,550	407,969	347,760
Costa Rica	297,643	271,169	300,851
Canada	776,038	519,821	254,450
Saudi Arabia	338,066	231,852	245,168
Peru	261,751	308,614	242,811
United Kingdom	326,895	289,920	156,232
France(*)	182,732	133,745	155,820
Philippines	167,058	135,392	134,081
Lebanon	75,242	78,364	124,773
India	2,353	17,114	122,245
Morocco	39,785	0	105,797
Algeria	0	30,105	98,057
Israel(*)	118,187	140,329	97,629
Rest of World	5,198,882	1,092,974	639,809
World Total	46,182,748	52,279,092	64,164,691

(*) Denotes a country that is a summarization of its component countries.
FAS, Office of Global Analysis, (202) 720–6301. Data Source: U.S. Census Bureau Trade Data.

Table 3-37.—Soybean oil: United States exports by country of destination, 2018–2020

Country of destination	2018	2019	2020
	Metric tons		
Korea, South	281,161	356,797	314,029
Dominican Republic	142,728	128,614	158,152
Mexico	149,136	134,293	111,298
Guatemala	75,475	84,870	109,986
Colombia	128,416	75,516	103,208
Morocco	11,798	0	82,900
Venezuela	48,857	11,428	70,251
Canada	21,825	19,821	41,269
India	110	123	36,141
Egypt	1	0	31,000
China	888	482	30,734
Peru	93,051	11,964	26,436
Jamaica	27,013	32,628	25,543
Algeria	0	0	22,878
El Salvador	7,565	11,859	12,421
Costa Rica	5,772	6,794	10,180
Nicaragua	15,737	8,434	9,574
Trinidad and Tobago	11,518	9,704	9,456
Tunisia	0	0	6,876
Saudi Arabia	3,589	6,150	5,242
Honduras	4,399	4,271	4,150
United Arab Emirates	4,391	4,038	3,538
Haiti	0	50	2,755
Japan	2,543	2,418	2,594
Panama	7,779	3,018	2,286
Kuwait	2,042	2,424	1,818
Bahamas, The	2,146	1,646	1,392
Qatar	865	1,625	1,206
Jordan	1,761	1,545	1,160
Vietnam	0	0	590
Rest of World	58,148	39,370	4,002
World Total	1,108,711	959,878	1,243,065

Users should use cautious interpretation on quantity reports using mixed units of measure. Quantity line items will only include statistics on the units of measure that are equal to, or are able to be converted to, the assigned unit of measure of the grouped commodities.
FAS, Office of Global Analysis, (202) 720–6301. Data Source: U.S. Census Bureau Trade Data.

Table 3-38.—Soybean cake and meal: United States exports by country of destination, 2017–2019

Country of destination	2017	2018	2019
	Metric tons		
Philippines	2,154,941	2,136,033	2,429,461
Mexico	1,781,852	1,783,625	1,789,043
Colombia	1,229,025	1,221,239	1,393,580
Canada	998,471	978,177	1,141,432
Ecuador	320,420	533,996	682,867
Dominican Republic	491,461	543,411	482,741
Morocco	553,234	328,033	464,856
Guatemala	430,002	462,828	459,871
Honduras	273,006	287,318	324,319
Peru	217,228	156,585	294,259
Indonesia	306,650	41,517	246,062
Venezuela	182,796	150,332	244,352
Burma	153,197	269,156	238,872
Japan	330,711	337,365	231,006
Spain	354,736	69,964	224,335
El Salvador	217,846	235,525	222,614
Libya	59,845	24,000	201,533
Panama	218,113	197,083	189,779
Vietnam	762,470	536,149	182,552
Sri Lanka	169,787	216,483	173,350
Nicaragua	107,284	123,479	133,016
Denmark(*)	36,437	46,788	113,855
United Kingdom	56,333	85,947	112,628
Jamaica	126,079	115,197	111,323
Israel(*)	53,657	144,501	107,278
Bangladesh	47,102	69,736	105,899
Costa Rica	108,712	100,936	101,573
Taiwan	22,556	42,038	83,490
Belgium-Luxembourg(*)	49,549	57,683	63,913
Ireland	99,962	23,646	46,925
Rest of World	1,095,961	948,685	487,049
World Total	13,009,424	12,267,453	13,083,830

(*) Denotes a country that is a summarization of its component countries. Users should use cautious interpretation on quantity reports using mixed units of measure. Quantity line items will only include statistics on the units of measure that are equal to, or are able to be converted to, the assigned unit of measure of the grouped commodities.
FAS, Office of Global Analysis, (202) 720–6301. Data Source: U.S. Census Bureau Trade Data.

Table 3-39.—International oil, soybean: Production in specified countries, 2017/2018–2019/2020

Country	2017/2018	2018/2019	2019/2020
		1,000 metric tons	
China	16,128	15,232	15,411
United States	10,783	10,976	11,018
Argentina	7,236	7,910	8,500
Brazil	8,485	8,150	8,400
European Union	2,841	2,945	3,021
India	1,386	1,730	1,495
Mexico	937	1,100	1,110
Russia	824	834	881
Paraguay	733	700	739
Egypt	582	620	656
Japan	468	468	474
Bolivia	425	470	470
Taiwan	383	401	420
Pakistan	375	375	410
Thailand	251	359	410
Bangladesh	222	293	370
Canada	355	396	360
Iran	486	288	324
Turkey	250	250	259
South Africa	220	220	238

FAS, Office of Global Analysis, (202) 720–6301. Prepared or estimated on the basis of official USDA production, supply, and distribution statistics from foreign governments.

Table 3-40.—International trade: Meal, soybean in specified countries, 2017/2018–2019/2020

Country	2017/2018	2018/2019	2019/2020
		1,000 metric tons	
Principle exporting countries:			
Argentina	26,265	28,832	30,000
Brazil	16,032	15,973	15,400
United States	12,715	12,296	11,975
Paraguay	2,625	2,333	2,550
Bolivia	1,651	1,725	1,750
India	1,863	2,200	1,450
China	1,198	932	975
Ukraine	365	777	700
Russia	403	371	400
Canada	357	425	325
European Union	395	374	300
Belarus	135	204	245
Norway	182	182	182
Vietnam	120	100	110
South Africa	91	85	85
Korea, South	41	60	65
Turkey	31	62	55
Nigeria	49	50	50
Malaysia	57	52	45
Serbia	38	30	35
Principle importing countries:			
European Union	18,354	18,699	18,700
Vietnam	4,850	5,400	5,450
Indonesia	4,486	4,575	4,750
Thailand	3,191	2,889	3,225
Philippines	2,625	2,900	2,850
Iran	1,514	2,700	2,100
Mexico	1,818	1,932	1,980
Korea, South	1,846	1,900	1,925
Japan	1,728	1,625	1,675
Colombia	1,373	1,425	1,500
Algeria	1,500	1,350	1,450
Malaysia	1,609	1,578	1,400
Peru	1,353	1,345	1,375
Ecuador	1,145	1,150	1,170
Australia	923	1,050	1,100
Canada	1,022	1,018	1,050
Chile	824	967	1,000
Saudi Arabia	922	915	925
Turkey	557	724	850
Morocco	602	615	650

FAS, Office of Global Analysis, (202) 720–6301. Prepared or estimated on the basis of official USDA production, supply, and distribution statistics from foreign governments.

Table 3-41.—International trade: Oil, soybean in specified countries, 2017/2018–2019/2020

Country	2017/2018	2018/2019	2019/2020
	1,000 metric tons		
Principle exporting countries:			
Argentina	4,164	5,261	5,800
Brazil	1,511	1,079	1,000
United States	1,108	881	953
European Union	902	788	850
Paraguay	702	654	710
Russia	568	564	620
Bolivia	380	350	370
Ukraine	192	334	240
Canada	157	169	165
China	211	197	150
Malaysia	124	123	125
Thailand	70	80	90
Turkey	58	85	90
Norway	62	67	66
South Africa	55	55	55
Serbia	43	66	50
Saudi Arabia	33	33	33
Egypt	25	25	25
Vietnam	40	25	25
Taiwan	7	17	19
Principle importing countries:			
India	2,984	3,100	3,500
China	481	783	1,100
Algeria	720	760	770
Bangladesh	859	1,038	700
Morocco	502	536	545
Peru	503	500	525
Colombia	355	375	390
European Union	284	416	375
Korea, South	276	300	295
United States	152	180	204
Venezuela	226	210	200
Dominican Republic	165	180	190
South Africa	150	175	185
Mexico	195	142	170
Iran	213	135	165
Egypt	227	83	150
Chile	67	100	115
Ecuador	105	110	110
Malaysia	88	100	110
Tunisia	95	106	108
Cuba	97	97	100
Korea, North	90	100	100
Pakistan	104	90	100

FAS, Office of Global Analysis, (202) 720–6301. Prepared or estimated on the basis of official USDA production, supply, and distribution statistics from foreign governments.

Table 3-42.—International trade: Oil, soybean local in specified countries, 2017/2018–2019/2020

Country	2017/2018	2018/2019	2019/2020
	1,000 metric tons		
Principle exporting countries:			
Argentina	4,567	5,400	5,900
Brazil	1,410	1,008	1,000
Principle importing countries:			
Brazil	41	35	30

FAS, Office of Global Analysis, (202) 720–6301. Prepared or estimated on the basis of official USDA production, supply, and distribution statistics from foreign governments.

Table 3-43.—International trade: Oilseed, soybean in specified countries, 2017/2018–2019/2020

Country	2017/2018	2018/2019	2019/2020
	1,000 metric tons		
Principle exporting countries:			
Brazil	76,136	74,594	77,000
United States	58,071	47,564	49,668
Argentina	2,132	9,104	8,200
Paraguay	6,029	4,901	5,900
Canada	4,925	5,258	4,700
Ukraine	2,757	2,531	2,450
Uruguay	1,250	2,750	2,130
Russia	892	797	950
European Union	276	179	250
India	217	178	150
Serbia	28	143	150
China	134	116	125
Ethiopia	93	95	80
Malaysia	17	30	35
Nigeria	28	30	30
Turkey	20	25	25
Bolivia	7	10	10
Chile	7	8	8
South Africa	34	5	5
Uganda	5	5	5
Principle importing countries:			
China	94,095	82,540	88,000
European Union	14,584	15,004	15,200
Mexico	4,873	5,908	6,000
Argentina	4,703	6,408	3,900
Egypt	3,550	3,350	3,700
Thailand	2,482	3,155	3,400
Japan	3,256	3,300	3,350
Indonesia	2,483	2,725	2,950
Taiwan	2,666	2,730	2,850
Turkey	2,777	2,600	2,800
Pakistan	2,300	1,719	2,200
Russia	2,237	2,066	2,200
Bangladesh	1,179	1,733	1,900
Iran	2,559	2,000	1,850
Vietnam	1,824	1,800	1,850
Korea, South	1,256	1,365	1,450
Canada	487	1,172	900
Malaysia	690	770	825
Tunisia	683	670	710
Saudi Arabia	590	585	640

FAS, Office of Global Analysis, (202) 720–6301.   Prepared or estimated on the basis of official USDA production, supply, and distribution statistics from foreign governments.

Table 3-44.—International trade: Oilseed, Soybeans local in specified countries, 2017/2018–2019/2020

Country	2017/2018	2018/2019	2019/2020
	1,000 metric tons		
Principle exporting countries:			
Brazil	83,729	73,234	77,000
Argentina	3,841	10,310	8,000
Principle importing countries:			
Argentina	7,256	3,850	3,900
Brazil	185	145	150

FAS, Office of Global Analysis, (202) 720–6301.   Prepared or estimated on the basis of official USDA production, supply, and distribution statistics from foreign governments.

Table 3-45.—Sunflower, all: Area, yield, production, and value, United States, 2011–2020

Year	Area planted	Area harvested	Yield per harvested acre	Production	Price per cwt	Value of production
	1,000 acres	1,000 acres	Pounds	1,000 pounds	Dollars	1,000 dollars
2011	1,543.0	1,457.8	1,398	2,038,275	29.10	589,282
2012	1,920.0	1,840.0	1,487	2,736,060	25.40	699,970
2013	1,575.5	1,464.6	1,380	2,021,765	21.40	443,296
2014	1,565.3	1,505.1	1,470	2,212,350	21.70	496,469
2015	1,860.1	1,800.4	1,625	2,925,030	19.60	574,481
2016	1,596.6	1,532.0	1,731	2,651,635	17.40	464,015
2017	1,403.0	1,333.8	1,603	2,137,750	17.20	375,077
2018	1,301.0	1,217.4	1,731	2,107,045	17.40	370,466
2019	1,350.0	1,253.5	1,560	1,956,035	17.90	386,346
2020	1,719.1	1,666.1	1,790	2,982,890	21.10	631,976

NASS, Crops Branch, (202) 720–2127.

Table 3-46.—Sunflower, oil varieties: Area, yield, production, and value, United States, 2011–2020

Year	Area planted	Area harvested	Yield per harvested acre	Production	Price per cwt.	Value of production
	1,000 acres	1,000 acres	Pounds	1,000 pounds	Dollars	1,000 dollars
2011	1,289.5	1,233.4	1,397	1,722,675	28.00	480,412
2012	1,658.0	1,589.8	1,484	2,359,775	24.40	580,404
2013	1,279.0	1,200.9	1,363	1,637,205	19.30	322,605
2014	1,174.0	1,134.5	1,461	1,657,390	19.30	322,163
2015	1,550.5	1,510.0	1,579	2,383,870	18.20	434,795
2016	1,418.0	1,368.5	1,731	2,369,015	16.90	403,850
2017	1,216.0	1,168.0	1,582	1,847,525	16.90	312,065
2018	1,164.0	1,094.0	1,725	1,887,260	16.70	320,867
2019	1,197.0	1,131.0	1,561	1,765,550	19.10	342,887
2020	1,490.0	1,452.5	1,802	2,617,340	20.40	537,186

NASS, Crops Branch, (202) 720–2127.

Table 3-47.—Sunflower, non-oil varieties: Area, yield, production, and value, United States, 2011–2020

Year	Area planted	Area harvested	Yield per harvested acre	Production	Price per cwt.	Value of production
	1,000 acres	1,000 acres	Pounds	1,000 pounds	Dollars	1,000 dollars
2011	253.5	224.4	1,406	315,600	33.80	108,870
2012	262.0	250.2	1,504	376,285	29.60	119,566
2013	296.5	263.7	1,458	384,560	31.30	120,691
2014	391.3	370.6	1,497	554,960	31.50	174,306
2015	309.6	290.4	1,863	541,160	26.60	139,686
2016	178.6	163.5	1,729	282,620	21.20	60,165
2017	187.0	165.8	1,750	290,225	21.00	63,012
2018	137.0	123.4	1,781	219,785	22.80	49,579
2019	153.6	122.5	1,555	190,485	22.60	43,459
2020	229.1	213.6	1,711	365,550	26.20	94,790

NASS, Crops Branch, (202) 720–2127.

Table 3-48.—Sunflower, all: Area, yield, production, and value, by type, State and United States, 2018–2019

Type and State	Area planted 2018	Area planted 2019	Area harvested 2018	Area harvested 2019	Yield per harvested acre 2018	Yield per harvested acre 2019
Oil:	*1,000 acres*	*1,000 acres*	*1,000 acres*	*1,000 acres*	*Pounds*	*Pounds*
California	58.0	49.0	57.0	49.0	1,300	1,400
Colorado	58.0	47.0	49.0	44.0	1,100	1,000
Kansas	43.0	37.0	41.0	32.0	1,500	1,400
Minnesota	45.0	53.0	44.0	51.0	2,250	1,850
Nebraska	25.0	28.0	24.0	26.0	1,420	1,300
North Dakota	395.0	470.0	380.0	430.0	1,750	1,500
South Dakota	520.0	485.0	480.0	460.0	1,830	1,700
Texas	20.0	28.00	19.0	26.0	1,120	1,300
United States	1,164.0	1,197.0	1,094	1,118.0	1,726	1,562
Non-oil:						
California	2.0	1.6	2.0	1.6	1,200	1,300
Colorado	8.0	12.0	7.0	11.0	1,150	1,400
Kansas	10.0	8.0	8.5	7.3	1,500	1,250
Minnesota	7.5	5.0	6.9	4.6	2,150	1,800
Nebraska	12.0	9.0	9.5	8.5	1,400	1,300
North Dakota	41.0	65.0	40.0	58.0	1,860	1,650
South Dakota	51.0	48.0	45.0	31.0	1,950	1,600
Texas	5.5	5.0	4.5	4.5	1,400	1,300
United States	137.0	153.6	123.4	126.5	1,781	1,562
Total:						
California	60.0	50.6	59.0	50.6	1,297	1,397
Colorado	66.0	59.0	56.0	55.0	1,106	1,080
Kansas	53.0	45.0	49.5	39.3	1,500	1,372
Minnesota	52.5	58.0	50.9	55.6	2,236	1,846
Nebraska	37.0	37.0	33.5	34.5	1,414	1,300
North Dakota	436.0	535.0	420.0	488.0	1,760	1,518
South Dakota	571.0	533.0	525.0	491.0	1,840	1,694
Texas	25.5	33.0	23.5	30.5	1,174	1,300
United States	1,301.0	1,350.6	1,217.4	1,244.5	1,731	1,562

Type and State	Production 2018	Production 2019	Marketing year average price per cwt 2018	Marketing year average price per cwt 2019[1]	Value of production 2018	Value of production 2019[1]
Oil:	*1,000 lbs*	*1,000 lbs*	*Dollars*	*Dollars*	*1,000 dollars*	*1,000 dollars*
California	74,100	68,600	(D)	27.10	(D)	18,591
Colorado	53,900	44,000	(D)	18.40	(D)	8,096
Kansas	61,500	44,800	(D)	(D)	(D)	(D)
Minnesota	99,000	94,350	(D)	(D)	(D)	(D)
Nebraska	34,080	33,800	15.50	17.00	5,282	5,746
North Dakota	665,000	645,000	17.10	17.50	113,715	112,875
South Dakota	878,400	782,000	(D)	(D)	(D)	(D)
Texas	21,280	33,800	18.00	18.00	3,830	6,084
Other States[2]	....	....	17.00	17.20	198,940	158,787
United States	1,887,260	1,746,350	16.70	17.40	320,867	310,179
Non-oil:						
California	2,400	2,080	(D)	24.20	(D)	503
Colorado	8,050	15,400	(D)	20.80	(D)	3,203
Kansas	12,750	9,125	(D)	(D)	(D)	(D)
Minnesota	14,835	8,280	(D)	(D)	(D)	(D)
Nebraska	13,300	11,050	25.60	21.00	3,405	2,321
North Dakota	74,400	95,700	23.40	23.90	17,410	22,872
South Dakota	87,750	49,600	(D)	(D)	(D)	(D)
Texas	6,300	5,850	24.00	20.00	1,512	1,170
Other States[2]	....	....	21.70	27.10	27,252	18,160
United States	219,785	197,085	22.80	22.40	49,579	48,229
Total:						
California	76,500	70,680	25.00	27.00	19,101	19,094
Colorado	61,950	59,400	17.30	19.00	10,692	11,299
Kansas	74,250	53,925	17.60	17.90	13,235	9,651
Minnesota	113,835	102,630	18.40	18.90	21,272	19,526
Nebraska	47,380	44,850	18.30	18.00	8,687	8,067
North Dakota	739,400	740,700	18.10	18.30	131,125	135,747
South Dakota	966,150	831,600	16.50	17.20	160,992	147,770
Texas	27,580	39,650	19.40	18.30	5,342	7,254
United States	2,107,045	1,943,435	17.40	17.80	370,446	358,408

(D) Withheld to avoid disclosing data for individual operations.   [1] Preliminary.   [2] Includes data withheld above.
NASS, Crops Branch, (202) 720–2127.

Table 3-49.—International Oilseed, sunflowerseed: Area and production in specified countries, 2017/2018–2019/2020

Country	Area			Production		
	2017/2018	2018/2019	2019/2020	2017/2018	2018/2019	2019/2020
	1,000 hectares			1,000 metric tons		
Ukraine	6,800	6,500	6,200	13,700	15,000	16,000
Russia	7,146	7,944	8,363	10,362	12,710	15,305
European Union	4,394	4,122	4,350	10,128	9,513	9,750
Argentina	1,678	1,876	1,590	3,538	3,825	3,400
China	1,171	921	1,250	3,149	2,494	3,250
Turkey	700	715	730	1,550	1,800	1,750
Kazakhstan	883	850	815	903	848	918
United States	540	493	504	970	956	882
Moldova	385	364	356	804	789	806
South Africa	602	515	610	862	680	750
Serbia	220	220	220	540	680	660
Burma	600	600	600	390	390	390
India	284	281	225	230	172	170
Pakistan	80	120	140	90	144	145
Brazil	96	65	80	142	111	120
Uruguay	50	56	60	78	90	100
Bolivia	109	115	120	121	80	90
Canada	26	27	29	58	57	63
Paraguay	41	31	30	65	49	51
Iran	40	40	40	43	43	43

FAS, Office of Global Analysis, (202) 720–6301. Prepared or estimated on the basis of official USDA production, supply, and distribution statistics from foreign governments.

Table 3-50—Sunflowerseed: United States exports by country of destination, 2018–2020

Country	2018	2019	2020
	Metric tons		
Canada	14,217	15,469	20,274
Spain	19,790	16,450	10,344
Mexico	14,053	11,472	5,776
Israel(*)	3,462	1,945	3,128
Korea, South	1,484	1,170	1,054
Greece	1,492	1,039	920
Bulgaria	479	0	648
Ukraine	201	0	588
Japan	526	483	553
Germany(*)	361	257	462
Romania	794	1,078	184
Ethiopia(*)	45	0	151
Poland	419	499	117
Singapore	91	91	94
Argentina	44	81	55
Hong Kong	0	15	44
Colombia	492	279	37
Philippines	27	26	35
Indonesia	14	339	28
Uruguay	0	0	22
Chile	116	112	21
United Kingdom	220	0	20
Netherlands	0	20	15
Trinidad and Tobago	4	5	12
Jamaica	0	9	9
Guatemala	3	13	9
Vietnam	40	0	5
Sri Lanka	0	0	5
Costa Rica	20	0	3
Barbados	0	2	3
Rest of World	4,125	1,757	3
World Total	62,517	52,611	44,619

(*) Denotes a country that is a summarization of its component countries.
FAS, Office of Global Analysis, (202) 720–6301. Data Source: U.S. Census Bureau Trade Data.

Table 3-51.—Sunflowerseed oil: United States exports by country of destination, 2018–2020

Country	2018	2019	2020
	Metric tons		
Canada	20,653	21,746	22,785
Mexico	16,209	16,349	8,287
Malaysia	2,322	6,420	2,151
Korea, South	257	1,162	1,740
Australia(*)	1,471	658	795
Japan	901	864	570
Taiwan	624	549	563
China	35	84	323
Netherlands	224	36	170
Italy(*)	62	100	154
India	45	198	141
Netherlands Antilles(*)	6	0	109
Colombia	14	49	109
Honduras	732	326	96
Indonesia	11	91	90
Vietnam	1,507	1,105	79
Kyrgyzstan	40	0	60
Spain	0	0	58
United Kingdom	0	38	44
Thailand	44	31	30
Gambia, The	0	0	24
France(*)	0	0	23
Bahamas, The	0	0	18
Uruguay	6	6	13
Peru	18	52	7
Dominican Republic	1	0	7
Brazil	8	8	6
New Zealand(*)	13	43	5
Jamaica	0	0	5
Iceland	0	0	4
Rest of World	531	6,044	5
World Total	45,733	55,960	38,468

(*) Denotes a country that is a summarization of its component countries.
FAS, Office of Global Analysis, (202) 720–6301.

Table 3-52.—International oil, sunflowerseed: Production in specified countries, 2017/2018–2019/2020

Country	2017/2018	2018/2019	2019/2020
	1,000 metric tons		
Ukraine	5,913	6,364	6,772
Russia	4,192	4,875	5,660
European Union	3,760	3,718	3,676
Argentina	1,385	1,425	1,350
Turkey	892	1,022	979
China	645	466	717
South Africa	352	293	335
Serbia	212	212	233
United States	197	201	187
Kazakhstan	213	138	169
Burma	131	131	131
Moldova	83	83	87
India	103	63	62
Pakistan	44	48	60
Iran	66	48	54
Brazil	57	49	51
Uruguay	31	36	40
Bolivia	52	34	39
Bosnia and Herzegovina	40	38	38
Egypt	37	37	35
Georgia	23	23	23
Belarus	10	22	20
Paraguay	23	18	18
Mexico	14	14	15
Morocco	17	10	13
Australia	10	13	8
Israel	8	8	8
Guatemala	7	7	7
Switzerland	7	7	7
Macedonia	6	4	5
Chile	3	3	3

FAS, Office of Global Analysis, (202) 720–6301.   Prepared or estimated on the basis of official USDA production, supply, and distribution statistics from foreign governments.

Table 3-53.—Mint oil: Production and value, by State and United States, 2017–2019

State	Production			Price per pound			Value of production		
	2017	2018	2019	2017	2018	2019[1]	2017	2018	2019[1]
	1,000 pounds	1,000 pounds	1,000 pounds	Dollars	Dollars	Dollars	1,000 dollars	1,000 dollars	1,000 dollars
Peppermint:									
California[2]	123	136	(NA)	22.80	(D)	(NA)	2,804	(D)	(NA)
Idaho	1,890	1,785	2,040	17.60	18.90	18.60	33,264	33,737	37,944
Indiana	383	350	307	21.50	21.50	22.30	8,235	7,525	6,846
Oregon	1,710	1,615	1,805	19.40	21.10	19.70	33,174	34,077	35,559
Washington	1,440	1,320	1,300	16.50	19.40	19.30	23,760	25,608	25,090
Wisconsin[2]	204	171	(NA)	18.50	(D)	(NA)	3,774	(D)	(NA)
Other States[3]	....	....	....	(X)	18.10	(X)	....	5,542	....
United States	5,750	5,377	5,452	18.30	19.80	19.30	105,011	106,489	105,439
Spearmint:									
Idaho	(D)	(D)	154	(D)	(D)	(D)	(D)	2,170	(D)
Indiana	167	216	281	17.00	(D)	(D)	2,839	(D)	(D)
Michigan[2]	(D)	(D)	(NA)	(D)	(D)	(NA)	(D)	(D)	(NA)
Oregon	263	313	313	19.50	17.40	15.90	5,129	5,446	4,977
Washington	2,100	1,748	1,665	15.60	16.70	17.40	32,832	29,229	28,995
Native	1,320	1,264	(D)	16.60	16.50	(D)	21,912	20,856	(D)
Scotch	780	484	(D)	14.00	17.30	(D)	10,920	8,373	(D)
Other States[3]	266	294	....	17.10	16.70	15.60	4,536	6,333	6,793
United States	2,796	2,571	2,413	16.20	16.80	16.90	45,336	43,178	40,765

(D) Withheld to avoid disclosing data for individual operations. (NA) Not available. (X) Not applicable. [1] Preliminary. [2] Estimates discontinued in 2019. [3] Includes data withheld above.
NASS, Crops Branch, (202) 720–2127.

Table 3-54.—Peppermint oil: Area, yield, production, and value, United States, 2010–2019

Year	Area harvested	Yield per harvested acre	Production	Price per pound	Value of production
	1,000 acres	Pounds	1,000 pounds	Dollars	1,000 dollars
2010	72.8	89	6,495	20.30	131,805
2011	75.5	89	6,700	23.10	154,626
2012	75.7	87	6,549	24.10	158,121
2013	70.0	90	6,273	23.80	149,557
2014	65.0	91	5,887	22.90	134,775
2015	64.9	91	5,876	21.80	127,956
2016	64.5	91	5,843	20.90	121,923
2017	60.8	95	5,750	18.30	105,011
2018	58.5	92	5,377	19.80	106,489
2019	52.4	104	5,452	19.30	105,439

NASS, Crops Branch (202), 720–2127.

Table 3-55.—Spearmint oil: Area, yield, production, and value, United States, 2010–2019

Year	Area harvested	Yield per harvested acre	Production	Price per pound	Value of production
	1,000 acres	*Pounds*	*1,000 pounds*	*Dollars*	*1,000 dollars*
2010	18.6	125	2,318	16.20	37,553
2011	17.3	132	2,286	18.60	42,438
2012	20.0	119	2,386	19.50	46,521
2013	24.5	119	2,926	19.10	55.829
2014	24.4	114	2,784	19.80	54,977
2015	25.8	114	2,930	18.30	53,664
2016	24.5	131	3,208	17.30	55,378
2017	22.3	125	2,796	16.20	45,336
2018	20.8	124	2,571	16.80	43,178
2019	18.5	130	2,413	16.90	40,765

NASS, Crops Branch, (202) 720–2127.

Table 3-56.—International oil, olive: Production in specified countries, 2017/2018–2019/2020

Country	2017/2018	2018/2019	2019/2020
	1,000 metric tons		
European Union	2,220	2,400	2,100
Tunisia	280	120	250
Turkey	263	183	250
Morocco	140	200	170
Syria	100	100	140
Algeria	83	76	80
Argentina	44	26	40
Jordan	25	24	24
Lebanon	17	24	20
Saudi Arabia	5	10	20
Libya	18	16	18
Australia	22	20	17
Chile	17	16	16
United States	16	16	16
Israel	15	15	14
China	5	4	4

FAS, Office of Global Analysis, (202) 720–6301. Prepared or estimated on the basis of official USDA production, supply, and distribution statistics from foreign governments.

Table 3-57.—Fats and oils: Wholesale price per pound, 2015–2019 [1]

Item and market	2015	2016	2017	2018	2019
	Cents	*Cents*	*Cents*	*Cents*	*Cents*
Coconut oil, crude, tanks, f.o.b. New York	52.27	69.12	80.36	50.18	35.32
Corn oil, crude, tank cars, f.o.b. Decatur	38.24	29.24	36.78	28.40	27.76
Cottonseed oil, crude, tank cars, f.o.b. Valley	47.01	45.81	38.53	30.68	37.01
Palm oil, U.S. ports, refined	32.10	34.39	35.67	31.26	29.63
Canola oil, Midwest	36.70	36.44	38.65	37.91	35.88
Soybean oil, crude, tank cars, f.o.b. Decatur	30.20	31.58	32.06	28.92	28.97
Sunflower oil, crude, Minneapolis	68.03	55.27	53.40	54.07	55.58
Tallow, edible, number 1 delivered Chicago	28.44	32.96	34.43	31.23	33.48

[1] All prices are calendar year average.
ERS, Market and Trade Economics Division, Field Crops Branch, (202) 694–5300. Compiled from the Chemical Marketing Reporter, Milling and Baking News, and the Agricultural Marketing Service.

CHAPTER IV

STATISTICS OF VEGETABLES AND MELONS

This chapter contains statistics on potatoes, sweet potatoes, and commercial vegetables and melons.

For potatoes and sweet potatoes, the estimates of area, production, value, and farm disposition pertain to the total crop and include quantities produced both for sale and for use on farms where grown. Potato statistics are shown on a within-year seasonal grouping of winter, spring, summer, and fall crops, by States. Some States have production in more than one seasonal group.

Commercial vegetables for fresh market include 26 principal vegetable and melon crops in the major producing States. These estimates relate to crops which are grown primarily for sale and do not include vegetables and melons produced in farm and non-farm gardens. The bulk of the production of the principal vegetable and melon crops is for consumption in the fresh state. The commercial estimates of these crops include local market production from areas near consuming centers as well as production from well recognized commercial areas which specialize in producing supplies for shipment to distant markets. For fresh market vegetables and melons, value per unit and total value are on an f.o.b. basis.

For processing vegetables, the estimates of area, production, and value for each of 10 crops relate to production used by commercial canners, freezers, and other processors, except dehydrators. These estimates include raw products grown by processors themselves and those grown under contract or purchased on the open market. This production and the actual area harvested are not duplicated in the fresh market estimates for the same commodities. The production of those vegetables used for processing for which regular processing estimates are not made is included in the fresh market estimates. The processed segment of production for asparagus, broccoli, and cauliflower, combined with fresh market production during the year, is published separately at the end of the season. For processed vegetables, value per unit and total value are at processing plant door.

Beginning in 2016, acreage and yield estimates for fresh market and processing utilizations were discontinued. Total production and utilized production are estimated for each crop. Harvested not sold estimates were added to the estimating program. This is defined as the difference between total production and total utilized production.

Table 4-1.—Vegetables, principal: Fresh Market and Processing, Area Harvested, Production, and Value, by State and United States, 2018–2020

State	Area harvested			Total production		
	2018	2019	2020	2018	2019	2020
	Acres	*Acres*	*Acres*	*1,000 cwt*	*1,000 cwt*	*1,000 cwt*
Alabama	5,900	(NA)	(NA)	619.5	(NA)	(NA)
Arizona	(D)	122,600	115,600	(D)	34,973.5	31,813.5
California	985,800	955,500	926,600	464,180.6	433,357.0	435,922.0
Colorado	(D)	2,700	3,300	(D)	1,147.5	1,452.0
Delaware	(D)	(NA)	(NA)	(D)	(NA)	(NA)
Florida	172,800	170,700	164,200	34,121.0	34,121.0	30,797.5
Georgia	95,400	92,800	90,700	17,731.3	21,267.0	17,909.4
Idaho	12,300	10,900	12,900	7,827.0	8,938.0	10,320.0
Illinois	38,850	38,100	41,000	7,980.0	7,464.8	8,628.3
Indiana	28,000	11,100	12,500	10,219.2	3,543.0	3,365.0
Maryland	(D)	(NA)	(NA)	(D)	(NA)	(NA)
Michigan	101,900	87,200	82,500	16,683.2	12,419.1	11,035.9
Minnesota	160,600	154,300	151,700	17,454.8	15,647.4	17,310.5
Mississippi	-	27,500	29,500	-	4,262.5	5,900.0
Missouri	(D)	(NA)	(NA)	(D)	(NA)	(NA)
New Jersey	28,500	10,600	11,100	3,533.3	1,606.0	1,582.4
New Mexico	15,000	15,300	14,700	5,611.0	5,254.5	5,514.0
New York	89,200	86,300	80,900	12,763.8	13,065.7	13,761.0
North Carolina	36,500	126,300	133,100	6,614.5	24,732.0	21,506.5
Ohio	21,500	3,500	3,600	4,913.0	437.5	378.0
Oregon	(D)	79,000	75,800	(D)	23,908.0	23,820.9
Pennsylvania	25,500	13,500	14,900	1,957.3	1,151.1	1,185.3
South Carolina	10,300	4,500	4,500	2,501.4	1,440.0	1,710.0
Tennessee	12,700	(NA)	(NA)	1,626.6	(NA)	(NA)
Texas	62,000	47,800	47,900	15,926.3	12,770.0	12,841.7
Virginia	7,500	5,600	5,400	1,491.7	924.0	972.0
Washington	144,100	140,300	146,300	40,206.3	37,515.2	39,329.9
Wisconsin	(D)	155,900	157,600	(D)	19,787.5	22,723.7
Other States [1]	430,750	-	-	89,653.4	-	-
United States	2,485,100	2,356,900	2,326,300	763,615.2	720,082.7	719,779.5

State	Utilized production			Value of utilized production		
	2018	2019	2020	2018	2019	2020
	1,000 cwt	*1,000 cwt*	*1,000 cwt*	*1,000 dollars*	*1,000 dollars*	*1,000 dollars*
Alabama	615.2	(NA)	(NA)	15,379	(NA)	(NA)
Arizona	(D)	34,973.5	31,813.5	(D)	1,628,351	1,154,644
California	461,897.6	431,684.3	433,773.9	7,327,501	7,744,144	7,676,076
Colorado	(D)	1,109.6	1,452.0	(D)	18,531	28,024
Delaware	(D)	(NA)	(NA)	(D)	(NA)	(NA)
Florida	33,363.7	34,253.4	29,828.6	1,121,981	1,222,850	1,168,155
Georgia	17,702.3	20,803.8	17,886.6	452,589	515,530	583,351
Idaho	7,808.6	8,893.3	10,268.4	60,831	65,815	68,331
Illinois	7,949.0	7,423.6	8,622.7	39,577	41,932	39,446
Indiana	10,206.6	3,539.3	3,321.8	97,104	52,276	63,295
Maryland	(D)	(NA)	(NA)	(D)	(NA)	(NA)
Michigan	16,633.1	12,352.7	10,803.6	273,314	217,138	196,907
Minnesota	17,430.1	15,477.7	17,293.2	116,288	76,579	89,658
Mississippi	-	4,262.5	5,900.0	-	75,021	121,540
Missouri	(D)	(NA)	(NA)	(D)	(NA)	(NA)
New Jersey	3,262.7	1,593.0	1,535.7	138,376	80,629	88,100
New Mexico	5,611.0	5,254.5	5,514.0	133,357	152,628	139,123
New York	12,528.2	12,763.2	13,676.3	209,911	226,905	222,273
North Carolina	6,506.4	23,478.1	21,380.5	145,025	449,681	469,399
Ohio	4,899.0	434.4	370.4	103,562	9,911	9,995
Oregon	(D)	23,712.9	23,634.6	(D)	194,586	202,153
Pennsylvania	1,905.7	1,136.0	1,159.8	59,224	25,389	30,653
South Carolina	2,495.3	1,402.6	1,691.2	68,470	16,130	31,118
Tennessee	1,584.1	(NA)	(NA)	66,984	(NA)	(NA)
Texas	15,803.7	12,591.5	12,734.9	298,047	184,896	215,990
Virginia	1,439.2	903.7	962.3	43,653	16,427	17,595
Washington	39,330.3	36,759.8	38,513.8	351,475	362,740	299,824
Wisconsin	(D)	19,711.1	22,655.8	(D)	128,310	150,694
Other States [1]	89,342.7	-	-	1,747,898	-	-
United States	758,314.5	714,490.5	714,793.6	12,869,883	13,556,399	13,066,344

(D) Withheld to avoid disclosing data for individual operations. (NA) Not available.   [1] Includes data withheld above.
NASS, Crops Branch, (202) 720–2127.

Table 4-2.— Artichokes for fresh market and processing: Area, yield, production, value, and total value, United States, 2011-2020

Year	Area harvested	Yield per acre	Utilized Production	Value	
				Per cwt	Total
	Acres	Cwt	1,000 cwt	Dollars	1,000 dollars
2011	7,400	135.0	999	51.10	51,049
2012	7,300	145.0	1,059	54.30	57,504
2013	7,100	135.0	959	61.00	58,499
2014	7,300	130.0	949	57.60	54,662
2015	6,800	135.0	918	87.80	80,600
2016	6,800	145.0	986	78.80	77,697
2017	7,200	130.0	936.0	70.00	65,520
2018	6,900	145.0	1,000.5	63.00	63,032
2019	6,600	145.0	956.0	78.00	74,568
2020	5,800	140.0	792.5	79.00	62,608

Note: Beginning in 2016, Acreage and Yield estimates for fresh market and processing utilizations were discontinued. Total Production and Utilized Production are estimated for each crop. Harvested Not Sold estimates were added to the estimating program. This is defined as the difference between Total Production and Total Utilized Production. Table 4-2, 2016-2018 includes utilized production.
NASS, Crops Branch, (202) 720–2127.

Table 4-3.—Asparagus for Fresh Market and Processing: Area planted and harvested, yield, production, price and value - State and United States, 2018–2020

State	Area planted			Area harvested		
	2018	2019	2020	2018	2019	2020
	Acres	Acres	Acres	Acres	Acres	Acres
California	6,200	5,000	4,000	6,000	4,900	4,000
Michigan	10,000	10,000	10,000	9,500	9,400	9,500
New Jersey	2,200	2,100	2,000	2,100	2,000	1,900
Washington	4,500	4,500	4,000	4,100	4,100	3,800
United States	22,900	21,600	20,000	21,700	20,400	19,200

State	Yield per acre			Utilized Production		
	2018	2019	2020	2018	2019	2020
	Cwt	Cwt	Cwt	1,000 cwt	1,000 cwt	1,000 cwt
California	30.0	35.0	33.0	178.2	171.5	132.0
Michigan	28.0	30.0	28.0	266.0	273.5	260.7
New Jersey	33.0	32.0	30.0	69.3	63.7	56.9
Washington	65.0	55.0	55.0	261.2	216.5	209.0
United States	36.0	36.4	34.6	774.7	725.2	658.6

State	Price per cwt			Value of Production		
	2018	2019	2020	2018	2019	2020
	Dollars	Dollars	Dollars	1,000 dollars	1,000 dollars	1,000 dollars
California	149.00	202.00	177.00	26,552	34,643	23,364
Michigan	87.50	94.60	91.50	23,275	25,875	23,856
New Jersey	167.00	256.00	262.00	11,562	16,302	14,896
Washington	100.00	98.10	111.00	26,195	21,242	23,168
United States	113.00	135.00	129.00	87,584	98,062	85,284

NASS, Crops Branch, (202) 720–2127.

Utilization and State	Utilized Production		
	2018	2019	2020
Fresh market	*1,000 cwt*	*1,000 cwt*	*1,000 cwt*
California	178.2	171.5	132.0
Michigan	133.0	152.3	143.6
New Jersey	(D)	(D)	(D)
Washington	(D)	(D)	(D)
Other States [1]	306.4	257.0	244.9
United States	617.6	580.8	520.5
Processing	*Tons*	*Tons*	*Tons*
California	-	-	-
Michigan	6,650	6,063	5,852
New Jersey	(D)	(D)	(D)
Washington	(D)	(D)	(D)
Other States [1]	1,202	1,160	1,051
United States	7,852	7,223	6,903

Utilization and State	Price per unit		
	2018	2019	2020
Fresh market	*Dollars per cwt*	*Dollars per cwt*	*Dollars per cwt*
California	149.00	202.00	177.00
Michigan	95.00	105.00	105.00
New Jersey	(D)	(D)	(D)
Washington	(D)	(D)	(D)
Other States [1]	117.00	139.00	149.00
United States	122.00	149.00	144.00
Processing	*Dollars per ton*	*Dollars per ton*	*Dollars per ton*
California	(X)	(X)	(X)
Michigan	1,600.00	1,630.00	1,500.00
New Jersey	(D)	(D)	(D)
Washington	(D)	(D)	(D)
Other States [1]	1,470.00	1,500.00	1,470.00
United States	1,580.00	1,610.00	1,500.00

Utilization and State	Value of utilized production		
	2018	2019	2020
Fresh market	*1,000 dollars*	*1,000 dollars*	*1,000 dollars*
California	26,552	34,643	23,364
Michigan	12,635	15,992	15,078
New Jersey	(D)	(D)	(D)
Washington	(D)	(D)	(D)
Other States [3]	35,988	35,801	36,514
United States	75,175	86,436	74,956
Processing	*1,000 dollars*	*1,000 dollars*	*1,000 dollars*
California [1]	-	-	-
Michigan	10,640	9,883	8,778
New Jersey [2]	(D)	(D)	(D)
Washington	(D)	(D)	(D)
Other States [3]	1,769	1,743	1,550
United States	12,409	11,626	10,328

(D) Withheld to avoid disclosing data for individual operations. (X) Not applicable. [1] Includes data withheld above.
NASS, Crops Branch, (202) 720–2127.

Table 4-5.—Snap Beans for Fresh Market and Processing: Area Harvested, Production, and Value - States and United States, 2018–2020

State	Area harvested			Total production		
	2018	2019	2020	2018	2019	2020
	Acres	*Acres*	*Acres*	*1,000 cwt*	*1,000 cwt*	*1,000 cwt*
California	7,900	6,900	5,900	908.5	655.5	619.5
Delaware	1,700	(NA)	(NA)	102.0	(NA)	(NA)
Florida	27,600	26,200	26,200	1,380.0	1,755.4	1,310.0
Georgia	11,900	10,200	9,400	559.3	612.0	432.0
Illinois	8,800	11,700	12,600	800.8	865.8	1,108.8
Indiana	2,600	(NA)	(NA)	187.2	(NA)	(NA)
Maryland	3,000	(NA)	(NA)	180.0	(NA)	(NA)
Michigan	18,200	17,600	19,100	1,365.0	1,601.6	1,699.9
Minnesota	2,800	3,400	3,900	215.6	323.0	370.5
New Jersey	2,700	(NA)	(NA)	118.8	(NA)	(NA)
New York	26,300	25,300	27,200	2,104.0	1,796.3	1,768.0
North Carolina	4,800	(NA)	(NA)	216.0	(NA)	(NA)
Oregon	11,500	12,200	10,000	1,437.5	1,830.0	1,350.0
Pennsylvania	7,400	7,200	7,900	436.6	489.6	450.3
Tennessee	7,100	(NA)	(NA)	269.8	(NA)	(NA)
Texas	2,800	(NA)	(NA)	196.0	(NA)	(NA)
Washington	3,200	(NA)	(NA)	246.4	(NA)	(NA)
Wisconsin	63,500	63,500	56,600	6,350.0	6,223.0	5,660.0
United States	213,800	184,200	178,800	17,073.5	16,152.2	14,769.4

State				Value of utilized production		
	2018	2019	2020	2018	2019	2020
	1,000 cwt	*1,000 cwt*	*1,000 cwt*	*1,000 dollars*	*1,000 dollars*	*1,000 dollars*
California	908.5	655.5	548.8	69,008	43,945	45,721
Delaware	102.0	(NA)	(NA)	2,385	(NA)	(NA)
Florida	1,373.1	1,755.4	1,264.2	58,702	68,866	69,580
Georgia	559.3	612.0	428.1	28,025	32,375	24,897
Illinois	800.8	831.2	1,108.8	9,294	9,315	8,339
Indiana	187.2	(NA)	(NA)	3,123	(NA)	(NA)
Maryland	180.0	(NA)	(NA)	3,456	(NA)	(NA)
Michigan	1,365.0	1,600.0	1,698.2	21,520	25,611	31,270
Minnesota	215.4	322.7	370.1	4,714	6,675	3,672
New Jersey	117.6	(NA)	(NA)	5,986	(NA)	(NA)
New York	2,104.0	1,783.7	1,766.2	34,023	32,052	24,259
North Carolina	214.3	(NA)	(NA)	8,020	(NA)	(NA)
Oregon	1,437.5	1,830.0	1,343.3	23,596	27,909	20,558
Pennsylvania	435.3	489.1	449.8	8,057	8,612	8,140
Tennessee	265.5	(NA)	(NA)	10,544	(NA)	(NA)
Texas	196.0	(NA)	(NA)	5,723	(NA)	(NA)
Washington	246.4	(NA)	(NA)	7,856	(NA)	(NA)
Wisconsin	6,337.3	6,223.0	5,631.7	47,877	42,254	35,291
United States	17,045.2	16,102.6	14,645.2	351,909	297,614	271,727

(NA) Not available.
NASS, Crops Branch, (202) 720–2127.

Table 4-6.—Broccoli, fresh market and processing: Area, yield, production, value per hundredweight and per ton, and total value, United States, 2014-2020 [1]

Year	Total crop				
	Area harvested	Yield per acre	Production	Value [2]	
				Per cwt	Total
	Acres	*Cwt*	*1,000 cwt*	*Dollars*	*1,000 dollars*
2014	126,400	163.0	20,600.0	40.00	824,961
2015	124,400	176.0	21,888.0	48.40	1,058,770
2016	131,300	171.0	22,466.0	37.70	846,595
2017	128,600	158.5	20,384.0	45.40	925,716
2018	113,900	151.7	17,273.0	42.80	738,527
2019	105,000	158.0	16,594.0	51.30	850,742
2020	100,300	157.8	15,832.0	55.50	874,959

Year	Fresh market			Processing		
	Utilized Production	Value [2]		Utilized Production	Value [3]	
		Per cwt	Total		Per ton	Total
	1,000 cwt	*Dollars*	*1,000 dollars*	*Tons*	*Dollars*	*1,000 dollars*
2014	19,910.0	40.70	809,608	34,500	445.00	15,353
2015	21,104.0	49.10	1,035,211	39,200	601.00	23,559
2016	21,548.0	38.20	824,103	45,903	490.00	22,492
2017	19,908.0	46.00	916,482	23,800	388.00	9,234
2018	16,778.1	43.10	722,789	24,746	636.00	15,738
2019	15,836.4	52.50	832,181	37,880	490.00	18,561
2020	15,259.2	56.50	862,680	25,060	490.00	12,279

[1] Sprouting broccoli only. Does not include broccoli rabe nor heading (cauliflower) broccoli.   [2] Price and value at point of first sale.   [3] Price and value at processing plant door.
NASS, Crops Branch, (202) 720–2127.

Table 4-7.—Broccoli: Area, production, and value, by State and United States, 2018–2020 [1]

State	Area harvested			Utilized production		
	2018	2019	2020	2018	2019	2020
	Acres			*1,000 cwt*		
Arizona	10,900	10,300	10,800	1,308.0	1,442.0	1,512.0
California	103,000	94,700	89,500	15,965.0	15,152.0	14,248.4
United States	113,900	105,000	100,300	17,273.0	16,594.0	15,760.4

State	Price per cwt			Value of utilized production		
	2018	2019	2020	2018	2019	2020
	Dollars			*1,000 dollars*		
Arizona	45.20	72.00	61.40	59,122	103,824	92,837
California	42.60	49.30	54.90	679,405	746,918	782,122
United States	42.80	51.30	55.50	738,527	850,742	874,959

Utilization and State	Utilized production			Price per unit			Value of utilized production		
	2018	2019	2020	2018	2019	2020	2018	2019	2020
	1,000 cwt			*Dollars per cwt*			*1,000 dollars*		
Fresh Market									
Arizona	1,308.0	1,442.0	(D)	42.20	72.00	(D)	59,122	103,824	(D)
California	15,470.1	14,394.4	(D)	42.90	50.60	(D)	663,667	728,357	(D)
Other States	-	-	15,259.2	(X)	(X)	56.50	-	-	862,680
United States	16,778.1	15,836.4	15,259.2	43.10	52.50	56.50	722,789	832,181	862,680
	Tons			*Dollars per ton*			*1,000 dollars*		
Processing									
Arizona	-	-	(D)	(X)	(X)	(D)	-	-	(D)
California	24,746	37,880	(D)	636.00	490.00	(D)	15,738	18,561	(D)
Other States	-	-	25,060	(X)	(X)	490.00	-	-	12,279
United States	24,746	37,880	25,060	636.00	490.00	490.00	15,738	18,561	12,279

(X) Not applicable. [1] Sprouting broccoli only. Does not include broccoli rabe nor heading (cauliflower) broccoli.
NASS, Crops Branch, (202) 720–2127.

Table 4-8.—Cabbage for fresh market and processing: Area Harvested, production, and value, by State and United States, 2018–2020

State	Area harvested			Total production		
	2018	2019	2020	2018	2019	2020
	Acres			1,000 cwt		
Arizona	3,300	(D)	3,800	1,650.0	(D)	1,748.0
California	14,200	15,800	14,300	4,828.0	6,478.0	5,863.0
Florida	8,900	8,200	8,800	3,204.0	2,952.0	2,464.0
Georgia	2,900	4,800	(D)	1,160.0	1,920.0	(D)
Michigan	3,700	4,500	4,000	1,295.0	1,530.0	1,520.0
New York	10,100	11,700	11,700	3,939.5	4,446.0	5,616.0
North Carolina ..	2,800	(NA)	(NA)	644.0	(NA)	(NA)
Texas	5,000	(D)	6,400	1,350.0	(D)	1,856.0
Wisconsin	3,300	5,000	(D)	1,336.5	1,325.0	(D)
Other States	-	10,400	9,600	-	3,588.0	4,608.0
United States	54,200	59,100	58,600	19,406.5	22,239.0	23,675.0

State	Utilized production			Value of utilized production		
	2018	2019	2020	2018	2019	2020
	1,000 cwt			1,000 dollars		
Arizona	1,650.0	(D)	1,748.0	33,495	(D)	32,163
California	4,828.0	6,478.0	5,863.0	181,533	204,057	148,042
Florida	3,172.0	2,922.5	2,439.4	62,806	58,394	49,852
Georgia	1,160.0	1,887.4	(D)	14,845	30,723	(D)
Michigan	1,295.0	1,526.9	1,520.0	14,327	18,684	16,751
New York	3,820.8	4,423.8	5,593.5	52,862	82,430	81,693
North Carolina ..	606.0	(NA)	(NA)	10,120	(NA)	(NA)
Texas	1,350.0	(D)	1,856.0	27,405	(D)	40,832
Wisconsin	1,336.5	1,325.0	(D)	10,698	15,598	(D)
Other States	-	3,588.0	4,608.0	-	100,854	58,649
United States	19,218.3	22,151.6	23,627.9	408,091	510,740	427,982

State	Utilized production			Price per unit			Value of utilized production		
	2018	2019	2020	2018	2019	2020	2018	2019	2020
	1,000 cwt			Dollars per cwt			1,000 dollars		
Fresh Market									
Arizona	(D)	(D)	1,748.0	(D)	(D)	18.40	(D)	(D)	32,163
California	4,828.0	(D)	4,983.6	37.60	(D)	27.80	181,533	(D)	138,544
Florida	3,172.0	(D)	(D)	19.80	(D)	(D)	62,806	(D)	(D)
Georgia	(D)	(D)	(D)	(D)	(D)	(D)	(D)	(D)	(D)
Michigan	686.4	608.9	851.2	14.00	19.00	13.00	9,610	11,569	11,066
New York	3,663.3	(D)	(D)	14.00	(D)	(D)	51,286	(D)	(D)
North Carolina ..	606.0	(NA)	(NA)	16.70	(NA)	(NA)	10,120	(NA)	(NA)
Texas	1,350.0	(D)	1,856.0	20.30	(D)	22.00	27,405	(D)	40,832
Wisconsin	(D)	(D)	(D)	(D)	(D)	(D)	(D)	(D)	(D)
Other States [1] ...	2,991.3	18,854.2	9,704.4	17.90	25.20	18.10	53,572	475,246	175,511
United States	17,297.0	19,463.1	19,143.2	22.90	25.00	20.80	396,332	486,815	398,116
	Tons			Dollars per ton			1,000 dollars		
Processing									
Arizona	(D)	(D)	43,973	(D)	(D)	(X)	(D)	(D)	-
California	-	(D)	43,973	(X)	(D)	216.00	-	(D)	9,498
Florida	-	(D)	(D)	(X)	(D)	(D)	-	(D)	(D)
Georgia	(D)	(D)	(D)	(D)	(D)	(D)	(D)	(D)	(D)
Michigan	30,433	45,900	33,440	155.00	155.00	170.00	4,717	7,115	5,685
New York	7,878	(D)	(D)	200.00	(D)	(D)	1,576	(D)	(D)
North Carolina ..	-	(NA)	(NA)	(X)	(NA)	(NA)	-	(NA)	(NA)
Texas	-	(D)	-	(X)	(D)	(X)	-	(D)	-
Wisconsin	(D)	(D)	(D)	(D)	(D)	(D)	(D)	(D)	(D)
Other States [1] ...	57,761	88,524	146,828	94.60	190.00	100.00	5,466	16,810	14,683
United States	96,072	134,424	224,241	122.00	178.00	133.00	11,759	23,925	29,866

(D) Withheld to avoid disclosing data for individual operations. (NA) Not available. [1] Includes data withheld above.
NASS, Crops Branch, (202) 720–2127.

Table 4-9.—Cantaloupes for fresh market: Area Harvested, production, and value, by State and United States, 2018–2020

State	Area harvested			Yield per acre		
	2018	2019	2020	2018	2019	2020
	Acres			1,000 cwt		
Arizona	16,300	14,000	13,000	230.0	225.0	235.0
California	31,500	27,800	21,900	265.0	245.0	330.0
Florida	(D)	2,300	1,900	(D)	210.0	240.0
Georgia	(D)	3,900	3,800	(D)	220.0	160.0
Indiana	1,700	(NA)	(NA)	225.0	(NA)	(NA)
North Carolina ..	1,200	(NA)	(NA)	255.0	(NA)	(NA)
Pennsylvania	900	(NA)	(NA)	120.0	(NA)	(NA)
South Carolina ..	(D)	(NA)	(NA)	(D)	(NA)	(NA)
Texas	2,000	(NA)	(NA)	110.0	(NA)	(NA)
Other States [1] ...	7,100	-	-	210.0	(X)	(X)
United States	60,700	48,000	40,600	240.6	235.5	279.5

State	Total production			Utilized production		
	2018	2019	2020	2018	2019	2020
	1,000 cwt			1,000 dollars		
Arizona	3,749.5	3,150.0	3,055.0	3,749.5	3,150.0	3,055.0
California	8,347.5	6,811.0	7,227.0	8,347.5	6,811.0	7,227.0
Florida	(D)	483.0	456.0	(D)	481.1	455.5
Georgia	(D)	858.0	608.0	(D)	852.9	608.0
Indiana	382.5	(NA)	(NA)	382.5	(NA)	(NA)
North Carolina ..	306.0	(NA)	(NA)	302.9	(NA)	(NA)
Pennsylvania	108.0	(NA)	(NA)	106.9	(NA)	(NA)
South Carolina ..	(D)	(NA)	(NA)	(D)	(NA)	(NA)
Texas	220.0	(NA)	(NA)	220.0	(NA)	(NA)
Other States [1] ...	1,494.0	-	-	1,494.0	-	-
United States	14,607.0	12,713.0	11,346.0	14,602.8	11,295.0	11,345.5

State	Price per cwt			Value of utilized production		
	2018	2019	2020	2018	2019	2020
	Dollars			1,000 dollars		
Arizona	23.20	25.60	27.00	86,977	80,640	82,485
California	22.50	19.50	25.50	187,819	132,815	184,289
Florida	(D)	19.30	30.20	(D)	9,285	13,756
Georgia	(D)	17.60	25.00	(D)	15,011	15,200
Indiana	22.50	(NA)	(NA)	8,606	(NA)	(NA)
North Carolina ..	15.00	(NA)	(NA)	4,544	(NA)	(NA)
Pennsylvania	38.80	(NA)	(NA)	4,148	(NA)	(NA)
South Carolina ..	(D)	(NA)	(NA)	(D)	(NA)	(NA)
Texas	23.00	(NA)	(NA)	5,060	(NA)	(NA)
Other States [1] ...	23.00	(X)	(X)	34,388	-	-
United States	22.70	21.00	26.10	331,542	237,751	295,730

(D) Withheld to avoid disclosing data for individual operations. (NA) Not available. (X) Not applicable. [1] Includes data withheld above.
NASS, Crops Branch, (202) 720–2127.

Table 4-10.—Carrot for fresh market and processing: Area Harvested, production, and value, by State and United States, 2018–2020

State	Area harvested			Total production		
	2018	2019	2020	2018	2019	2020
	Acres			1,000 cwt		
California	64,300	62,400	60,300	38,580.0	26,832.0	24,723.0
Michigan	4,000	(NA)	(NA)	1,520.0	(NA)	(NA)
Texas	1,600	(NA)	(NA)	400.0	(NA)	(NA)
Washington	5,900	6,400	5,900	3,658.0	4,864.0	4,602.0
Wisconsin	4,000	3,300	3,500	1,720.0	1,600.5	1,820.0
United States	79,800	72,100	69,700	45,878.0	33,296.5	31,145.0

State	Utilized production			Value of utilized production		
	2018	2019	2020	2018	2019	2020
	1,000 cwt			1,000 dollars		
California	38,464.3	26,832.0	24,723.0	687,631	730,769	685,198
Michigan	1,520.0	(NA)	(NA)	14,456	(NA)	(NA)
Texas	400.0	(NA)	(NA)	3,785	(NA)	(NA)
Washington	3,658.0	4,864.0	4,602.0	19,982	29,415	22,469
Wisconsin	1,714.8	1,600.5	1,803.6	7,092	6,977	8,483
United States	45,757.1	33,296.5	31,128.6	732,946	863,518	716,150

Utilization and State	Utilized production			Price per unit			Value of utilized production		
	2018	2019	2020	2018	2019	2020	2018	2019	2020
	1,000 cwt			Dollars per cwt			1,000 dollars		
Fresh Market									
California	(D)	(D)	(D)	(D)	(D)	(D)	(D)	(D)	(D)
Michigan	410.4	(NA)	(NA)	19.00	(NA)	(NA)	7,798	(NA)	(NA)
Texas	(D)	(NA)	(NA)	(D)	(NA)	(NA)	(D)	(NA)	(NA)
Washington	(D)	170.2	(D)	57.00	(D)	(D)	(D)	9,701	(D)
Wisconsin	3.4	(D)	14.6	138.00	(D)	116.00	469	(D)	1,694
Other States [1] ...	36,201.8	24,150.4	22,278.3	18.40	28.30	28.80	664,918	683,537	642,476
United States	36,615.6	24,320.6	22,292.9	18.40	28.50	28.90	673,185	693,238	644,170
	Tons			Dollars per ton			1,000 dollars		
Processing									
California	(D)	(D)	(D)	(D)	(D)	(D)	(D)	(D)	(D)
Michigan	55,480	(NA)	(NA)	120.00	(NA)	(NA)	6,658	(NA)	(NA)
Texas	(D)	(NA)	(NA)	(D)	(NA)	(NA)	(D)	(NA)	(NA)
Washington	(D)	234,688	(D)	84.00	(D)	(D)	(D)	19,714	(D)
Wisconsin	85,570	(D)	89,453	77.40	(D)	75.90	6,623	(D)	6,789
Other States [1] ...	316,023	214,105	352,334	147.00	253.00	185.00	46,480	54,209	65,191
United States	457,073	448,793	441,787	131.00	165.00	163.00	59,761	73,923	71,980

(D) Withheld to avoid disclosing data for individual operations. (NA) Not available. [1] Includes data withheld above.
NASS, Crops Branch, (202) 720–2127.

Table 4-11.—Cauliflower for fresh market and processing: Area harvested, yield, production, and value, United States, 2011-2020 [1]

Year	Area for harvest	Yield per acre	Production	Value [2]	
				Per cwt.	Total [3]
	Acres	1,000 cwt	cwt	Dollars	1,000 dollars
2011	36,430	183.0	6,649.0	46.00	305,539
2012	36,070	185.0	6,690.0	35.80	239,203
2013	36,830	181.0	6,662.0	44.30	295,450
2014	35,070	181.0	6,361.0	49.80	316,937
2015	37,210	176.0	6,559.0	61.30	401,747
2016	41,900	178.1	7,461.0	55.70	415,761
2017	45,800	198.1	9,074.5	45.90	415,737
2018	44,900	211.6	9,501.0	45.80	434,491
2019	45,200	222.9	10,076.0	45.70	459,988
2020	42,200	212.2	8,953.0	39.10	346,391

Note: Beginning in 2016, acreage and yield estimates for fresh market and processing utilizations were discontinued. Only total acreage and total yield will be published beginning in 2016. Total production and utilized production are estimated for each crop. Harvested not sold estimates were added to the estimating program. This is defined as the difference between total production and total utilized production.
[1] Includes heading (cauliflower) broccoli.   [2] Price and value at point of first sale.   [3] Beginning in 2016, value of utilized production.
NASS, Crops Branch, (202) 720–2127.

Table 4-12.—Cauliflower for fresh market and processing: Area harvested, production, and value, by State and United States, 2018–2020

State	Area harvested			Total Production		
	2018	2019	2020	2018	2019	2020
	Acres			1,000 cwt		
Arizona	6,100	6,400	6,000	1,159.0	1,152.0	1,170.0
California	38,800	38,800	36,200	8,342.0	8,924.0	7,783.0
United States	44,900	45,200	42,200	9,501.0	10,076.0	8,953.0

State	Utilized production			Value of total production		
	2018	2019	2020	2018	2019	2020
	1,000 cwt			1,000 dollars		
Arizona	1,159.0	1,152.0	1,170.0	79,739	93,658	79,209
California	8,333.7	8,915.1	7,681.8	354,752	366,330	267,182
United States	9,492.7	10,067.1	8,851.8	434,491	459,988	346,391

Utilization and State	Utilized production			Price per unit			Value of utilized production		
	2018	2019	2020	2018	2019	2020	2018	2019	2020
	1,000 cwt			Dollars per cwt			1,000 dollars		
Fresh Market									
Arizona	(D)	(D)	(D)	(D)	(D)	(D)	(D)	(D)	(D)
California	(D)	(D)	(D)	(D)	(D)	(D)	(D)	(D)	(D)
Other States [1]	9,309.1	10,058.2	8,797.3	46.00	45.70	39.20	428,563	459,703	344,639
United States	9,309.1	10,058.2	8,797.3	46.00	45.70	39.20	428,563	459,703	344,639
	Tons			Dollars per ton			1,000 dollars		
Processing									
Arizona	(D)	(D)	(D)	(D)	(D)	(D)	(D)	(D)	(D)
California	(D)	(D)	(D)	(D)	(D)	(D)	(D)	(D)	(D)
Other States [1]	9,176	446	2,724	646.00	639.00	643.00	5,928	285	1,752
United States	9,176	446	2,724	646.00	639.00	643.00	5,928	285	1,752

(D) Withheld to avoid disclosing data for individual operations. (X) Not applicable. [1] Includes data withheld above.
NASS, Crops Branch, (202) 720–2127.

Table 4-13.—Celery for fresh market and processing: Area harvested, yield, production, price, and value, United States, 2014–2020 [1]

Year	Area harvested	Yield per acre	Production	Value [2]	
				Per cwt	Total
	Acres	*Cwt*	*1,000 cwt*	*Dollars*	*1,000 dollars*
2014	28,900	636.0	18,393	17.10	314,134
2015	27,700	618.0	17,110	24.80	424,664
2016	33,100	534.0	17,676	18.10	319,321
2017	31,800	505.9	16,089	20.10	322,047
2018	30,200	580.0	17,516	25.00	436,818
2019	28,100	560.0	15,736	30.20	474,711
2020	28,800	560.0	16,128	22.30	358,579

Note: Beginning in 2016, acreage and yield estimates for fresh market and processing utilizations were discontinued. Only total acreage and total yield will be published beginning in 2016. Total production and utilized production are estimated for each crop. Harvested Not Sold estimates were added to the estimating program. This is defined as the difference between total production and total utilized production.
[1] Mostly for fresh market use, but includes quantities used for processing. [2] Price and value at point of first sale.
NASS, Crops Branch, (202) 720–2127.

Table 4-14.—Celery for fresh market and processing: Area harvested, production, price, and value, by State and United States, 2018–2020

State	Area harvested			Total Production		
	2018	2019	2020	2018	2019	2020
	Acres			*1,000 cwt*		
California	28,300	28,100	28,800	14,850.0	16,414.0	15,736.0
Michigan	1,900	(NA)	(NA)	1,239.0	1,102.0	(NA)
United States	30,200	28,100	28,800	16,089.0	17,516.0	15,736.0

State	Utilized production			Value of total production		
	2018	2019	2020	2018	2019	2020
	1,000 cwt			*1,000 dollars*		
California	16,397.6	15,720.3	16,111.9	417,347	474,711	358,579
Michigan	1,102.0	(NA)	(NA)	19,471	(NA)	(NA)
United States	17,499.6	15,720.3	16,111.9	436,818	474,711	358,579

Utilization and State	Utilized production			Price per unit			Value of utilized production		
	2018	2019	2020	2018	2019	2020	2018	2019	2020
	1,000 cwt			*Dollars per cwt*			*1,000 dollars*		
Fresh Market									
California	(D)	(D)	(D)	(D)	(D)	(D)	(D)	(D)	(D)
Michigan	(D)	(NA)	(NA)	(D)	(NA)	(NA)	(D)	(NA)	(NA)
Other States [1] ...	16,272.7	(D)	(D)	25.90	(D)	(D)	421,967	(D)	(D)
United States	16,272.7	(D)	(D)	25.90	(D)	(D)	315,484	(D)	(D)
	Tons			*Dollars per ton*			*1,000 dollars*		
Processing									
California	(D)	(D)	(D)	(D)	(D)	(D)	(D)	(D)	(D)
Michigan	(D)	(NA)	(NA)	(D)	(D)	(NA)	(D)	(NA)	(NA)
Other States [1] ...	61,344	(D)	(D)	242.00	242.00	(D)	6,563	14,954	(D)
United States	61,344	(D)	(D)	242.00	242.00	(D)	6,563	14,954	(D)

(D) Withheld to avoid disclosing data for individual operations. (NA) Not available. [1] Includes data withheld above.
NASS, Crops Branch, (202) 720–2127.

STATISTICS OF VEGETABLES AND MELONS

Table 4-15.—Sweet corn for fresh market and processing: Area harvested, production, price, and value, by State and United States, 2018–2020

State	Area harvested			Total Production		
	2018	2019	2020	2018	2019	2020
	Acres			1,000 cwt		
California	33,800	33,600	29,700	6,084.0	6,048.0	5,346.0
Delaware	11,200	(NA)	(NA)	1,512.0	(NA)	(NA)
Florida	39,700	41,000	36,000	4,764.0	4,715.0	4,320.0
Georgia	29,000	26,900	27,000	4,350.0	3,228.0	2,835.0
Idaho	3,900	(NA)	(NA)	351.0	(NA)	(NA)
Illinois	14,600	15,500	12,500	1,825.0	2,402.5	1,875.0
Indiana	4,100	(NA)	(NA)	389.5	(NA)	(NA)
Maryland	8,100	(NA)	(NA)	972.0	(NA)	(NA)
Michigan	9,100	(NA)	(NA)	837.2	(NA)	(NA)
Minnesota	110,600	99,100	96,200	15,484.0	13,874.0	15,392.0
New Jersey	6,400	(NA)	(NA)	556.8	(NA)	(NA)
New York	26,600	26,500	25,000	2,793.0	3,445.0	2,875.0
Ohio	9,100	(NA)	(NA)	864.5	(NA)	(NA)
Oregon	28,900	23,700	25,700	5,924.5	4,858.5	4,883.0
Pennsylvania	10,600	(NA)	(NA)	604.2	(NA)	(NA)
Washington	72,000	75,000	77,000	16,560.0	15,750.0	15,400.0
Wisconsin	56,400	49,400	57,100	9,588.0	8,645.0	9,992.5
United States	474,100	390,700	386,200	73,459.7	62,966.0	62,918.5

State	Utilized production			Value of total production		
	2018	2019	2020	2018	2019	2020
	1,000 cwt			1,000 dollars		
California	6,084.0	6,048.0	5,335.3	175,828	172,368	194,738
Delaware	1,512.0	(NA)	(NA)	16,633	(NA)	(NA)
Florida	4,764.0	4,696.1	4,142.9	142,920	140,883	136,716
Georgia	4,345.7	3,050.5	2,823.7	111,684	75,042	137,514
Idaho	347.5	(NA)	(NA)	12,163	(NA)	(NA)
Illinois	1,825.0	2,400.1	1,875.0	13,763	15,532	9,806
Indiana	389.5	(NA)	(NA)	8,959	(NA)	(NA)
Maryland	972.0	(NA)	(NA)	13,994	(NA)	(NA)
Michigan	837.2	(NA)	(NA)	19,256	(NA)	(NA)
Minnesota	15,468.5	13,707.5	15,376.6	81,899	50,431	62,820
New Jersey	542.9	(NA)	(NA)	13,868	(NA)	(NA)
New York	2,765.1	3,431.2	2,866.4	36,257	40,422	36,867
Ohio	864.5	(NA)	(NA)	23,342	(NA)	(NA)
Oregon	5,924.5	4,839.1	4,883.0	44,492	38,103	41,034
Pennsylvania	590.9	(NA)	(NA)	24,745	(NA)	(NA)
Washington	16,560.0	15,750.0	15,400.0	84,080	85,806	73,904
Wisconsin	9,588.0	8,575.8	9,992.5	40,181	33,470	49,507
United States	73,381.3	62,498.3	62,695.4	864,064	652,057	742,906

See footnote(s) at end of table.

Table 4-15.—Sweet corn for fresh market and processing: Area harvested, production, price, and value, by State and United States, 2018–2020—Continued

Utilization and State	Utilized production			Price per unit			Value of utilized production		
	2018	2019	2020	2018	2019	2020	2018	2019	2020
	1,000 cwt			*Dollars per cwt*			*1,000 dollars*		
Fresh Market									
California	6,084.0	6,048.0	5,335.3	28.90	28.50	36.50	175,828	172,368	194,738
Delaware	362.9	(NA)	(NA)	30.00	(NA)	(NA)	10,887	(NA)	(NA)
Florida	4,764.0	4,696.1	4,142.9	30.00	30.00	33.00	142,920	140,883	136,716
Georgia	4,345.7	3,050.5	2,823.7	25.70	24.60	48.70	111,684	75,042	137,514
Idaho	347.5	(NA)	(NA)	35.00	(NA)	(NA)	12,163	(NA)	(NA)
Illinois	310.3	235.4	176.3	27.00	31.50	29.70	8,378	7,415	5,236
Indiana	389.5	(NA)	(NA)	23.00	(NA)	(NA)	8,959	(NA)	(NA)
Maryland	335.3	(NA)	(NA)	33.00	(NA)	(NA)	11,065	(NA)	(NA)
Michigan	837.2	(NA)	(NA)	23.00	(NA)	(NA)	19,256	(NA)	(NA)
Minnesota	588.4	263.6	415.6	46.00	24.80	32.00	27,066	6,537	13,299
New Jersey	(D)	(NA)	(NA)	(D)	(NA)	(NA)	(D)	(NA)	(NA)
New York	1,027.8	809.6	819.4	28.60	37.30	35.00	29,395	30,198	28,679
Ohio	864.5	(NA)	(NA)	27.00	(NA)	(NA)	23,342	(NA)	(NA)
Oregon	521.4	685.0	698.3	27.30	25.00	27.90	14,234	17,125	19,483
Pennsylvania	(D)	(NA)	(NA)	(D)	(NA)	(NA)	(D)	(NA)	(NA)
Washington	447.1	630.0	308.0	43.90	34.20	51.30	19,628	21,546	15,800
Wisconsin	326.0	354.4	429.7	26.80	21.60	37.10	8,737	7,655	15,942
Other States [1] ...	996.8	....	....	38.00	(X)	(X)	37,910	....	....
United States	22,548.4	16,772.6	15,149.2	29.30	28.50	37.50	661,452	478,769	567,407
	Tons			*Dollars per ton*			*1,000 dollars*		
Processing									
California	....	....	....	(X)	(X)	(X)	....	....	....
Delaware	57,456	(NA)	(NA)	100.00	(NA)	(NA)	5,746	(NA)	(NA)
Florida	....	....	....	(X)	(X)	(X)	....	....	....
Georgia	....	....	....	(X)	(X)	(X)	....	....	....
Idaho	....	(NA)	(NA)	(X)	(NA)	(NA)	....	(NA)	(NA)
Illinois	75,738	108,233	84,938	71.10	75.00	53.80	5,385	8,117	4,570
Indiana	....	(NA)	(NA)	(X)	(NA)	(NA)	....	(NA)	(NA)
Maryland	31,833	(NA)	(NA)	92.00	(NA)	(NA)	2,929	(NA)	(NA)
Michigan	....	(NA)	(NA)	(X)	(NA)	(NA)	....	(NA)	(NA)
Minnesota	744,006	672,195	748,051	73.70	65.30	66.20	54,833	43,894	49,521
New Jersey	(D)	(NA)	(NA)	(D)	(NA)	(NA)	(D)	(NA)	(NA)
New York	86,862	131,082	102,350	79.00	78.00	80.00	6,862	10,224	8,188
Ohio	....	(NA)	(NA)	(X)	(NA)	(NA)	....	(NA)	(NA)
Oregon	270,157	207,701	209,237	112.00	101.00	103.00	30,258	20,978	21,551
Pennsylvania	(D)	(NA)	(NA)	(D)	(NA)	(NA)	(D)	(NA)	(NA)
Washington	805,644	756,000	754,600	80.00	85.00	77.00	64,452	64,260	58,104
Wisconsin	463,100	411,070	478,141	67.90	62.80	70.20	31,444	25,815	33,565
Other States [1] ...	6,850	....	....	103.00	(X)	(X)	703	....	....
United States	2,541,646	2,286,281	2,377,317	79.70	75.80	73.80	202,612	173,288	175,499

(D) Withheld to avoid disclosing data for individual operations. (NA) Not available. (X) Not applicable. [1] Includes data withheld above.

NASS, Crops Branch, (202) 720–2127.

Table 4-16.—Cucumbers for fresh market and processing: Area harvested, production, price, and value, by State and United States, 2017–2019

State	Area harvested			Total Production		
	2017	2018	2019	2017	2018	2019
	Acres			1,000 cwt		
Alabama	5,400	5,900	(NA)	756.0	619.5	(NA)
California	8,200	8,100	6,800	1,435.0	1,660.5	1,088.0
Delaware	(D)	(D)	(NA)	(D)	(D)	(NA)
Florida	25,900	24,900	23,000	5,309.5	4,233.0	3,450.0
Georgia	9,500	9,400	9,100	1,662.5	1,410.0	1,820.0
Michigan	37,500	34,400	39,600	5,625.0	4,128.0	5,940.0
New Jersey	2,900	2,600	(NA)	464.0	244.4	(NA)
North Carolina ..	10,500	9,600	11,400	1,680.0	1,488.0	1,653.0
Ohio	2,000	1,900	(NA)	340.0	294.5	(NA)
South Carolina ..	(D)	(D)	(NA)	(D)	(D)	(NA)
Texas	6,100	4,900	(D)	610.0	475.3	(D)
Wisconsin	5,900	5,100	(D)	737.5	612.0	(D)
Other States [1] ...	3,300	4,100	10,900	293.3	285.2	993.7
United States	117,200	110,900	100,800	18,912.8	15,450.4	14,944.7

State	Utilized production			Value of utilized production		
	2017	2018	2019	2017	2018	2019
	1,000 cwt			1,000 dollars		
Alabama	756.0	615.2	(NA)	16,659	15,379	(NA)
California	1,435.0	1,660.5	1,088.0	35,485	33,781	30,133
Delaware	(D)	(D)	(NA)	(D)	(D)	(NA)
Florida	5,309.5	4,233.0	3,443.1	137,601	118,524	89,277
Georgia	1,662.5	1,410.0	1,801.8	43,853	35,212	46,172
Michigan	5,625.0	4,123.9	5,928.1	79,739	55,418	70,560
New Jersey	463.1	240.7	(NA)	16,431	7,028	(NA)
North Carolina ..	1,664.9	1,482.0	1,653.0	28,699	25,582	25,478
Ohio	332.2	294.5	(NA)	5,376	4,983	(NA)
South Carolina ..	(D)	(D)	(NA)	(D)	(D)	(NA)
Texas	610.0	475.3	(D)	11,590	8,746	(D)
Wisconsin	736.0	603.4	(D)	11,531	12,913	(D)
Other States [1] ...	292.8	282.3	991.6	5,049	5,433	17,174
United States	18,887.0	15,420.8	14,905.6	392,013	322,999	278,794

Utilization and State	Utilized production			Price per unit			Value of utilized production		
	2017	2018	2019	2017	2018	2019	2017	2018	2019
	1,000 cwt			Dollars per cwt			1,000 dollars		
Fresh Market									
Alabama	(D)	(D)	(NA)	(D)	(D)	(NA)	(D)	(D)	(NA)
California	(D)	513.1	400.4	(D)	45.60	59.20	(D)	23,397	23,704
Delaware	(D)	(D)	(NA)	(D)	(D)	(NA)	(D)	(D)	(NA)
Florida	1,391.1	(D)	(D)	29.20	(D)	(D)	40,620	(D)	(D)
Georgia	(D)	(D)	(D)	(D)	(D)	(D)	(D)	(D)	(D)
Michigan	871.9	1,060.9	1,098.9	27.40	21.20	22.90	23,890	22,491	25,165
New Jersey	(D)	240.7	(NA)	(D)	29.20	(NA)	(D)	7,028	(NA)
North Carolina ..	445.2	626.4	271.1	22.00	22.40	16.50	9,794	14,031	4,473
Ohio	72.4	88.4	(NA)	32.10	27.80	(NA)	2,324	2,458	(NA)
South Carolina ..	(D)	(D)	(NA)	(D)	(D)	(NA)	(D)	(D)	(NA)
Texas	122.0	95.1	(D)	25.00	24.00	(D)	3,050	2,282	(D)
Wisconsin	(D)	(D)	(D)	(D)	(D)	(D)	(D)	(D)	(D)
Other States [1] ...	2,126.1	2,970.9	2,829.5	32.10	29.80	28.90	68,209	88,433	81,855
United States	5,028.7	5,595.5	4,599.9	29.40	28.60	29.40	147,887	160,120	135,197

See footnote(s) at end of table.

Table 4-16.—Cucumbers for fresh market and processing: Area harvested, production, price, and value, by State and United States, 2017–2019—Continued

Utilization and State	Utilized production			Price per unit			Value of utilized production		
	2017	2018	2019	2017	2018	2019	2017	2018	2019
	Tons			Dollars per ton			1,000 dollars		
Processing									
Alabama	(D)	(D)	(NA)	(D)	(D)	(NA)	(D)	(D)	(NA)
California	(D)	57,370	34,381	(D)	353.00	187.00	(D)	10,384	6,429
Delaware	(D)	(D)	(NA)	(D)	(D)	(NA)	(D)	(D)	(NA)
Florida	195,921	(D)	(D)	495.00	(D)	(D)	96,981	(D)	(D)
Georgia	(D)	(D)	(D)	(D)	(D)	(D)	(D)	(D)	(D)
Michigan	237,656	153,149	241,461	235.00	215.00	188.00	55,849	32,927	45,395
New Jersey	(D)	-	(NA)	(D)	(X)	(NA)	(D)	-	(NA)
North Carolina	60,984	42,780	69,095	310.00	270.00	304.00	18,905	11,551	21,005
Ohio	12,988	10,308	(NA)	235.00	245.00	(NA)	3,052	2,525	(NA)
South Carolina	(D)	(D)	(NA)	(D)	(D)	(NA)	(D)	(D)	(NA)
Texas	24,400	19,012	(D)	350.00	340.00	(D)	8,540	6,464	(D)
Wisconsin	(D)	(D)	(D)	(D)	(D)	(D)	(D)	(D)	(D)
Other States [1]	160,961	208,649	170,352	378.00	475.00	415.00	60,799	99,028	70,768
United States	692,910	491,268	515,289	313.00	352.00	279.00	244,126	162,879	143,597

(D) Withheld to avoid disclosing data for individual operations. (NA) Not available. (X) Not applicable. [1] Includes data withheld above.
NASS, Crops Branch, (202) 720–2127.

Table 4-17.—Garlic for fresh market and processing: Area harvested, production, price, and value, by State and United States, 2017–2019

State	Area harvested			Total Production		
	2017	2018	2019	2017	2018	2019
	Acres			1,000 cwt		
California	33,000	29,900	27,000	5,115.0	5,232.5	4,185.0
United States	33,000	29,900	27,000	5,115.0	5,232.5	4,185.0

State	Utilized production			Value of utilized production		
	2017	2018	2019	2017	2018	2019
	1,000 cwt			1,000 dollars		
California	5,115.0	5,232.5	4,185.0	390,021	412,587	327,277
United States	5,115.0	5,232.5	4,185.0	390,021	412,587	327,277

Utilization and State	Utilized production			Price per unit			Value of utilized production		
	2017	2018	2019	2017	2018	2019	2017	2018	2019
	1,000 cwt			Dollars per cwt			1,000 dollars		
Fresh Market									
California	1,754.4	1,831.4	1,464.8	184.00	190.00	190.00	322,810	347,966	278,312
United States	1,754.4	1,831.4	1,464.8	184.00	190.00	190.00	322,810	347,966	278,312
	Tons			Dollars per ton			1,000 dollars		
Processing									
California	168,028	170,056	136,013	400.00	380.00	360.00	67,211	64,621	48,965
United States	168,028	170,056	136,013	400.00	380.00	360.00	67,211	64,621	48,965

NASS, Crops Branch, (202) 720–2127.

STATISTICS OF VEGETABLES AND MELONS

Table 4-18.—Honeydew for fresh market: Area harvested, production, price, and value, by State and United States, 2017–2019

State	Area harvested			Yield per acre		
	2017	2018	2019	2017	2018	2019
	Acres			*Cwt*		
California	11,600	12,400	11,100	290.0	310.0	255.0
United States	11,600	12,400	11,100	290.0	310.0	255.0

State	Total production			Utilized production		
	2017	2018	2019	2017	2018	2019
	1,000 cwt			*1,000 cwt*		
California	3,364.0	3,844.0	2,830.5	3,364.0	3,844.0	2,830.5
United States	3,364.0	3,844.0	2,830.5	3,364.0	3,844.0	2,830.5

State	Price			Value of utilized production		
	2017	2018	2019	2017	2018	2019
	Dollars per cwt			*1,000 dollars*		
California	28.00	19.60	20.90	94,192	75,342	59,157
United States	28.00	19.60	20.90	94,192	75,342	59,157

NASS, Crops Branch, (202) 720–2127.

Table 4-19.—Head lettuce for fresh market: Area harvested, production, price, and value, by State and United States, 2017–2019

State	Area harvested			Yield per acre		
	2017	2018	2019	2017	2018	2019
	Acres			*Cwt*		
Arizona	39,200	38,600	37,300	315.0	310.0	335.0
California	101,500	81,700	77,200	365.0	350.0	375.0
United States	140,700	120,300	114,500	351.1	337.2	362.0

State	Total production			Utilized production		
	2017	2018	2019	2017	2018	2019
	1,000 cwt			*1,000 cwt*		
Arizona	12,348.0	11,966.0	12,495.5	12,348.0	11,966.0	12,495.5
California	37,047.5	28,595.0	28,950.0	37,047.5	28,595.0	28,950.0
United States	49,395.5	40,561.0	41,445.5	49,395.5	40,561.0	41,445.5

State	Price			Value of utilized production		
	2017	2018	2019	2017	2018	2019
	Dollars per cwt			*1,000 dollars*		
Arizona	45.90	37.90	86.90	566,773	453,511	1,085,859
California	32.60	26.80	30.20	1,207,749	766,346	874,290
United States	35.90	30.10	47.30	1,774,522	1,219,857	1,960,149

NASS, Crops Branch, (202) 720–2127.

Table 4-20.—Leaf lettuce for fresh market: Area harvested, production, price, and value, by State and United States, 2017–2019

State	Area harvested			Yield per acre		
	2017	2018	2019	2017	2018	2019
	Acres			Cwt		
Arizona	9,400	9,700	9,800	225.0	240.0	230.0
California	57,800	56,000	47,500	200.0	150.0	215.0
United States	67,200	65,700	57,300	203.5	163.3	217.6
State	Total production			Utilized production		
	2017	2018	2019	2017	2018	2019
	1,000 cwt			1,000 cwt		
Arizona	2,115.0	2,328.0	2,254.0	2,115.0	2,328.0	2,254.0
California	11,560.0	8,400.0	10,212.5	11,560.0	8,400.0	10,212.5
United States	13,675.0	10,728.0	12,466.5	13,675.0	10,728.0	12,466.5
State	Price			Value of utilized production		
	2017	2018	2019	2017	2018	2019
	Dollars per cwt			1,000 dollars		
Arizona	65.40	44.70	102.70	138,321	104,062	231,711
California	60.10	53.80	41.00	694,756	451,920	418,713
United States	60.90	51.80	52.20	833,077	555,982	650,424

NASS, Crops Branch, (202) 720–2127.

Table 4-21.—Romaine lettuce for fresh market: Area harvested, production, price, and value, by State and United States, 2017–2019

State	Area harvested			Yield per acre		
	2017	2018	2019	2017	2018	2019
	Acres			Cwt		
Arizona	27,200	26,900	23,900	340.0	330.0	330.0
California	90,200	72,700	64,000	300.0	280.0	305.0
United States	117,400	99,600	87,900	309.3	293.5	311.8
State	Total production			Utilized production		
	2017	2018	2019	2017	2018	2019
	1,000 cwt			1,000 cwt		
Arizona	9,248.0	8,877.0	7,887.0	9,248.0	8,877.0	7,887.0
California	27,060.0	20,356.0	19,520.0	27,060.0	20,152.4	19,324.8
United States	36,308.0	29,233.0	27,407.0	36,308.0	29,029.4	27,211.8
State	Price			Value of utilized production		
	2017	2018	2019	2017	2018	2019
	Dollars per cwt			1,000 dollars		
Arizona	55.50	37.50	44.30	513,264	332,888	349,394
California	41.20	28.20	27.50	1,114,872	568,298	531,432
United States	44.80	31.00	32.40	1,628,136	901,186	880,826

NASS, Crops Branch, (202) 720–2127.

Table 4-22.—Onions for fresh market and processing: Area harvested, production, price, and value, by State and United States, 2017–2019

State	Area harvested			Total Production		
	2017	2018	2019	2017	2018	2019
	Acres			1,000 cwt		
California	44,800	41,000	43,500	21,056.0	18,450.0	18,270.0
Colorado	3,600	2,600	2,500	1,656.0	1,170.0	1,147.5
Georgia	10,800	10,800	9,500	3,780.0	2,808.0	3,040.0
Idaho	12,500	8,400	10,900	9,062.5	7,476.0	8,938.0
New Mexico	7,100	7,100	6,600	4,828.0	4,189.0	3,993.0
New York	6,900	7,500	7,000	3,036.0	2,250.0	2,240.0
Oregon	24,500	19,300	20,300	16,163.5	15,494.0	14,921.0
Malheur County	13,700	11,800	12,500	9,521.5	9,794.0	9,500.0
All other counties	10,800	7,500	7,800	6,642.0	5,700.0	5,421.0
Texas	11,500	11,000	9,000	2,990.0	3,300.0	3,015.0
Washington	29,800	21,900	19,900	19,817.0	17,301.0	14,328.0
United States	151,500	129,600	129,400	82,389.0	72,438.0	69,892.5

State	Utilized production			Value of utilized production		
	2017	2018	2019	2017	2018	2019
	1,000 cwt			1,000 dollars		
California	21,056.0	18,154.9	18,270.0	291,568	240,220	294,676
Colorado	1,656.0	1,170.0	1,109.6	39,413	27,261	18,531
Georgia	3,685.5	2,794.0	2,973.1	128,301	110,519	144,181
Idaho	8,962.8	7,461.1	8,893.3	74,192	48,668	65,815
New Mexico	4,828.0	4,189.0	3,993.0	84,490	79,591	102,620
New York	2,620.1	2,196.0	2,047.4	50,682	42,752	36,140
Oregon	16,154.0	15,288.3	14,778.5	138,036	100,339	108,409
Malheur County	9,512.0	9,588.3	9,357.5	73,841	60,439	60,292
All other counties	6,642.0	5,700.0	5,421.0	64,195	39,900	48,117
Texas	2,990.0	3,234.0	2,954.7	73,913	61,380	51,038
Washington	18,608.2	16,436.0	13,625.9	161,495	176,211	180,576
United States	80,560.6	70,923.3	68,645.5	1,042,090	886,941	1,001,986

Utilization and State	Utilized production			Price per unit			Value of utilized production		
	2017	2018	2019	2017	2018	2019	2017	2018	2019
	1,000 cwt			Dollars per cwt			1,000 dollars		
Fresh Market									
California	15,328.8	8,542.4	9,719.6	14.50	19.40	23.50	222,268	165,723	228,411
Colorado	1,656.0	(D)	(D)	23.80	(D)	(D)	39,413	(D)	(D)
Georgia	(D)	(D)	(D)	(D)	(D)	(D)	(D)	(D)	(D)
Idaho	7,023.4	5,308.0	(D)	9.10	7.10	(D)	63,913	37,687	(D)
New Mexico	4,828.0	4,189.0	3,993.0	17.50	19.00	25.70	84,490	79,591	102,620
New York	2,529.0	(D)	1,953.3	19.50	(D)	17.90	49,316	(D)	34,964
Oregon	9,585.2	(D)	9,195.1	8.69	(D)	6.62	83,323	(D)	60,895
Malheur County	(D)	(D)	(D)	(D)	(D)	(D)	(D)	(D)	(D)
All other counties	(D)	(D)	(D)	(D)	(D)	(D)	(D)	(D)	(D)
Texas	(D)	(D)	(D)	(D)	(D)	(D)	(D)	(D)	(D)
Washington	(D)	11,764.7	(D)	(D)	12.00	(D)	(D)	141,176	(D)
Other States [1]	19,435.6	18,628.8	22,981.9	16.70	16.10	17.80	324,905	300,467	408,978
United States	60,386.0	48,432.9	47,842.9	14.40	15.00	17.50	867,628	724,644	835,868

See footnote(s) at end of table.

Table 4-22.—Onions for fresh market and processing: Area harvested, production, price, and value, by State and United States, 2017–2019—Continued

Utilization and State	Utilized production			Price per unit			Value of utilized production		
	2017	2018	2019	2017	2018	2019	2017	2018	2019
	Tons			Dollars per ton			1,000 dollars		
Processing									
California	286,362	480,623	427,518	242.00	155.00	155.00	69,300	74,497	66,265
Colorado	....	(D)	(D)	(X)	(D)	(D)	....	(D)	(D)
Georgia	(D)	(D)	(D)	(D)	(D)	(D)	(D)	(D)	(D)
Idaho	96,969	107,654	(D)	106.00	102.00	(D)	10,279	10,981	(D)
New Mexico	....	....	....	(X)	(X)	(X)	....	....	....
New York	4,554	(D)	4,704	300.00	(D)	250.00	1,366	(D)	1,176
Oregon	328,440	(D)	279,171	167.00	(D)	170.00	54,713	(D)	47,514
Malheur County	(D)	(D)	(D)	(D)	(D)	(D)	(D)	(D)	(D)
All other counties	(D)	(D)	(D)	(D)	(D)	(D)	(D)	(D)	(D)
Texas	(D)	(D)	(D)	(D)	(D)	(D)	(D)	(D)	(D)
Washington	(D)	233,564	(D)	(D)	150.00	(D)	(D)	35,035	(D)
Other States[1]	292,404	302,675	328,741	133.00	138.00	156.00	38,804	41,784	51,163
United States	1,008,729	1,124,516	1,040,134	173.00	144.00	160.00	174,462	162,297	166,118

(D) Withheld to avoid disclosing data for individual operations. (X) Not applicable. [1] Includes data withheld above.
NASS, Crops Branch, (202) 720–2127.

Table 4-23.—Green Peas for fresh market and processing: Area harvested, production, price, and value, by State and United States, 2017–2019

State	Area harvested			Total Production		
	2017	2018	2019	2017	2018	2019
	Acres			1,000 cwt		
Illinois	5,600	4,000	(NA)	207.2	168.0	(NA)
Minnesota	46,000	45,800	51,800	1,932.0	1,328.2	1,450.4
New York	8,900	6,700	(NA)	364.9	247.9	(NA)
Oregon	20,000	18,900	17,500	700.0	567.0	595.0
Washington	31,200	32,400	32,300	1,840.8	1,782.0	1,905.7
Wisconsin	22,500	23,300	26,500	967.5	978.6	1,086.5
United States	134,200	131,100	128,100	6,012.4	5,071.7	5,037.6

State	Utilized production			Value of utilized production		
	2017	2018	2019	2017	2018	2019
	1,000 cwt			1,000 dollars		
Illinois	207.2	168.0	(NA)	2,223	2,477	(NA)
Minnesota	1,932.0	1,326.9	1,447.5	24,651	17,306	19,473
New York	364.9	247.9	(NA)	6,760	3,351	(NA)
Oregon	700.0	567.0	595.0	8,706	7,190	6,896
Washington	1,840.8	1,780.2	1,903.8	28,772	22,766	30,157
Wisconsin	967.5	978.6	1,086.5	14,363	11,811	11,272
United States	6,012.4	5,068.6	5,032.8	85,475	64,901	67,798

Utilization and State	Utilized production			Price per unit			Value of utilized production		
	2017	2018	2019	2017	2018	2019	2017	2018	2019
	1,000 cwt			Dollars per cwt			1,000 dollars		
Fresh Market									
Illinois	(D)	(D)	(NA)	(D)	(D)	(NA)	(D)	(D)	(NA)
Minnesota	1.9	(D)	(D)	73.10	(D)	(D)	139	(D)	(D)
New York	20.1	5.5	(NA)	115.00	89.00	(NA)	2,312	490	(NA)
Oregon	(D)	(D)	(D)	(D)	(D)	(D)	(D)	(D)	(D)
Washington	(D)	(D)	(D)	(D)	(D)	(D)	(D)	(D)	(D)
Wisconsin	12.6	1.0	1.1	329.00	275.00	281.00	4,145	275	309
Other States[1] ...	66.1	3.9	25.0	75.60	173.00	185.00	4,999	675	4,618
United States	100.7	10.4	26.1	138.00	115.00	189.00	11,595	1,440	4,927

See footnote(s) at end of table.

Table 4-23.—Green Peas for fresh market and processing: Area harvested, production, price, and value, by State and United States, 2017–2019—Continued

Utilization and State	Utilized production			Price per unit			Value of utilized production		
	2017	2018	2019	2017	2018	2019	2017	2018	2019
	Tons			Dollars per ton			1,000 dollars		
Processing									
Illinois	(D)	(D)	(NA)	(D)	(D)	(NA)	(D)	(D)	(NA)
Minnesota	96,503	(D)	(D)	254.00	(D)	(D)	24,512	(D)	(D)
New York	17,242	12,122	(NA)	258.00	236.00	(NA)	4,448	2,861	(NA)
Oregon	(D)	(D)	(D)	(D)	(D)	(D)	(D)	(D)	(D)
Washington	(D)	(D)	(D)	(D)	(D)	(D)	(D)	(D)	(D)
Wisconsin	47,746	48,881	54,271	214.00	236.00	202.00	10,218	11,536	10,963
Other States [1]	134,093	191,913	196,068	259.00	256.00	265.00	34,702	49,064	51,908
United States	295,584	252,916	250,339	250.00	251.00	251.00	73,880	63,461	62,871

(D) Withheld to avoid disclosing data for individual operations. (NA) Not available. [1] Includes data withheld above.
NASS, Crops Branch, (202) 720–2127.

Table 4-24.—Bell peppers for fresh market and processing: Area harvested, production, price, and value, by State and United States, 2017–2019

State	Area harvested			Total Production		
	2017	2018	2019	2017	2018	2019
	Acres			1,000 cwt		
California	15,900	13,500	15,000	6,678.0	6,075.0	5,400.0
Florida	12,000	11,900	11,800	4,020.0	3,570.0	3,481.0
Georgia	3,400	3,200	3,600	986.0	848.0	1,116.0
Michigan	2,200	2,000	2,100	561.0	480.0	535.0
New Jersey	3,400	3,400	3,500	952.0	935.0	1,050.0
New York	900	1,400	(NA)	103.5	154.0	(NA)
North Carolina ..	2,100	2,000	2,300	567.0	400.0	552.0
Ohio	1,300	1,400	(NA)	292.5	280.0	(NA)
Pennsylvania	1,000	900	(NA)	230.0	153.0	(NA)
United States	42,200	39,700	38,300	14,390.0	12,895.0	12,134.5

State	Utilized production			Value of utilized production		
	2017	2018	2019	2017	2018	2019
	1,000 cwt			1,000 dollars		
California	6,504.4	6,075.0	5,400.0	282,452	210,007	181,400
Florida	4,020.0	3,570.0	3,481.0	188,940	180,642	234,968
Georgia	986.0	848.0	1,104.8	43,581	40,110	54,467
Michigan	561.0	480.0	531.8	15,318	18,220	19,674
New Jersey	951.0	929.4	1,042.7	39,381	39,726	45,854
New York	97.3	154.0	(NA)	5,196	8,455	(NA)
North Carolina ..	567.0	376.0	529.9	25,487	15,685	21,297
Ohio	292.5	280.0	(NA)	11,700	12,040	(NA)
Pennsylvania	213.9	151.8	(NA)	13,522	8,422	(NA)
United States	14,193.1	12,864.2	12,090.2	625,577	533,307	557,660

Utilization and State	Utilized production			Price per unit			Value of utilized production		
	2017	2018	2019	2017	2018	2019	2017	2018	2019
	1,000 cwt			Dollars per cwt			1,000 dollars		
Fresh Market									
California	4,480.9	4,835.7	2,970.0	54.50	39.20	50.40	244,209	189,559	149,688
Florida	4,020.0	3,570.0	3,481.0	47.00	50.60	67.50	188,940	180,642	234,968
Georgia	986.0	848.0	1,104.8	44.20	47.30	49.30	43,581	40,110	54,467
Michigan	(D)	(D)	(D)	(D)	(D)	(D)	(D)	(D)	(D)
New Jersey	(D)	865.8	924.0	(D)	44.80	47.50	(D)	38,788	43,890
New York	97.3	154.0	(NA)	53.40	54.90	(NA)	5,196	8,455	(NA)
North Carolina ..	(D)	(D)	(D)	(D)	(D)	(D)	(D)	(D)	(D)
Ohio	(D)	280.0	(NA)	(D)	43.00	(NA)	(D)	12,040	(NA)
Pennsylvania	(D)	(D)	(NA)	(D)	(D)	(NA)	(D)	(D)	(NA)
Other States [1] ...	2,419.7	981.1	1,023.7	42.40	42.30	39.00	102,575	41,468	39,930
United States	12,003.9	11,534.6	9,503.5	48.70	44.30	55.00	584,501	511,062	522,943

See footnote(s) at end of table.

Table 4-24.—Bell peppers for fresh market and processing: Area harvested, production, price, and value, by State and United States, 2017–2019—Continued

Utilization and State	Utilized production			Price per unit			Value of utilized production		
	2017	2018	2019	2017	2018	2019	2017	2018	2019
	Tons			Dollars per ton			1,000 dollars		
Processing									
California	101,172	61,965	121,500	378.00	330.00	261.00	38,243	20,448	31,712
Florida	....	....	....	(X)	(X)	(X)	....	....	....
Georgia	....	....	....	(X)	(X)	(X)	....	....	....
Michigan	(D)	(D)	(D)	(D)	(D)	(D)	(D)	(D)	(D)
New Jersey	(D)	3,179	5,933	(D)	295.00	331.00	(D)	938	1,964
New York	....	....	(NA)	(X)	(X)	(NA)	....	....	(NA)
North Carolina	(D)	(D)	(D)	(D)	(D)	(D)	(D)	(D)	(D)
Ohio	(D)	....	(NA)	(D)	(X)	(NA)	(D)	....	(NA)
Pennsylvania	(D)	(D)	(NA)	(D)	(D)	(NA)	(D)	(D)	(NA)
Other States[1]	8,293	1,336	1,899	342.00	643.00	548.00	2,833	859	1,041
United States	109,465	66,480	129,332	375.00	335.00	268.00	41,076	22,245	34,717

(D) Withheld to avoid disclosing data for individual operations. (NA) Not available. (X) Not applicable. [1] Includes data withheld above.
NASS, Crops Branch, (202) 720–2127.

Table 4-25.—Chili peppers for fresh market and processing: Area harvested, production, price, and value, by State and United States, 2017–2019

State	Area harvested			Total Production		
	2017	2018	2019	2017	2018	2019
	Acres			1,000 cwt		
Arizona	1,200	1,100	(NA)	78.0	66.0	(NA)
California	4,800	2,700	1,500	1,872.0	1,039.5	382.5
New Mexico	7,600	7,900	8,700	1,254.0	1,422.0	1,261.5
Texas	2,400	2,500	(NA)	132.0	137.5	(NA)
United States	16,000	14,200	10,200	3,336.0	2,665.0	1,644.0

State	Utilized production			Value of utilized production		
	2017	2018	2019	2017	2018	2019
	1,000 cwt			1,000 dollars		
Arizona	78.0	66.0	(NA)	2,039	2,660	(NA)
California	1,872.0	1,039.5	382.1	58,874	29,468	13,703
New Mexico	1,254.0	1,422.0	1,261.5	44,553	53,766	50,008
Texas	132.0	137.5	(NA)	8,096	8,873	(NA)
United States	3,336.0	2,665.0	1,643.6	113,562	94,767	63,711

Utilization and State	Utilized production			Price per unit			Value of utilized production		
	2017	2018	2019	2017	2018	2019	2017	2018	2019
	1,000 cwt			Dollars per cwt			1,000 dollars		
Fresh Market									
Arizona	(D)	(D)	(NA)	(D)	(D)	(NA)	(D)	(D)	(NA)
California	280.8	187.1	187.0	44.20	43.60	48.50	12,411	8,158	9,070
New Mexico	263.3	270.2	227.1	30.00	37.00	38.00	7,899	9,997	8,630
Texas	(D)	(D)	(NA)	(D)	(D)	(NA)	(D)	(D)	(NA)
Other States[1] ...	55.9	94.5	....	53.10	64.80	(X)	2,968	6,128	....
United States	600.0	551.8	414.1	38.80	44.00	42.70	23,278	24,283	17,700
	Tons			Dollars per ton			1,000 dollars		
Processing									
Arizona	(D)	(D)	(NA)	(D)	(D)	(NA)	(D)	(D)	(NA)
California	79,560	42,620	9,754	584.00	500.00	475.00	46,463	21,310	4,633
New Mexico	49,533	57,591	51,722	740.00	760.00	800.00	36,654	43,769	41,378
Texas	(D)	(D)	(NA)	(D)	(D)	(NA)	(D)	(D)	(NA)
Other States[1] ...	7,704	5,448	....	930.00	992.00	(X)	7,167	5,405	....
United States	136,797	105,659	61,476	660.00	667.00	748.00	90,284	70,484	46,011

(D) Withheld to avoid disclosing data for individual operations. (NA) Not available. (X) Not applicable. [1] Includes data withheld above.
NASS, Crops Branch, (202) 720–2127.

Table 4-26.—Potatoes: Area, yield, production, season average price, and value, United States, 2009–2018

Year	Area planted	Area harvested	Yield per harvested acre	Production	Season average price per cwt received by farmers	Value of production
	1,000 acres	1,000 acres	Cwt	1,000 cwt	Dollars	1,000 dollars
2009	1,071.2	1,044.0	414	432,601	8.25	3,557,574
2010	1,026.7	1,008.9	401	404,549	9.20	3,724,821
2011	1,100.7	1,078.5	399	430,037	9.41	4,044,869
2012	1,154.8	1,138.5	408	464,970	8.63	4,017,245
2013	1,063.9	1,050.9	414	434,652	9.75	4,237,284
2014	1,062.6	1,051.1	421	442,170	8.88	3,928,211
2015	1,066.1	1,054.4	418	441,205	8.76	3,865,538
2016	1,056.7	1,037.7	434	450,324	9.08	4,090,689
2017	1,052.6	1,044.5	432	450,921	9.17	4,133,073
2018	1,026.5	1,014.8	443	450,020	8.90	4,006,340

NASS, Crops Branch, (202) 720–2127.

Table 4-27.—Potatoes: Area harvested, yield, and production by seasonal group, by State and United States, 2016–2018

Season and State	Area harvested			Yield			Production		
	2016	2017	2018	2016	2017	2018	2016	2017	2018
	1,000 acres	1,000 acres	1,000 acres	Cwt	Cwt	Cwt	1,000 cwt	1,000 cwt	1,000 cwt
Spring:									
California	30.4	33.5	31.0	390	435	395	11,856	14,573	12,245
Florida	22.9	28.7	20.8	235	250	265	5,382	7,175	5,512
United States	53.3	62.2	51.8	323	350	343	17,238	21,748	17,757
Summer:									
Illinois	7.4	8.1	7.6	380	410	375	2,812	3,321	2,850
Kansas	4.2	4.1	3.3	300	380	430	1,260	1,558	1,419
Maryland	(D)	2.5	2.0	(D)	365	255	(D)	913	510
Missouri	7.9	8.5	7.4	305	285	225	2,410	2,423	1,665
New Jersey	(D)	2.0	2.0	(D)	300	265	(D)	600	530
North Carolina	13.6	15.1	12.2	220	230	190	2,992	3,473	2,318
Texas	21.0	22.8	17.5	395	390	425	8,295	8,892	7,438
Virginia	4.1	4.5	4.4	290	265	235	1,189	1,193	1,034
Other States [1]	4.6	....	....	313	....	....	1,440	....	....
United States	62.8	67.6	56.4	325	331	315	20,398	22,373	17,764
Fall:									
Alaska [2]	(X)	(X)	0.5	(X)	(X)	280	(X)	(X)	140
California	7.9	8.2	7.3	445	405	440	3,516	3,321	3,212
Colorado	57.1	55.6	55.0	389	382	395	22,236	21,220	21,722
San Luis Valley	51.5	51.5	51.6	385	375	390	19,828	19,313	20,124
All other areas	5.6	4.1	3.4	430	465	470	2,408	1,907	1,598
Idaho	324.0	310.0	315.0	430	435	450	139,320	134,850	141,750
Maine	46.5	47.5	48.5	325	320	310	15,113	15,200	15,035
Michigan	47.0	49.5	48.0	370	370	380	17,390	18,315	18,240
Minnesota	43.0	45.5	43.5	400	405	430	17,200	18,428	18,705
Montana	11.0	11.1	11.1	335	340	350	3,685	3,774	3,885
Nebraska	16.4	19.0	19.3	450	475	480	7,380	9,025	9,264
New York	14.8	14.4	13.4	240	280	290	3,552	4,032	3,886
North Dakota	72.0	74.0	73.0	300	330	325	21,600	24,420	23,725
Oregon	44.9	45.9	45.0	590	550	600	26,491	25,245	27,000
Washington	169.0	164.0	160.0	625	605	630	105,625	99,220	100,800
Wisconsin	68.0	70.0	67.0	435	425	405	29,580	29,750	27,135
United States [3]	921.6	914.7	906.6	448	445	457	412,688	406,800	414,499
All Potatoes:									
United States [3]	1,037.7	1,044.5	1,014.8	434	432	443	450,324	450,921	450,020

(D) Withheld to avoid disclosing data for individual operations. (X) Not applicable. [1] Includes data withheld above. [2] Previously included in Alaska table. [3] Beginning in 2018, United States total includes data for Alaska. NASS, Crops Branch, (202) 720–2127.

Table 4-28.—Fall potatoes: Stocks held by growers, local dealers, and processors [1] - 13 Fall States: 2017 and 2018 [1]

State	Current year	Following year		
	Dec. 1, 2017	Feb. 1, 2018	Apr. 1, 2018	June 1, 2018
	1,000 cwt			
California	2,600	1,800	1,100	(D)
Colorado	15,300	11,400	7,200	2,800
Idaho	96,000	75,000	52,000	27,000
Maine	11,500	8,500	5,000	1,700
Michigan	11,000	6,900	3,800	(D)
Minnesota	13,600	10,400	7,200	3,900
Montana	3,500	3,400	2,800	240
Nebraska	5,400	3,900	2,100	(D)
New York	2,300	1,300	800	300
North Dakota	20,600	15,300	9,600	4,000
Oregon	19,800	13,300	8,300	3,500
Washington	57,000	45,000	29,000	13,000
Wisconsin	19,300	14,400	9,900	5,300
Other States [2]				2,000
United States	277,900	210,600	138,800	63,740
Klamath Basin [3]	5,000	3,300	1,800	(D)

State	Current year	Following year		
	Dec. 1, 2018	Feb. 1, 2019	Apr. 1, 2019	June 1, 2019
	1,000 cwt			
California	2,200	(D)	900	(D)
Colorado	15,600	11,600	7,600	3,000
Idaho	101,000	79,000	57,000	34,000
Maine	10,900	7,800	4,700	1,500
Michigan	10,500	6,700	3,400	300
Minnesota	12,800	9,700	6,700	4,200
Montana	3,700	3,600	3,100	70
Nebraska	5,000	3,700	2,300	(D)
New York	2,000	(D)	800	400
North Dakota	17,000	11,700	6,900	2,800
Oregon	21,100	14,500	9,800	3,900
Washington	57,500	46,000	29,500	14,800
Wisconsin	20,000	15,700	12,000	4,700
Other States [2]		2,800		700
United States	279,300	212,800	144,700	70,370
Klamath Basin [3]	5,100	(D)	1,700	(D)

(D) Withheld to avoid disclosing data for individual operations. [1] Stocks are defined as the quantity (whether sold or not) remaining in storage for all purposes and uses, including seed potatoes that are not yet moved, and shrinkage, waste, and other losses that occur after the date of each estimate. [2] Includes data withheld above. [3] Includes potato stocks in California and Klamath County, Oregon.
NASS, Crops Branch, (202) 720–2127.

Table 4-29.—Fall potatoes: Production and total stocks held by growers and local dealers, 13 Major States, 2009–2018

Crop year	Production	Total stocks			
		Dec. 1	Following year		
			Feb. 1	Apr. 1	June 1
	1,000 cwt	*1,000 cwt*	*1,000 cwt*	*1,000 cwt*	*1,000 cwt*
2009	383,962	265,800	203,500	128,700	55,120
2010	357,467	240,200	180,300	111,000	41,320
2011	382,318	253,000	187,500	115,650	43,340
2012	410,367	271,500	204,600	(NA)	(NA)
2013	386,824	(NA)	(NA)	119,050	46,885
2014	396,798	265,700	200,800	128,700	56,335
2015	404,701	262,700	198,100	125,700	51,280
2016	450,324	275,800	213,000	142,600	67,570
2017	450,921	277,900	210,600	138,800	63,740
2018	450,020	279,300	212,800	144,700	70,370

(NA) Not available.
NASS, Crops Branch, (202) 720–2127.

Table 4-30.—Potatoes: Production, seed used, and disposition, United States, 2009–2018

| Year | Production | Total used for seed | Used on farms where produced | | Sold |
			For seed, feed, and household use	Shrinkage and loss	
			1,000 cwt		
2009	432,601	24,027	4,535	29,135	398,931
2010	404,549	25,100	4,227	24,996	375,326
2011	430,037	26,527	4,146	27,789	398,102
2012	464,970	25,656	4,850	28,505	431,615
2013	434,652	25,249	4,323	26,211	404,118
2014	442,170	26,259	4,192	26,762	411,216
2015	441,205	25,715	4,631	26,509	410,065
2016	450,324	26,167	4,437	26,883	419,004
2017	450,921	24,673	4,410	25,139	421,372
2018	450,020	24,973	4,047	25,526	420,447

NASS, Crops Branch, (202) 720–2127.

Table 4-31.—Potatoes: Utilization and processing, Program States, 2017 and 2018

Utilization items	2017	2018
	1,000 cwt	1,000 cwt
Sales		
Table stock	109,824	106,462
Processing	284,411	289,209
Other sales		
Livestock feed	1,913	697
Seed	25,224	24,079
Other Sales Total	27,137	24,776
Total sales	421,372	420,447
Non-sales		
Seed used on farms where grown	3,526	3,491
Household use and used for feed on farms where grown	884	556
Shrinkage and loss	25,139	25,526
Total non-sales	29,549	29,573
Total production	450,921	450,020

Processing - United States	2016	2017
	1,000 cwt	1,000 cwt
Processing		
Chips and shoestring	58,751	62,700
All Dehydrated (including starch and flour)	45,761	49,066
Frozen french fries	155,798	162,640
Other frozen products	13,803	15,956
Canned potatoes	1,152	1,113
Other canned products (hash, stews, soups)	703	758
Other (including fresh pack, potato salad, vodka, etc)	6,160	5,550
Total	282,128	297,783

NASS, Crops Branch, (202) 720–2127.

Table 4-32.—Potatoes: Production, seed use, and farm disposition, by seasonal groups, by States and United States, 2017 crop [1]

Season and State	Production	Total used for seed	Used on farms where produced		Sold
			For seed, feed, and household use	Shrinkage and loss	
			1,000 cwt		
Spring					
California	14,573	776	227	291	14,055
Florida	7,175	684	17	145	7,013
United States	21,748	1,460	244	436	21,068
Summer					
Illinois	3,321	127		33	3,288
Kansas	1,558	114			1,558
Maryland	913	(D)	(D)	(D)	(D)
Missouri	2,423	183			2,423
New Jersey	600	(D)	(D)	(D)	(D)
North Carolina	3,473	294	1	1	3,471
Texas	8,892	420	22		8,870
Virginia	1,193	93		4	1,189
Other States [2]		84	1	1	1,511
United States	22,373	1,315	24	39	22,310
Fall					
California	3,321	203		13	3,308
Colorado	21,220	1,383	981	1,550	18,689
Idaho	134,850	7,529	808	8,300	125,742
Maine	15,200	1,092	221	879	14,100
Michigan	18,315	1,344	379	623	17,313
Minnesota	18,428	880	86	1,071	17,271
Montana	3,774	264	275	189	3,310
Nebraska	9,025	546	259	640	8,126
New York	4,032	375	56	236	3,740
North Dakota	24,420	1,517	200	1,500	22,720
Oregon	25,245	882	271	1,575	23,399
Washington	99,220	4,208	263	6,040	92,917
Wisconsin	29,750	1,675	343	2,048	27,359
United States	406,800	21,898	4,142	24,664	377,994
All potatoes					
United States	450,921	24,673	4,4104	25,139	421,372

(D) Withheld to avoid disclosing data for individual operations. [1] Totals may not add due to rounding. [2] Includes data withheld above.
NASS, Crops Branch, (202) 720–2127.

Table 4-33.—Potatoes: Production, seed use, and farm disposition, by seasonal groups, by States and United States, 2018 crop [1]

Season and State	Production	Total used for seed	Used on farms where produced		Sold
			For seed, feed, and household use	Shrinkage and loss	
			1,000 cwt		
Spring					
California	12,245	748	4	495	11,746
Florida	5,512	564	1	82	5,429
United States	17,757	1,312	5	577	17,175
Summer					
Illinois	2,850	214	....	20	2,830
Kansas	1,419	92		....	1,419
Maryland	510	48	1	1	508
Missouri	1,665	163	....	210	1,455
New Jersey	530	33	....	1	529
North Carolina	2,318	391	....		2,318
Texas	7,438	401	28	25	7,385
Virginia	1,034	119	....	....	1,034
United States	17,764	1,461	29	257	17,478
Fall					
California	3,212	195	....	62	3,150
Colorado	21,722	1,350	945	1,616	19,161
Idaho	141,750	7,592	795	8,700	132,255
Maine	15,035	1,100	252	783	14,000
Michigan	18,240	1,400	373	680	17,187
Minnesota	18,705	738	67	1,028	17,610
Montana	3,885	289	202	190	3,493
Nebraska	9,264	566	217	825	8,222
New York	3,886	343	45	181	3,660
North Dakota	23,725	1,548	150	2,000	21,575
Oregon	27,000	1,148	341	1,680	24,979
Washington	100,800	4,241	258	5,800	94,742
Wisconsin	27,135	1,680	344	1,136	25,655
United States	414,499	22,200	4,013	24,692	385,794
All potatoes					
United States	450,020	24,973	4,047	25,526	420,447

[1] United States and totals may not add due to rounding.
NASS, Crops Branch, (202) 720–2127.

Table 4-34.—Potatoes, fresh & seed: United States exports by country of destination and imports by country of origin, 2017–2019

Country	2017	2018	2019
	Metric tons		
Imports			
Canada	501,679	486,399	412,260
Colombia	50	40	35
Ghana	9	0	23
China	0	4	15
Ecuador	30	32	14
Togo	0	0	4
Peru	1	3	1
Costa Rica	0	3	0
Netherlands	24	0	0
World Total	501,794	486,481	412,351
Exports			
Canada	265,211	207,226	278,047
Mexico	93,206	113,027	100,529
Japan	39,876	33,914	32,348
Taiwan	42,883	30,443	32,172
Philippines	22,271	12,090	20,150
Korea, South	20,974	22,639	14,229
Malaysia	12,355	9,725	13,769
Dominican Republic	6,230	8,207	8,609
Honduras	10,175	10,227	8,604
Thailand	3,057	5,630	7,447
Singapore	5,489	4,892	5,116
Hong Kong	3,648	3,346	4,293
Guatemala	3,032	2,411	3,892
Bahamas, The	1,531	1,495	2,316
Costa Rica	1,270	1,021	2,198
Vietnam	221	1,557	1,527
Leeward-Windward Islands(*)	1,212	1,741	1,459
Panama	3,139	2,981	1,398
Cayman Islands	743	968	968
Nicaragua	809	963	781
French Pacific Islands(*)	262	449	757
Trinidad and Tobago	807	601	733
United Arab Emirates	558	653	633
El Salvador	618	406	593
Netherlands Antilles(*)	285	389	517
Turks and Caicos Islands	171	275	475
Kuwait	81	70	361
Barbados	196	185	298
Chile	142	183	290
Bermuda	262	302	274
Rest of World	5,614	3,040	1,432
World Total	546,324	481,056	546,210

(*) Denotes a country that is a summarization of its component countries.
FAS, Office of Global Analysis, (202) 720-6301.

Table 4-35.—Potatoes (fresh market): Foreign trade, United States, 2010–2019 [1]

Year beginning July	Imports for consumption	Domestic exports
	1,000 cwt.	*1,000 cwt.*
2010/2011	10,384	9,294
2011/2012	9,041	9,348
2012/2013	7,375	10,467
2013/2014	10,833	10,001
2014/2015	8,514	9,369
2015/2016	10,103	10,135
2016/2017	11,265	11,308
2017/2018	10,487	10,890
2018/2019	9,517	11,685
2019/2020	10,336	11,172

[1] Includes seed.
ERS, (816) 412-5256. Based on data from U.S. Department of Commerce, U.S. Census Bureau.

Table 4-36.—Pumpkins for fresh market and processing: Area harvested, production, price, and value, by State and United States, 2017–2019 [1]

State	Area harvested			Total Production		
	2017	2018	2019	2017	2018	2019
	Acres			1,000 cwt		
California	4,400	4,900	4,700	1,452.0	1,347.5	1,198.5
Illinois	17,400	11,000	10,900	6,438.0	5,170.0	4,196.5
Indiana	6,000	5,500	5,000	960.0	1,265.0	1,225.0
Michigan	4,900	5,400	5,400	759.5	1,026.0	810.0
Minnesota	1,800	1,400	(NA)	162.0	427.0	(NA)
New Jersey	2,100	1,700	(NA)	199.5	110.5	(NA)
New York	5,600	5,700	5,700	588.0	467.4	410.4
North Carolina ..	2,700	2,300	3,100	567.0	253.0	713.0
Ohio	3,500	3,700	3,500	595.0	666.0	437.5
Oregon	2,500	2,500	1,900	450.0	675.0	598.5
Pennsylvania	6,900	5,700	6,300	1,138.5	655.5	661.5
Tennessee	1,400	1,600	(NA)	124.6	116.8	(NA)
Texas	4,500	4,900	(D)	877.5	1,617.0	(D)
Virginia	3,200	5,200	5,600	720.0	1,066.0	924.0
Washington	2,600	2,400	2,600	468.0	300.0	442.0
Wisconsin	2,800	3,700	(D)	420.0	244.2	(D)
Other States	....	....	6,500	....	....	1,834.0
United States	72,300	67,600	61,200	15,919.6	15,406.9	13,450.9

State	Utilized production			Value of utilized production		
	2017	2018	2019	2017	2018	2019
	1,000 cwt			1,000 dollars		
California	1,450.5	1,339.4	1,191.3	20,742	27,592	22,754
Illinois	6,302.8	5,139.0	4,192.3	24,421	13,751	17,085
Indiana	959.0	1,252.4	1,221.3	18,457	16,971	16,982
Michigan	758.0	1,010.6	806.8	8,314	14,947	12,909
Minnesota	139.3	419.3	(NA)	3,691	12,369	(NA)
New Jersey	198.1	108.8	(NA)	6,101	4,178	(NA)
New York	570.4	435.1	380.4	11,123	8,037	8,635
North Carolina ..	560.8	250.5	703.0	10,437	6,609	10,991
Ohio	586.7	652.0	434.4	7,968	11,024	9,911
Oregon	427.5	645.3	568.6	6,514	9,781	5,147
Pennsylvania	1,110.0	620.8	646.9	19,503	13,852	16,777
Tennessee	111.6	103.4	(NA)	2,132	2,264	(NA)
Texas	864.3	1,615.4	(D)	23,163	24,069	(D)
Virginia	718.6	1,024.4	903.7	10,348	15,366	16,427
Washington	446.5	296.1	399.6	12,604	11,844	15,544
Wisconsin	396.5	214.7	(D)	11,023	2,791	(D)
Other States	....	....	1,772.8	....	....	27,028
United States	15,600.6	15,127.2	13,221.1	196,541	195,445	180,190

See footnote(s) at end of table.

Table 4-36.—Pumpkins for fresh market: Area harvested, production, price, and value, by State and United States, 2017–2019 [1]—Continued

Utilization and State	Utilized production			Price per unit			Value of utilized production		
	2017	2018	2019	2017	2018	2019	2017	2018	2019
	1,000 cwt			Dollars per cwt			1,000 dollars		
Fresh Market									
California	1,450.5	1,339.4	1,191.3	14.30	20.60	19.10	20,742	27,592	22,754
Illinois	(D)	325.7	537.2	(D)	16.80	18.40	(D)	5,472	9,884
Indiana	(D)	(D)	(D)	(D)	(D)	(D)	(D)	(D)	(D)
Michigan	(D)	(D)	806.8	(D)	(D)	16.00	(D)	(D)	12,909
Minnesota	139.3	419.3	(NA)	26.50	29.50	(NA)	3,691	12,369	(NA)
New Jersey	198.1	108.8	(NA)	30.80	38.40	(NA)	6,101	4,178	(NA)
New York	570.4	(D)	380.4	19.50	(D)	22.70	11,123	(D)	8,635
North Carolina	(D)	(D)	(D)	(D)	(D)	(D)	(D)	(D)	(D)
Ohio	(D)	(D)	(D)	(D)	(D)	(D)	(D)	(D)	(D)
Oregon	(D)	276.1	139.5	(D)	25.80	20.90	(D)	7,123	2,916
Pennsylvania	(D)	(D)	(D)	(D)	(D)	(D)	(D)	(D)	(D)
Tennessee	111.6	103.4	(NA)	19.10	21.90	(NA)	2,132	2,264	(NA)
Texas	864.3	1,615.4	(D)	26.80	14.90	(D)	23,163	24,069	(D)
Virginia	718.6	1,024.4	(D)	14.40	15.00	(D)	10,348	15,366	(D)
Washington	(D)	296.1	399.6	(D)	40.00	38.90	(D)	11,844	15,544
Wisconsin	396.5	214.7	(D)	27.80	13.00	(D)	11,023	2,791	(D)
Other States [1]	5,234.5	4,154.9	5,615.7	18.10	17.00	17.30	94,540	70,771	97,424
United States	9,683.8	9,878.2	9,070.5	18.90	18.60	18.70	182,863	183,839	170,066
	Tons			Dollars per ton			1,000 dollars		
Processing									
California				(X)	(X)	(X)			
Illinois	(D)	240,664	182,758	(D)	34.40	39.40	(D)	8,279	7,201
Indiana	(D)	(D)	(D)	(D)	(D)	(D)	(D)	(D)	(D)
Michigan	(D)	(D)		(D)	(D)	(X)	(D)	(D)	
Minnesota			(NA)	(X)	(X)	(NA)			(NA)
New Jersey			(NA)	(X)	(X)	(NA)			(NA)
New York		(D)		(X)	(D)	(X)		(D)	
North Carolina	(D)	(D)	(D)	(D)	(D)	(D)	(D)	(D)	(D)
Ohio	(D)	(D)	(D)	(D)	(D)	(D)	(D)	(D)	(D)
Oregon	(D)	18,461	21,456	(D)	144.00	104.00	(D)	2,658	2,231
Pennsylvania	(D)	(D)	(D)	(D)	(D)	(D)	(D)	(D)	(D)
Tennessee			(NA)	(X)	(X)	(NA)			(NA)
Texas			(D)	(X)	(X)	(D)			(D)
Virginia			(D)	(X)	(X)	(D)			(D)
Washington	(D)			(D)	(X)	(X)	(D)		
Wisconsin			(D)	(X)	(X)	(D)			(D)
Other States [1]	295,841	3,325	3,324	46.20	201.00	208.00	13,678	669	692
United States	295,841	262,450	207,538	46.20	44.20	48.80	13,678	11,606	10,124

(D) Withheld to avoid disclosing data for individual operations. (NA) Not available. (X) Not applicable. [1] Includes data withheld above.

NASS, Crops Branch, (202) 720–2127.

Table 4-37.—Spinach for fresh market and processing: Area Harvested, production, price, and value, by State and United States, 2017–2019

State	Area harvested			Utilized production		
	2017	2018	2019	2017	2018	2019
	Acres			1,000 cwt		
Arizona	12,200	11,100	(D)	1,830.0	1,887.0	(D)
California	46,400	44,200	50,100	5,104.0	5,525.0	7,014.0
Colorado	(D)	(D)	(NA)	(D)	(D)	(NA)
Maryland	(D)	(D)	(NA)	(D)	(D)	(NA)
New Jersey	2,100	2,000	1,900	315.0	230.0	228.0
Texas	2,800	2,800	(D)	672.0	322.0	(D)
Other States [1]	1,230	1,350	13,800	169.6	138.5	2,364.0
United States	64,730	61,450	65,800	8,090.6	8,102.5	9,606.0

State	Price per cwt			Value of utilized production		
	2017	2018	2019	2017	2018	2019
	Dollars			1,000 dollars		
Arizona	53.30	44.40	(D)	97,539	83,783	(D)
California	67.20	57.30	55.40	342,809	316,699	388,741
Colorado	(D)	(D)	(NA)	(D)	(D)	(NA)
Maryland	(D)	(D)	(NA)	(D)	(D)	(NA)
New Jersey	28.70	22.70	29.20	9,039	5,230	6,658
Texas	28.80	19.10	(D)	19,369	6,138	(D)
Other States [1]	12.40	27.60	55.60	2,104	3,821	131,371
United States	58.20	49.90	54.80	470,860	415,671	526,770

State	Utilized production			Price per unit			Value of utilized production		
	2017	2018	2019	2017	2018	2019	2017	2018	2019
	1,000 cwt			Dollars per cwt			1,000 dollars		
Fresh Market									
Arizona	1,830.0	1,887.0	(D)	53.30	44.40	(D)	97,539	83,783	(D)
California	(D)	(D)	6,284.5	(D)	(D)	60.00	(D)	(D)	377,070
Colorado	(D)	(D)	(NA)	(D)	(D)	(NA)	(D)	(D)	(NA)
Maryland	(D)	(D)	(NA)	(D)	(D)	(NA)	(D)	(D)	(NA)
New Jersey	(D)	(D)	(D)	(D)	(D)	(D)	(D)	(D)	(D)
Texas	463.7	132.0	(D)	39.30	38.80	(D)	18,223	5,122	(D)
Other States [1]	4,339.9	4,724.4	2,420.4	78.50	66.10	56.60	340,801	312,356	137,111
United States	6,633.6	6,743.4	8,704.9	68.80	59.50	59.10	456,563	401,261	514,181
	Tons			Dollars per ton			1,000 dollars		
Processing									
Arizona	....	....	(D)	(X)	(X)	(X)	....	....	(D)
California	(D)	(D)	36,473	(D)	(D)	320.00	(D)	(D)	11,671
Colorado	(D)	(D)	(NA)	(D)	(D)	(NA)	(D)	(D)	(NA)
Maryland	(D)	(D)	(NA)	(D)	(D)	(NA)	(D)	(D)	(NA)
New Jersey	(D)	(D)	(D)	(D)	(D)	(D)	(D)	(D)	(D)
Texas	10,416	9,499	(D)	110.00	107.00	(D)	1,146	1,016	(D)
Other States [1]	62,434	58,457	8,580	211.00	229.00	107.00	13,151	13,394	918
United States	72,850	67,956	45,053	196.00	212.00	279.00	14,297	14,410	12,589

(D) Withheld to avoid disclosing data for individual operations. (NA) Not available. (X) Not applicable. [1] Includes data withheld above.
NASS, Crops Branch, (202) 720–2127.

Table 4-38.—Squash for fresh market and processing: Area Harvested, production, price, and value, by State and United States, 2017–2019

State	Area harvested			Total production		
	2017	2018	2019	2017	2018	2019
	Acres			1,000 cwt		
California	7,700	6,700	7,300	1,309.0	1,038.5	1,460.0
Florida	7,500	(D)	7,700	975.0	(D)	808.5
Georgia	3,300	(D)	3,700	511.5	(D)	444.0
Michigan	9,200	8,700	8,600	2,116.0	1,914.0	1,720.0
New Jersey	3,300	3,500	3,200	363.0	325.5	288.0
New York	5,400	4,900	5,200	810.0	808.5	728.0
North Carolina	2,800	3,500	4,400	271.6	612.5	572.0
Oregon	5,000	4,300	3,400	1,500.0	1,333.0	1,105.0
Texas	1,700	1,500	(NA)	153.0	88.5	(NA)
Other States [1]	....	11,700	....	....	1,272.0	....
United States	45,900	44,800	43,500	8,009.1	7,392.5	7,125.5

State	Utilized production			Value of utilized production		
	2017	2018	2019	2017	2018	2019
	1,000 cwt			1,000 dollars		
California	1,288.1	968.9	1,455.6	45,022	30,973	58,339
Florida	970.1	(D)	808.5	39,095	(D)	35,412
Georgia	506.4	(D)	424.0	22,180	(D)	16,343
Michigan	2,116.0	1,883.4	1,685.6	42,838	37,072	40,502
New Jersey	362.6	307.3	258.6	16,313	8,387	13,706
New York	802.7	805.3	696.7	30,737	24,174	27,226
North Carolina	271.1	611.3	561.7	12,313	18,306	20,311
Oregon	1,500.0	1,333.0	1,101.7	17,369	13,194	8,122
Texas	153.0	88.2	(NA)	9,746	3,481	(NA)
Other States [1]	....	1,252.9	....	....	57,335	....
United States	7,970.0	7,250.3	6,992.4	235,613	192,922	219,961

State	Utilized production			Price per unit			Value of utilized production		
	2017	2018	2019	2017	2018	2019	2017	2018	2019
	1,000 cwt			Dollars per cwt			1,000 dollars		
Fresh Market									
California	(D)	884.8	(D)	(D)	33.20	(D)	(D)	29,375	(D)
Florida	970.1	(D)	808.5	40.30	(D)	43.80	39,095	(D)	35,412
Georgia	506.4	(D)	(D)	43.80	(D)	(D)	22,180	(D)	(D)
Michigan	1,299.2	1,225.0	1,186.8	28.10	26.50	31.50	36,508	32,463	37,384
New Jersey	(D)	(D)	258.6	(D)	(D)	53.00	(D)	(D)	13,706
New York	(D)	(D)	587.5	(D)	(D)	41.50	(D)	(D)	24,381
North Carolina	(D)	(D)	(D)	(D)	(D)	(D)	(D)	(D)	(D)
Oregon	217.5	122.6	82.9	43.00	46.90	35.30	9,353	5,750	2,926
Texas	153.0	(D)	(NA)	63.70	(D)	(NA)	9,746	(D)	(NA)
Other States [1]	2,598.4	2,883.8	2,220.6	39.40	37.30	41.20	102,251	107,629	91,405
United States	5,744.6	5,116.2	5,144.9	38.10	34.20	39.90	219,133	175,217	205,214
	Tons			Dollars per ton			1,000 dollars		
Processing									
California	(D)	4,206	(D)	(D)	380.00	(D)	(D)	1,598	(D)
Florida	....	(D)	....	(X)	(D)	(X)	....	(D)	....
Georgia	....	(D)	(D)	(X)	(D)	(D)	....	(D)	(D)
Michigan	40,839	32,921	24,940	155.00	140.00	125.00	6,330	4,609	3,118
New Jersey	(D)	(D)	(D)	(D)	(D)	(X)	(D)	(D)	(D)
New York	(D)	(D)	5,460	(D)	(D)	521.00	(D)	(D)	2,845
North Carolina	(D)	(D)	(D)	(D)	(D)	(D)	(D)	(D)	(D)
Oregon	64,125	60,518	50,941	125.00	123.00	102.00	8,016	7,444	5,196
Texas	....	(D)	(NA)	(X)	(D)	(NA)	....	(D)	(NA)
Other States [1]	6,304	9,057	11,305	339.00	448.00	325.00	2,134	4,054	3,588
United States	111,268	106,702	92,376	148.00	166.00	160.00	16,480	17,705	14,747

(D) Withheld to avoid disclosing data for individual operations. (NA) Not available. (X) Not applicable. [1] Includes data withheld above.

NASS, Crops Branch, (202) 720–2127.

Table 4-39.—Sweet Potatoes: Area, yield, production, season average price per hundredweight received by farmers, and value, United States, 2010–2019

Year	Area harvested	Yield per acre	Production	Market year average price [1]	Value of production
	1,000 acres	*Cwt*	*1,000 cwt*	*Dollars*	*1,000 dollars*
2010	116.9	204.0	23,845.0	19.80	472,218
2011	129.7	208.0	26,964.0	18.80	505,938
2012	126.6	209.0	26,482.0	17.40	461,861
2013	113.2	219.0	24,785.0	24.10	· 597,217
2014	135.2	219.0	29,584.0	23.90	706,916
2015	153.1	203.0	31,016.0	21.80	675,583
2016	163.3	193.0	31,546.0	20.70	651,514
2017	159.3	224.0	35,646.0	18.40	657,021
2018	144.4	190.0	27,378.0	23.20	634,228
2019	146.7	217.9	31,972.5	18.50	588,125

[1] Obtained by weighting State prices by production.
NASS, Crops Branch, (202) 720–2127.

Table 4-40 .—Sweet Potatoes: Area harvested, production, season average price, and value, by State and United States, 2017–2019

State	Area harvested			Production		
	2017	2018	2019	2017	2018	2019
	1,000 Acres			*1,000 cwt*		
Arkansas	(D)	4.8	(NA)	(D)	1,056.0	(NA)
California	21.0	21.0	21.5	6,510.0	7,770.0	8,170.0
Florida	(D)	5.8	(NA)	(D)	812.0	(NA)
Louisiana	9.5	8.3	(NA)	2,185.0	2,200.0	(NA)
Mississippi	29.0	26.0	27.5	4,930.0	4,550.0	4,262.5
North Carolina ..	89.5	78.5	97.7	19,690.0	10,990.0	19,540.0
Other States [2] ...	10.3	....	....	2,331.0	....	....
United States	159.3	144.4	146.7	35,646.0	27,378.0	31,972.5

State	Price per cwt			Value of production		
	2017	2018	2019 [1]	2017	2018	2019 [1]
	Dollars			*1,000 dollars*		
Arkansas	(D)	23.20	(NA)	(D)	24,499	(NA)
California	23.70	23.60	23.30	154,287	183,372	189,236
Florida	(D)	47.90	(NA)	(D)	38,895	(NA)
Louisiana	19.90	20.00	(NA)	43,482	44,000	(NA)
Mississippi	18.50	18.00	17.60	91,205	81,900	75,021
North Carolina ..	15.30	23.80	16.60	301,257	261,562	323,868
Other States [2] ...	28.60	(X)	(X)	66,790	....	....
United States	18.40	23.20	18.50	657,021	634,228	588,125

(D) Withheld to avoid disclosing data for individual operations. (NA) Not available. (X) Not applicable. [1] Preliminary.
[2] Includes data withheld above.
NASS, Crops Branch, (202) 720–2127.

Table 4-41.—Tomatoes for fresh market and processing: Area Harvested, production, and value, by State and United States, 2017–2019

State	Area harvested			Total production		
	2017	2018	2019	2017	2018	2019
	Acres			1,000 cwt		
California	247,700	260,600	247,700	221,691.5	255,388.0	231,599.5
Florida	28,000	27,000	26,000	8,400.0	7,560.0	7,800.0
Indiana	7,800	7,600	(NA)	4,602.0	4,940.0	(NA)
Michigan	5,500	5,000	(NA)	3,080.0	2,750.0	(NA)
New Jersey	4,000	4,100	(NA)	1,120.0	943.0	(NA)
North Carolina	3,200	3,000	(NA)	1,056.0	870.0	(NA)
Ohio	5,500	5,400	(NA)	2,695.0	2,808.0	(NA)
South Carolina	2,800	3,200	(NA)	1,036.0	1,152.0	(NA)
Tennessee	3,600	4,000	(NA)	1,278.0	1,240.0	(NA)
Virginia	2,400	2,000	(NA)	696.0	420.0	(NA)
United States	310,500	321,900	273,700	245,654.5	278,071.0	239,399.5

State	Utilized production			Value of utilized production		
	2017	2018	2019	2017	2018	2019
	1,000 cwt			1,000 dollars		
California	216,592.6	253,855.7	230,209.9	1,075,824	1,197,642	1,174,395
Florida	7,988.4	6,917.4	7,729.8	262,020	344,131	425,912
Indiana	4,602.0	4,940.0	(NA)	30,519	31,530	(NA)
Michigan	3,067.7	2,750.0	(NA)	35,987	35,352	(NA)
New Jersey	1,118.9	716.7	(NA)	39,202	42,411	(NA)
North Carolina	999.0	863.9	(NA)	46,116	33,845	(NA)
Ohio	2,695.0	2,808.0	(NA)	48,626	52,173	(NA)
South Carolina	1,033.9	1,150.8	(NA)	34,429	44,881	(NA)
Tennessee	1,265.2	1,215.2	(NA)	61,719	54,176	(NA)
Virginia	692.5	409.1	(NA)	43,518	27,774	(NA)
United States	240,055.2	275,626.8	237,939.7	1,677,960	1,863,915	1,600,307

State	Utilized production			Price per unit			Value of utilized production		
	2017	2018	2019	2017	2018	2019	2017	2018	2019
	1,000 cwt			Dollars per cwt			1,000 dollars		
Fresh Market									
California	7,315.8	8,172.4	6,484.8	31.20	27.80	43.10	228,253	227,193	279,495
Florida	7,988.4	(D)	7,729.8	32.80	(D)	55.10	262,020	(D)	425,912
Indiana	32.2	49.4	(NA)	75.00	69.00	(NA)	2,415	3,409	(NA)
Michigan	406.6	495.0	(NA)	54.80	47.50	(NA)	22,282	23,513	(NA)
New Jersey	689.9	510.2	(NA)	53.90	80.90	(NA)	37,186	41,275	(NA)
North Carolina	(D)	(D)	(NA)	(D)	(D)	(NA)	(D)	(D)	(NA)
Ohio	649.5	561.6	(NA)	56.60	69.90	(NA)	36,762	39,256	(NA)
South Carolina	1,033.9	1,150.8	(NA)	33.30	39.00	(NA)	34,429	44,881	(NA)
Tennessee	(D)	(D)	(NA)	(D)	(D)	(NA)	(D)	(D)	(NA)
Virginia	(D)	(D)	(NA)	(D)	(D)	(NA)	(D)	(D)	(NA)
Other States [1]	2,853.4	8,683.1	....	52.10	50.00	(X)	148,744	442,090	....
United States	20,969.7	19,622.5	14,214.6	36.80	41.60	49.60	772,091	821,617	705,407
	Tons			Dollars per ton			1,000 dollars		
Processing									
California	10,463,839	12,284,163	11,186,256	81.00	79.00	80.00	847,571	970,449	894,900
Florida	....	(D)	....	(X)	(D)	(X)	....	(D)	(NA)
Indiana	228,489	244,530	(NA)	123.00	115.00	(NA)	28,104	28,121	(NA)
Michigan	133,056	112,750	(NA)	103.00	105.00	(NA)	13,705	11,839	(NA)
New Jersey	21,448	10,326	(NA)	94.00	110.00	(NA)	2,016	1,136	(NA)
North Carolina	(D)	(D)	(NA)	(D)	(D)	(NA)	(D)	(D)	(NA)
Ohio	102,275	112,320	(NA)	116.00	115.00	(NA)	11,864	12,917	(NA)
South Carolina	....	....	(NA)	(X)	(X)	(NA)	....	....	(NA)
Tennessee	(D)	(D)	(NA)	(D)	(D)	(NA)	(D)	(D)	(NA)
Virginia	(D)	(D)	(NA)	(D)	(D)	(NA)	(D)	(D)	(NA)
Other States [1]	5,160	28,566	....	506.00	624.00	(X)	2,609	17,836	....
United States	10,954,267	12,792,655	11,186,256	82.70	81.50	80.00	905,869	1,042,298	894,900

(D) Withheld to avoid disclosing data for individual operations. (NA) Not available. (X) Not applicable. [1] Includes data withheld above.

NASS, Crops Branch, (202) 720–2127.

Table 4-42.—Watermelon for fresh market and processing: Area harvested, production, and value, by State and United States, 2017–2019

State	Area harvested			Total production		
	2017	2018	2019	2017	2018	2019
	Acres			*1,000 cwt*		
Arizona	3,500	(D)	5,000	1,802.5	(D)	2,525.0
California	10,600	11,900	10,200	6,201.0	6,426.0	5,100.0
Delaware	3,900	3,800	(NA)	1,092.0	1,026.0	(NA)
Florida	22,000	22,500	24,500	8,690.0	8,100.0	9,056.0
Georgia	20,900	20,600	21,100	7,942.0	5,356.0	8,229.0
Indiana	6,200	6,500	6,100	2,573.0	3,055.0	2,318.0
Maryland	3,700	3,500	(NA)	1,110.0	1,050.0	(NA)
Missouri	3,000	(D)	(NA)	705.0	(D)	(NA)
North Carolina ..	7,100	7,300	7,400	2,130.0	1,825.0	1,702.0
South Carolina ..	4,900	4,300	4,500	2,156.0	989.0	1,440.0
Texas	22,000	23,000	23,000	6,380.0	7,820.0	6,670.0
Other States	....	8,000	....	....	3,698.0	....
United States	107,800	112,000	101,800	40,781.5	39,345.5	37,049.0

State	Utilized production			Value of utilized production		
	2017	2018	2019	2017	2018	2019
	1,000 cwt			*1,000 dollars*		
Arizona	1,802.5	(D)	2,525.0	42,359	(D)	34,593
California	6,176.2	6,393.9	5,100.0	117,348	116,369	105,060
Delaware	1,092.0	1,026.0	(NA)	8,736	11,286	(NA)
Florida	8,690.0	8,043.3	8,974.4	152,944	160,866	161,539
Georgia	7,727.6	5,345.3	8,097.3	84,231	76,438	101,216
Indiana	2,573.0	3,055.0	2,318.0	27,017	27,915	35,294
Maryland	1,110.0	1,039.5	(NA)	12,321	10,395	(NA)
Missouri	702.2	(D)	(NA)	8,445	(D)	(NA)
North Carolina ..	2,102.3	1,799.5	1,702.0	22,705	22,314	23,998
South Carolina ..	2,153.8	987.0	1,402.6	26,276	17,174	16,022
Texas	6,156.7	7,765.3	6,603.3	91,651	143,387	83,202
Other States	....	3,694.0	....	....	77,291	....
United States	40,286.3	39,148.8	36,722.6	594,033	663,435	560,924

State	Utilized production			Price per unit			Value of utilized production		
	2017	2018	2019	2017	2018	2019	2017	2018	2019
	1,000 cwt			*Dollars per cwt*			*1,000 dollars*		
Fresh Market									
Arizona	1,802.5	(D)	2,525.0	23.50	(D)	13.70	42,359	(D)	34,593
California	6,176.2	6,393.9	5,100.0	19.00	18.20	20.60	117,348	116,369	105,060
Delaware	1,092.0	1,026.0	(NA)	8.00	11.00	(NA)	8,736	11,286	(NA)
Florida	8,690.0	8,043.3	8,974.4	17.60	20.00	18.00	152,944	160,866	161,539
Georgia	7,727.6	5,345.3	8,097.3	10.90	14.30	12.50	84,231	76,438	101,216
Indiana	2,573.0	(D)	(D)	10.50	(D)	(D)	27,017	(D)	(D)
Maryland	1,110.0	1,039.5	(NA)	11.10	10.00	(NA)	12,321	10,395	(NA)
Missouri	(D)	(D)	(NA)	(D)	(D)	(NA)	(D)	(D)	(NA)
North Carolina	2,102.3	1,799.5	1,702.0	10.80	12.40	14.10	22,705	22,314	23,998
South Carolina	2,153.8	987.0	(D)	12.20	17.40	(D)	26,276	17,174	(D)
Texas	(D)	(D)	6,603.3	(D)	(D)	12.60	(D)	(D)	83,202
Other States [1]	6,606.0	14,345.9	3,664.2	15.10	17.20	14.00	99,782	247,360	51,132
United States ..	40,033.4	38,980.4	36,666.2	14.80	17.00	15.30	593,719	662,202	560,740
	Tons			*Dollars per ton*			*1,000 dollars*		
Processing									
Arizona	....	(D)	....	(X)	(D)	(X)	....	(D)	....
California	....	....	....	(X)	(X)	(X)	....	....	....
Delaware	....	....	(NA)	(X)	(X)	(NA)	....	....	(NA)
Florida	....	....	....	(X)	(X)	(X)	....	....	....
Georgia	....	....	....	(X)	(X)	(X)	....	....	....
Indiana	....	(D)	(D)	(X)	(D)	(D)	....	(D)	(D)
Maryland	....	....	(NA)	(X)	(X)	(NA)	....	....	(NA)
Missouri	(D)	(D)	(NA)	(D)	(D)	(NA)	(D)	(D)	(NA)
North Carolina	....	....	....	(X)	(X)	(X)	....	....	....
South Carolina	....	....	(D)	(X)	(X)	(D)	....	....	(D)
Texas	(D)	(D)	....	(D)	(D)	(X)	(D)	(D)	....
Other States [1]	12,646	8,420	2,815	24.80	146.00	146.00	314	1,233	184
United States ..	12,646	8,420	2,815	24.80	146.00	146.00	64	1,233	184

(D) Withheld to avoid disclosing data for individual operations. (NA) Not available. (X) Not applicable. [1] Includes data withheld above.

NASS, Crops Branch, (202) 720–2127.

Table 4-43.—Vegetables and melons, fresh: Total reported domestic rail, truck, and air shipments, 2020

Commodity	Jan.	Feb.	Mar.	Apr.	May	June	July
Vegetables:	1,000 cwt						
Artichokes	49	68	66	78	76	75	63
Artichokes-organic	3	2	2	4	3	5	5
Asparagus	...	...	...	33	101	82	...
Beans	192	176	194	191	202	122	31
Beans-organic	...	...	...	...	...	...	...
Beets	5	5	7	11	6	7	4
Beets-organic	...	...	...	2	4	4	4
Broccoli	461	505	524	653	656	448	559
Broccoli-organic	47	57	56	62	71	40	57
Brussels sprouts	61	42	29	31	43	65	113
Cabbage	977	871	1,147	594	313	203	347
Cabbage-organic	10	12	22	6	4	8	8
Carrots	630	606	665	679	678	656	724
Carrots-organic	246	230	245	237	225	262	300
Cauliflower	402	420	416	480	524	446	452
Cauliflower-organic	23	34	44	48	60	42	52
Celery	1,554	1,189	1,416	1,316	1,279	1,224	1,153
Celery-organic	86	93	84	102	82	131	130
Corn, sweet	384	337	630	1,262	1,971	1,128	560
Cucumbers	14	2	95	236	224	377	342
Cucumbers-organic	...	...	...	1	...	1	...
Eggplant	50	38	24	34	84	99	25
Eggplant-organic	1	1	1	2	...	...	...
Endive	13	12	12	8	3	2	2
Escarole	21	18	19	12	3	3	3
Greens	252	288	288	238	256	114	97
Greens-organic	14	10	8	13	17	20	17
Lettuce, iceberg	1,812	1,859	1,887	2,188	2,195	2,237	2,207
Lettuce, iceberg-organic	63	9	11	23	22	20	32
Lettuce, other	365	335	307	218	190	174	166
Lettuce, other-organic	12	13	19	8	9	8	8
Lettuce, romaine	1,763	1,763	1,662	1,655	1,692	1,679	1,517
Lettuce, romaine-organic	126	106	114	120	126	133	139
Lettuce processed	1,236	925	1,168	549	119	2	4
Lettuce processed-organic	4	...	1	...	...	...	...

Commodity	Aug.	Sep.	Oct.	Nov.	Dec.	Total
Artichokes	50	53	84	50	28	740
Artichokes-organic	3	2	2	1	...	32
Asparagus	...	...	...	...	...	216
Beans	64	43	86	150	83	1,534
Beans-organic	...	...	2	...	...	2
Beets	5	5	6	7	9	77
Beets-organic	4	4	4	2	...	28
Broccoli	490	397	492	354	388	5,927
Broccoli-organic	51	45	47	25	46	604
Brussels sprouts	143	184	229	265	210	1,415
Cabbage	469	485	522	620	784	7,332
Cabbage-organic	25	14	13	14	8	144
Carrots	588	538	600	796	724	7,884
Carrots-organic	231	81	84	76	83	2,300
Cauliflower	400	388	459	321	385	5,093
Cauliflower-organic	48	43	50	21	27	492
Celery	1,112	1,153	1,390	1,700	1,454	15,940
Celery-organic	123	117	134	124	97	1,303
Corn, sweet	449	216	228	319	126	7,610
Cucumbers	336	214	280	208	108	2,436
Cucumbers-organic	...	...	...	2	1	5
Eggplant	37	27	114	69	37	638
Eggplant-organic	...	...	...	...	1	6
Endive	2	2	2	3	6	67
Escarole	2	3	3	4	9	100
Greens	96	95	183	303	277	2,487
Greens-organic	16	14	14	9	14	166
Lettuce, iceberg	2,236	2,077	2,013	1,357	1,874	23,942
Lettuce, iceberg-organic	35	28	25	24	35	327
Lettuce, other	161	168	178	181	226	2,669
Lettuce, other-organic	8	7	10	4	13	119
Lettuce, romaine	1,502	1,507	1,455	1,380	1,554	19,129
Lettuce, romaine-organic	136	120	102	73	97	1,392
Lettuce processed	4	6	139	719	768	5,639
Lettuce, processed-organic	...	...	...	22	1	28

See footnote(s) at end of table.

Table 4-43.—Vegetables and melons, fresh: Total reported domestic rail, truck, and air shipments, 2020—Continued

Commodity	Jan.	Feb.	Mar.	Apr.	May	June	July
Vegetables:				*1,000 cwt*			
Onions, dry	4,231	3,614	3,961	3,454	4,500	3,744	3,890
Onions, dry-organic	1	1	1	11	14	9	5
Onions processed	412	480	362	367	522	431	438
Onions, green	18	20	20	25	34	31	32
Onions, green-organic							2
Parsley	41	38	35	47	42	41	41
Parsley-organic		1	2	2	2	2	2
Peas, green	1	1	1		1	1	2
Peppers, bell	279	244	255	418	622	654	657
Peppers, bell-organic	4	4	3	3		6	8
Peppers, other	30	26	25	12	35	5	9
Peppers, other-organic	4	4	3	3		6	8
Potatoes, table	7,186	6,262	8,491	6,737	7,095	7,032	7,115
Potatoes, table-organic	145	125	158	134	68	53	39
Potatoes, chipper	4,031	4,864	3,896	4,168	4,625	4,595	4,746
Potatoes, seed	124	1,363	4,005	5,633	1,168	179	
Radishes	86	78	75	71	57	44	43
Spinach	146	145	157	87	44	50	53
Spinach-organic	34	29	34	5	1	5	5
Squash	122	116	166	114	129	84	167
Squash-organic	7	7	6	5	3	1	
Sweet potatoes	631	739	787	717	736	538	569
Sweet potatoes-organic	13	8	6	4	1		
Tomatoes	996	875	711	724	763	849	834
Tomatoes, organic							
Tomatoes, greenhouse	60	103	83	101	152	118	111
Toms, Grape Type	100	105	79	76	97	112	43
Toms, Grape Type-greenhouse	17	22	18	18	25	18	20
Tomatoes, grape-organic	9	8	4	5	2		
Toms, Cherry	29	23	15	12	11	5	4
Toms, Cherry-greenhouse	2	2	3	2	3	2	3
Toms, Plum Type	329	262	232	250	256	82	304
Toms, Plum Type-greenhouse	2	2	2	3	3	3	4
Total	29,966	2,446	34,759	34,302	32,249	28,517	28,275

Commodity	Aug.	Sep.	Oct.	Nov.	Dec.	Total
Onions, dry	3,738	3,747	4,531	3,916	3,773	47,099
Onions, dry-organic	4	16	13	16	16	107
Onions processed	460	253	455	316	339	4,835
Onions, green	37	32	37	32	24	342
Onions, green-organic	3	3	3	4	2	17
Parsley	34	40	40	37	37	473
Parsley-organic	3	3	2	1	2	22
Peas, green	2	2	1	1		13
Peppers, bell	594	576	620	531	274	5,724
Peppers, bell-organic	2			3	4	37
Peppers, other	10	3	7	20	13	195
Peppers, other-organic	2			3	4	37
Potatoes, table	6,569	7,578	7,734	8,027	7,217	87,043
Potatoes, table-organic	75	109	128	153	139	1,326
Potatoes, chipper	4,997	4,424	5,116	4,320	4,677	54,459
Potatoes, seed		63	67	68	42	12,712
Radishes	34	42	47	43	42	662
Spinach	49	45	63	85	134	1,058
Spinach-organic	4	4	10	28	35	194
Squash	122	69	111	50	72	1,322
Squash-organic			2	3	3	37
Sweet potatoes	508	515	684	946	655	8,025
Sweet potatoes-organic		3	6	7	5	53
Tomatoes	1,094	968	713	774	834	10,135
Tomatoes-organic			1			1
Tomatoes, greenhouse	87	78	110	102	116	1,221
Tomatoes, Grape Type	46	28	67	80	24	857
Tomatoes, Grape Type-greenhouse	28	16	17	10	12	221
Tomatoes, Grape-organic	1	1		4	2	36
Toms, Cherry	6	4	9	12	5	135
Toms, Cherry-greenhouse	5	4	4	2	2	34
Toms, Plum Type	511	496	302	243	222	3,489
Toms, Plum Type-greenhouse	3	2	2	4	3	33
Total	27,854	27,160	29,852	29,044	28,202	359,777

See footnote(s) at end of table.

Table 4-43.—Vegetables and melons, fresh: Total reported domestic rail, truck, and air shipments, 2020–Continued

Commodity	Jan.	Feb.	Mar.	Apr.	May	June	July
Melons:				*1,000 cwt*			
Cantaloupe	....	....	1	5	704	1,612	1,749
Cantaloupe-organic	....	....	....	....	....	20	45
Honeydews	....	....	....	....	64	304	514
Honeydews-organic	....	....	....	....	....	9	15
Mixed & misc. melons	....	....	....	....	16	108	63
Mixed & misc. melons-organic	....	....	....	....	....	5	7
Watermelon, seedless	....	....	12	1,562	6,063	9,811	9,193
Watermelon, seedless-organic	....	....	....	....	12	41	176
Watermelon, seeded	....	....	....	174	402	612	600
Watermelon, seeded-organic	....	....	....	....	5	10	6
Total	....	....	13	1,741	7,266	12,532	12,368

Commodity	Aug.	Sep.	Oct.	Nov.	Dec.	Total	
Cantaloupe	1,816	1,133	852	304	....	8,176	
Cantaloupe-organic	41	11	6	....	....	123	
Honeydews	615	373	263	65	....	2,198	
Honeydews-organic	11	6	2	....	....	43	
Mixed & misc. melons	76	8	26	8	....	305	
Mixed & misc. melons-organic	5	1	....	....	....	18	
Watermelon, seedless	7,380	3,356	408	4	....	37,789	
Watermelon, seedless-organic	99	31	12	....	....	371	
Watermelon, seeded	315	70	11	....	....	2,184	
Watermelon, seeded-organic	....	....	....	....	....	21	
Total	10,358	4,989	1,580	381	....	51,228	

AMS, Fresh Fruit and Vegetable Specialty Crops, Market News Division, (301) 365-6701.

Table 4-44.—Commercially produced vegetables: Per capita utilization, United States, 2010–2019

Year	Farm weight equivalent						
	Total fresh and processed	Fresh [2]	Processed *ERR17*				
			Total	Canning	Freezing	Potatoes	Others [1]
	Pounds	*Pounds*	*Pounds*	*Pounds*	*Pounds*	*Pounds*	*Pounds*
2010	352.0	144.9	207.1	97.7	20.9	77.1	11.4
2011	342.2	142.2	200.3	89.6	22.0	76.4	12.3
2012	350.5	144.8	205.7	91.1	22.3	80.3	12.0
2013	341.1	141.2	199.9	90.3	19.6	79.0	11.0
2014	346.8	142.6	204.2	92.1	19.9	79.5	12.7
2015	337.2	141.9	195.3	80.6	20.5	81.3	12.9
2016	351.5	155.9	195.6	86.0	20.2	76.5	12.9
2017	358.1	157.1	201.0	83.3	21.4	82.9	13.4
2018	354.5	149.2	205.3	89.6	22.6	83.0	10.1
2019	365.7	153.3	212.4	92.6	21.6	84.7	13.4

Percentage of annual total

Year	Fresh[2]	Processed *ERR17*				
		Total	Canning	Freezing	Pota-toes	Others[1]
	Percent	Percent	Percent	Percent	Percent	Percent
2010	41.2	58.8	27.7	6.0	21.9	3.2
2011	41.5	58.5	26.2	6.4	22.3	3.6
2012	41.3	58.7	26.0	6.4	22.9	3.4
2013	41.4	58.6	26.5	5.7	23.2	3.2
2014	41.1	58.9	26.6	5.7	22.9	3.7
2015	42.1	57.9	23.9	6.1	24.1	3.8
2016	44.3	55.7	24.5	5.7	21.8	3.7
2017	43.9	56.1	23.3	6.0	23.2	3.7
2018	42.1	57.9	25.3	6.4	23.4	2.8
2019	41.9	58.1	25.3	5.9	23.2	3.7

[1] Others include mushrooms, sweet potatoes, and onions for dehydrating market.   [2] See table 4-45 for items included under Fresh category. Excludes melons.

ERS, Market and Trade Economics Division, (816) 412–5256.

Table 4-45.—Vegetables, fresh: Per capita civilian availability (farm-weight basis), United States, 2010–2019 [1]

Year	Asparagus	Snap beans	Broccoli	Cabbage	Carrots	Cauliflower
	Pounds	Pounds	Pounds	Pounds	Pounds	Pounds
2010	1.4	1.9	6.0	7.5	7.8	1.3
2011	1.4	1.7	6.0	6.6	7.5	1.2
2012	1.4	1.6	6.3	6.3	8.0	1.2
2013	1.4	1.6	6.9	6.9	8.0	1.3
2014	1.7	1.5	6.7	6.7	8.5	1.3
2015	1.5	1.6	7.4	6.3	8.8	1.6
2016	1.6	1.7	7.5	5.9	7.8	1.7
2017	1.6	1.6	7.1	6.2	7.4	2.4
2018	1.8	1.6	5.9	5.7	12.2	2.5
2019	1.8	1.8	6.1	6.5	13.6	3.0

Year	Celery	Sweet Corn	Cucumbers	Head lettuce	Leaf/romaine	Garlic
	Pounds	Pounds	Pounds	Pounds	Pounds	Pounds
2010	6.1	9.3	6.7	15.9	12.0	2.3
2011	6.0	8.2	6.4	15.8	11.7	2.3
2012	6.0	8.7	7.1	16.0	11.9	2.3
2013	5.5	8.9	7.3	14.1	11.4	2.3
2014	5.5	7.7	7.4	14.5	10.8	2.2
2015	5.1	8.6	7.6	13.6	11.9	2.4
2016	5.0	7.1	8.1	16.9	14.5	3.0
2017	4.7	7.2	7.4	15.3	15.1	3.0
2018	4.9	6.8	8.0	12.3	12.1	2.4
2019	5.3	6.8	8.0	12.7	12.3	1.9

Year	Onions	Bell peppers	Spinach	Tomatoes [2]	Others [3]	Total vegetables [4]
	Pounds	Pounds	Pounds	Pounds	Pounds	Pounds
2010	19.6	10.3	1.7	20.6	18.4	144.9
2011	19.1	10.6	1.8	21.0	18.8	142.2
2012	19.3	10.8	1.6	20.8	19.3	144.8
2013	18.5	10.0	1.6	20.3	18.8	141.2
2014	18.4	10.7	1.7	20.6	20.5	142.6
2015	18.3	10.7	1.7	20.6	18.3	141.9
2016	22.8	11.1	2.0	20.3	24.0	155.9
2017	25.1	11.3	1.9	20.1	24.6	157.1
2018	20.5	11.2	1.9	20.3	23.4	149.2
2019	20.4	11.3	2.5	20.3	23.4	153.3

[1] Fresh vegetable consumption computed for total commercial production for fresh market. Does not include production for home use. Consumption obtained by dividing the total apparent consumption by total July 1 population as reported by the Bureau of the Census. All data for calendar year. [2] After 1996, includes an ERS estimate of domestically produced hothouse tomatoes. Hothouse imports included in all years. [3] Includes artichokes, brussels sprouts, eggplant, endive/escarole, garlic, radishes, green limas, squash, spinach, okra, pumpkins, kale, collards, turnip greens, and mustard greens. [4] Excludes melons, mushrooms, potatoes, and sweet potatoes.
ERS, Market and Trade Economics Division, (816) 412–5256.

Table 4-46.—Vegetables, canning: Per capita availability (farm weight), United States, 2010–2019

Year	Cabbage	Asparagus	Snap beans	Carrots	Green peas
	Pounds	*Pounds*	*Pounds*	*Pounds*	*Pounds*
2010	1.0	0.1	3.7	0.8	1.1
2011	1.0	0.1	3.2	0.8	0.8
2012	1.2	0.1	2.9	0.8	0.8
2013	1.0	0.1	2.9	0.8	0.9
2014	1.0	0.1	2.8	0.7	0.7
2015	0.9	0.1	3.0	0.7	0.8
2016	1.0	0.1	3.2	1.1	0.8
2017	1.3	0.1	3.1	1.1	0.7
2018	0.8	0.1	2.9	1.0	0.6
2019	0.7	0.1	2.9	1.2	0.7

Year	Tomatoes	Sweet corn	Pickling Cucumbers	Other [1]	Total
	Pounds	*Pounds*	*Pounds*	*Pounds*	*Pounds*
2010	71.3	6.9	3.8	9.0	97.7
2011	65.8	5.8	2.8	9.3	89.6
2012	66.6	5.9	3.0	9.8	91.1
2013	66.0	5.8	3.2	9.6	90.3
2014	67.4	5.8	3.9	9.7	92.1
2015	56.3	5.3	3.4	10.1	80.6
2016	61.2	5.0	3.0	10.6	86.0
2017	57.9	5.0	3.7	10.4	83.3
2018	65.6	5.2	3.3	10.5	90.0
2019	68.0	5.3	3.4	10.4	92.6

[1] Includes beets, green limas, spinach, chile peppers, and miscellaneous imports.
ERS, Market and Trade Economics Division, (816) 412–5256.

Table 4-47.—Vegetables, freezing: Per capita utilization (farm weight basis), United States, 2010–2019

Year	Asparagus	Snap beans	Carrots	Peas	Broccoli
	Pounds	*Pounds*	*Pounds*	*Pounds*	*Pounds*
2010	0.1	2.0	1.5	1.5	2.5
2011	0.1	1.5	1.6	1.6	2.7
2012	0.1	1.9	1.2	1.9	2.6
2013	0.1	2.1	1.7	1.5	2.5
2014	0.1	1.8	1.2	1.6	2.6
2015	0.1	1.9	1.4	1.5	2.6
2016	0.2	2.0	1.9	1.0	2.6
2017	0.1	1.9	2.4	1.3	2.4
2018	0.1	1.9	2.4	1.3	2.5
2019	0.1	1.9	1.8	1.3	2.6

Year	Cauliflower	Sweet Corn	Other [1]	Total vegetables excluding potatoes
	Pounds	*Pounds*	*Pounds*	*Pounds*
2010	0.4	8.6	4.5	20.9
2011	0.4	9.8	4.3	22.0
2012	0.3	9.8	4.5	22.3
2013	0.3	7.0	4.3	19.6
2014	0.4	7.7	4.6	19.9
2015	0.3	8.0	4.7	20.5
2016	0.4	7.5	4.6	20.2
2017	0.5	8.0	4.8	21.4
2018	0.6	7.9	6.0	22.6
2019	0.7	6.9	6.4	21.6

[1] Includes green lima beans, spinach, and miscellaneous freezing vegetables.
ERS, Market and Trade Economics Division, (816) 412–5256.

Table 4-48.—Frozen Vegetables and potato products: Cold storage holdings, United States, 2018 and 2019

End of the month	Asparagus		Green beans, french cut		Green beans, Lima		Green beans, regular cut	
	2018	2019	2018	2019	2018	2019	2018	2019
				1,000 pounds				
January	9,690	7,694	14,738	12,622	49,217	34,443	172,503	143,960
February	8,119	7,136	13,923	12,025	45,506	29,861	155,853	130,780
March	6,989	6,419	13,402	11,534	42,315	26,059	128,304	117,427
April	6,036	5,714	12,230	11,471	37,826	18,879	109,337	110,140
May	7,767	5,807	10,651	10,112	36,335	17,010	93,324	87,598
June	10,855	7,220	11,184	9,879	33,421	14,441	81,164	82,556
July	10,971	7,297	12,886	16,571	29,161	29,161	115,005	125,225
August	10,120	6,454	14,413	21,160	33,072	33,072	172,836	163,225
September	9,358	6,372	15,847	20,285	44,301	44,301	202,123	203,481
October	8,933	6,344	15,328	19,950	47,691	47,691	190,921	185,412
November	8,364	6,257	13,793	17,143	42,601	42,601	173,687	173,403
December	8,106	6,002	13,747	14,887	38,647	38,647	152,495	155,713

End of the month	Broccoli, chopped & cut		Broccoli, spears		Brussels sprouts		Carrots, diced	
	2018	2019	2018	2019	2018	2019	2018	2019
				1,000 pounds				
January	30,206	36,913	25,814	26,337	21,121	15,728	128,815	120,219
February	31,302	39,476	29,513	28,628	20,636	13,164	121,470	116,148
March	33,530	37,688	31,806	34,710	20,900	12,916	114,872	109,514
April	36,759	35,876	34,494	40,829	20,736	13,341	108,053	105,619
May	35,108	32,798	38,616	39,849	19,317	12,501	98,881	110,909
June	34,532	32,061	45,339	43,927	17,361	12,774	84,708	100,442
July	38,981	36,520	44,166	45,936	17,102	12,930	65,564	84,444
August	41,735	43,555	44,250	48,278	15,536	12,823	53,967	72,505
September	43,080	45,550	37,705	47,694	13,257	12,237	48,927	62,579
October	41,796	39,750	35,174	46,109	13,410	12,982	86,070	113,935
November	39,422	37,303	30,802	43,369	13,940	12,505	129,184	171,712
December	37,761	34,048	26,691	41,991	15,680	13,254	125,994	173,673

End of the month	Carrots, other		Cauliflower		Sweet corn, cut		Sweet corn, cob	
	2018	2019	2018	2019	2018	2019	2018	2019
				1,000 pounds				
January	149,233	100,107	34,901	28,000	446,194	433,018	231,840	242,621
February	136,166	93,262	36,257	26,134	403,945	394,400	207,582	226,032
March	125,914	87,761	35,212	24,059	356,223	351,796	176,477	202,924
April	119,288	77,125	32,896	23,981	312,151	295,948	142,645	169,151
May	104,184	73,787	30,354	18,478	276,599	259,917	107,713	149,776
June	94,449	64,844	25,340	18,926	240,908	240,636	79,134	137,539
July	87,118	57,293	24,701	19,682	257,797	250,720	105,145	137,583
August	84,641	53,727	24,088	18,565	443,885	461,516	208,224	246,139
September	96,342	67,712	23,258	19,684	558,378	662,567	276,776	332,852
October	105,654	86,019	30,422	21,973	592,617	674,400	307,075	345,723
November	113,794	105,246	28,645	23,324	530,696	637,174	288,300	307,982
December	110,822	98,720	29,760	24,382	475,712	567,306	269,689	275,612

End of the month	Greens, southern		Okra		Onions, other		Onion rings	
	2018	2019	2018	2019	2018	2019	2018	2019
				1,000 pounds				
January	13,243	11,889	20,870	37,915	53,999	52,133	14,859	17,588
February	12,661	11,164	16,743	31,855	56,916	53,274	16,629	18,362
March	11,268	10,351	14,666	21,396	60,604	59,335	17,190	15,731
April	10,534	9,976	13,443	16,652	62,211	66,088	18,696	16,500
May	9,144	10,514	12,632	17,388	60,049	73,692	18,698	16,229
June	10,996	12,907	30,181	28,658	60,160	72,312	17,976	15,146
July	12,352	15,254	41,318	43,014	58,276	64,400	16,534	12,880
August	13,146	15,149	50,058	56,509	60,197	66,956	16,117	11,357
September	12,725	14,477	54,779	58,883	55,390	64,243	16,875	12,238
October	13,195	14,583	55,093	57,568	47,346	55,543	17,056	11,825
November	12,778	13,272	48,631	52,782	48,431	52,817	16,801	15,724
December	12,174	10,908	44,156	48,906	51,663	51,024	17,160	14,918

See footnote(s) at end of table.

Table 4-48.—Frozen Vegetables and potato products: Cold storage holdings, United States, 2018 and 2019—Continued

End of the month	Blackeye peas		Green peas		Peas & carrots mixed		Spinach	
	2018	2019	2018	2019	2018	2019	2018	2019
	1,000 pounds							
January	1,606	1,497	247,040	188,769	7,454	7,826	51,346	30,847
February	1,655	1,394	223,679	174,792	8,135	7,391	50,691	28,965
March	1,512	1,712	198,966	147,662	7,410	8,001	50,882	33,114
April	1,357	1,495	190,125	132,510	8,083	7,954	51,731	34,603
May	1,407	1,373	177,152	121,763	7,758	8,436	57,378	38,555
June	1,293	1,413	284,008	233,194	6,754	9,098	57,896	41,009
July	2,089	1,615	341,193	385,001	7,424	9,953	52,689	39,444
August	2,009	1,655	319,549	352,447	7,605	9,545	44,851	34,753
September	2,000	1,930	303,905	309,511	6,947	8,515	40,251	30,952
October	2,037	1,904	268,892	277,596	7,457	8,423	38,782	32,030
November	1,790	1,332	244,288	250,797	6,928	8,567	35,439	32,739
December	1,479	1,227	207,808	212,684	7,262	9,058	30,994	33,492

End of the month	Squash		Vegetables, mixed		Vegetables, other		Total frozen vegetables	
	2018	2019	2018	2019	2018	2019	2018	2019
	1,000 pounds							
January	65,820	55,342	59,410	52,405	563,016	535,862	2,412,935	2,193,735
February	59,535	55,155	60,105	54,958	504,878	510,354	2,221,899	2,064,710
March	54,323	52,618	53,310	53,253	461,985	476,131	2,018,060	1,902,111
April	50,724	48,370	52,886	55,753	406,018	440,646	1,838,259	1,738,621
May	48,427	43,275	54,013	48,189	376,945	377,702	1,682,452	1,575,658
June	44,881	40,456	56,417	47,214	377,555	355,236	1,706,512	1,621,888
July	44,933	37,843	60,139	52,260	422,205	354,953	1,867,749	1,821,909
August	46,032	45,421	66,995	50,131	502,853	384,582	2,276,179	2,191,605
September	48,877	46,079	63,700	47,185	569,778	423,955	2,544,579	2,530,067
October	61,029	55,609	60,301	50,241	623,597	458,115	2,669,876	2,615,705
November	60,200	58,825	56,423	41,737	606,165	455,499	2,548,102	2,555,201
December	60,482	56,884	53,845	41,323	582,039	435,111	2,374,166	2,354,632

End of the month	Frozen potatoes					
	French fries		Other frozen potatoes		Total frozen potatoes	
	2018	2019	2018	2019	2018	2019
	1,000 pounds					
January	1,001,232	1,030,263	257,077	234,970	1,258,309	1,265,233
February	997,602	1,052,280	267,617	246,684	1,265,219	1,298,964
March	964,870	1,038,225	260,942	253,586	1,225,812	1,291,811
April	938,695	969,089	254,107	242,123	1,192,802	1,211,212
May	889,808	932,737	266,879	240,164	1,156,687	1,172,901
June	941,336	945,264	270,621	239,233	1,211,957	1,184,497
July	859,456	907,021	237,286	227,235	1,096,742	1,134,256
August	898,725	935,993	242,029	226,265	1,140,754	1,162,258
September	932,954	921,903	252,068	238,779	1,185,022	1,160,682
October	1,002,221	942,518	248,025	228,186	1,250,246	1,170,704
November	962,841	954,826	235,592	226,101	1,198,433	1,180,927
December	944,230	948,850	230,329	207,080	1,174,559	1,155,930

NASS, Livestock Branch, (202) 720–3570.

CHAPTER V

STATISTICS OF FRUITS, TREE NUTS, AND HORTICULTURAL SPECIALTIES

For most fruits, production is estimated at two levels—total and utilized. Total production is the quantity of fruit harvested plus quantities which would have been acceptable for fresh market or processing but were not harvested or utilized because of economic and other reasons. Utilized production is the amount sold plus the quantities used on farms where grown and quantities held in storage. The difference between total and utilized production is the quantity of marketable fruit not harvested and fruit harvested but not sold or utilized because of economic and other reasons. Production relates to the crop produced on all farms, except for apples and strawberries. In accordance with Congressional enactment, the Department's estimates of apple production since 1938 have related only to commercial production. The estimates for strawberries cover production on area grown primarily for sale. Statistics on utilization of fruit by commercial processors refer to first utilization, not necessarily final utilization. For example, frozen fruit includes fruit which may later be used for preserves.

The price shown for each crop is a marketing year average price for all methods of sales. Prices for most fresh fruit are the average prices producers received at the point of first sale, commonly referred to as the "average price as sold." Since the point of first sale is not the same for all producers, prices for the various methods of sale are weighted by the proportionate quantity sold. For example, if in a given State part of the fruit crop is sold f.o.b. packed by growers, part sold as bulk fruit at the packinghouse door, and some sold retail at roadside stands, the fresh fruit average price as sold is a weighted average of the average price for each method of sale.

The annual estimates are checked and adjusted at the end of each marketing season on the basis of shipment and processing records from transportation agencies, processors, cooperative marketing associations, and other industry organizations. The estimates are reviewed (and revised if necessary) at 5-year intervals, when the Census of Agriculture data become available. The Department's available statistics are limited to the major tree fruits and nuts and to grapes, cranberries, and strawberries, and exclude some States where census data indicate production is of only minor importance.

Table 5-1.—Fruits and planted nuts: Bearing area, United States, 2009–2018

Year	Citrus fruits [1]	Major deciduous fruits [2]	Miscellaneous Noncitrus [3]	Nuts [4]	Total
			Acres		
2009	844,800	1,739,670	306,280	1,159,700	4,050,450
2010	825,200	1,750,300	309,995	1,206,000	4,091,495
2011	809,200	1,744,240	315,510	1,261,500	4,130,450
2012	801,800	1,734,600	260,710	1,316,000	4,113,110
2013	791,200	1,757,980	347,950	1,409,000	4,306,130
2014	777,700	1,742,290	368,955	1,487,000	4,375,945
2015	764,900	1,729,230	371,150	1,533,000	4,398,280
2016	737,800	1,693,970	367,460	1,971,200	4,770,430
2017	709,800	1,680,250	351,680	2,076,800	4,818,530
2018	697,900	1,551,800	329,460	2,174,800	4,753,960

[1] Grapefruit, lemons, oranges, tangelos, and tangerines. [2] Commercial apples, apricots, cherries, grapes, nectarines, peaches, pears, plums, and prunes. [3] Avocados, bananas, berries, coffee, cranberries, dates, figs, guavas, kiwifruit, olives, papayas, and strawberries. [4] Almonds, hazelnuts, macadamia nuts, pistachios, and walnuts. Bearing acreage estimates for pecans began in 2016.
NASS, Crops Branch, (202) 720–2127.

FRUITS, TREE NUTS, AND HORTICULTURAL SPECIALTIES

Table 5-2.—Fruits: Total production in tons, United States, 2010–2019 [1]

Year	Apples, commercial crop [2]	Pears	Grapes (fresh basis)	Sweet cherries	Tart cherries	Apricots
	Tons					
2010	4,641,050	813,600	7,432,120	313,220	95,200	66,380
2011	4,719,800	965,720	7,408,740	334,415	115,900	66,650
2012	4,496,150	851,240	7,530,883	424,000	42,600	60,800
2013	5,261,700	877,130	8,631,790	332,090	147,100	61,035
2014	5,931,550	831,610	7,883,830	363,640	152,100	64,928
2015	5,051,250	816,520	7,621,150	335,480	126,250	45,657
2016	5,747,500	738,770	7,697,030	350,240	164,650	64,050
2017	5,776,850	737,450	7,383,850	437,550	129,750	45,650
2018	5,120,000	805,500	7,596,000	344,400	149,150	39,550
2019	5,509,000	729,000	6,871,000	354,300	131,000	51,300

Year	Figs [3] (CA) (fresh basis)	Plums (CA)	Prunes (dry basis) (CA)	Olives (CA)	Strawberries	Avocados [4]
	Tons					
2010	40,910	142,000	130,000	206,000	1,426,000	174,330
2011	38,660	160,000	137,000	71,200	1,450,800	262,950
2012	35,200	115,000	138,000	160,000	1,526,000	(NA)
2013	33,000	100,600	85,000	166,000	1,523,500	182,920
2014	33,400	104,000	108,000	95,000	1,511,850	172,940
2015	31,700	92,500	112,000	179,000	1,532,750	228,990
2016	32,700	108,800	54,000	164,900	1,480,345	138,050
2017	31,200	117,900	105,000	192,300	1,360,400	187,680
2018	(NA)	107,500	88,000	53,600	1,304,995	185,770
2019	(NA)	101,500	90,190	167,500	1,126,000	135,620

Year	Nectarines	Oranges [5]	Tangerines and Mandarins [5][6]	Grapefruit [5]	Lemons [5]	Tangelos [5][7] (FL)
	Tons					
2010	233,200	8,243,000	596,000	1,238,000	882,000	41,000
2011	225,200	8,905,000	657,000	1,264,000	920,000	52,000
2012	188,900	8,982,000	644,000	1,153,000	850,000	52,000
2013	162,100	8,268,000	682,000	1,204,000	912,000	45,000
2014	187,300	6,768,000	732,000	1,047,000	824,000	40,000
2015	159,500	6,353,000	863,000	910,000	904,000	30,000
2016	151,350	6,088,000	935,000	803,000	904,000	18,000
2017	141,850	5,088,000	1,029,000	698,000	882,000	(NA)
2018	120,500	3,875,000	804,000	509,000	888,000	(NA)
2019	134,000	5,427,000	1,107,000	604,000	1,002,000	(NA)

Year	Bananas [3]	Kiwifruit (CA)	Dates	Papayas (HI) [8]	Peaches	Cranberries
	Tons					
2010	8,900	32,700	29,000	15,050	1,149,430	340,410
2011	8,700	37,700	33,300	14,300	1,071,270	385,685
2012	(NA)	29,600	31,100	(NA)	968,070	402,250
2013	7,250	27,600	30,500	12,100	905,371	447,870
2014	6,000	28,500	33,400	11,750	852,799	420,000
2015	4,530	20,900	39,000	12,600	844,780	428,150
2016	2,775	28,300	37,340	9,875	791,940	481,370
2017	3,330	33,600	43,320	11,125	700,770	419,703
2018	(NA)	37,800	41,050	5,145	651,500	446,300
2019	(NA)	51,500	61,400	5,290	681,600	395,850

(NA) Not available.   [1] For some crops in certain years, production includes some quantities unharvested for economic reasons or excess cullage fruit.   [2] Estimates of the commercial crop refer to production in orchards of 100 or more bearing-age trees.   [3] Estimates discontinued in 2018.   [4] Year of bloom.   [5] Year harvest was complete.   [6] Beginning in 2015, tangerine and mandarin estimates are discontinued for Arizona.   [7] Beginning in 2016, tangelos are included in tangerines and mandarins.   [8] Utilized production.

NASS, Crops Branch, (202) 720–2127.

Table 5-3.—Apples, commercial crop: Production and season average price per pound, by State and United States, 2017–2019

State	Total production			Utilized production			Price per pound for crop of—		
	2017	2018	2019	2017	2018	2019	2017	2018	2019
	Million pounds						Dollars		
California	230.0	248.0	305.0	225.0	243.0	302.0	0.333	0.272	0.241
Connecticut [1]	29.5	(NA)	(NA)	29.3	(NA)	(NA)	0.679	(NA)	(NA)
Idaho [1]	47.4	(NA)	(NA)	45.0	(NA)	(NA)	0.181	(NA)	(NA)
Illinois [1]	22.4	(NA)	(NA)	21.4	(NA)	(NA)	0.647	(NA)	(NA)
Maine [1]	39.2	(NA)	(NA)	37.5	(NA)	(NA)	0.439	(NA)	(NA)
Maryland [1]	48.4	(NA)	(NA)	48.0	(NA)	(NA)	0.193	(NA)	(NA)
Massachusetts [1]	49.6	(NA)	(NA)	48.5	(NA)	(NA)	0.382	(NA)	(NA)
Michigan	900.0	1,035.0	946.0	899.0	1,034.0	945.1	0.303	0.276	0.274
Minnesota [1]	25.7	(NA)	(NA)	24.2	(NA)	(NA)	0.864	(NA)	(NA)
New Jersey [1]	38.5	(NA)	(NA)	37.0	(NA)	(NA)	0.943	(NA)	(NA)
New York	1,350.0	1,395.0	1,320.0	1,330.0	1,376.8	1,318.6	0.269	0.191	0.209
North Carolina [1] ..	104.0	(NA)	(NA)	102.0	(NA)	(NA)	0.247	(NA)	(NA)
Ohio [1]	58.9	(NA)	(NA)	58.4	(NA)	(NA)	0.474	(NA)	(NA)
Oregon	175.2	170.0	150.0	175.0	169.0	148.0	0.221	0.327	0.262
Pennsylvania	528.0	488.0	507.0	526.0	484.1	506.0	0.223	0.222	0.210
Vermont [1]	30.9	(NA)	(NA)	30.7	(NA)	(NA)	0.742	(NA)	(NA)
Virginia	225.0	204.0	190.0	224.0	201.9	188.1	0.217	0.185	0.184
Washington	7,500.0	6,700.0	7,600.0	7,200.0	6,365.0	7,220.0	0.338	0.336	0.271
West Virginia [1]	102.0	(NA)	(NA)	101.0	(NA)	(NA)	0.179	(NA)	(NA)
Wisconsin [1]	49.0	(NA)	(NA)	47.9	(NA)	(NA)	0.549	(NA)	(NA)
United States	11,553.7	10,240.0	11,018.0	11,209.9	9,873.8	10,627.8	0.321	0.299	0.258

-Represents zero. (NA) Not available. [1] Estimates discontinued in 2018.
NASS, Crops Branch, (202) 720–2127.

Table 5-4.—Apples: Production and value, United States, 2010–2019

Year	Apples, commercial crop			
	Total production	Utilized production	Marketing year average price [1]	Value
	Million pounds	Million pounds	Cents per pound	1,000 dollars
2010	9,282.1	9,205.0	25.1	2,310,982
2011	9,439.6	9,328.8	30.3	2,830,784
2012	8,992.3	8,926.5	37.1	3,314,996
2013	10,523.4	10,431.7	30.2	3,147,435
2014	11,863.1	11,269.9	25.6	2,886,900
2015	10,102.5	10,022.9	33.6	3,365,665
2016	11,495.0	11,045.6	31.6	3,492,607
2017	11,553.7	11,209.9	32.1	3,601,447
2018	10,240.0	9,873.8	29.9	2,954,219
2019	11,018.0	10,627.8	25.8	2,746,225

[1] Fresh fruit prices are equivalent packinghouse-door returns for California, Michigan, New York, Pennsylvania, and Washington; prices at point of first sale for other States. Processing prices are equivalent at processing plant door.
NASS, Crops Branch, (202) 720–2127.

Table 5-5.—International Apples, fresh: Production, 2016/2017–2018/2019

Country	2016/2017	2017/2018	2018/2019
	metric tons		
China	40,393,000	41,390,000	31,000,000
European Union	12,722,620	10,013,600	14,008,570
United States	5,010,201	5,084,727	5,048,000
Turkey	2,900,000	2,750,000	3,000,000
Iran	2,799,200	2,799,200	2,799,200
India	2,258,000	1,920,000	2,300,000
Russia	1,509,148	1,359,580	1,503,100
Chile	1,310,000	1,330,000	1,264,000
Ukraine	1,099,200	1,099,200	1,099,200
Brazil	1,049,300	1,049,300	1,049,300
South Africa	902,130	790,000	840,000
Japan	765,000	765,000	765,000
Mexico	716,930	714,149	660,000
Argentina	560,000	560,000	590,000
New Zealand	523,000	575,500	561,000
Belarus	509,300	509,300	509,300
Canada	408,404	345,568	395,300
Serbia	328,400	328,400	328,400
Australia	308,300	308,300	308,300
Azerbaijan	254,300	254,300	254,300
Kazakhstan	188,100	188,100	188,100
Kyrgyzstan	135,600	135,600	135,600
Uruguay	37,700	37,700	37,700
Guatemala	26,500	26,500	26,500
Norway	12,400	12,400	12,400
Colombia	2,300	2,300	2,300
Taiwan	1,483	1,451	1,500
World Total	76,730,516	74,350,175	68,687,070

FAS, Office of Global Analysis, (202) 720-6301. Prepared or estimated on the basis of official USDA production, supply, and distribution statistics from foreign governments.

Table 5-6.—Apples, commercial crop: Production and utilization, United States, 2009–2018

Crop of—	Total production	Utilized production	Utilization				
			Fresh	Processed (fresh basis)			
				Canned	Dried	Frozen	Juice, cider & other [1]
	Million pounds						
2009	9,687.7	9,435.6	6,296.4	1,158.2	161.2	236.2	1,583.6
2010	9,282.1	9,205.0	6,248.8	1,088.3	175.5	206.0	1,486.4
2011	9,439.6	9,328.8	6,312.9	1,123.7	183.5	190.5	1,517.8
2012	8,992.3	8,926.5	6,594.9	748.9	223.0	66.6	1,292.8
2013	10,523.4	10,431.7	6,918.7	1,311.2	161.0	249.3	1,791.0
2014	11,863.1	11,269.9	7,909.0	1,161.5	171.0	250.5	1,767.8
2015	10,102.5	10,022.9	6,928.1	1,121.1	179.0	187.5	1,527.5
2016	11,495.0	11,045.6	7,745.1	1,211.1	339.2	137.5	1,478.6
2017	11,553.7	11,209.9	7,815.8	1,161.9	370.0	119.0	1,574.8
2018	10,257.0	9,890.8	6,865.1	(NA)	(NA)	(NA)	(NA)

[1] Includes vinegar, wine, and slices for pie making.
NASS, Crops Branch, (202) 720-2127.

Table 5-7.—Apples, commercial crop: Production and utilization, by State and United States, crop of 2017 and 2018

State	Total production	Utilized production	Utilization				
			Fresh	Processed (fresh basis)			
				Canned	Dried	Frozen	Juice, cider & other [1]
			2017				
			Million pounds				
California	230.0	225.0	(D)	....	....	....	....
Connecticut	29.5	29.3	25.9	....	....	....	....
Idaho	47.4	45.0	24.6	....	....	....	....
Illinois	22.4	21.4	(D)	....	....	....	....
Maine	39.2	37.5	27.5	....	....	....	....
Maryland	48.4	48.0	16.4	....	....	....	....
Massachusetts	49.6	48.5	31.0	....	....	....	....
Michigan	900.0	899.0	490.0	210.0	....	....	75.0
Minnesota	25.7	24.2	22.0	....	....	....	....
New Jersey	38.5	37.0	28.0	....	....	....	....
New York	1,350.0	1,330.0	735.0	252.0	....	....	284.0
North Carolina	104.0	102.0	52.0	....	....	....	....
Ohio	58.9	58.4	48.5	....	....	....	....
Oregon	175.2	175.0	148.0	....	....	....	....
Pennsylvania	528.0	526.0	236.0	220.0	....	....	38.0
Vermont	30.9	30.7	24.3	....	....	....	....
Virginia	225.0	224.0	91.0	....	....	....	....
Washington	7,500.0	7,200.0	5,650.0	(D)	....	....	(D)
West Virginia	102.0	101.0	36.0	....	....	....	....
Wisconsin	49.0	47.9	37.0	....	....	....	....
Other States [2]	....	....	92.6	479.9	....	....	997.8
United States	11,553.7	11,209.9	7,815.8	1,161.9	370.0	123.0	1,574.8

State	Total production	Utilized production	Fresh
	2018		
	Million pounds		
California	250.0	245.0	(D)
Connecticut [3]	(NA)	(NA)	(NA)
Idaho [3]	(NA)	(NA)	(NA)
Illinois [3]	(NA)	(NA)	(NA)
Maine [3]	(NA)	(NA)	(NA)
Maryland [3]	(NA)	(NA)	(NA)
Massachusetts [3] ...	(NA)	(NA)	(NA)
Michigan	1,050.0	1,049.0	545.0
Minnesota [3]	(NA)	(NA)	(NA)
New Jersey [3]	(NA)	(NA)	(NA)
New York	1,395.0	1,376.8	747.7
North Carolina [3] ...	(NA)	(NA)	(NA)
Ohio [3]	(NA)	(NA)	(NA)
Oregon	170.0	169.0	(D)
Pennsylvania	488.0	484.1	233.8
Vermont [3]	(NA)	(NA)	(NA)
Virginia	204.0	201.9	83.6
Washington	6,700.0	6,365.0	5,025.0
West Virginia [3]	(NA)	(NA)	(NA)
Wisconsin [3]	(NA)	(NA)	(NA)
Other States [2]	-	-	230.0
United States	10,257.0	9,890.8	6,865.1

(D) Data withheld to avoid disclosing data for individual operations. [1] Includes vinegar, wine, and slices for pie making. [2] Includes data withheld above and/or data for States not listed in this table. [3] Estimates discontinued in 2018.
NASS, Crops Branch, (202) 720–2127.

Table 5-8.—Fruits, fresh: United States exports by country of destination, 2018–2020

Country	2018	2019	2020
	Metric tons		
Fresh fruits, deciduous:			
Mexico	462,750	424,823	401,600
Canada	351,061	340,355	337,734
Taiwan	81,052	116,027	74,962
Vietnam	53,007	70,956	63,263
India	152,783	58,589	43,009
Hong Kong	58,057	49,165	38,825
Korea, South	41,164	31,844	36,108
Indonesia	35,029	39,692	33,431
Japan	23,349	24,401	27,011
Dominican Republic	24,949	25,787	26,224
Guatemala	16,871	18,386	22,244
China	31,984	25,676	20,981
Thailand	21,778	26,779	18,888
Saudi Arabia	20,865	20,140	18,582
United Arab Emirates	24,636	16,988	17,979
Colombia	13,385	11,841	17,016
Israel(*)	14,478	10,871	14,848
Australia(*)	20,729	20,667	14,339
Philippines	23,227	24,366	13,863
El Salvador	11,609	11,223	12,307
Malaysia	18,989	11,094	11,610
Honduras	9,322	10,713	11,603
Singapore	13,096	12,645	10,640
Costa Rica	12,511	8,768	9,695
Peru	4,697	7,064	9,557
New Zealand(*)	9,864	9,799	8,567
Panama	7,319	6,119	8,552
Ecuador	6,100	7,006	4,956
Trinidad and Tobago	4,832	4,961	4,339
Chile	3,734	3,990	3,898
Rest of World	40,840	35,274	40,376
World Total	1,614,064	1,486,008	1,377,007

(*) Denotes a country that is a summarization of its component countries. All zeroes for a data item may show that statistics exist in the other import type. Consumption or General. Users should use cautious interpretation on Quantity reports using mixed units of measure. Quantity line items will only include statistics on the units of measure that are equal to, or are able to be converted to, the assigned unit of measure of the grouped commodities.

FAS, Office of Global Analysis, (202) 720-6301. Data Source: U.S. Census Bureau Trade Data.

Table 5-9.—Apples: Foreign trade, United States, 2010–2019 [1]

Year beginning October	Imports, fresh and dried, in terms of fresh	Domestic exports	
		Fresh	Dried, in terms of fresh [1]
	Metric tons	Metric tons	Metric tons
2010	184,475	817,906	26,802
2011	219,305	856,819	28,492
2012	243,093	908,751	22,282
2013	243,875	848,671	23,741
2014	209,498	1,057,853	26,092
2015	233,564	746,893	27,894
2016	220,426	880,567	25,397
2017	181,398	996,529	18,652
2018	193,081	742,829	13,172
2019	149,149	858,658	9,362

[1] Dried converted to terms of fresh apples on following basis; 1 pound dried is equivalent to 8 pounds fresh. No re-exports reported.

ERS, Crops Branch, (816) 412–4162.

Table 5-10.—Apricots: Production and value, United States, 2010–2019

Year	Total production	Utilized production	Market year average price per ton	Value
	Tons	Tons	Dollars	1,000 dollars
2010	66,380	66,350	722.00	47,876
2011	66,650	66,620	616.00	41,056
2012	60,800	60,770	673.00	40,879
2013	61,035	61,028	737.00	44,987
2014	64,928	64,918	818.00	53,096
2015	45,657	45,507	1,010.00	45,889
2016	64,050	63,950	898.00	57,402
2017	45,650	45,500	979.00	44,556
2018	39,550	39,380	1,210.00	47,469
2019	51,300	51,180	1,000.00	51,392

NASS, Crops Branch, (202) 720–2127.

Table 5-11.—Apricots: Production and marketing year average price per ton, by State and United States, 2017–2019

State	Total production			Utilized production			Price for crop of—		
	2017	2018	2019	2017	2018	2019	2017	2018	2019
	Tons	Tons	Tons	Tons	Tons	Tons	Dollars	Dollars	Dollars
California	37,000	31,700	43,900	36,900	31,570	43,810	945.00	1,210.00	923.00
Washington	8,650	7,850	7,400	8,600	7,810	7,370	1,130.00	1,210.00	1,490.00
United States ..	45,650	39,550	51,300	45,500	39,380	51,180	979.00	1,210.00	1,000.00

NASS, Crops Branch, (202) 720–2127.

Table 5-12.—Apricots: Production and utilization, United States, 2009–2018

Crop of—	Total production	Utilized production	Utilization of quantities sold		
			Fresh	Processed [1]	
				Canned	Dried (fresh basis)
	Tons	*Tons*	*Tons*	*Tons*	*Tons*
2009	68,720	68,690	25,170	23,120	9,000
2010	66,380	66,350	23,510	20,340	10,000
2011	66,650	66,620	23,990	17,230	12,000
2012	60,800	60,770	23,130	16,640	9,500
2013	61,035	61,028	25,228	14,550	10,000
2014	64,928	64,918	25,812	17,550	9,500
2015	45,657	45,507	19,104	9,000	9,000
2016	64,050	63,950	28,500	13,350	11,000
2017	45,650	45,500	22,300	8,400	(D)
2018	39,550	39,370	23,870	(NA)	(NA)

(D) Withheld to avoid disclosure of individual operations. (NA) Not available. [1] California only. Estimates discontinued in 2018.
NASS, Crops Branch, (202) 720–2127.

Table 5-13.—Apricots: Production and utilization, by State and United States, crop of 2018

State	Total production	Utilized production	Utilization	
			Fresh	Processed
			Tons	
California	31,700	31,570	(D)	(D)
Washington	7,850	7,800	(D)	(D)
Other States [1]	....	....	23,870	15,500
United States	39,550	39,370	23,870	15,500

(D) Withheld to avoid disclosure of individual operations. [1] Includes data withheld above.
NASS, Crops Branch, (202) 720–2127.

Table 5-14.—Apricots: Foreign trade, United States, 2010–2019

Year beginning October	Domestic exports				
	Fresh	Canned [1]	Dried [1]	Dried, in fruit salad [2]	Total, in terms of fresh [3]
	Metric tons	*Metric tons*	*Metric tons*	*Metric tons*	*Metric tons*
2010	5,646	1,389	708	470	10,283
2011	7,459	660	634	519	11,191
2012	7,774	646	533	547	10,978
2013	6,859	755	473	504	9,831
2014	5,402	621	370	409	7,749
2015	7,249	508	668	214	11,045
2016	7,775	718	894	163	12,887
2017	4,458	666	749	88	8,784
2018	5,010	560	859	106	9,828
2019	3,878	484	1,230	71	10,549

[1] Net processed weight. [2] Dried apricots are 12⅓ percent of total dried fruit for salad. [3] Dried fruit converted to unprocessed dry weight by dividing by 1.07. Unprocessed dry weight converted to terms of fresh fruit on the basis that 1 pound dried equals 5.5 pounds fresh. Canned apricots converted to terms of fresh on the basis that 1 pound canned equals 0.717 pounds fresh.
ERS, Crops Branch, (816) 412–4162.

Table 5-15.—Avocados: Foreign trade, United States, 2010–2019

Year beginning October	Imports
	Metric tons
2010	385,434
2011	475,630
2012	565,127
2013	699,388
2014	832,841
2015	874,209
2016	877,043
2017	1,017,273
2018	1,083,929
2019	1,097,343

ERS, Crops Branch, (816) 412–4162.

Table 5-16.—Avocados: Total production, marketing year average price per ton, and value of utilized production, by State and United States, 2010/2011 to 2019/2020

Season	California			Florida		
	Production	Price per ton	Value	Production	Price per ton	Value
	Tons	*Dollars*	*1,000 dollars*	*Tons*	*Dollars*	*1,000 dollars*
2010/2011	151,500	3,040.00	460,560	22,500	800.00	18,000
2011/2012	231,500	1,650.00	381,975	31,100	756.00	23,512
2012/2013	(NA)	(NA)	(NA)	(NA)	(NA)	(NA)
2013/2014	149,000	2,240.00	333,760	33,400	796.00	26,586
2014/2015	140,000	2,170.00	303,800	32,500	656.00	21,320
2015/2016	201,000	2,050.00	412,050	27,300	745.00	20,339
2016/2017	113,000	3,140.00	351,240	24,100	798.00	19,080
2017/2018	170,000	2,260.00	382,460	16,900	477.00	8,014
2018/2019	171,000	2,270.00	383,485	13,900	1,120.00	15,278
2019/2020	109,000	3,440.00	373,185	25,800	923.00	23,565

Season	Hawaii			United States		
	Production	Price per ton	Value	Production	Price per ton	Value
	Tons	*Dollars*	*1,000 dollars*	*Tons*	*Dollars*	*1,000 dollars*
2010/2011	330	1,540.00	508	174,330	2,750.00	479,068
2011/2012	350	1,600.00	560	262,950	1,540.00	406,047
2012/2013	(NA)	(NA)	(NA)	(NA)	(NA)	(NA)
2013/2014	520	2,000.00	1,040	182,920	1,980.00	361,386
2014/2015	440	2,860.00	1,258	172,940	1,890.00	326,378
2015/2016	690	2,310.00	1,481	228,990	1,900.00	433,870
2016/2017	950	2,150.00	1,934	138,050	2,720.00	372,254
2017/2018	780	2,080.00	1,538	187,680	2,100.00	392,012
2018/2019	870	2,040.00	1,591	185,770	2,180.00	400,354
2019/2020	820	2,450.00	1,787	135,620	2,960.00	398,537

(NA) Not available.
NASS, Crops Branch, (202) 720–2127.

Table 5-17.—Bananas: Bearing acreage, yield, utilized production, marketing year average price, and value, Hawaii, 2008–2017 [1]

Year	Bearing acreage	Yield per acre	Utilized Production	Price per pound	Value
	Acres	1,000 pounds	1,000 pounds	Cents	1,000 dollars
2008	1,100	15.8	17,400	46.0	8,004
2009	1,100	16.8	18,500	55.0	10,175
2010	1,100	16.2	17,800	60.0	10,680
2011	1,000	17.4	17,400	65.0	11,310
2012	(NA)	(NA)	(NA)	(NA)	(NA)
2013	1,250	11.6	14,500	90.0	13,050
2014	1,210	9.9	12,000	82.0	9,840
2015	1,150	8.0	9,060	91.2	8,265
2016	1,050	5.3	5,550	101.0	5,592
2017	950	7.0	6,610	91.2	6,028

(NA) Not available.   [1] Estimates discontinued in 2018.
NASS, Crops Branch, (202) 720–2127.

Table 5-18.—Kiwifruit: Area, yield, utilized production, marketing year average price, and value, California, 2010–2019

Year	Bearing acreage	Yield [1]	Utilized Production	Price per ton	Value
	Acres	Tons	Tons	Dollars	1,000 dollars
2010	4,200	7.79	32,500	768	24,961
2011	4,000	8.98	36,700	775	28,439
2012	3,700	8.00	27,100	1,020	27,508
2013	3,800	7.26	26,900	1,110	29,812
2014	3,700	7.70	27,900	1,190	33,333
2015	3,500	5.97	20,900	1,470	30,723
2016	3,900	7.26	28,300	1,570	44,431
2017	3,600	9.33	33,200	1,050	34,860
2018	3,900	9.70	37,800	1,470	55,566
2019	4,400	11.70	51,190	1,680	85,999

[1] Yield based on total production.
NASS, Crops Branch, (202) 720-2127.

Table 5-19.—Cherries: Foreign trade, United States, 2010–2019

Year beginning October	Imports		Domestic exports	
	Fresh	Dried and preserved	Fresh	Canned
	Metric tons	Metric tons	Metric tons	Metric tons
2010	23,126	5,076	71,542	13,544
2011	17,250	6,289	101,073	16,127
2012	10,362	6,350	66,937	14,491
2013	12,033	6,614	87,626	17,761
2014	16,096	10,517	74,707	19,035
2015	11,463	8,067	75,952	17,465
2016	12,422	8,054	111,772	17,107
2017	14,512	8,477	86,648	18,805
2018	10,002	8,978	84,291	12,812
2019	9,902	8,055	66,919	10,270

ERS, Crops Branch, (816) 412–4162.

Table 5-20.—Sweet cherries: Production and value, United States, 2010–2019

Year	Total production	Utilized production	Marketing year average price per ton [1]	Value
	Tons	Tons	Dollars	1,000 dollars
2010	313,220	307,630	2,330.00	715,684
2011	334,415	330,290	2,530.00	834,585
2012	424,000	418,415	2,020.00	843,313
2013	332,090	295,950	2,610.00	771,798
2014	363,640	358,910	2,140.00	766,551
2015	335,480	333,886	2,250.00	751,122
2016	350,240	343,090	2,250.00	773,021
2017	437,550	433,020	2,060.00	891,652
2018	344,400	342,070	1,860.00	637,700
2019	354,300	348,770	1,890.00	659,781

[1] Fresh fruit prices are equivalent packinghouse-door returns for Western States, and the average price as sold for other States. Quantities processed are priced at the equivalent processing plant door level.
NASS, Crops Branch, (202) 720–2127.

Table 5-21.—Tart cherries: Production and value, United States, 2010–2019

Year	Total production	Utilized production	Marketing year average price per pound [1]	Value
	Million pounds	Million pounds	Dollars	1,000 dollars
2010	190.4	183.2	0.222	40,741
2011	231.8	230.3	0.300	69,072
2012	85.2	85.0	0.594	50,520
2013	294.2	291.1	0.359	104,395
2014	304.2	300.6	0.355	106,810
2015	252.5	251.1	0.347	87,037
2016	329.3	318.7	0.274	87,335
2017	259.5	254.1	0.224	56,868
2018	298.3	288.8	0.196	56,635
2019	262.0	263.3	0.151	35,747

[1] Fresh fruit prices are equivalent packinghouse-door returns for Western States, and the average price as sold for other States. Quantities processed are priced at the equivalent processing plant door level.
NASS, Crops Branch, (202) 720–2127.

Table 5-22.—Sweet cherries: Production and season average price, by State and United States, 2017–2019

State	Total production			Utilized production			Price [1]		
	2017	2018	2019	2017	2018	2019	2017	2018	2019
	Tons	Tons	Tons	Tons	Tons	Tons	Dollars per ton	Dollars per ton	Dollars per ton
California	97,800	44,800	58,100	95,000	44,170	54,300	3,480.00	3,180.00	3,520.00
Michigan [2]	21,300	(NA)	(NA)	21,020	(NA)	(NA)	765.00	(NA)	(NA)
Oregon	55,900	54,600	57,200	55,400	54,100	56,630	1,270.00	1,310.00	1,330.00
Washington	262,550	245,000	239,000	261,600	243,800	237,810	1,810.00	1,750.00	1,660.00
United States	437,550	437,550	354,300	433,020	342,070	348,770	2,060.00	1,860.00	1,890.00

(NA) Not available. [1] Fresh fruit prices are equivalent packinghouse-door returns for California, Oregon, and Washington, and the average price as sold for other States. Quantities processed are priced at the equivalent processing plant door level. [2] Estimates discontinued in 2018.
NASS, Crops Branch, (202) 720–2127.

Table 5-23.—Tart cherries: Production and season average price, by State and United States, 2017–2019

State	Total production			Utilized production			Price [1]		
	2017	2018	2019	2017	2018	2019	2017	2018	2019
	Million pounds	Million pounds	Million pounds	Million pounds	Million pounds	Million pounds	Dollars per Lb.	Dollars per Lb.	Dollars per Lb.
Michigan	189.2	201.0	170.0	188.0	198.2	157.6	0.211	0.191	0.143
New York	8.0	(D)	4.3	7.7	(D)	4.3	0.316	(D)	0.172
Utah	26.0	45.0	54.0	25.0	41.0	42.7	0.304	0.222	0.156
Washington	25.0	(D)	24.6	24.0	(D)	23.1	0.210	(D)	0.211
Wisconsin	11.3	10.9	9.1	9.4	10.0	8.6	0.224	0.193	0.109
Other States	....	41.4	....	....	39.6	....	(X)	0.194	(X)
United States	259.5	298.3	262.0	254.1	288.8	236.3	0.224	0.196	0.151

(D) Withheld to avoid disclosing data for individual operations. (X) Not applicable. [1] Fresh fruit prices are equivalent packinghouse-door returns for Oregon and Washington, and the average price as sold for other States. Quantities processed are priced at the equivalent processing plant door level.
NASS, Crops Branch, (202) 720–2127.

Table 5-24.—Sweet cherries: Production and utilization, by State and United States, crop of 2018 [1]

State	Total production	Utilized production	Utilization		
			Fresh [1]	Processed [2]	
				Canned	Brined
			Tons		
California	44,800	44,170	35,660	....	....
Michigan [2]	(NA)	(NA)	(NA)	....	....
Oregon	54,600	54,100	41,000	....	(NA)
Washington	245,000	243,800	214,400	(NA)	(NA)
United States	344,400	343,090	291,060	(NA)	(NA)

- Represents zero. (NA) Not available. [1] Includes "Home use." [2] Estimates discontinued in 2018.
NASS, Crops Branch, (202) 720–2127.

Table 5-25.—Tart cherries: Production and utilization, by State and United States, crop of 2018 [1]

State	Total production	Utilized production	Utilization		
			Fresh [1]	Processed	
				Canned [2]	Frozen [2]
			Million pounds		
Michigan	201.0	198.2	0.2	(NA)	(NA)
New York	(D)	(D)	(D)	....	....
Utah	45.0	41.0	....	....	....
Washington	(D)	(D)	(D)	....	....
Wisconsin	10.9	10.0	0.3	....	....
Other States [3]	41.4	39.6	0.3	(NA)	(NA)
United States	298.3	288.8	0.8	(NA)	(NA)

(D) Withheld to avoid disclosing data for individual operations. (NA) Not available. [1] Includes "Home use." [2] Estimates discontinued in 2018. [3] Includes data withheld above and/or data for States not listed in this table.
NASS, Crops Branch, (202) 720–2127.

Table 5-26.—Sweet cherries: Production and utilization, United States, 2009–2018

Crop of—	Total production	Utilized production	Utilization of quantities sold		
			Fresh [1]	Processed	
				Other [2]	Brined
			Tons		
2009	442,870	385,625	296,750	29,053	51,571
2010	313,220	307,630	244,340	21,905	38,234
2011	334,415	330,290	258,920	25,495	39,625
2012	424,000	418,415	332,555	35,795	47,065
2013	332,090	295,950	217,950	28,535	44,945
2014	363,640	358,910	268,010	40,360	47,041
2015	335,480	333,886	250,806	....	43,090
2016	350,240	343,090	257,860	....	51,600
2017	437,550	433,020	348,920	....	51,850
2018	344,400	342,070	291,060	....	....

[1] Includes "Home use."   [2] Includes canned utilization and other processed utilizations from all States.
NASS, Crops Branch, (202) 720–2127.

Table 5-27.—Tart cherries: Production and utilization, United States, 2009–2018

Crop of—	Total production	Utilized production	Utilization of quantities sold		
			Fresh [1]	Processed	
				Other [2]	Frozen
			Million pounds		
2009	359.2	320.8	1.3	35.3	232.0
2010	190.4	183.2	0.8	21.2	125.9
2011	231.8	230.3	0.5	37.3	154.1
2012	85.2	85.0	0.4	18.3	59.8
2013	294.2	291.1	1.2	92.4	158.4
2014	304.2	300.6	1.9	63.3	198.9
2015	252.5	251.1	1.2	....	175.4
2016	329.3	318.7	0.6	....	240.6
2017	259.5	254.1	0.8	....	169.8
2018	298.3	288.8	0.8	....	....

[1] Includes "Home use."   [2] Includes canned utilization and other processed utilizations from all states.
NASS, Crops Branch, (202) 720–2127.

Table 5-28.—Citrus fruit: Utilized production and value, United States, for season of 2010/2011 to 2019/2020

Season [1]	Production	Marketing year average returns per box [2]	Value	Quantities processed
	Oranges [3]			
	1,000 boxes	*Dollars*	*1,000 dollars*	*1,000 boxes*
2010/2011	204,949	10.90	2,230,412	148,237
2011/2012	206,119	12.70	2,621,620	149,972
2012/2013	189,893	10.85	2,073,638	134,799
2013/2014	155,977	14.29	2,254,303	109,376
2014/2015	146,602	13.29	1,963,353	102,388
2015/2016	141,891	13.55	1,927,270	91,791
2016/2017	118,520	16.30	1,943,678	74,437
2017/2018	91,130	19.82	1,830,445	50,081
2018/2019	126,550	14.43	1,765,347	84,380
2019/2020	121,940	14.06	1,714,690	75,312
	Grapefruit			
2010/2011	30,360	9.29	283,597	14,276
2011/2012	27,650	10.08	279,033	13,121
2012/2013	28,950	8.87	256,524	14,340
2013/2014	25,200	9.60	241,686	12,389
2014/2015	21,950	9.85	216,258	9,755
2015/2016	19,400	13.09	254,318	8,794
2016/2017	16,960	15.12	256,917	7,123
2017/2018	12,480	16.71	207,970	5,136
2018/2019	14,810	13.69	202,712	7,889
2019/2020	13,050	16.03	199,621	4,113
	Lemons			
2010/2011	23,000	16.80	386,514	7,987
2011/2012	21,250	21.12	448,698	4,869
2012/2013	22,800	17.56	400,295	7,394
2013/2014	20,600	31.13	641,259	4,840
2014/2015	22,600	30.83	696,835	7,302
2015/2016	22,600	33.41	755,086	5,224
2016/2017	22,050	34.62	763,446	4,535
2017/2018	22,200	32.24	715,761	5,195
2018/2019	25,050	29.92	730,843	6,620
2019/2020	27,500	24.43	671,929	8,500
	Tangerines and Mandarins [4]			
2010/2011	15,550	20.87	330,503	3,260
2011/2012	15,290	22.34	349,167	3,029
2012/2013	16,440	25.60	426,101	2,785
2013/2014	17,750	31.05	557,357	2,869
2014/2015	21,135	22.13	468,083	5,614
2015/2016	23,115	21.23	490,217	7,657
2016/2017	25,420	22.35	568,084	8,366
2017/2018	19,950	28.86	575,976	4,664
2018/2019	27,490	25.50	700,977	8,647
2019/2020	23,020	35.28	812,199	5,382

[1] The crop year begins with the bloom of the first year shown and ends with completion of harvest the following year. [2] Equivalent packing-house door returns. [3] Includes small quantities of tangerines in Texas and Temples in Florida. [4] Arizona and California tangelos and tangors included. Beginning in 2016/2017, Florida includes tangelos.
NASS, Crops Branch, (202) 720–2127.

Table 5-29.—Citrus fruit: Utilized production and marketing year average returns per box, by State, 2018/2019 and 2019/2020 [1]

Crop and State	Utilized production		Market year average price [2]	
	2018/2019	2019/2020	2018/2019	2019/2020
	1,000 boxes [3]	*1,000 boxes* [3]	*Dollars*	*Dollars*
Oranges				
Early, midseason, and Navel varieties:				
California	42,000	44,300	14.19	15.26
Florida	30,400	29,650	12.86	11.60
Texas	2,210	1,150	8.96	10.70
Total	74,610	75,100	11.19	13.74
Valencia:				
California	10,200	9,000	10.14	17.29
Florida	41,450	37,650	15.67	13.91
Texas	290	190	16.62	21.63
Total	51,940	46,840	15.30	13.88
All oranges:				
California	52,200	53,300	13.40	15.59
Florida	71,850	67,300	14.48	12.89
Texas	2,500	1,340	9.85	12.25
United States	126,550	121,940	14.43	14.06
Grapefruit				
California	4,200	3,800	13.46	17.25
Florida, all	4,510	4,850	17.95	13.45
Red	3,740	4,060	18.02	13.92
White [4]	770	790	17.61	11.05
Texas	6,100	4,400	10.69	10.69
United States	14,810	13,050	13.69	16.03
Lemons				
Arizona	1,350	1,800	31.61	27.77
California	23,700	25,700	29.04	24.20
United States	25,050	27,500	29.92	24.43
Tangerines and Mandarins				
California [5]	26,500	22,000	25.65	35.77
Florida	990	1,020	21.55	24.83
United States	27,490	23,020	25.50	35.28

[1] The crop year begins with the bloom of the first year shown and ends with completion of harvest the following year.   [2] Equivalent packinghouse-door returns.   [3] Net lbs. per box: oranges—California, 80; Florida, 90; and Texas, 85; grapefruit—California, 80, Florida, 95; Florida, 85; Texas, 80; lemons—80; tangerines and mandarins—California, 80.   [4] Includes seedy grapefruit.   [5] Includes tangelos and tangors.
NASS, Crops Branch, (202) 720–2127.

Table 5-30.—International Citrus, fresh: Production in specified countries, 2017/2018-2019/2020

Country	Production		
	2017/2018	2018/2019	2019/2020
	1,000 metric tons		
Grapefruit:			
China	4,800	4,900	4,930
United States	462	512	582
Mexico	418	456	468
South Africa	403	390	420
Turkey	260	250	300
Israel	144	139	155
European Union	107	108	89
Japan	26	26	26
Lemons/limes:			
Mexico	2,311	2,401	2,422
Argentina	1,770	1,800	1,600
European Union	1,472	1,684	1,470
Turkey	1,000	1,100	1,000
United States	806	876	740
South Africa	446	498	530
Israel	65	68	75
Japan	50	42	51
Morocco	36	45	40
United Arab Emirates	5	5	5
Oranges:			
Brazil	15,953	19,380	15,100
China	7,300	7,200	7,300
European Union	6,270	6,505	5,840
United States	3,560	4,833	4,898
Mexico	4,737	4,389	4,417
Egypt	3,120	3,600	3,000
Turkey	1,905	1,900	1,800
South Africa	1,586	1,500	1,560
Morocco	1,021	1,183	815
Vietnam	770	770	770
Argentina	750	800	720
Australia	525	510	500
Costa Rica	315	295	310
Guatemala	180	180	180
Israel	76	68	76
Iraq	75	75	75
Mozambique	68	68	68
Bangladesh	21	21	21
Malaysia	13	13	13
Japan	6	6	6
Tangerines/mandarins:			
China	21,200	22,000	23,000
European Union	2,913	3,213	2,643
Turkey	1,550	1,650	1,500
Japan	968	994	952
Morocco	1,185	1,375	910
United States	729	986	844
Korea, South	577	608	645
South Africa	356	390	420
Argentina	350	450	390
Israel	162	198	200
Thailand	135	135	135
Philippines	13	13	13

FAS, Office of Global Analysis, (202) 720-6301. Prepared or estimated on the basis of official USDA production, supply, and distribution statistics from foreign governments.

Table 5-31.—Fresh fruits, citrus: United States exports by country of destination, 2018–2020

Country of destination	2018	2019	2020
	Metric tons		
Canada	162,499	167,099	178,831
Korea, South	164,211	155,093	161,711
Japan	110,963	118,838	105,437
Hong Kong	94,187	81,733	81,554
Mexico	25,460	39,323	36,548
Australia(*)	16,872	19,911	25,251
China	42,197	24,700	25,056
Taiwan	9,091	16,154	12,280
Singapore	10,104	9,970	11,565
Malaysia	9,388	9,570	9,055
New Zealand(*)	10,133	8,974	7,815
Netherlands	9,856	6,816	7,482
France(*)	6,935	8,909	7,470
Chile	6,918	5,845	4,831
Indonesia	1,371	2,188	3,344
Philippines	3,790	3,967	3,276
Vietnam	113	729	3,222
Peru	2,394	2,599	2,347
Ecuador	891	1,766	2,205
Cayman Islands	299	540	1,736
Dominican Republic	1,411	1,586	1,638
Bahamas, The	1,564	1,707	1,636
Belgium-Luxembourg(*)	1,071	1,170	1,519
Thailand	1,537	1,034	1,277
Guatemala	984	960	1,174
Barbados	577	555	1,108
Panama	595	641	763
Other Pacific Islands, NEC(*)	281	517	579
United Kingdom	833	832	568
Germany(*)	775	52	509
Rest of World	2,613	2,608	2,627
World Total	699,910	696,384	704,413

(*) Denotes a country that is a summarization of its component countries.   Users should use cautious interpretation on quantity reports using mixed units of measure.   Quantity line items will only include statistics on the units of measure that are equal to, or are able to be converted to, the assigned unit of measure of the grouped commodities.
     FAS, Office of Global Analysis,(202) 720–6301.   Data Source: U.S. Census Bureau Trade Data.

Table 5-32.—Fresh citrus fruits: Foreign trade, United States, 2010–2019

Year [1]	Oranges		Grapefruit		Lemons		Limes		Tangerines	
	Imports	Domestic exports	Imports	Domestic exports	Imports	Domestic exports	Imports	Domestic exports	Imports	Domestic exports
	Metric tons	*Metric tons*	*Metric tons*	*Metric tons*	*Metric tons*	*Metric tons*	*Metric tons*	*Metric tons*	*Metric tons*	*Metric tons*
2010	92,159	752,613	7,103	225,836	56,278	97,275	352,956	2,550	6,101	30,419
2011	131,519	694,530	2,869	207,537	50,939	92,081	423,350	3,434	4,202	22,786
2012	130,812	679,660	11,862	182,725	38,152	104,031	438,830	4,389	3,614	23,529
2013	156,261	507,665	13,777	146,673	56,996	122,420	438,273	4,569	2,573	17,628
2014	152,211	523,345	9,291	140,729	85,519	109,663	499,221	3,954	4,565	18,713
2015	166,074	655,187	21,931	123,458	83,851	107,338	542,152	4,433	7,882	12,837
2016	172,345	615,187	26,845	108,030	110,252	106,831	602,749	4,846	2,250	12,916
2017	219,023	511,830	10,216	57,647	110,827	88,565	605,356	5,342	3,550	11,749
2018	195,774	477,218	15,190	57,366	135,860	90,234	643,425	6,734	4,003	11,531
2019	195,470	511,232	14,541	55,109	145,927	86,430	698,638	6,433	3,009	11,616

[1] Year beginning October for all commodities.
ERS, Crops Branch, (816) 412–4162.

Table 5-33.—Concentrated citrus juices: Annual packs, Florida, 2009–2018

Season beginning December	Frozen concentrated juice [1]		
	Orange [2]	Grapefruit [2]	Tangerine
	1,000 gallons	*1,000 gallons*	*1,000 gallons*
2009	82,260	7,904	740
2010	82,106	9,297	1,374
2011	106,432	9,059	1,083
2012	76,132	7,437	928
2013	35,655	5,745	825
2014	28,878	4,504	1,046
2015	22,269	3,275	276
2016	17,916	2,187	....
2017	9,948	600	....
2018	21,012	696	....

[1] Net pack. [2] Frozen orange juice reported in 42.0° Brix; Grapefruit 40.0° Brix. Includes concentrated juice for manufacture.
ERS, Crops Branch, (816) 412–4162.

Table 5-34.—Dates: Area, yield, total production, marketing year average price per ton, and value, California, 2010–2019

Year	Bearing acreage	Yield per acre	Production	Price per ton	Value
	Acres	Tons	Tons	Dollars	1,000 dollars
2010	7,700	3.77	29,000	1,270	36,830
2011	8,400	3.96	33,300	1,320	43,956
2012	8,800	3.53	31,100	1,340	41,674
2013	8,200	3.72	30,500	1,220	37,210
2014	10,000	3.34	33,400	1,510	50,434
2015	10,200	3.82	39,000	1,560	60,840
2016	12,300	3.04	37,340	2,020	75,156
2017	13,400	3.23	43,320	3,510	150,959
2018	15,000	2.74	41,050	3,800	152,175
2019	15,400	3.99	61,400	3,650	223,778

NASS, Crops Branch, (202) 720–2127.

Table 5-35.—Dates: Foreign trade, United States, 2010–2019

Year beginning October	Imports
	Metric tons
2010	20,113
2011	22,875
2012	23,945
2013	28,974
2014	32,189
2015	27,939
2016	21,900
2017	35,839
2018	27,834
2019	21,314

ERS, Crops Branch, (816) 412–4162.

Table 5-36.—Cranberries: Area, yield, production, season average price per barrel, value and quantities processed, United States, 2010–2019 [1]

Year	Area harvested	Yield per acre [2]	Total production [3]	Utilized production	Price [4]	Value	Quantities processed [5]
	Acres	Barrels [6]	Barrels [6]	Barrels [6]	Dollars	1,000 dollars	Barrels [6]
2010	38,500	176.8	6,808,200	6,808,200	43.90	299,123	6,589,000
2011	38,500	200.4	7,713,700	7,713,700	44.80	345,561	7,473,200
2012	40,300	199.6	8,045,000	8,045,000	47.90	385,506	7,791,000
2013	42,000	211.4	8,957,400	8,880,700	32.40	287,322	8,559,300
2014	40,600	202.9	8,400,000	8,236,000	30.90	254,412	7,968,000
2015	40,900	206.7	8,563,000	8,455,000	31.00	261,853	8,004,800
2016	41,500	230.0	9,627,400	9,544,000	30.60	292,292	9,083,900
2017	39,900	209.1	8,394,050	8,343,150	30.20	252,088	8,010,250
2018	39,300	227.1	8,926,000	8,846,560	27.80	245,762	8,578,900
2019	38,500	205.6	7,917,000	7,827,580	28.70	224,843	7,557,100

[1] Estimates relate to Massachusetts, New Jersey, Oregon, Washington, and Wisconsin. [2] Derived from utilized production. [3] Differences between utilized and total production are quantities unharvested for economic reasons or excess cullage and/or set-aside production under provisions of the Cranberry Marketing Order. [4] Average price of utilized production. Equivalent returns at first delivery point, screened basis of utilized production. [5] Mainly for canning. [6] Barrels of 100 pounds.
NASS, Crops Branch, (202) 720–2127.

Table 5-37.—Cranberries: Area, yield, production, and season average price per barrel, by State and United States, 2017–2019

State	Area harvested			Yield per acre [1]		
	2017	2018	2019	2017	2018	2019
	Acres	Acres	Acres	Bbl.	Bbl.	Bbl.
Massachusetts	12,300	12,700	12,300	154.0	180.4	175.6
New Jersey	2,700	3,100	2,700	178.8	165.3	196.0
Oregon	2,800	2,800	2,700	173.0	206.7	206.8
Washington [2]	1,500	(NA)	(NA)	98.4	(NA)	(NA)
Wisconsin	20,600	20,700	20,800	259.5	267.8	224.4
United States	39,900	39,300	38,500	209.1	209.1	205.6

State	Total production			Price per barrel [3]		
	2017	2018	2019	2017	2018	2019
	Bbl.	Bbl.	Bbl.	Dollars	Dollars	Dollars
Massachusetts	1,911,400	2,290,000	2,160,000	31.50	27.10	27.80
New Jersey	473,300	512,300	529,000	36.60	29.30	29.60
Oregon	489,700	579,700	558,000	26.40	26.20	26.60
Washington [2]	147,650	(NA)	(NA)	42.50	(NA)	(NA)
Wisconsin	5,372,000	5,545,000	4,670,000	29.20	28.10	29.30
United States	8,394,050	8,926,000	7,917,000	30.20	27.80	28.70

[1] 2017 yield is based upon utilized production. 2018 yield is based upon total production. [2] Estimates discontinued in 2018. [3] Average price of utilized production. Equivalent returns at first delivery point, screened basis of utilized production. NASS, Crops Branch, (202) 720–2127.

Table 5-38.—Figs: Total production, marketing year average price per ton, and value, California, 2008–2017 [1]

Year	Dried				Total		
	Production (dry basis)			Price per ton	Production	Price per ton	Value
	Total	Standard	Substandard				
	Tons	1,000 tons	Tons	Dollars	Tons	Dollars	1,000 dollars
2008	13,100	11,800	1,300	1,200	43,300	599	25,954
2009	13,300	12,000	1,300	1,540	43,750	695	30,422
2010	12,320	10,900	1,420	1,220	40,910	542	22,185
2011	11,560	10,140	1,420	1,230	38,660	526	20,336
2012	10,400	9,600	800	1,350	35,200	555	19,520
2013	9,300	8,600	700	1,500	33,000	610	20,143
2014	9,470	8,840	630	1,640	33,400	719	23,998
2015	8,940	8,320	620	1,760	31,700	799	25,333
2016	9,260	8,720	540	1,870	32,700	911	29,779
2017	9,100	8,570	530	1,490	31,200	916	28,568

[1] Estimates discontinued in 2018.
NASS, Crops Branch, (202) 720–2127.

Table 5-39.—Figs, dried: Foreign trade, United States, 2010–2019

Year beginning October	Imports for consumption	Domestic exports
	Metric tons	Metric tons
2010	4,042	5,065
2011	4,236	5,449
2012	5,816	4,895
2013	10,294	4,537
2014	7,137	4,670
2015	11,821	3,964
2016	9,983	4,295
2017	12,427	3,353
2018	10,955	2,657
2019	13,910	1,867

ERS, Crops Branch, (816) 412–4162.

Table 5-40.—Grapes: Production, price, and value, United States, 2010–2019

Year	Grapes			
	Production (fresh basis)		Market year average price per ton [1]	Value
	Total	Utilized		
	Tons	*Tons*	*Dollars*	*1,000 dollars*
2010	7,432,120	7,429,490	542.00	4,023,967
2011	7,408,740	7,401,370	576.00	4,262,945
2012	7,530,883	7,524,443	752.00	5,661,096
2013	8,631,790	8,620,810	712.00	6,135,301
2014	7,883,830	7,871,580	740.00	5,822,250
2015	7,621,150	7,621,080	776.00	5,914,468
2016	7,697,030	7,694,900	818.00	6,294,150
2017	7,383,850	7,383,160	881.00	6,507,849
2018	7,596,000	7,596,000	872.00	6,621,258
2019	6,871,000	6,791,000	842.00	5,719,758

[1] Fresh fruit prices are equivalent packinghouse-door returns for California and Washington, and the average price as sold for other States. Quantities processed are priced at the equivalent processing plant door level.
NASS, Crops Branch, (202) 720–2127.

Table 5-41.—Grapes: Production and marketing year average price per ton, by State and United States, 2017–2019

State	Total production			Utilized production		
	2017	2018	2019	2017	2018	2019
	Tons	*Tons*	*Tons*	*Tons*	*Tons*	*Tons*
California	6,507,000	7,130,000	6,480,000	6,507,000	7,130,000	6,400,000
Raisin [1]	1,301,000	1,545,000	1,300,000	1,301,000	1,545,000	1,300,000
Table [1]	1,190,000	1,300,000	1,180,000	1,190,000	1,300,000	1,180,000
Wine	4,016,000	4,285,000	4,000,000	4,016,000	4,285,000	3,920,000
Michigan [2]	63,600	(NA)	(NA)	63,500	(NA)	(NA)
Missouri [2]	6,130	(NA)	(NA)	6,100	(NA)	(NA)
New York [2]	187,000	(NA)	(NA)	187,000	(NA)	(NA)
North Carolina [2]	7,210	(NA)	(NA)	7,200	(NA)	(NA)
Ohio [2]	4,640	(NA)	(NA)	4,600	(NA)	(NA)
Oregon [2]	77,000	(NA)	(NA)	77,000	(NA)	(NA)
Pennsylvania [2]	91,700	(NA)	(NA)	91,300	(NA)	(NA)
Texas [2]	11,760	(NA)	(NA)	11,660	(NA)	(NA)
Virginia [2]	8,810	(NA)	(NA)	8,800	(NA)	(NA)
Washington	419,000	466,000	391,000	419,000	466,000	391,000
Juice	190,000	205,000	190,000	190,000	205,000	190,000
Wine	229,000	261,000	201,000	229,000	261,000	201,000
United States	7,383,850	7,596,000	6,871,000	7,383,160	7,596,000	6,791,000

State	Price per ton [3]		
	2017	2018	2019
	Dollars	*Dollars*	*Dollars*
California	899.00	878.00	846.00
Raisin [1]	414.00	428.00	296.00
Table [1]	1,330.00	978.00	1,030.00
Wine	927.00	1,010.00	971.00
Michigan [2]	379.00	(NA)	(NA)
Missouri [2]	702.00	(NA)	(NA)
New York [2]	369.00	(NA)	(NA)
North Carolina [2]	734.00	(NA)	(NA)
Ohio [2]	644.00	(NA)	(NA)
Oregon [2]	2,230.00	(NA)	(NA)
Pennsylvania [2]	281.00	(NA)	(NA)
Texas [2]	1,620.00	(NA)	(NA)
Virginia [2]	2,170.00	(NA)	(NA)
Washington	761.00	774.00	788.00
Juice	220.00	220.00	225.00
Wine	1,210.00	1,210.00	1,320.00
United States	881.00	872.00	842.00

(NA) Not available. [1] Fresh equivalent of dried and not dried. [2] Estimates discontinued in 2018. [3] Fresh fruit prices are equivalent packinghouse-door returns for California and Washington, and the average price as sold for other States. Quantities processed are priced at the equivalent processing plant door level.
NASS, Crops Branch, (202) 720–2127.

Table 5-42.—Grapes: Production and utilization, United States, 2009–2018

Crop of—	Total production [1]	Utilized production	Utilization of quantities sold				
			Fresh	Processed			
				Canned	Dried (fresh basis)	Crushed for wine	Crushed for juice, etc. [2]
			Tons				
2009	7,267,890	7,240,310	898,940	20,000	1,510,000	4,373,070	438,300
2010	7,432,120	7,429,490	953,290	25,000	1,777,000	4,270,300	403,900
2011	7,408,740	7,401,370	944,740	25,000	1,807,000	4,154,530	470,100
2012	7,530,883	7,524,443	963,483	20,000	1,488,000	4,706,470	346,490
2013	8,631,790	8,620,810	1,116,940	22,000	1,909,000	5,067,610	504,160
2014	7,883,830	7,871,580	1,053,040	21,000	1,721,000	4,526,020	549,920
2015	7,621,150	7,621,080	1,043,970	22,000	1,864,000	4,254,330	435,780
2016	7,697,030	7,694,900	1,039,950	19,000	1,478,000	4,667,830	488,420
2017	7,383,850	7,383,160	1,030,310	16,000	1,221,000	4,662,950	451,900
2018	7,596,000	7,596,000	1,098,900	(NA)	(NA)	(NA)	(NA)

[1] Total production includes utilized production plus production not harvested and harvested not sold. [2] Mostly juice, but includes some quantities used for jam, jelly, etc.
NASS, Crops Branch, (202) 720–2127.

Table 5-43.—Grapes: Production and utilization, by State and United States, crop of 2018

State	Total production	Utilized production	Utilization	
			Fresh	Processed
			Tons	
California	7,130,000	7,130,000	1,098,900	6,031,100
Raisin	1,545,000	1,545,000	10,800	1,534,200
Table	1,300,000	1,300,000	1,088,100	211,900
Wine	4,285,000	4,285,000	....	4,285,000
Michigan [1]	(NA)	(NA)	(NA)	(NA)
Missouri [1]	(NA)	(NA)	(NA)	(NA)
New York [1]	(NA)	(NA)	(NA)	(NA)
North Carolina [1]	(NA)	(NA)	(NA)	(NA)
Ohio [1]	(NA)	(NA)	(NA)	(NA)
Oregon [1]	(NA)	(NA)	(NA)	(NA)
Pennsylvania [1]	(NA)	(NA)	(NA)	(NA)
Texas [1]	(NA)	(NA)	(NA)	(NA)
Virginia [1]	(NA)	(NA)	(NA)	(NA)
Washington	466,000	466,000	....	466,000
Juice	205,000	205,000	....	205,000
Wine	261,000	261,000	....	261,000
United States	7,596,000	7,596,000	1,098,900	6,497,100

(NA) Not available. [1] Estimates discontinued in 2018.
NASS, Crops Branch, (202) 720–2127.

Table 5-44.—Grapes and raisins: Foreign trade, United States, 2010–2019

Year beginning October	Grapes		Raisins [1]	
	Imports, fresh	Domestic exports, fresh	Imports for consumption	Domestic exports
	Metric tons			
2010	557,397	334,609	18,813	154,541
2011	557,310	378,504	19,336	142,997
2012	566,038	366,088	17,102	131,980
2013	500,977	421,560	14,904	174,024
2014	554,674	366,143	20,588	132,274
2015	532,383	329,973	25,421	124,775
2016	625,371	330,271	14,753	136,454
2017	580,062	333,961	46,411	104,550
2018	643,957	371,172	29,380	84,051
2019	646,586	310,556	15,430	87,000

[1] Raisins converted to sweatbox or production basis by multiplying by 1.08.
ERS, Crops Branch, (816) 412–4162.

Table 5-45.—Nectarines: Total Production, utilization, and value, United States, 2010–2019

Year	Total Production	Utilization		Marketing year average price per ton	Value
		Fresh	Processed (fresh basis)		
	Tons	Tons	Tons	Dollars	1,000 dollars
2010	233,200	233,200	(NA)	553.00	129,075
2011	225,200	225,200	(NA)	582.00	130,973
2012	188,900	188,900	(NA)	767.00	144,906
2013	162,100	148,300	13,800	772.00	125,113
2014	187,300	170,000	9,300	866.00	162,221
2015	159,500	150,600	6,600	910.00	143,061
2016	151,350	145,600	5,600	885.00	133,791
2017	141,850	135,200	5,600	911.00	128,255
2018	120,500	(D)	(D)	874.00	104,626
2019	134,000	(D)	(D)	980.00	129,300

(D) Withheld to avoid disclosing data for individual operations. (NA) Not available
NASS, Crops Branch, (202) 720–2127.

Table 5-46.—Olives: Total production, marketing year average price, value, and processed utilization, California, 2010–2019

Year	Total Production	Marketing year average price per ton	Value	Processed utilization			
				Crushed for oil	Canned	Limited	Undersized
	Tons	Dollars	1,000 dollars	Tons	Tons	Tons	Tons
2010	206,000	664	136,796	36,000	125,000	37,000	8,000
2011	71,200	733	52,168	42,000	26,500	2,200	500
2012	160,000	813	130,038	74,000	78,500	6,400	1,100
2013	166,000	813	134,881	75,000	78,800	10,500	1,700
2014	95,000	774	73,559	45,000	30,500	5,900	900
2015	179,000	894	160,043	101,000	60,000	14,600	3,400
2016	164,900	860	141,761	97,700	54,000	11,100	2,000
2017	192,300	974	186,649	101,000	70,000	17,300	3,400
2018	53,600	766	40,523	35,500	14,920	2,060	420
2019	167,500	791	130,218	77,710	54,830	26,340	5,770

NASS, Crops Branch, (202) 720–2127.

Table 5-47.—Olives and olive oil: Foreign trade, United States, 2010–2019

Year beginning October	Imports			
	Olives		Olive oil	
	In brine	Dried	Edible	Inedible
	Metric tons			
2010	117,915	206	290,226	258
2011	118,614	145	314,937	788
2012	119,035	131	296,029	379
2013	118,734	202	311,142	351
2014	119,442	130	310,110	163
2015	127,273	48	330,323	153
2016	121,986	47	315,493	156
2017	121,918	75	321,496	215
2018	140,082	123	355,132	214
2019	109,156	110	395,606	222

ERS, Crops Branch, (816) 412–4162.

Table 5-48.—Papayas: Area, utilized production, utilization, marketing year average price, and value, Hawaii, 2010–2019

Year	Area harvested	Utilized production	Utilization		Price per pound	Value
			Fresh	Processed		
	Acres	1,000 pounds	1,000 pounds	1,000 pounds	Cents	dollars
2010	1,350	30,100	29,200	900	37.0	11,123
2011	1,300	28,600	27,700	900	34.0	9,722
2012	(NA)	(NA)	(NA)	(NA)	(NA)	(NA)
2013	700	24,200	23,000	1,200	34.4	8,316
2014	900	23,500	23,000	500	48.0	11,285
2015	900	25,200	(D)	(D)	41.9	10,570
2016	700	19,750	(D)	(D)	49.2	9,713
2017	1,100	22,250	(D)	(D)	42.2	9,400
2018	800	10,290	7,000	3,290	55.4	5,702
2019	690	10,580	(D)	(D)	46.7	4,943

(D) Withheld to avoid disclosing data for individual operations.   (NA) Not available.
NASS, Crops Branch, (202) 720–2127.

Table 5-49.—Peaches: Production and value, United States, 2010–2019

Year	Total production	Utilized production	Marketing year average price [1]	Value
	1,000 tons	1,000 tons	Dollars per ton	1,000 dollars
2010	1,149,430	1,129,770	547	617,459
2011	1,071,270	1,042,340	563	587,228
2012	968,070	955,890	647	618,369
2013	905,371	890,181	618	550,243
2014	852,799	837,907	750	628,846
2015	844,780	823,005	732	602,214
2016	791,940	775,230	803	622,624
2017	700,770	694,220	864	599,862
2018	651,500	638,020	801	511,226
2019	681,600	658,830	788	518,876

[1] Fresh fruit prices are equivalent packinghouse-door returns for California and Washington except equivalent returns for bulk fruit at the first delivery point for California Clingstone, and the average price as sold for other States. Quantities processed are priced at the equivalent processing plant door level.
NASS, Crops Branch, (202) 720–2127.

Table 5-50.—Peaches: Production and utilization, United States, 2009–2018

Year	Total production [1]	Utilized production	Utilization of quantities sold				
			Fresh [2]	Processed (fresh basis)			
				Canned [3]	Dried	Frozen [3]	Other [4]
			Tons				
2009	1,103,520	1,082,420	502,920	463,740	7,100	92,000	16,850
2010	1,149,430	1,129,770	566,400	428,470	12,700	104,400	17,800
2011	1,071,270	1,042,340	531,050	387,190	4,600	100,600	18,900
2012	968,070	955,890	480,750	364,640	9,800	90,210	10,490
2013	905,371	890,181	398,470	369,751	4,200	103,740	14,020
2014	852,799	837,907	393,200	330,220	4,200	95,290	14,497
2015	844,780	823,005	355,335	339,530	(NA)	108,400	(NA)
2016	791,940	775,230	333,350	322,350	(NA)	100,320	(NA)
2017	700,770	694,220	314,600	301,460	(NA)	62,500	(NA)
2018	651,500	638,020	279,790	(NA)	(NA)	(NA)	(NA)

[1] Includes harvested not sold and unharvested production for California Clingstone peaches. [2] Includes "Home use." [3] Estimated discontinued in 2018. [4] Used for jams, preserves, pickles, wine, brandy, baby food, etc. Includes small quantities frozen for some years.
NASS, Crops Branch, (202) 720–2127.

Table 5-51.—Peaches: Foreign trade, United States, 2010–2019

Year beginning October	Domestic exports				
	Fresh	Canned	Canned, in fruit salad [1]	Dried, in fruit salad [2] [3]	Total, in terms of fresh [4]
	Metric tons	Metric tons	Metric tons	Metric tons	Metric tons
2010	103,523	25,636	15,568	801	149,175
2011	95,798	28,295	17,605	884	146,609
2012	102,140	25,526	21,811	931	154,648
2013	80,241	20,847	20,144	859	126,004
2014	84,680	18,007	20,098	696	126,653
2015	77,769	10,689	18,698	364	109,179
2016	54,845	7,378	19,441	278	83,207
2017	63,966	9,451	20,433	150	94,683
2018	73,543	5,848	19,752	181	100,148
2019	64,038	3,409	21,478	121	89,584

[1] Canned peaches are 40 percent of total canned fruit for salad. [2] Net processed weight. [3] Dried peaches are 21 percent of total dried fruit for salad. [4] Dried fruit converted to unprocessed dry weight by dividing by 1.08. Unprocessed dry weight converted to terms of fresh fruit on the basis that 1 pound dried equals 6.0 pounds fresh. Canned peaches converted to terms of fresh on basis that 1 pound canned equals about 1 pound fresh.
ERS, Crops Branch, (816) 412–4162.

Table 5-52.—Peaches: Production and season average price, by State and United States, 2017–2019

State	Total production			Utilized production			Price per ton [1]		
	2017	2018	2019	2017	2018	2019	2017	2018	2019
	Tons	Tons	Tons	Tons	Tons	Tons	Dollars	Dollars	Dollars
Alabama [2]	1,500	(NA)	(NA)	1,500	(NA)	(NA)	2,750.00	(NA)	(NA)
California	553,000	479,000	498,000	550,000	475,870	495,100	701.00	639.00	598.00
Clingstone ...	297,000	259,000	264,000	296,000	256,950	263,200	474.00	480.00	470.00
Freestone ...	256,000	220,000	234,000	254,000	218,920	231,900	966.00	826.00	743.00
Colorado	10,750	15,000	14,300	10,160	14,550	13,300	2,070.00	1,930.00	2,300.00
Georgia	10,000	26,000	39,100	9,600	23,400	33,780	1,820.00	1,020.00	1,120.00
Idaho [2]	5,220	(NA)	(NA)	5,120	(NA)	(NA)	1,290.00	(NA)	(NA)
Illinois [2]	6,030	(NA)	(NA)	5,880	(NA)	(NA)	1,460.00	(NA)	(NA)
Maryland [2]	4,060	(NA)	(NA)	4,000	(NA)	(NA)	1,320.00	(NA)	(NA)
Michigan	9,600	12,000	4,800	9,500	11,940	4,800	1,140.00	1,060.00	1,110.00
Missouri [2]	2,230	(NA)	(NA)	2,230	(NA)	(NA)	2,340.00	(NA)	(NA)
New Jersey	24,580	23,000	19,500	24,570	23,000	17,980	1,560.00	1,780.00	1,430.00
New York [2]	4,810	(NA)	(NA)	4,720	(NA)	(NA)	1,720.00	(NA)	(NA)
North Carolina [2]	1,740	(NA)	(NA)	1,740	(NA)	(NA)	1,540.00	(NA)	(NA)
Ohio [2]	4,730	(NA)	(NA)	4,680	(NA)	(NA)	1,720.00	(NA)	(NA)
Pennsylvania ...	21,400	17,400	19,750	21,000	16,970	19,080	1,180.00	1,220.00	1,280.00
South Carolina	11,000	65,800	75,000	10,400	59,220	63,750	1,700.00	1,210.00	1,350.00
Texas [2]	2,700	(NA)	(NA)	2,500	(NA)	(NA)	2,500.00	(NA)	(NA)
Utah [2]	3,400	(NA)	(NA)	3,370	(NA)	(NA)	1,460.00	(NA)	(NA)
Virginia [2]	4,650	(NA)	(NA)	3,950	(NA)	(NA)	1,450.00	(NA)	(NA)
Washington	12,770	13,300	11,150	12,700	13,070	11,040	963.00	696.00	1,200.00
West Virginia [2]	6,600	(NA)	(NA)	6,600	(NA)	(NA)	940.00	(NA)	(NA)
United States ...	700,770	651,500	681,600	694,220	638,020	658,830	864.00	801.00	788.00

(NA) Not available. [1] Fresh fruit prices are equivalent packing house-door returns for California and Washington except equivalent returns for bulk fruit at the first delivery point for California Clingstone, and the average price as sold for other States. Quantities processed are priced at the equivalent processing plant door level. [2] Estimates discontinued in 2018.
NASS, Crops Branch, (202) 720–2127.

Table 5-53.—Peaches: Production and utilization, by State and United States, crop of 2019

State	Total production	Utilized production [1]	Utilization	
			Fresh [2]	Processed (fresh basis)
	Tons			
California	498,000	495,100	114,900	380,200
Clingstone	264,000	263,200	-	263,200
Freestone	234,000	231,900	114,900	117,000
Colorado	14,300	13,300	(D)	(D)
Georgia	39,100	33,780	(D)	(D)
Michigan	4,800	4,800	(D)	(D)
New Jersey	19,500	17,980	(D)	(D)
Pennsylvania	19,750	19,080	16,830	2,250
South Carolina	75,000	63,750	(D)	(D)
Washington	11,150	11,040	(D)	(D)
Other States [3]	....	....	131,030	13,620
United States	681,600	658,830	262,760	396,070

- Represents zero. (D) Withheld to avoid disclosing data for individual operations. (NA) Not available. [1] Difference between total and utilized production is harvested not sold and unharvested production. [2] Includes "Home use." [3] Includes data withheld above.
NASS, Crops Branch, (202) 720–2127.

Table 5-54.—Pears: Foreign trade, United States, 2010–2019

Year beginning October	Imports for consumption, fresh	Domestic exports				
		Fresh [1]	Canned	Dried, in fruit salad [1][2]	Canned, in fruit salad [3]	Total, in terms of fresh fruit [4]
	Metric tons	Metric tons	Metric tons	Metric tons	Metric tons	Metric tons
2010	77,992	154,025	7,958	635	13,622	179,615
2011	64,000	197,633	8,681	702	15,404	226,146
2012	79,034	186,855	7,535	739	19,084	218,137
2013	81,586	200,928	6,283	682	17,626	229,139
2014	89,741	174,774	4,425	553	17,586	200,271
2015	79,523	148,454	5,824	289	16,361	172,464
2016	74,356	123,088	7,473	220	17,011	148,963
2017	79,843	120,719	7,428	119	17,879	146,777
2018	74,373	148,686	3,412	144	17,283	170,287
2019	72,529	121,093	3,450	96	18,784	143,931

[1] Net processed weight.　[2] Dried pears are 16⅔ percent of total dried fruit for salad.　[3] Canned pears are 35 percent of total canned fruit for salad.　[4] Dried converted to unprocessed dry weight by dividing by 1.03. Unprocessed dry weight converted to terms of fresh on the basis that 1 pound dried equals about 6.5 pounds fresh. Canned converted to terms of fresh on basis that 1 pound of canned equals about 1 pound fresh.
ERS, Crops Branch, (816) 412–4162.

Table 5-55.—Pears: Production and value, United States 2010–2019

Year	Total production	Utilized production	Marketing year average price [1]	Value
	Tons	Tons	Dollars per ton	1,000 dollars
2010	813,600	813,400	476.00	386,955
2011	965,720	965,110	380.00	366,552
2012	851,240	851,130	509.00	432,988
2013	877,130	876,520	491.00	430,660
2014	831,610	831,250	562.00	467,194
2015	816,520	803,130	615.00	494,190
2016	738,770	735,870	660.00	485,763
2017	737,450	731,350	710.00	519,290
2018	805,500	800,260	536.00	428,940
2019	729,000	724,820	435.00	315,145

[1] Fresh fruit prices are equivalent packinghouse-door returns for California, Oregon, and Washington, and the average price as sold for other States. Quantities processed are priced at the equivalent processing plant door level.
NASS, Crops Branch, (202) 720–2127.

Table 5-56.—Pears: Production and season average price per ton, by State and United States, 2017–2019

State and Variety	Total production			Utilized production			Price per ton [1]		
	2017	2018	2019	2017	2018	2019	2017	2018	2019
	Tons	Tons	Tons	Tons	Tons	Tons	Dollars	Dollars	Dollars
California	195,000	161,500	163,500	192,000	161,000	161,370	501.00	480.00	380.00
Bartlett [2]	162,000	(NA)	(NA)	160,000	(NA)	(NA)	420.00	(NA)	(NA)
Other [2]	33,000	(NA)	(NA)	32,000	(NA)	(NA)	905.00	(NA)	(NA)
Oregon	226,050	246,000	236,000	224,950	245,260	234,110	785.00	575.00	465.00
Bartlett [2]	53,850	(NA)	(NA)	52,850	(NA)	(NA)	776.00	(NA)	(NA)
Other [2]	172,200	(NA)	(NA)	172,100	(NA)	(NA)	788.00	(NA)	(NA)
Washington	316,400	398,000	330,000	314,400	394,000	329,340	784.00	535.00	440.00
Bartlett [2]	125,400	(NA)	(NA)	124,400	(NA)	(NA)	838.00	(NA)	(NA)
Other [2]	191,000	(NA)	(NA)	190,000	(NA)	(NA)	748.00	(NA)	(NA)
United States ..	737,450	805,500	729,000	731,350	800,260	724,820	710.00	536.00	435.00

(NA) Not available. [1] Fresh fruit prices are equivalent packinghouse-door returns for California, Oregon, and Washington, and the average price as sold for other States. Quantities processed are priced at the equivalent processing plant door level.
[2] Estimates discontinued in 2018.
NASS, Crops Branch, (202) 720–2127.

Table 5-57.—Pears: Production and utilization, by State and United States, crop of 2019

State and variety	Total production	Utilized production	Utilization	
			Fresh [1]	Processed
		Tons		
California	163,000	161,370	69,440	91,930
Bartlett [2]	(NA)	(NA)	(NA)	(NA)
Other [2]	(NA)	(NA)	(NA)	(NA)
Oregon	236,000	234,110	192,100	42,010
Bartlett [2]	(NA)	(NA)	(NA)	(NA)
Other [2]	(NA)	(NA)	(NA)	(NA)
Washington	330,000	329,340	262,350	66,990
Bartlett [2]	(NA)	(NA)	(NA)	(NA)
Other [2]	(NA)	(NA)	(NA)	(NA)
United States [3]	729,000	724,820	523,890	200,930

(NA) Not available.   [1] Includes "Home use."   [2] Estimates discontinued in 2018.   [3] Mostly canned, but includes small quantities dried, juiced, and other uses.
NASS, Crops Branch, (202) 720–2127.

Table 5-58.—Pears: Production and utilization, United States, 2010–2019

Crop of—	Total production	Utilized production	Utilization of quantities sold—Fresh [1]
		Tons	
2010	813,600	813,400	531,430
2011	965,720	965,110	643,710
2012	851,240	851,130	551,820
2013	877,130	876,520	584,730
2014	831,610	831,250	550,080
2015	816,520	803,130	514,780
2016	738,770	735,870	505,000
2017	737,450	731,350	486,150
2018	805,500	800,260	557,700
2019	729,000	724,820	523,890

[1] Includes "Home use."
NASS, Crops Branch, (202) 720–2127.

Table 5-59.—Plums: Production, value, and utilization, California, 2010–2019

Season	Total production	Utilized production	Marketing year average price per ton	Value
	Tons	Tons	Dollars	1,000 dollars
2010	142,000	142,000	555	78,810
2011	160,000	160,000	402	64,320
2012	115,000	115,000	695	79,940
2013	100,600	98,600	665	65,527
2014	104,000	104,000	912	94,842
2015	92,500	91,500	996	91,125
2016	108,800	107,800	811	87,460
2017	117,900	114,900	1,000	114,897
2018	107,500	106,450	935	99,537
2019	101,500	97,850	1,180	115,889

NASS, Crops Branch, (202) 720–2127.

Table 5-60.—Prunes (dried basis): Production, price and value, California, 2010–2019

Season	Total production	Utilized production	Marketing year average price per ton	Value
	Tons	Tons	Dollars	1,000 dollars
2010	130,000	130,000	1,350.00	175,500
2011	137,000	137,000	1,310.00	179,470
2012	138,000	138,000	1,330.00	183,540
2013	85,000	85,000	2,000.00	170,000
2014	108,000	108,000	2,470.00	266,760
2015	112,000	110,000	2,050.00	225,500
2016	54,000	54,000	2,180.00	117,720
2017	105,000	105,000	1,980.00	207,900
2018	88,000	88,000	1,910.00	168,080
2019	91,100	90,100	1,510.00	136,187

NASS, Crops Branch, (202) 720–2127.

Table 5-61.—Prunes: Foreign trade, United States, 2010–2019

Year beginning October	Imports				Domestic exports			
	Fresh prunes and plums	Otherwise prepared or preserved	Dried prunes[1]	Total, in terms of fresh[2]	Fresh prunes and plums	Dried prunes[1]	Dried, in fruit salad[1][3]	Total, in terms of fresh[2]
	Metric tons							
2010	29,768	831	497	31,805	59,653	69,110	1,639	243,328
2011	24,105	822	565	26,311	56,788	67,529	1,810	236,801
2012	30,417	680	1,159	34,036	52,426	68,642	1,906	235,579
2013	13,625	821	6,844	32,129	41,741	48,498	1,759	172,216
2014	25,259	798	11,514	55,869	36,506	48,026	1,426	164,891
2015	26,533	985	19,183	77,221	29,660	38,342	746	131,139
2016	22,631	1,094	15,069	62,733	25,533	33,159	569	113,095
2017	22,432	1,038	9,642	48,398	31,024	37,281	307	128,608
2018	26,661	989	3,699	34,153	29,149	31,973	370	113,118
2019	19,079	1,045	1,495	23,900	23,539	31,408	247	105,721

[1] Net processed weight. [2] Exports and imports of dried prunes converted to unprocessed dry weight by dividing by 1.04. Unprocessed dry weight converted to terms of fresh fruit on the basis that 1 pound dried equals 2.7 pounds fresh. "Otherwise prepared or preserved" converted to terms of fresh fruit on the basis that 1 pound equals 0.899 pound fresh. [3] Dried prunes in salad estimated at 43 percent of total dried fruit for salad.
ERS, Crops Branch, (816) 412–4162.

Table 5-62.—Strawberries, commercial crop: Production and value per hundredweight, by State and United States, 2017–2019

Utilization, season, and State	Utilized Production			Value per unit		
	2017	2018	2019	2017	2018	2019
	1,000 cwt	1,000 cwt	1,000 cwt	Dollars per cwt	Dollars per cwt	Dollars per cwt
Fresh market:						
California	18,996.1	17,846.3	(D)	123.00	104.00	(D)
Florida	(D)	2,450.0	(D)	(D)	115.00	(D)
New York	(D)	(D)	(NA)	(D)	(D)	(NA)
North Carolina	126.0	125.0	(NA)	168.00	171.00	(NA)
Oregon	32.8	(D)	(NA)	195.00	(D)	(NA)
Washington	(D)	(D)	(NA)	(D)	(D)	(NA)
Other States[1]	2,217.1	58.1	17,530.0	143.00	211.00	129.00
United States	21,372.0	20,479.4	17,530.0	125.00	106.00	129.00
Processing:						
California	5,553.8	5,451.7	(D)	35.00	42.20	(D)
Florida	(D)	(D)	(D)	(D)	(X)	(D)
New York	(D)	(D)	(NA)	(D)	(D)	(NA)
North Carolina	2.7	-	(NA)	51.90	(X)	(NA)
Oregon	167.4	(D)	(NA)	93.50	(D)	(NA)
Washington	(D)	(D)	(NA)	(D)	(D)	(NA)
Other States[1]	78.8	167.6	4,970.0	69.10	88.30	52.80
United States	5,802.7	5,619.3	4,970.0	37.20	43.60	52.80

(D) Withheld to avoid disclosing data for individual operations. (X) Not applicable. [1] Includes data withheld above.
NASS, Crops Branch, (202) 720–2127.

Table 5-63.—Strawberries, commercial crop: Area, yield, production, value per hundred weight, and total value, United States, 2010–2019

Year	Area for harvest	Yield per acre	Total production	Value [2]	
				Per cwt	Total
	Acres	*Cwt*	*1,000 cwt*	*Dollars per cwt*	*1,000 dollars*
2010 ...	56,890	501.0	28,520.0	79.30	2,260,733
2011 ...	57,250	507.0	29,016.0	82.40	2,391,406
2012 ...	58,310	523.0	30,520.0	80.40	2,453,039
2013 ...	60,410	504.0	30,470.0	85.60	2,609,038
2014 ...	59,895	505.0	30,237.0	93.30	2,821,854
2015 ...	58,010	528.0	30,655.0	73.00	2,239,301
2016 ...	53,760	550.7	29,606.9	110.00	3,243,711
2017 ...	53,200	511.4	27,208.0	107.00	2,895,813
2018 ...	48,720	535.7	26,099.9	92.60	2,416,285
2019 ...	44,800	503.0	22,520.0	112.00	2,528,520

Year	Fresh market [1]			Processing		
	Production	Value [2]		Production	Value [2]	
		Per cwt	Total		Per cwt	Total
	1,000 cwt	*Dollars per cwt*	*1,000 dollars*	*1,000 cwt*	*Dollars per cwt*	*1,000 dollars*
2010 ...	23,196.0	90.80	2,105,492	5,324.0	29.20	155,241
2011 ...	23,324.0	94.00	2,193,379	5,692.0	34.80	198,027
2012 ...	24,552.0	91.80	2,253,854	5,968.0	33.40	199,185
2013 ...	25,085.0	96.50	2,421,370	5,385.0	34.90	187,668
2014 ...	24,543.0	105.00	2,579,425	5,694.0	42.60	242,429
2015 ...	24,372.0	79.90	1,946,121	6,283.0	46.70	293,180
2016 ...	23,023.8	127.00	2,931,642	6,554.8	47.60	312,069
2017 ...	21,372.0	125.00	2,680,189	5,802.7	37.20	215,624
2018 ...	20,479.4	106.00	2,171,428	5,619.3	43.60	244,857
2019 ...	17,530.0	129.00	2,265,910	4,970.0	52.80	262,610

[1] Fresh market price and value at point of first sale. Processing price and value at processing plant door.   [2] Mostly for fresh market, but includes some quantities used for processing in States for which processing estimates are not prepared.
NASS, Crops Branch, (202) 720–2127.

Table 5-64.—Strawberries, commercial crop: Area harvested, production, value per hundred weight, by State and United States, 2017–2019 [1]

Season and State	Area harvested			Total production			Value per unit		
	2017	2018	2019	2017	2018	2019	2017	2018	2019
	Acres			*1,000 cwt*			*Dollars per cwt*		
California	38,100	35,300	35,400	24,574.5	23,298.0	20,500.0	103.00	89.50	108.00
Florida	9,500	9,800	9,400	2,137.5	2,450.0	2,020.0	140.00	115.00	152.00
New York	1,200	700	(NA)	46.8	30.8	(NA)	229.00	204.00	(NA)
North Carolina	1,000	1,000	(NA)	135.0	125.0	(NA)	166.00	171.00	(NA)
Oregon	2,200	1,100	(NA)	200.2	110.0	(NA)	110.70	107.00	(NA)
Washington ...	1,200	820	(NA)	114.0	86.1	(NA)	107.00	107.00	(NA)
United States	53,200	48,720	44,800	27,208.0	26,099.9	22,520.0	107.00	92.60	112.00

(NA) Not available. [1] Includes quantities used for fresh market and processing.
NASS, Crops Branch, (202) 720–2127.

Table 5-65.—Fruits, noncitrus: Production, utilization, and value,
United States, 2009–2018 [1]

Year	Utilized production	Fresh [2]	Processed						Value of utilized production
			Canned	Dried	Juice	Frozen	Wine	Other	
	1,000 tons	*1,000 tons*	*1,000 tons*	*1,000 tons*	*1,000 tons*	*1,000 tons*	*1,000 tons*	*1,000 tons*	*1,000 dollars*
2009	18,069	7,562	1,394	2,148	1,235	742	4,373	269	11,811,298
2010	17,879	7,458	1,386	2,318	1,103	706	4,270	298	12,367,607
2011	18,147	7,702	1,301	2,399	1,153	737	4,154	316	13,910,375
2012	17,635	7,443	1,100	2,091	1,213	707	4,707	374	15,611,441
2013	19,433	7,718	1,373	2,321	1,630	827	5,068	497	16,220,440
2014	19,151	8,267	1,208	2,194	1,617	857	4,526	483	16,410,049
2015	18,334	7,702	1,252	2,323	1,391	881	4,255	530	16,602,493
2016	18,690	8,042	1,234	1,858	1,519	890	4,668	479	17,865,364
2017	18,455	8,107	1,188	1,754	1,477	731	4,665	531	18,589,066
2018 [3]	(NA)	(NA)	(NA)	(NA)	(NA)	(NA)	(NA)	(NA)	(NA)

(NA) Not available. [1] Includes the following crops: Apples, apricots, avocados, bananas, berries, cherries, cranberries, dates, figs, grapes, guavas, kiwifruit, nectarines, olives, papayas, peaches, pears, pineapples, plums, prunes, and strawberries. [2] Includes local and roadside sales. [3] Estimates discontinued.
NASS, Crops Branch, (202) 720–2127.

Table 5-66.—Fruits, fresh: Total reported domestic rail, truck,
and air shipments, 2020

Commodity	Jan.	Feb.	Mar.	Apr.	May	Jun.	Jul.
Citrus:	*1,000 cwt*						
Grapefruit	692	695	519	603	478	467	224
Grapefruit-organic	22	22	22	20	20	20	26
Lemons	2,395	2,371	2,427	2,015	1,976	1,963	847
Lemons-organic	43	38	38	123	123	123	35
Oranges	7,472	6,178	6,157	4,777	4,747	4,471	1,322
Oranges-organic	141	141	141	101	94	101	68
Tangelos	380	342	337	31	31	31	....
Tangelos-organic	7	7	7	....	....	....	....
Tangerines	2,555	2,524	2,474	1,076	1,072	1,072	....
Tangerines-organic	41	41	41	....	....	....	....
Temples	2	10	1	....	....	....	....
Total	13,750	12,369	12,164	8,746	8,541	8,248	2,522

Commodity	Aug.	Sep.	Oct.	Nov.	Dec.	Total
	1,000 cwt					
Grapefruit	227	244	512	542	581	5,784
Grapefruit-organic	26	26	....	....	....	204
Lemons	835	1,023	1,128	1,142	1,153	19,275
Lemons-organic	35	35	74	74	74	815
Oranges	1,310	1,328	2,791	2,790	2,858	46,201
Oranges-organic	68	68	102	101	102	1,228
Tangelos	....	....	....	....	4	1,156
Tangelos-organic	....	....	....	....	....	21
Tangerines	....	11	128	104	160	11,176
Tangerines-organic	....	....	....	....	....	123
Temples	....	....	....	....	....	13
Total	2,501	2,735	4,735	4,753	4,932	85,996

See footnote(s) at end of table.

Table 5-66.—Fruits, fresh: Total reported domestic rail, truck, and air shipments, 2020—Continued

Commodity	Jan.	Feb.	Mar.	Apr.	May	Jun.	Jul.
Noncitrus:				*1,000 cwt*			
Apples	4,728	6,205	6,063	4,246	5,586	4,089	3,763
Apples-organic	593	773	753	505	647	382	273
Apricots	...	...	...	...	18	382	273
Apricots-organic	...	...	...	...		28	23
Avocados	39	217	305	426	785	656	613
Blueberries	...	...	50	211	403	467	514
Blueberries-organic	7	19	22	56	131	91	164
Cherries	...	...	...	24	1,065	2,080	2,130
Cherries-organic	...	...	...	...	12	61	38
Cranberries	...	...	...	...	...	...	...
Cranberries-organic	...	...	...	...	...	...	...
Grapes	163	...	...	...	24	318	1,591
Grapes-organic	...	...	...	...	30	66	2
Kiwifruit	84	108	69	57	64	22	3
Nectarines	...	...	...	...	103	326	448
Peaches	...	...	...	...	257	745	919
Peaches-organic	...	...	...	...	...	...	8
Pears	855	1,055	666	458	600	314	333
Pears-organic	99	56	25	6	15	10	5
Persimmons	...	...	...	...	...	...	...
Plums	...	...	...	...	12	138	279
Pomegranates	...	...	...	...	...	...	...
Prunes	...	...	...	...	...	...	...
Raspberries	23	18	18	17	71	210	122
Raspberries-organic	11	18	30	29	35	51	36
Strawberries	646	1,289	1,359	2,020	2,823	2,212	1,758
Strawberries-organic	27	34	30	119	321	297	287
Total	7,275	9,792	9,390	8,174	13,002	12,563	13,318

Commodity	Aug.	Sep.	Oct.	Nov.	Dec.	Total
Noncitrus:				*1,000 cwt*		
Apples	4,878	4,449	6,160	5,055	4,599	59,821
Apples-organic	357	478	695	577	559	6,592
Apricots	1	...	...	...	...	70
Apricots-organic	...	...	...	...	...	9
Avocados	568	374	241	97	54	4,375
Blueberries	278	91	10	...	...	2,024
Blueberries-organic	79	27	6	4	5	611
Cherries	233	2	...	...	...	5,534
Cherries-organic	2	...	...	...	...	113
Cranberries	...	13	66	102	18	199
Cranberries-organic	...	...	...	2	...	2
Grapes	3,178	3,171	3,274	2,764	1,660	16,143
Grapes-organic	...	...	...	...	...	98
Kiwifruit	...	...	67	62	58	594
Nectarines	424	135	1	...	...	1,437
Peaches	710	278	58	...	...	2,967
Peaches-organic	53	20	...	...	...	81
Pears	388	633	1,110	872	812	8,096
Pears-organic	42	104	165	112	100	739
Persimmons	...	...	4	22	16	42
Plums	184	109	34	...	...	756
Pomegranates	...	59	164	99	42	364
Prunes	15	1	...	...	...	16
Raspberries	173	130	49	22	18	871
Raspberries-organic	51	38	21	11	9	340
Strawberries	1,722	1,316	1,126	644	538	17,453
Strawberries-organic	259	173	113	76	48	1,784
Total	13,595	11,601	13,364	10,521	8,536	131,131

AMS, Fruit and Vegetable Programs, Market News Division, (301) 365-6701.

Table 5-67.—Fruits, dried: Production (dry basis), California, 2009–2018

Year	Apricots	Figs [1]	Peaches [2]	Prunes	Grapes [3]
			Tons		
2009	1,090	13,300	850	166,000	335,500
2010	1,400	12,320	2,010	130,000	394,800
2011	1,810	11,560	470	137,000	384,300
2012	1,210	10,400	1,230	138,000	345,900
2013	1,080	9,300	420	85,000	406,100
2014	1,500	9,470	610	108,000	366,200
2015	1,050	8,940	880	110,000	388,500
2016	1,280	9,260	(NA)	54,000	335,900
2017	(D)	9,100	(NA)	105,000	271,300
2018 [4]	(NA)	(NA)	(NA)	(NA)	(NA)

(NA) Not available. [1] Standard and substandard. [2] Freestone only. Discontinued in 2015. [3] Raisin and table type. [4] Estimates discontinued in 2018.
NASS, Crops Branch, (202) 720–2127.

Table 5-68.—International Raisins: Production in specified countries, 2016/2017–2018/2019

Country	2016/2017	2017/2018	2018/2019
	Metric tons		
Turkey	310,000	306,000	280,000
United States	304,723	241,402	263,000
China	165,000	180,000	190,000
Iran	170,000	110,000	150,000
South Africa	62,300	70,500	73,000
Uzbekistan	71,000	65,000	70,000
Chile	53,700	57,000	60,000
Argentina	31,000	41,000	42,000
Afghanistan	26,000	36,500	38,000
Australia	18,000	20,000	20,000
Other	19,000	22,000	19,000

FAS, Office of Global Analysis, (202) 720-6301. Prepared or estimated on the basis of official USDA production, supply, and distribution statistics from foreign governments.

Table 5-69.—Fruits: Per capita consumption, United States, 2009–2018 [1]

Year	Fruits used fresh		Canned fruits [4]	Juice [5]	Frozen fruit [6]	Dried fruits [7]
	Citrus fruit [2]	Noncitrus fruits [3]				
	Pounds	*Pounds*	*Pounds*	*Gallons*	*Pounds*	*Pounds*
2009	20.7	77.4	13.6	7.1	5.1	2.1
2010	21.6	80.9	13.1	7.2	5.7	2.3
2011	22.8	82.4	12.1	6.1	5.3	2.3
2012	23.5	85.1	11.5	6.4	5.0	2.3
2013	23.9	87.9	13.0	6.2	5.3	2.4
2014	23.3	90.7	11.8	5.9	6.5	2.3
2015	22.7	89.7	12.4	5.8	6.5	2.4
2016	24.1	91.3	11.7	5.6	5.3	2.4
2017	23.8	92.9	11.4	5.4	6.1	2.3
2018	24.0	91.2	10.1	5.2	6.0	1.0

[1] Fresh citrus fruits, canned fruit, and fruit juices are on a crop-year basis. Dried fruits are on a pack-year basis. The per capita consumption was obtained by dividing the total consumption by total population. [2] Oranges and temples, tangerines and tangelos, lemons, limes, and grapefruit. [3] Apples, apricots, avocados, bananas, cherries, cranberries, grapes, kiwifruit, mangoes, peaches and nectarines, pears, pineapples, papayas, plums and prunes, and strawberries. [4] Apples, apricots, cherries, olives, peaches, pears, pineapples, and plums and prunes. [5] Orange, grapefruit, lemon, lime, apple, grape, pineapple, prune, and cranberry. [6] Blackberries, blueberries, raspberries, strawberries, other berries, apples, apricots, cherries, and peaches. [7] Apples, apricots, dates, figs, peaches, pears, prunes, and raisins. Dried data in terms of processed weight.
ERS, Crops Branch, (816) 926–6007.

Table 5-70.—Fruit: Exports, 2016–2018

Country	2016	2017	2018
	Metric tons		
Fruit, processed:			
Canada	81,103	77,039	76,946
China	19,958	43,280	26,182
Netherlands	35,738	33,160	22,349
Mexico	20,691	26,442	22,223
Korea, South	7,398	7,926	7,454
Japan	7,271	6,168	6,450
Australia(*)	5,580	4,972	5,351
United Kingdom	3,376	4,538	4,670
Hong Kong	2,191	2,374	4,140
Poland	2,766	3,498	3,461
Taiwan	3,790	4,120	3,239
Germany(*)	1,302	1,314	2,591
India	2,158	2,629	2,579
Israel(*)	4,479	3,869	2,541
Indonesia	1,585	1,662	2,347
Malaysia	1,929	2,120	2,268
Switzerland(*)	682	230	2,265
Russia	1,186	1,661	2,071
Thailand	3,035	3,040	1,958
Vietnam	1,066	1,819	1,634
Singapore	1,323	1,954	1,525
New Zealand(*)	1,920	1,415	1,308
Colombia	1,110	1,073	1,244
Belgium-Luxembourg(*)	3,149	3,749	1,210
Philippines	1,283	1,383	1,157
Turkey	1,826	2,228	1,021
Panama	795	841	955
France(*)	415	1,825	848
Italy(*)	1,264	879	810
Greece	898	709	747
Rest of World	9,856	8,727	8,007
World Total	231,120	256,641	221,553
Fruit, prepared, misc:			
Canada	75,277	77,340	72,441
Mexico	8,079	10,638	9,679
Netherlands	507	347	8,569
China	7,497	5,832	3,862
Japan	3,347	2,634	3,023
Australia(*)	5,958	1,538	1,876
Korea, South	9,018	2,916	1,858
Hong Kong	3,784	6,258	1,382
Philippines	1,056	939	1,242
Saudi Arabia	5,999	1,248	1,218
Panama	981	1,081	1,005
Dominican Republic	863	555	1,000
Germany(*)	278	251	954
Malaysia	880	605	731
Taiwan	1,230	614	708
Bahamas, The	471	779	679
Thailand	1,230	671	674
Singapore	795	601	610
Turkey	113	36	583
United Arab Emirates	923	794	578
Trinidad and Tobago	567	301	568
Israel(*)	398	295	472
Costa Rica	548	660	465
United Kingdom	748	963	414
Netherlands Antilles(*)	534	238	370
Indonesia	643	250	360
Chile	793	626	333
Jordan	227	268	314
Vietnam	4,081	85	310
France(*)	540	1,415	302
Rest of World	9,417	6,068	3,885
World Total	146,780	126,845	120,463

(*) Denotes a country that is a summarization of its component countries. All zeroes for a data item may show that statistics exist in the other import type. Consumption or General. Users should use cautious interpretation on Quantity reports using mixed units of measure. Quantity line items will only include statistics on the units of measure that are equal to, or are able to be converted to, the assigned unit of measure of the grouped commodities.

FAS, Office of Global Analysis, (202) 720-6301. Data Source: Department of Commerce, U.S. Census Bureau, Foreign Trade Statistics.

Table 5-71.—International Fruits, fresh: Production in specified countries, 2017/2018-2019/2020

Country	Production		
	2017/2018	2018/2019	2019/2020
	Metric tons		
Apples:			
China	41,390,000	33,000,000	41,000,000
European Union	10,004,642	15,030,401	11,476,790
United States	5,084,727	4,486,393	4,820,690
Turkey	2,750,000	3,000,000	3,000,000
India	1,920,000	2,371,000	2,370,000
Iran	2,096,700	2,096,700	2,096,700
Russia	1,359,580	1,610,990	1,713,600
Brazil	1,300,900	1,300,900	1,300,900
Chile	1,330,000	1,210,000	1,143,650
Ukraine	1,076,200	1,076,200	1,076,200
South Africa	835,873	893,846	942,203
Japan	735,200	735,200	735,200
Mexico	714,149	547,382	678,765
New Zealand	575,500	576,850	593,000
Argentina	560,000	550,000	480,000
Moldova	400,000	400,000	400,000
Serbia	378,600	378,600	378,600
Canada	364,763	385,290	369,900
Belarus	317,100	317,100	317,100
Australia	313,700	313,700	313,700
Azerbaijan	275,100	275,100	275,100
Kyrgyzstan	147,600	147,600	147,600
Kazakhstan	188,100	188,100	118,100
Uruguay	45,100	45,100	45,100
Guatemala	25,100	25,100	25,100
Norway	12,700	12,700	12,700
Colombia	2,000	2,000	2,000
Taiwan	1,451	1,619	1,500
Cherries, sweet and sour:			
European Union	809,000	824,000	865,000
Turkey	620,103	834,938	647,516
United States	508,087	441,318	450,000
China	380,000	340,000	420,000
Russia	245,900	245,900	245,900
Ukraine	243,100	243,100	243,100
Chile	206,741	201,000	231,000
Uzbekistan	193,700	193,700	193,700
Serbia	119,000	119,000	119,000
Syria	68,500	68,500	68,500
Azerbaijan	46,400	46,400	46,400
Belarus	28,900	28,900	28,900
Canada	16,000	17,000	18,000
Japan	19,100	18,100	17,000
Australia	12,300	12,300	12,300
Argentina	7,100	7,100	7,100
Kyrgyzstan	5,200	5,200	5,200
Peaches & nectarines:			
China	14,300,000	13,500,000	15,000,000
European Union	4,345,594	3,880,624	4,138,180
Turkey	771,500	790,000	830,000
United States	757,518	687,347	814,000
Brazil	248,600	248,600	248,600
Argentina	89,700	226,200	226,200
Uzbekistan	193,300	193,300	193,300
South Africa	183,700	183,700	183,700
Mexico	163,800	163,800	163,800
Chile	159,302	157,600	161,500
Japan	124,900	113,200	101,500
Australia	92,000	94,000	96,000
Russia	32,200	32,200	32,200
Canada	27,500	27,500	27,500
Ukraine	19,900	19,900	19,900
Taiwan	23,254	22,506	17,000
Kazakhstan	1,900	1,900	1,900
Switzerland	200	200	200

See footnote(s) at end of table.

Table 5-71.—International Fruits, fresh: Production in specified countries, 2017/2018-2019/2020—Continued

Country	Production 2017/2018	2018/2019	2019/2020
	Metric tons		
Pears, fresh:			
China	16,410,000	14,000,000	17,000,000
European Union	2,384,265	2,591,806	2,184,475
United States	663,470	725,984	657,546
Argentina	580,000	600,000	550,000
Turkey	420,000	450,000	490,000
South Africa	408,146	413,245	407,455
India	280,000	340,000	340,000
Japan	274,500	274,500	274,500
Russia	218,065	243,438	244,735
Chile	262,000	252,000	227,000
Korea, South	265,757	203,166	210,000
Taiwan	118,600	118,600	118,600
Australia	105,000	105,000	105,000
Switzerland	39,800	39,800	39,800
Belarus	32,100	32,100	32,100
Mexico	27,930	29,940	27,049
Brazil	22,100	22,100	22,100
New Zealand	13,812	12,585	13,150
Canada	8,622	8,982	8,800

FAS, Office of Global Analysis, (202) 720-6301. Prepared or estimated on the basis of official USDA production, supply, and distribution statistics from foreign governments.

Table 5-72.—All tree nuts: Supply and utilization, United States, 2010/2011–2019/2020

Market year[1]	Beginning stocks	Marketable production [2]	Imports	Total supply	Exports	Ending stocks	Domestic consumption Total	Per capita Pounds
	—Million pounds (shelled)—							
2010/2011	422.1	2,482.2	485.1	3,389.4	1,786.1	407.4	1,195.9	3.85
2011/2012	407.4	2,787.2	449.2	3,643.9	1,977.1	480.2	1,186.6	3.79
2012/2013	480.2	2,762.3	515.6	3,753.1	1,979.6	462.1	1,316.5	4.17
2013/2014	462.1	2,806.7	582.1	3,758.1	2,075.2	505.5	1,270.1	4.00
2014/2015	505.5	2,738.4	666.9	3,910.9	2,025.2	585.2	1,300.5	4.07
2015/2016	585.2	2,665.8	668.1	3,919.1	2,035.2	575.5	1,308.4	4.06
2016/2017	575.5	3,328.2	697.2	4,601.0	2,381.8	647.4	1,571.9	4.85
2017/2018	647.4	3,187.4	738.8	4,573.6	2,395.2	536.1	1,642.3	5.03
2018/2019	536.1	3,469.7	720.2	4,726.0	2,486.1	536.6	1,703.4	5.20
2019/2020	536.5	3,632.3	749.9	4,918.7	2,445.0	683.5	1,790.2	5.44

[1] Marketing season begins July 1 for hazelnuts and macadamias; August 1 for almonds and walnuts; September 1 for pistachios; and October 1 for pecans. [2] Utilized production (NASS data) minus inedibles and noncommercial useage.
ERS, Crops Branch, (816) 412–4162.

Table 5-73.—International Nuts, Almonds: Production in specified countries, 2017/2018–2019/2020

Country	2017/2018	2018/2019	2019/2020
	Metric tons		
United States	1,029,650	1,034,190	997,900
European Union	109,500	123,800	121,000
Australia	76,000	92,000	95,000
China	43,000	43,000	45,000
Turkey	15,000	16,000	15,000
Chile	9,500	11,000	11,500
India	4,000	4,500	4,500

FAS, Office of Global Analysis, (202) 720-6301. Prepared or estimated on the basis of official USDA production, supply, and distribution statistics from foreign governments.

Table 5-74.—Almonds (shelled basis): Bearing acreage, yield, production, price, and value, California, 2010–2019 [1]

Year	Bearing Acreage	Yield per acre [2]	Utilized production	Price per pound	Value
	Acres	*Pounds*	*1,000 pounds*	*Dollars*	*1,000 dollars*
2010	770,000	2,220	1,640,000	1.79	2,903,380
2011	800,000	2,540	2,030,000	1.99	4,007,860
2012	820,000	2,310	1,890,000	2.58	4,816,860
2013	880,000	2,280	2,010,000	3.21	6,384,690
2014	930,000	2,010	1,870,000	4.00	7,388,000
2015	950,000	2,000	1,900,000	3.13	5,868,750
2016	970,000	2,210	2,140,000	2.39	5,052,460
2017	1,030,000	2,200	2,215,000	2.53	5,603,950
2018	1,090,000	2,090	2,241,000	2.50	5,602,500
2019	1,180,000	2,160	2,508,000	2.43	6,094,440

[1] Price and value are based on edible portion of the crop only. Production includes inedible quantities of no value as follows (million pounds): 2009-20.0; 2010-18.0; 2011-16.0; 2012-23.0; 2013-21.0; 2014-23.0; 2015-25.0; 2016-26.0; 2017-55.0; 2018-39.0. [2] Yield is based on utilized production.
NASS, Crops Branch, (202) 720–2127.

Table 5-75.—Almonds (shelled basis): Foreign trade, United States, 2010–2019 [1]

Year beginning October	Imports	Domestic exports
	Metric tons	*Metric tons*
2010	2,391	527,228
2011	5,729	615,275
2012	15,653	579,553
2013	14,724	581,398
2014	10,026	546,116
2015	9,501	562,036
2016	7,638	640,207
2017	10,306	667,255
2018	11,621	686,111
2019	6,846	752,711

[1] Imports of unshelled nuts converted to shelled basis at ratio of 1.67 to 1. Exports of unshelled nuts converted to shelled basis at ratio of 1.67 to 1.0.
ERS, Crops Branch, (816) 412–4162.

Table 5-76.—Hazelnuts (in-shell basis): Bearing acreage, yield, production, price, and value, Oregon, 2010–2019

Year	Bearing Acreage	Yield per acre	Utilized production	Price per ton	Value
	Acres	Tons	Tons	Dollars	1,000 dollars
2010	29,000	1.00	28,000	2,410	67,480
2011	28,500	1.00	38,500	2,330	89,705
2012	29,000	1.22	35,500	1,830	64,965
2013	30,000	1.50	45,000	2,680	120,600
2014	30,000	1.20	36,000	3,600	129,600
2015	34,000	0.91	31,000	2,800	86,800
2016	37,000	1.19	44,000	2,700	118,800
2017	40,000	0.80	32,000	2,300	73,600
2018	44,000	1.16	51,000	1,800	91,800
2019	50,000	0.88	44,000	1,920	84,480

NASS, Crops Branch, (202) 720–2127.

Table 5-77.—Hazelnuts (shelled basis): Foreign trade, United States, 2010–2019 [1]

Year beginning October	Imports	Domestic exports
	Metric tons	Metric tons
2010	4,417	7,691
2011	3,118	10,031
2012	5,392	11,243
2013	4,747	14,862
2014	1,761	20,309
2015	2,748	8,766
2016	3,333	11,634
2017	5,443	8,850
2018	5,646	9,966
2019	5,040	9,659

[1] Imports of unshelled nuts converted to shelled basis at ratio of 2.22 to 1. Exports of unshelled nuts converted to shelled basis at ratio of 2.50 to 1.
ERS, Crops Branch, (816) 412–4162.

Table 5-78.—Macadamia nuts (in-shell basis): Bearing acreage, yield, production, price, and value, Hawaii, 2010–2019

Year	Bearing Acreage	Yield per acre	Utilized production	Price per pound	Value
	Acres	Pounds	1,000 pounds	Cents	1,000 dollars
2010	15,000	2,670	40,000	75.0	30,000
2011	15,000	3,270	49,000	78.0	38,220
2012	15,000	2,930	44,000	80.0	35,200
2013	16,000	2,560	41,000	87.0	35,670
2014	16,000	2,880	46,000	87.0	40,020
2015	16,000	2,940	47,000	97.0	45,590
2016	16,500	2,550	42,000	100.0	42,000
2017	17,000	2,880	49,000	110.0	53,900
2018	16,900	2,090	35,300	119.0	42,007
2019	16,900	2,410	40,700	120.0	48,840

NASS, Crops Branch, (202) 720–2127.

Table 5-79.—Pecans (in-shell basis): Production, price per pound, and value, United States, 2010–2019

Year	Improved varieties [1]			Native and seedling			All pecans		
	Utilized production	Price per pound	Value	Utilized production	Price per pound	Value	Utilized production	Price per pound	Value
	1,000 pounds	Dollars	1,000 dollars	1,000 pounds	Dollars	1,000 dollars	1,000 pounds	Dollars	1,000 dollars
2010	232,560	2.490	578,149	61,180	1.580	96,679	293,740	2.300	674,828
2011	227,030	2.590	587,064	42,670	1.610	68,825	269,700	2.430	655,889
2012	247,100	1.730	427,473	55,200	0.879	48,518	302,300	1.570	475,991
2013	220,000	1.900	417,758	46,330	0.920	42,632	266,330	1.730	460,390
2014	227,410	2.120	482,323	36,740	0.933	34,268	264,150	1.960	516,591
2015	225,180	2.310	520,529	29,110	1.360	39,687	254,290	2.200	560,216
2016	249,970	2.660	663,746	18,800	1.760	33,060	268,770	2.590	696,806
2017	278,600	2.400	667,858	26,250	1.580	41,360	304,850	2.330	709,218
2018	226,470	1.790	405,007	14,460	1.140	16,524	240,930	1.750	421,531
2019	231,140	1.910	442,299	24,460	1.170	28,700	255,600	1.840	470,999

[1] Budded, grafted or topworked varieties.
NASS, Crops Branch, (202) 720–2127.

Table 5-80.—Pecans (in-shell basis): Production and marketing year average price per pound, by State and United States, 2017–2019

Item and State	Utilized production			Price per pound		
	2017	2018	2019	2017	2018	2019
	1,000 pounds	*1,000 pounds*	*1,000 pounds*	*Dollars*	*Dollars*	*Dollars*
Improved Varieties [1]						
Alabama	1,600	1,490	(NA)	2.030	1.500	(NA)
Arizona	28,000	27,900	36,100	2.500	1.870	1.890
California	5,000	3,700	(NA)	2.300	2.000	(NA)
Georgia	107,000	70,000	73,000	2.400	1.620	1.880
Louisiana	3,000	2,510	(NA)	2.000	1.250	(NA)
New Mexico	92,000	89,100	87,800	2.400	1.900	1.880
Oklahoma	3,000	2,970	4,240	2.100	2.250	1.360
Texas	39,000	28,800	30,000	2.390	1.760	2.200
United States	278,600	226,470	231,140	2.400	1.790	1.910
Native and Seedling						
Alabama	250	110	(NA)	1.520	1.190	(NA)
Louisiana	5,000	3,520	(NA)	1.250	0.800	(NA)
Oklahoma	11,000	6,030	16,960	1.630	1.360	1.250
Texas	10,000	4,800	7,500	1.680	1.120	1.000
United States	26,250	14,4600	24,460	1.580	1.140	1.170
All Pecans						
Alabama	1,850	1,600	(NA)	1.960	1.480	(NA)
Arizona	28,000	27,900	36,100	2.500	1.870	1.890
California	5,000	3,700	(NA)	2.300	2.000	(NA)
Georgia	107,000	70,000	73,000	2.400	1.620	1.880
Louisiana	8,000	6,030	(NA)	1.530	0.990	(NA)
New Mexico	92,000	89,100	87,800	2.400	1.900	1.880
Oklahoma	14,000	9,000	21,200	1.730	1.650	1.270
Texas	49,000	33,600	37,500	2.250	1.670	1.960
United States	304,850	240,930	255,600	2.330	1.750	1.840

[1] Budded, grafted or topworked varieties.
NASS, Crops Branch, (202) 720–2127.

Table 5-81.—Pecans (shelled basis): Foreign trade, United States, 2010–2019 [1]

Year beginning October	Imports	Domestic exports
	Metric tons	*Metric tons*
2010	35,906	25,531
2011	30,449	31,141
2012	33,525	37,873
2013	39,000	33,098
2014	43,736	40,727
2015	46,612	35,721
2016	52,830	42,987
2017	58,230	47,689
2018	70,118	41,632
2019	65,204	39,250

[1] Imports of unshelled nuts converted to shelled basis at ratio of 2.50 to 1. Exports of unshelled nuts converted to shelled basis at ratio of 2.50 to 1.
ERS, Crops Branch, (816) 412–4162.

Table 5-82.—Pistachios (in-shell basis): Bearing acreage, yield, production, price, and value, California, 2010–2019

Year	Bearing Acreage	Yield per acre	Utilized production	Price per pound	Value
	Acres	Pounds	1,000 pounds	Dollars	1,000 dollars
2010	137,000	3,810	522,000	2.00	1,158,840
2011	153,000	2,900	444,000	2.00	879,120
2012	182,000	3,030	551,000	2.61	1,438,110
2013	203,000	2,320	470,000	3.48	1,635,600
2014	221,000	2,330	514,000	3.57	1,834,980
2015	233,000	1,160	270,000	3.29	888,300
2016	239,000	3,750	896,500	1.68	1,506,120
2017	250,000	2,400	600,300	1.69	1,014,507
2018	264,000	3,740	987,000	2.65	2,615,550
2019	289,000	2,560	740,000	2.62	1,938,800

NASS, Crops Branch, (202) 720–2127.

Table 5-83.—Walnuts, English (in-shell basis): Bearing acreage, yield, production, price, and value, California, 2010–2019

Year	Bearing Acreage	Yield per acre [1]	Utilized production	Price per ton	Value
	Acres	Tons	Tons	Dollars	1,000 dollars
2010	255,000	1.98	504,000	2,040	1,028,160
2011	265,000	1.74	461,000	2,900	1,336,900
2012	270,000	1.84	497,000	3,030	1,505,910
2013	280,000	1.76	492,000	3,710	1,825,320
2014	290,000	1.97	571,000	3,340	1,907,140
2015	300,000	2.02	606,000	1,670	1,012,020
2016	315,000	2.19	689,000	1,850	1,274,650
2017	335,000	1.88	630,000	2,490	1,568,700
2018	350,000	1.94	679,000	1,350	916,650
2019	365,000	1.79	653,000	1,970	1,286,410

[1]Yield is based on utilized production.
NASS, Crops Branch, (202) 720–2127.

Table 5-84.—Walnuts (shelled basis): Foreign trade, United States, 2010–2019 [1]

Year beginning October	Imports	Domestic exports
	Metric tons	Metric tons
2010	186	133,868
2011	2,442	117,031
2012	3,957	133,049
2013	5,266	134,379
2014	9,780	158,186
2015	5,319	188,467
2016	6,495	191,336
2017	5,618	176,058
2018	1,334	182,881
2019	1,129	173,281

[1]Imports of unshelled nuts converted to shelled basis at ratio of 2.50 to 1. Exports of unshelled nuts converted to shelled basis at ratio of 2.50 to 1.
ERS, Crops Branch, (816) 412–4162.

Table 5-85.—Coffee, green: International trade, 2017/2018-2019/2020

Country of origin	2017/2018	2018/2019	2019/2020
	1,000 60-Kg bags		
Principle exporting countries:			
Brazil	30,450	39,720	36,820
Vietnam	27,900	27,200	28,300
Colombia	12,725	13,400	13,400
Indonesia	8,010	6,150	7,845
Honduras	7,225	6,700	6,200
India	6,148	5,540	5,555
Peru	4,185	4,260	4,300
Ethiopia	3,893	3,980	4,000
Uganda	4,500	4,600	4,000
Mexico	3,220	3,220	3,340
Guatemala	3,465	3,405	3,300
Malaysia	3,050	3,100	3,100
Nicaragua	2,520	2,415	2,215
European Union	2,130	2,400	2,200
China	1,885	1,770	1,920
Cote d'Ivoire	1,150	1,615	1,725
Switzerland	1,225	1,300	1,300
Tanzania	1,030	1,230	1,230
Costa Rica	1,210	1,110	1,160
Principle importing countries:			
European Union	47,430	49,000	48,500
United States	24,790	26,600	26,950
Japan	7,720	8,500	8,200
Philippines	6,100	6,200	6,150
Canada	4,750	4,720	4,900
Russia	4,465	4,450	4,575
China	2,705	2,750	2,900
Korea South	2,645	2,700	2,800
Switzerland	2,750	2,700	2,800
Algeria	2,300	2,340	2,440
Australia	1,875	1,875	1,965
Malaysia	1,550	1,800	1,700
Mexico	1,545	1,670	1,580
India	1,472	1,341	1,322
Ukraine	1,095	1,280	1,300
Morocco	825	1,020	1,220
Indonesia	1,751	1,676	1,215
Vietnam	1,060	1,160	1,210
Turkey	875	1,080	1,025
Argentina	775	780	860

FAS, Office of Global Analysis, (202) 720-6301. Prepared or estimated on the basis of official USDA production, supply, and distribution statistics from foreign governments. Data Source: Department of Commerce, U.S. Census Bureau, Foreign Trade Statistics.

Table 5-86.—Coffee: Area, yield, production, marketing year average price, and value, Hawaii, 2010/2011–2019/2020 [1]

Year	Area Harvested	Yield per acre	Utilized production	Price per pound	Value
	Acres	Pounds	1,000 pounds	Dollars	1,000 dollars
2010/2011	7,500	1,170	8,800	3.25	33,440
2011/2012	7,700	990	7,600	4.15	31,540
2012/2013	7,900	890	7,000	5.90	41,300
2013/2014	8,200	1,020	8,400	6.20	52,080
2014/2015	7,800	4,720	36,408	1.72	62,622
2015/2016	6,900	4,600	30,137	1.55	46,712
2016/2017	7,000	4,180	28,571	1.71	48,856
2017/2018	7,200	3,530	24,592	1.78	43,774
2018/2019	7,100	3,845	26,400	1.90	50,160
2019/2020	6,900	3,952	26,880	2.02	54,298

[1] For 2009/2010 season thru 2013/2014 season, all data in a parchment basis. Beginning with the 2014/2015 season, all data is for a cherry basis.
NASS, Crops Branch, (202) 720–2127.

Table 5-87.—Coffee and tea: U.S. Imports, Area/Partners of Origin, 2017-2019

Country	2017	2018	2019
	Metric tons		
Coffee and coffee products:			
Brazil	372,634	384,482	478,530
Colombia	346,419	343,509	357,835
Vietnam	237,138	213,639	175,194
Guatemala	85,458	67,828	88,141
Mexico	80,054	73,017	87,234
Nicaragua	76,933	82,788	84,266
Honduras	78,364	82,190	78,498
Peru	64,167	64,827	63,039
Indonesia	75,129	58,596	62,326
Canada	50,635	50,876	48,566
Costa Rica	37,056	36,102	37,865
Germany(*)	29,509	36,200	30,590
Ethiopia(*)	26,294	25,531	25,804
Uganda	12,066	15,884	20,363
El Salvador	16,359	14,869	16,389
Papua New Guinea	11,512	11,659	13,533
Italy(*)	11,862	13,493	11,862
China	10,816	9,265	10,802
Switzerland(*)	6,599	8,044	10,362
Kenya	8,975	6,843	6,556
Rwanda	4,181	5,819	6,400
Tanzania	5,980	5,152	5,077
India	1,584	1,612	3,764
Venezuela	1,708	2,735	3,661
Spain	4,969	5,601	3,168
Belgium-Luxembourg(*)	0	4,274	3,114
Malaysia	1,333	1,580	2,184
Korea, South	1,306	1,582	1,809
Burundi	1,060	805	1,355
Rest of World	15,899	14,123	14,592
World Total	1,676,000	1,642,924	1,752,877
Tea, including herbal tea:			
Canada	53,532	48,977	54,420
Argentina	52,918	49,990	47,471
China	20,611	21,186	22,643
India	16,859	14,610	15,050
Sri Lanka	5,456	6,143	7,518
Malawi	7,458	5,671	6,543
Vietnam	6,897	6,602	5,418
Indonesia	3,639	3,358	4,993
Nigeria	1,490	4,644	4,111
Germany(*)	4,517	4,938	3,953
Kenya	5,779	3,133	2,789
Taiwan	1,801	2,234	2,662
Zimbabwe	1,867	2,439	2,494
Chile	2,101	1,816	2,147
Mexico	3,616	3,094	2,006
Japan	1,877	1,986	1,961
Poland	473	622	1,803
Egypt	565	686	1,556
Thailand	1,299	1,589	1,540
United Kingdom	1,059	1,299	1,444
Brazil	929	734	1,047
Pakistan	590	674	623
Korea, South	433	716	545
Ecuador	620	584	501
Ireland	297	336	371
South Africa	344	470	297
United Arab Emirates	313	285	297
France(*)	274	267	270
Mozambique	246	66	232
Rest of World	4,217	3,969	4,012
World Total	202,078	193,117	200,715

(*) Denotes a country that is a summarization of its component countries. All zeroes for a data item may show that statistics exist in the other import type. Consumption or General. Users should use cautious interpretation on Quantity reports using mixed units of measure. Quantity line items will only include statistics on the units of measure that are equal to, or are able to be converted to, the assigned unit of measure of the grouped commodities.

FAS, Office of Global Analysis, (202) 720-6301. Data Source: USDA FAS Global Agricultural Trade System (GATS)-BICO-HS10.

Table 5-88.—Specialty mushrooms: Number of growers, total production, volume of sales, price per pound, and value of sales, United States: 2017/2018-2019/2020

Year and variety	Growers [1]	Total Production [2]	All sales		
			Volume of sales [3]	Price per pound [4]	Value of sales
	Number	*1,000 pounds*	*1,000 pounds*	*Dollars*	*1,000 dollars*
2017/2018					
Shiitake	185	10,429	10,112	4.44	44,883
Oyster	116	11,268	10,842	3.13	33,890
Other	64	5,690	5,050	5.33	26,923
United States	229	27,387	26,004	4.06	105,696
2018/2019					
Shiitake	(NA)	6,987	6,726	3.20	21,515
Oyster	(NA)	8,941	8,623	3.10	26,695
Other	(NA)	3,970	3,906	4.62	18,041
United States	(NA)	19,898	19,255	3.44	66,251
2019/2020 [5]					
Shiitake	(NA)	7,298	7,013	3.44	24,091
Oyster	(NA)	8,642	8,517	2.70	23,032
Other	(NA)	4,652	4,475	4.54	20,323
United States	(NA)	20,592	20,005	3.37	67,446

(NA) Not available. [1] Growers counted only once for United States total if growing more than one specialty type mushroom. Growers growing Agaricus and specialty mushrooms are included. Estimates discontinued in 2018-2019. [2] Total production includes all fresh market and processing sales plus amount harvested but not sold (shrinkage, cullage, dumped, etc.). [3] Virtually all specialty mushroom sales are for fresh market. [4] Prices for mushrooms are the average prices producers receive at the point of first sale, commonly referred to as the average price as sold. For example, if in a given State, part of the fresh mushrooms are sold F.O.B. packed by growers, part are sold bulk to brokers or repackers, and some are sold retail at roadside stands, the mushroom average price as sold is a weighted average of the average price for each method of sale. [5] Beginning in 2018-2019, includes California, Florida, Illinois, Maryland, Oklahoma, Pennsylvania, Tennessee, and Texas.
NASS, Crops Branch, (202) 720–2127.

Table 5-89.—Agaricus mushrooms: Area, volume of sales, marketing year average price, and value of sales, United States: 2010-2019 [1]

Year	Area in production Total fillings	Volume of sales	Price per pound	Value of sales		
				Total	Fresh market	Processing
	1,000 sq. ft.	*1,000 pounds*	*Dollars*	*1,000 dollars*	*1,000 dollars*	*1,000 dollars*
2010/2011	134,266	845,951	1.140	964,192	887,839	76,353
2011/2012	139,331	881,857	1.180	1,039,159	969,847	69,312
2012/2013	139,846	869,625	1.190	1,038,541	969,278	69,263
2013/2014	134,685	882,075	1.190	1,049,972	971,521	78,451
2014/2015	143,292	907,191	1.230	1,118,371	1,054,652	63,719
2015/2016	142,147	919,012	1.200	1,098,745	1,035,106	63,639
2016/2017	143,497	906,593	1.240	1,122,821	1,060,281	62,540
2017/2018	140,563	891,231	1.270	1,127,886	1,070,316	57,570
2018/2019 [2]	119,185	812,469	1.290	1,048,459	1,004,062	44,397
2019/2020	135,084	796,362	1.360	1,085,850	1,045,857	39,993

[1] Marketing year begins July 1 and ends June 30 the following year. [2] Beginning in 2018-2019, includes California, Florida, Illinois, Maryland, Oklahoma, Pennsylvania, Tennessee, and Texas.
NASS, Crops Branch, (202) 720–2127.

Table 5-90.—Cut flowers: Sales and wholesale value for operations with $100,000+ sales, Surveyed States, 2008–2019

Year	Quantity sold	Wholesale price	Value of sales at wholesale[1]	Quantity sold	Wholesale price	Value of sales at wholesale[1]	Quantity sold	Wholesale price	Value of sales at wholesale[1]
	Alstroemeria			Carnations, standard			Chrysanthemums pompon		
	1,000 stems	Cents per stem	1,000 dollars	1,000 stems	Cents per stem	1,000 dollars	1,000 bunches	Cents per bunch	1,000 dollars
2008 ...	10,774	17.9	1,927	3,343	17.0	567	10,058	1.34	13,428
2009 ...	8,800	18.5	1,629	2,837	16.9	480	7,920	1.43	11,298
2010 ...	9,868	16.7	1,650	1,893	16.7	317	8,347	1.40	11,705
2011 ...	8,764	19.1	1,676	1,441	16.2	233	7,823	1.41	11,048
2012 ...	10,964	21.0	2,307	715	23.4	167	9,167	1.43	13,115
2013 ...	10,164	20.7	2,104	624	24.5	153	9,009	1.53	13,816
2014 ...	8,890	19.1	1,702	797	30.6	244	6,677	1.73	11,518
2015 ...	7,747	19.6	1,517	896	30.5	273	7,777	1.48	11,524
2018 ...	(NA)	(NA)	(NA)	(NA)	(NA)	(NA)	6,880	1.52	10,459
2019 ...	(NA)	(NA)	(NA)	(NA)	(NA)	(NA)	3,668	1.51	5,535
	Delphinium & Larkspur			Gerbera Daisies			Gladioli		
	1,000 stems	Cents per stem	1,000 dollars	1,000 stems	Cents per stem	1,000 dollars	1,000 spikes	Cents per spike	1,000 dollars
2008 ...	31,221	24.0	7,505	120,836	29.8	35,976	76,850	25.9	19,935
2009 ...	22,373	27.1	6,071	106,805	30.9	33,027	94,951	24.1	22,880
2010 ...	27,173	26.5	7,193	107,678	30.4	32,737	89,672	25.4	22,801
2011 ...	19,639	30.5	5,981	113,655	28.5	32,385	60,167	27.1	16,299
2012 ...	19,448	37.4	7,265	107,899	30.6	33,067	60,747	25.3	15,349
2013 ...	16,929	38.6	6,542	98,535	31.0	30,552	59,435	34.1	20,244
2014 ...	17,091	35.3	6,030	105,028	31.4	32,987	61,724	32.7	20,193
2015 ...	12,671	41.0	5,199	106,680	30.4	32,423	60,778	32.3	19,608
2018 ...	(NA)	(NA)	(NA)	90,999	35.1	31,930	61,647	32.7	20,175
2019 ...	(NA)	(NA)	(NA)	96,889	29.6	28,648	49,880	34.7	17,287
	Iris			Lilies, all			Lisianthus		
	1,000 stems	Cents per stem	1,000 dollars	1,000 stems	Cents per stem	1,000 dollars	1,000 stems	Cents per stem	1,000 dollars
2008 ...	92,404	22.1	20,462	116,797	67.3	78,609	15,180	35.6	5,406
2009 ...	64,114	24.3	15,550	101,339	63.5	64,392	8,689	38.3	3,327
2010 ...	57,576	25.2	14,518	93,373	65.5	61,165	7,650	38.8	2,966
2011 ...	62,414	26.1	16,303	141,337	56.5	79,798	7,502	42.1	3,160
2012 ...	55,025	24.5	13,477	99,743	66.7	66,553	9,846	43.1	4,240
2013 ...	54,635	24.4	13,356	87,094	68.4	59,558	9,216	45.2	4,167
2014 ...	45,682	26.4	12,078	79,432	77.6	61,661	8,484	45.2	3,839
2015 ...	43,787	26.4	11,554	82,551	75.4	62,235	9,010	45.0	4,055
2018 ...	36,466	27.7	10,107	72,435	102.6	74,321	(NA)	(NA)	(NA)
2019 ...	32,340	28.6	9,240	80,946	72.2	58,460	(NA)	(NA)	(NA)
	Orchids, all			Roses, all			Snapdragons		
	1,000 blooms	Cents per bloom	1,000 dollars	1,000 stems	Cents per stem	1,000 dollars	1,000 spikes	Cents per spike	1,000 dollars
2008 ...	7,882	98.2	7,737	57,999	38.8	22,481	42,696	27.6	11,790
2009 ...	7,637	185.1	14,133	42,031	42.0	17,662	37,473	27.0	10,118
2010 ...	7,852	99.8	7,834	39,497	42.9	16,950	31,475	27.1	8,524
2011 ...	7,166	83.0	5,949	37,004	48.4	17,912	34,777	25.1	8,744
2012 ...	6,498	90.9	5,909	32,736	49.4	16,184	35,061	29.7	10,396
2013 ...	5,846	163.6	9,564	28,626	56.3	16,105	42,013	25.4	10,652
2014 ...	6,737	245.6	16,546	30,555	56.2	17,178	41,467	24.8	10,274
2015 ...	4,682	170.5	7,983	27,812	61.3	17,039	43,863	29.5	12,933
2018 ...	3,628	169.4	6,146	29,774	64.4	19,168	28,218	26.1	7,368
2019 ...	3,047	181.7	5,536	17,265	77.1	13,317	22,839	34.5	7,869

Year	Tulips			Other cut flowers
	1,000 stems	Cents per stem	1,000 dollars	1,000 dollars
2008 ...	170,854	37.6	64,285	126,990
2009 ...	150,228	38.1	57,185	103,687
2010 ...	155,667	36.6	56,900	129,466
2011 ...	169,219	35.3	59,788	99,824
2012 ...	161,802	37.2	60,172	171,159
2013 ...	161,926	36.8	59,535	116,509
2014 ...	160,990	35.5	57,198	112,006
2015 ...	167,378	34.6	57,840	130,135
2018 ...	173,247	38.4	66,489	112,778
2019 ...	182,205	37.1	67,613	88,913

(NA) Not available. [1] Equivalent wholesale value of all sales.
NASS, Crops Branch, (202) 720–2127.

Table 5-91.—Cut Cultivated Greens: Sales and wholesale value for operations with $100,000+ sales, Surveyed States, 2008–2019

Year	Leatherleaf Ferns			Other cut cultivated greens
	Quantity sold	Wholesale price	Value of sales at wholesale [1]	Value of sales at wholesale [1]
	1,000 bunches	*Dollars per bunch*	*1,000 dollars*	*1,000 dollars*
2008	34,761	0.98	33,924	57,824
2009	31,800	0.94	29,942	43,993
2010	28,474	1.03	29,312	47,713
2011	26,277	0.97	25,499	46,537
2012	32,063	0.99	31,706	43,811
2013	32,209	1.02	32,779	42,706
2014	32,385	0.99	32,209	40,974
2015	33,319	1.02	33,853	46,573
2018	29,650	1.35	40,115	61,882
2019	24,584	1.59	39,151	50,086

[1] Equivalent wholesale value of all sales.
NASS, Crops Branch, (202) 720–2127.

Table 5-92.—Foliage Plants for Indoor or Patio Use: Sales and Wholesale value for operations with $100,000+ sales, Surveyed States, 2007–2018

Year	Foliage, Hanging Baskets			Foliage, Pots
	Quantity Sold	Wholesale price	Value of sales at wholesale	Value of sales at wholesale
	1,000 baskets	*Dollars per basket*	*1,000 dollars*	*1,000 dollars*
2008	11,003	4.90	53,949	456,362
2009	12,072	5.29	63,881	493,148
2010	14,530	5.39	78,247	507,882
2011	14,483	5.42	78,438	534,943
2012	10,323	6.12	63,158	576,778
2013	11,493	5.92	67,996	544,562
2014	10,199	6.19	63,103	559,779
2015	11,556	5.85	67,562	646,127
2018	13,071	6.26	81,785	571,294
2019	10,865	6.42	69,773	545,882

NASS, Crops Branch, (202) 720–2127.

Table 5-93.— Potted Flowering Plants for Indoor or Patio Use: Sales and wholesale value for operations with $100,000+ sales, Surveyed States, 2008–2019

Year	Quantity sold		Wholesale price		Value of sales at wholesale [1]
	Less than 5 inches	5 inches or more	Less than 5 inches	5 inches or more	

			African violets [2]		
	1,000 pots	*1,000 pots*	*Dollars per pot*	*Dollars*	*1,000 dollars*
2007	4,357	430	1.37	1.95	6,809
2008	2,946	9	1.35	3.34	3,993
2009	2,313	38	1.49	3.48	3,580
2010	2,727	23	1.31	1.88	3,614
2011	2,582	51	1.25	3.84	3,414
2012	2,632	27	1.55	2.38	4,150
2013	2,572	33	1.47	2.53	3,870
2014	2,595	9	1.55	4.13	4,063
2015	2,641	8	1.56	3.85	4,161
2018	(NA)	(NA)	(NA)	(NA)	(NA)

			Florist azaleas [2]		
	1,000 pots	*1,000 pots*	*Dollars per pot*	*Dollars per pot*	*1,000 dollars*
2007	1,514	5,081	2.34	4.90	28,435
2008	1,095	7,188	2.24	4.65	35,897
2009	2,345	5,214	2.30	4.92	31,044
2010	1,348	3,289	2.59	5.67	22,138
2011	1,266	3,012	2.32	6.01	21,022
2012	1,129	3,544	2.68	5.28	21,734
2013	1,109	3,313	2.48	5.05	19,471
2014	22	4,063	4.25	4.65	18,977
2015	103	3,587	5.26	4.96	18,343
2018	(NA)	(NA)	(NA)	(NA)	(NA)

			Florist chrysanthemums		
	1,000 pots	*1,000 pots*	*Dollars per pot*	*Dollars*	*1,000 dollars*
2007	1,810	11,363	1.65	3.15	38,777
2008	1,927	9,902	1.57	3.21	34,762
2009	1,314	6,181	1.90	3.61	24,842
2010	2,225	4,526	1.82	3.97	22,029
2011	1,351	5,210	2.43	3.54	21,720
2012	1,654	4,400	2.00	4.14	21,535
2013	613	5,343	2.82	3.99	23,045
2014	1,239	4,673	3.02	3.96	22,238
2015	457	4,119	2.02	3.83	16,699
2018	2,185	5,495	1.84	4.55	28,999

			Easter lilies		
	1,000 pots	*1,000 pots*	*Dollars per pot*	*Dollars per pot*	*1,000 dollars*
2007	....	6,546	....	4.05	26,512
2008	31	5,824	4.05	4.33	25,335
2009	93	6,196	3.16	4.38	27,405
2010	147	5,891	3.29	4.29	25,764
2011	99	5,094	2.73	4.35	22,436
2012	37	5,011	3.48	4.36	21,958
2013	295	5,901	2.80	4.23	25,758
2014	785	5,099	3.90	4.59	26,460
2015	155	5,370	2.54	4.45	24,317
2018	1,098	4,935	4.58	4.54	27,453

			Potted Orchids		
	1,000 pots	*1,000 pots*	*Dollars per pot*	*Dollars per pot*	*1,000 dollars*
2007	10,661	6,655	6.95	9.89	139,960
2008	10,689	5,415	7.16	9.23	126,509
2009	12,503	7,135	7.36	9.70	161,208
2010	13,395	7,933	7.10	9.71	172,196
2011	15,415	8,520	6.78	10.19	191,306
2012	15,915	12,389	7.01	9.62	230,695
2013	18,934	12,750	7.34	8.83	251,559
2014	19,085	14,474	7.65	8.80	273,481
2015	19,393	16,983	7.25	8.70	288,284
2018	20,546	14,142	7.59	9.71	293,399

See footnote(s) at end of table.

Table 5-93.—Potted flowering for indoor or patio use: Sales and wholesale value for operations with $100,000+ sales, Surveyed States, 2007–2018—Continued

Year	Quantity sold		Wholesale price		Value of sales at wholesale [1]
	Less than 5 inches	5 inches or more	Less than 5 inches	5 inches or more	
	Poinsettias				
	1,000 pots	*1,000 pots*	*Dollars per pot*	*Dollars per pot*	*1,000 dollars*
2007	7,130	31,901	2.07	4.60	161,409
2008	6,373	28,922	2.07	4.82	152,611
2009	6,679	28,649	2.13	4.69	148,579
2010	7,710	26,942	2.02	4.65	140,841
2011	7,470	27,259	1.84	4.60	139,274
2012	6,620	27,301	2.12	4.77	144,309
2013	6,610	26,797	2.06	4.82	142,805
2014	6,338	27,263	2.15	4.77	143,715
2015	6,509	25,459	2.14	4.94	139,710
2018	8,479	25,720	2.22	5.05	148,760
	Potted florist roses				
	1,000 pots	*1,000 pots*	*Dollars per pot*	*Dollars*	*1,000 dollars*
2007	6,834	2,364	1.94	5.16	25,425
2008	7,252	1,064	2.74	5.34	25,569
2009	6,924	1,031	2.57	5.14	23,115
2010	5,599	2,167	2.50	5.83	26,669
2011	5,183	2,550	2.16	4.87	23,619
2012	5,729	2,828	2.18	5.74	28,741
2013	5,976	2,750	2.40	6.14	31,214
2014	7,751	934	3.26	6.41	31,282
2015	6,341	1,784	2.42	5.25	24,696
2018	8,353	2,478	1.91	4.88	28,069
	Potted spring flowering bulbs				
	1,000 pots	*1,000 pots*	*Dollars per pot*	*Dollars*	*1,000 dollars*
2007	10,073	8,624	1.91	3.66	50,861
2008	13,317	10,958	1.69	3.56	61,532
2009	4,689	11,234	1.74	3.43	46,662
2010	9,766	12,382	1.46	3.52	57,903
2011	8,162	11,637	1.52	3.54	53,638
2012	5,095	11,434	1.74	3.63	50,376
2013	4,623	11,013	1.96	3.77	50,614
2014	5,018	10,791	1.78	3.86	50,561
2015	5,548	16,865	2.19	3.38	69,115
2018	6,347	16,502	2.42	3.27	69,376
	Other flowering				
	1,000 pots	*1,000 pots*	*Dollars per pot*	*Dollars per pot*	*1,000 dollars*
2007	27,176	36,862	2.09	4.51	223,111
2008	22,529	31,482	2.10	4.91	201,962
2009	19,531	29,173	2.13	4.62	176,570
2010	17,162	25,695	2.71	5.00	175,006
2011	24,663	21,896	1.88	5.36	163,903
2012	22,670	25,625	2.57	5.99	211,766
2013	24,868	26,835	2.67	5.87	223,931
2014	25,569	32,190	2.70	5.29	239,162
2015	23,575	29,889	1.93	5.99	224,335
2018	31,310	40,991	2.48	4.95	280,698

(NA) Not available. [1] Equivalent wholesale value of all sales except for potted foliage which is value of sales less cost of plant material purchased from other growers for growing on. [2] Estimates discontinued in 2018.
NASS, Crops Branch, (202) 720–2127.

Table 5-94.—Annual Bedding and Garden Hanging Baskets: Sales and wholesale value for operations with $100,000+ sales, Surveyed States, 2007–2018

Year	Quantity sold	Wholesale price	Value of sales at wholesale [1]	Quantity sold	Wholesale price	Value of sales at wholesale [1]
	Begonias			Geraniums from vegetative cuttings		
	1,000 baskets	Dollars	1,000 dollars	1,000 baskets	Dollars	1,000 dollars
2007	1,701	5.76	9,796	3,296	6.87	22,640
2008	1,707	5.80	9,899	3,056	7.32	22,366
2009	1,531	5.84	8,944	3,564	7.44	26,523
2010	1,650	5.96	9,839	3,753	7.10	26,659
2011	1,622	5.99	9,723	3,561	7.13	25,390
2012	1,823	5.94	10,830	3,280	7.49	24,562
2013	2,016	6.33	12,770	3,126	7.39	23,113
2014	1,849	6.00	11,089	3,320	7.56	25,089
2015	1,960	6.25	12,250	3,310	7.43	24,586
2018	1,954	7.38	14,424	4,005	7.63	30,561
	Geraniums from seeds [2]			Impatiens, Other		
	1,000 baskets	Dollars	1,000 dollars	1,000 baskets	Dollars	1,000 dollars
2007	316	5.63	1,778	2,597	5.22	13,548
2008	267	6.05	1,616	2,375	5.29	12,561
2009	455	5.95	2,708	2,098	5.79	12,146
2010	286	7.01	2,005	2,534	5.63	14,260
2011	337	6.61	2,227	2,385	5.72	13,639
2012	475	6.56	3,115	2,479	5.44	13,494
2013	415	7.28	3,020	2,065	5.33	11,015
2014	460	7.46	3,432	2,021	5.32	10,750
2015	438	7.39	3,237	2,098	5.45	11,432
2018	(NA)	(NA)	(NA)	2,124	5.44	11,560
	New Guinea Impatiens			Marigolds		
	1,000 baskets	Dollars	1,000 dollars	1,000 baskets	Dollars	1,000 dollars
2007	2,987	6.96	20,797	184	6.08	1,118
2008	2,668	7.23	19,280	202	6.30	1,272
2009	2,556	7.09	18,122	55	6.33	348
2010	2,615	7.11	18,581	83	6.01	499
2011	2,456	7.14	17,526	77	5.77	444
2012	2,380	7.32	17,420	87	4.92	428
2013	2,254	7.37	16,613	117	4.38	513
2014	2,294	7.31	16,764	137	5.88	805
2015	2,388	7.39	17,637	139	5.99	833
2018	2,123	7.51	15,936	192	5.10	979
	Pansies/Violas			Petunias		
	1,000 baskets	Dollars	1,000 dollars	1,000 baskets	Dollars	1,000 dollars
2007	694	5.02	3,485	4,011	5.99	24,017
2008	695	5.20	3,612	3,969	5.98	23,752
2009	1,077	5.43	5,848	4,186	6.38	26,711
2010	911	5.59	5,091	5,066	6.16	31,225
2011	941	5.83	5,483	5,047	6.29	31,767
2012	1,096	5.75	6,299	5,028	6.21	31,240
2013	1,085	5.62	6,096	4,986	6.11	30,459
2014	1,182	5.92	7,002	5,557	6.28	34,906
2015	1,111	6.23	6,920	5,294	6.27	33,196
2018	1,077	6.51	7,006	6,154	5.97	36,712
	Other flowering hanging baskets and foliar					
	1,000 baskets		Dollars		1,000 dollars	
2007	15,153		6.95		105,330	
2008	14,718		6.92		101,856	
2009	14,451		7.36		106,323	
2010	13,483		7.67		103,399	
2011	12,759		7.56		96,500	
2012	14,865		7.33		109,030	
2013	14,797		7.73		114,409	
2014	13,259		8.23		109,117	
2015	15,269		7.67		117,065	
2018	15,269		8.20		124,587	

(NA) Not available. [1] Equivalent wholesale value of all sales. [2] Estimates discontinued in 2018.
NASS, Crops Branch, (202) 720–2127.

Table 5-95.—Annual bedding garden plants flats: Sales and wholesale value for operations with $100,000+ sales, Surveyed States, 2007–2018

Year	Quantity sold	Wholesale price	Value of sales at wholesale [1]	Quantity sold	Wholesale price	Value of sales at wholesale [1]
	Begonias			Geraniums from vegetative cuttings		
	1,000 flats	*Dollars*	*1,000 dollars*	*1,000 flats*	*Dollars*	*1,000 dollars*
2007	4,094	8.17	33,444	417	12.32	5,138
2008	4,360	8.49	36,999	396	12.57	4,979
2009	4,055	8.75	35,490	353	15.09	5,326
2010	4,218	8.13	34,313	306	13.12	4,015
2011	3,983	7.97	31,738	264	14.08	3,716
2012	3,865	8.56	33,005	237	13.57	3,215
2013	3,758	8.15	30,640	325	11.65	3,785
2014	3,970	8.62	34,208	252	14.03	3,535
2015	3,819	8.33	31,813	248	12.83	3,182
2018	4,240	8.53	36,182	556	13.72	7,626
	Geraniums from seeds [2]			Impatients, other		
	1,000 flats	*Dollars*	*1,000 dollars*	*1,000 flats*	*Dollars*	*1,000 dollars*
2007	380	11.54	4,387	8,915	8.11	72,320
2008	384	11.00	4,223	8,547	8.52	72,815
2009	424	9.23	3,915	7,973	8.67	69,093
2010	465	10.29	4,784	8,641	8.24	71,160
2011	332	10.62	3,526	8,353	7.96	66,519
2012	394	9.81	3,866	6,852	9.08	62,230
2013	475	7.51	3,565	5,055	8.17	41,300
2014	372	9.26	3,445	4,775	8.38	40,034
2015	425	8.07	3,431	4,404	8.78	38,647
2018	(NA)	(NA)	(NA)	4,896	8.45	41,357
	New Guinea Impatiens			Marigolds		
	1,000 flats	*Dollars*	*1,000 dollars*	*1,000 flats*	*Dollars*	*1,000 dollars*
2007	243	11.09	2,696	3,694	8.39	31,001
2008	218	11.55	2,518	3,933	8.69	34,190
2009	290	10.77	3,124	3,976	8.98	35,713
2010	276	9.69	2,675	4,100	8.89	36,444
2011	190	10.56	2,006	3,884	8.45	32,807
2012	226	9.86	2,229	3,436	8.49	29,188
2013	335	10.01	3,355	3,488	8.24	28,733
2014	625	9.84	6,148	3,671	8.36	30,706
2015	368	9.76	3,592	3,587	8.20	29,425
2018	547	9.93	5,432	3,495	9.24	32,282
	Pansies/Violas			Petunias		
	1,000 flats	*Dollars*	*1,000 dollars*	*1,000 flats*	*Dollars*	*1,000 dollars*
2007	8,047	8.33	67,050	7,023	8.52	59,808
2008	8,169	8.82	72,036	7,402	8.80	65,129
2009	7,430	9.15	67,957	7,006	9.32	65,317
2010	7,538	8.88	66,916	7,448	8.92	66,404
2011	7,266	8.66	62,936	7,227	8.56	61,891
2012	7,343	9.02	66,245	6,667	8.64	57,618
2013	6,369	8.94	56,926	6,581	8.36	55,034
2014	7,272	8.45	61,441	6,896	9.11	62,822
2015	6,297	8.91	56,113	6,448	8.76	56,509
2018	5,269	9.72	51,195	5,751	9.62	55,348
	Other flowering and foliar plants			Vegetable type plants		
	1,000 flats	*Dollars*	*1,000 dollars*	*1,000 flats*	*Dollars*	*1,000 dollars*
2007	21,350	8.70	185,788	4,135	9.39	38,822
2008	19,441	9.00	175,027	4,545	10.25	46,573
2009	16,331	9.45	154,342	5,025	10.53	52,911
2010	17,898	9.40	168,261	4,862	10.20	49,603
2011	17,836	9.50	169,484	5,102	10.53	53,740
2012	16,934	9.10	154,089	6,297	9.64	60,714
2013	16,275	8.71	141,740	4,998	10.18	50,858
2014	14,788	9.38	138,683	4,861	10.82	52,616
2015	14,811	8.87	131,358	5,453	10.60	57,808
2018	14,488	10.00	144,925	7,330	11.73	86,013

(NA) Not available. [1] Equivalent wholesale value of all sales. [2] Estimates discontinued in 2018.
NASS, Crops Branch, (202) 720–2127.

Table 5-96.—Potted annual bedding and garden plants: Sales and wholesale value for operations with $100,000+ sales, Surveyed States, 2007–2018

Year	Quantity sold		Wholesale price		Value of sales at wholesale [1]
	Less than 5 inches	5 inches or more	Less than 5 inches	5 inches or more	

	Begonias				
	1,000 pots	*1,000 pots*	*Dollars*	*Dollars*	*1,000 dollars*
2007	16,748	3,683	0.84	2.06	21,645
2008	16,481	4,296	0.91	2.17	24,293
2009	17,821	3,272	0.86	2.34	22,907
2010	14,709	3,163	0.92	2.22	20,617
2011	14,763	3,374	0.91	2.24	20,973
2012	15,837	3,323	0.91	2.40	22,340
2013	18,296	4,118	0.94	2.58	27,922
2014	16,901	3,619	1.02	2.48	26,248
2015	16,853	4,757	1.05	2.82	31,023
2018	16,923	5,958	1.03	2.91	34,772

	Geraniums from cuttings				
	1,000 pots	*1,000 pots*	*Dollars*	*Dollars*	*1,000 dollars*
2007	22,785	13,253	1.66	3.35	82,364
2008	23,094	13,050	1.76	3.35	84,300
2009	22,985	14,209	1.79	3.18	86,303
2010	23,339	13,431	1.81	3.54	89,770
2011	21,156	12,844	1.85	3.57	85,031
2012	21,563	13,560	1.85	3.38	85,842
2013	20.429	11,554	1.88	3.62	80,293
2014	21,093	11,119	1.93	3.70	81,970
2015	19,821	11,724	1.92	3.66	80,989
2018	20,587	11,701	1.82	3.77	81,641

	Geraniums from seed [2]				
	1,000 pots	*1,000 pots*	*Dollars*	*Dollars*	*1,000 dollars*
2007	28,897	343	0.83	2.86	25,071
2008	25,114	367	0.87	3.31	23,186
2009	24,622	495	0.92	2.78	23,923
2010	18,748	1,248	1.03	4.67	25,097
2011	23,673	1,648	0.93	5.20	30,680
2012	16,449	728	0.88	3.42	16,988
2013	17,825	393	1.12	3.49	21,604
2014	17,230	340	1.11	4.06	20,552
2015	13,336	1,119	1.00	3.58	17,297
2018	(NA)	(NA)	(NA)	(NA)	(NA)

	Other impatiens				
	1,000 pots	*1,000 pots*	*Dollars*	*Dollars*	*1,000 dollars*
2007	19,575	5,575	0.81	1.69	25,267
2008	20,606	4,973	0.78	1.91	25,663
2009	21,923	5,075	0.76	1.87	26,065
2010	21,955	4,033	0.77	2.43	26,702
2011	20,480	4,220	0.77	2.25	25,334
2012	13,941	4,834	0.82	2.11	21,678
2013	8,825	3,629	0.94	1.90	15,245
2014	7,115	3,776	0.95	1.88	13,880
2015	6,754	3,614	1.00	2.25	14,911
2018	7,786	2,104	1.38	2.78	16,608

	New guinea impatiens				
	1,000 pots	*1,000 pots*	*Dollars*	*Dollars*	*1,000 dollars*
2007	11,885	4,735	1.58	2.83	32,180
2008	12,630	4,283	1.57	3.18	33,459
2009	12,439	3,834	1.59	3.25	32,177
2010	10,919	3,961	1.50	3.28	29,376
2011	9,794	3,658	1.59	3.44	28,130
2012	11,640	4,236	1.47	3.27	30,956
2013	13,325	4,045	1.51	3.46	34,105
2014	12,971	4,160	1.59	3.39	34,762
2015	12,864	4,024	1.52	3.63	34,158
2018	13,989	4,679	1.78	3.20	39,857

See footnote(s) at end of table.

Table 5-96.—Potted annual bedding and garden plants: Sales and wholesale value for operations with $100,000+ sales, Surveyed States, 2007–2018—Continued

Year	Quantity sold		Wholesale price		Value of sales at wholesale [1]
	Less than 5 inches	5 inches or more	Less than 5 inches	5 inches or more	
	Marigolds				
	1,000 pots	1,000 pots	Dollars	Dollars	1,000 dollars
2007	8,372	2,150	0.68	1.59	9,125
2008	7,600	1,704	0.72	1.61	8,185
2009	8,837	1,826	0.78	1.76	10,124
2010	7,901	2,463	0.76	1.88	10,621
2011	7,180	2,272	0.81	1.82	9,947
2012	8,871	1,792	0.79	2.10	10,762
2013	8,637	1,819	0.80	2.09	10,688
2014	9,264	1,273	0.97	2.32	11,922
2015	9,100	1,745	0.97	2.14	12,596
2018	8,020	2,357	1.09	2.39	14,366
	Pansies/violas				
	1,000 pots	1,000 pots	Dollars	Dollars	1,000 dollars
2007	28,021	6,145	0.74	2.13	33,788
2008	25,980	5,989	0.75	2.09	31,966
2009	27,054	5,529	0.74	2.06	31,363
2010	23,394	6,159	0.80	2.02	31,035
2011	24,573	6,130	0.80	2.12	32,692
2012	23,416	6,918	0.81	2.19	34,078
2013	21,953	6,155	0.86	2.19	32,308
2014	22,813	6,273	0.86	2.17	33,116
2015	23,029	6,418	0.89	2.17	34,518
2018	14,732	7,522	1.03	2.33	32,646
	Petunias				
	1,000 pots	1,000 pots	Dollars	Dollars	1,000 dollars
2007	18,551	6,935	0.98	2.37	34,558
2008	16,310	6,796	1.01	2.27	31,852
2009	18,088	7,527	0.98	2.20	34,301
2010	19,152	9,142	1.07	2.11	39,732
2011	18,212	8,843	1.12	2.07	38,629
2012	20,830	8,651	1.14	2.30	43,546
2013	18,713	8,251	1.23	2.64	44,844
2014	17,627	7,763	1.27	2.70	43,273
2015	17,664	7,815	1.28	2.68	43,536
2018	16,681	10,173	1.30	2.75	49,646
	Other flowering and foliar plants				
	1,000 pots	1,000 pots	Dollars	Dollars	1,000 dollars
2007	117,723	50,605	1.13	3.08	288,890
2008	108,251	55,789	1.20	2.65	278,250
2009	93,289	48,271	1.18	3.06	257,709
2010	104,633	57,937	1.26	3.04	301,479
2011	108,661	54,133	1.25	2.96	296,030
2012	127,328	64,961	1.20	3.02	348,961
2013	111,363	50,025	1.32	3.30	309,160
2014	98,436	45,668	1.35	3.33	284,313
2015	106,082	47,534	1.38	3.39	307,799
2018	115,900	64,616	1.45	3.56	398,531
	Vegetable type plants [3]				
	1,000 pots	1,000 pots	Dollars	Dollars	1,000 dollars
2007	27,676	3,874	1.01	2.22	36,668
2008	35,998	7,497	1.06	2.49	56,697
2009	38,534	12,794	1.07	2.51	73,307
2010	38,453	14,155	1.12	2.64	80,411
2011	40,176	7,478	1.29	3.19	75,761
2012	31,100	12,211	1.22	2.98	74,478
2013	31,816	10,057	1.24	3.16	71,249
2014	44,491	10,531	1.47	3.21	99,356
2015	36,402	8,174	1.33	2.73	70,721
2018	37,663	7,998	1.43	4.15	87,023

(NA) Not available. [1] Equivalent wholesale value of all sales. [2] Estimates discontinued in 2018. [3] Does not include vegetable transplants grown for use in commercial vegetable production.
NASS, Crops Branch, (202) 720–2127.

Table 5-97.—Potted herbaceous perennial plants: Sales and wholesale value for operations with $100,000+ sales, Surveyed States, 2007–2018

Year	Quantity sold		Wholesale price		Value of sales at wholesale [1]
	Less than 5 inches	5 inches or more	Less than 5 inches	5 inches or more	
	Hardy/Garden Chrysanthemums				
	1,000 pots	1,000 pots	Dollars	Dollars	1,000 dollars
2007	9,763	35,148	1.06	2.66	103,831
2008	9,217	34,689	1.10	2.61	100,868
2009	8,049	35,833	1.25	2.81	110,747
2010	11,352	34,531	1.10	2.93	113,620
2011	11,962	36,634	1.03	2.77	113,747
2012	13,327	35,792	1.03	3.08	124,097
2013	15,558	33,176	1.08	2.89	112,552
2014	14,727	33,907	1.04	3.08	119,888
2015	9,326	37,885	1.12	2.99	123,677
2018	15,810	37,243	1.46	3.34	147,494

Year	Quantity sold			Wholesale price			Value of sales at wholesale [1]
	Less than 1 gallon	1-2 gallons	2 gallons or more	Less than 1 gallon	1-2 gallons	2 gallons or more	
	Hosta						
	1,000 pots	1,000 pots	1,000 pots	Dollars	Dollars	Dollars	1,000 dollars
2007	4,374	6,589	271	1.74	3.50	7.69	32,723
2008	4,451	6,793	173	1.91	3.43	9.10	33,391
2009	4,279	6,340	582	2.15	3.36	6.47	34,283
2010	1,448	6,783	337	2.11	3.26	7.54	27,704
2011	2,112	6,270	281	2.27	3.19	8.53	27,195
2012	2,365	5,535	363	2.34	3.40	8.04	27,240
2013	2,511	5,898	382	2.64	3.39	7.98	29,671
2014	5,362	3,870	398	2.73	3.75	7.78	32,242
2015	5,195	4,419	419	2.70	3.92	8.35	34,869
2018	5,128	3,521	162	2.85	4.35	9.11	31,391
	Other Herbaceous Perennials						
	1,000 pots	1,000 pots	1,000 pots	Dollars	Dollars	Dollars	1,000 dollars
2007	68,640	69,843	6,442	1.71	3.33	6.84	394,407
2008	65,928	74,574	7,533	1.59	3.43	6.65	410,867
2009	50,229	80,234	4,975	1.68	3.42	6.92	392,847
2010	53,613	86,180	6,257	1.63	3.38	7.11	423,266
2011	56,970	83,944	5,459	1.75	3.35	7.43	421,276
2012	56,936	65,596	10,001	1.77	3.78	7.33	422,282
2013	62,721	72,430	6,983	1.90	3.90	8.41	460,375
2014	62,508	60,111	5,823	2.19	3.90	8.47	420,547
2015	57,666	62,449	4,271	2.17	4.01	8.75	412,866
2018	69,491	63,028	14,100	2.05	4.06	6.53	489,931

[1] Equivalent wholesale value of all sales.
NASS, Crops Branch, (202) 720–2127.

Table 5-98.—Floriculture: Number of Producers and Area Used for Production by Type of Cover, operations with $10,000+ sales, 15 Program States: 2015 and 2018

State	Total number of producers		Glass greenhouses		Fiberglass and other rigid greenhouses		Film plastic (single/ multi) greenhouses	
	2015	2018	2015	2018	2015	2018	2015	2018
	Number		*1,000 square feet*					
Alaska[1]	(NA)	51	(NA)	(D)	(NA)	(D)	(D)	253
California	685	850	10,748	10,387	30,042	30,091	30,091	64,726
Colorado[1]	(NA)	121	(NA)	(D)	(NA)	(D)	(D)	3,854
Connecticut[1]	(NA)	216	(NA)	2,533	(NA)	1,560	1,560	10,067
Florida	710	680	3,054	3,800	8,159	5,468	5,468	34,499
Hawaii[2]	301	(NA)	(D)	(NA)	(D)	(NA)	(NA)	(NA)
Illinois	273	241	2,966	2,695	2,249	1,701	1,701	9,058
Maryland[2]	153	(NA)	1,644	(NA)	1,375	(NA)	(NA)	(NA)
Michigan	556	569	3,458	3,126	3,773	2,926	2,926	41,861
New Jersey	273	303	4,675	4,350	1,031	548	548	13,213
New York	615	585	3,816	3,114	1,223	1,467	1,467	15,156
North Carolina	294	257	6,652	7,662	529	265	265	13,486
Ohio	472	481	8,860	9,455	1,767	2,272	2,272	15,337
Oregon	283	259	2,835	2,367	2,691	2,485	2,485	12,054
Pennsylvania	727	683	2,585	2,616	3,808	3,613	3,613	16,135
South Carolina[2]	72	(NA)	(D)	(NA)	(D)	(NA)	(NA)	(NA)
Texas	251	254	1,361	1,221	3,696	4,977	4,977	25,844
Virginia[1]	(NA)	190	(NA)	574	(NA)	68	68	12,233
Washington	248	277	2,317	1,860	1,099	894	894	5,771
Wisconsin[1]	(NA)	369	(NA)	793	(NA)	1,457	1,457	8,148
Other States[3]	....	....	27	1,326	1,704	3,647	3,647	....
Total	5,913	6,386	54,998	57,879	63,146	63,439	63,439	301,695

State	Total greenhouse cover		Shade and temporary cover		Total covered area		Open ground[4]	
	2015	2018	2015	2018	2015	2018	2015	2018
	1,000 square feet						*Acres*	
Alaska[1]	(NA)	1,063	(NA)	-	(NA)	1,063	(NA)	54
California	104,779	105,204	37,148	30,386	141,927	135,590	9,399	13,327
Colorado[1]	(NA)	8,017	(NA)	188	(NA)	8,205	(NA)	169
Connecticut[1]	(NA)	14,160	(NA)	211	(NA)	14,371	(NA)	503
Florida	51,673	43,767	289,184	392,386	340,857	436,153	6,853	6,527
Hawaii[2]	(D)	(NA)	(D)	(NA)	17,940	(NA)	914	(NA)
Illinois	14,604	13,454	664	619	15,268	14,073	4,272	1,179
Maryland[2]	9,274	(NA)	360	(NA)	9,634	(NA)	618	(NA)
Michigan	46,278	47,913	711	1,742	46,989	49,655	2,063	2,359
New Jersey	23,236	18,111	493	227	23,729	18,338	4,826	2,890
New York	20,760	19,737	433	377	21,193	20,114	722	943
North Carolina	21,640	21,413	1,244	251	22,884	21,664	912	644
Ohio	26,632	27,064	956	538	27,588	27,602	385	431
Oregon	18,861	16,906	2,275	2,408	21,136	19,314	3,903	3,047
Pennsylvania	20,959	22,364	262	187	21,221	22,551	778	802
South Carolina[2]	(D)	(NA)	(D)	(NA)	5,921	(NA)	396	(NA)
Texas	33,109	32,042	6,485	5,694	39,594	37,736	1,215	1,789
Virginia[1]	(NA)	12,875	(NA)	430	(NA)	13,305	(NA)	582
Washington	10,118	8,525	917	286	11,035	8,811	2,786	2,132
Wisconsin[1]	(NA)	10,398	(NA)	431	(NA)	10,829	(NA)	980
Other States[3]	7,425	....	16,436	....	....	....	....	....
Total	409,348	423,013	357,568	436,361	766,916	859,374	40,042	38,358

(D) Withheld to avoid disclosure of individual operations.   (NA) Not available.   [1] Estimates began in 2018.   [2] Estimates discontinued in 2018.   [3] Includes data withheld above.   [4] Totals may not add due to rounding.
NASS, Crops Branch, (202) 720-2127.

Table 5-99.—Floriculture Crops: Wholesale value of all sales by category, operations with $100,000+ sales: 2015 and 2018

State	Annual bedding/ garden plants		Herbaceous perennial plants		Total bedding/ garden plants [1]	
	2015	2018	2015	2018	2015	2018
	1,000 dollars					
Alaska [2]	(NA)	4,136	(NA)	336	(NA)	4,472
California	193,209	205,623	72,361	126,603	265,570	332,226
Colorado [2]	(NA)	61,486	(NA)	23,647	(NA)	85,133
Connecticut [2]	(NA)	74,025	(NA)	40,683	(NA)	114,708
Florida	96,402	140,090	37,023	63,539	133,425	203,629
Hawaii [3]	2,199	(NA)	1,587	(NA)	3,786	(NA)
Illinois	38,595	40,612	25,619	35,375	64,214	75,987
Maryland [3]	64,704	(NA)	37,527	(NA)	102,231	(NA)
Michigan	208,727	224,469	61,939	69,390	270,666	293,859
New Jersey	77,016	71,187	56,641	49,562	133,657	120,749
New York	86,189	72,076	24,608	21,276	110,797	93,352
North Carolina	140,596	84,195	42,873	58,199	183,469	142,394
Ohio	81,126	69,016	51,844	40,933	132,970	109,949
Oregon	52,586	71,514	30,667	37,857	83,253	109,371
Pennsylvania	67,574	77,783	22,593	31,025	90,167	108,808
South Carolina [3]	8,036	(NA)	46,786	(NA)	54,822	(NA)
Texas	136,112	98,708	32,118	29,868	168,230	128,576
Virginia [2]	(NA)	76,269	(NA)	24,254	(NA)	100,523
Washington	33,511	39,586	27,226	38,449	60,737	78,035
Wisconsin [2]	(NA)	46,440	(NA)	16,595	(NA)	63,035
Other States [4]			(NA)		(NA)	
Total	1,286,582	1,457,215	571,412	707,591	1,857,994	2,164,806

State	Potted flowering plants		Foliage plants for indoor or patio use		Cut flowers	
	2015	2018	2015	2018	2015	2018
	1,000 dollars					
Alaska [2]	(NA)	(D)	(NA)	(D)	(NA)	163
California	273,537	299,573	114,599	155,649	293,737	288,356
Colorado [2]	(NA)	9,149	(NA)	1,446	(NA)	2,724
Connecticut [2]	(NA)	8,460	(NA)	(D)	(NA)	66
Florida	201,212	151,957	543,447	413,873	2,289	(D)
Hawaii [3]	15,079	(NA)	9,612	(NA)	7,014	(NA)
Illinois	23,875	25,070	1,121	1,746	1,103	(D)
Maryland [3]	7,060	(NA)	(D)	(NA)	470	(NA)
Michigan	31,147	70,435	6,305	8,849	5,312	(D)
New Jersey	29,368	50,723	(D)	12,996	14,675	(D)
New York	29,537	33,433	(D)	2,266	885	(D)
North Carolina	27,545	18,494	(D)	18,078	4,981	(D)
Ohio	68,163	75,458	4,207	7,559	(D)	800
Oregon	14,809	17,186	1,170	4,695	13,350	13,231
Pennsylvania	44,954	47,996	(D)	(D)	(D)	8,513
South Carolina [3]	8,221	(NA)	(D)	(NA)	(D)	(NA)
Texas	27,165	26,040	(D)	14,010	(D)	3,533
Virginia [2]	(NA)	30,130	(NA)	835	(NA)	2,026
Washington	7,988	7,028	(D)	6,486	20,457	21,571
Wisconsin [2]	(NA)	(D)	(NA)	(D)	(NA)	2,799
Other States [4]		5,622	33,228	4,591	10,045	31,162
Total	809,660	876,754	713,689	653,079	374,318	374,944

See footnote(s) at end of table.

Table 5-99.—Floriculture Crops: Wholesale value of all sales by category, operations with $100,000+ sales: 2015 and 2018–Continued

State	Cut cultivated greens		Propagative floriculture material		Total wholesale value of all plant categories	
	2015	2018	2015	2018	2015	2018
	1,000 dollars					
Alaska [2]	(NA)	....	(NA)	....	(NA)	5,602
California	15,762	21,105	107,076	102,488	1,070,281	1,199,397
Colorado [2]	(NA)	....	(NA)	27,516	(NA)	125,968
Connecticut [2]	(NA)	....	(NA)	(D)	(NA)	123,667
Florida	61,080	(D)	86,828	90,893	1,028,281	938,886
Hawaii [3]	323	(NA)	1,352	(NA)	37,166	(NA)
Illinois	....	10	1,359	1,633	91,672	105,372
Maryland [3]	....	(NA)	(D)	(NA)	111,163	(NA)
Michigan	(D)	(D)	(D)	96,208	398,113	474,977
New Jersey	(D)	(D)	18,271	21,122	197,001	221,597
New York	(D)	(D)	16,522	17,712	160,167	148,014
North Carolina	....	(D)	(D)	3,432	234,168	188,269
Ohio	....	(D)	(D)	3,142	210,102	196,923
Oregon	2,465	3,318	14,292	10,925	129,339	158,726
Pennsylvania	(D)	(D)	(D)	27,864	169,962	195,620
South Carolina [3] ..	....	(NA)	(D)	(NA)	63,199	(NA)
Texas	(D)	....	(D)	4,925	216,429	177,084
Virginia [2]	(NA)	(D)	(NA)	(D)	(NA)	140,093
Washington	(D)	44	21,920	13,655	112,761	126,819
Wisconsin [2]	(NA)	(D)	(NA)	2,995	(NA)	75,691
Other States [4]	796	77,520	126,097	6,615	....	....
Total	80,426	101,997	393,717	431,125	4,229,804	4,602,705

- Represents zero.   (D) Withheld to avoid disclosure of individual operations.(NA) Not available.   [1] Includes Annual Bedding Plants and Herbaceous Perennials.   [2] Estimates began in 2018.   [3] Estimates discontinued in 2018.   [4] Includes data withheld above.
NASS, Crops Branch, (202) 720-2127.

Table 5-100.—Nuts, Pecans: Cold storage holdings, end of month, United States, 2018 and 2019

Month	Pecans			
	Shelled		In-shell	
	2018	2019	2018	2019
	1,000 pounds			
January	45,662	58,036	162,210	140,859
February	46,991	64,498	196,988	170,017
March	51,950	65,269	184,869	177,727
April	57,156	65,869	161,330	164,069
May	60,151	65,899	136,556	145,807
June	63,314	69,135	111,349	124,677
July	65,379	69,020	89,383	98,245
August	70,019	69,614	57,796	69,011
September	64,493	69,602	33,667	42,677
October	55,475	58,894	25,476	31,633
November	53,219	54,329	47,970	37,229
December	54,259	52,466	94,823	75,123

NASS, Livestock Branch, (202) 720-3570.

Table 5-101.—Fruit and orange juice: Cold storage holdings, end of month, United States, 2018 and 2019

Month	Apples		Apricots		Blackberries, IQF		Blackberries, pails & tubs	
	2018	2019	2018	2019	2018	2019	2018	2019
					1,000 pounds			
January	34,420	31,785	4,295	4,762	14,018	15,312	1,747	1,500
February	35,915	35,345	3,616	4,248	11,789	14,208	1,502	1,316
March	36,968	35,219	2,974	3,432	10,188	14,127	1,518	1,137
April	35,087	35,149	2,275	2,270	9,329	12,150	1,184	972
May	32,441	28,196	1,664	2,082	7,962	9,889	1,133	1,117
June	33,715	28,122	8,301	3,760	8,924	8,830	1,106	1,058
July	30,609	26,479	9,538	3,819	25,723	23,622	1,681	1,451
August	24,822	22,539	8,843	3,528	22,340	24,430	1,320	1,358
September	22,366	20,286	8,148	3,237	22,247	23,037	1,344	1,402
October	21,602	20,326	7,549	6,689	21,081	21,165	1,678	1,414
November	23,141	21,713	6,640	6,054	18,770	18,259	1,635	1,269
December	28,276	27,323	6,458	5,294	17,059	16,065	1,420	1,494

Month	Blackberries, barrels		Blackberries, concentrate		Blackberries, total		Blueberries	
	2018	2019	2018	2019	2018	2019	2018	2019
					1,000 pounds			
January	4,356	5,237	1,281	754	21,402	22,803	192,354	178,750
February	3,735	4,339	1,179	731	18,205	20,594	162,564	148,696
March	3,210	3,625	1,266	680	16,182	19,569	134,469	129,739
April	2,976	3,551	1,262	704	14,751	17,377	116,387	112,147
May	2,416	2,462	1,023	790	12,534	14,258	96,891	92,992
June	3,519	2,041	932	735	14,481	12,664	99,912	93,422
July	10,207	6,252	1,103	832	38,714	32,157	175,163	174,711
August	8,707	4,921	1,080	800	33,447	31,509	244,902	280,464
September	7,665	4,660	1,038	565	32,294	29,664	247,396	290,020
October	6,417	4,643	922	632	30,098	27,854	228,308	278,570
November	5,900	3,794	764	667	27,069	23,989	199,883	262,652
December	5,389	3,438	771	744	24,639	21,741	182,857	246,625

Month	Boysenberries		Cherries, Tart (RTP)		Cherries, Sweet		Grapes	
	2018	2019	2018	2019	2018	2019	2018	2019
					1,000 pounds			
January	412	772	125,530	126,955	16,935	13,640	2,859	4,242
February	589	387	115,381	120,147	14,840	12,387	2,853	5,178
March	437	423	108,226	114,474	14,400	12,370	3,015	5,684
April	430	407	98,931	111,041	13,710	12,942	2,525	5,572
May	347	1,170	88,879	94,508	12,447	11,538	3,055	4,447
June	835	1,294	74,151	84,115	10,877	10,117	4,464	4,351
July	1,044	2,046	167,724	117,089	16,941	14,008	3,719	4,349
August	897	1,618	184,463	162,132	22,197	18,525	5,798	3,320
September	868	1,323	169,664	152,361	20,896	17,361	4,831	5,158
October	933	794	156,443	145,276	16,924	15,943	3,785	4,445
November	794	612	145,503	139,349	14,646	14,067	4,417	5,820
December	722	667	141,203	128,711	15,147	12,628	4,772	5,429

Month	Peaches		Raspberries, Black		Red Raspberries, IQF		Red Raspberries, pails & tubs	
	2018	2019	2018	2019	2018	2019	2018	2019
					1,000 pounds			
January	68,986	58,556	1,756	1,170	33,313	31,230	6,428	6,672
February	60,036	54,491	1,677	1,088	32,545	26,539	6,678	5,932
March	54,899	52,611	1,703	904	29,636	23,738	6,369	5,243
April	46,756	43,830	1,423	793	27,388	22,545	5,934	5,131
May	40,717	41,729	1,306	822	24,831	19,892	5,671	4,766
June	35,517	38,043	2,081	998	26,870	18,124	5,419	4,776
July	37,622	39,840	2,718	1,694	55,768	45,790	9,483	8,262
August	47,951	47,955	1,992	1,430	53,168	48,388	9,225	7,901
September	69,188	65,860	1,796	1,437	47,645	43,293	8,784	7,514
October	69,577	66,485	1,625	1,362	43,591	39,276	8,483	7,350
November	64,956	57,342	1,513	1,164	39,721	34,923	7,913	6,073
December	62,532	52,109	1,467	890	37,341	31,877	7,627	5,484

See footnotes(s) at end of table.

Table 5-101.—Fruit and orange juice: Cold storage holdings, end of month, United States, 2018 and 2019—Continued

Month	Red Raspberries, barrels		Red Raspberries, concentrate		Red Raspberries, total		Strawberries, IQF & Poly	
	2018	2019	2018	2019	2018	2019	2018	2019
	1,000 pounds							
January	26,466	32,368	1,027	1,640	67,234	71,910	110,933	73,708
February	23,695	25,547	2,037	1,419	64,955	59,437	95,498	69,538
March	19,891	19,970	2,107	1,349	58,003	50,300	95,820	67,405
April	20,758	17,371	2,126	1,078	56,206	46,125	90,021	84,122
May	18,483	17,700	1,912	1,393	50,897	43,751	111,245	100,640
June	14,062	15,087	2,211	1,611	48,562	39,598	141,526	111,976
July	46,228	30,869	1,978	2,858	113,457	87,960	138,909	108,787
August	46,080	30,583	1,896	2,271	110,369	89,143	129,037	98,212
September ...	44,888	31,578	1,882	2,013	103,199	84,398	126,616	91,230
October	41,770	27,549	1,540	2,224	95,384	76,399	108,659	77,629
November	38,648	24,550	1,519	2,220	87,801	67,766	90,907	72,842
December	38,240	23,662	1,566	1,631	84,774	62,254	86,344	63,015

Month	Strawberries, pails & tubs		Strawberries, barrels & drums		Strawberries, juice stock		Strawberries, total	
	2018	2019	2018	2019	2018	2019	2018	2019
	1,000 pounds							
January	83,607	64,900	46,853	46,215	11,626	9,028	253,019	193,851
February	70,208	58,624	36,151	35,947	14,226	8,335	216,083	172,444
March	57,643	54,694	28,576	28,709	13,841	7,025	195,880	157,833
April	56,735	56,989	27,743	34,275	12,480	7,208	186,979	182,594
May	82,692	82,258	43,875	37,569	11,716	8,371	249,528	228,838
June	126,678	101,099	95,690	43,433	13,339	12,982	377,233	269,490
July	122,929	101,987	100,883	48,335	10,475	18,851	373,196	277,960
August	111,697	89,761	98,137	69,725	11,748	17,617	350,619	275,315
September ...	94,959	75,756	95,479	66,234	11,123	17,057	328,177	250,277
October	84,202	63,667	81,553	54,908	11,796	14,881	286,210	211,085
November	81,755	56,167	69,646	47,341	10,870	12,497	253,178	188,847
December	73,196	47,069	57,780	36,812	10,113	10,492	227,433	157,388

Month	Other fruit		Total frozen fruit		Orange juice	
	2018	2019	2018	2019	2018	2019
	1,000 pounds					
January	595,561	598,220	1,390,288	1,390,589	517,105	604,674
February	554,544	547,960	1,256,166	1,195,128	500,973	633,535
March	487,759	501,052	1,119,005	1,095,484	563,125	704,400
April	462,212	457,599	1,041,047	1,039,599	632,626	795,383
May	399,596	399,196	992,928	974,599	730,886	884,215
June	404,649	357,543	1,117,468	953,677	733,849	859,757
July	395,232	335,751	1,379,068	1,128,294	691,110	822,305
August	361,493	318,388	1,417,408	1,267,929	633,390	808,049
September ...	398,684	332,966	1,425,149	1,266,403	608,983	809,639
October	700,422	668,223	1,677,206	1,535,305	566,387	757,808
November	709,259	645,653	1,556,323	1,446,413	528,895	725,568
December	666,624	592,537	1,449,406	1,325,111	547,910	766,191

NASS, Livestock Branch, (202) 720–3570.

STATISTICS OF HAY, SEEDS, AND MINOR FIELD CROPS

Chapter VI deals with hay, pasture, seeds, and various minor field crops.

Table 6-1.—Hay, all: Area, yield, and production, by State and United States, 2018–2020

State	Area harvested			Yield per harvested acre			Production		
	2018	2019	2020	2018	2019	2020	2018	2019	2020
	1,000 acres	*1,000 acres*	*1,000 acres*	*Tons*	*Tons*	*Tons*	*1,000 tons*	*1,000 tons*	*1,000 tons*
Alabama	850	700	750	2.80	2.50	3.10	2,380	1,750	2,325
Alaska [1]	22	22	22	1.30	1.30	1.10	29	29	24
Arizona	300	325	310	7.82	1.72	7.94	2,346	2,509	2,460
Arkansas	1,203	1,253	1,273	1.80	2.20	2.10	2,168	2,760	2,677
California	980	1,010	825	5.80	5.74	5.59	5,682	5,795	4,610
Colorado	1,420	1,460	1,380	2.55	2.78	2.39	3,621	4,052	3,298
Connecticut	47	47	46	2.34	1.72	1.80	110	81	83
Delaware	13	14	14	2.62	2.21	2.43	34	31	34
Florida	280	270	280	3.10	2.90	3.00	868	783	840
Georgia	600	560	570	2.90	2.75	3.00	1,740	1,540	1,710
Idaho	1,340	1,300	1,300	3.75	3.93	4.05	5,019	5,111	5,270
Illinois	470	420	490	2.79	2.71	3.02	1,309	1,140	1,479
Indiana	510	520	500	2.71	2.48	2.56	1,382	1,290	1,282
Iowa	940	1,020	1,160	3.19	3.05	3.19	2,998	3,116	3,697
Kansas	2,360	2,280	2,590	2.02	2.77	2.28	4,760	6,315	5,893
Kentucky	1,895	1,945	2,195	2.68	2.27	2.47	5,088	4,424	5,428
Louisiana	380	390	400	2.20	2.50	2.40	836	975	960
Maine	110	110	104	1.89	2.15	1.76	208	236	183
Maryland	195	189	200	2.83	2.68	2.16	552	507	432
Massachusetts	79	51	60	1.48	2.25	1.77	117	115	106
Michigan	810	780	780	2.24	2.38	2.56	1,812	1,858	2,000
Minnesota	1,220	1,100	1,230	2.52	2.70	2.88	3,077	2,966	3,546
Mississippi	590	610	650	2.10	2.30	2.50	1,239	1,403	1,625
Missouri	3,070	3,360	3,070	1.76	2.19	2.10	5,408	7,367	6,437
Montana	2,900	3,000	2,860	1.93	2.08	2.07	4,740	5,595	6,225
Nebraska	2,700	2,450	2,740	2.59	2.48	2.32	6,985	6,085	6,370
Nevada	365	435	320	3.17	3.60	3.58	1,158	1,565	1,147
New Hampshire	39	49	42	1.77	1.69	1.83	69	83	77
New Jersey	114	91	106	1.93	2.05	1.85	220	187	196
New Mexico	250	245	225	3.73	3.89	3.65	932	954	822
New York	1,220	1,180	1,060	2.25	1.90	1.61	2,744	2,240	1,710
North Carolina	816	816	665	2.71	2.30	2.40	2,210	1,877	1,598
North Dakota	2,670	2,420	2,220	1.66	1.70	1.62	4,419	4,116	3,596
Ohio	970	920	860	2.43	2.32	2.44	2,356	2,137	2,102
Oklahoma	3,230	3,005	2,790	1.59	1.98	1.92	5,121	5,935	5,364
Oregon	1,000	970	960	3.06	3.47	3.10	3,056	3,362	2,976
Pennsylvania	1,190	1,210	1,335	2.30	2.47	2.43	2,739	2,986	3,297
Rhode Island	6	5	5	2.00	1.40	1.60	12	7	8
South Carolina	270	270	310	2.50	2.10	2.40	675	567	744
South Dakota	3,250	3,350	3,050	1.78	2.09	1.76	5,788	7,003	5,365
Tennessee	1,720	1,763	1,749	2.46	2.31	2.37	4,231	4,073	4,140
Texas	4,740	4,920	5,010	1.77	1.87	1.92	8,374	9,216	9,604
Utah	650	680	730	3.38	3.85	3.48	2,195	2,618	2,540
Vermont	170	160	167	2.15	1.86	1.88	366	298	314
Virginia	1,140	1,145	1,135	2.23	2.23	2.39	2,540	2,555	2,711
Washington	760	640	690	3.64	3.83	3.79	2,764	2,448	2,616
West Virginia	535	515	540	1.72	1.74	1.92	922	894	1,035
Wisconsin	1,360	1,300	1,370	2.17	2.14	2.54	2,953	2,784	3,483
Wyoming	1,090	1,150	1,080	2.20	2.17	2.49	2,393	2,496	2,690
United States [2]	52,839	52,425	52,238	2.34	2.46	2.43	123,600	128,864	128,812

(X) Not applicable. [1] Previously was included in the Alaska table. For 2017 data please refer to the Alaska table. [2] Beginning in 2018, United States total includes data for Alaska.
NASS, Crops Branch, (202) 720–2127.

Table 6-4.—Hay, all other: Area, yield, and production, by State and United States, 2018–2020

State	Area harvested			Yield per harvested acre			Production		
	2018	2019	2020	2018	2019	2020	2018	2019	2020
	1,000 acres	*1,000 acres*	*1,000 acres*	Tons	Tons	Tons	*1,000 tons*	*1,000 tons*	*1,000 tons*
Alabama [1]	850	700	750	2.80	2.50	3.10	2,380	1,750	2,325
Alaska [1] [2]	22	22	22	1.30	1.30	1.10	29	29	24
Arizona	40	45	45	4.80	4.70	5.00	188	185	250
Arkansas	1,200	1,250	1,270	1.80	2.20	2.10	2,160	2,750	2,667
California	360	430	350	3.90	3.90	3.40	1,404	1,677	1,190
Colorado	690	730	680	1.65	1.85	1.35	1,139	1,351	918
Connecticut	40	40	40	2.30	1.70	1.80	92	68	72
Delaware	9	11	10	2.40	2.00	2.40	22	22	24
Florida [1]	280	270	280	3.10	2.90	3.00	868	783	840
Georgia [1]	600	560	570	2.90	2.75	3.00	1,740	1,540	1,710
Idaho	290	290	290	2.10	2.30	2.50	609	667	725
Illinois	220	220	270	2.20	2.00	2.30	484	440	621
Indiana	270	300	280	2.45	2.10	2.30	662	630	644
Iowa	320	320	330	2.20	2.30	2.40	704	736	792
Kansas	1,750	1,650	2,050	1.50	2.30	1.90	2,625	3,795	3,895
Kentucky	1,750	1,800	2,050	2.65	2.20	2.40	4,638	3,960	4,920
Louisiana [1]	380	390	400	2.20	2.50	2.40	836	975	960
Maine	100	100	95	1.85	2.15	1.70	185	215	162
Maryland	155	155	165	2.40	2.50	2.00	372	388	330
Massachusetts	70	45	55	1.40	2.20	1.80	98	99	99
Michigan	220	230	230	1.80	2.10	2.00	396	483	460
Minnesota	500	370	490	2.05	1.90	1.80	1,025	703	882
Mississippi [1]	590	610	650	2.10	2.30	2.50	1,239	1,403	1,625
Missouri	2,800	3,100	2,850	1.70	2.15	2.05	4,760	6,665	5,843
Montana	1,000	900	960	1.70	2.15	1.80	1,700	1,710	1,728
Nebraska	1,850	1,500	1,880	1.55	1.80	1.65	3,330	2,475	3,102
Nevada	180	210	145	1.60	2.20	2.60	288	462	377
New Hampshire	35	45	37	1.70	1.70	1.80	60	77	67
New Jersey	105	80	90	1.80	1.90	1.70	189	152	153
New Mexico	90	85	95	2.00	2.00	1.40	180	170	133
New York	920	890	760	2.20	1.80	1.50	2,024	1,602	1,140
North Carolina	810	810	660	2.70	2.30	2.40	2,187	1,863	1,584
North Dakota	1,200	1,200	1,000	1.60	1.60	1.40	1,920	1,920	1,400
Ohio	620	590	560	2.05	2.00	2.20	1,271	1,180	1,232
Oklahoma	3,000	2,800	2,600	1.50	1.90	1.80	4,500	5,320	4,680
Oregon	580	570	600	2.30	2.60	2.20	1,334	1,482	1,320
Pennsylvania	890	920	960	2.10	2.30	2.20	1,869	2,116	2,112
Rhode Island	5	4	4	1.90	1.30	1.60	10	5	6
South Carolina [1]	270	270	310	2.50	2.10	2.40	675	567	744
South Dakota	1,500	1,450	1,250	1.35	1.75	1.70	2,025	2,538	2,125
Tennessee	1,700	1,750	1,730	2.45	2.30	2.35	4,165	4,025	4,066
Texas	4,600	4,800	4,900	1.65	1.80	1.85	7,590	8,640	9,065
Utah	150	170	180	2.30	2.50	2.50	345	425	450
Vermont	150	140	150	2.20	1.80	1.90	330	252	285
Virginia	1,100	1,100	1,100	2.20	2.20	2.35	2,420	2,420	2,585
Washington	410	310	280	2.90	3.00	2.90	1,189	930	812
West Virginia	520	500	530	1.70	1.70	1.90	884	850	1,007
Wisconsin	540	420	530	1.90	1.60	1.50	1,026	672	795
Wyoming	500	530	470	1.60	1.55	1.70	800	822	799
United States [2]	36,3231	35,682	36,490	1.96	2.07	2.05	70,966	73,989	73,745

(X) Not applicable. [1] Alfalfa and alfalfa mixtures included in all other hay. [2] Beginning in 2018, United States total includes data for Alaska.
NASS, Crops Branch, (202) 720–2127.

Table 6-5.—Hay, all: Stocks on farms, United States, 2010–2019

Crop year	Dec. 1	May 1 [1]
2011	89,723	22,217
2012	75,175	21,381
2013	89,394	14,156
2014	92,172	19,186
2015	94,928	24,537
2016	95,924	25,155
2017	89,422	24,400
2018	79,055	15,348
2019	84,488	14,906
2020	84,020	20,426

[1] Following year.
NASS, Crops Branch, (202) 720–2127.

Table 6-6.—Hay, all: Marketing year average price and value of production, by State and United States, 2018–2020

State	Marketing year average price per ton, baled [1]			Value of production		
	2018	2019	2020 [2]	2018	2019	2020 [2]
	Dollars	*Dollars*	*Dollars*	*1,000 dollars*	*1,000 dollars*	*1,000 dollars*
Alabama	95.00	87.00	96.00	226,100	152,250	223,200
Alaska [3]	355.00	350.00	370.00	10,295	10,150	8,880
Arizona	209.00	204.00	183.00	488,622	513,420	450,930
Arkansas	108.00	108.00	108.00	234,816	298,920	289,956
California	191.00	192.00	180.00	1,083,312	1,091,622	824,880
Colorado	220.00	231.00	212.00	794,138	931,959	700,298
Connecticut	172.00	177.00	184.00	18,960	14,325	15,270
Delaware	168.00	160.00	161.00	5,650	4,972	5,460
Florida	153.00	151.00	154.00	132,804	118,233	129,360
Georgia	82.00	84.00	99.00	142,680	129,360	169,290
Idaho	154.00	157.00	156.00	773,241	798,867	816,515
Illinois	149.00	161.00	152.00	194,260	179,520	219,138
Indiana	154.00	178.00	177.00	211,026	230,100	226,752
Iowa	131.00	124.00	124.00	394,170	385,208	437,044
Kansas	153.00	127.00	128.00	635,950	724,710	667,626
Kentucky	159.00	149.00	152.00	770,610	616,200	786,148
Louisiana	102.00	103.00	101.00	85,272	100,425	96,960
Maine	133.00	134.00	161.00	28,121	31,688	29,415
Maryland	163.00	157.00	158.00	91,092	79,822	68,046
Massachusetts	182.00	165.00	173.00	21,662	18,931	18,300
Michigan	147.00	160.00	168.00	271,980	313,375	348,840
Minnesota	136.00	142.00	121.00	410,294	424,580	431,946
Mississippi	97.00	95.00	99.00	120,183	133,285	160,875
Missouri	121.00	120.00	111.00	631,392	866,514	694,493
Montana	145.00	143.00	131.00	800,860	893,595	772,944
Nebraska	107.00	103.00	103.00	706,705	608,815	629,852
Nevada	174.00	175.00	183.00	202,644	272,027	209,901
New Hampshire	114.00	164.00	170.00	8,103	13,579	13,055
New Jersey	186.00	187.00	185.00	41,032	35,048	36,177
New Mexico	231.00	223.00	215.00	211,832	212,044	176,390
New York	150.00	163.00	165.00	423,976	382,006	295,260
North Carolina	123.00	113.00	118.00	271,897	211,624	188,310
North Dakota	87.00	83.00	86.00	357,969	319,968	294,844
Ohio	145.00	165.00	165.00	354,888	365,213	357,352
Oklahoma	103.00	106.00	108.00	539,127	637,165	589,644
Oregon	195.00	197.00	195.00	590,414	657,580	569,160
Pennsylvania	182.00	184.00	189.00	502,203	569,036	660,183
Rhode Island	140.00	171.00	180.00	1,684	1,199	1,440
South Carolina	139.00	142.00	120.00	93,825	80,514	89,280
South Dakota	104.00	102.00	104.00	588,941	697,950	536,120
Tennessee	120.00	112.00	117.00	510,353	457,093	483,574
Texas	143.00	130.00	146.00	1,078,326	1,118,592	1,354,997
Utah	171.00	181.00	181.00	364,058	460,326	445,730
Vermont	138.00	167.00	150.00	50,412	49,634	47,125
Virginia	139.00	126.00	131.00	347,540	323,185	354,377
Washington	186.00	193.00	191.00	519,277	468,306	500,740
West Virginia	127.00	114.00	119.00	116,446	101,948	123,195
Wisconsin	153.00	185.00	156.00	441,450	513,504	544,296
Wyoming	167.00	176.00	171.00	387,596	426,294	458,685
United States [3]	166.00	163.00	156.00	17,288,215	18,039,795	17,552,253

(NA) Not available. [1] Baled hay. [2] Preliminary. [3] Beginning in 2018, United States total includes data for Alaska.
NASS, Crops Branch, (202) 720–2127.

Table 6-7.—Hay: Area and production, by type, United States, 2011–2020

Year	Area harvested			Production		
	Alfalfa	All other hay	All hay	Alfalfa	All other hay	All hay
	1,000 acres	*1,000 acres*	*1,000 acres*	*1,000 tons*	*1,000 tons*	*1,000 tons*
2011	19,044	36,160	55,204	64,815	65,065	129,880
2012	16,795	37,858	54,653	50,600	66,472	117,072
2013	17,699	40,274	57,973	57,307	77,891	135,198
2014	18,406	38,747	57,153	61,487	78,632	140,119
2015	17,810	36,719	54,529	59,060	75,608	134,668
2016	17,029	36,156	53,185	58,601	75,481	134,082
2017	17,007	35,770	52,777	55,812	72,395	128,207
2018	16,608	36,231	52,839	52,634	70,966	123,600
2019	16,743	35,682	52,425	54,875	73,989	128,864
2020	16,230	36,008	52,238	53,067	73,745	126,812

NASS, Crops Branch, (202) 720–2127.

Table 6-8.—Hay: Supply and disappearance, prices, and number of animal units fed annually, United States, 2009–2018 [1]

Year beginning May	Farm carryover May 1	Production	Total supply	Disappear-ance	Roughage-consuming animal units	Supply per animal unit	Disappear-ance per animal unit	Price received per ton
	Million tons	*Million tons*	*Million tons*	*Million tons*	*Million tons*	*Tons*	*Tons*	*Dollars*
2009 [2]	22.1	146.6	170.0	148.8	70	2.41	2.11	108
2010	20.9	143.5	166.0	143.7	69	2.39	2.07	114
2011	22.2	140.3	152.2	130.7	68	2.24	1.92	178
2012	21.4	126.1	138.7	124.3	68	2.05	1.84	191
2013	14.2	132.7	149.5	130.0	67	2.24	1.95	176
2014	19.2	137.0	159.4	134.6	67	2.36	2.00	172
2015	24.5	134.5	159.3	133.9	69	2.29	1.93	145
2016	25.1	133.8	160.1	135.5	71	2.26	1.91	129
2017	....	....	....	....	....	....	....	142
2018	....	....	....	....	....	....	....	164

[1] Excludes trade. [2] Beginning in 2009, supply includes imports.
ERS, Market and Trade Economics Division, (202) 694-5313.

Forage production is the sum of all dry hay production and haylage/greenchop production after converting the haylage/greenchop production to a dry equivalent basis (13 percent moisture) by multiplying the green weight (weight at harvest) by 0.4943. The conversion factor (0.4943) is based on the assumption that one ton of dry hay is 0.87 ton of dry matter, one ton of haylage is 0.45 ton dry matter and one ton of greenchop is 0.25 ton dry matter. The total haylage/greenchop production is assumed to be comprised of 90 percent haylage and 10 percent greenchop. Therefore, the conversion factor used to adjust haylage/greenchop production to a dry equivalent basis = ((0.45*0.9)+(0.25*0.1))/0.87 = 0.4943. The factors assumed here may vary by State and can be adjusted. Adjustments would result in a slightly different conversion factor.

Table 6-9.—All forage: Area harvested, yield, and production, by State and 17 State total, 2018–2020 [1]

State	Area harvested			Yield		
	2018	2019	2020	2018	2019	2020
	1,000 acres	1,000 acres	1,000 acres	Tons	Tons	Tons
California	1,180	1,190	960	5.98	5.93	6.02
Idaho	1,380	1,380	1,390	4.00	4.35	4.35
Illinois	485	450	515	2.92	2.86	3.19
Iowa	995	1,115	1,225	3.31	3.15	3.27
Kansas	2,460	2,345	2,665	2.09	2.85	2.33
Michigan	1,010	990	985	2.70	2.99	3.16
Minnesota	1,380	1,330	1,505	2.73	2.82	3.05
Missouri	3,170	3,490	3,145	1.81	2.20	2.11
Nebraska	2,730	2,505	2,770	2.59	2.50	2.36
New York	1,740	1,640	1,550	3.01	2.52	2.35
Ohio	1,035	970	900	2.66	2.62	2.69
Pennsylvania	1,465	1,430	1,625	2.77	2.98	2.73
South Dakota	3,330	3,505	3,105	1.83	2.10	1.79
Texas	4,845	5,045	5,190	1.84	1.98	2.03
Vermont	295	265	275	3.76	3.54	3.14
Washington	830	670	725	4.07	4.02	4.18
Wisconsin	2,210	2,330	2,360	2.93	2.63	3.07
17 State Total	30,540	30,650	30,890	2.61	2.71	2.66

State	Production		
	2018	2019	2020
	1,000 tons	1,000 tons	1,000 tons
California	7,053	7,060	5,780
Idaho	5,516	6,000	6,045
Illinois	1,417	1,285	1,641
Iowa	3,289	3,517	4,006
Kansas	5,140	6,690	6,222
Michigan	2,729	2,959	3,113
Minnesota	3,763	3,745	4,588
Missouri	5,737	7,661	6,644
Nebraska	7,084	6,258	6,544
New York	5,233	4,130	3,635
Ohio	2,757	2,546	2,421
Pennsylvania	4,065	4,265	4,439
South Dakota	6,110	7,365	5,562
Texas	8,910	9,965	10,519
Vermont	1,110	939	864
Washington	3,382	2,694	3,029
Wisconsin	6,479	6,135	7,242
17 State Total	79,774	83,214	82,294

[1] All forage production is the sum of the following dry equivalents: alfalfa hay harvested as dry hay, all other hay harvested as dry hay, alfalfa haylage and greenchop, all other hay haylage and greenchop; after converting alfalfa and all other haylage and greenchop to a dry equivalent basis.
NASS, Crops Branch, (202) 720–2127.

Table 6-10.—All alfalfa forage: Area harvested, yield, and production, by State and 17 State total, 2018–2020 [1]

State	Area harvested			Yield		
	2018	2019	2020	2018	2019	2020
	1,000 acres	*1,000 acres*	*1,000 acres*	*Tons*	*Tons*	*Tons*
California	670	610	515	6.75	7.06	7.09
Idaho	1,080	1,060	1,060	4.43	4.86	4.75
Illinois	260	220	235	3.47	3.68	4.15
Iowa	655	765	865	3.84	3.52	3.56
Kansas	620	645	545	3.54	4.05	3.74
Michigan	780	750	745	2.94	3.20	3.44
Minnesota	850	930	980	3.13	3.20	3.68
Missouri	290	290	225	2.68	2.69	2.84
Nebraska	870	990	880	4.26	3.75	3.84
New York	650	530	570	3.95	3.47	3.25
Ohio	390	370	330	3.66	3.44	3.37
Pennsylvania	465	380	535	3.65	4.37	3.48
South Dakota	1,800	2,000	1,845	2.21	2.34	1.83
Texas	145	125	115	5.52	4.90	4.85
Vermont	45	35	45	4.27	4.94	4.16
Washington	355	350	430	4.72	4.63	4.61
Wisconsin	1,590	1,680	1,660	3.29	3.00	3.65
17 State Total	11,515	11,730	11,580	3.64	3.61	3.62

State	Production		
	2018	2019	2020
	1,000 tons	*1,000 tons*	*1,000 tons*
California	4,523	4,308	3,651
Idaho	4,788	5,155	5,038
Illinois	902	810	976
Iowa	2,514	2,690	3,083
Kansas	2,194	2,613	2,083
Michigan	2,290	2,403	2,566
Minnesota	2,657	2,975	3,607
Missouri	778	781	638
Nebraska	3,704	3,711	3,382
New York	2,566	1,840	1,851
Ohio	1,428	1,273	1,112
Pennsylvania	1,698	1,661	1,860
South Dakota	3,985	4,682	3,373
Texas	801	613	558
Vermont	192	173	187
Washington	1,676	1,619	1,982
Wisconsin	5,239	5,036	6,053
17 State Total	41,935	42,343	41,955

[1] All alfalfa forage production is the sum of alfalfa harvested as dry hay; and alfalfa haylage and greenchop production after converting it to a dry equivalent basis.
NASS, Crops Branch, (202) 720–2127.

Table 6-11.—All haylage and greenchop: Area harvested, yield, and production, by State and 17 State total, 2018–2020 [1]

State	Area harvested			Yield		
	2018	2019	2020	2018	2019	2020
	1,000 acres	*1,000 acres*	*1,000 acres*	*Tons*	*Tons*	*Tons*
California	250	210	185	11.10	12.19	12.80
Idaho	105	155	165	9.57	11.60	9.50
Illinois	38	49	54	5.74	5.96	6.06
Iowa	80	140	95	7.36	5.80	6.59
Kansas	120	85	105	6.42	8.92	6.33
Michigan	285	290	280	6.51	7.68	8.04
Minnesota	220	265	315	6.31	5.95	6.69
Missouri	155	190	125	4.29	3.13	3.36
Nebraska	40	75	55	5.05	4.67	6.42
New York	710	610	670	7.09	6.27	5.81
Ohio	135	125	110	6.00	6.62	5.87
Pennsylvania	410	390	370	6.54	6.64	6.24
South Dakota	120	190	80	5.44	3.85	5.00
Texas	145	190	250	7.48	7.97	7.40
Vermont	185	165	175	8.14	7.85	6.36
Washington	119	85	90	10.50	5.85	9.28
Wisconsin	1,120	1,290	1,130	6.37	5.26	6.73
17 State Total	4,237	4,504	4,254	6.99	6.44	6.90

State	Production		
	2018	2019	2020
	T31,000 tons		
California	2,774	2,559	2,368
Idaho	1,005	1,798	1,568
Illinois	218	292	327
Iowa	589	812	626
Kansas	770	758	665
Michigan	1,856	2,227	2,252
Minnesota	1,388	1,576	2,108
Missouri	665	595	420
Nebraska	202	350	353
New York	5,035	3,824	3,894
Ohio	810	828	646
Pennsylvania	2,683	2,588	2,310
South Dakota	653	731	400
Texas	1,085	1,515	1,851
Vermont	1,505	1,296	1,113
Washington	1,249	497	835
Wisconsin	7,132	6,780	7,606
17 State Total	29,619	29,026	29,342

[1] Includes all types of forage harvested as haylage or greenchop (green weight). Forage harvested as dry hay and corn and sorghum silage/greenchop are not included.
NASS, Crops Branch, (202) 720–2127.

Table 6-12.—Alfalfa haylage and greenchop: Area harvested, yield, and production, by State and 17 State total, 2018–2020 [1]

State	Area harvested			Yield		
	2018	2019	2020	2018	2019	2020
	1,000 acres	*1,000 acres*	*1,000 acres*	*Tons*	*Tons*	*Tons*
California	80	60	60	6.20	6.40	7.80
Idaho	85	115	105	9.00	12.50	9.50
Illinois	24	30	35	6.50	7.40	6.80
Iowa	55	95	50	8.10	6.60	7.20
Kansas	20	25	15	6.00	7.50	5.30
Michigan	260	260	250	6.80	8.00	8.30
Minnesota	180	225	265	6.80	6.40	7.20
Missouri	35	40	15	7.50	4.00	6.00
Nebraska	25	50	35	4.00	4.10	6.60
New York	450	320	360	8.30	7.60	7.20
Ohio	90	90	70	7.70	7.10	7.00
Pennsylvania	250	200	195	6.70	8.00	7.00
South Dakota	75	125	60	6.00	3.50	4.50
Texas	5	10	5	7.00	7.50	7.50
Vermont	45	35	45	7.00	7.30	7.10
Washington	24	40	40	8.50	5.10	9.00
Wisconsin	1,000	1,020	920	6.70	5.80	7.40
17 State Total	2,703	2,740	2,525	7.08	6.68	7.40

State	Production		
	2018	2019	2020
	1,000 tons	*1,000 tons*	*1,000 tons*
California	496	384	4,680
Idaho	765	1,438	9,980
Illinois	156	222	2,380
Iowa	446	627	3,600
Kansas	120	188	800
Michigan	1,768	2,080	20,750
Minnesota	1,224	1,440	19,080
Missouri	263	160	900
Nebraska	100	205	2,310
New York	3,735	2,432	25,920
Ohio	693	639	4,900
Pennsylvania	1,675	1,600	13,650
South Dakota	450	438	2,700
Texas	35	75	380
Vermont	315	256	3,200
Washington	204	204	3,600
Wisconsin	6,700	5,916	8,080
17 State Total	19,145	18,304	18,691

NASS, Crops Branch, (202) 720–2127.

Table 6-13.—Beans, dry edible (clean basis): Production, by classes, United States, 2017–2019 [1]

Class	2017	2018 [1]	2019
	1,000 cwt	*1,000 cwt*	*1,000 cwt*
Navy (pea beans)	4,161	4,191	3,029
Great northern	1,403	1,188	1,040
Small white	171	155	105
Pinto	13,617	8,778	6,769
Red kidney, light	899	897	915
Red kidney, dark	1,099	1,625	1,489
Pink	332	398	291
Small red	438	701	567
Cranberry	185	244	161
Black	5,120	5,212	5,069
Large lima	255	234	197
Baby lima	204	275	278
Blackeye	437	528	259
Small chickpeas (Garbanzo)	1,969	3,346	1,423
Large chickpeas (Garbanzo)	5,088	9,441	4,814
Chickpeas, all (Garbanzo)	7,057	12,787	6,237
Other [2]	583	532	642
Total	35,961	37,745	20,811

[1] Excludes beans grown for garden seed. [2] Data are included in "Other" class to avoid disclosing data for individual operations.
NASS, Crops Branch, (202) 720–2127.

Table 6-14.—Beans, dry edible: Area, yield, and production, by State and United States, 2017–2019 [1]

State	Area planted			Area harvested		
	2017	2018	2019	2017	2018	2019
	1,000 acres	*1,000 acres*	*1,000 acres*	*1,000 acres*	*1,000 acres*	*1,000 acres*
California	50.0	48.0	27.4	49.7	47.7	27.4
Colorado	58.0	42.0	37.0	54.5	30.5	33.8
Idaho	180.0	185.0	47.0	178.0	183.0	45.0
Michigan	220.0	195.0	185.0	218.5	193.0	180.0
Minnesota	170.0	185.0	210.0	163.0	178.0	201.0
Montana [2]	275.0	395.0	(NA)	265.0	386.0	(NA)
Nebraska	180.0	140.2	120.0	155.0	131.2	97.0
North Dakota	705.0	635.0	615.0	685.0	615.0	550.0
Texas [2]	22.0	20.3	(NA)	20.0	18.3	(NA)
Washington	196.0	218.0	25.0	195.0	217.0	25.0
Wyoming	41.0	31.0	21.0	39.0	28.5	17.3
United States	2,097.0	2,094.5	1,287.4	2,022.7	2,028.2	1,176.5

State	Yield per acre (clean basis)			Production (clean basis)		
	2017	2018	2019	2017	2018	2019
	Pounds	Pounds	Pounds	*1,000 cwt*	*1,000 cwt*	*1,000 cwt*
California	2,100	2,490	2,660	1,045	1,190	729
Colorado	2,000	2,120	1,840	1,092	647	623
Idaho	1,610	1,710	2,370	2,873	3,127	1,067
Michigan	2,010	2,400	2,030	4,394	4,635	3,662
Minnesota	2,190	2,360	2,040	3,567	4,200	4,101
Montana [2]	1,000	1,350	(NA)	2,643	5,214	(NA)
Nebraska	2,520	2,480	1,940	3,901	3,254	1,883
North Dakota	1,810	1,760	1,400	12,392	10,806	7,691
Texas [2]	1,100	1,150	(NA)	220	210	(NA)
Washington	1,490	1,780	2,660	2,901	3,857	665
Wyoming	2,390	2,120	2,250	933	605	390
United States	1,778	1,861	1,769	35,961	37,745	20,811

(NA) Not available. [1] Excludes beans grown for garden seed. Beginning 2019, chickpeas are excluded. [2] Estimates discontinued in 2019.
NASS, Crops Branch, (202) 720–2127.

Table 6-15.—Beans, dry edible: Area, yield, production, price, and value, United States, 2010–2019[1]

Year	Area planted	Area harvested	Yield per acre[2]	Production[2]	Marketing year average price per 100 pounds received by farmers	Value of production
	1,000 acres	*1,000 acres*	*Pounds*	*1,000 cwt.*	*Dollars*	*1,000 dollars*
2010	1,911.4	1,842.7	1,726	31,801	28.00	899,258
2011	1,217.9	1,167.9	1,703	19,890	42.10	851,131
2012	1,742.5	1,690.4	1,889	31,925	38.00	1,235,255
2013	1,361.8	1,315.0	1,868	24,567	39.10	982,385
2014	1,703.1	1,648.6	1,754	28,910	32.30	980,622
2015	1,766.7	1,708.4	1,759	30,057	27.30	866,222
2016	1,664.0	1,558.1	1,842	28,703	29.20	863,431
2017	2,097.0	2,022.7	1,778	35,961	26.70	1,006,353
2018	2,094.5	2,028.2	1,861	37,745	25.40	951,047
2019	1,287.4	1,176.5	1,769	20,811	29.10	608,870

[1] Excludes beans grown for garden seed.   [2] Clean basis.
NASS, Crops Branch, (202) 720–2127.

Table 6-16.—Beans, dry edible ((clean basis): Marketing year average price and value of production, by State and United States, 2017–2019

States	Marketing year average price per cwt.			Value of production		
	2017	2018	2019[1]	2017	2018	2019[1]
	Dollars	*Dollars*	*Dollars*	*1,000 dollars*	*1,000 dollars*	*1,000 dollars*
California	61.20	69.20	53.30	63,954	82,348	38,856
Colorado	28.90	31.20	33.20	31,559	20,186	20,684
Idaho	27.80	23.50	22.40	79,869	73,485	23,901
Michigan	29.30	27.60	29.80	128,744	127,926	109,128
Minnesota	27.40	26.70	31.90	97,736	112,140	130,822
Montana[2]	33.80	19.30	(NA)	89,333	100,630	(NA)
Nebraska	25.50	(D)	28.50	99,476	(D)	53,666
North Dakota	24.10	22.90	25.70	298,647	247,457	197,659
Texas[2]	34.60	(D)	(NA)	7,612	(D)	(NA)
Washington	29.10	22.70	35.70	84,419	87,554	23,741
Wyoming	26.80	25.90	26.70	25,004	15,670	10,413
United States	26.70	25.40	29.10	1,006,353	951,047	608,870

(D) Withheld to avoid disclosing data for individual operations. (NA) Not available. [1] Preliminary. [2] Estimates discontinued in 2019.
NASS, Crops Branch, (202) 720–2127.

Table 6-17.—Beans, dry edible: Season average price [1] per 100 pounds, 2010–2019

Year beginning September	Lima	Garbanzo	Blackeye	Pinto	Great northern	Small red	Pea bean (Navy)	Black	Red kidney
					Dollars				
2010	40.13	49.69	42.47	36.08	41.81	47.74	41.94	41.81	48.25
2011	57.88	58.42	69.57	62.72	54.75	61.25	58.61	54.75	69.30
2012	48.14	52.32	54.75	45.54	53.96	53.36	45.57	53.96	63.32
2013	53.45	40.63	55.19	45.76	(NA)	52.17	55.25	(NA)	68.88
2014	56.50	38.54	70.00	32.41	48.46	55.10	38.85	48.46	64.84
2015	58.75	45.20	70.00	33.14	32.47	39.80	32.19	32.47	38.37
2016	50.49	47.98	56.86	38.34	40.53	38.00	38.72	40.53	45.04
2017	58.08	63.67	65.62	31.05	33.79	37.25	34.40	33.79	44.67
2018	58.61	28.50	64.16	28.86	36.47	38.38	33.43	36.47	49.00
2019	(NA)	(NA)	(NA)	46.87	65.75	45.88	44.94	39.19	57.50

(NA) Not available.   [1] Free-on-board (f.o.b.) dealer prices as reported by USDA, Bean Market News.
ERS, Specialty Crops Branch, (816) 412–5256. Compiled from the Bean Market Summary, Agricultural Marketing Service, U.S. Department of Agriculture, Greeley, Colorado.

Table 6-18.—Beans, dry edible: United States exports to specified countries, 2018–2020 [1]

Country	2018	2019	2020
	Metric tons		
Mexico	98,855	82,014	93,666
Canada	45,486	49,458	47,266
Italy(*)	38,754	46,312	42,302
Dominican Republic	22,968	26,592	37,795
United Kingdom	28,241	25,344	31,679
Haiti	7,888	14,138	19,771
Costa Rica	2,476	4,218	15,251
Australia(*)	4,846	5,620	6,083
Panama	5,926	4,944	5,735
Japan	7,637	8,003	5,675
Germany(*)	4,009	3,998	5,668
El Salvador	3,850	4,077	5,073
United Arab Emirates	1,965	2,024	4,624
Colombia	9,759	7,875	4,584
Belgium-Luxembourg(*)	3,690	6,036	3,726
Jamaica	3,184	3,242	3,689
Yemen(*)	0	10,797	3,578
China	834	1,009	3,500
Peru	3,500	1,669	3,294
Spain	5,034	4,698	3,242
Guatemala	5,615	2,994	2,915
Korea, South	3,901	2,524	2,363
French West Indies(*)	1,152	1,047	2,269
Philippines	1,710	987	2,017
France(*)	4,394	3,165	1,715
Pakistan	796	1,043	1,564
Turkey	1,006	6,022	1,406
Saudi Arabia	0	19,117	1,364
Tanzania	1,157	1,060	1,329
Chile	1,515	456	1,163
Rest of World	19,506	18,771	15,153
World Total	339,655	369,252	379,457

(*) Denotes a country that is a summarization of its component countries.   [1] Excluding seed bean exports.
FAS, Office of Global Analysis, (202) 720-6301. Data Source: U.S. Census Bureau Trade Data.

Table 6-19.—Chickpeas & lentils, dried: United States exports by class and quantity, 2018–2020 [1]

Country	2018	2019	2020
	Metric tons		
Dried chickpeas:			
Pakistan	14,744	40,916	48,582
Spain	19,709	21,916	24,116
Canada	15,163	34,498	22,998
United Arab Emirates	1,041	2,662	7,382
Portugal	3,206	13,760	7,124
Italy(*)	1,663	5,938	6,988
Sri Lanka	1,122	1,473	5,072
Algeria	1,688	724	3,393
Colombia	263	2,593	2,575
Turkey	1,271	,1,094	2,422
Peru	1,841	1,562	2,278
Korea, South	526	649	2,096
Nepal	0	0	1,529
India	4,323	6,784	1,306
Israel(*)	545	1,197	1,251
New Zealand(*)	760	1,560	986
Lebanon	1,515	1,402	971
Jordan	1,180	1,315	954
Egypt	485	46	828
Japan	652	397	814
Taiwan	554	486	637
Chile	24	0	545
China	474	173	483
Philippines	500	232	471
Dominican Republic	432	685	374
Malaysia	111	207	279
Costa Rica	185	305	253
Singapore	0	23	230
Belgium-Luxembourg(*)	472	15	201
France(*)	927	46	185
Rest of World	2,314	1,626	1,144
World Total	77,689	144,283	148,466
Dried lentils:			
Canada	16,306	77,664	90,527
Spain	22,216	31,536	32,133
Mexico	11,698	20,222	30,280
India	8,272	56,969	28,573
Sudan(*)	21,747	16,700	28,465
Colombia	8,967	9,381	20,318
Peru	9,650	11,491	15,381
China	6,280	9,661	13,238
Turkey	838	375	10,418
United Arab Emirates	414	1,044	7,003
Pakistan	1,215	966	5,920
Italy(*)	2,862	4,261	5,330
Egypt	0	0	2,759
Togo	0	0	2,614
Brazil	0	0	2,572
Belgium-Luxembourg(*)	1,244	1,974	2,541
Dominican Republic	918	924	2,229
Morocco	0	165	1,923
Greece	2,427	2,222	1,492
Laos	240	240	1,049
Chile	0	403	1,047
Germany(*)	837	495	1,042
Sri Lanka	0	78	959
Ecuador	328	566	861
Algeria	240	476	712
Korea, South	490	314	630
French Pacific Islands(*)	524	493	630
Burkina Faso	0	450	480
Nepal	0	0	473
Netherlands	515	667	453
Rest of World	7,798	5,689	4,141
World Total	126,026	255,423	316,188

(*) Denotes a country that is a summarization of its component countries.   [1] Excluding seed pea exports.
FAS, Office of Global Analysis, (202) 720-6301. Data Source: U.S. Census Bureau Trade Data.

Table 6-20.—Peas, dry: United States exports to specified countries, 2018–2020 [1]

Country	2018	2019	2020
	Metric tons		
China	13,550	14,365	107,352
Canada	15,422	63,398	89,613
Yemen(*)	30,781	0	34,622
Ethiopia(*)	25,912	22,433	33,366
Peru	17,675	16,467	27,448
Philippines	16,791	19,933	25,504
Kenya	11,718	10,964	12,991
Cameroon	4,170	10,488	12,592
Djibouti	11,642	11,545	11,643
Zimbabwe	0	551	9,611
Mexico	10,685	7,931	8,930
Congo (Kinshasa)	160	3,365	7,311
Sudan(*)	2,156	1,795	6,806
Pakistan	1,340	2,964	6,744
Colombia	897	3,906	6,098
India	15,421	13,332	5,947
Belgium-Luxembourg(*)	485	3,308	5,767
Nepal	0	1,009	5,538
Togo	1,994	2,584	5,306
South Africa	7,295	8,918	3,560
Saudi Arabia	2,657	4,750	3,466
United Arab Emirates	258	4,655	3,425
Mali	150	148	2,907
Turkey	411	2,213	2,648
Taiwan	2,861	2,338	2,615
Korea, South	284	1,237	2,609
Dominican Republic	155	452	2,534
Madagascar	0	1,132	2,501
Somalia	6,364	7,872	1,974
TanzaniaSudan(*)	26,150	6,358	1,704
Rest of World	8,066	9,906	14,859
World Total	235,451	260,316	467,994

(*) Denotes a country that is a summarization of its component countries.   [1] Excluding seed pea exports.
FAS, Office of Global Analysis, (202) 720-6301. Data Source: U.S. Census Bureau Trade Data.

Table 6-21.—Hops: Area, yield, production, price, value, and Sept. stocks, United States, 2010–2019 1A[1]

Year	Area harvested	Yield per acre	Production	Marketing year average price per pound received by farmers	Value of production	Stocks Sept. 1	Stocks Mar. 1
	1,000 acres	Pounds	1,000 pounds	Dollars per pound	1,000 dollars	1,000 pounds	1,000 pounds
2010	31.3	2,093	65,493	3.28	214,589	83,000	102,000
2011	29.8	2,175	64,782	3.14	203,378	87,000	121,000
2012	29.7	1,985	58,911	3.17	186,876	96,000	120,000
2013	35.3	1,962	69,246	3.35	232,308	(NA)	115,000
2014	38.0	1,868	70,996	3.67	260,627	90,000	121,000
2015	43.6	1,807	78,846	4.38	345,388	83,000	119,000
2016	50.9	1,713	87,140	5.72	498,420	85,000	128,000
2017	54.0	1,956	105,622	5.60	591,375	98,000	140,000
2018	55.0	1,943	106,907	5.46	583,444	113,000	169,000
2019	56.5	1,981	112,041	5.68	636,580	....	....

(NA) Not available.
NASS, Crops Branch, (202) 720–2127.

Table 6-22.—Hops: Area, yield, and production, by State and United States, 2017–2019

State	Area harvested			Yield per acre			Production		
	2017	2018	2019	2017	2018	2019	2017	2018	2019
	1,000 acres	*1,000 acres*	*1,000 acres*	*Pounds*	*Pounds*	*Pounds*	*1,000 pounds*	*1,000 pounds*	*1,000 pounds*
Idaho	7,125	8,140	8,358	1,974	1,995	2,034	14,067.3	16,242.8	17,003.1
Oregon	8,216	7,725	7,306	1,518	1,675	1,783	12,470.4	12,936.2	13,023.2
Washington	38,648	39,170	40,880	2,046	1,984	2,006	79,083.8	77,727.7	82,014.9
United States ...	53,989	55,035	56,544	1,956	1,943	1,981	105,621.5	106,906.7	112,041.2

NASS, Crops Branch, (202) 720–2127.

Table 6-23.—Hops: Marketing year average price and value of production, by State and United States, 2017–2019

State	Marketing year average price per pound			Value of production		
	2017	2018	2019 [1]	2017	2018	2019 [1]
	Dollars	*Dollars*	*Dollars*	*1,000 dollars*	*1,000 dollars*	*1,000 dollars*
Idaho	5.00	5.30	5.25	70,337	86,087	89,266
Oregon	5.00	5.40	5.50	62,352	69,855	71,628
Washington	5.80	5.50	5.80	458,686	427,502	475,686
United States ...	5.60	5.46	5.68	591,375	583,444	636,580

[1] Preliminary.
NASS, Crops Branch, (202) 720–2127.

Table 6-24.—Hops, including extract: United States exports by country of destination, 2018–2020

Country	2018	2019	2020
	Metric tons		
Canada	1,748	2,431	2,372
Germany(*)	1,754	1,895	2,354
Belgium-Luxembourg(*)	2,563	2,520	2,197
United Kingdom	2,100	2,224	1,810
Brazil	1,489	1,766	1,561
China	1,472	600	1,062
Argentina	593	526	908
Australia(*)	869	836	785
Mexico	923	726	519
Japan	469	432	477
Vietnam	270	322	296
Hong Kong	125	106	286
Korea, South	254	227	259
Chile	155	171	222
New Zealand(*)	99	194	167
Colombia	593	450	161
Netherlands	14	94	102
Russia	98	99	102
Peru	251	225	100
Dominican Republic	96	98	97
Philippines	190	156	97
Sweden	5	38	73
Uruguay	20	15	61
Ecuador	97	111	59
South Africa	113	104	58
Ireland	23	84	54
Guatemala	48	51	46
Taiwan	34	28	39
Panama	69	61	39
Paraguay	15	29	36
Rest of World	582	557	312
World Total	17,129	17,176	16,710

(*) Denotes a country that is a summarization of its component countries.
FAS, Office of Global Analysis, (202) 720-6301. Data Source: U.S. Census Bureau Trade Data

CHAPTER VII

STATISTICS OF CATTLE, HOGS, AND SHEEP

This chapter contains information about most kinds of farm livestock and livestock products, with the exception of dairy and poultry. The information relates to inventories, production, disposition, prices, and income for farm animals, and to livestock slaughter, meat production, and market statistics for meat animals.

Table 7-1.—All cattle and calves: Inventory, and value, United States, Jan. 1, 2010-2019

Year	Inventory	Value	
		Per head	Total
	Thousands	Dollars	1,000 dollars
2010	94,081	833	78,335,410
2011	92,887	947	87,988,337
2012	91,160	1,111	101,252,540
2013	90,095	1,139	101,731,742
2014	88,243	1,223	107,921,189
2015	89,173	1,584	141,250,032
2016	91,888	1,410	129,562,080
2017	93,625	1,109	103,829,681
2018	94,298	1,146	108,065,508
2019	94,805	1,031	97,746,846

NASS, Livestock Branch, (202) 720–3570.

Table 7-2.—All cattle and calves: Number by class, United States, Jan. 1, 2010–2019

Year	All cattle and calves [1]	Cows and heifers that have calved		500 pounds and over					Calves under 500 pounds
				Heifers					
		Beef cows	Milk cows	Beef cow replacements	Milk cow replacements	Other	Steers	Bulls	
	Thousands	Thousands	Thousands	Thousands	Thousands	Thousands	Thousands	Thousands	Thousands
2010	94,081	31,440	9,087	5,443	4,551	9,784	16,568	2,190	15,019
2011	92,887	30,913	9,156	5,135	4,577	9,938	16,394	2,165	14,610
2012	91,160	30,282	9,236	5,281	4,618	9,546	15,957	2,100	14,141
2013	90,095	29,631	9,221	5,429	4,546	9,281	15,931	2,074	13,983
2014	88,243	28,956	9,208	5,556	4,539	8,824	15,623	2,038	13,498
2015	89,173	29,332	9,312	6,086	4,710	8,469	15,630	2,109	13,523
2016	91,888	30,164	9,312	6,335	4,814	8,753	16,305	2,137	14,067
2017	93,625	31,171	9,369	6,363	4,754	8,995	16,374	2,244	14,356
2018	94,298	31,466	9,432	6,108	4,768	9,341	16,528	2,252	14,401
2019	94,805	31,691	9,353	5,885	4,702	9,624	16,758	2,253	14,540

[1] Totals may not add due to rounding.
NASS, Livestock Branch, (202) 720–3570.

STATISTICS OF CATTLE, HOGS, AND SHEEP

Table 7-3.—All cattle and calves: Inventory and value, by State and United States, Jan. 1, 2018–2019

State	Inventory		Value			
			Value per head		Total value	
	2018	2019	2018	2019	2018	2019
	Thousands	*Thousands*	*Dollars*	*Dollars*	*1,000 dollars*	*1,000 dollars*
Alabama	1,340.0	1,300.0	930	840	1,246,200	1,092,000
Alaska	15.0	16.0	1,280	1,280	19,200	20,480
Arizona	1,020.0	1,020.0	1,100	940	1,122,000	958,800
Arkansas	1,760.0	1,780.0	1,010	890	1,777,600	1,584,200
California	5,200.0	5,150.0	1,230	980	6,396,000	5,047,000
Colorado	2,850.0	2,850.0	1,230	1,100	3,505,500	3,163,500
Connecticut	50.0	47.0	1,210	1,070	60,500	50,290
Delaware	17.0	15.0	1,080	980	18,360	14,700
Florida	1,630.0	1,680.0	1,100	1,000	1,793,000	1,680,000
Georgia	1,060.0	1,070.0	950	950	1,007,000	1,016,500
Hawaii	144.0	142.0	750	700	108,000	99,400
Idaho	2,420.0	2,500.0	1,250	1,050	3,025,000	2,625,000
Illinois	1,150.0	1,190.0	1,220	1,020	1,403,000	1,213,800
Indiana	860.0	880.0	1,070	920	920,200	809,600
Iowa	4,000.0	3,950.0	1,200	1,130	4,800,000	4,463,500
Kansas	6,300.0	6,400.0	1,110	1,070	6,993,000	6,848,000
Kentucky	2,160.0	2,130.0	960	850	2,073,600	1,810,500
Louisiana	820.0	800.0	1,090	950	893,800	760,000
Maine	81.0	78.0	1,190	980	96,390	76,440
Maryland	193.0	197.0	1,070	930	206,510	183,210
Massachusetts	38.0	37.0	1,130	920	42,940	34,040
Michigan	1,160.0	1,160.0	1,140	950	1,322,400	1,102,000
Minnesota	2,350.0	2,320.0	1,080	940	2,538,000	2,180,800
Mississippi	930.0	900.0	950	860	883,500	774,000
Missouri	4,350.0	4,250.0	1,060	970	4,611,000	4,122,500
Montana	2,550.0	2,500.0	1,350	1,310	3,442,500	3,275,000
Nebraska	6,800.0	6,800.0	1,260	1,210	8,568,000	8,228,000
Nevada	465.0	470.0	1,270	1,180	590,550	554,600
New Hampshire	36.0	33.0	1,160	980	41,760	32,340
New Jersey	29.0	30.0	1,160	1,100	33,640	33,000
New Mexico	1,510.0	1,480.0	1,310	1,010	1,978,100	1,494,800
New York	1,480.0	1,450.0	1,130	990	1,672,400	1,435,500
North Carolina	800.0	800.0	900	730	720,000	584,000
North Dakota	1,860.0	1,830.0	1,450	1,340	2,697,600	2,452,200
Ohio	1,300.0	1,310.0	1,090	860	1,417,000	1,126,600
Oklahoma	5,100.0	5,300.0	1,100	1,010	5,610,000	5,353,000
Oregon	1,270.0	1,310.0	1,210	1,090	1,536,700	1,427,900
Pennsylvania	1,620.0	1,600.0	1,060	910	1,717,200	1,456,000
Rhode Island	5.0	4.7	1,280	1,180	6,400	5,546
South Carolina	340.0	350.0	960	820	326,400	287,000
South Dakota	4,000.0	4,050.0	1,350	1,240	5,400,000	5,022,000
Tennessee	1,830.0	1,800.0	940	890	1,720,200	1,602,000
Texas	12,500.0	13,000.0	1,080	990	13,500,000	12,870,000
Utah	790.0	810.0	1,270	1,150	1,003,300	931,500
Vermont	260.0	255.0	1,270	1,000	330,200	255,000
Virginia	1,480.0	1,440.0	940	860	1,391,200	1,238,400
Washington	1,160.0	1,180.0	1,200	930	1,392,000	1,097,400
West Virginia	395.0	390.0	1,000	870	395,000	339,300
Wisconsin	3,500.0	3,450.0	1,140	950	3,990,000	3,277,500
Wyoming	1,320.0	1,300.0	1,330	1,260	1,755,600	1,638,000
United States	94,298.0	94,804.7	1,146	1,031	108,065,508	97,746,846

NASS, Livestock Branch, (202) 720–3570.

Table 7-4.—Cattle and calves, January 1: Number by class, State and United States, 2018–2019

State	Cows and heifers that have calved				Heifers, 500 pounds and over					
	Beef cows		Milk cows		Beef cow replacements		Milk cow replacements		Other	
	2018	2019	2018	2019	2018	2019	2018	2019	2018	2019
	1,000 head									
Alabama	714.0	705.0	6.0	5.0	125.0	116.0	3.0	2.0	37.0	37.0
Alaska	6.1	6.8	0.3	0.2	1.4	1.4	0.1	0.1	0.5	0.7
Arizona	200.0	215.0	210.0	205.0	36.0	35.0	105.0	115.0	29.0	20.0
Arkansas	924.0	935.0	6.0	5.0	160.0	156.0	4.0	4.0	71.0	75.0
California	670.0	630.0	1,740.0	1,730.0	125.0	115.0	780.0	760.0	175.0	215.0
Colorado	812.0	792.0	168.0	178.0	175.0	170.0	100.0	110.0	550.0	570.0
Connecticut	5.0	4.5	20.0	19.5	2.0	1.5	9.5	9.0	1.5	1.5
Delaware	2.5	2.0	5.0	4.5	0.7	0.6	2.0	1.6	0.4	0.3
Florida	886.0	914.0	124.0	116.0	115.0	130.0	40.0	35.0	30.0	25.0
Georgia	485.0	499.0	85.0	81.0	95.0	90.0	25.0	30.0	25.0	30.0
Hawaii	75.0	75.5	2.0	1.5	12.0	11.5	1.0	1.0	5.0	5.0
Idaho	510.0	506.0	600.0	614.0	120.0	110.0	310.0	340.0	210.0	220.0
Illinois	397.0	405.0	93.0	85.0	70.0	70.0	47.0	45.0	98.0	95.0
Indiana	208.0	204.0	187.0	181.0	50.0	45.0	75.0	80.0	45.0	50.0
Iowa	950.0	930.0	220.0	220.0	165.0	155.0	135.0	125.0	550.0	560.0
Kansas	1,504.0	1,529.0	156.0	161.0	280.0	280.0	140.0	170.0	1,490.0	1,420.0
Kentucky	1,033.0	1,017.0	57.0	53.0	145.0	120.0	45.0	45.0	115.0	130.0
Louisiana	473.0	459.0	12.0	11.0	90.0	83.0	4.0	4.0	20.0	23.0
Maine	10.0	11.0	30.0	29.0	4.0	3.0	15.0	14.0	3.0	3.0
Maryland	46.0	50.0	47.0	44.0	12.0	13.0	28.0	30.0	10.0	8.0
Massachusetts	6.5	7.0	11.5	10.5	2.0	2.0	7.0	6.5	1.0	1.0
Michigan	102.0	108.0	428.0	422.0	24.0	25.0	176.0	160.0	30.0	40.0
Minnesota	365.0	370.0	455.0	450.0	100.0	95.0	290.0	255.0	175.0	170.0
Mississippi	501.0	477.0	9.0	8.0	92.0	90.0	7.0	5.0	40.0	40.0
Missouri	2,086.0	2,059.0	84.0	81.0	355.0	335.0	40.0	40.0	205.0	205.0
Montana	1,497.0	1,448.0	13.0	12.0	390.0	380.0	7.0	8.0	223.0	232.0
Nebraska	1,910.0	1,941.0	60.0	59.0	375.0	365.0	15.0	15.0	1,520.0	1,530.0
Nevada	238.0	242.0	32.0	33.0	42.0	42.0	12.0	11.0	30.0	29.0
New Hampshire	4.5	4.0	12.5	12.0	1.5	1.3	7.0	6.5	0.5	0.7
New Jersey	9.0	9.5	6.0	5.5	2.1	2.5	3.2	3.3	1.2	0.7
New Mexico	483.0	480.0	332.0	325.0	105.0	95.0	130.0	125.0	95.0	85.0
New York	105.0	105.0	625.0	625.0	45.0	40.0	350.0	335.0	50.0	45.0
North Carolina	370.0	367.0	45.0	43.0	63.0	60.0	17.0	20.0	22.0	20.0
North Dakota	964.0	975.0	16.0	15.0	191.0	197.0	9.0	8.0	240.0	210.0
Ohio	296.0	307.0	264.0	253.0	70.0	70.0	121.0	125.0	59.0	55.0
Oklahoma	2,088.0	2,150.0	42.0	40.0	410.0	400.0	25.0	20.0	510.0	520.0
Oregon	536.0	535.0	124.0	125.0	95.0	110.0	70.0	65.0	100.0	115.0
Pennsylvania	215.0	225.0	525.0	505.0	60.0	65.0	310.0	290.0	60.0	55.0
Rhode Island	1.6	1.4	0.8	0.7	0.5	0.6	0.5	0.5	0.2	0.2
South Carolina	174.0	186.0	15.0	14.0	28.0	37.0	6.0	5.0	9.0	8.0
South Dakota	1,751.0	1,818.0	119.0	122.0	435.0	385.0	45.0	40.0	500.0	550.0
Tennessee	910.0	914.0	40.0	36.0	135.0	145.0	25.0	25.0	80.0	75.0
Texas	4,520.0	4,655.0	530.0	545.0	800.0	740.0	250.0	260.0	1,470.0	1,690.0
Utah	338.0	340.0	97.0	100.0	70.0	70.0	50.0	50.0	60.0	65.0
Vermont	15.0	14.0	128.0	126.0	5.0	4.5	57.0	55.0	6.0	6.5
Virginia	633.0	631.0	87.0	79.0	100.0	93.0	40.0	37.0	70.0	61.0
Washington	235.0	230.0	275.0	280.0	52.0	57.0	123.0	123.0	115.0	126.0
West Virginia	203.0	198.0	7.0	7.0	37.0	32.0	3.0	3.0	18.0	20.0
Wisconsin	285.0	290.0	1,275.0	1,270.0	80.0	80.0	700.0	680.0	50.0	60.0
Wyoming	714.0	714.0	6.0	6.0	160.0	160.0	4.0	4.0	136.0	126.0
United States	31,466.2	31,690.7	9,432.1	9,353.4	6,108.2	5,884.9	4,768.3	4,701.5	9,341.3	9,623.6

See footnote(s) at end of table.

Table 7-4.—Cattle and calves, January 1: Number by class, State and United States, 2018–2019—Continued

State	Steers, 500 pounds and over		Bulls, 500 pounds and over		Calves under 500 pounds	
	2018	2019	2018	2019	2018	2019
	Thousands	Thousands	Thousands	Thousands	Thousands	Thousands
Alabama	40.0	45.0	50.0	45.0	365.0	345.0
Alaska	0.5	0.7	2.4	3.0	3.7	3.1
Arizona	275.0	295.0	20.0	20.0	145.0	115.0
Arkansas	110.0	115.0	60.0	60.0	425.0	430.0
California	620.0	610.0	70.0	60.0	1,020.0	1,030.0
Colorado	810.0	830.0	55.0	55.0	180.0	145.0
Connecticut	2.0	1.5	0.5	0.5	9.5	9.0
Delaware	2.1	2.6	0.3	0.4	4.0	3.0
Florida	20.0	20.0	55.0	60.0	360.0	380.0
Georgia	35.0	37.0	35.0	33.0	275.0	270.0
Hawaii	11.0	10.5	4.0	4.0	34.0	33.0
Idaho	310.0	320.0	40.0	40.0	320.0	350.0
Illinois	195.0	245.0	25.0	25.0	225.0	220.0
Indiana	104.0	115.0	16.0	17.0	175.0	188.0
Iowa	1,390.0	1,390.0	70.0	70.0	520.0	500.0
Kansas	2,020.0	2,060.0	95.0	95.0	615.0	685.0
Kentucky	195.0	225.0	70.0	70.0	500.0	470.0
Louisiana	23.0	27.0	31.0	30.0	167.0	163.0
Maine	4.0	4.0	1.5	1.5	13.5	12.5
Maryland	17.0	14.0	4.0	5.0	29.0	33.0
Massachusetts	2.0	2.0	1.0	1.0	7.0	7.0
Michigan	180.0	180.0	15.0	15.0	205.0	210.0
Minnesota	475.0	485.0	35.0	35.0	455.0	460.0
Mississippi	48.0	52.0	38.0	38.0	195.0	190.0
Missouri	410.0	395.0	120.0	125.0	1,050.0	1,010.0
Montana	210.0	240.0	105.0	100.0	105.0	80.0
Nebraska	2,480.0	2,380.0	110.0	110.0	330.0	400.0
Nevada	40.0	39.0	15.0	15.0	56.0	59.0
New Hampshire	2.0	1.5	0.5	0.5	7.5	6.5
New Jersey	2.1	2.5	1.0	1.0	4.4	5.0
New Mexico	130.0	130.0	40.0	35.0	195.0	205.0
New York	47.0	47.0	18.0	18.0	240.0	235.0
North Carolina	33.0	35.0	30.0	30.0	220.0	225.0
North Dakota	260.0	255.0	70.0	65.0	110.0	105.0
Ohio	210.0	215.0	30.0	30.0	250.0	255.0
Oklahoma	990.0	1,050.0	155.0	180.0	880.0	940.0
Oregon	145.0	160.0	40.0	40.0	160.0	160.0
Pennsylvania	130.0	135.0	25.0	25.0	295.0	300.0
Rhode Island	0.5	0.4	0.1	0.1	0.8	0.8
South Carolina	10.0	10.0	16.0	14.0	82.0	76.0
South Dakota	730.0	730.0	110.0	105.0	310.0	300.0
Tennessee	150.0	130.0	60.0	65.0	430.0	410.0
Texas	2,620.0	2,720.0	340.0	340.0	1,970.0	2,050.0
Utah	80.0	85.0	25.0	25.0	70.0	75.0
Vermont	4.0	4.0	3.0	3.0	42.0	42.0
Virginia	160.0	155.0	40.0	39.0	350.0	345.0
Washington	200.0	200.0	20.0	20.0	140.0	150.0
West Virginia	41.0	42.0	15.0	14.0	71.0	74.0
Wisconsin	380.0	360.0	30.0	30.0	700.0	680.0
Wyoming	175.0	150.0	40.0	40.0	85.0	100.0
United States	16,528.2	16,757.7	2,252.3	2,253.0	14,401.0	14,539.9

NASS, Livestock Branch, (202) 720–3570.

Table 7-5.—Cows and calf crop: Cows and heifers that have calved, Jan. 1, 2018–2019, and calves born, by State and United States, 2017–2018

State	Cows and heifers that have calved		Calves born	
	Jan. 1		2017	2018
	2018	2019		
	Thousands	Thousands	Thousands	Thousands
Alabama	720.0	710.0	630.0	620.0
Alaska	6.4	7.0	4.5	5.0
Arizona	410.0	420.0	310.0	320.0
Arkansas	930.0	940.0	790.0	800.0
California	2,410.0	2,360.0	1,880.0	1,860.0
Colorado	980.0	970.0	830.0	840.0
Connecticut	25.0	24.0	17.5	16.5
Delaware	7.5	6.5	7.0	6.0
Florida	1,010.0	1,030.0	790.0	820.0
Georgia	570.0	580.0	480.0	510.0
Hawaii	77.0	77.0	60.0	60.0
Idaho	1,110.0	1,120.0	960.0	960.0
Illinois	490.0	490.0	420.0	430.0
Indiana	395.0	385.0	340.0	350.0
Iowa	1,170.0	1,150.0	1,090.0	1,100.0
Kansas	1,660.0	1,690.0	1,430.0	1,500.0
Kentucky	1,090.0	1,070.0	990.0	970.0
Louisiana	485.0	470.0	370.0	360.0
Maine	40.0	40.0	30.0	29.0
Maryland	93.0	94.0	70.0	75.0
Massachusetts	18.0	17.5	17.0	16.0
Michigan	530.0	530.0	410.0	420.0
Minnesota	820.0	820.0	790.0	800.0
Mississippi	510.0	485.0	400.0	385.0
Missouri	2,170.0	2,140.0	1,960.0	1,940.0
Montana	1,510.0	1,460.0	1,480.0	1,440.0
Nebraska	1,970.0	2,000.0	1,700.0	1,790.0
Nevada	270.0	275.0	220.0	220.0
New Hampshire	17.0	16.0	13.5	12.0
New Jersey	15.0	15.0	9.5	10.0
New Mexico	815.0	805.0	630.0	620.0
New York	730.0	730.0	550.0	550.0
North Carolina	415.0	410.0	365.0	365.0
North Dakota	980.0	990.0	960.0	940.0
Ohio	560.0	560.0	490.0	490.0
Oklahoma	2,130.0	2,190.0	1,950.0	2,050.0
Oregon	660.0	660.0	630.0	620.0
Pennsylvania	740.0	730.0	600.0	610.0
Rhode Island	2.4	2.1	2.2	2.2
South Carolina	189.0	200.0	147.0	164.0
South Dakota	1,870.0	1,940.0	1,840.0	1,880.0
Tennessee	950.0	950.0	850.0	860.0
Texas	5,050.0	5,200.0	4,400.0	4,650.0
Utah	435.0	440.0	375.0	385.0
Vermont	143.0	140.0	105.0	102.0
Virginia	720.0	710.0	640.0	630.0
Washington	510.0	510.0	440.0	440.0
West Virginia	210.0	205.0	195.0	190.0
Wisconsin	1,560.0	1,560.0	1,430.0	1,420.0
Wyoming	720.0	720.0	660.0	670.0
United States	40,898.3	41,044.1	35,758.2	36,312.7

NASS, Livestock Branch, (202) 720–3570.

Table 7-6.—Cattle and calves: All cattle on feed, United States, Jan. 1, 2010–2019 [1]

Year	Inventory
	Thousands
2010	13,727.6
2011	14,131.5
2012	14,355.3
2013	13,703.3
2014	12,949.3
2015	13,024.8
2016	13,156.7
2017	13,108.4
2018	14,146.0
2019	14,367.9

[1] Cattle and calves on feed are steers and heifers for slaughter market being fed a ration of grain or other concentrates and are expected to produce a carcass that will grade select or better.
NASS, Livestock Branch, (202) 720–3570.

Table 7-7.—Cattle and calves: Total number on feed by State and United States, Jan. 1, 2018–2019

State	2018	2019
	1,000 head	*1,000 head*
Arizona	274.0	297.0
California	490.0	535.0
Colorado	1,000.0	1,050.0
Idaho	265.0	295.0
Illinois	220.0	250.0
Indiana	90.0	100.0
Iowa	1,300.0	1,320.0
Kansas	2,450.0	2,430.0
Kentucky	17.0	16.0
Maryland	9.0	9.0
Michigan	140.0	150.0
Minnesota	430.0	410.0
Missouri	80.0	100.0
Montana	45.0	40.0
Nebraska	2,800.0	2,750.0
Nevada	3.0	4.0
New York	22.0	22.0
North Dakota	58.0	59.0
Ohio	140.0	150.0
Oklahoma	330.0	330.0
Oregon	90.0	90.0
Pennsylvania	85.0	100.0
South Dakota	470.0	425.0
Texas	2,650.0	2,750.0
Utah	20.0	23.0
Virginia	18.0	15.0
Washington	215.0	230.0
West Virginia	4.0	4.0
Wisconsin	280.0	280.0
Wyoming	70.0	65.0
Other States [1]	81.0	68.9
United States	14,146.0	14,367.9

[1] Individual state estimates not available for states not shown, but are included in Other States.
NASS, Livestock Branch, (202) 720–3570.

Table 7-8.—Cattle: Average price per 100 pounds, by grades, at Nebraska Direct, Worthing, SD and Louisville, KY, 2010–2019

Year	Nebraska		Worthing, SD		Louisville, KY	
	Choice		Cows [1]		Cows	
	Steers [2]	Heifers [3]	Commercial	Breaking utility	Breaking utility	85-95% Lean
	Dollars	*Dollars*	*Dollars*	*Dollars*	*Dollars*	*Dollars*
2010	95.81	95.41	(NA)	61.49	53.98	41.70
2011	111.52	111.55	74.25	71.34	67.20	53.92
2012	123.11	124.18	83.95	78.90	76.55	62.71
2013	127.13	127.37	84.83	78.52	79.22	71.00
2014	154.03	154.67	108.79	109.08	105.26	83.56
2015	148.71	148.09	100.39	104.29	99.14	78.27
2016	117.74	119.69	82.14	76.40	(NA)	(NA)
2017	121.43	121.92	83.72	71.65	(NA)	(NA)
2018	116.42	117.62	79.15	68.45	(NA)	(NA)
2019	118.47	118.05	84.32	(NA)	(NA)	(NA)

(NA) Not available. [1] All weights; simple average of price range. [2] 1,100 to 1,500 pound weight range; weighted average of price range. [3] 1,000 to 1,300 pound weight range; simple average of price range.
AMS, Livestock and Grain Market News, (202) 720–7316.

Table 7-9.—Cattle and calves: Production, disposition, cash receipts, and gross income, United States, 2009-2018

Year	Calf crop [1]	Death loss		Marketings [2]		Inshipments [3]	Farm slaughter
		Cattle	Calves	Cattle	Calves		Cattle and calves
	1,000 head	*1,000 head*	*1,000 head*	*1,000 head*	*1,000 head*	*1,000 head*	*1,000 head*
2010	35,740	1,736	2,265	44,658	8,874	20,757	157
2011	35,357	1,787	2,230	44,875	8,401	20,357	148
2012	34,469	1,752	2,171	43,578	8,337	20,443	139
2013	33,630	1,730	2,140	43,453	7,996	19,965	128
2014	33,522	1,720	2,130	41,243	7,819	20,443	124
2015	34,087	1,736	2,144	40,487	7,397	20,508	116
2016	35,063	1,736	2,140	41,756	7,656	20,084	123
2017	35,758	1,784	2,144	43,644	7,777	20,380	116
2018	36,313	1,786	2,205	45,031	7,602	20,937	119
2019	36,060	1,865	2,300	45,040	7,541	20,418	123

Year	Production (live weight) [4]	Value of production	Cash receipts [5]	Value of home consumption	Gross income [6]	Average price per 100 pounds received by farmers	
						Cattle	Calves
	1,000 pounds	*1,000 dollars*	*1,000 dollars*	*1,000 dollars*	*1,000 dollars*	*Dollars*	*Dollars*
2010	41,379,839	36,850,474	51,246,136	405,789	51,651,925	92.20	117.00
2011	41,483,945	45,059,200	62,321,217	478,871	62,800,088	113.00	142.00
2012	40,920,479	48,059,904	66,090,126	525,630	66,615,756	121.00	172.00
2013	40,781,761	48,595,712	67,849,440	509,175	68,358,615	125.00	181.00
2014	40,268,012	60,141,507	81,076,720	610,833	81,687,553	152.00	261.00
2015	41,503,073	60,080,918	78,252,807	588,216	78,841,023	147.00	247.00
2016	42,694,001	48,572,501	63,691,327	472,478	64,163,805	119.00	158.00
2017	44,197,461	50,398,374	66,936,726	455,988	67,392,714	120.00	168.00
2018	45,677,452	49,147,588	67,038,059	431,071	67,469,130	116.00	170.00
2019	44,820,270	48,223,046	66,239,043	436,788	66,675,831	116.00	159.00

[1] Calves born during the year. [2] Includes custom slaughter for use on farms where produced and State outshipments, but excludes interfarm sales within the State. [3] Includes cattle shipped in from other States, but excludes cattle for immediate slaughter. [4] Adjustments made for changes in inventory and for inshipments. [5] Receipts from marketings and sale of farm slaughter. [6] Cash receipts from sales of cattle, calves, beef, and veal plus value of cattle and calves slaughtered for home consumption.

NASS, Livestock Branch, (202) 720–3570.

Table 7-10.—Cattle: Weighted average weight and price per 100 pounds, Texas-Oklahoma, Kansas, Colorado, Nebraska, Iowa-So. Minnesota Feedlots, 2010–2019 [1]

Year	Steers SE/CH 65-80%			Steers SE/CH 35-65%		
	Price	Average Weight	Number of Head	Price	Average Weight	Number of Head
	Dollars	*Pounds*		*Dollars*	*Pounds*	
2010 ...	95.00	1,359	561,173	95.95	1,301	1,329,021
2011 ...	114.45	1,364	518,689	114.92	1,304	1,101,808
2012 ...	122.84	1,402	458,382	123.06	1,312	743,859
2013 ...	126.27	1,408	384,642	126.35	1,338	517,782
2014 ...	154.25	1,410	548,667	152.15	1,339	386,051
2015 ...	147.64	1,432	341,078	149.00	1,366	228,126
2016 ...	120.04	1,429	735,708	121.29	1,369	276,086
2017 ...	122.85	1,454	845,341	123.13	1,313	235,130
2018 ...	117.06	1,401	704,101	119.06	1,312	195,726
2019 ...	117.87	1,390	456,517	115.45	1,322	108,332

Year	Heifers SE/CH 65-80%			Heifers SE/CH 35-65%		
	Price	Average Weight	Number of Head	Price	Average Weight	Number of Head
	Dollars	*Pounds*		*Dollars*	*Pounds*	
2010 ...	95.41	1,227	562,788	96.22	1,166	1,159,191
2011 ...	114.05	1,222	508,487	114.64	1,167	928,633
2012 ...	123.38	1,255	412,483	123.31	1,173	577,535
2013 ...	126.09	1,266	320,285	126.36	1,198	335,205
2014 ...	154.37	1,279	322,272	152.18	1,204	218,658
2015 ...	148.20	1,289	220,073	147.73	1,235	97,078
2016 ...	120.99	1,288	400,528	121.67	1,231	103,739
2017 ...	122.87	1,251	404,560	123.25	1,194	86,001
2018 ...	117.74	1,247	353,713	118.80	1,206	73,320
2019 ...	116.62	1,248	246,807	114.29	1,207	38,108

[1] Sales FOB the feedyard. Estimated net weights after 3-4% shrink.
AMS, Livestock and Grain Market News, (202) 720–7316.

Table 7-11.—Cattle: Receipts at selected markets, 2010–2019

Year	Oklahoma City	Fort Collins	Tulia [1]	South St. Joseph	Sioux Falls
	Thousands	*Thousands*	*Thousands*	*Thousands*	*Thousands*
2010	492	63	74	105	153
2011	468	30	60	94	104
2012	399	72	43	121	153
2013	409	46	35	90	156
2014	382	42	37	86	140
2015	368	43	21	88	139
2016	368	51	34	91	179
2017	369	15	39	98	174
2018	388	31	26	91	139
2019	415	32	91	77	203

[1] Changed from Amarillo, Texas to Tulia, Texas
AMS, Livestock & Grain Market News, (202) 720–7316.

Table 7-12.—Cattle and calves: Number slaughtered, United States, 2010–2019

Year	Cattle slaughter					Calf slaughter				
	Commercial			Farm	Total	Commercial			Farm	Total
	Federally inspected	Other	Total [1]			Federally inspected	Other	Total [1]		
	1,000 head									
2010 ...	33,702	547	34,249	124	34,373	864	14	879	33	912
2011 ...	33,555	532	34,087	119	34,205	839	14	853	30	882
2012 ...	32,426	525	32,951	112	33,062	760	12	772	27	800
2013 ...	31,947	515	32,462	103	32,565	751	11	762	26	788
2014 ...	29,682	486	30,168	98	30,266	558	8	566	26	591
2015 ...	28,296	455	28,752	92	28,844	446	7	453	24	476
2016 ...	30,114	464	30,578	98	30,676	480	8	488	25	513
2017 ...	31,704	485	32,189	91	32,281	503	9	512	25	537
2018 ...	32,518	487	33,005	95	33,100	571	9	580	23	604
2019 ...	33,069	486	33,555	101	33,656	579	8	587	22	609

[1] Totals are based on unrounded numbers.
NASS, Livestock Branch, (202) 720-3570.

Table 7-13.—Cattle and calves: Number slaughtered under Federal inspection, and average live weight, 2010–2019

Year	Cattle		Calves	
	Number slaughtered	Average live weight [1]	Number slaughtered	Average live weight [1]
	Thousands	*Pounds*	*Thousands*	*Pounds*
2010	33,702	1,282	864	260
2011	33,555	1,280	839	260
2012	32,426	1,305	760	257
2013	31,947	1,317	751	248
2014	29,682	1,333	558	281
2015	28,296	1,364	446	309
2016	30,114	1,365	480	264
2017	31,704	1,351	503	248
2018	32,518	1,352	571	224
2019	33,069	1,347	579	219

[1] Excludes postmortem condemnations.
NASS, Livestock Branch, (202) 720-3570.

Table 7-14.—Cattle and calves: Number slaughtered commercially, total and average live weight, by State and United States, 2019[1]

State	Cattle			Calves		
	Number slaughtered	Total live weight[2]	Average live weight[2]	Number slaughtered	Total live weight[2]	Average live weight[2]
	Thousands	1,000 pounds	Pounds	Thousands	1,000 pounds	Pounds
Alabama	5.9	6,168	1,037	(Y)	(Y)	(Y)
Alaska	0.6	698	1,130	(D)	(D)	(D)
Arizona	551.3	752,983	1,368	(D)	(D)	(D)
Arkansas	5.3	5,068	957	(Y)	(Y)	(Y)
California	1,531.1	2,002,936	1,317	82.0	8,365	104
Colorado	2,469.3	3,384,389	1,372	(D)	(D)	(D)
Delaware-Maryland	37.7	51,736	1,373	(D)	(D)	(D)
Florida	(D)	(D)	(D)	0.8	310	392
Georgia	(D)	(D)	(D)	1.3	575	442
Hawaii	13.4	14,509	1,087	(D)	(D)	(D)
Idaho	503.5	642,342	1,288	40.3	3,545	89
Illinois	(D)	(D)	(D)	1.0	379	383
Indiana	34.2	40,024	1,170	4.5	1,353	300
Iowa	(D)	(D)	(D)	(D)	(D)	(D)
Kansas	6,436.7	8,642,515	1,343	0.5	202	445
Kentucky	39.1	40,870	1,053	(D)	(D)	(D)
Louisiana	5.5	4,356	788	0.2	69	423
Michigan	(D)	(D)	(D)	1.2	369	302
Minnesota	(D)	(D)	(D)	(Y)	(Y)	(Y)
Mississippi	4.4	3,777	863	(D)	(D)	(D)
Missouri	47.6	55,305	1,161	0.3	119	447
Montana	21.7	29,198	1,349	(Y)	(Y)	(Y)
Nebraska	7,666.0	10,727,535	1,401	(D)	(D)	(D)
Nevada	1.4	1,558	1,085	(D)	(D)	(D)
New England[3]	28.4	32,839	1,156	3.2	714	222
New Jersey	41.9	46,537	1,114	22.6	8,568	379
New Mexico	4.9	4,976	1,014	(Y)	(Y)	(Y)
New York	39.6	46,819	1,200	101.1	8,960	89
North Carolina	79.9	98,205	1,234	0.7	213	301
North Dakota	8.8	11,341	1,290	(D)	(D)	(D)
Ohio	64.5	83,771	1,301	154.7	22,345	145
Oklahoma	31.0	33,006	1,065	0.3	142	429
Oregon	17.3	19,443	1,124	(D)	(D)	(D)
Pennsylvania	1,124.4	1,357,158	1,211	108.9	46,209	424
South Carolina	228.7	280,833	1,234	(D)	(D)	(D)
South Dakota	496.1	699,472	1,416	(D)	(D)	(D)
Tennessee	16.8	16,532	997	0.2	86	410
Texas	5,858.5	7,604,107	1,302	2.2	946	423
Utah	699.0	938,615	1,345	(D)	(D)	(D)
Virginia	16.0	16,995	1,060	(D)	(D)	(D)
Washington	1,145.6	1,579,384	1,383	5.8	456	78
West Virginia	10.8	10,695	990	(D)	(D)	(D)
Wisconsin	1,379.4	1,894,776	1,382	50.9	23,598	465
Wyoming	5.4	5,947	1,111	(D)	(D)	(D)
United States	33,555.3	45,011,509	1,344	587.0	128,804	221

(D) Withheld to avoid disclosing data for individual operations.   (Y) Less than level of precision shown.   [1] Includes slaughter in federally inspected and other slaughter plants; excludes animals slaughtered on farms.   Average live weight is based on unrounded numbers.   Totals may not add due to rounding.   [2] Excludes postmortem condemnations.   [3] New England includes Connecticut, Maine, Massachusetts, New Hampshire, Rhode Island, and Vermont.
NASS, Livestock Branch, (202) 720-3570.

Table 7-15.—Cattle and calves: Production, disposition, cash receipts, and gross income, by State and United States, 2019

State	Marketings[1]		Inship-ments[2]	Farm slaugh-ter[3]	Production (live weight)[4]	Value of production	Cash receipts[5]	Value of home con-sump-tion	Gross income[6]
	Cattle	Calves							
	1,000 head	*1,000 head*	*1,000 head*	*1,000 head*	*1,000 pounds*	*1,000 dollars*	*1,000 dollars*	*1,000 dollars*	*1,000 dollars*
Alabama	526.0	52.0	18.0	2.0	592,458	402,396	406,929	2,106	409,035
Alaska	2.7	0.1	0.4	0.4	4,443	4,884	3,424	441	3,865
Arizona	533.5	95.1	337.0	1.4	484,789	543,422	783,923	2,269	786,192
Arkansas	633.0	234.0	115.0	1.0	510,641	360,750	452,034	3,579	455,613
California	2,027.0	311.0	740.0	7.0	2,312,271	2,426,684	3,064,300	10,074	3,074,374
Colorado	2,364.5	102.5	1,709.0	2.0	1,861,346	1,796,196	3,625,741	13,157	3,638,898
Connecticut	7.4	7.5	1.6	0.2	12,223	13,250	17,255	827	12,413
Delaware	4.0	1.8	0.5	0.1	4,808	5,115	7,497	637	5,638
Florida	220.0	565.5	40.0	1.5	430,506	439,933	507,755	2,862	477,872
Georgia	301.0	162.5	17.0	1.5	398,613	311,266	335,319	2,057	303,448
Hawaii	15.6	42.2		0.2	35,038	41,387	45,781	448	43,200
Idaho	1,165.0	160.0	450.0	3.0	1,259,900	1,405,115	1,725,717	10,120	1,745,760
Illinois	492.0	79.0	135.0	7.0	556,181	660,003	595,677	16,656	834,533
Indiana	323.0	122.0	109.0	5.0	283,810	282,568	353,897	14,816	408,778
Iowa	2,403.0	100.5	1,570.0	2.5	2,075,108	2,536,003	4,074,878	14,583	3,946,525
Kansas	5,344.0	4.0	4,200.0	2.0	4,425,147	4,651,116	8,285,905	15,790	8,406,456
Kentucky	551.0	383.0	73.0	3.0	594,091	648,279	738,867	11,167	703,175
Louisana	131.5	217.5	8.0	1.0	202,545	202,975	234,660	1,612	205,903
Maine	12.7	14.1	3.0	0.2	15,242	16,504	20,514	1,684	18,746
Maryland	60.5	21.0	4.1	0.6	73,049	76,424	68,955	2,838	94,487
Massachusetts	9.0	8.0	0.8	0.3	8,092	8,596	9,482	632	11,379
Michigan	377.0	41.0	70.0	3.0	487,465	486,956	553,716	14,249	562,046
Minnesota	1,366.5	105.5	800.0	4.0	1,395,147	1,422,743	2,063,652	18,475	2,014,746
Mississippi	228.0	110.0	15.0	2.0	245,638	191,007	215,709	3,286	175,272
Missouri	903.0	895.0	115.0	7.0	1,445,831	1,880,552	2,170,559	24,470	1,893,181
Montana	1,290.0	150.5	124.0	3.5	1,115,068	1,254,311	1,365,683	13,010	1,368,143
Nebraska	6,408.0	85.0	4,965.0	2.0	5,586,250	5,424,191	10,583,711	15,871	10,562,966
Nevada	215.0	95.0	110.0	1.0	210,394	232,289	326,304	2,386	322,126
New Hampshire	5.9	6.3	0.6	0.4	7,439	8,272	9,696	948	9,826
New Jersey	7.0	5.1	1.4	0.4	7,334	8,080	5,804	1,654	10,984
New Mexico	892.7	101.2	390.0	1.1	632,851	715,030	919,041	4,337	997,630
New York	202.6	300.4	18.5	3.5	261,505	276,247	344,279	12,798	289,042
North Carolina	208.5	119.5	6.0	1.0	291,217	222,816	247,857	2,822	222,057
North Dakota	870.3	103.7	140.0	1.0	794,993	943,461	1,028,871	9,720	993,144
Ohio	475.0	21.0	50.0	6.0	585,650	594,916	575,463	27,365	650,715
Oklahoma	2,332.0	355.0	900.0	3.0	2,117,748	2,578,360	3,308,434	19,133	3,293,410
Oregon	515.0	194.0	140.0	5.0	547,700	625,158	701,269	12,650	749,610
Pennsylvania	410.0	210.7	36.0	7.3	513,029	553,687	586,422	20,313	636,223
Rhode Island	1.1	1.1	0.2	0.2	1,086	1,174	902	493	1,721
South Carolina	141.0	16.0	4.0	2.0	167,087	115,360	125,693	2,159	124,321
South Dakota	1,889.0	500.0	584.0	1.0	1,720,157	2,123,392	2,726,006	10,760	2,739,338
Tennessee	482.0	323.0	30.0	3.0	585,786	476,175	548,804	7,647	495,312
Texas	5,428.0	257.5	1,650.0	4.5	6,181,230	7,256,724	8,624,064	16,041	8,440,074
Utah	376.0	35.5	58.0	1.5	403,998	446,167	449,991	6,405	498,907
Vermont	39.3	61.2	3.4	0.9	55,927	62,520	65,525	2,957	70,574
Virginia	341.5	221.5	12.0	3.0	439,952	347,309	412,529	5,168	349,751
Washington	564.0	6.0	210.0	6.0	658,905	698,751	748,635	13,183	867,111
West Virginia	112.5	76.5	20.0	2.0	145,668	157,535	173,634	5,154	165,886
Wisconsin	1,027.0	375.2	163.0	4.8	1,499,119	1,590,916	1,752,726	31,022	1,693,324
Wyoming	786.0	85.5	270.0	0.5	575,768	695,811	942,966	3,963	892,101
United States	45,040.3	7,541.2	20,417.5	122.5	44,820,270	48,233,046	67,105,197	431,231	66,675,831

[1] Includes custom slaughter for use on farms where produced and State outshipments, but excludes interfarm sales within the State.　[2] Includes cattle shipped in from other states, but excludes cattle for immediate slaughter.　[3] Excludes custom slaughter for farmers at commercial establishments.　[4] Adjustments made for changes in inventory and for inshipments.　[5] Includes receipts from marketings and sales of farm-slaughter.　[6] Includes cash receipts from sales of cattle, calves, beef, and veal plus value of cattle and calves slaughtered for home consumption.
NASS, Livestock Branch, (202) 720–3570.

Table 7-16.—Cattle and calves: Inventory Jan 1, 2018–2019, and number of operations, 2017, by State and United States [1]

State	January 1 Cattle inventory		Operations with cattle [2]
	2018	2019	2017
	1,000 head	*1,000 head*	*Number*
Alabama	1,340.0	1,000.0	22,046
Alaska	15.0	16.0	118
Arizona	1,020.0	1,020.0	7,057
Arkansas	1,760.0	1,780.0	25,372
California	5,200.0	5,150.0	13,694
Colorado	2,850.0	2,850.0	14,914
Connecticut	50.0	47.0	1,158
Delaware	17.0	15.0	301
Florida	1,630.0	1,680.0	21,469
Georgia	1,060.0	1,070.0	17,387
Hawaii	144.0	142.0	1,218
Idaho	2,420.0	2,500.0	10,076
Illinois	1,150.0	1,190.0	16,269
Indiana	860.0	880.0	17,014
Iowa	4,000.0	3,950.0	25,367
Kansas	6,300.0	6,400.0	26,740
Kentucky	2,160.0	2,130.0	38,657
Louisana	820.0	800.0	13,449
Maine	81.0	78.0	1,756
Maryland	193.0	197.0	3,322
Massachusetts	38.0	37.0	1,267
Michigan	1,160.0	1,160.0	12,221
Minnesota	2,350.0	2,320.0	20,969
Mississippi	930.0	900.0	15,980
Missouri	4,350.0	4,250.0	53,497
Montana	2,550.0	2,500.0	11,400
Nebraska	6,800.0	6,800.0	20,430
Nevada	465.0	470.0	1,621
New Hampshire	36.0	33.0	903
New Jersey	29.0	30.0	1,246
New Mexico	1,510.0	1,480.0	10,880
New York	1,480.0	1,450.0	12,796
North Carolina	800.0	800.0	18,413
North Dakota	1,860.0	1,830.0	8,777
Ohio	1,300.0	1,310.0	25,224
Oklahoma	5,100.0	5,300.0	52,048
Oregon	1,270.0	1,310.0	13,880
Pennsylvania	1,620.0	1,600.0	22,729
Rhode Island	5.0	4.7	214
South Carolina	340.0	350.0	7,868
South Dakota	4,000.0	4,050.0	13,928
Tennessee	1,830.0	1,800.0	37,288
Texas	12,500.0	13,000.0	152,882
Utah	790.0	810.0	8,026
Vermont	260.0	255.0	2,317
Virginia	1,480.0	1,440.0	21,880
Washington	1,160.0	1,180.0	11,311
West Virginia	395.0	390.0	11,774
Wisconsin	3,550.0	3,450.0	27,777
Wyoming	1,320.0	1,300.0	5,762
United States	94,298.0	94,804.7	882,692

[1] An operation is any place having one or more head of cattle on hand on December 31. [2] State level estimates only available in conjunction with the Census of Agriculture every 5 years.
NASS, Livestock Branch, (202) 720–3570.

Table 7-17.—Cattle: Number slaughtered under Federal inspection and percentage distribution, by classes, 2010–2019 [1]

Year	Number						Percentage of total					
	Steers	Heif-ers	Cows			Bulls	Steers	Heif-ers	Cows			Bulls
			Dairy cows	Other cows	Total cows				Dairy cows	Other cows	Total cows	
	Thousands						Percent					
2010 ...	16,596	10,047	2,807	3,630	6,437	622	49.2	29.8	8.3	10.8	19.1	1.8
2011 ...	16,539	9,726	2,914	3,798	6,712	579	49.3	29.0	8.7	11.3	20.0	1.7
2012 ...	16,160	9,269	3,102	3,344	6,446	551	49.8	28.6	9.6	10.3	19.9	1.7
2013 ...	16,003	9,132	3,125	3,130	6,255	557	50.1	28.6	9.8	9.8	19.6	1.7
2014 ...	15,378	8,377	2,816	2,565	5,380	548	51.8	28.2	9.5	8.6	18.1	1.8
2015 ...	15,331	7,351	2,915	2,236	5,151	462	54.2	26.0	10.3	7.9	18.2	1.6
2016 ...	16,495	7,698	2,886	2,543	5,428	494	54.8	25.6	9.6	8.4	18.0	1.6
2017 ...	16,771	8,611	2,988	2,784	5,773	550	52.9	27.2	9.4	8.8	18.2	1.7
2018 ...	16,637	9,167	3,153	3,024	6,177	538	51.2	28.2	9.7	9.3	19.0	1.7
2019 ...	16,298	9,819	3,224	2,784	6,414	539	49.3	29.7	9.7	8.4	19.4	1.6

[1] Totals and percentages based on unrounded data and may not equal sum of classes due to rounding.
NASS, Livestock Branch, (202) 720-3570.

Table 7-18.—Cattle and calves: Average dressed weight under Federal inspection, 2010–2019 [1]

Year	Cattle					Calves
	All cattle	Steers	Heifers	Cows	Bulls	
	Pounds					
2010	773	835	768	607	875	154
2011	773	841	773	596	868	154
2012	790	859	792	608	877	152
2013	796	863	794	620	880	146
2014	808	872	800	627	898	166
2015	829	892	818	644	915	183
2016	829	891	822	643	901	155
2017	817	877	812	642	896	145
2018	818	880	817	645	889	130
2019	813	878	813	639	878	127

[1] Excludes postmortem condemnations.
NASS, Livestock Branch, (202) 720-3570.

Table 7-19.—Beef cows: Inventory Jan 1, 2018 and 2019, and number of operations, 2017, by State and United States [1]

State	January 1 beef cow inventory		Operations with beef cows [2]
	2018	2019	2017
	1,000 head	*1,000 head*	*Number*
Alabama	714.0	705.0	20,004.0
Alaska	6.1	6.8	92.0
Arizona	200.0	215.0	5,560.0
Arkansas	924.0	935.0	23,036.0
California	670.0	630.0	10,254.0
Colorado	812.0	792.0	12,407.0
Connecticut	5.0	4.5	860.0
Delaware	2.5	2.0	235.0
Florida	886.0	914.0	18,493.0
Georgia	485.0	499.0	14,869.0
Hawaii	75.0	75.5	1,047.0
Idaho	510.0	506.0	8,149.0
Illinois	397.0	405.0	13,139.0
Indiana	208.0	204.0	11,753.0
Iowa	950.0	930.0	19,171.0
Kansas	1,504.0	1,529.0	23,682.0
Kentucky	1,033.0	1,017.0	33,864.0
Louisana	473.0	459.0	12,051.0
Maine	10.0	11.0	1,141.0
Maryland	46.0	50.0	2,486.0
Massachusetts	6.5	7.0	879.0
Michigan	102.0	108.0	7,445.0
Minnesota	365.0	370.0	13,339.0
Mississippi	501.0	477.0	14,752.0
Missouri	2,086.0	2,059.0	48,122.0
Montana	1,497.0	1,448.0	10,290.0
Nebraska	1,910.0	1,941.0	17,707.0
Nevada	238.0	242.0	1,356.0
New Hampshire	4.5	4.0	602.0
New Jersey	9.0	9.5	941.0
New Mexico	483.0	480.0	8,991.0
New York	105.0	105.0	7,310.0
North Carolina	370.0	367.0	16,407.0
North Dakota	964.0	975.0	8,245.0
Ohio	296.0	307.0	17,733.0
Oklahoma	2,088.0	2,150.0	46,080.0
Oregon	536.0	535.0	11,548.0
Pennsylvania	215.0	225.0	13,176.0
Rhode Island	1.6	1.4	163.0
South Carolina	174.0	186.0	6,917.0
South Dakota	1,751.0	1,818.0	12,613.0
Tennessee	910.0	914.0	32,960.0
Texas	4,520.0	4,655.0	134,250.0
Utah	338.0	340.0	6,508.0
Vermont	15.0	14.0	1,399.0
Virginia	633.0	631.0	18,453.0
Washington	235.0	230.0	9,295.0
West Virginia	203.0	198.0	10,336.0
Wisconsin	285.0	290.0	13,954.0
Wyoming	714.0	714.0	4,982.0
United States	31,466.2	31,690.7	729,046.0

[1] An operation is any place having one or more beef cows on hand on December 31.　　[2] State level estimates only available in conjunction with the Census of Agriculture every 5 years.

NASS, Livestock Branch, (202) 720–3570.

Table 7-20.—Hogs and pigs: Inventory and value, Dec. 1, 2018–2019, and number of operations, 2017, by State and United States

State	Inventory		Value				Operations [1]
	2018	2019	Value per head		Total value		2017
			2018	2019	2018	2019	
	Thousands	Thousands	Dollars	Dollars	1,000 dollars	1,000 dollars	Number
Alabama	33.0	36.0	112	110	3,696	3,960	1,074
Alaska	1.9	1.9	221	220	420	418	64
Arizona	170.0	161.0	115	110	19,550	17,710	521
Arkansas	130.0	117.0	110	105	14,300	12,285	1,021
California	101.0	106.0	145	145	14,645	15,370	1,389
Colorado	750.0	760.0	110	105	82,500	78,750	1,227
Connecticut	3.7	4.0	145	145	537	580	214
Delaware	6.5	7.0	110	110	715	770	55
Florida	13.0	10.0	110	112	1,430	1,120	1,810
Georgia	72.0	62.0	100	100	7,200	6,200	1,091
Hawaii	9.0	11.0	170	170	1,530	1,870	226
Idaho	32.0	35.0	110	110	3,520	3,850	606
Illinois	5,400.0	5,500.0	97	102	523,800	545,700	2,153
Indiana	4,250.0	4,450.0	97	102	412,250	438,600	2,570
Iowa	23,600.0	25,100.0	96	102	2,265,600	2,529,600	5,660
Kansas	2,050.0	2,160.0	100	102	205,000	214,000	943
Kentucky	285.0	435.0	95	93	27,075	40,455	1,805
Louisiana	6.0	6.0	112	110	672	660	874
Maine	4.4	4.6	120	120	528	552	429
Maryland	19.0	20.0	120	120	2,280	2,400	562
Massachusetts	8.0	8.0	105	105	840	840	337
Michigan	1,180.0	1,240.0	95	99	112,100	120,780	2,017
Minnesota	9,100.0	9,500.0	97	102	882,700	938,400	3,225
Mississippi	190.0	190.0	108	106	20,520	20,140	784
Missouri	3,650.0	3,400.0	99	103	361,350	334,750	2,687
Montana	192.0	210.0	113	113	21,696	23,730	452
Nebraska	3,550.0	3,850.0	100	103	355,000	386,250	1,230
Nevada	6.0	5.0	121	120	726	600	70
New Hampshire	3.5	3.4	115	115	403	391	281
New Jersey	8.5	7.5	120	120	1,020	900	347
New Mexico	1.3	2.0	115	115	150	230	353
New York	46.0	53.0	105	105	4,830	5,565	1,739
North Carolina	9,200.0	9,500.0	91	96	837,200	883,200	2,426
North Dakota	145.0	142.0	103	100	14,935	14,200	156
Ohio	2,550.0	2,950.0	103	104	272,850	291,200	3,484
Oklahoma	2,200.0	2,280.0	120	116	264,000	263,320	2,264
Oregon	9.0	11.0	115	115	1,035	1,265	1,177
Pennsylvania	1,310.0	1,330.0	95	100	124,450	131,300	2,777
Rhode Island	1.7	1.6	120	120	204	192	60
South Carolina	210.0	195.0	96	95	20,160	18,525	1,005
South Dakota	1,750.0	2,010.0	100	102	175,000	202,980	571
Tennessee	225.0	250.0	91	93	20,475	23,250	1,898
Texas	1,110.0	1,140.0	115	114	127,650	128,820	5,894
Utah	710.0	960.0	105	105	74,550	100,800	561
Vermont	3.7	3.6	135	135	500	486	353
Virginia	345.0	340.0	94	96	32,430	32,640	1,461
Washington	17.0	17.0	115	115	1,955	1,955	1,126
West Virginia	4.0	3.0	112	105	448	315	892
Wisconsin	320.0	340.0	97	101	31,040	36,865	2,198
Wyoming	88.0	94.0	105	110	9,240	10,340	320
United States	75,070.2	79,047.6	98	102	7,356,703	7,888,779	66,439

(D) Withheld to avoid disclosing data for individual operations. [1] State level estimates only available in conjunction with the Census of Agriculture every 5 years. An operation is any place having one or more hogs and pigs on hand December 31. Totals may not add due to rounding.
NASS, Livestock Branch, (202) 720–3570.

Table 7-21.—Hogs and pigs: Operations, inventory and value, United States, Dec. 1, 2010–2019

Year	Inventory	Value	
		Per head	Total
	Thousands	Dollars	1,000 dollars
2010	64,725	106.00	6,880,179
2011	66,259	123.00	8,145,169
2012	66,224	116.00	7,683,152
2013	64,775	138.00	8,920,314
2014	67,626	144.00	9,731,521
2015	69,019	96.00	6,635,688
2016	71,345	92.00	6,578,419
2017	73,145	99.00	7,206,965
2018	75,070	98.00	7,356,703
2019	79,048	102.00	7,888,779

NASS, Livestock Branch, (202) 720–3570.

Table 7-22.—Sows farrowing and pig crop: Number, United States 2010-2019

Year	Sows farrowing		Pig crop		
	Dec.-May	June-Nov.	Dec.-May	June-Nov.	Total
	Thousands	Thousands	Thousands	Thousands	Thousands
2010	5,749	5,824	55,770	57,358	113,128
2011	5,694	5,846	56,469	58,616	115,085
2012	5,759	5,810	57,749	58,906	116,655
2013	5,595	5,670	57,020	58,115	115,135
2014	5,573	5,975	53,821	60,933	114,754
2015	5,749	5,949	59,219	62,221	121,441
2016	5,898	6,098	61,256	64,651	125,907
2017	6,008	6,209	63,026	66,403	129,429
2018	6,041	6,377	64,053	68,515	132,568
2019	6,233	6,540	67,617	72,575	140,192

NASS, Livestock Branch, (202) 720–3570.

Table 7-23.—Hogs and pigs: Number for breeding and market, United States, 2010–2019

Year	All hogs and pigs	Kept for breeding	Market hogs by weight groups				
			Under 50 pounds	50 to 119 pounds	120 to 179 pounds	180 pounds and over	Total
June 1							
	Thousands	Thousands	Thousands	Thousands	Thousands	Thousands	Thousands
2010	64,650	5,788	19,224	16,832	12,154	10,653	58,862
2011	65,320	5,803	19,423	17,241	12,254	10,599	59,517
2012	66,469	5,862	19,746	17,924	12,243	10,694	60,607
2013	65,188	5,884	19,145	17,068	12,414	10,678	59,304
2014	61,468	5,855	18,254	15,801	11,471	10,086	55,613
2015	67,065	5,926	19,365	17,461	12,935	11,379	61,140
2016	69,281	5,979	20,356	18,198	13,291	11,456	63,302
2017	71,210	6,109	20,647	18,841	13,696	11,917	65,101
2018	72,231	6,320	21,081	18,846	13,898	12,085	65,911
2019	75,725	6,109	22,210	19,693	14,396	13,017	69,316
Dec. 1							
	Thousands	Thousands	Thousands	Thousands	Thousands	Thousands	Thousands
2010	64,725	5,778	18,864	16,519	12,183	11,381	58,947
2011	66,259	5,803	19,447	16,618	12,473	11,918	60,456
2012	66,224	5,819	19,299	16,752	12,614	11,741	60,405
2013	64,775	5,757	18,389	16,080	12,576	11,972	59,018
2014	67,626	5,939	19,746	17,296	13,000	11,646	61,688
2015	69,019	6,002	20,038	17,262	13,440	12,276	63,017
2016	71,345	6,110	20,862	18,077	13,711	12,585	65,235
2017	73,145	6,179	21,407	18,544	13,925	13,089	66,966
2018	75,020	6,326	21,858	19,369	14,323	13,195	68,745
2019	79,048	6,471	22,648	20,691	15,321	13,916	72,577

NASS, Livestock Branch, (202) 720–3570.

Table 7-24.—Cattle and swine: Production, 2018–2020

Country	2018	2019	2020
	1,000 head		
Cattle:			
India	68,600	69,000	69,400
Brazil	49,500	50,490	51,500
China	47,500	48,500	49,500
United States	36,403	36,300	36,200
European Union	28,800	28,350	28,300
Argentina	14,650	14,780	14,900
Australia	9,100	8,700	8,300
Mexico	7,700	7,900	8,105
Russia	6,566	6,590	6,650
New Zealand	4,895	4,915	4,875
Canada	4,292	4,325	4,400
Uruguay	2,750	2,700	2,810
Ukraine	2,104	2,020	1,950
Egypt	1,930	1,940	1,940
Belarus	1,400	1,400	1,400
Japan	1,224	1,225	1,230
Korea, South	968	991	1,028
Turkey	3,930	0	0
Swine:			
China	685,000	490,000	412,000
European Union	267,000	266,500	270,000
United States	132,568	138,032	142,790
Russia	49,500	50,915	52,600
Brazil	40,954	42,500	44,000
Canada	28,027	28,450	28,900
Mexico	18,750	19,600	20,200
Korea, South	19,118	19,530	19,415
Japan	16,690	17,000	17,030
Ukraine	8,816	8,740	8,750
Belarus	5,050	4,825	4,725

FAS, Office of Global Analysis, (202) 720-6301. Prepared or estimated on the basis of official USDA production, supply, and distribution statistics from foreign governments.

Table 7-25.—Hogs: Number slaughtered, United States, 2010–2019

Year	Commercial			Farm	Total
	Federally inspected	Other	Total [1]		
	Thousands				
2010	109,315	945	110,260	107	110,367
2011	109,956	904	110,860	96	110,956
2012	112,265	898	113,163	83	113,247
2013	111,248	829	112,077	84	112,161
2014	106,123	753	106,876	82	106,958
2015	114,616	810	115,425	87	115,512
2016	117,388	832	118,220	84	118,304
2017	120,516	801	121,317	73	121,390
2018	123,693	739	124,432	76	124,508
2019	129,211	702	129,913	73	129,989

[1] Totals are based on unrounded number.
NASS, Livestock Branch, (202) 720-3570.

Table 7-26.—Sows farrowing and pig crop: Number by State and United States, 2018–2019

State	Sows farrowing							
	December[1]–February		March–May		June–August		September–November	
	2018	2019	2018	2019	2018	2019	2018	2019
	Thousands							
Colorado	72	78	75	78	79	79	75	76
Illinois	254	270	275	275	265	290	280	285
Indiana	130	125	110	120	125	120	130	125
Iowa	530	530	550	530	575	550	570	540
Kansas	79	86	76	86	87	90	85	92
Michigan	53	56	52	54	57	55	54	56
Minnesota	290	300	305	295	300	300	310	310
Missouri	220	245	240	242	255	260	255	265
Nebraska	180	185	190	200	185	194	195	195
North Carolina ..	445	455	455	460	485	500	475	480
Ohio	91	93	88	98	89	102	99	104
Oklahoma	200	205	205	215	210	230	205	220
Pennsylvania	48	55	50	54	51	51	52	57
South Dakota ...	113	119	110	123	117	129	127	138
Texas	55	66	64	66	68	71	67	68
Utah	36	40	34	43	39	44	37	41
Other States[2] ...	181	191	185	194	185	210	189	213
United States[3]	2,977	3,099	3,064	3,133	3,172	3,275	3,205	3,265

State	Pig crop							
	December[1]–February		March–May		June–August		September–November	
	2018	2019	2018	2019	2018	2019	2018	2019
	Thousands							
Colorado	698	718	720	835	751	845	720	806
Illinois	2,692	2,876	2,943	2,956	2,822	3,176	2,982	3,121
Indiana	1,359	1,275	1,133	1,284	1,313	1,320	1,378	1,313
Iowa	5,830	5,936	6,105	6,069	6,440	6,243	6,384	6,129
Kansas	806	912	768	920	948	981	927	989
Michigan	567	610	567	594	616	611	567	608
Minnesota	3,248	3,480	3,416	3,496	3,345	3,585	3,534	3,674
Missouri	2,233	2,585	2,448	2,577	2,665	2,886	2,703	2,942
Nebraska	2,106	2,137	2,147	2,300	2,091	2,260	2,233	2,282
North Carolina ..	4,406	4,505	4,596	4,830	4,996	5,250	4,821	5,064
Ohio	983	995	968	1,098	970	1,153	1,049	1,186
Oklahoma	2,120	2,183	2,194	2,268	2,237	2,507	2,173	2,387
Pennsylvania	509	594	525	599	546	576	572	638
South Dakota ...	1,294	1,410	1,287	1,470	1,299	1,529	1,480	1,656
Texas	545	673	627	693	687	774	697	707
Utah	277	368	258	460	429	484	370	472
Other States[2] ...	1,824	1,906	1,854	2,005	1,864	2,189	1,906	2,231
United States[3]	31,497	33,163	32,556	34,454	34,019	36,369	34,496	36,205

[1] December preceding year.   [2] Individual State estimates not available for the 34 other States.   [3] Totals may not add due to rounding.
NASS, Livestock Branch, (202) 720–3570.

Table 7-27.—Hogs: Production, disposition, cash receipts, and gross income, United States, 2010–2019

Year	Mar-ketings [1]	Inship-ments [2]	Farm slaugh-ter [3]	Production (live weight) [4]	Value of produc-tion [5]	Cash receipts [6]	Value of home consump-tion	Gross income	Average price per 100 pounds received by farmers
	1,000 head	1,000 head	1,000 head	1,000 pounds	1,000 dollars	1,000 dollars	1,000 dollars	1,000 dollars	Dollars
2010	144,362	40,004	107	30,284,630	16,012,200	17,898,063	38,306	17,936,369	55.10
2011	145,420	40,522	96	30,836,171	20,014,277	21,631,894	44,004	21,675,898	66.50
2012	151,835	44,027	83	32,060,619	20,285,027	22,092,108	40,007	22,132,115	64.20
2013	154,923	47,864	73	32,524,986	21,611,356	23,706,457	37,428	23,743,885	67.20
2014	149,097	47,185	82	32,126,235	24,183,766	26,489,394	43,550	26,532,944	77.10
2015	159,724	50,146	87	34,739,292	18,814,459	20,552,958	31,982	20,584,940	53.50
2016	165,538	52,954	84	35,898,712	17,363,044	19,037,752	28,797	19,066,549	49.60
2017	171,320	55,266	73	36,962,875	19,159,248	21,038,034	29,273	21,067,307	53.60
2018	180,251	61,619	76	38,498,011	18,769,964	20,881,335	27,267	20,908,602	49.90
2019	187,648	63,297	76	40,509,010	19,826,838	22,015,189	28,146	22,043,335	51.90

[1] Includes custom slaughter for use on farms where produced and State outshipments, but excludes interfarm sales within the State. [2] Includes hogs and pigs shipped in from other states but excludes animals for immediate slaughter. [3] Excludes custom slaughter for farmers at commercial establishments. [4] Adjustments made for changes in inventory and for inshipments. [5] Includes allowance for higher average price of State inshipments and outshipments of feeder pigs. [6] Receipts from marketings and sale of farm slaughter.
NASS Livestock Branch, (202) 720–3570.

Table 7-28.—Hogs: Direct receipts at interior markets, 2010–2019

Year	All receipts (live and carcass basis)			
	National	Iowa/ Southern Minnesota [1]	Western Region	Eastern Region
	Thousands	Thousands	Thousands	Thousands
2010	75,104	40,143	48,413	22,896
2011	75,514	41,479	49,649	22,643
2012	75,459	42,343	50,607	22,192
2013	71,599	40,744	48,202	20,929
2014	73,182	41,687	49,180	21,341
2015	78,212	44,997	53,076	22,298
2016	80,716	26,315	32,247	15,922
	Number	Number	Number	Number
2017	2,912,345	1,607,503	1,763,741	1,145,350
2018	3,163,846	1,675,816	1,521,595	1,068,483
2019 [2]	2,845,278	(NA)	(NA)	(NA)

(NA) Not available. [1] Iowa / Southern Minnesota is a subset of the Western Region. [2] Due to confidentiality rules, these numbers are now only tracked on a national basis.
AMS, Livestock & Grain Market News, (202) 720–7316.

Table 7-29.—Hogs and corn: Hog-corn price ratio and average price received by farmers for corn, United States, 2010–2019 [1][2]

Year	Hog-corn price ratio [1]	Price of corn per bushel [2]
		Dollars
2010	14.4	3.83
2011	11.0	6.02
2012	9.6	6.67
2013	11.3	6.15
2014	18.9	4.11
2015	14.5	3.70
2016	14.2	3.48
2017	15.9	3.36
2018	14.4	3.47
2019	13.8	3.75

[1] Number of bushels of corn equal in value to buy 100 pounds of live hogs at local markets, based on average prices received by farmers for hogs and corn. Annual average is a simple average of monthly ratios for the calendar year. [2] Annual average is a simple average of monthly prices for the calendar year.
NASS, Environmental, Economics, and Demographics Branch, (202) 720–6146.

Table 7-30.—Hogs: Production, disposition, cash receipts, and gross income, by State and United States, 2019

State	Mar-ketings [1]	Inship-ments [2]	Farm slaugh-ter [3]	Production (live weight) [4]	Value of production [5]	Cash receipts [5][6]	Value of home consump-tion	Gross income
	1,000 head	1,000 head	1,000 head	1,000 pounds	1,000 dollars	1,000 dollars	1,000 dollars	1,000 dollars
Alabama	211.0	43.0	0.5	27,958	16,595	20,170	283	18,369
Alaska	3.2	1.3	0.8	982	539	324	109	615
Arizona	276.5	3.0	1.0	67,654	39,957	36,790	294	40,853
Arkansas	1,040.0	21.0	1.0	65,205	51,980	60,345	392	57,411
California	181.0	144.0	3.0	39,830	18,393	27,453	612	27,191
Colorado	3,208.0	140.0	2.0	293,229	176,024	140,519	302	183,910
Connecticut	5.2	1.2	0.1	1,384	672	397	25	693
Delaware	40.0	1.0	0.1	9,869	5,084	3,808	47	5,058
Florida	31.5	9.0	0.5	3,729	1,994	1,836	150	2,415
Georgia	552.0	202.0	2.0	57,982	30,776	39,986	538	36,827
Hawaii	1.7	0.1	1.6	1,044	613	485	180	478
Idaho	108.1	29.2	1.0	28,333	15,854	16,056	294	17,268
Illinois	12,880.0	1,394.0	3.0	2,196,434	1,184,193	1,209,683	825	1,228,867
Indiana	10,063.0	5,493.0	2.0	2,235,725	1,029,649	1,199,559	839	1,239,617
Iowa	54,732.0	35,800.0	5.0	14,455,917	6,651,649	7,616,470	2,099	7,772,961
Kansas	5,245.0	2,023.0	1.0	1,048,275	485,277	518,816	429	549,481
Kentucky	1,003.0	243.0	4.0	194,995	110,057	114,816	1,208	115,567
Louisiana	6.0	4.0	0.5	919	509	865	71	689
Maine	5.8	1.5	0.1	1,436	686	1,088	58	792
Maryland	48.1	13.5	0.1	9,917	4,839	6,809	38	5,939
Massachusetts ..	15.0	2.5	0.1	3,236	1,608	1,825	25	1,673
Michigan	2,476.0	198.0	2.0	635,011	325,244	502,505	590	330,083
Minnesota	22,302.0	9,600.0	3.0	4,777,656	2,328,552	2,514,681	1,202	2,724,246
Mississippi	995.0	4.0	4.0	61,289	41,421	59,299	695	41,783
Missouri	12,240.9	1,548.9	2.0	1,656,302	866,479	788,932	1,060	927,228
Montana	668.0	5.0	2.0	120,614	69,822	56,717	476	70,255
Nebraska	8,805.0	604.0	3.0	1,509,174	853,620	813,183	1,352	873,673
Nevada	3.4	2.3	0.1	648	289	181	28	530
New Hampshire	6.2	1.5	0.1	1,656	796	866	73	883
New Jersey	13.4	7.5	0.1	1,027	229	616	76	743
New Mexico	5.9	3.8	0.2	957	464	680	52	614
New York	88.3	54.0	0.5	1,432	2,285	6,851	224	6,374
North Carolina ..	17,968.0	660.0	1.0	4,361,099	2,076,752	2,129,121	626	2,174,162
North Dakota	937.6	143.1	0.3	44,904	41,872	56,962	84	60,660
Ohio	4,916.0	1,100.0	6.0	1,331,230	623,182	667,969	2,973	677,872
Oklahoma	9,433.0	725.0	2.0	2,035,654	921,129	938,522	408	976,075
Oregon	7.3	2.0	1.0	2,170	1,849	1,624	283	1,180
Pennsylvania ...	2,402.7	225.0	3.3	642,821	272,183	275,440	787	330,148
Rhode Island	2.6	0.1	0.1	638	277	275	22	322
South Carolina	215.0	77.0	1.0	40,077	17,800	17,153	873	24,115
South Dakota ...	6,860.0	1,250.0	2.0	1,153,511	530,360	585,716	1,385	731,300
Tennessee	648.0	170.0	2.0	160,384	72,280	79,520	574	89,496
Texas	3,232.0	685.0	6.0	487,749	225,405	230,092	2,151	244,389
Utah	1,413.8	73.3	0.5	292,364	128,244	123,783	136	166,359
Vermont	6.1	1.0	0.2	1,624	1,057	1,095	91	867
Virginia	451.0	430.0	2.0	109,527	29,561	43,580	647	61,929
Washington	25.9	1.5	1.0	6,706	4,270	3,972	416	4,016
West Virginia	6.0	0.4	0.2	1,549	750	795	102	885
Wisconsin	1,158.5	155.0	1.0	218,375	112,135	122,706	683	150,741
Wyoming	704.0	1.0	1.0	108,809	57,287	57,122	307	65,674
United States ...	187,647.7	63,296.7	76.0	40,509,010	19,060,203	21,098,058	21,794	22,043,335

- Represents zero. (D)Withheld to avoid disclosing data for individual operations. [1] Includes custom slaughter for use on farms where produced and State outshipments,but excludes interfarm sales within the State. [2] Includes hogs and pigs shipped in from other states but excludes animals for immediate slaughter. [3] Excludes custom slaughter for farmers at commercial establishments. [4] Adjustments made for changes in inventory and for inshipments. [5] Includes allowance for higher average price of State inshipments and outshipments of feeder pigs. [6] Receipts from marketings and sale of farm-slaughter.

NASS, Livestock Branch, (202) 720–3570.

Table 7-31.—Hogs: Number slaughtered commercially, total and average live weight, by State and United States, 2019[1]

State	Number slaughtered	Total live weight[2]	Average live weight[2]
	Thousands	*1,000 pounds*	*Pounds*
Alabama	23.0	9,002	392
Alaska	1.2	337	274
Arizona	1.7	460	269
Arkansas	6.5	1,805	279
California	2,415.2	618,886	257
Colorado	18.4	4,460	243
Delaware & Maryland	18.2	4,729	260
Florida	62.3	8,156	131
Georgia	65.5	15,938	243
Hawaii	4.1	1,054	260
Idaho	173.5	46,779	270
Illinois	12,420.7	3,555,598	286
Indiana	8,542.5	2,391,121	280
Iowa	39,115.6	11,128,200	285
Kansas	(D)	(D)	(D)
Kentucky	(D)	(D)	(D)
Louisiana	8.2	1,773	217
Michigan	2,814.2	827,692	294
Minnesota	11,929.7	3,289,204	276
Mississippi	35.6	5,639	159
Missouri	8,752.7	2,562,179	293
Montana	16.1	4,533	282
Nebraska	8,012.1	2,274,615	284
Nevada	0.7	171	257
New England[3]	33.7	8,710	259
New Jersey	105.0	10,144	97
New Mexico	2.6	704	267
New York	24.6	5,915	241
North Carolina	(D)	(D)	(D)
North Dakota	3.1	923	302
Ohio	923.3	260,018	282
Oklahoma	5,072.3	1,582,889	278
Oregon	166.1	44,786	270
Pennsylvania	3,329.9	932,733	280
South Carolina	30.5	7,341	241
South Dakota	(D)	(D)	(D)
Tennessee	861.6	391,048	454
Texas	311.0	64,034	206
Utah	59.5	8,724	147
Virginia	(D)	(D)	(D)
Washington	12.8	3,307	259
West Virginia	7.7	2,224	288
Wisconsin	731.5	316,360	434
Wyoming	3.1	824	269
United States[4]	129,913.0	37,023,920	285

(D) Withheld to avoid disclosing data for individual operations. [1] Includes slaughter in federally inspected and other slaughter plants; excludes animals slaughtered on farms. Average live weight is based on unrounded numbers. Totals may not add due to rounding. [2] Excludes postmortem condemnations. [3] Connecticut, Maine, Massachusetts, New Hampshire, Rhode Island, and Vermont. [4] States with no data printed are still included in US total. Data are not printed to avoid disclosing individual operations.

NASS, Livestock Branch, (202) 720-3570.

Table 7-32.—Hogs: Number slaughtered, average dressed and live weights, Federally inspected, 2010–2019 [1]

| Year | Federally inspected | | | | | |
| | Barrows and gilts | | | Sows | | |
	Head	Percent of total	Avg. dressed weight [2]	Head	Percent of total	Avg. dressed weight [2]
	1,000		*Pounds*	*1,000*		*Pounds*
2010	105,983	97.0	201	2,966	2.7	305
2011	106,600	96.9	203	3,027	2.8	305
2012	108,912	97.0	203	3,009	2.7	306
2013	107,965	97.0	205	2,932	2.6	304
2014	102,998	97.1	212	2,788	2.6	305
2015	111,488	97.3	210	2,852	2.5	309
2016	114,184	97.3	209	2,885	2.5	310
2017	117,195	97.2	209	2,952	2.4	308
2018	120,303	97.3	209	3,015	2.4	305
2019	125,844	97.4	211	3,012	2.3	304

| Year | Boars | | | Total | | |
	Head	Percent of total	Avg. dressed weight [2]	Head	Avg. dressed weight [2]	Avg. live weight [2]
	1,000		*Pounds*	*1,000*	*Pounds*	*Pounds*
2010	366	0.3	200	109,315	204	273
2011	329	0.3	210	109,956	206	275
2012	344	0.3	208	112,265	206	275
2013	351	0.3	204	111,248	207	277
2014	337	0.3	204	106,123	214	285
2015	276	0.2	207	114,616	213	283
2016	319	0.3	206	117,388	211	282
2017	370	0.3	201	120,516	211	283
2018	376	0.3	192	123,693	212	283
2019	354	0.3	196	129,211	213	285

[1] All weights calculated using unrounded totals.　Totals and percentages based on unrounded data and may not equal sum of classes due to rounding.　[2] Excludes postmortem condemnations.
NASS, Livestock Branch, (202) 720-3570.

Table 7-33.—Lard: Supply and disappearance, United States, 2010–2019

| Calendar year | Supply | | | | Disappearance | | |
	Stocks Jan 1	Production	Imports	Total	Domestic	Exports	Total
	Million lbs	*Million lbs*	*Million lbs*	*Million lbs*	*Million lbs*	*Million lbs*	*Million lbs*
2010	18	840	15	873	776	72	847
2011	26	852	13	891	794	77	871
2012	20	871	14	905	830	55	885
2013	20	867	14	901	816	65	881
2014	20	852	16	888	821	47	868
2015	20	915	14	949	897	44	941
2016	9	932	10	951	901	42	943
2017	8	959	13	980	935	38	973
2018	8	987	15	1,010	962	37	999
2019	8	1,037	14	1,058	1,003	50	1,052

ERS, Market and Trade Economics Division, Field Crops Branch, (202) 694–5300.

Table 7-34.—Lard: United States exports by country of destination, 2018–2020

Country	2018	2019	2020
	Metric tons		
Mexico	16,173	22,115	17,515
Guatemala	0	0	209
Canada	264	259	191
Ireland	98	63	117
Micronesia	4	3	44
Marshall Islands	118	55	12
Singapore	12	10	10
Brazil	1	0	0
Chile	14	0	0
Guyana	24	0	0
Norway(*)	72	0	0
Netherlands Antilles(*)	2	0	0
Philippines	37	0	0
Spain	5	0	0
Leeward-Windward Islands(*)	3	0	0
World Total	16,825	22,506	22,506

(*) Denotes a country that is a summarization of its component countries.
FAS, Office of Global Analysis, (202) 720-6301. Data Source: U.S. Census Bureau Trade Data

Table 7-35.—Sheep and lambs: Inventory and value, United States, Jan. 1, 2010–2019

Year	Inventory	Value	
		Per head	Total
	1,000 head	Dollars	1,000 dollars
2010	5,620	135.00	761,115
2011	5,470	170.00	929,453
2012	5,375	221.00	1,187,730
2013	5,360	177.00	951,020
2014	5,235	188.00	982,316
2015	5,270	214.00	1,127,157
2016	5,295	202.00	1,071,467
2017	5,270	203.00	1,067,857
2018	5,265	204.00	1,071,378
2019	5,270	203.00	1,061,498

NASS, Livestock Branch, (202) 720–3570.

Table 7-36.—Sheep and lambs: Number by class, United States, Jan. 1, 2010–2019

Year	All sheep and lambs	Breeding sheep			
		Total [1]	Replacement lambs	1 year and over	
				Ewes	Rams
	1,000 head	1,000 head	1,000 head	1,000 head	1,000 head
2010	5,620	4,185	655	3,335	195
2011	5,470	4,070	665	3,215	190
2012	5,375	3,995	660	3,165	170
2013	5,360	3,985	670	3,135	180
2014	5,235	3,890	635	3,080	175
2015	5,270	3,925	650	3,100	175
2016	5,295	3,940	665	3,100	175
2017	5,270	3,894	666	3,058	170
2018	5,265	3,865	662	3,033	170
2019	5,270	3,820	650	3,000	170

[1] Categories may not add to total due to rounding.
NASS, Livestock Branch, (202) 720–3570.

Table 7-37.—Lamb mutton, goat, etc. meat: U.S. imports, 2018–2020

Country	2018	2019	2020
	Metric tons		
Australia(*)	97,356	100,918	107,504
New Zealand(*)	26,010	24,465	23,392
Canada	1,200	1,031	1,035
Chile	539	504	840
Mexico	370	917	779
Uruguay	197	188	393
Iceland	203	1	1
China	26	0	0
Denmark(*)	-	0	0
Mozambique	19	0	0
Netherlands	0	0	0
World Total	125,919	128,023	133,944

(*) Denotes a country that is a summarization of its component countries. Users should use cautious interpretation on quantity reports using mixed units of measure. Quantity line items will only include statistics on the units of measure that are equal to, or are able to be converted to, the assigned unit of measure of the grouped commodities.
FAS, Office of Global Analysis, (202) 720-6301. Data Source: U.S. Census Bureau Trade Data.

Table 7-38.—Breeding sheep: Number by class, State and United States, Jan. 1, 2018–2019

State	Under one year old		One year and over			
	Replacement lambs		Ewes		Rams	
	2018	2019	2018	2019	2018	2019
	1,000 head					
Arizona	18.0	19.0	67.0	63.0	5.0	4.0
California	45.0	45.0	260.0	250.0	10.0	10.0
Colorado	33.0	29.0	156.0	150.0	6.0	6.0
Idaho	39.0	35.0	141.0	130.0	5.0	5.0
Illinois	8.0	8.0	36.0	35.0	2.0	2.0
Indiana	8.0	8.0	38.0	40.0	4.0	4.0
Iowa	19.0	19.0	91.0	80.0	5.0	4.0
Kansas	6.0	7.5	34.0	37.0	2.0	2.5
Kentucky	8.0	9.5	36.0	37.0	2.0	2.5
Michigan	13.0	14.0	41.0	45.0	3.0	3.0
Minnesota	12.0	12.0	74.0	74.0	4.0	4.0
Missouri	14.0	14.0	63.0	63.0	3.0	3.0
Montana	39.0	36.0	150.0	141.0	6.0	6.0
Nebraska	9.0	8.0	55.0	53.0	3.0	3.0
Nevada	9.0	9.0	43.0	44.0	2.0	2.0
New England [1]	8.0	7.0	30.0	30.0	2.0	3.0
New Mexico	16.0	15.0	58.0	61.0	6.0	5.0
New York	13.0	13.0	55.0	51.0	3.0	3.0
North Carolina	3.0	3.0	16.0	18.0	2.0	2.0
North Dakota	8.0	7.0	39.0	36.0	2.0	2.0
Ohio	16.0	16.0	73.0	72.0	6.0	6.0
Oklahoma	8.0	6.0	31.0	30.0	3.0	3.0
Oregon	20.0	19.0	94.0	95.0	6.0	6.0
Pennsylvania	13.0	12.0	60.0	60.0	5.0	5.0
South Dakota	31.0	31.0	153.0	157.0	6.0	6.0
Tennessee	7.0	6.0	29.0	29.0	2.0	3.0
Texas	100.0	100.0	465.0	455.0	35.0	35.0
Utah	42.0	41.0	200.0	210.0	8.0	9.0
Virginia	9.0	10.0	45.0	48.0	3.0	3.0
Washington	6.0	7.0	27.0	28.0	2.0	2.0
West Virginia	4.0	4.0	23.0	21.0	1.0	1.0
Wisconsin	12.0	12.0	48.0	48.0	3.0	3.0
Wyoming	43.0	43.0	210.0	215.0	7.0	7.0
Other States [2]	23.0	25.0	92.0	92.0	6.0	5.0
United States	662.0	650.0	3,033.0	3,000.0	170.0	170.0

[1] New England includes Connecticut, Maine, Massachusetts, New Hampshire, Rhode Island, and Vermont. [2] Individual state estimates not available for states not shown, but are included in Other States.
NASS, Livestock Branch, (202) 720-3570.

Table 7-39.—Sheep and lambs: Average price per 100 pounds at San Angelo, 2010–2019 [1]

Year	Sheep			Slaughter lambs choice & prime			
	Good	Utility	Cull	Wooled		Shorn	
				90-110 lbs	110-130 1bs	90-110 lbs	110-130 1bs
2010	59.51	59.50	41.12	114.66	115.12	115.18	115.68
2011	66.22	66.62	41.43	161.09	161.08	161.53	161.24
2012	64.30	65.80	42.84	113.64	114.01	114.56	114.68
2013	47.68	49.68	28.21	107.34	107.50	107.44	107.69
2014	65.66	67.88	43.76	157.08	157.14	157.19	157.30
2015	79.11	80.63	54.70	143.97	143.97	144.02	144.12
2016	72.12	75.37	45.63	135.18	135.28	135.24	135.58
2017	76.86	77.14	47.63	140.98	140.74	141.07	141.01
2018	65.13	67.16	40.52	126.58	125.48	134.63	133.50
2019	72.96	74.84	42.64	133.03	133.71	133.03	133.67

[1] Simple average of monthly bulk-of-sales prices from data of the livestock reporting service.
AMS, Livestock & Grain Market News, (202) 720–7316.

Table 7-40.—Sheep and lambs: Number of breeding and market sheep, by State and United States, Jan. 1, 2018–2019

State	Breeding sheep and lambs		Market sheep and lambs	
	2018	2019	2018	2019
	1,000 head	*1,000 head*	*1,000 head*	*1,000 head*
Arizona	90.0	86.0	35.0	29.0
California	315.0	305.0	255.0	245.0
Colorado	195.0	185.0	250.0	235.0
Idaho	184.0	170.0	50.0	50.0
Illinois	46.0	45.0	9.0	8.0
Indiana	50.0	52.0	7.0	8.0
Iowa	115.0	103.0	50.0	50.0
Kansas	42.0	47.0	25.0	25.0
Kentucky	46.0	49.0	12.0	15.0
Michigan	57.0	62.0	23.0	24.0
Minnesota	90.0	90.0	40.0	35.0
Missouri	80.0	80.0	20.0	20.0
Montana	195.0	183.0	30.0	32.0
Nebraska	67.0	64.0	13.0	11.0
Nevada	54.0	55.0	7.0	8.0
New England [1]	40.0	40.0	9.0	8.0
New Mexico	80.0	81.0	16.0	19.0
New York	71.0	67.0	14.0	13.0
North Carolina	21.0	23.0	6.0	6.0
North Dakota	49.0	45.0	21.0	27.0
Ohio	95.0	94.0	24.0	27.0
Oklahoma	42.0	39.0	12.0	11.0
Oregon	120.0	120.0	45.0	55.0
Pennsylvania	78.0	77.0	18.0	18.0
South Dakota	190.0	194.0	60.0	61.0
Tennessee	38.0	38.0	8.0	10.0
Texas	600.0	590.0	150.0	160.0
Utah	250.0	260.0	25.0	30.0
Virginia	57.0	61.0	18.0	18.0
Washington	35.0	37.0	10.0	13.0
West Virginia	28.0	26.0	7.0	6.0
Wisconsin	63.0	63.0	12.0	12.0
Wyoming	260.0	265.0	85.0	85.0
Other States [2]	121.0	124.0	34.0	36.0
United States	3,865.0	3,820.0	1,400.0	1,410.0

[1] New England includes Connecticut, Maine, Massachusetts, New Hampshire, Rhode Island, and Vermont.   [2] Includes data for States not published in this table.
NASS, Livestock Branch, (202) 720–3570.

Table 7-41.—Lamb crop: Per 100 ewes 1+, number and percent of previous year, by State and United States, 2018–2019

State	Breeding ewes 1 year & older, Jan. 1		Lambs per 100 ewes, Jan. 1		Lamb crop [1]		
	2018	2019	2018	2019	2018	2019	2019 as % of 2018
	1,000 head	1,000 head	Number	Number	1,000 head	1,000 head	Percent
Arizona	67	63	66	56	44	35	80
California	260	250	90	94	235	235	100
Colorado	156	150	119	123	185	185	100
Idaho	141	130	113	123	160	160	100
Illinois	36	35	114	120	41	42	102
Indiana	38	40	121	110	46	44	96
Iowa	91	80	121	144	110	115	105
Kansas	34	37	129	127	44	47	107
Kentucky	36	37	103	108	37	40	108
Michigan	41	45	122	120	50	54	108
Minnesota	74	74	122	122	90	90	100
Missouri	63	63	124	125	78	79	101
Montana	150	141	120	122	180	172	96
Nebraska	55	53	118	134	65	71	109
Nevada	43	44	88	86	38	38	100
New England [2]	30	30	117	123	35	37	106
New Mexico	58	61	83	67	48	41	85
New York	55	51	104	112	57	57	100
North Carolina	16	18	106	89	17	16	94
North Dakota	39	36	115	139	45	50	111
Ohio	73	72	121	132	88	95	108
Oklahoma	31	30	103	110	32	33	103
Oregon	94	95	120	111	113	105	93
Pennsylvania	60	60	110	112	66	67	102
South Dakota	153	157	131	124	200	195	98
Tennessee	29	29	114	117	33	34	103
Texas	465	455	78	81	365	370	101
Utah	200	210	118	110	235	230	98
Virginia	45	48	131	121	59	58	98
Washington	27	28	119	125	32	35	109
West Virginia	23	21	113	133	26	28	108
Wisconsin	48	48	119	129	57	62	109
Wyoming	210	215	114	105	240	225	94
Other States [3]	92	94	91	91	84	84	101
United States	3,033	3,000	107	108	3,235	3,230	100

[1] Lamb crop is defined as lambs born in the Eastern States and lambs docked or branded in the Western States.   [2] New England includes Connecticut, Maine, Massachusetts, New Hampshire, Rhode Island, and Vermont.   [3] Includes data for States not published in this table.
NASS, Livestock Branch, (202) 720–3570.

Table 7-42.—Sheep and lambs: Receipts at selected markets, 2010–2019

Year	Sioux Falls, SD	Billings, MT	San Angelo, TX	New Holland,PA
	Thousands	Thousands	Thousands	Thousands
2010	41	48	143	92
2011	38	42	156	94
2012	35	53	89	101
2013	48	52	110	109
2014	52	49	107	107
2015	82	63	110	117
2016	57	54	129	133
2017	62	61	141	123
2018	69	52	143	142
2019	55	56	160	38

AMS, Livestock & Grain Market News, (202) 720–7316.

Table 7-43.—Sheep and lambs: Number slaughtered, United States, 2010–2019

Year	Commercial			Farm	Total
	Federally inspected	Other	Total [1]		
	Thousands	*Thousands*	*Thousands*	*Thousands*	*Thousands*
2010	2,261	196	2,458	95	2,553
2011	2,000	164	2,164	93	2,258
2012	2,012	171	2,183	93	2,275
2013	2,120	199	2,319	94	2,412
2014	2,105	205	2,310	95	2,404
2015	1,998	225	2,224	95	2,319
2016	2,010	228	2,238	95	2,333
2017	1,937	241	2,178	96	2,274
2018	2,000	265	2,265	92	2,357
2019	2,020	301	2,322	92	2,413

[1] Totals are based on unrounded numbers.
NASS, Livestock Branch, (202) 720–3570.

Table 7-44.—Sheep and lambs: Number slaughtered, average dressed and live weights, percentage distribution, by class, Federally inspected, 2010–2019 [1]

Year	Federally inspected								
	Lambs and yearlings			Mature sheep			Total		
	Head	Percent of total	Avg. dressed weight [2]	Head	Percent of total	Avg. dressed weight [2]	Head	Avg. dressed weight [2]	Avg. live weight [2]
	1,000		*Pounds*	*1,000*		*Pounds*	*1,000*	*Pounds*	
2010	2,105	93.1	69	156	6.9	65	2,261	68	137
2011	1,860	93.0	71	141	7.0	66	2,000	70	141
2012	1,869	92.9	74	143	7.1	64	2,012	74	147
2013	1,988	93.7	69	133	6.3	64	2,120	69	137
2014	1,968	93.5	69	136	6.5	66	2,105	69	137
2015	1,885	94.3	70	113	5.7	67	1,998	70	139
2016	1,902	94.6	69	108	5.4	67	2,010	69	137
2017	1,836	94.8	68	102	5.2	67	1,937	68	136
2018	1,893	94.7	70	107	5.3	67	2,000	70	139
2019	1,906	93.2	66	115	6.8	65	2,020	66	132

[1] All percents and weights calculated using unrounded totals.   [2] Excludes postmortem condemnations.
NASS, Livestock Branch, (202) 720–3570.

Table 7-45.—Sheep and lambs: Number slaughtered commercially, total and average live weight, by State and United States, 2019 [1]

State	Number slaughtered	Total live weight	Average live weight [2]
	Thousands	1,000 pounds	Pounds
Alabama	0.4	32	81
Alaska	0.1	11	137
Arizona	4.5	595	133
Arkansas	0.5	48	103
California	315.6	46,346	147
Colorado	742.1	117,594	159
Delaware-Maryland	37.6	3,531	94
Florida	17.8	1,010	57
Georgia	28.9	1,962	68
Hawaii	1.2	132	110
Idaho	2.0	258	131
Illinois	58.7	5,210	89
Indiana	56.6	6,065	107
Iowa	2.2	338	154
Kansas	4.9	469	95
Kentucky	16.7	1,995	119
Louisiana	4.5	246	55
Michigan	(D)	(D)	(D)
Minnesota	5.5	524	95
Mississippi	11.3	683	60
Missouri	10.9	932	86
Montana	4.8	667	139
Nebraska	0.7	80	114
Nevada	0.9	127	135
New England [3]	40.5	3,928	97
New Jersey	167.9	13,039	78
New Mexico	6.7	950	143
New York	58.9	5,704	97
North Carolina	19.3	1,323	69
North Dakota	0.6	80	136
Ohio	59.7	9,457	158
Oklahoma	10.3	995	97
Oregon	48.3	6,633	137
Pennsylvania	88.2	8,787	100
South Carolina	(D)	(D)	(D)
South Dakota	4.4	586	134
Tennessee	12.3	794	64
Texas	175.2	14,831	85
Utah	22.8	3,060	134
Virginia	9.0	695	77
Washington	18.0	2,422	135
West Virginia	(D)	(D)	(D)
Wisconsin	27.4	4,209	154
Wyoming	1.0	137	142
United States	2,321.7	297,205	128

(D) Withheld to avoid disclosing data for individual operations. (Y) Less than level of precision shown. [1] Includes slaughter in federally inspected and in other slaughter plants; exludes animals slaughtered on farms. Excludes postmortem condemnations. [2] Averages are based on unrounded data. [3] New England includes Connecticut, Maine, Massachusetts, New Hampshire, Rhode Island, and Vermont.

NASS, Livestock Branch, (202) 720–3570.

Table 7-46.—Sheep and lambs: Inventory Jan 1, 2018–2019, and number of operations, 2017, by State and United States [1]

State	January 1 Sheep inventory		Operations with sheep [2]
	2018	2019	2017
	1,000 head	*1,000 head*	*Number*
Alabama			1,062
Alaska			49
Arizona	125	115	7,509
Arkansas			1,053
California	570	550	3,807
Colorado	445	420	1,731
Connecticut			428
Delaware			89
Florida			1,666
Georgia			1,208
Hawaii			548
Idaho	235	220	1,447
Illinois	55	53	1,870
Indiana	57	60	2,316
Iowa	165	153	2,801
Kansas	67	72	1,234
Kentucky	58	64	2,818
Louisiana			785
Maine			738
Maryland			925
Michigan	80	86	728
Minnesota	130	125	2,483
Mississippi			2,248
Missouri	100	100	748
Montana	225	215	3,103
Nebraska	80	75	1,383
Nevada	61	63	1,153
New England [3]	49	48	328
New Hampshire			502
New Jersey			1,047
New Mexico	96	100	4,047
New York	85	80	2,113
North Carolina	27	29	1,679
North Dakota	70	72	573
Ohio	119	121	4,123
Oklahoma	54	50	2,216
Oregon	165	175	3,263
Pennsylvania	96	95	3,749
Rhode Island			108
South Carolina			738
South Dakota	250	255	1,337
Tennessee	46	48	2,503
Texas	750	750	14,672
Utah	275	290	1,898
Vermont			704
Virginia	75	79	2,646
Washington	45	50	2,281
West Virginia	35	32	1,226
Wisconsin	75	75	2,845
Wyoming	345	350	859
Other States [4]	155	160	
United States	5,265	5,230	101,387

[1] An operation is any place having one or more head of sheep on hand December 31. [2] State level estimates only available in conjunction with the Census of Agriculture every 5 years. [3] New England includes Connecticut, Maine, Massachusetts, New Hampshire, Rhode Island, and Vermont. [4] Includes data for States not published in this table.
NASS, Livestock Branch, (202) 720–3570.

Table 7-47.—Wool: Number of sheep shorn, weight per fleece, production, average price per pound received by farmers, value of production, exports, imports, total new supply of apparel wool, and imports of carpet wool, United States, 2010–2019

Year	Sheep and lambs shorn [1]	Weight per fleece	Shorn wool production	Price per pound [2]	Value of production [3]
	Thousands	*Pounds*	*1,000 pounds*	*Cents*	*1,000 dollars*
2010	4,180	7.3	30,360	1.15	35,013
2011	4,030	7.3	29,280	1.67	48,920
2012	3,790	7.3	27,630	1.52	41,972
2013	3,700	7.3	26,990	1.45	39,209
2014	3,680	7.3	26,680	1.46	38,909
2015	3,675	7.4	27,015	1.45	39,205
2016	3,585	7.3	26,050	1.45	37,721
2017	3,435	7.2	24,810	1.48	36,774
2018	3,372	7.2	24,400	1.75	42,772
2019	3,320	7.2	24,010	1.89	45,364

Year	Shorn wool production	Raw wool supply (clean)				
		Domestic production [4]	Exports [5]	Imports for consumption		Total new supply [8]
				48's and Finer [6]	Not Finer than 46's [7]	
	1,000 pounds	*1,000 pounds*	*1,000 pounds*	*1,000 pounds*	*1,000 pounds*	
2010	30,360	16,035	9,973	3,108	4,928	14,098
2011	29,280	15,465	9,586	3,791	4,694	14,364
2012	27,630	14,467	7,741	4,564	4,551	15,841
2013	26,990	14,251	9,998	3,858	3,746	11,857
2014	26,680	14,087	7,916	3,917	3,363	13,247
2015	27,015	14,264	7,847	3,980	3,321	13,718
2016	26,050	13,754	7,826	3,909	2,178	12,015
2017	24,810	13,100	11,002	3,396	2,285	7,779
2018	24,400	12,883	12,250	3,050	2,350	6,033
2019	24,010	11,294	10,207	3,306	2,046	5,439

[1] Includes sheep shorn at commercial feeding yards.   [2] Price computed by weighting State average prices for all wool sold during the year by sales of shorn wool.   [3] Production by States multiplied by annual average price.   [4] Conversion factor from grease basis to clean basis are as follows: Shorn wool production—52.8 percent (Stat. Bull. 616) from 1987-1997.   [5] Includes carpet wool exports.   [6] Prior to 1989, known as dutiable imports.   [7] Prior to 1989, known as duty-free imports. In 1994 includes 24,645,306 pounds of imported raw wool not finer than 46's and 2,182,576 pounds of miscellaneous imported raw wool.   [8] Production minus exports plus imports; stocks not taken into consideration.
NASS, Livestock Branch, (202) 720–3570 and ERS, Field Crops Branch, (202) 694–5300.   Imports and exports from reports of the U.S. Department of Commerce.

Table 7-48.—Wool: Price-support operations, United States, 2011–2020 [1]

Year	Program price levels per pound		Put under loan		Acquired by CCC under loan program [2]	Owned by CCC at end of marketing year
	Graded wool loan	Nongraded loan	Quantity	Percentage of production		
	Dollars	*Dollars*	*1,000 pounds*	*Percent*	*1,000 pounds*	*1,000 pounds*
2011	1.15	0.40	0.0	0.00	0.0	0.0
2012	1.15	0.40	0.0	0.00	0.0	0.0
2013	1.15	0.40	14.0	0.05	0.0	0.0
2014	1.15	0.40	11.0	0.04	0.0	0.0
2015	1.15	0.40	0.0	0.00	0.0	0.0
2016	1.15	0.40	0.0	0.00	0.0	0.0
2017	1.15	0.40	10.0	0.04	0.0	0.0
2018	1.15	0.40	0.0	0.00	0.0	0.0
2019	1.15	0.40	0.0	0.00	0.0	0.0
2020	1.15	0.40	49.7	0.20	0.0	0.0

[1] Nonrecourse Marketing Loan Program authorized by the Food, Conservation, and Energy Act of 2008, as amended, for marketing years 2008-2013, and the Agricultural Act of 2014, as amended, for marketing years 2014-2018.   [2] Projected acquisitions as of March 11, 2021.
FPAC-BC, Commodity Analysis Branch, (202) 720-4284.

Table 7-49.—Wool: United States imports of raw wool for mill use, clean yield[1], 2017–2020

Year	Finer-than-58s[2]	48s-and-finer[2]	Not-finer-than-46s[3]	Grand total[4]	Share finer-than-58s of grand total raw wool imports
I40(3)*1,000 pounds*	*Percent*				
2017	2,114	3,396	2,285	5,681	37.2
2018	1,996	3,116	2,348	5,463	36.5
2019	3,643	4,790	2,714	7,504	48.5
2020	2,515	3,122	2,814	5,936	42.4

[1] Wool not advanced in any way or by any process of manufacture beyond washed, scoured, or carbonized condition. Imports for consumption include entries for immediate consumption and warehouse withdrawals for consumption.   [2] Formerly "Dutiable".   [3] Formerly "Duty-free".   [4] Grand total includes "48s-and-finer" and "Not-finer-than-46s".
ERS, Field Crops Branch, (202) 694–5300. Source: U.S. Department of Commerce, U.S. Census Bureau.

Table 7-50.—U.S. raw wool imports by country of origin, clean yield, 2018–2020

Country of origin	Not-finer-than 46s			48s-and-finer		
	2018	2019	2020	2018	2019	2020
	1,000 pounds					
Australia	32.6	--	--	1,681.9	2,004.4	848.4
Belgium	--	107.7	17.5	--	--	--
Canada	43.6	--	--	176.8	172.3	482.6
China	167.2	--	0.3	125.9	39.0	42.7
Italy	0.2	0.0	--	98.5	185.6	410.7
Germany	--	72.0	--	--	--	--
Mexico	--	--	--	59.7	17.4	7.5
New Zealand	1,456.7	1,563.8	2,215.9	435.8	802.5	631.4
Pakistan	90.6	0.1	--	--	--	--
South Africa	82.8	104.2	94.1	74.6	118.0	82.1
Spain	42.3	10.2	134.0	107.3	377.7	53.8
United Kingdom	270.7	619.6	293.2	0.2	36.8	4.6
Uruguay	--	--	--	355.0	1004.0	558.0
Other	160.9	236.1	59.3	0.2	32.1	0.1
Total	2,347.6	2,713.7	2,814.3	3,115.7	4,789.8	3,121.9

(--) No imports. 0.0 = Less than 100 pounds.
ERS, Field Crops Branch, (202) 694–5300. Source: U.S. Department of Commerce, U.S. Census Bureau.

Table 7-51.—Wool: Graded territory shorn wool, and Australian offering prices, 2011–2020[1]

Year	Graded territory shorn wool, clean[1]		Australian offering prices, clean[2]
	64s staple 2-3/4" & up	58s staple 3-1/4" & up	Grade 64s type 63
	U.S. dollars per pound		
2011	4.25	4.07	6.30
2012	2.81	3.46	5.90
2013	4.23	3.01	5.34
2014	4.17	3.00	4.89
2015	3.58	3.04	4.50
2016	3.94	3.21	4.89
2017	4.36	3.24	5.50
2018	6.04	4.43	7.23
2019	5.75	3.90	6.47
2020	3.08	1.83	4.28

[2] Refers to wool principally produced in Texas and the Rocky Mountain States.   [2] Free on board (f.o.b.) Australian Wool Corporation's South Carolina warehouse in bond. A duty of 10 cents per pound, clean, should be added to these prices.
ERS, Field Crops Branch, (202) 694–5300. Sources: USDA and International Wool Textile Organization.

Table 7-52.—Wool: Number of sheep shorn, weight per fleece, and production, by State and United States, 2018–2019

State	Sheep		Weight per fleece		Shorn wool production	
	2018	2019	2018	2019	2018	2019
	1,000 head	*1,000 head*	*Pounds*	*Pounds*	*1,000 pounds*	*1,000 pounds*
Arizona	83.0	67.0	6.9	7.0	570	470
California	380.0	390.0	6.3	6.2	2,400	2,400
Colorado	315.0	335.0	7.0	7.0	2,200	2,350
Idaho	170.0	170.0	8.8	8.8	1,500	1,500
Illinois	32.0	29.0	6.3	5.9	200	170
Indiana	42.0	41.0	6.0	6.0	250	245
Iowa	140.0	130.0	5.4	5.7	760	740
Kansas	43.0	42.0	6.4	6.1	275	255
Kentucky	11.0	11.0	6.8	6.4	75	70
Michigan	55.0	61.0	5.9	6.1	325	375
Minnesota	102.0	98.0	6.3	6.3	640	620
Missouri	40.0	37.0	5.8	5.8	230	215
Montana	180.0	170.0	8.9	8.9	1,610	1,510
Nebraska	58.0	61.0	7.1	7.2	410	440
Nevada	47.0	48.0	9.6	9.2	450	440
New England [1]	27.0	27.0	6.7	7.0	180	188
New Mexico	82.0	80.0	7.6	7.6	625	610
New York	46.0	49.0	5.9	5.9	270	290
North Carolina	6.0	7.0	5.5	5.0	33	35
North Dakota	59.0	62.0	6.9	7.5	410	465
Ohio	79.0	87.0	5.8	5.8	460	505
Oklahoma	19.0	17.0	5.5	5.6	105	95
Oregon	130.0	130.0	6.4	6.2	830	800
Pennsylvania	46.0	48.0	6.7	6.7	310	320
South Dakota	230.0	225.0	7.6	7.5	1,750	1,690
Tennessee	10.0	9.0	5.0	5.0	50	45
Texas	240.0	230.0	7.3	7.4	1,760	1,700
Utah	245.0	240.0	9.1	8.9	2,220	2,140
Virginia	24.0	23.0	6.0	5.9	145	135
Washington	33.0	36.0	8.0	7.8	265	280
West Virginia	17.0	16.0	5.4	5.4	92	87
Wisconsin	50.0	49.0	6.6	6.9	330	340
Wyoming	285.0	250.0	8.4	8.8	2,400	2,200
Other States [2]	46.0	45.0	5.9	6.3	270	285
United States	3,372.0	3,320.0	7.2	7.2	24,400	24,010

[1] New England includes Connecticut, Maine, Massachusetts, New Hampshire, Rhode Island, and Vermont.   [2] Includes data for States not published in this table.
NASS, Livestock Branch, (202) 720–3570.

Table 7-53.—Wool: Price and value, by State and United States, 2018–2019

State	Price per pound		Value[1]	
	2018	2019	2018	2019
	Dollars	Dollars	1,000 Dollars	1,000 dollars
Arizona	1.20	1.10	684	517
California	2.00	2.20	4,800	5,280
Colorado	2.10	2.60	4,620	6,110
Idaho	2.02	2.78	3,030	4,170
Illinois	0.65	0.55	130	94
Indiana	0.55	0.69	138	169
Iowa	0.59	0.45	448	333
Kansas	0.95	0.80	261	204
Kentucky	0.80	0.90	60	63
Michigan	0.65	0.68	211	255
Minnesota	0.67	0.50	429	310
Missouri	0.60	0.40	138	86
Montana	2.50	2.50	4,025	3,775
Nebraska	0.88	0.88	361	387
Nevada	2.20	2.30	990	1,012
New England[2]	0.85	0.85	153	160
New Mexico	2.10	2.10	1,313	1,281
New York	0.90	0.80	243	232
North Carolina	1.20	1.10	40	39
North Dakota	1.32	1.35	541	628
Ohio	0.40	0.48	184	242
Oklahoma	0.70	0.75	74	71
Oregon	1.65	1.45	1,370	1,160
Pennsylvania	0.60	0.60	186	192
South Dakota	1.83	1.87	3,203	3,160
Tennessee	0.80	0.80	40	36
Texas	1.80	1.90	3,168	3,230
Utah	2.00	2.10	4,440	4,494
Virginia	1.40	1.20	203	162
Washington	2.10	2.95	557	826
West Virginia	1.40	1.50	129	131
Wisconsin	0.60	0.55	198	187
Wyoming	2.50	2.70	6,000	5,940
Other States[3]	1.50	1.50	405	428
United States	1.75	1.89	42,772	45,364

[1] Production multiplied by marketing year average price. United States value is the summation of State values.   [2] New England includes Connecticut, Maine, Massachusetts, New Hampshire, Rhode Island, and Vermont.   [3] Includes data for States not published in this table.

NASS, Livestock Branch, (202) 720–3570.

Table 7-54.—Mohair: Price-support operations, United States, 2011–2020 [1]

Year	Program price levels per pound	Put under loan		Acquired by CCC under loan program [2]	Owned by CCC at end of marketing year
	Loan	Quantity	Percentage of production		
	Dollars	*1,000 pounds*	*Percent*	*1,000 pounds*	*1,000 pounds*
2011	4.20	0.0	0.0	0.0	0.0
2012	4.20	0.0	0.0	0.0	0.0
2013	4.20	0.0	0.0	0.0	0.0
2014	4.20	0.0	0.0	0.0	0.0
2015	4.20	0.0	0.0	0.0	0.0
2016	4.20	0.0	0.0	0.0	0.0
2017	4.20	0.0	0.0	0.0	0.0
2018	4.20	0.0	0.0	0.0	0.0
2019	4.20	0.0	0.0	0.0	0.0
2020	4.20	0.0	0.0	0.0	0.0

[1] Nonrecourse Marketing Loan Program authorized by the Food , Conservation, and Energy Act of 2008, as amended, for marketing years 2008-2013, and the Agricultural Act of 2014, as amended, for marketing years 2014-2018.　[2] Projected acquisitions as of March 11, 2021.
FPAC-BC, Commodity Analysis Branch, (202) 720-4284.

Table 7-55.—Mohair: Goats clipped, production, price, and value, by State and United States, 2018–2019

State	Goats clipped		Average clip per goat		Production		Price per pound		Value [1]	
	2018	2019	2018	2019	2018	2019	2018	2019	2018	2019
	Head	*Head*	*Pounds*	*Pounds*	*1,000 pounds*	*1,000 pounds*	*Dollars*	*Dollars*	*1,000 dollars*	*1,000 dollars*
Arizona	28,000	21,000	4.5	4.5	125	95	1.30	1.30	163	124
California	2,000	(NA)	5.0	(NA)	10	(NA)	6.00	(NA)	60	(NA)
New Mexico ...	7,000	7,000	4.3	3.6	30	25	1.60	1.30	48	33
Texas	75,000	75,000	6.2	6.3	465	470	7.20	8.70	3,348	4,089
Other States [2]	21,000	24,000	6.0	5.8	125	140	2.75	2.90	344	406
United States	133,000	127,000	5.7	5.7	755	730	5.25	6.37	3,963	4,652

[1] Production multiplied by marketing year average price.　U.S. value is summation of State values.　[2] Includes data for States not published in this table.
NASS, Livestock Branch, (202) 720–3570.

STATISTICS OF CATTLE, HOGS, AND SHEEP

Table 7-56—Angora goats: Inventory Jan 1, 2018–2019, and number of operations, 2017, by State and United States [1]

State	January 1 angora goats inventory		Operations with angora goats [2]
	2018	2019	2017
	Head	*Head*	*Number*
Alabama			202
Alaska			6
Arizona	30,000	27,000	2,185
Arkansas			25
California	3,500	3,000	363
Colorado			217
Connecticut			70
Delaware			5
Florida			284
Georgia			236
Hawaii			57
Idaho			107
Illinois			82
Indiana			126
Iowa			113
Kansas			75
Kentucky			266
Louisiana			95
Maine			49
Maryland			114
Massachusetts			85
Michigan			238
Minnesota	(NA)	(NA)	157
Mississippi			44
Missouri	(NA)	(NA)	192
Montana			86
Nebraska			61
Nevada			17
New Hampshire			50
New Jersey			129
New Mexico	9,500	9,000	1,196
New York			211
North Carolina			273
North Dakota			20
Ohio			241
Oklahoma			181
Oregon	(NA)	(NA)	295
Pennsylvania			290
Rhode Island			16
South Carolina			147
South Dakota			39
Tennessee			35
Texas	75,000	75,000	1,514
Utah			272
Vermont			65
Virginia			201
Washington			267
West Virginia			93
Wisconsin	(NA)	(NA)	168
Wyoming			33
Other States	26,000	23,000	33
United States	144,000	137,000	11,293

(NA) Not available.   [1] An operation is any place having one or more head of angora goats on hand December 31.   [2] State level estimates only available in conjunction with the Census of Agriculture every 5 years.   [3] New England includes Connecticut, Maine, Massachusetts, New Hampshire, Rhode Island, and Vermont.   [4] Includes data for States not published in this table.
    NASS, Livestock Branch, (202) 720–3570.

Table 7-57.—Milk goats: Inventory Jan 1, 2018–2019, and number of operations, 2017, by State and United States [1]

| State | January 1 milk goats inventory | | Operations with milk goats [2] |
	2018	2019	2017
	Head	Head	Number
Alabama	3,500	4,000	547
Alaska	(NA)	(NA)	39
Arizona	(NA)	(NA)	499
Arkansas	4,000	4,000	709
California	40,000	42,000	1,372
Colorado	9,000	10,000	1,124
Connecticut	(NA)	(NA)	280
Delaware	(NA)	(NA)	34
Florida	10,000	8,500	1,410
Georgia	7,100	8,500	809
Hawaii	(NA)	(NA)	93
Idaho	8,000	7,000	598
Illinois	10,000	11,000	585
Indiana	11,000	12,000	1,120
Iowa	31,000	32,000	753
Kansas	4,400	4,000	525
Kentucky	6,000	6,000	1,078
Louisiana	(NA)	(NA)	368
Maine	(NA)	(NA)	395
Maryland	(NA)	(NA)	343
Massachusetts	(NA)	(NA)	335
Michigan	11,000	12,000	1,246
Minnesota	14,000	13,000	698
Mississippi	(NA)	(NA)	431
Missouri	12,000	12,000	1,382
Montana	(NA)	(NA)	400
Nebraska	3,500	4,000	419
Nevada	(NA)	(NA)	104
New England [3]	17,000	19,000	....
New Hampshire	(NA)	(NA)	231
New Jersey	(NA)	(NA)	286
New Mexico	(NA)	(NA)	564
New York	13,000	12,000	1,033
North Carolina	7,000	6,000	849
North Dakota	(NA)	(NA)	164
Ohio	12,000	12,000	1,504
Oklahoma	7,000	8,000	1,142
Oregon	14,000	13,000	1,216
Pennsylvania	15,000	15,000	1,240
Rhode Island	(NA)	(NA)	59
South Carolina	3,500	3,000	479
South Dakota	(NA)	(NA)	235
Tennessee	7,500	7,000	981
Texas	29,000	27,000	3,630
Utah	(NA)	(NA)	397
Vermont	(NA)	(NA)	270
Virginia	5,500	5,000	867
Washington	7,000	8,000	982
West Virginia	(NA)	(NA)	523
Wisconsin	67,000	72,000	1,029
Wyoming	(NA)	(NA)	305
Other States [4]	31,000	33,000	....
United States	420,000	430,000	35,682

(NA) Not available.　[1] An operation is any place having one or more head of angora goats on hand December 31.　[2] State level estimates only available in conjunction with the Census of Agriculture every 5 years.　[3] New England includes Connecticut, Maine, Massachusetts, New Hampshire, Rhode Island, and Vermont.　[4] Includes data for States not published in this table.

NASS, Livestock Branch, (202) 720–3570.

Table 7-58.—Meat and other goats: Inventory Jan 1, 2018–2019, and number of operations, 2017, by State and United States [1]

State	January 1 meat and other goats inventory		Operations with Meat goats [2]
	2018	2019	2017
	Head	Head	Number
Alabama	47,000	45,000	1,549
Alaska	(NA)	(NA)	18
Arizona	30,000	33,000	390
Arkansas	31,000	32,000	1,111
California	85,000	90,000	1,343
Colorado	23,000	24,000	1,008
Connecticut	(NA)	(NA)	123
Delaware	(NA)	(NA)	44
Florida	45,000	50,000	1,526
Georgia	60,000	59,000	1,893
Hawaii	(NA)	(NA)	194
Idaho	(NA)	(NA)	585
Illinois	25,000	23,000	867
Indiana	36,000	34,000	1,154
Iowa	40,000	37,000	1,183
Kansas	41,000	44,000	1,093
Kentucky	57,000	52,000	1,768
Louisiana	15,000	15,000	504
Maine	(NA)	(NA)	82
Maryland	(NA)	(NA)	362
Massachusetts	(NA)	(NA)	141
Michigan	(NA)	(NA)	691
Minnesota	24,000	25,000	758
Mississippi	20,000	21,000	837
Missouri	70,000	72,000	1,724
Montana	(NA)	(NA)	256
Nebraska	(NA)	(NA)	657
Nevada	(NA)	(NA)	126
New Hampshire	(NA)	(NA)	83
New Jersey	(NA)	(NA)	361
New Mexico	(NA)	(NA)	535
New York	16,000	17,000	592
North Carolina	47,000	49,000	1,658
North Dakota	(NA)	(NA)	117
Ohio	44,000	45,000	1,942
Oklahoma	82,000	80,000	2,477
Oregon	29,000	27,000	1,048
Pennsylvania	38,000	38,000	1,351
Rhode Island	(NA)	(NA)	18
South Carolina	34,000	32,000	1,216
South Dakota	(NA)	(NA)	282
Tennessee	96,000	89,000	2,875
Texas	765,000	740,000	12,511
Utah	(NA)	(NA)	385
Vermont	(NA)	(NA)	63
Virginia	41,000	42,000	1,356
Washington	19,000	21,000	723
West Virginia	21,000	19,000	809
Wisconsin	(NA)	(NA)	582
Wyoming	(NA)	(NA)	256
Other States [4]	194,000	200,000	....
United States	2,075,000	2,055,000	53,227

(NA) Not available. [1] An operation is any place having one or more head of angora goats on hand December 31. [2] State level estimates only available in conjunction with the Census of Agriculture every 5 years. [3] New England includes Connecticut, Maine, Massachusetts, New Hampshire, Rhode Island, and Vermont. [4] Includes data for States not published in this table.
NASS, Livestock Branch, (202) 720–3570.

Table 7-59.—All goats: Number of operations, 2017, by State and United States [1]

State	2017 [2]
	Number
Alabama	3,279
Alaska	73
Arizona	4,721
Arkansas	2,488
California	3,938
Colorado	2,803
Connecticut	592
Delware	121
Florida	4,366
Georgia	4,063
Hawaii	609
Idaho	1,556
Illinios	2,028
Indiana	2,833
Iowa	2,400
Kansas	2,010
Kentucky	4,330
Louisiana	1,501
Maine	583
Maryland	1,085
Massachusetts	719
Michigan	2,614
Minnesota	1,996
Mississippi	2,048
Missouri	4,132
Montana	908
Nebraska	1,341
Nevada	339
New Hampshire	427
New Jersey	969
New Mexico	2,770
New York	2,192
North Carolina	4,084
North Dakota	335
Ohio	4,841
Oklahoma	5,398
Oregon	3,289
Pennsylvania	3,749
Rhode Island	102
South Carolina	2,905
South Dakota	721
Tennessee	5,802
Texas	26,143
Utah	1,392
Vermont	480
Virginia	3,449
Washington	2,609
West Virginia	2,040
Wisconsin	2,586
Wyoming	683
United States	136,442

[1] An operation is any place having one or more head of goats on hand December 31.   [2] State level estimates only available in conjunction with the Census of Agriculture every 5 years.   [3] New England includes Connecticut, Maine, Massachusetts, New Hampshire, Rhode Island, and Vermont.
    NASS, Livestock Branch, (202) 720–3570.

**Table 7-60.—Red meat: Production, by class of slaughter,
United States, 2010–2019**

Year	Commercial		Farm	Total
	Federally inspected	Total		
			Beef	
			Million pounds	
2010	25,954	26,305	84	26,389
2011	25,854	26,195	75	26,270
2012	25,573	25,913	76	25,989
2013	25,385	25,720	70	25,790
2014	23,932	24,249	66	24,315
2015	23,395	23,698	63	23,760
2016	24,908	25,221	67	25,288
2017	25,856	26,188	63	26,251
2018	26,536	26,873	66	26,939
2019	26,821	27,155	69	27,224
			Pork, excluding lard	
			Million pounds	
2010	22,275	22,437	19	22,456
2011	22,599	22,758	17	22,775
2012	23,090	23,253	15	23,268
2013	23,040	23,187	16	23,203
2014	22,710	22,843	15	22,858
2015	24,355	24,501	16	24,517
2016	24,789	24,941	16	24,957
2017	25,437	25,584	14	25,598
2018	26,177	26,315	14	26,329
2019	27,507	27,637	14	27,652
			Veal	
			Million pounds	
2010	131	134	8	143
2011	126	130	7	136
2012	115	118	7	125
2013	109	111	6	117
2014	92	94	6	100
2015	81	83	5	88
2016	74	76	6	81
2017	73	74	6	80
2018	74	76	5	81
2019	73	74	5	79
			Lamb and Mutton	
			Million pounds	
2010	154	164	5	168
2011	141	149	5	153
2012	148	156	5	161
2013	146	156	5	161
2014	145	156	5	161
2015	139	151	5	156
2016	138	150	5	155
2017	132	145	5	150
2018	140	153	5	158
2019	134	149	5	153
			All meat, excluding lard	
			Million pounds	
2010	48,514	49,039	116	49,155
2011	48,721	49,232	103	49,335
2012	48,925	49,440	103	49,543
2013	48,679	49,174	97	49,271
2014	46,879	47,342	91	47,433
2015	47,970	48,432	89	48,520
2016	49,909	50,388	93	50,481
2017	51,497	51,991	88	52,079
2018	52,927	53,417	90	53,507
2019	54,535	55,015	93	55,108

NASS, Livestock Branch, (202) 720–3570.

Table 7-61.—Meat: United States exports and imports into the United States, carcass weight equivalent, 2010–2019 [1]

Year	Exports				Imports			
	Beef and veal	Lamb and mutton	Pork [2]	All meat	Beef & veal	Lamb and mutton	Pork [2]	All meat
	Million pounds							
2010	2,300	16	4,223	6,539	2,298	166	859	3,323
2011	2,785	19	5,196	8,000	2,057	162	803	3,022
2012	2,452	11	5,379	7,842	2,220	154	802	3,175
2013	2,588	7	4,986	7,582	2,250	173	880	3,302
2014	2,574	7	5,092	7,672	2,947	195	1,011	4,153
2015	2,267	4	5,010	7,282	3,368	214	1,116	4,698
2016	2,557	5	5,239	7,801	3,012	216	1,091	4,319
2017	2,859	6	5,632	8,497	2,993	252	1,116	4,361
2018	3,160	6	5,877	9,042	2,998	273	1,042	4,313
2019	3,026	6	6,321	9,353	3,058	272	945	4,275

[1] Carcass weight equivalent of all meat, including the meat content of minor meats and of mixed products.   Shipments to U.S. Territories are included in domestic consumption.   [2] The pork series has been revised to a dressed weight equivalent rather than "Pork, excluding lard."

ERS, Market and Trade Economics Division, Animal Products and Cost of Production Branch, (202) 694–5409. Data on imports and commercial exports are computed from records of the U.S. Department of Commerce, those on exports by the U.S. Department of Agriculture are separately estimated from deliveries and stocks.

Table 7-62.—International Meat: Production, 2017–2019

Country	2017	2018	2019
	1,000 metric tons		
Beef and veal:			
United States	11,943	12,257	12,383
Brazil	9,550	9,900	10,200
European Union	7,869	8,003	7,928
China	6,346	6,440	6,670
India	4,230	4,240	4,305
Argentina	2,840	3,050	3,125
Australia	2,149	2,306	2,432
Mexico	1,925	1,980	2,030
Pakistan	1,780	1,800	1,820
Russia	1,325	1,357	1,369
Canada	1,201	1,265	1,340
South Africa	1,046	1,027	1,019
Colombia	758	773	770
New Zealand	654	672	713
Uruguay	594	596	562
Swine:			
China	54,518	54,040	42,550
European Union	23,660	24,082	23,960
United States	11,611	11,943	12,543
Brazil	3,725	3,763	3,975
Russia	2,959	3,155	3,321
Vietnam	2,741	2,811	2,380
Canada	1,958	1,955	2,020
Philippines	1,563	1,601	1,585
Mexico	1,267	1,321	1,408
Korea, South	1,280	1,329	1,364
Japan	1,272	1,284	1,279
Taiwan	811	829	820
Ukraine	769	732	745
Argentina	565	621	630
Chile	489	534	530

FAS, Office of Global Analysis, (202) 720-6301.   Data Source: USDA FAS PSD Online.

Table 7-63.—Meat: U.S. exports, 2018–2020

Country	2018	2019	2020
	Metric tons		
Beef & veal, prep/pres:			
Canada	25,595	23,987	24,918
Hong Kong	1,958	5,408	4,856
China	12	15	3,039
Mexico	905	1,726	1,341
Vietnam	0	0	649
Guatemala	143	210	250
Dominican Republic	86	186	186
Philippines	176	146	162
Sri Lanka	0	0	120
Panama	218	68	96
Suriname	0	11	93
Trinidad and Tobago	67	116	72
Senegal	0	0	71
Micronesia	39	60	66
Ireland	0	18	63
Ecuador	0	0	58
Bermuda	23	40	48
United Arab Emirates	24	28	42
Chile	168	89	41
Bahamas, The	43	61	36
El Salvador	21	31	36
Belize	2	15	33
Costa Rica	60	27	30
Netherlands Antilles(*)	20	52	29
Leeward-Windward Islands(*)	31	43	28
Honduras	41	9	25
Haiti	0	8	25
New Zealand(*)	103	10	23
Nigeria	0	0	15
Venezuela	0	14	14
Rest of World	1,313	971	134
World Total	31,047	33,347	36,600
Beef & veal, fr/ch/fz:			
Japan	278,823	248,955	259,400
Korea, South	224,729	242,007	235,787
Mexico	141,591	134,315	101,655
Canada	78,206	67,777	74,649
Hong Kong	101,309	73,257	70,027
Taiwan	59,630	63,647	63,699
China	7,189	10,492	36,879
Indonesia	7,411	10,904	11,003
Philippines	12,043	13,832	10,248
Vietnam	12,118	12,271	9,941
Netherlands	10,771	9,927	9,734
Chile	9,227	9,408	6,722
Guatemala	4,965	5,080	5,298
United Arab Emirates	5,638	5,615	3,888
Dominican Republic	5,979	6,187	3,282
Singapore	2,943	3,423	3,174
Colombia	3,262	3,865	2,779
Kuwait	2,715	2,541	2,376
Bahamas, The	3,188	3,295	2,373
Costa Rica	2,320	2,460	2,212
Netherlands Antilles(*)	2,512	2,766	1,950
Italy(*)	4,811	3,899	1,875
Panama	1,346	1,947	1,493
Thailand	961	1,499	1,480
Cayman Islands	1,563	1,456	1,383
Germany(*)	2,963	2,173	1,320
Trinidad and Tobago	928	999	1,188
Peru	1,360	1,600	1,131
Qatar	1,105	1,096	1,130
Saudi Arabia	1,222	1,539	1,125
Rest of World	18,958	16,599	11,158
World Total	1,011,781	964,831,	940,357

See footnote(s) at end of table.

Table 7-63.—Meat: U.S. exports, 2018–2020—Continued

Country	2018	2019	2020
	Metric tons		
Pork, fr/ch/fz:			
China	104,991	378,085	732,825
Mexico	621,672	552,569	565,429
Japan	366,606	343,874	349,941
Korea, South	220,401	188,898	144,133
Canada	105,434	119,183	141,134
Australia(*)	72,014	97,646	74,043
Colombia	91,718	94,963	61,077
Chile	26,585	32,419	37,104
Dominican Republic	38,087	30,136	36,619
Honduras	28,940	31,575	35,885
Philippines	20,631	21,786	24,580
Vietnam	5,496	3,541	21,509
Taiwan	13,091	12,204	17,320
Hong Kong	18,197	15,391	17,273
Guatemala	14,191	15,265	14,399
Panama	9,511	12,038	10,442
New Zealand(*)	6,162	8,299	10,060
Nicaragua	6,419	7,456	9,158
El Salvador	6,784	7,034	7,249
Costa Rica	4,692	6,191	6,235
Peru	5,499	4,962	4,401
Bahamas, The	4,023	4,063	3,943
Singapore	2,601	3,726	3,310
Trinidad and Tobago	1,964	2,499	2,746
Leeward-Windward Islands(*)	1,826	2,192	1,841
Albania	852	1,240	1,599
North Macedonia	78	0	1,214
Netherlands Antilles(*)	1,227	1,535	1,013
United Kingdom	1,087	923	945
Ukraine	1	49	888
Rest of World	7,123	7,533	6,537
World Total	1,807,900	2,007,272	2,344,852
Pork, hams/shldrs,cured:			
Canada	17,705	16,563	17,187
Panama	2,437	2,788	2,427
Mexico	1,387	1,435	1,115
Korea, South	123	303	1,011
Albania	587	913	996
Trinidad and Tobago	620	457	723
Belize	734	782	611
Netherlands Antilles(*)	529	509	502
Colombia	538	402	470
Japan	118	63	460
China	523	0	432
Australia(*)	863	262	382
Bahamas, The	397	422	319
Hong Kong	299	262	236
Leeward-Windward Islands(*)	138	167	214
Barbados	160	217	210
Guatemala	63	176	121
Taiwan	1	0	94
El Salvador	51	65	75
Haiti	32	46	72
Singapore	0	9	71
Honduras	63	59	45
Spain	22	4	42
Costa Rica	14	47	27
Congo (Brazzaville)	74	0	25
Guyana	4	13	17
Dominican Republic	60	134	13
Turks and Caicos Islands	11	17	12
Suriname	0	0	12
New Zealand(*)	10	24	10
Rest of World	219	342	21
World Total	27,780	26,478	27,948

See footnote(s) at end of table.

Table 7-63.—Meat: U.S. exports, 2018–2020—Continued

Country	2018	2019	2020
	Metric tons		
Pork, bacon, cured:			
Mexico	12,283	13,289	9,503
Canada	7,399	5,870	9,276
Japan	3,316	3,554	3,774
Korea, South	3,195	3,848	2,426
Australia(*)	1,853	1,447	1,286
New Zealand(*)	777	1,304	997
French Pacific Islands(*)	1,152	1,247	885
Dominican Republic	823	643	387
Hong Kong	387	474	359
Samoa	444	393	345
Guatemala	344	382	339
Chile	345	413	244
Costa Rica	298	292	233
Bahamas, The	368	406	223
Panama	160	282	204
Bermuda	102	137	189
Singapore	281	232	187
Colombia	421	343	173
Cayman Islands	101	162	126
Leeward-Windward Islands(*)	101	159	112
Netherlands Antilles(*)	134	232	87
El Salvador	125	174	79
Taiwan	0	47	77
Peru	41	28	66
Philippines	42	72	54
Guyana	30	37	53
Honduras	107	154	51
Vietnam	0	2	47
Malaysia	0	76	32
Turks and Caicos Islands	49	61	30
Rest of World	233	180	114
World Total	34,908	35,937	31,957
Pork, prep/pres, nt/cn:			
Canada	56,856	55,309	41,713
Japan	5,899	6,648	21,310
Mexico	11,787	10,622	6,776
Korea, South	1,092	1,429	2,011
Chile	620	635	601
Panama	306	509	353
Philippines	423	514	315
Australia(*)	67	631	287
Micronesia	227	252	250
Costa Rica	164	226	233
Dominican Republic	136	267	220
Peru	101	1,681	215
Colombia	685	736	166
Hong Kong	289	172	116
El Salvador	79	115	110
Marshall Islands	47	84	87
Netherlands Antilles(*)	57	68	85
Albania	0	0	74
Bahamas, The	60	47	70
New Zealand(*)	12	27	69
Singapore	10	31	69
Honduras	62	49	63
Trinidad and Tobago	19	39	54
Guatemala	78	86	54
Leeward-Windward Islands(*)	44	31	28
Haiti	11	10	20
Other Pacific Islands, NEC(*)	23	1	19
Nicaragua	11	16	12
Cayman Islands	5	11	9
Venezuela	0	5	9
Rest of World	106	142	33
World Total	79,276	80,393	75,427

See footnote(s) at end of table.

Table 7-63.—Meat: U.S. exports, 2018–2020—Continued

Country	2018	2019	2020
	Metric tons		
Pork, prep/pres, canned:			
Philippines	8,854	6,220	9,051
Japan	6,234	5,364	5,445
Australia(*)	3,896	3,764	3,146
Panama	1,573	1,889	2,062
Dominican Republic	2,639	1,578	1,913
Hong Kong	1,476	1,580	1,673
Korea, South	1,998	1,697	1,114
Singapore	408	442	584
Colombia	521	572	308
Costa Rica	326	524	302
Guatemala	148	161	256
Chile	111	227	246
New Zealand(*)	644	360	243
United Arab Emirates	89	134	206
Taiwan	81	171	179
Netherlands Antilles(*)	179	214	128
Vietnam	127	175	116
Trinidad and Tobago	94	103	114
El Salvador	98	171	105
Indonesia	41	83	100
Canada	15	62	99
Mexico	501	302	80
Malaysia	40	43	73
French Pacific Islands(*)	45	75	50
Jamaica	48	46	49
Honduras	80	88	44
Nicaragua	52	57	41
Palau	4	6	39
Belize	19	32	30
Bahamas, The	18	38	23
Rest of World	133	123	89
World Total	30,491	26,301	27,903
Lamb & mutton; fr/ch/fz:			
Mexico	684	765	7,610
Bahamas, The	219	178	101
Bermuda	67	65	97
Trinidad and Tobago	95	123	79
Canada	132	101	66
Japan	69	20	64
Hong Kong	3	6	55
Egypt	0	25	45
Leeward-Windward Islands(*)	108	60	43
Netherlands Antilles(*)	83	90	39
Panama	13	58	27
Bahrain	0	18	27
Turks and Caicos Islands	58	32	22
Dominican Republic	74	104	21
Barbados	41	39	21
Guatemala	23	34	20
Jamaica	95	39	18
Nicaragua	0	0	15
Philippines	19	25	13
Singapore	31	12	13
Spain	19	31	12
French Pacific Islands(*)	3	1	5
Honduras	0	4	5
Kuwait	5	4	5
Guyana	7	12	5
Australia(*)	4	1	3
Cayman Islands	2	3	3
Equatorial Guinea	0	10	2
Taiwan	30	20	2
Costa Rica	43	23	2
Rest of World	498	395	11
World Total	2,426	2,294	8,449

See footnote(s) at end of table.

Table 7-63.—Meat: U.S. exports, 2018–2020—Continued

Country	2018	2019	2020
	Metric tons		
Sausages & bologna:			
Canada	42,967	43,346	39,212
Japan	23,444	24,090	20,887
Mexico	10,437	9,991	9,437
Korea, South	5,910	6,267	7,281
Philippines	3,980	3,481	2,926
Guatemala	1,021	1,483	1,986
Hong Kong	1,506	1,759	1,816
Belize	1,134	1,646	1,624
Taiwan	275	658	710
United Kingdom	589	746	667
Dominican Republic	609	621	643
Bahamas, The	413	463	603
Panama	721	556	577
Chile	528	716	570
Australia(*)	114	448	554
Singapore	337	452	518
China	253	25	471
Netherlands Antilles(*)	427	472	436
Honduras	209	369	405
Costa Rica	386	291	391
Colombia	393	547	382
El Salvador	405	389	247
Marshall Islands	246	215	202
Peru	210	239	188
United Arab Emirates	108	92	132
Bermuda	113	128	129
New Zealand(*)	30	62	122
Leeward-Windward Islands(*)	76	168	120
Micronesia	140	117	111
Thailand	84	65	109
Rest of World	1,117	1,078	736
World Total	98,182	100,981	94,189
Other meat products, prp/ps:			
Canada	2,876	2,401	2,545
Mexico	1,962	2,138	2,540
Vietnam	0	2	1,174
Philippines	432	587	546
Guatemala	152	461	394
Korea, South	79	265	207
Colombia	137	179	201
Taiwan	76	92	131
Australia(*)	103	117	115
Dominican Republic	15	8	85
Ecuador	103	68	63
Kuwait	37	29	50
New Zealand(*)	20	31	45
Brazil	0	2	41
Trinidad and Tobago	59	44	39
Thailand	44	43	37
El Salvador	24	7	35
Netherlands Antilles	39	19	32
Japan	144	144	32
Leeward-Windward Islands(*)	37	72	31
Haiti	6	18	27
Bermuda	35	8	26
Panama	372	286	24
Costa Rica	13	0	22
Bolivia	0	0	18
Belize	32	26	16
Gabon	0	0	16
Honduras	19	25	15
Senegal	0	0	14
Bahamas, The	30	19	14
Rest of World	279	441	112
World Total	7,124	7,532	8,647

See footnote(s) at end of table.

Table 7-63.—Meat: U.S. exports, 2018–2020—Continued

Country	2018	2019	2020
	Metric tons		
Variety meats, beef:			
Mexico	96,612	100,645	89,952
Egypt	61,623	63,534	49,177
Japan	51,602	62,805	46,729
South Africa	12,448	11,197	16,075
Hong Kong	19,173	14,248	11,106
Korea, South	14,141	13,543	10,436
Canada	10,144	8,040	8,661
Indonesia	6,700	12,689	7,991
Peru	6,481	5,879	7,894
Angola	3,303	3,550	3,429
Jamaica	4,326	4,153	3,353
Gabon	1,986	2,276	3,060
China	97	131	2,896
Cote d'Ivoire	1,661	690	2,496
Philippines	5,721	4,485	2,271
Chile	1,776	1,881	1,943
Colombia	2,911	2,837	1,769
Trinidad and Tobago	759	894	1,015
Dominican Republic	782	1,649	817
Ecuador	990	713	797
Honduras	991	753	662
Ethiopia(*)	0	0	607
El Salvador	680	456	521
Vietnam	420	479	506
Nicaragua	273	534	503
Mozambique	355	723	425
Costa Rica	776	482	380
Guatemala	686	575	329
United Arab Emirates	68	26	264
Guinea	141	355	259
Rest of World	2,165	2,385	1,478
World Total	309,788	322,604	277,800
Variety meats, pork:			
China	80,974	155,399	222,668
Mexico	112,758	112,792	87,060
Hong Kong	111,637	72,775	19,943
Canada	17,522	16,466	15,392
Philippines	17,273	10,970	11,936
Chile	2,728	8,555	11,188
Japan	13,968	10,331	5,609
Colombia	2,033	2,757	4,876
Korea, South	12,297	8,556	4,070
Guatemala	3,056	4,393	3,529
Vietnam	9,343	10,045	3,506
Taiwan	4,822	3,610	2,812
Panama	2,343	2,065	2,094
Trinidad and Tobago	1,221	1,095	1,737
Honduras	1,341	1,447	1,128
Dominican Republic	902	1,541	591
Leeward-Windward Islands(*)	434	512	564
Haiti	538	324	504
South Africa	487	113	445
Denmark(*)	0	0	269
El Salvador	283	325	237
Albania	27	119	218
Costa Rica	361	404	209
Singapore	289	218	167
Australia(*)	297	423	133
Turks and Caicos Islands	43	84	126
Bahamas, The	135	75	109
Malaysia	0	0	90
Jamaica	27	0	81
Nicaragua	102	137	80
Rest of World	789	1,047	157
World Total	398,028	426,578	401,527

See footnote(s) at end of table.

Table 7-63.—Meat: U.S. exports, 2018–2020—Continued

Country	2018	2019	2020
	Metric tons		
Other meat products, fr/ch/fz:			
Vietnam	21	99	106
Leeward-Windward Islands(*)	72	153	81
Hong Kong	0	0	26
Jamaica	0	28	19
Bermuda	3	8	15
Mexico	75	59	13
Cayman Islands	2	11	11
Turks and Caicos Islands	5	1	10
Dominican Republic	0	10	7
Germany(*)	0	0	5
Panama	0	12	1
Singapore	1	1	1
Netherlands Antilles(*)	1	1	1
Bahamas, The	3	2	0
Barbados	26	0	0
United Arab Emirates	0	8	0
Australia(*)	28	0	0
Denmark(*)	0	1	0
Estonia	0	1	0
El Salvador	19	0	0
France(*)	3	0	0
Italy(*)	1	30	0
Japan	6	0	0
Korea, South	5	17	0
Netherlands	11	1	0
Nicaragua	1	0	0
Saudi Arabia	0	2	0
Spain	0	0	0
Trinidad and Tobago	0	12	0
Venezuela	0	28	0
World Total	281	484	295

(*)Denotes a country that is a summarization of its component countries. Users should use cautious interpretation on quantity reports using mixed units of measure. Quantity line items will only include statistics on the units of measure that are equal to, or are able to be converted to, the assigned unit of measure of the grouped commodities.
FAS, Office of Global Analysis, (202) 720-6301. Data Source: U.S. Census Bureau Trade Data, as of February 25, 2021.

Table 7-64.—Meat, beef, veal, and swine: International trade, imports and exports, 2018–2020

Country	2018	2019	2020
	1,000 metric tons		
Principle exporters, beef and veal:			
Brazil	2,082	2,356	2,580
India	1,556	1,600	1,700
United States	1,434	1,372	1,499
Australia	1,662	1,825	1,470
Argentina	507	765	840
New Zealand	633	649	642
Canada	502	560	610
Uruguay	466	470	468
Mexico	310	355	390
European Union	352	370	360
Paraguay	365	320	350
Belarus	220	195	195
Nicaragua	158	160	160
Pakistan	66	70	75
Ukraine	60	57	52
Principle importers, beef and veal:			
China	1,467	2,300	2,900
United States	1,360	1,388	1,306
Japan	862	870	890
Korea, South	582	610	625
Russia	495	440	430
Chile	317	380	395
European Union	373	357	355
Hong Kong	541	350	350
Egypt	300	310	320
Canada	245	215	215
Mexico	202	200	205
Taiwan	176	190	200
Malaysia	215	210	195
Israel	132	145	155
Saudi Arabia	134	140	145
Principle exporters, swine:			
European Union	2,933	3,650	3,900
United States	2,665	2,856	3,221
Canada	1,331	1,330	1,400
Brazil	730	860	1,000
Chile	200	240	270
Mexico	178	215	250
China	203	130	100
Russia	45	60	80
Australia	47	40	42
Serbia	14	18	20
South Africa	17	17	17
Argentina	8	11	12
Belarus	14	12	10
Vietnam	35	15	10
Norway	5	6	5
Principle importers, swine:			
China	1,561	2,600	3,700
Japan	1,481	1,510	1,490
Mexico	1,188	1,200	1,235
Korea, South	753	685	695
United States	473	434	401
Hong Kong	423	335	300
Philippines	287	240	300
Canada	233	250	260
Australia	216	260	240
Colombia	129	155	175
Chile	98	130	150
Singapore	125	123	124
Taiwan	109	107	105
Russia	87	130	80
Vietnam	20	50	75

FAS, Office of Global Analysis, (202) 720-6301. Prepared or estimated on the basis of official USDA production, supply, and distribution statistics from foreign governments.

Table 7-65.—Meats: Production and consumption, United States, 2010–2019 [1]

Year	Beef			Veal			Lamb and mutton		
	Production	Consumption		Produc-tion	Consumption		Produc-tion	Consumption	
		Total	Per capita		Total	Per capita		Total	Per capita
	Million pounds	Million pounds	Pounds	Million pounds	Million pounds	Pounds	Million pounds	Million pounds	Pounds
2010	26,412	26,390	85.2	145	150	0.5	168	318	1.0
2011	26,281	25,538	81.8	136	137	0.4	153	295	0.8
2012	25,989	25,748	81.9	125	123	0.4	161	299	1.0
2013	25,790	25,476	80.5	117	119	0.4	161	324	1.0
2014	24,316	24,682	77.4	100	98	0.3	161	340	1.1
2015	23,760	24,769	77.2	88	88	0.3	155	357	1.1
2016	25,288	25,669	79.4	81	73	0.2	155	381	1.2
2017	26,250	26,492	81.5	80	78	0.2	150	396	1.2
2018	26,942	26,767	81.9	80	89	0.3	158	415	1.3
2019	27,221	27,272	83.0	79	81	0.2	153	422	1.3

Year	Pork			All meats		
	Production	Consumption		Production	Consumption	
		Total	Per capita		Total	Per capita
	Million pounds	Million pounds	Pounds	Million pounds	Million pounds	Pounds
2010	22,456	19,076	61.6	49,181	45,934	148
2011	22,775	18,382	58.9	49,232	44,351	142
2012	23,268	18,607	59.2	49,543	44,778	142
2013	23,203	19,104	60.4	49,271	45,022	142
2014	22,858	18,836	59.1	47,435	43,955	138
2015	24,517	20,592	64.6	48,520	45,806	143
2016	24,957	20,892	64.6	50,388	47,015	145
2017	25,598	21,034	64.7	51,991	48,000	148
2018	26,330	21,490	65.7	53,417	48,758	149
2019	27,652	22,188	67.5	55,015	49,966	152

[1] Carcass weight equivalent or dressed weight. Beginning 1977, pork production was no longer reported as "pork, exclud-ing lard." This series has been revised to reflect pork production in prior years on a dressed weight basis that is comparable with the method used to report beef, veal, and lamb and mutton. Edible offals are excluded. Shipments to the U.S. terri-tories are included in domestic consumption.
ERS, Animal Products and Cost of Production Branch, (202) 694–5409.

Table 7-66.—Hides, packer: Average price per piece, Central U.S., 2010–2019

Year	Steers				Heifers	
	Heavy native	Heavy Texas	Butt branded	Colorado branded	Heavy native	Branded
	Dollars	Dollars	Dollars	Dollars	Dollars	Dollars
2010	71.93	72.30	70.77	67.31	63.44	67.57
2011	82.17	81.70	80.77	76.42	74.39	71.17
2012	84.53	84.23	84.28	79.83	71.77	70.19
2013	98.73	95.74	98.56	94.38	84.68	82.90
2014	110.98	106.37	108.95	103.05	93.45	89.68
2015	84.29	77.13	82.57	75.98	65.00	59.76
2016	73.88	68.02	72.37	60.11	58.39	53.00
2017	67.05	59.13	65.21	(NA)	51.77	42.76
2018	68.19	39.29	50.98	39.36	38.17	33.72
2019	24.57	36.96	28.61	21.94	16.00	16.46

(NA) Not available.
AMS, Livestock & Grain Market News, (202) 720–7316.

Table 7-67.—Hides and skins: United States imports by country of origin, 2018–2020

Country of origin	2018	2019	2020
	Number		
Furskins:			
Canada	915,358	1,169,297	1,134,417
Ukraine	207,500	358,000	308,956
Czech Republic	0	230,000	163,200
Finland	64,193	47,243	52,892
Belgium-Luxembourg(*)	200,362	8,889	8,216
China	672	349	3,200
Denmark(*)	6,493	7,415	2,143
Sweden	732	0	674
Australia(*)	0	0	170
Italy(*)	463	95	108
France(*)	1,742	47	102
Spain	0	25,000	18
Netherlands	2,741	955	9
Mexico	12,163	30	6
Greenland	0	0	1
Germany(*)	183	0	1
South Africa	4	1	1
United Arab Emirates	715	23	0
Armenia	25	0	0
Argentina	0	0	0
Bulgaria	12	0	0
Ireland	0	111	0
Greece	891	718	0
Hong Kong	8	54	0
India	60	0	0
Japan	4	0	0
Korea, South	101	0	0
Latvia	1,524	2,139	0
Lithuania	532	891	0
Slovakia	11	0	0
Rest of World	91,469	67,083	0
World Total	1,507,958	1,918,340	1,918,494
	Pieces		
Hides and skins:			
Mexico	9,235	31,822	333,401
Canada	653,668	347,052	267,176
Brazil	19,641	14,560	45,313
Belgium-Luxembourg(*)	196,535	118,831	30,155
Italy(*)	10,563	6,920	21,109
United Kingdom	426,434	342,439	20,422
Thailand	4,747	7,923	15,915
Slovenia	0	0	14,338
Spain	13,096	375	9,831
Colombia	13,694	2,016	6,848
Cote d'Ivoire	2,139	4,411	6,248
New Zealand(*)	16,504	3,855	4,605
France(*)	6,549	2,669	2,843
Argentina	15,211	2,719	1,597
Australia(*)	3,429	8,080	1,430
Germany(*)	0	22	1,214
China	4,939	211	1,156
Turkey	32	5,778	857
Singapore	21	300	789
Senegal	401	770	200
Indonesia	364	101	175
Honduras	0	0	82
Zimbabwe	4	628	36
Poland	1	26	31
South Africa	41	108	27
Denmark(*)	32	614	2
India	411	557	1
Azerbaijan	0	0	0
Austria	0	262	0
Dominican Republic	0	1,326	0
Rest of World	6,770	8,056	0
World Total	1,404,461	912,431	785,801

(*) Denotes a country that is a summarization of its component countries.
FAS, Office of Global Analysis, (202) 720–6301. Data as of February 25, 2021.

Table 7-68.—Hides: U.S. trade exports, 2018–2020

Country	2018	2019	2020
	Pieces		
Bovine hides, whole:			
China	8,882,126	8,808,907	13,003,691
Korea, South	1,669,958	2,022,979	4,284,933
Mexico	2,473,837	2,685,087	1,441,624
Thailand	1,496,653	923,431	370,106
Taiwan	374,302	385,011	248,641
Japan	159,598	164,067	236,178
Brazil	114,151	42,311	97,673
Indonesia	30,249	62,831	86,459
Netherlands	0	23,730	67,440
Vietnam	192,279	98,076	58,054
Italy(*)	183,274	60,333	45,263
India	175,111	181,501	42,028
Turkey	11,744	14,005	30,571
Cambodia	633	21,189	15,511
Ethiopia(*)	16,837	2,399	10,050
Hong Kong	64,156	71,727	10,000
Bosnia and Herzegovina	45,512	43,868	9,386
Slovenia	0	9,325	6,696
Egypt	0	0	3,200
Germany(*)	0	0	1,895
Belgium-Luxembourg(*)	0	920	1,855
Austria	55,347	11,208	1,777
Israel(*)	3,110	4,178	1,620
Colombia	4,760	97	1,610
Spain	0	0	540
Philippines	1,211	3,213	529
Portugal	0	3,166	234
Bahamas, The	0	0	115
Ecuador	0	123	99
Haiti	0	0	40
Rest of World	92,381	20,695	0
World Total	16,047,229	15,664,377	20,077,818
Other cattle hides:			
China	36,095	19,613	38,696
Thailand	65,130	29,731	19,361
Vietnam	7,459	3,541	18,786
Spain	38,133	35,892	17,043
Japan	33,131	35,151	15,477
Hong Kong	12,465	20,748	9,646
Korea, South	9,210	10,717	3,131
Netherlands	1,120	0	3,015
Italy(*)	630	3,199	2,518
United Kingdom	7,396	963	2,126
Germany(*)	4,327	0	1,918
Mexico	1,573,810	363,402	1,804
Israel(*)	0	0	837
India	1,077	935	436
Taiwan	7,210	567	374
Cambodia	0	1,070	203
Portugal	0	944	145
Dominican Republic	167	0	139
Switzerland(*)	0	0	107
Austria	247	1,669	0
Bangladesh	199	0	0
Brazil	26	0	0
Indonesia	64	0	0
Philippines	0	116	0
Sweden	734	1,039	0
World Total	1,798,630	529,297	135,762

See footnote(s) at end of table.

Table 7-68.—Hides: U.S. trade exports, 2018–2020—Continued

Country	2018	2019	2020
	Pieces		
Horse hides, whole:			
China	98,244	25,616	30,925
Korea, South	69,395	23,746	19,627
Mexico	21,326	88	1,229
Canada	8,965	1,762	1,100
Israel(*)	3,507	0	514
Colombia	0	0	400
Togo	24	349	281
United Kingdom	0	0	174
New Zealand(*)	2,000	0	140
United Arab Emirates	0	0	126
Ireland	333	0	0
Germany(*)	1	0	0
Honduras	1,757	0	0
Indonesia	9,852	31	0
Liberia	112	0	0
Nigeria	351	82	0
Netherlands	0	2,675	0
Sweden	223	0	0
Taiwan	14,608	0	0
Vietnam	5,418	0	0
World Total	236,116	54,349	54,516
Calf skins, whole:			
China	1,685,359	1,496,510	1,484,399
Korea, South	690,135	316,701	199,272
Mexico	393,267	329,255	195,728
Thailand	125,508	186,439	157,696
Italy(*)	114,591	218,480	105,322
Indonesia	0	32,823	80,135
Netherlands	0	45,228	74,894
Israel(*)	46,744	27,109	58,163
Spain	0	12,724	32,408
Cambodia	0	19,810	26,930
Turkey	13,892	1,800	17,005
India	32,319	25,739	2,690
Kuwait	85	56	2,639
Pakistan	5,752	0	900
El Salvador	0	0	763
Germany(*)	20,765	1,926	574
Dominican Republic	0	1,530	411
Nigeria	0	119	37
Vietnam	5,092	15,844	27
Brazil	4,628	1,600	5
Belgium-Luxembourg(*)	0	1,360	0
Bahamas, The	96	0	0
Sri Lanka	0	174	0
Colombia	0	3,849	0
Costa Rica	75,133	28,894	0
France(*)	150	11	0
Ghana	424	1,129	0
Guatemala	0	558	0
Haiti	1,820	0	0
Hong Kong	8,481	12,000	0
Rest of World	21,410	2,726	0
World Total	3,245,651	2,784,394	2,439,998
Sheep & lamb skins:			
China	635,279	483,942	452,025
Brazil	13,109	19,515	18,111
Turkey	116,840	55,153	13,175
Germany(*)	11,683	8,000	8,300
Canada	2,987	3,929	3,244
Mexico	18,615	18,331	1,142
Sweden	0	0	815
Italy(*)	0	0	438
Uruguay	0	0	108
Bolivia	0	120	0
Pakistan	748	243	0
Poland	28,310	2,473	0
Russia	55,860	22,650	0
Spain	2,685	3,990	0
United Kingdom	2,800	0	0
World Total	888,916	618,346	497,358

See footnote(s) at end of table.

Table 7-68.—Hides: U.S. trade exports, 2018–2020—Continued

Country	2018	2019	2020
	Pieces		
Other hides & skins:			
China	1,437,489	675,774	1,717,655
Mexico	1,643,008	1,140,446	473,105
Thailand	1,285,795	512,405	419,136
Korea, South	500,102	287,340	213,572
France(*)	195,216	179,197	165,575
Taiwan	396,557	66,416	140,435
United Kingdom	106,135	103,746	104,000
Singapore	105,229	103,713	90,682
Vietnam	52,284	302,451	89,719
Germany(*)	65,039	91,136	64,991
Italy(*)	156,409	75,557	55,569
Pakistan	2,449	453	31,143
Cambodia	189,891	242	28,973
Indonesia	35,479	22,919	17,930
Canada	17,397	8,212	10,861
Hong Kong	9,131	0	3,012
India	0	4,124	2,877
Brazil	17,374	647	1,550
Japan	12,864	1,739	1,263
Colombia	0	0	826
Ecuador	0	0	705
Malaysia	5,973	1,885	630
Portugal	2,985	10,606	320
Turkey	0	0	159
Peru	0	0	30
Australia(*)	0	0	0
Barbados	395	0	0
Belgium-Luxembourg(*)	515	0	0
Bangladesh	0	0	0
Bosnia and Herzegovina	160	126	0
Rest of World	32,431	6,995	0
World Total	6,270,307	3,596,129	3,634,718
	Number		
Other furskins:			
Canada	853,684	872,982	514,925
China	427,458	374,809	386,803
Cambodia	19,878	125,363	91,544
Hong Kong	154,208	132,831	69,827
Portugal	45,015	42,789	38,888
Greece	1,625	2,005	9,096
Belgium-Luxembourg(*)	41,077	9,687	6,400
Thailand	0	3,156	2,354
Poland	0	0	1,542
France(*)	3,697	767	428
United Kingdom	157	0	294
Germany(*)	24,168	3,730	200
Australia(*)	0	0	100
Malaysia	0	0	100
Chile	0	4	0
Finland	500	600	0
Haiti	0	0	0
Indonesia	685	0	0
Italy(*)	23,707	2,891	0
Latvia	0	0	0
Lithuania	0	1,005	0
Mexico	0	768	0
Pakistan	15,900	53,063	0
Spain	259	0	0
Switzerland(*)	200	0	0
Turkey	416	1,200	0
Taiwan	0	0	0
Vietnam	3,449	1,362	0
Rest of World			
World Total	1,616,083	1,629,012	1,122,501

(*) Denotes a country that is a summarization of its component countries.
FAS, Office of Global Analysis, (202) 720-6301. Data Source: U.S. Census Bureau Trade Data, as of February 25, 2021.

Table 7-69.—Mink: Farms, pelts produced, average price, and value, United States, 2010–2019

Year	Mink farms	Pelts produced	Average marketing price	Value of mink pelts
	Number	*Number*	*Dollars*	*Dollars*
2010	265	2,840,200	81.90	232,612,380
2011	268	3,091,470	94.30	291,525,621
2012 [1]	(NA)	(NA)	(NA)	(NA)
2013	(NA)	3,544,610	56.30	199,561,543
2014	(NA)	3,741,150	57.70	215,864,355
2015	(NA)	3,682,960	32.00	117,854,720
2016	(NA)	3,454,410	34.70	119,868,027
2017	(NA)	3,400,080	36.10	122,742,888
2018	(NA)	3,169,560	26.60	84,310,296
2019	(NA)	2,704,200	21.90	122,742,888

(NA) Not available.   [1] Due to sequestration the Mink report was suspended.
NASS, Livestock Branch, (202) 720–3570.

Table 7-70.—Mink pelts: Pelts produced by color class, selected States, and United States, 2019

State	Black	Demi/Wild	Pastel	Sapphire	Blue Iris	Mahogany
	Number	*Number*	*Number*	*Number*	*Number*	*Number*
Idaho	88,000	(D)	14,000	13,000	(D)	136,000
Illinois	25,000	-	-	-	-	(D)
Iowa	35,000	-	(D)	(D)	(D)	36,000
Michigan	49,000	-	400	4,100	(D)	(D)
Minnesota	(D)	(D)	3,200	-	(D)	(D)
Montana	(D)	(D)	(D)	(D)	(D)	(D)
Ohio	(D)	(D)	(D)	(D)	(D)	(D)
Oregon	182,000	-	-	1,500	(D)	(D)
Pennsylvania	28,000	(D)	(D)	1,500	(D)	(D)
Utah	185,000	33,000	36,000	40,000	(D)	196,000
Washington	27,000	-	-	-	-	-
Wisconsin	630,000	-	(D)	42,000	81,000	47,000
Other States [1]	155,600	57,440	30,740	53,030	37,540	53,680
United States	1,404,600	90,440	84,340	155,130	118,540	468,680

State	Pearl	Lavender	Violet	White	Other	Total [2]
	Number	*Number*	*Number*	*Number*	*Number*	*Number*
Idaho	-	(D)	(D)	-	(D)	267,740
Illinois	(D)	-	-	(D)	-	33,200
Iowa	-	-	-	(D)	-	80,450
Michigan	-	(D)	1,900	6,000	(D)	65,020
Minnesota	-	-	(D)	17,500	(D)	141,950
Montana	(D)	(D)	(D)	(D)	(D)	(D)
Ohio	(D)	(D)	(D)	(D)	(D)	(D)
Oregon	-	(D)	(D)	-	-	202,920
Pennsylvania	-	(D)	(D)	-	(D)	46,270
Utah	(D)	-	(D)	(D)	(D)	556,710
Washington	-	-	-	-	-	27,000
Wisconsin	-	15,500	(D)	149,000	720	1,016,220
Other States [1]	79,000	10,290	54,890	36,530	11,140	266,720
United States	79,000	25,790	56,790	209,030	11,860	2,704,200

- Represents zero.   (D) Withheld to avoid disclosing data for individual operations.   [1] Other States include New Hampshire, New Jersey, New York, North Carolina, South Dakota, and some pelts from the above listed States that were not published to avoid disclosing individual operations.   [2] Published color classes may not add to the State total to avoid disclosing individual operations.
NASS, Livestock Branch, (202) 720–3570.

Table 7-71.—Livestock: Inventory and value, United States, Jan. 1, 2017–2019

Class of livestock and poultry	Inventory			Value					
				Per head [1]			Total		
	2017	2018	2019	2017	2018	2019	2017	2018	2019
	1,000	*1,000*	*1,000*	*Dollars*	*Dollars*	*Dollars*	*1,000 Dollars*	*1,000 Dollars*	*1,000 Dollars*
Angora goats [2]	152	144	137	130	124	132	16,827	14,584	15,021
Cattle	93,625	94,298	94,805	1,109	1,146	1,031	103,829,681	108,065,508	97,746,846
Chickens [3]	514,838	533,891	532,498	4.20	4.32	4.43	2,162,545	2,308,002	2,361,628
Hogs [3]	73,145	75,070	78,228	99	98	102	7,206,965	7,356,703	7,888,779
Sheep and lambs	5,270	5,265	5,230	203	204	203	1,067,857	1,071,378	1,061,498

[1] Based on reporters' estimates of average price per head in their localities. [2] Four-State total for angora goats (Arizona, California, New Mexico, Texas). [3] Dec. 1 of preceding year.
NASS, Livestock Branch, (202) 720–3570.

Table 7-72.—Livestock: Market year for specified commodities

Cattle market year average price received: United States marketing years 2010–2019 [1]

Year	Cows [2]	Steers and heifers	Calves	Beef cattle [3]	Milks cows [4]
	Dollars	*Dollars*	*Dollars*	*Dollars*	*Dollars*
2010	54.80	97.70	117.00	92.20	1,330.00
2011	71.20	117.00	142.00	113.00	1,420.00
2012	81.70	123.00	172.00	121.00	1,430.00
2013	82.30	126.00	181.00	125.00	1,380.00
2014	107.00	153.00	261.00	152.00	1,830.00
2015	103.00	148.00	247.00	147.00	1,990.00
2016	74.30	121.00	158.00	119.00	1,760.00
2017	69.10	122.00	168.00	120.00	1,620.00
2018	63.50	117.00	170.00	115.00	1,360.00
2019	62.00	118.00	159.00	160.00	1,200.00

Hog market year average price received: United States marketing years 2010–2019 [5]

Year	Barrows and gilts	Sows	All Hogs
	Dollars	*Dollars*	*Dollars*
2010	54.40	48.70	54.10
2011	65.70	57.50	65.30
2012	64.60	51.30	64.20
2013	67.30	62.90	67.20
2014	76.50	77.70	76.50
2015	55.70	44.90	55.30
2016	49.60	40.70	49.30
2017	53.50	44.50	53.10
2018	50.50	41.30	50.20
2019	51.70	41.10	51.40

[1] Market year for cattle January 1-December 31 for United States and all States. [2] Cows includes beef cows and cull dairy cows sold for slaughter. [3] All beef includes steer and heifers combined and cows. [4] Milk cow prices are calendar year average. [5] Market year for hogs December 1-November 30 for United States and all States.
NASS, Livestock Branch, (202) 720–3570.

**Table 7-74.—Frozen meat: Cold storage holdings, end of month,
United States, 2018–2019**

Month	Boneless beef		Beef bone-in		Total beef	
	2018	2019	2018	2019	2018	2019
	1,000 pounds					
January	458,749	477,496	42,995	32,718	501,744	510,214
February	416,438	445,621	42,901	28,358	459,339	473,979
March	426,232	422,310	37,725	29,630	463,957	451,940
April	435,196	396,550	35,964	33,672	471,160	430,222
May	426,089	372,708	38,565	32,443	464,654	405,151
June	407,131	372,195	41,454	33,450	448,585	405,645
July	444,089	418,924	40,159	35,540	484,248	454,464
August	457,392	433,698	43,923	36,178	501,315	469,876
September ...	458,904	434,191	48,262	34,790	507,166	468,981
October	468,424	430,033	47,150	36,233	515,574	466,266
November	473,863	445,529	40,835	32,732	514,698	478,261
December	462,072	449,990	33,552	30,126	495,624	480,116

Month	Picnics		Bellies		Butts	
	2018	2019	2018	2019	2018	2019
	1,000 pounds					
January	7,074	7,067	43,810	53,736	25,477	20,527
February	8,644	6,742	49,012	53,771	22,503	25,290
March	11,314	8,019	59,202	58,783	20,629	26,271
April	10,094	9,926	64,563	61,110	20,904	21,164
May	10,110	7,561	61,234	64,124	15,313	21,189
June	7,268	7,920	53,279	56,468	15,734	17,218
July	8,157	7,940	38,556	52,647	13,218	18,363
August	8,874	10,063	34,805	45,723	11,498	16,200
September ...	8,375	8,582	30,354	40,543	13,282	15,494
October	7,879	9,923	26,690	45,414	17,014	20,676
November	6,644	7,506	36,859	54,416	17,623	25,933
December	6,832	7,669	42,251	66,647	16,749	20,457

	Hams					
Month	Bone-in		Boneless		Total	
	2018	2019	2018	2019	2018	2019
	1,000 pounds					
January	35,572	37,242	82,835	75,418	118,407	112,660
February	36,932	38,139	85,811	89,547	122,743	127,740
March	24,234	29,174	72,105	74,312	96,339	103,486
April	23,694	29,606	88,451	91,725	112,145	121,331
May	41,898	53,746	97,397	96,363	139,295	150,109
June	54,794	64,578	93,863	104,021	148,657	168,599
July	71,184	72,816	96,379	109,739	167,563	182,555
August	91,764	80,648	112,999	121,806	204,763	202,454
September ...	93,281	90,628	121,347	110,630	214,628	201,628
October	76,417	76,256	99,692	97,548	176,109	173,804
November	37,122	38,815	59,253	71,820	96,375	110,635
December	15,714	21,138	57,404	63,857	73,118	85,995

	Loins					
Month	Bone-in		Boneless		Total	
	2018	2019	2018	2019	2018	2019
	1,000 pounds					
January	14,276	12,322	26,497	22,627	40,773	34,949
February	14,638	14,414	24,102	24,241	38,740	38,655
March	13,081	17,110	26,472	24,522	39,553	41,632
April	12,958	18,999	26,872	24,126	39,830	43,125
May	12,205	22,103	24,314	23,687	36,519	45,790
June	9,889	22,133	22,060	24,545	31,949	46,678
July	7,261	20,761	19,353	25,566	26,614	46,327
August	9,810	19,837	20,765	22,534	30,575	42,371
September ...	11,130	17,703	22,633	21,992	33,763	39,695
October	9,790	18,357	24,426	23,629	34,216	41,986
November	10,279	22,153	23,644	26,566	33,923	48,719
December	11,221	21,924	22,871	27,199	34,092	49,123

See footnote(s) at end of table.

**Table 7-74.—Frozen meat: Cold storage holdings, end of month,
United States, 2018–2019—Continued**

Month	Ribs		Trimmings		Other frozen pork	
	2018	2019	2018	2019	2018	2019
	1,000 pounds					
January	114,366	127,107	48,602	47,104	104,544	78,254
February	131,600	142,603	51,186	51,317	97,215	83,644
March	143,957	140,779	56,318	55,835	93,548	85,359
April	143,717	146,859	57,490	48,237	90,657	81,809
May	119,286	127,769	56,969	47,948	92,610	80,851
June	88,871	101,647	45,132	47,862	85,049	89,917
July	84,171	84,866	40,372	47,546	86,046	87,129
August	77,803	79,353	42,253	42,008	86,905	85,780
September ...	83,403	85,287	38,499	38,736	81,592	83,900
October	101,369	100,850	42,156	41,699	79,323	88,918
November	108,324	110,333	43,033	41,581	81,265	86,792
December	124,310	120,877	48,441	53,435	78,855	89,965

Month	Variety meats		Unclassified pork		Total pork	
	2018	2019	2018	2019	2018	2019
	1,000 pounds					
January	30,735	35,023	46,926	46,306	580,714	562,733
February	33,161	34,829	55,009	51,083	209,813	615,674
March	35,875	32,782	54,278	55,433	611,013	608,379
April	36,544	31,946	58,778	55,949	634,722	621,456
May	34,681	31,495	57,708	52,120	623,725	628,956
June	34,438	31,184	51,502	51,961	561,879	619,454
July	34,439	31,186	52,893	53,133	552,029	611,692
August	34,307	32,743	49,730	50,089	581,513	606,784
September ...	37,030	32,436	48,477	52,819	589,403	598,750
October	36,193	31,443	49,968	57,203	570,917	611,916
November	36,001	29,534	47,621	59,391	507,668	574,840
December	34,009	32,984	46,630	53,312	505,287	580,464

Month	Veal		Lamb & mutton		Total red meat	
	2018	2019	2018	2019	2018	2019
	1,000 pounds					
January	19,912	8,614	26,790	38,376	1,129,160	1,119,937
February	21,158	9,332	28,280	35,503	1,118,590	1,134,488
March	20,780	4,574	28,615	31,026	1,124,365	1,095,919
April	20,033	5,463	33,992	40,949	1,159,907	1,098,090
May	18,206	5,243	35,591	38,484	1,142,176	1,077,834
June	14,954	4,257	38,678	40,025	1,064,096	1,069,381
July	18,096	4,717	42,129	43,052	1,096,502	1,113,925
August	14,179	5,386	39,386	46,642	1,136,393	1,128,688
September ...	13,736	5,727	40,466	41,648	1,150,771	1,115,106
October	9,842	5,659	39,321	37,805	1,135,654	1,121,646
November	9,106	5,461	37,859	34,022	1,069,331	1,092,584
December	8,238	6,171	36,454	34,752	1,045,603	1,101,503

NASS, Livestock Branch, (202) 720–3570.

CHAPTER VIII

DAIRY AND POULTRY STATISTICS

Dairy statistics in this chapter include series relating to many phases of production, movement, prices, stocks, and consumption of milk and its products. Two series of number of milk cows on farms are included in this publication. One series is an inventory number of a specific classification estimated as one of the major groups making up the total cattle population on January 1. The other series identified as "milk cows" is an annual average number of milk cows during the year (excluding any not yet fresh) and is used in estimating milk production.

In comparing the several series of milk prices, it is important to note that prices received by farmers for all whole milk sold are for milk or milkfat content as actually sold, while certain prices paid by dealers for milk for fluid purposes or for specified manufacturing purposes may be quoted on a 3.5 percent butterfat basis, or for some types of manufacturing milk on the test of the milk used for that particular purpose.

Poultry and poultry products statistics include inventory numbers of chickens by classes; the production, disposition, cash receipts, and gross income from chickens and eggs; poultry and egg receipts at principal markets; commercial broiler production; turkey production, disposition, and gross income; poultry and eggs under Federal inspection; and the National Poultry Improvement Plan. Estimates relating to inventories, production, and income exclude poultry and eggs produced on places not classified as farms.

Table 8-1.—Milk cows and heifers: Number that have calved and heifers 500 pounds and over kept for milk cow replacements, United States, Jan. 1, 2010–2019

Year	Milk cows and heifers that have calved	Heifers 500 pounds and over kept for milk cow replacements
	Thousands	*Thousands*
2010	9,087	4,551
2011	9,156	4,577
2012	9,236	4,618
2013	9,221	4,546
2014	9,209	4,539
2015	9,312	4,710
2016	9,312	4,814
2017	9,369	4,754
2018	9,432	4,768
2019	9,353	4,702

NASS, Livestock Branch, (202) 720–3570.

Table 8-2.—Milk cows and heifers: Number that have calved and heifers 500 pounds and over kept for milk cow replacements, by State and United States, Jan. 1, 2018 and 2019

State	Milk cows and heifers that have calved		Heifers 500 pounds and over kept for milk cow replacements	
	2018	2019	2018	2019
	Thousands	*Thousands*	*Thousands*	*Thousands*
Alabama	6.0	5.0	3.0	2.0
Alaska	0.3	0.2	0.1	0.1
Arizona	210.0	205.0	105.0	115.0
Arkansas	6.0	5.0	4.0	4.0
California	1,740.0	1,730.0	780.0	760.0
Colorado	168.0	178.0	100.0	110.0
Connecticut	20.0	19.5	9.5	9.0
Delaware	5.0	4.5	2.0	1.6
Florida	124.0	116.0	40.0	35.0
Georgia	85.0	81.0	25.0	30.0
Hawaii	2.0	1.5	1.0	1.0
Idaho	600.0	614.0	310.0	340.0
Illinois	93.0	85.0	47.0	45.0
Indiana	187.0	181.0	75.0	80.0
Iowa	220.0	220.0	135.0	125.0
Kansas	156.0	161.0	140.0	170.0
Kentucky	57.0	53.0	45.0	45.0
Louisiana	12.0	11.0	4.0	4.0
Maine	30.0	29.0	15.0	14.0
Maryland	47.0	44.0	28.0	30.0
Massachusetts	11.5	10.5	7.0	6.5
Michigan	428.0	422.0	176.0	160.0
Minnesota	455.0	450.0	290.0	255.0
Mississippi	9.0	8.0	7.0	5.0
Missouri	84.0	81.0	40.0	40.0
Montana	13.0	12.0	7.0	8.0
Nebraska	60.0	59.0	15.0	15.0
Nevada	32.0	33.0	12.0	11.0
New Hampshire	12.5	12.0	7.0	6.5
New Jersey	6.0	5.5	3.2	3.3
New Mexico	332.0	325.0	130.0	125.0
New York	625.0	625.0	350.0	335.0
North Carolina	45.0	43.0	17.0	20.0
North Dakota	16.0	15.0	9.0	8.0
Ohio	264.0	253.0	121.0	125.0
Oklahoma	42.0	40.0	25.0	20.0
Oregon	124.0	125.0	70.0	65.0
Pennsylvania	525.0	505.0	310.0	290.0
Rhode Island	0.8	0.7	0.5	0.5
South Carolina	15.0	14.0	6.0	5.0
South Dakota	119.0	122.0	45.0	40.0
Tennessee	40.0	36.0	25.0	25.0
Texas	530.0	545.0	250.0	260.0
Utah	97.0	100.0	50.0	50.0
Vermont	128.0	126.0	57.0	55.0
Virginia	87.0	79.0	40.0	37.0
Washington	275.0	280.0	123.0	123.0
West Virginia	7.0	7.0	3.0	3.0
Wisconsin	1,275.0	1,270.0	700.0	680.0
Wyoming	6.0	6.0	4.0	4.0
United States	9,432.1	9,353.4	4,768.3	4,701.5

NASS, Livestock Branch, (202) 720–3570.

Table 8-3.—Milk and milkfat production: Number of milk cows, production per cow, and total quantity produced, by State and United States, 2018 [1]

State	Number of milk cows [2]	Production of milk and milkfat [3]				
		Per milk cow		All milk percent of fat	Total	
		Milk	Milkfat		Milk	Milkfat
	Thousands	Pounds	Pounds	Percent	Million pounds	Million pounds
Alabama	5.0	14,600	566	3.88	73.0	2.8
Alaska	0.3	9,333	367	3.93	2.8	0.1
Arizona	208.0	23,909	875	3.66	4,978.0	182.2
Arkansas	6.0	12,333	467	3.79	74.0	2.8
California	1,734.0	23,301	909	3.90	40,413.0	1,576.1
Colorado	176.0	25,892	968	3.74	4,557.0	170.4
Connecticut	19.0	22,474	890	3.96	427.0	16.9
Delaware	4.8	19,063	732	3.84	91.5	3.5
Florida	120.0	19,833	730	3.68	2,381.0	87.6
Georgia	83.0	21,277	774	3.64	1,766.0	64.3
Hawaii	2.0	16,950	585	3.46	34.0	1.2
Idaho	609.0	24,870	985	3.96	15,149.0	599.9
Illinois	90.0	20,867	812	3.89	1,878.0	73.1
Indiana	183.0	22,574	860	3.78	4,161.0	157.3
Iowa	220.0	23,955	944	3.94	5,268.0	207.6
Kansas	159.0	23,321	900	3.86	3,708.0	143.1
Kentucky	55.0	18,345	695	3.79	1,009.0	38.2
Louisiana	11.0	13,818	558	4.04	152.0	6.1
Maine	30.0	20,600	797	3.87	618.0	23.9
Maryland	45.0	20,556	785	3.82	925.0	35.3
Massachusetts	11.0	18,364	731	3.98	202.0	8.0
Michigan	423.0	26,409	1,009	3.82	11,168.0	426.6
Minnesota	453.0	21,784	867	3.98	9,868.0	392.7
Mississippi	9.0	14,333	579	4.04	129.0	5.2
Missouri	83.0	14,386	573	3.98	1,194.0	47.5
Montana	12.0	22,833	868	3.80	274.0	10.4
Nebraska	60.0	24,000	926	3.86	1,440.0	55.6
Nevada	32.0	22,938	906	3.95	734.0	29.0
New Hampshire	12.0	20,750	811	3.91	249.0	9.7
New Jersey	6.0	18,333	697	3.80	110.0	4.2
New Mexico	330.0	25,106	929	3.70	8,285.0	306.5
New York	623.0	23,888	922	3.86	14,882.0	574.4
North Carolina	44.0	21,295	803	3.77	937.0	35.3
North Dakota	15.0	22,267	875	3.93	334.0	13.1
Ohio	259.0	21,359	831	3.89	5,532.0	215.2
Oklahoma	40.0	18,125	692	3.82	725.0	27.7
Oregon	123.0	20,577	835	4.06	2,531.0	102.8
Pennsylvania	519.0	20,534	782	3.81	10,665.0	406.3
Rhode Island	0.7	16,429	662	4.03	11.7	0.5
South Carolina	14.0	17,286	666	3.85	242.0	9.3
South Dakota	121.0	22,364	933	4.17	2,705.0	112.8
Tennessee	37.0	17,135	649	3.79	634.0	24.0
Texas	537.0	23,948	984	4.11	12,852.0	528.2
Utah	100.0	23,220	899	3.87	2,322.0	89.9
Vermont	127.0	21,126	824	3.90	2,680.0	104.5
Virginia	83.0	19,699	745	3.78	1,635.0	61.8
Washington	277.0	24,318	987	4.06	6,736.0	273.5
West Virginia	7.0	15,857	606	3.82	111.0	4.2
Wisconsin	1,274.0	24,002	934	3.89	30,579.0	1,189.5
Wyoming	6.0	23,700	863	3.64	142.2	5.2
United States	9,398.0	23,150	901	3.89	217,575.0	8,466.0

[1] May not add due to rounding.   [2] Average number during year, excluding heifers not yet fresh.   [3] Excludes milk sucked by calves.

NASS, Livestock Branch, (202) 720–3570.

Table 8-4.—Milk and milkfat production: Number of milk cows, production per cow, and total quantity produced, by State and United States, 2019 [1]

State	Number of milk cows [2]	Production of milk and milkfat [3]				
		Per milk cow		All milk percent of fat	Total	
		Milk	Milkfat		Milk	Milkfat
	Thousands	*Pounds*	*Pounds*	*Percent*	*Million pounds*	*Million pounds*
Alabama	5.0	12,000	466	3.88	60.0	2.3
Arizona	197.0	24,208	905	3.74	4,769.0	178.4
Arkansas	5.0	13,400	505	3.77	67.0	2.5
California	1,726.0	23,502	912	3.88	40,564.0	1,573.9
Colorado	186.0	25,844	985	3.81	4,807.0	183.1
Connecticut	19.0	22,526	892	3.96	428.0	16.9
Delaware	4.1	17,976	706	3.93	73.7	2.9
Florida	116.0	20,224	740	3.66	2,346.0	85.9
Georgia	82.0	21,598	790	3.66	1,771.0	64.8
Idaho	625.0	25,010	995	3.98	15,631.0	622.1
Illinois	83.0	21,010	830	3.94	1,748.0	68.9
Indiana	178.0	22,882	874	3.82	4,073.0	155.6
Iowa	218.0	24,271	966	3.98	5,291.0	210.6
Kansas	163.0	23,429	925	3.95	3,819.0	150.9
Kentucky	50.0	18,820	717	3.81	941.0	35.9
Louisiana	10.0	13,500	525	3.89	135.0	5.3
Maine	29.0	21,414	837	3.91	621.0	24.3
Maryland	43.0	19,535	758	3.88	840.0	32.6
Massachusetts	10.0	19,200	766	3.99	192.0	7.7
Michigan	426.0	26,725	1,024	3.83	11,385.0	436.0
Minnesota	448.0	22,167	898	4.05	9,931.0	402.2
Mississippi	8.0	15,750	663	4.21	126.0	5.3
Missouri	78.0	14,103	568	4.03	1,100.0	44.3
Montana	12.0	21,583	824	3.82	259.0	9.9
Nebraska	58.0	24,293	933	3.84	1,409.0	54.1
Nevada	33.0	23,091	898	3.89	762.0	29.6
New Hampshire	11.0	21,636	850	3.93	238.0	9.4
New Jersey	5.0	20,000	766	3.83	100.0	3.8
New Mexico	326.0	25,113	947	3.77	8,187.0	308.6
New York	627.0	24,118	938	3.89	15,122.0	588.2
North Carolina	42.0	21,476	816	3.80	902.0	34.3
North Dakota	15.0	21,733	898	4.13	326.0	13.5
Ohio	251.0	21,614	847	3.92	5,425.0	212.7
Oklahoma	41.0	17,829	704	3.95	731.0	28.9
Oregon	124.0	20,903	853	4.08	2,592.0	105.8
Pennsylvania	490.0	20,629	796	3.86	10,108.0	390.2
Rhode Island	0.7	15,143	601	3.97	10.6	0.4
South Carolina	12.0	17,167	647	3.77	206.0	7.8
South Dakota	125.0	22,480	955	4.25	2,810.0	119.4
Tennessee	32.0	17,219	656	3.81	551.0	21.0
Texas	565.0	24,513	1,022	4.17	13,850.0	577.5
Utah	98.0	23,082	907	3.93	2,262.0	88.9
Vermont	126.0	21,405	845	3.95	2,697.0	106.5
Virginia	75.0	19,867	753	3.79	1,490.0	56.5
Washington	280.0	24,225	988	4.08	6,783.0	276.7
West Virginia	6.0	15,000	576	3.84	90.0	3.5
Wisconsin	1,267.0	24,152	942	3.90	30,601.0	1,193.4
United States	9,336.0	23,391	917	3.92	218,382.0	8,558.4

[1] May not add due to rounding.   [2] Average number during year, excluding heifers not yet fresh.   [3] Excludes milk sucked by calves.

NASS, Livestock Branch, (202) 720–3570.

Table 8-5.—Milk: Quantities used and marketed by producers, by State and United States, 2018 [1]

State	Milk used where produced			Milk marketed by producers	
	Fed to calves [2]	Used for milk cream & butter	Total	Total quantity [3]	Fluid grade [4]
	Million pounds	Million pounds	Million pounds	Million pounds	Percent
Alabama	0.7	0.3	1.0	72.0	100
Alaska	0.2	0.3	0.5	2.3	100
Arizona	14.0	1.0	15.0	4,963.0	100
Arkansas	1.7	0.3	2.0	72.0	100
California	26.0	4.0	30.0	40,383.0	97
Colorado	21.0	1.0	22.0	4,535.0	100
Connecticut	2.5	0.5	3.0	424.0	100
Delaware	0.9	0.1	1.0	90.5	100
Florida	5.0	1.0	6.0	2,375.0	100
Georgia	7.0	1.0	8.0	1,758.0	100
Hawaii	0.1	0.1	0.2	33.8	100
Idaho	33.0	1.0	32.0	15,115.0	100
Illinois	10.0	2.0	12.0	1,866.0	98
Indiana	23.0	4.0	27.0	4,134.0	100
Iowa	16.0	1.0	17.0	5,251.0	100
Kansas	14.0	1.0	15.0	3,693.0	100
Kentucky	6.0	1.0	7.0	1,002.0	100
Louisiana	2.0	1.0	3.0	149.0	100
Maine	3.0	1.0	4.0	614.0	100
Maryland	7.0	1.0	8.0	917.0	100
Massachusetts	1.5	0.5	2.0	200.0	100
Michigan	34.0	2.0	36.0	11,132.0	100
Minnesota	95.0	4.0	99.0	9,769.0	99
Mississippi	1.0	1.0	2.0	127.0	100
Missouri	17.0	4.0	21.0	1,173.0	97
Montana	2.0	2.0	5.0	270.0	100
Nebraska	6.5	0.5	7.0	1,433.0	100
Nevada	5.0	1.0	6.0	728.0	100
New Hampshire	1.5	0.5	2.0	247.0	100
New Jersey	1.5	0.5	2.0	108.0	100
New Mexico	60.0	3.0	63.0	8,222.0	100
New York	55.0	2.0	57.0	14,825.0	100
North Carolina	5.0	1.0	6.0	931.0	100
North Dakota	3.5	0.5	4.0	330.0	98
Ohio	24.0	5.0	29.0	5,503.0	97
Oklahoma	6.0	1.0	7.0	718.0	100
Oregon	20.0	1.0	21.0	2,510.0	100
Pennsylvania	58.0	12.0	70.0	10,595.0	100
Rhode Island	0.1	-	0.1	11.6	100
South Carolina	2.0	1.0	3.0	239.0	100
South Dakota	7.0	1.0	8.0	2,697.0	100
Tennessee	4.0	1.0	5.0	629.0	100
Texas	27.0	1.0	28.0	12,824.0	100
Utah	13.0	1.0	14.0	2,308.0	100
Vermont	14.0	2.0	16.0	2,664.0	100
Virginia	8.0	2.0	10.0	1,625.0	100
Washington	17.0	1.0	18.0	6,718.0	100
West Virginia	1.0	1.0	2.0	109.0	100
Wisconsin	245.0	14.0	259.0	30,320.0	99
Wyoming	1.3	0.2	1.5	140.7	100
United States	929.0	89.0	1,017.0	216,556.0	99

- Represents zero.   [1] May not add due to rounding.   [2] Excludes milk sucked by calves.   [3] Milk sold to plants and dealers as whole milk and equivalent amounts of milk for cream.   Includes milk produced by dealers' own herds and milk sold directly to consumers.   Also includes milk produced by institutional herds.   [4] Percentage of milk sold that is eligible for fluid use (Grade A in most States).   Includes fluid grade milk used in manufacturing dairy products.
NASS, Livestock Branch, (202) 720–3570.

DAIRY AND POULTRY STATISTICS

Table 8-6.—Milk: Quantities used and marketed by producers, by State and United States, 2019 [1]

State	Milk used where produced			Milk marketed by producers	
	Fed to calves [2]	Used for milk cream & butter	Total	Total quantity [3]	Fluid grade [4]
	Million pounds	*Million pounds*	*Million pounds*	*Million pounds*	*Percent*
Alabama	0.7	0.3	1.0	72.0	100
Alaska	0.2	0.3	0.5	2.3	100
Arizona	14.0	1.0	15.0	4,963.0	100
Arkansas	1.7	0.3	2.0	72.0	100
California	26.0	4.0	30.0	40,383.0	97
Colorado	21.0	1.0	22.0	4,535.0	100
Connecticut	2.5	0.5	3.0	424.0	100
Delaware	0.9	0.1	1.0	90.5	100
Florida	5.0	1.0	6.0	2,375.0	100
Georgia	7.0	1.0	8.0	1,758.0	100
Hawaii	0.1	0.1	0.2	33.8	100
Idaho	33.0	1.0	34.0	15,115.0	100
Illinois	10.0	2.0	12.0	1,866.0	98
Indiana	23.0	4.0	27.0	4,134.0	100
Iowa	16.0	1.0	17.0	5,251.0	100
Kansas	14.0	1.0	15.0	3,693.0	100
Kentucky	6.0	1.0	7.0	1,002.0	100
Louisiana	2.0	1.0	3.0	149.0	100
Maine	3.0	1.0	4.0	614.0	100
Maryland	7.0	1.0	8.0	917.0	100
Massachusetts	1.5	0.5	2.0	200.0	100
Michigan	34.0	2.0	36.0	11,132.0	100
Minnesota	95.0	4.0	99.0	9,769.0	99
Mississippi	1.0	1.0	2.0	127.0	100
Missouri	17.0	4.0	21.0	1,173.0	97
Montana	2.0	2.0	4.0	270.0	100
Nebraska	6.5	0.5	7.0	1,433.0	100
Nevada	5.0	1.0	6.0	728.0	100
New Hampshire	1.5	0.5	2.0	247.0	100
New Jersey	1.5	0.5	2.0	108.0	100
New Mexico	60.0	3.0	63.0	8,222.0	100
New York	55.0	2.0	57.0	14,825.0	100
North Carolina	5.0	1.0	6.0	931.0	100
North Dakota	3.5	0.5	4.0	330.0	98
Ohio	24.0	5.0	29.0	5,503.0	97
Oklahoma	6.0	1.0	7.0	718.0	100
Oregon	20.0	1.0	21.0	2,510.0	100
Pennsylvania	58.0	12.0	70.0	10,595.0	100
Rhode Island	0.1	-	0.1	11.6	100
South Carolina	2.0	1.0	3.0	239.0	100
South Dakota	7.0	1.0	8.0	2,697.0	100
Tennessee	4.0	1.0	5.0	629.0	100
Texas	27.0	1.0	28.0	12,824.0	100
Utah	13.0	1.0	14.0	2,308.0	100
Vermont	14.0	2.0	16.0	2,664.0	100
Virginia	8.0	2.0	10.0	1,625.0	100
Washington	17.0	1.0	18.0	6,718.0	100
West Virginia	1.0	1.0	2.0	109.0	100
Wisconsin	245.0	14.0	259.0	30,320.0	99
Wyoming	1.3	0.2	1.5	140.7	100
United States	929.0	89.0	1,018.0	216,556.0	99

- Represents zero. [1] May not add due to rounding. [2] Excludes milk sucked by calves. [3] Milk sold to plants and dealers as whole milk and equivalent amounts of milk for cream. Includes milk produced by dealers' own herds and milk sold directly to consumers. Also includes milk produced by institutional herds. [4] Percentage of milk sold that is eligible for fluid use (Grade A in most States). Includes fluid grade milk used in manufacturing dairy products.
NASS, Livestock Branch, (202) 720–3570.

Table 8-7.—Milk and cream: Marketings and income, by State and United States, 2017 [1]

State	Milk utilized	All milk Average returns per cwt [2]	Returns per lb milkfat	Cash receipts from marketings
	Million pounds	Dollars	Dollars	1,000 dollars
Alabama	89.0	18.60	4.82	16,554
Alaska	2.5	22.00	5.61	550
Arizona	5,019.0	16.70	4.61	838,173
Arkansas	78.0	18.70	5.03	14,586
California	39,768.0	16.50	4.29	6,561,720
Colorado	4,167.0	18.10	4.91	754,227
Connecticut	417.0	18.60	4.72	77,562
Delaware	91.8	17.60	4.56	16,157
Florida	2,490.0	21.50	5.83	535,350
Georgia	1,832.0	19.00	5.23	348,080
Hawaii	38.7	28.60	8.64	11,068
Idaho	14,601.0	17.20	4.40	2,511,372
Illinois	1,917.0	18.30	4.77	350,811
Indiana	4,228.0	17.70	4.73	748,356
Iowa	5,163.0	18.10	4.68	934,503
Kansas	3,485.0	16.90	4.49	588,965
Kentucky	1,035.0	18.90	5.03	195,615
Louisiana	158.0	18.70	4.82	29,546
Maine	626.0	19.50	5.06	122,070
Maryland	948.0	17.80	4.66	168,744
Massachusetts ..	209.0	18.80	4.76	39,292
Michigan	11,196.0	16.40	4.41	1,836,144
Minnesota	9,768.0	17.80	4.58	1,738,704
Mississippi	135.0	18.90	4.92	25,515
Missouri	1,220.0	18.70	4.76	228,140
Montana	283.0	17.50	4.67	49,525
Nebraska	1,438.0	18.20	4.74	261,716
Nevada	703.0	17.90	4.58	125,837
New Hampshire	271.0	18.50	4.76	50,135
New Jersey	117.0	18.30	4.79	21,411
New Mexico	8,167.0	16.30	4.48	1,331,221
New York	14,872.0	18.20	4.73	2,706,704
North Carolina ..	946.0	18.80	5.01	177,848
North Dakota	340.0	17.60	4.60	59,840
Ohio	5,590.0	18.40	4.77	1,028,560
Oklahoma	721.0	19.20	5.11	138,432
Oregon	2,508.0	19.80	4.95	496,584
Pennsylvania	10,818.0	18.60	4.86	2,012,148
Rhode Island	12.9	18.50	4.67	2,387
South Carolina ..	245.0	19.10	4.96	46,795
South Dakota	2,610.0	18.80	4.61	490,680
Tennessee	688.0	18.90	5.03	130,032
Texas	12,028.0	18.40	4.55	2,213,152
Utah	2,202.0	17.70	4.66	389,754
Vermont	2,713.0	18.60	4.81	504,618
Virginia	1,726.0	19.40	5.17	334,844
Washington	6,513.0	18.20	4.55	1,185,366
West Virginia	124.0	18.00	4.75	22,320
Wisconsin	30,080.0	18.10	4.74	5,444,480
Wyoming	136.7	17.90	4.92	24,469
United States	214,535.0	17.69	4.61	37,940,662

[1] May not add due to rounding.   [2] Cash receipts divided by milk or milkfat in combined marketings.
NASS, Livestock Branch, (202) 720–3570.

Table 8-8.—Milk and cream: Marketings and income, by State and United States, 2018 [1]

State	Milk utilized	All milk Average returns per cwt [2]	Returns per lb milkfat	Cash receipts from marketings
	Million pounds	*Dollars*	*Dollars*	*1,000 dollars*
Alabama	72.0	16.60	4.28	11,952
Alaska	2.3	22.00	5.60	506
Arizona	4,963.0	15.50	4.23	769,265
Arkansas	72.0	17.00	4.49	12,240
California	40,383.0	15.78	4.05	6,372,437
Colorado	4,535.0	16.70	4.47	757,345
Connecticut	424.0	17.10	4.32	72,504
Delaware	90.5	16.10	4.19	14,571
Florida	2,375.0	19.90	5.41	472,625
Georgia	1,758.0	17.10	4.70	300,618
Hawaii	33.8	28.00	8.09	9,464
Idaho	15,115.0	15.70	3.96	2,373,055
Illinois	1,866.0	16.50	4.24	307,890
Indiana	4,134.0	15.70	4.15	649,038
Iowa	5,251.0	16.50	4.19	866,415
Kansas	3,693.0	15.30	3.96	565,029
Kentucky	1,002.0	17.50	4.62	175,350
Louisiana	149.0	17.20	4.26	25,628
Maine	614.0	18.10	4.68	111,134
Maryland	917.0	16.20	4.24	148,554
Massachusetts ..	200.0	17.40	4.37	34,800
Michigan	11,132.0	14.90	3.90	1,658,668
Minnesota	9,769.0	16.50	4.15	1,611,885
Mississippi	127.0	17.10	4.23	21,717
Missouri	1,173.0	16.90	4.25	198,237
Montana	270.0	16.00	4.21	43,200
Nebraska	1,433.0	16.20	4.20	232,146
Nevada	728.0	16.40	4.15	119,392
New Hampshire ..	247.0	17.00	4.35	41,990
New Jersey	108.0	16.20	4.26	17,496
New Mexico	8,222.0	14.70	3.97	1,208,634
New York	14,825.0	16.70	4.33	2,475,775
North Carolina ..	931.0	17.30	4.59	161,063
North Dakota	330.0	16.20	4.12	53,460
Ohio	5,503.0	16.40	4.22	902,492
Oklahoma	718.0	17.80	4.66	127,804
Oregon	2,510.0	18.70	4.61	469,370
Pennsylvania	10,595.0	16.80	4.41	1,779,960
Rhode Island	11.6	17.20	4.27	1,995
South Carolina ..	239.0	17.40	4.52	41,586
South Dakota	2,697.0	17.30	4.15	466,581
Tennessee	629.0	17.40	4.59	109,446
Texas	12,824.0	16.90	4.11	2,167,256
Utah	2,308.0	16.10	4.16	371,588
Vermont	2,664.0	17.10	4.38	455,544
Virginia	1,625.0	17.50	4.63	284,375
Washington	6,718.0	16.80	4.14	1,128,624
West Virginia	109.0	16.40	4.29	17,876
Wisconsin	30,320.0	16.50	4.24	5,002,800
Wyoming	140.7	16.30	4.48	22,934
United States	216,556.0	16.28	4.19	35,244,314

[1] May not add due to rounding.   [2] Cash receipts divided by milk or milkfat in combined marketings.
NASS, Livestock Branch, (202) 720–3570.

Table 8-9.—Milk production: Value, by State and United States, 2018 [1]

State	Used for milk, cream, & butter by producers		Gross producer income [3]	Value of milk produced [2][4]
	Milk utilized	Value [2]		
	Million pounds	1,000 dollars	1,000 dollars	1,000 dollars
Alabama	0.3	56	16,610	16,740
Alaska	0.2	44	594	638
Arizona	1.0	167	838,340	840,511
Arkansas	0.3	56	14,642	14,960
California	4.0	660	6,562,380	6,566,670
Colorado	1.0	181	754,408	758,209
Connecticut	0.5	93	77,655	78,120
Delaware	0.1	18	16,175	16,333
Florida	1.0	215	535,565	536,640
Georgia	1.0	190	348,270	349,600
Hawaii	0.1	29	11,097	11,125
Idaho	1.0	172	2,511,544	2,516,876
Illinois	2.0	366	351,177	353,007
Indiana	4.0	708	749,064	753,135
Iowa	1.0	181	934,684	937,399
Kansas	1.0	169	589,134	591,331
Kentucky	1.0	189	195,804	196,938
Louisiana	1.0	187	29,733	30,107
Maine	1.0	195	122,265	122,850
Maryland	1.0	178	168,922	170,168
Massachusetts	0.5	94	39,386	39,668
Michigan	2.0	328	1,836,472	1,841,884
Minnesota	4.0	712	1,739,416	1,756,326
Mississippi	1.0	189	25,704	25,893
Missouri	4.0	748	228,888	232,067
Montana	2.0	350	49,875	50,400
Nebraska	0.5	91	261,807	262,808
Nevada	1.0	179	126,016	126,911
New Hampshire	0.5	93	50,228	50,505
New Jersey	0.5	92	21,503	21,777
New Mexico	3.0	489	1,331,710	1,338,556
New York	2.0	364	2,707,068	2,717,078
North Carolina	1.0	188	178,036	178,976
North Dakota	0.5	88	59,928	60,720
Ohio	5.0	920	1,029,480	1,033,896
Oklahoma	1.0	192	138,624	139,776
Oregon	1.0	198	496,782	500,742
Pennsylvania	14.0	2,604	2,014,752	2,026,098
Rhode Island	-	-	2,387	2,405
South Carolina	1.0	191	46,986	47,368
South Dakota	1.0	188	490,868	492,184
Tennessee	1.0	189	130,221	130,977
Texas	1.0	184	2,213,336	2,217,936
Utah	1.0	177	389,931	392,055
Vermont	2.0	372	504,990	507,594
Virginia	2.0	388	335,232	336,784
Washington	1.0	182	1,185,548	1,188,642
West Virginia	1.0	180	22,500	22,860
Wisconsin	14.0	2,534	5,447,014	5,490,273
Wyoming	0.2	36	24,505	24,738
United States	91.0	16,594	37,957,256	38,119,254

- Represents zero.   [1] May not add due to rounding.   [2] Value at average returns per 100 pounds of milk in combined marketings of milk and cream.   [3] Cash receipts from marketings of milk and cream plus value of milk used for home consumption.   [4] Includes value of milk fed to calves.

NASS, Livestock Branch, (202) 720–3570.

Table 8-10.—Milk production: Value, by State and United States, 2019 [1]

State	Used for milk, cream, & butter by producers		Gross producer income [3]	Value of milk produced [2] [4]
	Milk utilized	Value [2]		
	Million pounds	1,000 Dollars	1,000 Dollars	1,000 Dollars
Alabama	0.3	50	12,002	12,118
Alaska	0.3	66	572	616
Arizona	1.0	155	769,420	771,590
Arkansas	0.3	51	12,291	12,580
California	4.0	631	6,373,068	6,377,171
Colorado	1.0	167	757,512	761,019
Connecticut	0.5	86	72,590	73,017
Delaware	0.1	16	14,587	14,732
Florida	1.0	199	472,824	473,819
Georgia	1.0	171	300,789	301,986
Hawaii	0.1	28	9,492	9,520
Idaho	1.0	157	2,373,212	2,378,393
Illinois	2.0	330	308,220	309,870
Indiana	4.0	628	649,666	653,277
Iowa	1.0	165	866,580	869,220
Kansas	1.0	153	565,182	567,324
Kentucky	1.0	175	175,525	176,575
Louisiana	1.0	172	25,800	26,144
Maine	1.0	181	111,315	111,858
Maryland	1.0	162	148,716	149,850
Massachusetts	0.5	87	34,887	35,148
Michigan	2.0	298	1,658,966	1,664,032
Minnesota	4.0	660	1,612,545	1,628,220
Mississippi	1.0	171	21,888	22,059
Missouri	4.0	676	198,913	201,786
Montana	2.0	320	43,520	43,840
Nebraska	0.5	81	232,227	233,280
Nevada	1.0	164	119,556	120,376
New Hampshire	0.5	85	42,075	42,330
New Jersey	0.5	81	17,577	17,820
New Mexico	3.0	441	1,209,075	1,217,895
New York	2.0	334	2,476,109	2,485,294
North Carolina	1.0	173	161,236	162,101
North Dakota	0.5	81	53,541	54,108
Ohio	5.0	820	903,312	907,248
Oklahoma	1.0	178	127,982	129,050
Oregon	1.0	187	469,557	473,297
Pennsylvania	12.0	2,016	1,781,976	1,791,720
Rhode Island	-	-	1,995	2,012
South Carolina	1.0	174	41,760	42,108
South Dakota	1.0	173	466,754	467,965
Tennessee	1.0	174	109,620	110,316
Texas	1.0	169	2,167,425	2,171,988
Utah	1.0	161	371,749	373,842
Vermont	2.0	342	455,886	458,280
Virginia	2.0	350	284,725	286,125
Washington	1.0	168	1,128,792	1,131,648
West Virginia	1.0	164	18,040	18,204
Wisconsin	14.0	2,310	5,005,110	5,045,535
Wyoming	0.2	33	22,967	23,179
United States	89.0	14,814	35,259,128	35,411,485

- Represents zero.   [1] May not add due to rounding.   [2] Value at average returns per 100 pounds of milk in combined marketings of milk and cream.   [3] Cash receipts from marketings of milk and cream plus value of milk used for home consumption.   [4] Includes value of milk fed to calves.
NASS, Livestock Branch, (202) 720–3570.

Table 8-11.—Milk cows, milk, and fat in cream: Average prices received by farmers, United States, 2010–2019

Year	Milk cows, per head [1]	Milk per 100 pounds [2]					
		Eligible for fluid market [3]		Of manufacturing grade		All milk wholesale	
		Price per 100 lb.	Fat test	Price per 100 lb.	Fat test	Price per 100 lb.	Fat test
	Dollars	Dollars	Percent	Dollars	Percent	Dollars	Percent
2010	1,330.00	16.37	3.65	14.56	4.00	16.35	3.66
2011	1,420.00	(NA)	(NA)	(NA)	(NA)	20.24	3.71
2012	1,430.00	(NA)	(NA)	(NA)	(NA)	18.56	3.72
2013	1,380.00	(NA)	(NA)	(NA)	(NA)	20.11	3.76
2014	1,830.00	(NA)	(NA)	(NA)	(NA)	24.07	3.74
2015	1,990.00	(NA)	(NA)	(NA)	(NA)	17.21	3.75
2016	1,760.00	(NA)	(NA)	(NA)	(NA)	16.34	3.79
2017	1,620.00	(NA)	(NA)	(NA)	(NA)	17.69	3.84
2018	1,360.00	(NA)	(NA)	(NA)	(NA)	16.28	3.89
2019	1,390.00	12.94	3.67	12.03	4.00	12.93	3.67

(NA) Not available.   [1] Simple average of quarterly prices, by States, weighted by the number of milk cows on farms Jan. 1 of the current year.   [2] Average price at average fat test for all milk sold at wholesale to plants and dealers, based on reports from milk-market administrators, cooperative milk-market associations, whole-milk distributors, and milk-products manufacturing plants, f.o.b. plant or receiving station (whichever is the customary place for determining prices) before hauling costs are deducted and including all premiums.   [3] Includes fluid milk surplus diverted to manufacturing.
NASS, Livestock Branch, (202) 720–3570.

Table 8-12—Milk-feed price ratios: All milk price; Dairy feed price, 16% protein; Milk-feed price ratios, United States, annual 2010–2019

Year	All milk price	Dairy feed price 16% protein [1]	Milk-feed price ratio [2]
	Dollars/cwt	Dollars/ton	Pounds
2010	16.35	274	2.26
2011	20.24	369	1.90
2012	18.56	442	1.52
2013	20.11	481	1.75
2014	24.07	502	2.54
2015	17.21	(NA)	2.14
2016	16.34	(NA)	2.26
2017	17.69	(NA)	2.42
2018	16.28	(NA)	2.05
2019	12.93	293	1.78

[1] Commercially prepared 16%protein dairy ration price collected from March annual Prices Paid Survey.   Discontinued beginning 2015.   [2] Annual ratios based on average of monthly ratios.   Pounds of 16% protein mixed dairy feed equal in value to one pound of whole milk.   Feed price component (16% protein) calculated using U.S. price received for corn (51 lbs), soybeans (8 lb), and alfalfa hay (41 lbs).
NASS, Environmental, Economics, and Demographics Branch, (202) 720–6146.

Table 8-13.—Fluid beverage milk: Total and per capita consumption, United States, 2010–2019

Year	Consumption [1]	
	Total	Per capita
	Million pounds	Pounds
2010	54,981	178
2011	54,040	173
2012	53,183	169
2013	52,026	165
2014	50,461	159
2015	49,741	155
2016	49,444	153
2017	48,360	149
2018	47,340	145
2019	46,511	142

[1] Includes estimated fluid milk sales plus farm home consumption.
ERS, Animal Products and Cost of Production Branch, (202) 694–5171.

Table 8-14.—Federal milk order markets [1]: Measures of growth, 2013–2019 [2]

Year	Population of Federal milk marketing areas	Number of handlers [3]	Number of producers [4]	Receipts of producer milk	Producer milk used in Class I	Percentage of producer milk used in Class I
	Thousands	*Number*	*Number*	*Million pounds*	*Million pounds*	*Percent*
2013	251,201	225	40,043	132,100	42,742	32.4
2014	255,184	223	39,146	129,420	41,420	32.0
2015	256,526	214	36,112	126,126	41,206	32.7
2016	258,172	216	34,689	133,846	41,140	30.7
2017	262,240	217	32,981	135,502	40,642	30.0
2018	302,089	233	32,061	141,684	40,945	28.9
2019	303,067	230	29,474	156,510	43,882	28.0

Year	Prices at 3.5 percent butterfat content per hundredweight [5]		Receipts as percentage of milk sold to plants and dealers		Daily deliveries of milk per producer	Gross value of receipts of producer milk [6]	
	Class I	Blend	Fluid grade	All milk		Per producer	All producer
	Dollars	*Dollars*	*Percent*	*Percent*	*Pounds*	*Dollars*	*1,000 dollars*
2013	21.80	19.44	67	66	9,039	641,295	25,682,588
2014	26.14	23.54	63	63	9,074	793,728	30,472,016
2015	19.21	16.70	61	61	9,559	583,173	21,063,042
2016	17.70	15.38	64	64	10,557	593,364	20,585,571
2017	19.31	16.96	64	63	11,244	696,651	22,981,139
2018	17.70	15.51	66	65	12,449	685,389	21,974,258
2019	19.74	17.35	33	72	14,507	921,305	27,154,539

[1] The California Federal Milk Marketing Order became effective on November 1, 2018. [2] Over this period, handler selected periodically not to pool substantial volumes of milk that normally would have been pooled under Federal orders. This decision resulted from disadvantageous blend/class price relationships and qualification circumstances. This fact should be kept in mind if year-to-year comparisons are made using the various "producer deliveries" measures of growth. [3] End of year. [4] Average for year. [5] Prices are weighted averages. [6] Based on blend (uniform) price adjusted for butterfat content, and in later years, other milk components of producer milk.
AMS, Dairy Programs, (202) 720–7461.

Table 8-15.—Milk production: Marketings, income and value, United States, 2010–2019

Year	Combined marketings of milk and cream				Used for milk, cream, and butter on farms where produced		Gross farm income from dairy products [3]	Farm value of all milk produced [2] [4]
	Milk utilized	Average returns [1]		Cash receipts from marketings	Milk utilized	Value [2]		
		Per 100 pounds milk	Per pound milkfat					
	Million pounds	*Dollars*	*Dollars*	*1,000 dollars*	*Million pounds*	*1,000 dollars*	*1,000 dollars*	*1,000 dollars*
2010	191,897	16.35	4.47	31,372,346	107	18,269	31,390,615	31,535,575
2011	195,290	20.24	5.46	39,531,306	98	20,561	39,551,867	39,730,346
2012	199,687	18.56	4.99	37,064,731	98	18,779	37,083,510	37,247,542
2013	200,283	20.11	5.35	40,282,881	100	20,629	40,303,510	40,482,699
2014	205,083	24.07	6.44	49,351,199	92	22,699	49,373,898	49,588,283
2015	207,536	17.21	4.59	35,716,849	91	16,291	35,733,140	35,888,595
2016	211,457	16.34	4.31	34,546,316	94	15,784	34,562,100	34,712,099
2017	214,535	17.69	4.61	37,940,662	91	16,594	37,957,256	38,119,254
2018	216,556	16.28	4.19	35,244,314	89	14,814	35,259,128	35,411,485
2019	188,189	12.93	3.52	24,321,032	112	15,224	24,336,256	24,455,900

[1] Cash receipts divided by milk or milkfat represented in combined marketings. [2] Valued at average returns per 100 pounds of milk in combined marketings of milk and cream. [3] Cash receipts from marketings of milk and cream plus value of milk used for home consumption. [4] Includes value of milk fed to calves.
NASS, Livestock Branch, (202) 720–3570.

Table 8-16.—Official Dairy Herd Information test plans: Numbers of herds and cows and milk, fat, and protein production, United States, 2010–2019

Year	Herds	Cows	Cows per herd	Average production			Cows with protein information	Average protein production	Average protein production
				Milk	Fat	Fat			
	Number	Number	Number	Pounds	Percent	Pounds	Percent	Percent	Pounds
2010 ...	15,067	3,746,177	248.6	22,765	3.66	836	98	3.09	706
2011 ...	14,490	3,800,410	262.3	22,961	3.71	855	98	3.11	714
2012 ...	13,894	3,762,925	270.8	23,328	3.72	871	98	3.12	728
2013 ...	13,329	3,712,080	278.5	23,695	3.77	894	98	3.13	742
2014 ...	13,043	3,829,273	293.6	24,101	3.76	907	98	3.14	757
2015 ...	12,440	3,822,370	307.3	24,403	3.75	917	98	3.13	764
2016 ...	11,745	3,836,074	326.6	24,651	3.79	934	98	3.13	773
2017 ...	10,932	3,809,695	348.5	24,776	3.84	951	99	3.16	783
2018 ...	9,787	3,715,872	379.7	24,660	3.87	956	99	3.16	781
2019 ...	8,710	3,636,877	417.6	24,787	3.91	970	100	3.18	789

Council on Dairy Cattle Breeding, (240) 334–4164, https://www.uscdcb.com.

Table 8-17.—Milk and milkfat production: Number of producing cows, production per cow, and total quantity produced, United States, 2010–2019

Year	Number of milk cows [1]	Production of milk and milkfat [2]				
		Per milk cow		Percentage of fat in all milk produced	Total	
		Milk	Milkfat		Milk	Milkfat
	Thousands	Pounds	Pounds	Percent	Million pounds	Million pounds
2010	9,123	21,142	774	3.66	192,877	7,054
2011	9,199	21,334	791	3.71	196,255	7,284
2012	9,237	21,722	808	3.72	200,642	7,463
2013	9,224	21,819	820	3.76	201,260	7,558
2014	9,261	22,249	832	3.74	206,048	7,698
2015	9,320	22,372	839	3.75	208,508	7,810
2016	9,334	22,761	863	3.79	212,451	8,054
2017	9,406	22,914	880	3.84	215,527	8,272
2018	9,399	23,149	900	3.89	217,575	8,466
2019	9,202	20,561	755	3.67	189,202	6,944

[1] Average number during year, excluding heifers not yet fresh. [2] Excludes milk sucked by calves.
NASS, Livestock Branch, (202) 720–3570.

Table 8-18.—Milk: Quantities used and marketed by farmers, United States, 2010–2019

Year	Milk used on farms where produced			Milk marketed by producers	
	Fed to calves [1]	Consumed as fluid milk or cream	Total	Total [2]	Fluid grade [3]
	Million pounds	Million pounds	Million pounds	Million pounds	Percent
2010	873	107	980	191,897	98
2011	867	98	965	195,290	99
2012	858	98	956	199,687	99
2013	877	100	977	200,283	99
2014	874	92	966	205,083	99
2015	880	91	971	207,536	99
2016	900	94	994	211,457	99
2017	901	91	992	214,535	99
2018	929	89	1,018	216,556	99
2019	901	112	1,013	188,189	98

[1] Excludes milk sucked by calves. [2] Milk sold to plants and dealers as whole milk and equivalent amounts of milk for cream. Includes milk produced by dealers' own herds and small amounts sold directly to consumers. Also includes milk produced by institutional herds. [3] Percentage of milk sold that is eligible for fluid use (Grade A in most States). Includes fluid-grade milk used in manufacturing dairy products.
NASS, Livestock Branch, (202) 720–3570.

Table 8-19.—Milk markets under Federal order program: Whole milk and fat-reduced milk products sold for fluid consumption within defined marketing areas, 2017–2019 [1]

Federal milk order marketing area	Whole milk products [2]		Fat-reduced milk products [3]		Total fluid milk products	
	Quantity	Butterfat content	Quantity	Butterfat content	Quantity	Butterfat content
	Million pounds	Percent	Million pounds	Percent	Million pounds	Percent
2017						
Northeast	3,249	3.27	4,782	1.18	8,031	2.03
Appalachian	1,157	3.29	2,005	1.34	3,162	2.05
Florida	1,152	3.23	1,579	1.31	2,731	2.12
Southeast	1,692	3.30	2,651	1.33	4,343	2.10
Upper Midwest	698	3.29	2,864	1.23	3,562	1.64
Central	1,164	3.30	2,918	1.30	4,082	1.87
Mideast	1,468	3.30	3,787	1.35	5,255	1.89
Pacific Northwest	596	3.33	1,307	1.36	1,903	1.98
Southwest	1,735	3.32	2,650	1.33	4,385	2.12
Arizona	346	3.29	671	1.31	1,017	1.99
Combined areas	13,256	3.29	25,214	1.29	38,471	1.98
2018						
Northeast	3,306	3.28	4,539	1.21	7,846	2.08
Appalachian	1,206	3.29	1,960	1.36	3,166	2.10
Florida	1,161	3.19	1,515	1.36	2,676	2.15
Southeast	1,704	3.31	2,517	1.36	4,221	2.15
Upper Midwest	712	3.29	2,715	1.25	3,427	1.67
Central	1,197	3.30	2,773	1.34	3,970	1.93
Mideast	1,514	3.30	3,685	1.37	5,209	1.94
California [4]	334	3.38	556	1.44	890	2.17
Pacific Northwest	613	3.32	1,229	1.37	1,842	2.02
Southwest	1,775	3.28	2,528	1.35	4,303	2.15
Arizona	363	3.29	657	1.33	1,020	2.03
Combined areas	13,886	3.29	24,673	1.32	38,568	2.03
2019						
Northeast	3,313	3.28	4,070	1.22	7,382	2.15
Appalachian	1,220	3.30	1,785	1.37	3,005	2.16
Florida	1,170	3.24	1,392	1.37	2,562	2.22
Southeast	1,707	3.32	2,255	1.38	3,962	2.22
Upper Midwest	733	3.30	2,460	1.27	3,194	1.73
Central	1,215	3.26	2,499	1.36	3,714	1.98
Mideast	1,579	3.31	3,467	1.41	5,046	2.01
California [4]	2,001	3.44	3,067	1.42	5,069	2.22
Pacific Northwest	613	3.32	1,077	1.38	1,690	2.08
Southwest	1,787	3.30	2,392	1.36	4,179	2.19
Arizona	360	3.31	596	1.37	956	2.10
Combined areas	15,699	3.31	25,060	1.35	40,759	2.10

[1] In-area sales include total sales in each of the areas by handlers regulated under the respective order, by handlers regulated under other orders, by partially regulated handlers, by exempt handlers, and by producer-handlers. Sales routes of handlers may extend outside defined marketing areas; therefore, some handlers' in-area sales are partially estimated. [2] Plain, organic, flavored, and miscellaneous whole milk products, and eggnog. [3] Plain, fortified, organic, and flavored reduced fat milk (2%), low fat milk (1%), and fat-free milk (skim), and miscellaneous fat-reduced milk products, and buttermilk. [4] The California Federal Milk Order became effective November 1, 2018.

AMS, Dairy Programs, (202) 720–7461.

Table 8-20.—Milk markets under Federal order program: Uniform and Class I milk prices at 3.5 percent fat test, number of producers, producer milk receipts, producer milk used in Class I, Class I percentage, daily milk deliveries per producer, average fat test of producer milk receipts, by markets, 2017–2019

Federal milk order marketing area	Class I $ / cwt [1]	Uniform $ / cwt [1] [2]	Average number of producers	Receipts of producer milk	Producer milk used in Class I	Class I utilization	Daily milk deliveries per producer	Average fat test of producer milk
	Dollars	Dollars	Number	Million pounds	Million pounds	Percent	Pounds	Percent
				2017				
Northeast [3]	19.71	17.43	11,170	27,397	8,799	32.1	6,722	3.85
Appalachian [4]	19.87	18.79	1,990	5,801	4,002	69.0	8,002	3.76
Florida [5]	21.87	20.92	143	2,602	2,169	83.3	49,877	3.69
Southeast [6]	20.27	19.13	1,672	5,451	3,767	69.1	8,936	3.74
Upper Midwest [7] [8]	18.26	16.28	9,431	32,312	3,244	10.0	9,345	3.84
Central [8] [9]	18.46	16.35	2,565	15,879	4,839	30.5	16,967	3.82
Mideast [8] [10]	18.46	16.56	4,968	20,241	6,430	31.8	11,160	3.78
Pacific Northwest [8] [11]	18.36	16.18	467	7,661	1,891	24.7	44,854	3.99
Southwest [8] [12]	19.46	17.16	486	13,092	4,217	32.2	73,541	3.86
Arizona [13]	18.81	16.39	89	5,065	1,284	25.4	155,410	3.62
All markets combined	19.31	16.96	32,981	135,502	40,642	30.0	11,244	3.82
				2018				
Northeast [3]	18.10	16.09	10,574	27,109	8,701	32.1	7,026	3.86
Appalachian [4]	18.25	17.29	1,704	5,735	3,984	69.5	9,243	3.79
Florida [5]	20.24	19.37	143	2,565	2,144	83.6	49,152	3.68
Southeast [6]	18.64	17.71	1,672	5,204	3,705	71.2	8,541	3.80
Upper Midwest [7] [8]	16.63	14.75	8,883	33,323	2,990	9.0	10,263	3.92
Central [8] [9]	16.85	14.87	2,433	16,613	4,792	28.8	18,722	3.89
Mideast [8] [10]	16.86	15.21	4,513	19,603	6,374	32.5	11,905	3.84
California [11]	17.39	15.18	1,081	4,117	927	22.5	62,481	4.01
Pacific Northwest [12]	16.76	14.86	495	8,558	1,851	21.6	47,288	4.07
Southwest [8] [13]	17.86	15.77	482	13,727	4,221	30.8	77,613	3.94
Arizona [14]	17.19	15.09	81	5,133	1,265	24.6	173,295	3.66
All markets combined	17.70	15.51	32,061	141,687	40,954	28.9	12,449	3.88
				2019				
Northeast [3]	20.23	18.11	9,760	26,752	8,283	31.0	7,510	3.89
Appalachian [4]	20.38	19.38	1,552	5,327	3,746	70.3	9,414	3.80
Florida [5]	22.35	21.39	125	2,510	2,091	83.3	55,174	3.66
Southeast [6]	20.76	19.75	1,540	4,903	3,438	70.1	8,733	3.80
Upper Midwest [7] [8]	18.79	16.70	7,981	32,310	2,720	8.4	10,961	3.93
Central [8] [9]	18.96	16.70	2,370	15,260	4,605	30.2	17,595	3.92
Mideast [8] [10]	18.99	17.20	4,164	18,942	6,560	34.6	12,456	3.86
California [11]	19.08	16.79	993	24,272	5,321	21.9	66,953	3.86
Pacific Northwest [12]	18.88	16.74	458	8,496	1,728	20.3	50,847	4.08
Southwest [8] [13]	19.97	17.40	457	12,900	4,147	32.2	77,184	3.99
Arizona [14]	19.35	17.23	74	4,840	1,241	25.6	177,338	3.74
All markets combined	19.74	17.35	29,474	156,510	43,882	28.0	14,507	3.90

[1] Prices are for milk of 3.5 percent butterfat content and for the principal pricing point of the market. See footnotes 3-13. [2] For those orders that use the component pricing system for paying producers (orders 1, 30, 32, 33, 124,and 126), the figures are the statistical uniform price (the sum of the producer price differential and the Class III price). For those orders that use the skim milk/butterfat pricing system for paying producers (orders 5, 6, 7, and 131), the figures are the uniform price (the sum of the uniform butterfat price times 3.5 and the uniform skim milk price times 0.965). [3] Suffolk Co. (Boston), MA. [4] Mecklenburg Co. (Charlotte), NC. [5] Hillsborough Co. (Tampa), FL. [5] Fulton Co. (Atlanta), GA. [7] Cook Co. (Chicago), IL. [8] Due to the disadvantageous intraorder class and uniform price relationships in some months in these markets, handlers elected not to pool milk that normally would have been pooled under these orders. [9] Jackson Co. (Kansas City), MO. [10] Cuyahoga Co. (Cleveland), OH. [11] The California Federal Milk Marketing Order became effective on November 1, 2018. [12] King Co. (Seattle), WA. [13] Dallas Co. (Dallas), TX. [14] Maricopa Co. (Phoenix), AZ.
AMS, Dairy Programs, (202) 720–7461.

Table 8-21.—Dairy products: Quantities manufactured, United States, 2014–2018

Product	2014	2015	2016	2017	2018
	1,000 pounds				
Butter	1,855,315	1,849,519	1,839,399	1,847,473	1,891,007
Cheese:					
American types	4,588,023	4,694,471	4,768,888	5,072,129	5,253,833
Cheddar	3,317,038	3,393,111	3,434,498	3,721,468	3,802,508
Other American	1,270,985	1,301,360	1,334,390	1,350,661	1,451,325
Blue and Gorgonzola	92,845	94,489	90,872	91,316	94,648
Brick	2,942	3,449	2,845	2,424	2,276
Cream and Neufchatel	851,713	876,286	908,972	918,071	914,824
Feta	105,622	112,424	126,849	122,470	129,823
Gouda	55,911	58,364	58,601	65,400	65,252
Hispanic	249,579	254,291	264,941	286,521	311,916
Italian types	4,950,235	5,081,826	5,304,355	5,395,248	5,556,850
Mozzarella	3,924,925	3,988,936	4,117,746	4,167,492	4,351,361
Parmesan	301,848	339,003	407,319	450,640	424,491
Provolone	361,088	379,316	401,589	393,792	397,786
Ricotta	245,284	243,464	252,231	245,912	249,461
Romano	45,021	55,034	52,448	58,302	58,058
Other Italian types	72,069	76,073	73,022	79,110	75,693
Muenster cheese	163,650	177,540	181,354	189,167	191,269
Swiss cheese	297,802	312,015	311,977	316,654	332,303
All other types	153,783	166,240	161,889	180,562	171,593
Total cheese [1]	11,512,105	11,831,395	12,181,543	12,639,962	13,024,587
Cottage cheese:					
Curd [2]	381,146	400,634	406,428	390,409	402,362
Creamed [3]	303,113	317,531	329,444	330,484	352,785
Lowfat [4]	364,614	363,004	367,815	344,421	342,084
Sour cream	1,302,900	1,325,629	1,374,059	1,387,149	1,403,411
Yogurt plain & flavored	4,756,562	4,645,594	4,458,399	4,478,204	4,388,088
Bulk condensed milk:					
Skim, sweetened	43,593	52,935	77,158	90,157	120,873
Skim, unsweetened	1,661,446	1,672,557	1,651,169	1,570,819	1,468,374
Whole, sweetened	88,607	99,867	116,563	142,602	144,659
Whole, unsweetened	65,596	173,701	97,204	62,259	66,023
Condensed or evaporated buttermilk	109,044	105,676	105,968	113,035	109,612
Canned milk:					
Evaporated and condensed whole [5] ...	315,290	452,780	456,695	379,193	412,599
Evaporated skim	27,856	43,940	16,897	9,156	15,144
Dry milk products:					
Dry buttermilk, total	111,097	98,364	109,641	112,904	118,075
Dry skim milk animal	11,303	9,953	9,287	11,862	14,071
Dry whole milk	103,122	108,522	98,174	122,397	143,654
Milk protein concentrate, total	126,017	157,309	125,685	139,047	145,632
Nonfat dry milk, human	1,764,632	1,822,348	1,752,634	1,835,277	1,773,540
Skim milk powder, total [6]	543,504	446,324	559,175	529,633	566,504
Dry whey, total	869,701	977,568	955,141	1,035,414	999,356
	1,000 gallons				
Ice cream, regular, total	865,753	896,688	906,680	871,157	840,028
Ice cream, lowfat, total [7]	411,701	438,991	435,868	461,414	451,103
Ice cream, nonfat, total	18,303	13,575	12,438	11,427	11,266
Sherbet, total	48,353	44,743	44,262	42,975	40,206
Frozen yogurt, total	66,456	74,229	66,814	62,911	50,277

[1] Excluding cottage cheese.　[2] Mostly used for processing into creamed or lowfat cottage cheese.　[3] Fat content 4 percent or more.　[4] Fat content less than 4 percent.　[5] Combined to avoid disclosing individual plant operations.　[6] Includes protein standardized and blends.　[7] Includes freezer-made milkshake.
NASS, Livestock Branch, (202) 720–3570.

Table 8-22.—Dairy Products: Factory production of specified items, by State and United States, 2017–2018

State	Butter		Total American cheese [1]		Total cheese [2]	
	2017	2018	2017	2018	2017	2018
	1,000 pounds	1,000 pounds	1,000 pounds	1,000 pounds	1,000 pounds	1,000 pounds
California	534,378	578,624	632,677	630,164	2,513,336	2,543,368
Idaho			605,555	625,427	958,687	991,239
Illinois					82,389	82,288
Iowa			155,111	182,094	256,737	296,396
Minnesota			589,516	622,884	712,988	740,601
New Jersey					57,727	59,087
New Mexico					766,804	895,779
New York	27,581	24,688	132,273	139,560	829,410	802,331
Ohio					222,044	239,267
Oregon			205,733	208,767	206,679	209,829
Pennsylvania	92,329	86,062			411,552	433,750
South Dakota					282,304	293,455
Vermont					142,941	146,953
Wisconsin			1,016,702	1,025,766	3,376,769	3,422,895
Other States [3]	1,193,185	1,201,633	1,734,562	1,819,161	1,819,595	1,867,349
United States	1,847,473	1,891,007	5,072,129	5,253,833	12,639,962	13,024,587

State	Ice cream, regular (hard)		Nonfat dry milk for human food	
	2017	2018	2017	2018
	1,000 Gallons	1,000 Gallons	1,000 Pounds	1,000 Pounds
California	73,643	66,328	562,017	587,059
Connecticut	12,206	12,614		
Missouri	32,404	37,350		
New Jersey	1,390	1,183		
New York	38,422	29,547		
Ohio	26,122	27,984		
Oregon	12,104	14,380		
Pennsylvania	41,064	37,595	183,766	181,158
Tennessee	25,711	22,704		
Utah	26,283	29,667		
Wisconsin	19,211	9,798		
Other States [3]	422,602	429,382	1,089,494	1,005,323
United States	731,162	718,532	1,835,277	1,773,540

[1] Includes Cheddar, Colby, washed curd, stirred curd, Monterey, and Jack.   [2] Excluding cottage cheese.   [3] States not shown when fewer than 3 plants reported or individual plant operations could be disclosed.
NASS, Livestock Branch, (202) 720–3570.

Table 8-23.—Dairy products: Average price per pound for specified products, 2016–2020

Item and market	2016	2017	2018	2019	2020
	Dollars	Dollars	Dollars	Dollars	Dollars
Butter, Chicago Mercantile Exchange, Grade AA:					
High [1]	2.3675	2.7375	2.4175	2.4350	2.0150
Low [1]	1.7550	2.0625	2.0675	1.9150	1.1000
Butter, Agricultural Marketing Service, Grade AA: [2]	2.0777	2.3303	2.2572	2.2431	1.5808
Cheese, Cheddar, Chicago Mercantile Exchange, Barrels:					
High [1]	1.8800	1.7600	1.6675	2.3900	2.5300
Low [1]	1.2700	1.3375	1.2345	1.1600	1.0000
Cheese, Cheddar, Chicago Mercantile Exchange, 40-lb blocks:					
High [1]	1.9425	1.8500	1.6905	2.2375	3.0000
Low [1]	1.2700	1.3600	1.3540	1.3700	1.0000
Cheese, Cheddar, Agricultural Marketing Service, Barrels: [3]	1.5961	1.5860	1.4659	1.7038	1.7745
Cheese, Cheddar, Agricultural Marketing Service, 40-lb blocks: [3]	1.5897	1.6513	1.5825	1.7826	2.0442
Nonfat dry milk, Agricultural Marketing Service:					
Low/medium heat [2]	0.8292	0.8666	0.7945	1.0419	1.0417
Dry whey, Agricultural Marketing Service:					
Edible nonhygroscopic [2]	0.2875	0.4437	0.3422	0.3799	0.3621

[1] Figures are the high and low prices for any trading day during the year.   [2] Simple average of the product prices from the Class and Component Prices Announcement.   [3] Simple average of the block and barrel prices used in the calculation of the cheese price on the Class and Component Prices Announcement. Historical data are available at: https://www.ams.usda.gov/rules-regulations/mmr/dmr.
AMS, Dairy Programs, (202) 720–4392.

Table 8-24.—Dairy products: Total disappearance, and total and per capita consumption, United States, 2010–2019 [1]

Year	Cheese [2]		
	Total disappearance	Consumption	
		Total	Per capita
	Million pounds	Million pounds	Pounds
2010	10,605	10,136	32.7
2011	10,893	10,300	33.0
2012	11,123	10,461	33.3
2013	11,364	10,580	33.4
2014	11,784	10,887	34.2
2015	12,049	11,268	35.1
2016	12,492	11,776	36.4
2017	12,861	12,018	37.0
2018	13,278	12,420	38.0
2019	13,468	12,589	38.3

Year	Butter			Ice cream (product weight)		
	Total disappearance	Consumption		Total disappearance	Consumption	
		Total	Per capita		Total	Per capita
	Million pounds	Million pounds	Pounds	Million pounds	Million pounds	Pounds
2010	1,623	1,521	4.9	6,399	6,329	20.4
2011	1,795	1,676	5.4	6,213	6,131	19.7
2012	1,829	1,730	5.5	6,438	6,335	20.2
2013	1,915	1,732	5.5	6,172	6,038	19.1
2014	1,887	1,753	5.5	6,094	5,951	18.7
2015	1,841	1,800	5.6	6,347	6,216	19.4
2016	1,881	1,843	5.7	6,376	6,248	19.3
2017	1,903	1,853	5.7	6,324	6,185	19.0
2018	2,037	1,975	6.0	6,235	6,079	18.6
2019	2,068	2,024	6.2	6,287	6,136	18.7

Year	Condensed and evaporated whole milk [3]			Dry skim milk products [4]		
	Total disappearance	Consumption		Total disappearance	Consumption (human use)	
		Total	Per capita		Total	Per capita
	Million pounds	Million pounds	Pounds	Million pounds	Million pounds	Pounds
2010	718	610	2.0	1,874	1,003	3.2
2011	711	600	1.9	1,934	947	3.0
2012	715	629	2.0	2,141	1,141	3.6
2013	722	597	1.9	2,168	924	2.9
2014	537	451	1.4	2,221	1,002	3.1
2015	782	701	2.2	2,316	1,057	3.3
2016	741	662	2.0	2,301	966	3.0
2017	662	570	1.8	2,285	909	2.8
2018	706	624	1.9	2,384	780	2.4
2019	713	615	1.9	2,473	901	2.7

Year	Dry whey			Whey protein concentrate		
	Total disappearance	Consumption (human use)		Total disappearance	Consumption (human use)	
		Total	Per capita		Total	Per capita
	Million pounds	Million pounds	Pounds	Million pounds	Million pounds	Pounds
2010	1,009	432	1.4	448	154	0.5
2011	1,011	433	1.4	444	193	0.6
2012	986	479	1.5	478	198	0.6
2013	950	409	1.3	532	272	0.9
2014	867	357	1.1	583	356	1.1
2015	970	566	1.8	546	313	1.0
2016	962	526	1.6	553	235	0.7
2017	1,003	517	1.6	536	213	0.7
2018	1,027	530	1.6	602	270	0.8
2019	977	628	1.9	560	278	0.8

[1] Total disappearance is based on production, imports, and change in stocks during the year. Production statistics for these commodities appear in other tables in this chapter. The total apparent consumption was obtained by subtracting ending stocks, shipments total exports, and animal use (when applicable) from the total supply. Per capita consumption was obtained by dividing the total apparent consumption by the number of persons. [2] Includes all kinds of cheese except cottage cheese. [3] Includes both bulk and canned goods. [4] Total disappearance includes nonfat dry milk, skim milk powders, and dry skim milk for animal use.

ERS, Animal Products and Cost of Production Branch, (202) 694–5171.

Table 8-25.—Dairy products: December 31 stocks, United States, 2012–2019

Year	Butter [1]	Cheese [2]	Canned milk	Dry whole milk	Dry whey	Whey Protein Concentrate	Dry skim milk products [3]
				Million pounds			
2012	153	1,023	38	7	60	51	184
2013	112	1,009	37	8	63	50	137
2014	105	1,018	32	23	65	66	242
2015	155	1,146	43	11	73	73	206
2016	166	1,198	42	13	66	62	227
2017	169	1,280	37	31	98	85	322
2018	179	1,345	42	16	71	65	293
2019	190	1,322	36	12	71	67	260

[1] Includes anhydrous milkfat and butter oil. [2] Excludes cottage cheese. [3] Includes nonfat dry milk and dry skim milk for animal use.
ERS, Animal Products and Cost of Production Branch, (202) 694–5171.

Table 8-26.—Dairy products: Manufacturers' stocks, end of month, United States, 2018–2019 [1]

Month	Evaporated and condensed whole milk [2]		Dry whole milk		Nonfat dry milk, human	
	2018	2019	2018	2019	2018	2019
			1,000 pounds			
January	43,940	51,472	18,034	33,232	227,052	300,828
February	55,613	48,558	21,660	37,328	263,021	296,991
March	50,777	49,050	22,284	46,035	246,484	297,296
April	63,792	53,147	23,060	47,243	267,375	273,346
May	69,730	73,770	22,961	59,625	280,078	270,489
June	76,890	73,123	21,224	56,604	297,773	303,301
July	79,138	79,064	21,864	51,876	295,906	317,447
August	82,905	88,565	15,948	42,387	312,929	280,494
September	75,947	79,977	20,608	32,589	320,765	261,646
October	61,202	64,953	22,070	18,733	316,826	252,648
November	41,983	43,053	27,878	17,559	316,969	289,199
December	37,191	42,112	31,007	15,573	320,046	276,527

[1] Stocks held by manufacturers at all points and in transit. [2] Combined to avoid disclosing individual plant operations.
NASS, Livestock Branch, (202) 720–3570.

Table 8-27.—International dairy: Butter production, 2018–2020

Country	2018	2019	2020
	1,000 metric tons		
India	5,600	5,850	6,100
European Union	2,345	2,425	2,410
United States	858	861	885
New Zealand	530	530	525
Russia	256	254	255
Mexico	228	231	233
Canada	116	112	115
Belarus	115	110	105
China	99	102	104
Ukraine	106	103	90

FAS, Office of Global Analysis, (202) 720-6301. Prepared or estimated on the basis of official USDA production, supply, and distribution statistics from foreign governments.

Table 8-28.—International dairy: Cheese production, 2018–2020

Country	2018	2019	2020
	1,000 metric tons		
European Union	10,160	10,275	10,350
United States	5,908	5,950	6,100
Russia	970	970	970
Brazil	760	780	795
Canada	510	519	525
Argentina	444	439	455
Mexico	419	436	454
Australia	367	370	375
New Zealand	355	360	365
Belarus	275	300	325
China	272	281	287
Ukraine	192	195	197
Japan	45	45	46
Korea, South	37	40	43
Philippines	2	2	2

FAS, Office of Global Analysis, (202) 720-6301. Prepared or estimated on the basis of official USDA production, supply, and distribution statistics from foreign governments.

Table 8-29.—Dairy products: United States imports by country of origin, 2018–2020

Commodity and country of origin	2018	2019	2020
	Metric tons		
Licensed cheese items 1:			
Netherlands	6,493	6,905	8,563
United Kingdom	5,418	5,257	3,479
Ireland	2,366	3,061	2,592
Germany(*)	1,383	1,349	1,387
Australia(*)	1,711	1,815	1,374
New Zealand(*)	1,459	1,708	1,291
Denmark(*)	1,940	1,791	1,278
Canada	1,243	787	1,220
Jamaica	498	450	560
Italy(*)	408	395	339
France(*)	307	286	313
Bahrain	138	157	182
Dominican Republic	193	183	140
Finland	185	137	127
Poland	39	43	86
Belgium-Luxembourg(*)	1	13	76
Estonia	85	25	70
Chile	1	9	31
Lithuania	33	21	25
Spain	62	45	22
India	115	75	12
Jordan	22	0	11
Philippines	7	20	10
Portugal	3	2	4
Croatia	1	3	2
Egypt	1	0	1
Norway(*)	20	0	1
Mexico	0	3	1
Japan	1	1	1
Greece	9	12	0
Rest of World	0	1	0
World Total	24,140	24,554	23,196
Licensed cheese items 2:			
Italy(*)	20,164	21,367	17,396
France(*)	19,742	18,543	16,236
Switzerland(*)	9,130	8,733	9,409
Nicaragua	5,957	6,312	7,756
Netherlands	7,380	7,827	6,611
Canada	4,395	3,877	4,839
Ireland	4,155	4,886	4,629
Norway(*)	6,506	6,074	4,427
Denmark(*)	6,327	5,217	4,204
Lithuania	1,964	5,000	4,150
Mexico	3,386	3,308	3,850
Germany(*)	7,803	6,792	3,843
Argentina	461	2,145	3,158
Finland	2,804	2,368	2,306
United Kingdom	1,916	2,033	2,128
Poland	1,647	1,716	2,083
Spain	5,583	4,159	1,823
Austria	1,273	1,233	1,142
Uruguay	1,365	887	1,090
Greece	533	488	959
Egypt	741	643	929
India	171	379	880
Colombia	621	588	809
Turkey	522	540	747
Belgium-Luxembourg(*)	749	802	716
Australia(*)	412	282	563
El Salvador	465	571	485
Estonia	371	472	443
Brazil	252	321	378
New Zealand(*)	40	329	372
Rest of World	1,991	2,254	2,262
World Total	118,824	120,144	110,623

See footnote(s) at end of table.

Table 8-29.—Dairy products: United States imports by country of origin, 2018–2020—Continued

Commodity and country of origin	2018	2019	2020
	Metric tons		
Non-licensed cheese:			
Italy(*)	11,963	15,398	11,460
Spain	5,778	6,016	6,782
Greece	3,598	4,002	4,424
Bulgaria	2,802	2,558	2,934
France(*)	3,941	3,190	2,550
Cyprus	516	467	854
Israel(*)	584	617	695
Turkey	397	345	450
Norway(*)	383	364	392
Romania	301	366	313
United Kingdom	385	432	291
Germany(*)	4	8	203
Albania	0	81	176
Netherlands	160	211	168
Switzerland(*)	214	82	165
Mexico	0	180	104
Jordan	114	66	88
Egypt	77	14	77
El Salvador	357	90	72
Portugal	26	25	31
Kuwait	0	1	30
Armenia	15	23	21
North Macedonia	11	18	21
United Arab Emirates	0	0	14
Hungary	10	19	9
Pakistan	0	0	7
Georgia	34	23	6
Austria	6	6	3
Poland	1	1	2
Croatia	20	14	2
Rest of World	1,542	15	2
World Total	33,237	34,628	32,345
Casein:			
New Zealand(*)	23,161	22,933	22,049
Ireland	7,456	10,703	10,602
Netherlands	8,149	6,965	6,464
France(*)	4,306	5,339	5,786
Denmark(*)	3,701	3,293	4,119
Argentina	3,568	2,180	3,329
Poland	2,442	4,053	2,983
Australia(*)	0	1,466	1,070
Uganda	476	353	1,004
Germany(*)	1,482	1,700	976
India	2,249	2,136	671
Italy(*)	4	0	5
Belgium-Luxembourg(*)	54	15	0
Russia	0	0	0
Japan	0	-	0
Mexico	2	0	0
Sweden	0	0	0
Switzerland(*)	24	15	0
United Kingdom	19	0	0
Ukraine	0	20	0
World Total	57,092	61,172	59,059

See footnote(s) at end of table.

Table 8-29.—Dairy products: United States imports by country of origin, 2018–2020—Continued

Commodity and country of origin	2018	2019	2020
		Metric tons	
Non-licensed dairy, misc.:			
Canada	10,233	16,334	15,175
Chile	14,280	14,189	14,627
Mexico	8,541	6,071	9,714
France(*)	3,245	4,524	5,129
New Zealand(*)	5,677	4,981	3,230
Netherlands	965	1,505	2,077
Ukraine	431	448	1,377
Denmark(*)	2,104	2,046	1,225
Ireland	1,300	1,593	1,121
United Kingdom	244	1,120	1,051
Brazil	496	655	966
Germany(*)	973	1,069	368
Colombia	202	336	326
China	-	100	311
Iceland	145	316	310
Lithuania	48	73	288
Belgium-Luxembourg(*)	196	227	259
Norway(*)	1,238	1,929	238
Italy(*)	1,845	1,312	216
India	72	67	193
Peru	11,973	7,441	162
Israel(*)	215	318	114
Russia	95	137	105
Poland	112	75	99
Australia(*)	87	214	95
Singapore	0	0	75
Greece	80	50	59
Argentina	98	156	59
Malaysia	83	256	58
Bangladesh	12	10	41
Rest of World	223	123	183
World Total	65,209	67,672	59,250
Misc. Dairy Quota:			
Canada	186,218	197,831	173,423
New Zealand(*)	38,842	43,447	44,672
Mexico	20,338	21,313	24,481
Nicaragua	11,464	12,391	17,872
Italy(*)	13,437	14,023	17,155
Korea, South	10,029	11,432	12,243
Germany(*)	5,305	9,107	10,657
United Arab Emirates	1	0	7,143
France(*)	6,238	5,518	5,733
Ireland	5,262	5,374	5,380
Taiwan	946	1,182	5,208
Belgium-Luxembourg(*)	4,920	5,149	3,710
India	2,385	2,556	3,108
Russia	202	768	2,847
Austria	1,844	1,765	2,524
Thailand	3,082	2,772	2,309
South Africa	1,263	1,192	1,875
Australia(*)	2,740	1,368	1,515
Malaysia	1,129	1,126	1,258
Singapore	742	849	1,124
Israel(*)	831	775	1,104
Brazil	365	466	931
Japan	515	636	798
Netherlands	2,691	3,219	775
Hungary	2,094	552	719
Lithuania	590	503	586
Switzerland(*)	755	477	501
Uruguay	399	706	403
Spain	174	284	398
Turkey	161	226	397
Rest of World	11,459	11,410	5,747
World Total	336,420	358,414	356,597

See footnote(s) at end of table.

Table 8-29.—Dairy products: United States imports by country of origin, 2018–2020—Continued

Commodity and country of origin	2018	2019	2020
	Metric tons		
Licensed dairy, misc :			
Mexico	21,884	45,746	51,736
Canada	29,326	28,032	19,607
Netherlands	2,231	1,710	3,778
Chile	6,753	2,423	2,545
Ireland	2,690	940	1,802
New Zealand(*)	1,129	928	1,651
Denmark(*)	864	1,003	1,229
Germany(*)	2,127	3,636	783
Belgium-Luxembourg(*)	742	1,063	672
Honduras	351	477	624
Peru	306	461	386
Italy(*)	570	459	327
Korea, South	662	356	294
Colombia	174	193	284
India	452	64	244
Malaysia	0	102	235
Ecuador	12	0	218
Brazil	185	188	201
France(*)	426	⸱ 345	172
Singapore	33	76	143
Argentina	142	135	113
Australia(*)	270	754	105
United Arab Emirates	122	8	92
United Kingdom	46	19	52
Switzerland(*)	16	72	48
Venezuela	3	14	46
Costa Rica	71	32	43
Poland	11	30	39
Egypt	1	0	32
Yemen(*)	0	0	32
Rest of World	1,022	196	160
World Total	72,621	89,461	87,690
Lactose:			
Germany(*)	1,853	1,394	1,679
Canada	203	1,035	779
Netherlands	421	735	669
New Zealand(*)	127	177	44
China	24	11	17
Moldova	0	0	8
Belarus	3	5	2
Japan	1	1	1
Mexico	0	0	1
Denmark(*)	0	0	1
South Africa	1	0	1
Ireland	0	0	0
Argentina	5	0	0
Australia(*)	0	7	0
Belgium-Luxembourg(*)	3	0	0
Bosnia and Herzegovina	3	0	0
France(*)	45	0	0
India	0	80	0
Italy(*)	11	0	0
Lithuania	2	0	0
Singapore	3	0	0
Switzerland(*)	1	0	0
Ukraine	0	5	0
World Total	2,704	3,450	3,202

(*) Denotes a country that is a summarization of its component countries.   Note: All zeroes for a data item may show that statistics exist in the other import type.   Consumption or General.   Users should use cautious interpretation on quantity reports using mixed units of measure.   Quantity line items will only include statistics on the units of measure that are equal to, or are able to be converted to the assigned unit of measure of the grouped commodities.
FAS, (202) 720-6301.   Data Source: U.S. Census Bureau Trade Data.

Table 8-30.—Dairy products: United States exports by country of destination, 2018–2020

Commodity and country of destination	2018	2019	2020
	Metric tons		
Condensed & evap milk:			
Mexico	6,115	6,070	2,373
Canada	878	1,510	1,200
Cayman Islands	54	695	1,008
Dominican Republic	2,113	2,357	915
Bahamas, The	817	796	694
China	369	360	623
Korea, South	431	348	519
Panama	385	379	500
Nigeria	1	2	470
Belize	103	19	333
Sweden	241	42	315
Malaysia	201	92	252
Hong Kong	205	372	209
Bermuda	88	152	146
El Salvador	657	529	114
Venezuela	3	21	107
Guatemala	112	157	87
Netherlands Antilles(*)	228	231	82
Leeward-Windward Islands(*)	86	82	75
Taiwan	27	30	75
Netherlands	3	1	65
Trinidad and Tobago	370	584	60
Costa Rica	98	66	57
Jamaica	415	323	54
Marshall Islands	34	23	50
Honduras	117	93	49
Peru	173	182	47
Micronesia	16	28	45
Iceland	0	10	43
Philippines	120	109	35
Rest of World	2,509	1,409	270
World Total	16,967	17,070	10,867
Non-fat dry milk:			
Mexico	346,686	329,298	287,118
Philippines	85,353	70,649	116,213
Indonesia	55,684	67,283	98,683
Vietnam	35,506	54,209	52,529
Malaysia	31,252	25,292	41,082
Colombia	10,716	24,488	29,144
China	21,131	9,050	26,609
Egypt	2,278	5,575	19,959
Peru	14,068	14,211	16,147
Japan	7,729	6,313	10,589
Chile	11,042	12,019	10,562
Thailand	4,015	6,538	10,069
Pakistan	17,904	9,350	7,938
New Zealand(*)	7,998	6,119	7,718
Dominican Republic	5,503	6,007	7,512
Singapore	3,403	3,028	6,294
Honduras	8,310	3,644	5,121
Korea, South	8,640	6,287	5,071
Algeria	1,829	0	4,565
Bangladesh	2,218	3,456	4,173
Panama	1,878	2,947	3,880
Ghana	544	1,876	3,453
Saudi Arabia	1,053	1,246	3,236
Nicaragua	2,164	1,766	2,995
Canada	4,332	3,356	2,498
Sri Lanka	4,054	5,990	2,474
Guatemala	1,200	1,650	2,261
Afghanistan	877	3,118	2,227
Morocco	694	1,028	2,052
El Salvador	2,132	2,150	2,040
Rest of World	11,812	12,967	18,473
World Total	712,007	700,910	812,683

See footnote(s) at end of table.

Table 8-30.—Dairy products: United States exports by country of destination, 2018–2020—Continued

Commodity and country of destination	2018	2019	2020
	Liters		
Fluid milk and cream:			
Taiwan	37,675,729	46,792,302	52,785,045
Canada	22,869,422	32,444,553	38,631,146
Mexico	38,189,834	38,098,256	28,190,489
Bahamas, The	1,383,635	1,306,898	1,437,432
Dominican Republic	6,390,531	3,261,452	1,403,551
Singapore	421,368	564,736	1,241,415
Hong Kong	1,869,960	1,723,910	831,283
Philippines	365,236	757,494	732,268
Cayman Islands	417,979	768,693	567,168
Turks and Caicos Islands	650,111	742,323	543,789
China	193,365	361,527	432,391
Korea, South	553,294	574,535	324,831
Leeward-Windward Islands(*)	316,014	274,634	230,109
Panama	93,939	28,065	177,052
Bermuda	140,888	174,940	156,593
Thailand	83,312	395,479	139,292
Vietnam	910,394	302,312	111,811
Micronesia	124,384	136,819	108,179
Colombia	125,043	48,531	83,127
Algeria	0	0	76,000
Costa Rica	56,974	137,065	63,303
Guyana	0	770	53,724
Marshall Islands	23,616	38,227	46,216
Venezuela	2,860	0	40,865
Germany(*)	0	0	33,333
Netherlands Antilles(*)	21,056	83,664	29,211
Barbados	156,524	84,233	27,869
Peru	0	0	23,094
Jamaica	8,841	28,596	20,860
Belize	0	4,906	20,740
Rest of World	2,163,088	1,517,650	176,617
World Total	115,207,397	130,652,570	128,738,803
	Metric tons		
Whey:			
China	197,030	97,568	209,795
Mexico	64,424	67,401	44,635
Canada	30,833	29,315	34,716
Philippines	36,612	37,719	31,114
Indonesia	18,027	24,298	30,234
New Zealand(*)	20,559	30,326	28,861
Vietnam	21,568	14,802	24,071
Japan	30,450	22,248	21,447
Korea, South	14,512	14,808	12,940
Thailand	11,312	12,811	12,514
Malaysia	12,045	12,029	11,995
Singapore	7,835	10,164	8,692
Egypt	6,612	6,471	6,779
Australia(*)	4,182	6,419	5,585
Colombia	5,149	4,651	5,342
Taiwan	5,990	7,107	4,388
Chile	3,573	4,856	4,052
Algeria	0	292	3,558
Bangladesh	134	1,071	3,148
Guatemala	3,359	3,413	2,876
Costa Rica	1,435	1,638	2,442
El Salvador	2,758	2,222	2,336
Belgium-Luxembourg(*)	3,352	2,907	2,257
Peru	2,682	2,410	2,219
Dominican Republic	2,340	2,238	1,992
Brazil	359	742	1,928
Morocco	6,203	1,037	1,887
Nicaragua	1,630	1,342	1,488
Honduras	1,979	1,396	1,342
Pakistan	528	1,067	1,309
Rest of World	19,482	10,668	12,745
World Total	536,957	435,435	538,687

(*) Denotes a country that is a summarization of its component countries.   Note: Users should use cautious interpretation on quantity reports using mixed units of measure.   Quantity line items will only include statistics on the units of measure that are equal to, or are able to be converted to, the assigned unit of measure of the grouped commodities.
FAS, Office of Global Analysis, (202) 720-6301.   Data Source: U.S. Census Bureau Trade Data.

Table 8-31.—Chickens: Layers, pullets, and other chickens, by State and United States, December 1, 2018 and 2019

State	Total layers		Total pullets		Other Chickens	
	2018	2019	2018	2019	2018	2019
	Thousands	Thousands	Thousands	Thousands	Thousands	Thousands
Alabama	9,348	9,962	5,792	6,342	973	1,071
Arkansas	14,175	14,690	8,372	8,596	1,009	1,060
California	14,582	15,021	3,237	4,025	54	54
Colorado	4,635	5,141	1,254	1,124	36	55
Florida	7,383	7,352	2,087	1,618	20	25
Georgia	20,134	20,222	8,822	9,644	1,101	894
Illinois	5,635	6,476	433	365	22	19
Indiana	34,082	34,631	9,202	9,693	72	49
Iowa	56,337	58,188	13,243	14,313	107	78
Kentucky	5,644	5,942	2,541	2,418	214	216
Louisiana	2,014	2,078	735	637	75	99
Maryland	2,858	2,831	1,400	1,260	9	8
Massachusetts	140	154	9	30	-	-
Michigan	14,737	16,149	3,655	3,476	4	4
Minnesota	10,458	11,174	3,427	2,974	33	37
Mississippi	5,684	5,536	3,531	3,651	501	508
Missouri	10,509	12,537	4,527	5,600	191	199
Montana	942	1,000	244	236	-	-
Nebraska	7,670	8,453	1,814	1,711	52	28
New York	5,626	5,628	1,095	996	6	11
North Carolina	15,294	13,434	7,319	7,399	894	851
Ohio	35,542	32,967	8,395	10,632	51	1
Oklahoma	2,951	3,105	1,103	1,192	232	179
Oregon	2,404	2,279	553	725	-	-
Pennsylvania	29,391	28,758	4,737	5,161	165	182
South Carolina	4,055	4,263	1,399	1,334	156	125
South Dakota	2,682	2,665	882	777	-	-
Tennessee	1,872	1,658	915	1,019	170	147
Texas	22,549	22,747	6,559	6,533	404	349
Utah	5,036	4,713	1,178	1,139	-	-
Vermont	202	190	20	6	-	2
Virginia	2,675	2,735	1,011	1,283	151	165
Washington	6,770	6,772	1,721	1,339	-	-
West Virginia	1,251	1,207	770	632	99	93
Wisconsin	7,383	7,284	1,679	1,509	22	25
Other States [1]	18,156	18,928	3,512	4,746	36	34
United States	390,806	396,870	117,173	124,135	6,859	6,568

- Represents zero.   [1] Alaska, Arizona, Connecticut, Delaware, Hawaii, Idaho, Kansas, Maine, New Hampshire, New Jersey, New Mexico, Nevada, North Dakota, Rhode Island, and Wyoming combined to avoid disclosing individual operations.
NASS, Livestock Branch, (202) 720–3570.

Table 8-32.—Chickens: Inventory number and value, United States, Dec. 1, 2010–2019 [1]

Year	Total layers	Total pullets	Other chickens	All chickens	Value per head	Total value
	Thousands	Thousands	Thousands	Thousands	Dollars	1,000 dollars
2010	342,782	107,025	7,390	457,197	3.58	1,637,016
2011	343,283	104,159	6,922	454,364	3.79	1,721,671
2012	354,977	105,140	6,827	466,944	4.04	1,885,904
2013	367,356	108,919	6,853	483,128	4.15	2,007,374
2014	374,880	108,044	6,403	489,327	4.13	2,020,748
2015	356,312	120,007	7,211	483,530	4.38	2,115,982
2016	380,610	113,239	6,759	500,608	4.23	2,115,245
2017	390,806	117,173	6,859	514,838	4.20	2,162,545
2018	396,870	124,135	6,568	527,573	4.33	2,284,164
2019	342,058	104,069	8,487	454,614	3.32	1,510,038

[1] Excludes commercial broilers.
NASS Livestock Branch, (202) 720-3570.

Table 8-33.—Chicken inventory: Number, value per head, and total value, by State and United States, December 1, 2018 and 2019[1]

State	Number		Value per bird		Total value	
	2018	2019	2018	2019	2018	2019
	1,000 Head	*1,000 Head*	*Dollars*	*Dollars*	*1,000 Dollars*	*1,000 Dollars*
Alabama	16,113	17,375	7.40	9.20	119,236	159,850
Arkansas	23,556	24,346	7.90	8.50	186,092	206,941
California	17,873	19,100	3.70	3.80	66,130	72,580
Colorado	5,925	6,320	2.50	2.40	14,813	15,168
Florida	9,490	8,995	2.30	2.70	21,827	24,287
Georgia	30,057	30,760	6.20	6.60	186,353	203,016
Illinois	6,090	6,860	2.70	2.60	16,443	17,836
Indiana	43,356	44,373	1.90	2.30	82,376	102,058
Iowa	69,687	72,579	2.30	2.40	160,280	174,190
Kentucky	8,399	8,576	4.80	5.00	40,315	42,880
Louisiana	2,824	2,814	5.20	5.50	14,685	15,477
Maryland	4,267	4,099	4.00	3.90	17,068	15,986
Massachusetts	149	184	7.50	9.50	1,118	1,748
Michigan	18,396	19,629	2.20	2.60	40,471	51,035
Minnesota	13,918	14,185	2.30	2.30	32,011	32,626
Mississippi	9,716	9,695	8.80	8.60	85,501	83,377
Missouri	15,227	18,336	4.10	4.20	62,431	77,011
Montana	1,186	1,236	5.70	8.60	6,760	10,630
Nebraska	9,536	10,192	3.70	4.10	35,283	41,787
New York	6,727	6,635	2.40	2.90	16,145	19,242
North Carolina	23,507	21,684	7.70	8.70	181,004	188,651
Ohio	43,988	43,600	4.40	3.80	193,547	165,680
Oklahoma	4,286	4,476	7.00	7.50	30,002	33,570
Oregon	2,957	3,004	5.00	4.90	14,785	14,720
Pennsylvania	34,293	34,101	4.20	3.60	144,031	122,764
South Carolina	5,610	5,722	4.70	5.00	26,367	28,610
South Dakota	3,564	3,442	3.50	3.50	12,474	12,047
Tennessee	2,957	2,824	9.40	9.10	27,796	25,698
Texas	29,512	29,629	4.40	4.80	129,853	142,219
Utah	6,214	5,852	2.20	2.30	13,671	13,460
Vermont	222	198	8.60	7.20	1,909	1,426
Virginia	3,837	4,183	7.30	6.50	28,010	27,190
Washington	8,491	8,111	3.90	4.20	33,115	34,066
West Virginia	2,120	1,932	7.50	7.90	15,900	15,263
Wisconsin	9,084	8,818	2.40	2.50	21,802	22,045
Other States[2]	21,704	23,708	3.82	2.91	82,941	69,030
United States	514,838	527,573	4.20	4.33	2,162,545	2,284,164

Totals may not add due to rounding.   [1] Excludes commercial broilers.   [2] Alaska, Arizona, Connecticut, Delaware, Hawaii, Idaho, Kansas, Maine, New Hampshire, New Jersey, New Mexico, Nevada, North Dakota, Rhode Island and Wyoming combined to avoid disclosing data for individual operations.
NASS, Livestock Branch, (202) 720-3570.

Table 8-34.—Mature chickens: Lost, sold for slaughter, price, and value, United States, 2010–2019[1]

Year	Number		Pounds (live weight) sold[3]	Price per pound live weight[3]
	Lost[2]	Sold[3]		
	1,000 head	*1,000 head*	*1,000 pounds*	*1,000 dollars*
2010	108,356	173,404	903,750	73,099
2011	106,361	182,153	943,142	81,110
2012	103,758	179,162	901,411	79,208
2013	102,105	186,486	940,635	89,497
2014	106,166	192,334	970,852	96,840
2015	132,625	198,648	1,010,070	104,828
2016	106,166	207,923	1,060,677	87,949
2017	125,941	189,841	1,001,685	46,999
2018	136,698	189,603	1,019,695	49,365
2019	99,596	176,266	910,333	65,381

[1] Annual estimates cover the period December 1 previous year through November 30.   Excludes broilers.   [2] Includes rendered, died, destroyed, composted, or disappeared for any reason (excluding sold for slaughter) during the 12-month period.
NASS, Livestock Branch, (202) 720–3570.

Table 8-35.—Chickens: Lost, sold for slaughter, and value of sales, by State and United States, 2018 and 2019 [1]

State	Number lost [2]		Number sold		Pounds sold		Value of sales	
	2018	2019	2018	2019	2018	2019	2018	2019
	1,000 head				1,000 pounds		1,000 dollars	
Alabama	3,195.9	3,476.2	11,002.1	11,650.7	87,466.7	92,856.1	6,472.5	7,057.1
Arkansas	3,474.2	3,513.9	16,212.7	15,524.2	121,595.3	115,034.3	8,633.3	8,282.5
California	5,978.1	7,143.7	3,013.3	2,671.1	11,058.8	9,909.8	132.7	109.0
Colorado	2,313.7	2,240.8	1,553.0	1,286.7	7,873.7	6,973.9	338.6	341.7
Florida	5,378.0	5,022.6	380.5	401.7	2,891.8	3,000.7	214.0	216.1
Georgia	6,131.3	6,425.8	15,484.6	17,214.4	108,701.9	118,262.9	7,283.0	7,805.4
Illinois	1,221.4	1,487.4	1,911.5	2,505.2	7,301.9	9,519.8	109.5	123.8
Indiana	14,310.9	13,820.0	11,245.3	12,441.1	39,246.1	44,041.5	196.2	220.2
Iowa	28,024.3	31,854.6	6,376.6	9,608.6	22,063.0	33,534.0	110.3	100.6
Kentucky	992.6	1,085.1	4,506.6	5,181.5	26,138.3	30,260.0	1,437.6	1,664.3
Louisiana	315.0	403.5	1,879.4	1,930.1	11,953.0	12,410.5	729.1	769.5
Maryland	280.0	809.6	1,525.3	508.1	5,613.1	2,118.8	67.4	50.9
Massachusetts	9.2	89.2	75.4	0.2	254.1	0.7	(Z)	(Z)
Michigan	1,069.5	3,959.0	9,756.2	5,674.0	32,976.0	19,518.6	33.0	19.5
Minnesota	3,902.3	4,729.9	4,058.2	3,571.8	15,705.2	15,394.5	267.0	431.0
Mississippi	1,399.8	1,406.8	5,525.2	5,812.7	40,555.0	43,072.1	2,798.3	3,058.1
Missouri	3,209.7	2,418.0	8,703.9	6,790.5	41,865.8	34,971.1	1,632.8	1,573.7
Montana	322.6	629.9	52.3	5.1	176.3	17.5	(Z)	(Z)
Nebraska	791.9	1,272.1	5,814.8	4,035.2	19,886.6	14,042.5	59.7	28.1
New York	509.2	586.4	3,903.2	4,532.3	13,192.8	15,681.8	13.2	15.7
North Carolina	4,056.5	4,059.9	14,993.5	17,210.5	103,305.2	112,900.9	6,818.1	7,112.8
Ohio	10,930.4	11,193.0	12,950.4	12,662.9	46,491.9	46,219.6	371.9	416.0
Oklahoma	736.2	775.1	2,562.1	2,251.2	20,112.5	18,144.7	1,488.3	1,397.1
Oregon	1,625.6	1,710.8	14.1	14.9	47.5	51.3	(Z)	(Z)
Pennsylvania	2,781.9	2,855.3	11,201.6	11,911.9	41,670.0	45,146.1	541.7	632.0
South Carolina	1,961.7	1,993.0	1,916.2	2,269.1	12,608.6	15,611.4	807.0	1,046.0
South Dakota	904.6	1,091.5	1,072.3	140.3	3,613.7	481.2	3.6	0.5
Tennessee	521.1	467.9	1,802.3	1,917.2	14,076.0	14,800.8	1,041.6	1,095.3
Texas	4,156.5	3,686.8	14,270.9	14,350.6	69,784.7	72,470.5	2,861.2	3,116.2
Utah	1,598.2	1,127.0	2,648.0	2,271.9	8,923.8	7,815.3	8.9	7.8
Vermont	19.2	25.2	103.2	142.2	390.1	594.4	5.9	14.3
Virginia	1,536.5	1,326.4	2,116.9	2,092.1	17,041.0	16,841.4	1,278.1	1,279.9
Washington	4,852.1	5,113.0	33.3	36.3	112.2	129.6	(Z)	(Z)
West Virginia	286.7	276.3	1,690.7	1,740.5	13,153.6	13,680.3	973.4	1,026.0
Wisconsin	1,093.4	2,951.1	2,540.6	2,157.1	9,781.3	9,340.2	166.3	261.5
Other States [3]	6,050.5	5,670.9	6,944.5	7,088.7	24,057.8	24,845.7	104.2	90.9
United States	125,940.7	136,697.7	189,840.7	189,602.6	1,001,685.3	1,019,694.5	46,999.0	49,364.4

(Z) Less than half of the unit shown.　[1] Annual estimates cover the period December 1 previous year through November 30.　Exclude broilers.　Totals may not add due to rounding.　[2] Includes rendered, died, destroyed, composted, or disappeared for any reason except sold during the 12-month period.　[3] Alaska, Arizona, Connecticut, Delaware, Hawaii, Idaho, Kansas, Maine, Nevada, New Hampshire, New Jersey, New Mexico, North Dakota, Rhode Island, and Wyoming combined to avoid disclosing data for individual operations.
NASS, Livestock Branch, (202) 720–3570.

Table 8-36.—Chickens: Production, commercial storage, exports, and consumption, United States, 2011–2020

Year	Production			Commercial storage at beginning of year	Exports	Commercial storage at end of year	Consumption	
	Commercial broilers	Other chickens	Total [1]				Total [1][2]	Per capita
	Million pounds							Pounds
2011	36,804	521	37,325	777	7,069	592	30,549	98
2012	36,643	516	37,159	592	7,363	652	29,850	95
2013	37,425	523	37,948	652	7,453	675	30,597	97
2014	38,153	521	38,673	675	7,406	683	31,378	98
2015	39,620	522	40,142	683	6,465	840	33,652	105
2016	40,261	548	40,809	840	6,803	786	34,194	106
2017	41,217	535	41,751	786	6,916	861	34,889	107
2018	42,145	539	42,684	861	7,153	850	35,683	109
2019	43,435	528	43,963	850	7,185	942	36,820	112
2020	44,106	549	44,655	942	7,446	834	37,464	113

[1] Totals may not add due to rounding.　[2] Shipments to territories now included in total consumption.
ERS Markets and Trade Economics Division, Animal Products and Cost of Production Branch, (202) 694–5308. Data as of March 12, 2021.

Table 8-37.—Broilers: Production and value, United States, 2010–2019 [1] [2] [3]

Year	Number produced	Pounds produced	Value of production
	1,000 head	*1,000 pounds*	*1,000 dollars*
2010	8,623,600	49,152,600	23,691,553
2011	8,607,600	50,082,400	22,987,822
2012	8,463,000	49,655,600	24,827,800
2013	8,533,800	50,678,200	30,761,669
2014	8,545,000	51,378,700	32,728,234
2015	8,688,700	53,376,200	28,716,398
2016	8,776,700	54,259,100	25,935,852
2017	8,913,800	55,573,900	30,232,203
2018	9,037,100	56,791,100	31,746,230
2019	8,550,200	47,752,300	21,822,804

[1] December 1, previous year through November 30, current year.   [2] Broiler production including other domestic meat-type strains.   [3] Excludes States producing less than 500,000 broilers.
NASS, Livestock Branch, (202) 720–3570.

Table 8-38.—Broilers: Production and value, States and United States, 2018 and 2019 [1]

State	2018			2019		
	Number produced	Pounds produced	Value of production	Number produced	Pounds produced	Value of production
	1,000 head	*1,000 pounds*	*1,000 dollars*	*1,000 head*	*1,000 pounds*	*1,000 dollars*
Alabama	1,095,400	6,134,200	3,337,005	1,123,700	6,180,400	3,454,844
Arkansas	1,059,000	6,989,400	3,802,234	1,092,000	7,316,400	4,089,868
Delaware	259,800	1,870,600	1,017,606	263,600	1,924,300	1,075,684
Florida	65,200	371,600	202,150	65,400	385,900	215,718
Georgia	1,363,400	8,044,100	4,375,990	1,361,400	8,168,400	4,566,136
Kentucky	295,800	1,893,100	1,029,846	303,300	1,971,500	1,102,069
Maryland	306,700	1,840,200	1,001,069	289,400	1,736,400	970,648
Minnesota	59,700	358,200	194,861	59,100	360,500	201,520
Mississippi	741,100	4,743,000	2,580,192	747,800	4,711,100	2,633,505
Missouri	291,100	1,426,400	775,962	293,100	1,465,500	819,215
North Carolina	830,800	6,563,300	3,570,435	873,600	6,901,400	3,857,883
Ohio	99,300	526,300	286,307	107,900	561,100	313,655
Oklahoma	204,500	1,370,200	745,389	196,800	1,318,600	737,097
Pennsylvania	185,200	1,037,100	564,182	200,100	1,140,600	637,595
South Carolina	243,100	1,798,900	978,602	237,800	1,807,300	1,010,281
Tennessee	171,500	909,000	494,496	177,300	939,700	525,292
Texas	651,200	4,102,600	2,231,814	653,500	4,247,800	2,374,520
Virginia	277,400	1,608,900	875,242	278,900	1,673,400	935,431
West Virginia	86,100	335,800	182,675	83,300	316,500	176,924
Wisconsin	53,800	226,000	122,944	55,800	228,800	127,899
Other States [2]	573,700	3,425,000	1,863,202	573,300	3,435,500	1,920,446
United States	8,913,800	55,573,900	30,232,203	9,037,100	56,791,100	31,746,230

[1] Annual estimates cover the period December 1 previous year through November 30.   Broiler production including other domestic meat-type strains.   Excludes States producing less than 500,000 broilers.   [2] Includes State estimates not shown and States whithheld to avoid disclosing data for individual operations.
NASS, Livestock Branch, (202) 720–3570.

Table 8-39.—Poultry: Slaughtered under Federal inspection, by class, United States, 2017–2019

Class	Number slaughtered			Total live weight		
	2017	2018	2019	2017	2018	2019
	Thousands	*Thousands*	*Thousands*	*Thousands*	*Thousands*	*Thousands*
Young chickens	8,768,399	8,916,083	9,034,504	54,036,929	55,314,913	56,541,518
Mature chickens	140,587	134,619	126,406	848,287	822,578	816,199
Total chickens	8,908,986	9,050,702	9,160,910	54,885,216	56,137,491	57,357,717
Young turkeys	241,418	240,014	235,198	7,412,058	7,420,122	7,310,114
Old turkeys	1,837	1,666	1,662	51,966	48,973	48,981
Total turkeys	243,255	241,680	236,860	7,464,024	7,469,095	7,359,095
Ducks	27,268	26,628	27,647	186,715	184,338	192,980
Other poultry [1]	(NA)	(NA)	(NA)	4,054	4,211	3,872
Total poultry	(NA)	(NA)	(NA)	62,540,009	63,795,135	64,913,664

Class	Pounds condemned					
	Ante-mortem (live weight)			Post-mortem (Carcass and parts)		
	2017	2018	2019	2017	2018	2019
	Thousands	*Thousands*	*Thousands*	*Thousands*	*Thousands*	*Thousands*
Young chickens	124,994	124,241	130,452	356,808	342,149	322,994
Mature chickens	10,156	9,563	8,167	30,365	25,923	20,727
Total chickens	135,150	133,804	138,619	387,173	368,072	343,721
Young turkeys	18,680	18,798	19,090	86,939	84,726	82,278
Old turkeys	662	543	494	1,900	2,025	1,944
Total turkeys	19,342	19,341	19,584	88,839	86,751	84,222
Ducks	528	592	797	3,633	3,531	3,667
Other poultry [2]	4	5	5	28	40	35
Total poultry	155,024	153,742	159,005	479,673	458,394	431,645

Class	Pounds certified (ready-to-cook)		
	2017	2018	2019
	Thousands	*Thousands*	*Thousands*
Young chickens	40,696,114	41,662,394	42,600,735
Mature chickens	548,567	535,291	539,362
Total chickens	41,244,681	42,197,685	43,140,097
Young turkeys	5,942,076	5,943,827	5,841,082
Old turkeys	39,025	36,750	37,009
Total turkeys	5,981,101	5,980,577	5,878,091
Ducks	135,821	134,313	140,936
Other poultry [2]	2,655	2,727	2,563
Total poultry	47,364,258	48,315,302	49,161,687

(NA) Not available. [1] Includes geese, guineas, ostriches, emus, rheas, and squab. [2] Includes geese, guineas, and squab.
NASS, Livestock Branch, (202) 720–3570.

Table 8-45.—Turkeys: Poults hatched by commercial hatcheries, United States by Month, 2018–2019

Month	2017	2018	Percent of Previous Year
	Thousands	*Thousands*	*Percent*
January	25,412	24,406	96
February	23,679	22,654	96
March	25,812	24,180	94
April	23,278	23,482	101
May	24,169	23,503	97
June	25,125	23,337	93
July	24,691	25,730	104
August	24,868	23,888	96
September	23,530	22,443	95
October	24,393	24,295	100
November	24,532	29,089	119
December	22,272	23,176	104
Total	291,761	290,183	99

NASS, Livestock Branch, (202) 720–3570.

Table 8-46.—Eggs: Supply, distribution, and per capita consumption, United States, 2011–2020 [1]

Year	Total egg production	Storage at beginning of the year [1]	Imports [2]	Exports [2]	Storage at end of the year [2]	Eggs used for hatching	Consumption Total [3]	Consumption Per capita
	Million dozen							*Number*
2011	7,715	20	21	305	28	950	6,472	249
2012	7,884	28	19	336	21	941	6,633	253
2013	8,233	21	17	425	24	964	6,859	260
2014	8,509	24	35	414	24	981	7,149	269
2015	8,144	24	132	342	32	996	6,931	259
2016	8,668	32	130	304	28	1,010	7,488	278
2017	8,947	28	34	355	23	1,035	7,596	280
2018	9,205	23	18	333	23	1,058	7,833	287
2019	9,442	23	15	334	32	1,081	8,033	293
2020	9,283	32	15	344	25	1,078	7,884	287

[1] Calendar years. [2] Shell eggs and the approximate shell-egg equivalent of egg product. [3] Shipments to territories now included in total consumption.
ERS Markets and Trade Economics Division, Animal Products and Cost of Production Branch, (202) 694–5409. Data as of March 12, 2021.

Table 8-47.—Eggs, shell: Average price per dozen on consumer Grade A cartoned white eggs to volume buyers, store-door delivery, New York, 2010–2019

Year	Large
	Cents
2010	106.29
2011	115.31
2012	117.46
2013	124.69
2014	142.33
2015	181.74
2016	85.70
2017	100.96
2018	137.58
2019	94.00

AMS, Livestock, Poultry and Seed Programs, Livestock, Poultry and Grain Market News Division, (515) 284-4460.

Table 8-48.—Total layers and egg production: Annual average number of layers, eggs per layer, and total production, by State and United States, 2017–2018 [1]

State	Average number of layers		Eggs per layer [2]		Total egg production	
	2017	2018	2017	2018	2017	2018
	Thousands	Thousands	Number	Number	Millions	Millions
Alabama	9,112	9,556	227	223	2,072.3	2,133.3
Arkansas	14,147	14,668	243	241	3,431.0	3,534.7
California	13,202	14,542	285	295	3,759.6	4,294.6
Colorado	4,642	4,866	305	305	1,414.5	1,482.9
Florida	7,587	7,340	276	273	2,095.7	2,005.4
Georgia	19,565	19,607	256	248	5,010.6	4,871.1
Illinois	5,088	6,004	295	294	1,500.4	1,764.1
Indiana	33,553	33,794	294	286	9,869.7	9,658.6
Iowa	55,867	57,614	289	282	16,155.2	16,273.8
Kentucky	5,190	5,690	262	252	1,360.5	1,434.4
Louisiana	1,984	2,004	242	258	480.8	517.5
Maryland	2,852	2,689	295	290	840.1	780.6
Massachusetts	124	142	324	304	40.2	43.1
Michigan	14,272	15,387	296	296	4,225.5	4,548.1
Minnesota	10,462	10,812	294	290	3,070.7	3,131.8
Mississippi	5,587	5,673	249	250	1,392.8	1,418.6
Missouri	10,764	11,937	292	291	3,146.3	3,473.9
Montana	523	900	294	325	153.8	292.5
Nebraska	8,167	7,829	305	305	2,489.1	2,388.8
New York	5,660	5,553	303	298	1,717.8	1,656.5
North Carolina	15,295	14,573	259	254	3,956.2	3,705.4
Ohio	33,773	32,848	289	285	9,754.6	9,364.9
Oklahoma	2,931	3,051	236	228	691.8	697.1
Oregon	2,369	2,382	314	307	744.6	732.4
Pennsylvania	28,232	28,477	295	296	8,337.3	8,423.1
South Carolina	3,922	4,331	272	267	1,068.3	1,156.2
South Dakota	2,701	2,603	290	307	784.3	797.9
Tennessee	1,642	1,798	229	216	376.6	388.8
Texas	21,781	22,563	267	271	5,820.3	6,108.5
Utah	5,153	4,793	294	293	1,512.9	1,403.4
Vermont	158	201	292	307	46.1	61.7
Virginia	2,698	2,676	265	268	716.0	716.7
Washington	6,994	6,959	301	302	2,103.7	2,102.1
West Virginia	1,244	1,284	221	230	274.7	295.9
Wisconsin	6,428	7,271	289	286	1,860.1	2,077.8
Other States [3]	17,506	18,894	284	289	4,967.5	5,455.9
United States	381,175	391,311	281	279	107,241.6	109,192.1

[1] Annual estimates cover the period December 1 previous year through November 30. Totals may not add due to rounding. [2] Total egg production divided by average number of layers on hand. [3] Alaska, Arizona, Connecticut, Delaware, Hawaii, Idaho, Kansas, Maine, New Hampshire, New Jersey, New Mexico, Nevada, North Dakota, Rhode Island, and Wyoming combined to avoid disclosing data for individual operations.
NASS, Livestock Branch, (202) 720–3570.

Table 8-49.—Eggs: Broken under Federal inspection, United States, 2017–2018

Item	Quantity	
	2017	2018
	1,000 dozen	1,000 dozen
Shell eggs broken	2,307,023	2,399,762
	1,000 pounds	1,000 pounds
Edible product from shell eggs broken		
Whole	1,837,087	1,911,501
White	771,207	788,037
Yolk	383,655	390,716
Total	2,991,949	3,090,254
Inedible product from shell eggs broken	239,584	260,875

NASS, Livestock Branch, (202) 720–3570.

Table 8-40.—Poultry: Feed-price ratios, United States, 2010–2019

Year	Ratios [1]		
	Egg-feed	Broiler-feed	Turkey-feed
	Pounds	Pounds	Pounds
2010	7.5	4.5	6.2
2011	6.0	3.1	4.9
2012	5.4	3.1	4.7
2013	6.5	3.7	4.6
2014	10.2	5.0	6.3
2015	17.1	5.0	8.5
2016	5.9	4.7	9.2
2017	7.7	5.4	7.2
2018	11.3	5.6	5.5
2019	7.2	4.1	5.0

[1] Number of pounds of poultry feed equivalent in value at local market prices to 1 dozen market eggs, or 1 pound of broiler or 1 pound of turkey live weight. Simple average of monthly feed-price ratios. Egg feed= corn (75 lbs) and soybeans (25 lbs); broiler feed= corn (58 lbs); soybeans (42 lbs); turkey feed= corn (51 lbs), soybeans (28 lbs), and wheat (21 lbs). Monthly equivalent prices of commercial prepared feeds are based on current U.S. prices received for corn, soybeans, and wheat.
NASS, Environmental, Economics, and Demographics Branch, (202) 720–6146.

Table 8-41.—Turkeys: Production, commercial storage, exports, and consumption, United States, 2011–2020

Year	Production	Commercial storage at beginning of year	Exports	Commercial storage at end of year	Consumption	
					Total [1][2]	Per capita
	Million pounds					Pounds
2011	5,715	192	703	211	5,013	16
2012	5,889	211	797	296	5,028	16
2013	5,729	296	741	237	5,068	16
2014	5,756	237	775	193	5,052	16
2015	5,627	193	529	201	5,135	16
2016	5,981	201	569	279	5,384	17
2017	5,981	279	622	310	5,352	16
2018	5,878	310	611	303	5,293	16
2019	5,818	303	639	233	5,261	16
2020	5,743	233	571	223	5,203	16

[1] Totals may not add due to rounding. [2] Shipments to territories now included in consumption.
ERS Markets and Trade Economics Division, Animal Products and Cost of Production Branch, (202) 694–5409. Data as of March 12, 2021.

Table 8-42.—Turkeys: Production and value, United States, 2010–2019

Year	Number raised	Pounds (live weight) produced	Value of production [1]
	1,000 head	1,000 pounds	1,000 dollars
2010	244,188	7,108,222	4,372,438
2011	248,500	7,313,205	4,987,608
2012	253,500	7,561,905	5,452,135
2013	240,000	7,277,536	4,839,562
2014	237,500	7,217,006	5,304,501
2015	233,100	7,038,136	5,707,928
2016	244,000	7,486,978	6,184,247
2017	245,200	7,554,397	4,873,677
2018	244,750	7,598,289	3,875,131
2019	247,359	7,149,314	3,573,324

NASS, Livestock Branch, (202) 720–3570.

Table 8-50.—Eggs: Number, rate of lay, production, and value, United States, 2009–2018 [1]

Year	Layers average number	Eggs per layer [2]	Total egg production	Value of production
	Thousands	Number	Millions	1,000 dollars
2009	338,846	268	90,737	6,191,040
2010	341,505	269	91,811	6,553,087
2011	340,598	271	92,450	7,355,873
2012	394,844	274	94,364	7,929,104
2013	358,313	275	98,481	8,745,404
2014	368,193	277	101,816	10,342,687
2015	356,370	276	98,291	13,762,519
2016	369,949	279	103,202	6,591,359
2017	381,175	281	107,242	7,635,001
2018	391,311	279	109,192	10,586,262

[1] Annual estimates cover the period December 1 previous year through November 30.   [2] Total egg production divided by average number of layers on hand.
NASS, Livestock Branch, (202) 720–3570.

Table 8-51.—Total Eggs: Production and value by State and United States, 2017–2018 [1]

State	Eggs produced		Value of production	
	2017	2018	2017	2018
	Millions	Millions	1,000 dollars	1,000 dollars
Alabama	2,072.3	2,133.3	349,437	382,196
Arkansas	3,431.0	3,534.7	482,651	527,651
California	3,759.6	4,294.6	267,690	503,663
Colorado	1,414.5	1,482.9	77,227	113,657
Florida	2,095.7	2,005.4	112,225	154,784
Georgia	5,010.6	4,871.1	587,500	656,656
Illinois	1,500.4	1,764.1	87,784	147,870
Indiana	9,869.7	9,658.6	543,793	796,467
Iowa	16,155.2	16,273.8	868,838	1,327,106
Kentucky	1,360.5	1,434.4	122,051	158,458
Louisiana	480.8	517.5	53,102	63,196
Maryland	840.1	780.6	45,389	60,686
Massachusetts	40.2	43.1	2,023	3,194
Michigan	4,225.5	4,548.1	220,431	364,078
Minnesota	3,070.7	3,131.8	171,173	262,646
Mississippi	1,392.8	1,418.6	211,051	230,685
Missouri	3,146.3	3,473.9	207,485	297,684
Montana	153.8	292.5	11,192	33,674
Nebraska	2,489.1	2,388.8	130,912	198,202
New York	1,717.8	1,656.5	90,433	127,359
North Carolina	3,956.2	3,705.4	461,195	509,017
Ohio	9,754.6	9,364.9	524,196	762,538
Oklahoma	691.8	697.1	80,090	92,177
Oregon	744.6	732.4	50,436	85,154
Pennsylvania	8,337.3	8,423.1	482,082	673,940
South Carolina	1,068.3	1,156.2	92,746	118,383
South Dakota	784.3	797.9	40,556	63,795
Tennessee	376.6	388.8	68,552	70,558
Texas	5,820.3	6,108.5	395,521	546,249
Utah	1,512.9	1,403.4	102,395	163,332
Vermont	46.1	61.7	2,787	5,218
Virginia	716.0	716.7	91,300	100,668
Washington	2,103.7	2,102.1	141,321	240,515
West Virginia	274.7	295.9	50,249	54,681
Wisconsin	1,860.1	2,077.8	108,619	176,103
Other States [2]	4,967.5	5,455.9	300,569	514,040
United States	107,241.6	109,192.1	7,635,001	10,586,262

Totals may not add due to rounding.   [1] Annual estimates cover the period December 1 previous year through November 30.   Includes hatching and market (table) eggs.   [2] Alaska, Arizona, Connecticut, Delaware, Hawaii, Idaho, Kansas, Maine, Nevada, New Hampshire, New Jersey, New Mexico, North Dakota, Rhode Island, and Wyoming combined to avoid disclosing individual operations.
NASS, Livestock Branch, (202) 720–3570.

CHAPTER IX

FARM RESOURCES, INCOME, AND EXPENSES

The statistics in this chapter deal with farms, farm resources, farm income, and expenses. Many of the series are estimates developed in connection with economic research activities of the Department.

Table 9-1.—Economic trends: Data relating to agriculture, United States, 2010–2019

Year	Prices paid by farmers [1]			Farm income [2]		
	Total including interest, taxes, and wage rates (PPITW)	Production items	Prices received by farmers [1]	Gross farm income [3]	Production expenses	Net farm income
	Index numbers 2011=100	Index numbers 2011=100	Index numbers 2011=100	Billion dollars	Billion dollars	Billion dollars
2010	89.0	87.7	86.8	356.5	279.4	77.1
2011	100.0	100.0	100.0	420.4	306.9	113.5
2012	104.8	105.4	105.0	449.8	353.4	96.4
2013	106.7	107.4	107.0	484.1	360.4	123.7
2014	113.1	114.1	107.9	483.3	391.0	92.2
2015	111.6	112.0	99.2	440.8	359.2	81.7
2016	105.7	104.7	90.2	412.3	349.9	62.3
2017	106.1	104.5	93.4	425.4	350.3	75.1
2018	108.7	106.4	90.5	425.1	343.8	81.3
2019	110.0	107.2	90.4	431.9	348.7	83.1

Year	National income [4]	Personal income [4]	Industrial production [5]	Consumer prices all items [6]	Producer prices consumer foods [6]
	Billion dollars	Billion dollars	Index numbers 2012=100	Index numbers 1982–84=100	Index numbers 1982=100
2010	12,736.8	12,551.6	94.1	218.1	182.4
2011	13,361.3	13,326.8	97.1	224.9	193.9
2012	14,093.1	14,010.1	100.0	229.6	199.1
2013	14,491.3	14,181.1	102.0	233.0	203.5
2014	15,239.9	14,991.7	105.2	236.7	212.5
2015	15,784.6	15,724.2	104.1	237.0	209.8
2016	16,082.7	16,160.7	102.1	240.0	204.7
2017	16,853.9	16,948.6	104.4	245.1	207.2
2018	17,689.6	17,851.8	108.6	251.1	207.4
2019	18,269.1	18,551.5	109.5	255.7	211.6

[1] U.S. Department of Agriculture - NASS. [2] U.S. Department of Agriculture - ERS. [3] Includes cash receipts from farm marketings, government payments, nonmoney income (gross rental value of dwelling and value of home consumption), other income (machine hire custom work and recreational income), and value of change in farm inventories. [4] Department of Commerce, Bureau of Economic Analysis. [5] Major Industry groups Federal Reserve Board. [6] U.S. Department of Labor, Bureau of Labor Statistics retrieved from FRED, Federal Reserve Bank of St. Louis.
ERS, Farm Economy Branch, (202) 694–5476. E-mail contact is Dipak Subedi at dipak.subedi@usda.gov.

Table 9-2.—Farms: Number, land in farms, and average size of farm, United States, 2010–2019

Year	Farms [1]	Land in farms	Average size farm
	Number	1,000 acres	Acres
2010	2,149,520	915,660	426
2011	2,131,240	914,420	429
2012	2,109,810	914,600	433
2013	2,100,350	911,720	434
2014	2,082,440	908,920	436
2015	2,063,890	905,790	439
2016	2,055,340	902,680	439
2017	2,042,000	900,370	441
2018	2,029,200	899,500	443
2019	2,023,400	897,400	444

[1] A farm is any establishment from which $1,000 or more of agricultural products were produced and sold or normally would have been sold during the year.
NASS, Environmental, Economics, and Demographics Branch, (202) 720–6146.

Table 9-3.—Farms: Percent of farms and land in farms, and average size, by economic sales class, United States, 2018–2019

Economic sales class	Percent of total				Average size farm	
	Farms		Land in farms		2018	2019
	2018	2019	2018	2019		
	Percent	Percent	Percent	Percent	Acres	Acres
$ 1,000 - $ 9,999	51.0	51.1	9.4	9.4	81	81
$ 10,000 - $ 99,999	30.5	30.4	20.8	20.8	302	304
$100,000 - $249,999	6.7	6.7	14.8	14.7	987	976
$250,000 - $499,999	4.4	4.4	14.3	14.3	1,450	1,448
$500,000 - $999,999	3.6	3.5	15.4	15.4	1,925	1,940
$1,000,000 or more	3.9	3.9	25.3	25.4	2,897	2,910
Total [1]	100.0	100.0	100.0	100.0	443	444

[1] May not add due to rounding.
NASS, Environmental, Economics, and Demographics Branch, (202) 720–6146.

Table 9-4.—Land in farms: Classification by tenure of operator, United States, 1935–2012

Year	Land in farms	Tenure of operator			
		Full owners	Part owners	Managers	All tenants
	Acres	Percent	Percent	Percent	Percent
1935 [1]	1,054,515,111	37.1	25.2	5.8	31.9
1940	1,065,113,774	35.9	28.2	6.5	29.4
1945 [1]	1,141,615,364	36.1	32.5	9.3	22.0
1950	1,161,419,720	36.1	36.4	9.2	18.3
1954 [1]	1,158,191,511	34.2	40.7	8.6	16.5
1959	1,123,507,574	31.0	44.0	9.8	14.8
1964	1,110,187,000	28.7	48.0	10.2	13.1
1969	1,062,892,501	35.3	51.8	....	13.0
1974	1,017,030,357	35.3	52.6	....	12.0
1978	1,014,777,234	32.7	55.3	....	12.0
1982	986,796,579	34.7	53.8	....	11.5
1987	964,470,625	32.9	53.9	....	13.2
1992	945,531,506	31.3	55.7	....	13.0
1997	931,795,255	33.9	54.5	....	11.6
2002 [2]	938,279,056	38.0	52.8	....	9.2
2007 [2]	922,095,843	37.3	53.8	....	8.9
2012 [2]	914,527,657	36.8	53.7	....	9.5

[1] Excludes Alaska and Hawaii.   [2] The 2002 Census of Agriculture introduced new methodology to account for all farms in the United States.   All 2002 published census items were reweighted for undercoverage.   Strictly speaking, data for 2002 and subsequent years are not fully comparable with data from earlier years.
ERS, Resource and Rural Economics Division, (202) 694–5572.   Data from the Census of Agriculture, National Agricultural Statistics Service.

Table 9-5.—Number of farms and land in farms by economic sales class by State and United States, 2018–2019

State	Economic Sales Class: $1,000-$9,999			
	Number of Farms		Land in Farms	
	2018	2019	2018	2019
	Number	*Number*	*1,000 Acres*	*1,000 Acres*
Alabama	22,600	21,800	2,100	1,900
Alaska	540	590	80	80
Arizona	14,300	14,200	4,800	4,800
Arkansas	20,700	20,500	1,800	1,750
California	26,400	27,200	1,400	1,300
Colorado	21,900	22,000	2,100	2,200
Connecticut	3,650	3,650	130	130
Delaware	820	820	20	20
Florida	29,000	28,900	1,300	1,300
Georgia	23,300	23,200	2,300	2,300
Hawaii	4,250	4,250	70	70
Idaho	13,500	13,300	700	650
Illinois	27,900	27,700	1,200	1,200
Indiana	25,800	26,100	900	1,000
Iowa	25,400	25,000	900	900
Kansas	21,800	21,300	2,000	1,900
Kentucky	44,300	44,000	3,100	3,000
Louisiana	15,300	15,400	1,100	1,100
Maine	4,800	4,800	390	390
Maryland	6,700	6,700	260	260
Massachusetts	4,500	4,500	190	190
Michigan	24,000	24,500	1,200	1,250
Minnesota	25,400	24,900	1,600	1,600
Mississippi	19,700	19,600	2,300	2,200
Missouri	44,400	44,500	3,300	3,200
Montana	11,600	11,400	1,900	2,000
Nebraska	11,500	11,300	800	800
Nevada	1,700	1,700	500	520
New Hampshire	2,750	2,750	170	170
New Jersey	6,400	6,400	160	160
New Mexico	16,800	17,000	5,100	5,000
New York	15,400	15,500	1,100	1,100
North Carolina	26,100	25,900	1,500	1,400
North Dakota	7,200	7,400	1,100	1,200
Ohio	40,400	41,400	1,600	1,900
Oklahoma	39,800	40,300	4,100	4,200
Oregon	23,400	23,500	1,000	1,100
Pennsylvania	25,000	24,900	1,300	1,300
Rhode Island	630	630	20	20
South Carolina	16,500	16,400	1,600	1,500
South Dakota	7,200	7,000	900	1,000
Tennessee	43,800	43,600	2,700	2,700
Texas	156,500	156,500	15,600	15,200
Utah	11,000	10,800	600	600
Vermont	3,750	3,750	280	280
Virginia	24,100	24,100	1,700	1,700
Washington	21,800	21,700	800	800
West Virginia	17,000	16,600	1,600	1,500
Wisconsin	28,800	29,000	1,800	1,900
Wyoming	5,600	5,600	1,200	1,200
United States	1,035,690	1,034,540	84,370	83,940

See footnote(s) at end of table.

Table 9-5.—Number of farms and land in farms by economic sales class by State and United States, 2018–2019—Continued

State	Economic Sales Class: $10,000-$99,999			
	Number of Farms		Land in Farms	
	2018	2019	2018	2019
	Number	Number	1,000 Acres	1,000 Acres
Alabama	12,500	12,500	3,200	3,200
Alaska	360	360	450	450
Arizona	3,550	3,450	5,300	5,200
Arkansas	14,700	14,500	3,700	3,700
California	22,500	22,600	4,000	4,300
Colorado	11,200	10,800	7,100	7,000
Connecticut	1,400	1,400	100	100
Delaware	510	510	50	50
Florida	13,500	13,500	2,100	2,100
Georgia	11,500	11,500	2,700	2,700
Hawaii	2,500	2,500	200	200
Idaho	6,500	6,500	1,800	1,800
Illinois	20,200	20,000	2,600	2,500
Indiana	16,600	16,100	1,800	1,700
Iowa	26,200	25,800	3,700	3,600
Kansas	21,300	21,500	7,100	7,200
Kentucky	24,200	24,200	4,400	4,500
Louisiana	8,800	8,700	1,900	1,900
Maine	2,050	2,050	350	350
Maryland	3,300	3,300	390	390
Massachusetts	1,950	1,950	160	160
Michigan	14,400	14,000	1,700	1,600
Minnesota	20,400	20,500	3,600	3,600
Mississippi	10,700	10,600	3,000	3,000
Missouri	37,200	37,300	8,600	8,600
Montana	8,000	8,100	10,400	10,300
Nebraska	14,500	14,300	5,000	4,900
Nevada	970	980	500	530
New Hampshire	1,100	1,100	170	170
New Jersey	2,350	2,350	170	170
New Mexico	6,100	6,000	10,400	10,200
New York	11,400	11,500	1,800	1,800
North Carolina	12,700	12,700	1,800	1,800
North Dakota	7,400	7,300	4,000	4,100
Ohio	23,000	22,000	2,700	2,900
Oklahoma	29,000	28,500	11,400	11,400
Oregon	9,000	8,900	3,000	2,900
Pennsylvania	16,700	16,700	2,200	2,200
Rhode Island	340	340	20	20
South Carolina	5,900	6,000	1,300	1,400
South Dakota	9,300	9,400	4,600	4,500
Tennessee	21,700	21,600	3,900	3,800
Texas	72,800	72,800	38,300	39,000
Utah	5,100	5,000	1,900	1,900
Vermont	1,950	1,950	310	310
Virginia	14,000	13,900	2,800	2,800
Washington	8,300	8,300	1,800	1,700
West Virginia	5,600	5,500	1,400	1,400
Wisconsin	20,100	20,200	2,900	2,900
Wyoming	3,700	3,800	4,000	4,100
United States	619,030	615,340	186,770	187,100

See footnote(s) at end of table.

Table 9-5.—Number of farms and land in farms by economic sales class by State and United States, 2018–2019—Continued

State	Economic Sales Class: $100,000-$249,999			
	Number of Farms		Land in Farms	
	2018	2019	2018	2019
	Number	*Number*	*1,000 Acres*	*1,000 Acres*
Alabama	1,050	1,150	750	810
Alaska	40	40	210	210
Arizona	530	510	10,300	10,400
Arkansas	1,350	1,400	950	950
California	6,450	6,500	3,200	3,200
Colorado	2,550	2,600	5,900	5,800
Connecticut	190	190	30	30
Delaware	130	130	40	40
Florida	1,900	1,900	1,200	1,100
Georgia	1,450	1,400	690	710
Hawaii	270	270	130	130
Idaho	1,700	1,700	1,700	1,700
Illinois	8,000	8,000	2,700	2,700
Indiana	5,000	5,200	1,700	1,600
Iowa	11,100	11,000	3,600	3,600
Kansas	6,300	6,100	6,600	6,500
Kentucky	2,900	3,000	1,200	1,200
Louisiana	950	950	790	790
Maine	320	320	100	100
Maryland	720	720	210	210
Massachusetts	340	340	40	40
Michigan	3,150	3,200	1,200	1,300
Minnesota	7,700	7,700	2,900	2,900
Mississippi	920	940	610	620
Missouri	5,800	5,800	3,500	3,500
Montana	3,100	3,150	10,200	10,300
Nebraska	6,400	6,500	5,700	5,900
Nevada	220	220	900	960
New Hampshire	(D)	(D)	(D)	(D)
New Jersey	450	450	110	110
New Mexico	820	810	6,300	6,200
New York	3,000	2,850	880	880
North Carolina	1,650	1,700	600	700
North Dakota	3,100	3,200	4,700	4,600
Ohio	6,400	6,500	2,200	2,000
Oklahoma	4,250	4,250	6,300	6,400
Oregon	1,850	1,800	2,600	2,500
Pennsylvania	5,100	5,000	1,100	1,100
Rhode Island	(D)	(D)	(D)	(D)
South Carolina	630	630	320	300
South Dakota	4,450	4,500	6,800	6,900
Tennessee	1,800	1,800	850	850
Texas	7,500	7,400	20,200	19,200
Utah	900	890	1,300	1,300
Vermont	470	470	140	140
Virginia	1,750	1,700	950	950
Washington	1,800	1,800	3,100	3,000
West Virginia	370	370	270	270
Wisconsin	6,900	7,000	2,100	2,100
Wyoming	1,200	1,200	5,400	5,300
Other States [1]	190	190	40	40
United States	135,110	135,440	133,310	132,140

See footnote(s) at end of table.

Table 9-5.—Number of farms and land in farms by economic sales class by State and United States, 2018–2019—Continued

State	Economic Sales Class: $250,000-$499,999			
	Number of Farms		Land in Farms	
	2018	2019	2018	2019
	Number	*Number*	*1,000 Acres*	*1,000 Acres*
Alabama	650	650	560	580
Alaska	(D)	(D)	(D)	(D)
Arizona	210	200	1,700	1,600
Arkansas	1,050	1,100	750	800
California	3,900	4,000	2,300	2,200
Colorado	1,450	1,500	5,700	5,800
Connecticut	110	110	20	20
Delaware	110	110	50	50
Florida	1,000	1,000	850	850
Georgia	1,050	1,100	610	690
Hawaii	120	120	170	170
Idaho	1,200	1,200	1,500	1,500
Illinois	6,200	6,100	4,000	4,000
Indiana	3,350	3,250	2,000	2,000
Iowa	8,900	9,200	5,500	5,500
Kansas	4,050	4,150	7,600	7,500
Kentucky	1,450	1,400	900	900
Louisiana	540	570	610	610
Maine	180	180	100	100
Maryland	490	490	230	230
Massachusetts	(D)	(D)	(D)	(D)
Michigan	2,200	2,150	1,200	1,300
Minnesota	5,800	5,800	3,900	4,000
Mississippi	600	580	590	580
Missouri	2,950	2,950	2,900	2,900
Montana	2,300	2,250	13,400	13,300
Nebraska	5,000	5,100	7,800	7,900
Nevada	240	200	1,000	900
New Hampshire	70	70	30	30
New Jersey	280	280	80	80
New Mexico	390	390	6,400	6,300
New York	1,750	1,700	780	780
North Carolina	1,250	1,250	700	700
North Dakota	3,000	3,000	6,500	6,600
Ohio	3,300	3,000	1,900	1,600
Oklahoma	2,050	2,100	4,600	4,600
Oregon	1,150	1,150	2,900	2,800
Pennsylvania	3,150	3,100	980	980
Rhode Island	(D)	(D)	(D)	(D)
South Carolina	280	280	270	230
South Dakota	3,700	3,800	8,700	8,800
Tennessee	1,000	1,000	660	660
Texas	3,650	3,600	14,700	14,800
Utah	520	510	2,000	2,000
Vermont	320	320	130	130
Virginia	910	960	680	680
Washington	1,250	1,250	2,100	2,200
West Virginia	130	130	120	110
Wisconsin	4,300	4,250	2,000	2,100
Wyoming	810	810	6,200	6,100
Other States [1]	250	250	130	130
United States	88,610	88,660	128,500	128,390

See footnote(s) at end of table.

Table 9-5.—Number of farms and land in farms by economic sales class by State and United States, 2018–2019—Continued

State	Economic Sales Class: $500,000-$999,999			
	Number of Farms		Land in Farms	
	2018	2019	2018	2019
	Number	*Number*	*1,000 Acres*	*1,000 Acres*
Alabama	1,200	1,100	690	660
Alaska	30	30	20	20
Arizona	200	220	1,000	1,000
Arkansas	1,350	1,400	1,200	1,200
California	3,550	3,200	2,200	2,300
Colorado	900	920	4,500	4,700
Connecticut	70	70	20	20
Delaware	260	260	110	110
Florida	900	900	650	650
Georgia	1,800	1,850	1,400	1,400
Hawaii	70	70	210	210
Idaho	800	800	1,800	1,750
Illinois	5,300	5,200	6,100	6,000
Indiana	2,450	2,500	2,800	2,700
Iowa	8,000	7,900	7,800	7,800
Kansas	3,000	2,900	9,200	9,200
Kentucky	1,000	1,000	900	900
Louisiana	710	730	1,050	1,050
Maine	110	110	70	70
Maryland	520	520	330	330
Massachusetts	140	140	30	30
Michigan	1,550	1,500	1,500	1,400
Minnesota	4,800	4,800	5,100	5,100
Mississippi	880	880	900	900
Missouri	2,400	2,400	3,700	3,700
Montana	1,300	1,250	12,200	12,100
Nebraska	4,400	4,300	9,400	9,200
Nevada	140	110	700	640
New Hampshire	30	30	10	10
New Jersey	200	200	90	90
New Mexico	260	260	6,300	6,200
New York	930	930	640	640
North Carolina	1,450	1,450	900	900
North Dakota	2,800	2,700	9,100	8,800
Ohio	2,550	2,650	2,300	2,200
Oklahoma	1,150	1,100	3,600	3,600
Oregon	850	870	2,800	2,800
Pennsylvania	1,700	1,650	750	750
Rhode Island	20	20	10	10
South Carolina	410	380	400	400
South Dakota	2,700	2,600	8,900	8,800
Tennessee	830	830	890	890
Texas	3,000	3,100	14,500	14,800
Utah	310	320	1,000	1,000
Vermont	140	140	80	80
Virginia	830	850	670	670
Washington	1,100	1,100	2,300	2,300
West Virginia	150	150	100	110
Wisconsin	2,550	2,400	1,900	1,800
Wyoming	390	380	6,100	6,100
United States	72,180	71,170	138,920	138,090

See footnote(s) at end of table.

Table 9-5.—Number of farms and land in farms by economic sales class by State and United States, 2018–2019—Continued

State	Economic Sales Class: $1,000,000 or more			
	Number of Farms		Land in Farms	
	2018	2019	2018	2019
	Number	*Number*	*1,000 Acres*	*1,000 Acres*
Alabama	1,700	1,600	1,200	1,150
Alaska	(D)	(D)	(D)	(D)
Arizona	410	420	3,100	3,200
Arkansas	3,350	3,400	5,500	5,600
California	6,600	6,400	11,200	11,000
Colorado	900	880	6,500	6,300
Connecticut	80	80	80	80
Delaware	470	470	260	260
Florida	1,200	1,200	3,600	3,700
Georgia	2,500	2,450	2,400	2,400
Hawaii	90	90	320	320
Idaho	1,100	1,100	4,100	4,100
Illinois	4,400	4,400	10,400	10,600
Indiana	2,900	2,850	5,800	5,900
Iowa	6,400	6,400	9,100	9,200
Kansas	2,450	2,550	13,300	13,400
Kentucky	1,250	1,200	2,400	2,400
Louisiana	1,100	1,050	2,550	2,550
Maine	140	140	290	290
Maryland	670	670	580	580
Massachusetts	(D)	(D)	(D)	(D)
Michigan	1,700	1,650	3,000	2,950
Minnesota	4,400	4,300	8,400	8,300
Mississippi	1,900	1,900	3,000	3,100
Missouri	2,250	2,250	5,700	5,700
Montana	600	650	9,900	10,000
Nebraska	4,100	4,200	16,300	16,200
Nevada	130	140	2,500	2,550
New Hampshire	(D)	(D)	(D)	(D)
New Jersey	220	220	140	140
New Mexico	330	340	6,000	6,100
New York	920	920	1,700	1,700
North Carolina	3,250	3,200	2,900	2,900
North Dakota	2,600	2,500	13,900	14,000
Ohio	2,150	2,250	3,200	3,000
Oklahoma	1,050	1,050	4,200	4,200
Oregon	950	980	3,700	3,700
Pennsylvania	1,350	1,350	970	970
Rhode Island	(D)	(D)	(D)	(D)
South Carolina	880	910	910	970
South Dakota	2,250	2,300	13,300	13,200
Tennessee	870	870	1,900	1,900
Texas	3,550	3,600	23,700	23,500
Utah	270	280	3,900	3,900
Vermont	170	170	260	260
Virginia	910	890	1,000	1,000
Washington	1,450	1,450	4,600	4,600
West Virginia	150	150	110	110
Wisconsin	2,150	2,050	3,600	3,500
Wyoming	200	210	6,100	6,200
Other States [1]	120	120	60	60
United States	78,580	78,250	227,630	227,740

(D) Withheld to avoid disclosing data for individual operations.   [1] Includes data withheld above.
NASS, Environmental, Economics, and Demographics Branch, (202) 720–6146.

Table 9-6.—Number of farms and land in farms by State and United States, 2018–2019

State	Number of Farms [1]		Land in farms		Average farm size	
	2018	2019	2018	2019	2018	2019
	Number	Number	1,000 acres	1,000 acres	Acres	Acres
Alabama	39,700	38,800	8,500	8,300	214	214
Alaska	1,000	1,050	850	850	850	810
Arizona	19,200	19,000	26,200	26,200	1,365	1,379
Arkansas	42,500	42,300	13,900	14,000	327	331
California	69,400	69,900	24,300	24,300	350	348
Colorado	38,900	38,700	31,800	31,800	817	822
Connecticut	5,500	5,500	380	380	69	69
Delaware	2,300	2,300	530	530	230	230
Florida	47,500	47,400	9,700	9,700	204	205
Georgia	41,600	41,500	10,100	10,200	243	246
Hawaii	7,300	7,300	1,100	1,100	151	151
Idaho	24,800	24,600	11,600	11,500	468	467
Illinois	72,000	71,400	27,000	27,000	375	378
Indiana	56,100	56,000	15,000	14,900	267	266
Iowa	86,000	85,300	30,600	30,600	356	359
Kansas	58,900	58,500	45,800	45,700	778	781
Kentucky	75,100	74,800	12,900	12,900	172	172
Louisiana	27,400	27,400	8,000	8,000	292	292
Maine	7,600	7,600	1,300	1,300	171	171
Maryland	12,400	12,400	2,000	2,000	161	161
Massachusetts	7,200	7,200	500	500	69	69
Michigan	47,000	47,000	9,800	9,800	209	209
Minnesota	68,500	68,000	25,500	25,500	372	375
Mississippi	34,700	34,500	10,400	10,400	300	301
Missouri	95,000	95,200	27,700	27,600	292	290
Montana	26,900	26,800	58,000	58,000	2,156	2,164
Nebraska	45,900	45,700	45,000	44,900	980	982
Nevada	3,400	3,350	6,100	6,100	1,794	1,821
New Hampshire	4,100	4,100	430	430	105	105
New Jersey	9,900	9,900	750	750	76	76
New Mexico	24,700	24,800	40,500	40,000	1,640	1,613
New York	33,400	33,400	6,900	6,900	207	207
North Carolina	46,400	46,200	8,400	8,400	181	182
North Dakota	26,100	26,100	39,300	39,300	1,506	1,506
Ohio	77,800	77,800	13,900	13,600	179	175
Oklahoma	77,300	77,300	34,200	34,400	442	445
Oregon	37,200	37,200	16,000	15,800	430	425
Pennsylvania	53,000	52,700	7,300	7,300	138	139
Rhode Island	1,100	1,100	60	60	55	55
South Carolina	24,600	24,600	4,800	4,800	195	195
South Dakota	29,600	29,600	43,200	43,200	1,459	1,459
Tennessee	70,000	69,700	10,900	10,800	156	155
Texas	247,000	247,000	127,000	126,500	514	512
Utah	18,100	17,800	10,700	10,700	591	601
Vermont	6,800	6,800	1,200	1,200	176	176
Virginia	42,500	42,400	7,800	7,800	184	184
Washington	35,700	35,600	14,700	14,600	412	410
West Virginia	23,400	22,900	3,600	3,500	154	153
Wisconsin	64,800	64,900	14,300	14,300	221	220
Wyoming	11,900	12,000	29,000	29,000	2,437	2,417
United States	2,029,200	2,023,400	899,500	897,400	443	444

[1] A farm is any establishment from which $1,000 or more of agricultural products were produced and sold or would normally have been sold during the year.
NASS, Environmental, Economics, and Demographics Branch, (202) 720–6146.

Table 9-7.—Farms: Classification by tenure of operator, United States, 1940–2017

Year	Farms	Tenure of operator			
		Full owners	Part owners	Managers	All tenants
	Number	Percent	Percent	Percent	Percent
1940	6,102,417	50.6	10.1	0.6	38.8
1945 [1]	5,859,169	56.4	11.3	0.7	31.7
1950	5,388,437	57.4	15.3	0.4	26.9
1954 [1]	4,783,021	57.4	18.2	0.4	24.0
1959	3,710,503	57.1	21.9	0.6	20.5
1964	3,157,857	57.6	24.8	0.6	17.1
1969	2,730,250	62.5	24.6	....	12.9
1974	2,314,013	61.5	27.2	....	11.3
1978	2,257,775	57.5	30.2	....	12.3
1982	2,240,976	59.2	29.3	....	11.6
1987	2,087,759	59.3	29.2	....	11.5
1992	1,925,300	57.7	31.0	....	11.3
1997	1,911,859	60.0	30.0	....	10.0
2002 [2]	2,128,982	67.1	25.9	....	7.0
2007 [2]	2,204,792	69.0	24.6	....	6.4
2012 [2]	2,109,303	67.7	25.3	....	7.0
2017	2,042,220	69.0	24.1	....	6.9

[1] Excludes Alaska and Hawaii.   [2] The 2002 Census of Agriculture introduced new methodology to account for all farms in the United States.   All 2002 published census items were reweighted for undercoverage.   Strictly speaking, data for 2002 and subsequent years are not fully comparable with data from earlier years.
NASS, Environmental, Economics, and Demographics Branch, (202) 720-6146.

Table 9-8.—Farmland Rented: Classification by tenants and part owners, United States, 1920–2017

Year	Land in farms	Land rented by tenure of operator [1]			Percentage of land rented
		Tenants	Part owners	Total	
	Million acres	Million acres	Million acres	Million acres	Percent
1920	958.7	[3]265.0	[4]54.7	319.7	33.3
1925	924.3	264.9	96.3	361.2	39.1
1930	990.1	307.3	125.2	432.5	43.7
1935	1,054.5	336.8	134.3	471.1	44.7
1940	1,065.1	313.2	155.9	469.1	44.0
1945	1,141.6	251.6	178.9	430.5	37.7
1950	1,161.4	212.2	196.2	408.4	35.2
1954	1,158.2	192.6	212.3	404.9	35.0
1959	1,123.0	166.8	234.1	400.9	35.7
1964	1,110.2	144.9	248.1	[5]393.0	35.4
1969	1,063.3	137.6	241.8	379.4	35.7
1974	1,017.0	122.3	258.4	380.7	37.4
1978	1,029.7	124.1	282.2	406.2	39.4
1982	986.2	113.6	269.9	383.5	38.9
1987	964.5	126.9	275.4	402.3	41.7
1992	945.5	122.7	282.2	404.9	42.8
1997	931.8	108.1	270.0	378.1	40.6
2002 [6]	938.3	86.5	266.8	353.3	37.7
2007 [6]	922.1	81.8	269.0	350.8	38.0
2012 [6]	914.5	87.0	268.1	355.1	38.8
2017	900.2	86.9	274.2	361.1	39.4

[1] Columns 3, 4, and 5 refer only to land rented from others and operated, so subleased land is not included.   Acres of land rented are comparable in the same year, but definitions change over time.   Basic sources are 1969 Census of Agriculture, table 5, p.14; 1974 Census of Agriculture, table 3, pp.1-6; 1978 Census of Agriculture, vol. 1, part 51, table 5, pp. 124-127; 1982 Census of Agriculture, vol. 1, part 51, table 48, p. 49; 1987 Census of Agriculture vol. 1 part 51, table 48, p. 49; 1992 Census of Agriculture, vol. 1, part 51, table 46, p. 53; 1997 Census of Agriculture, vol. 1, part 51, chapter 1, table 46, p. 57; 2002 Census of Agriculture, vol. 1, part 51, chapter 1, table 61, p. 214; 2007 Census of Agriculture, vol. 1, part 51, chapter 1, table 65, p. 262; 2012 Census of Agriculture, vol. 1, part 51, table 70, p. 231; and earlier census volumes as noted.   [2] Assumes land leased by part-owners is the difference between the average size of full-owner and part-owner farms.   Acreage leased by part-owners is this difference times the number of part-owners.   1910 Census of Agriculture, chapter 11, table 1 and 3, pp.97-99.   [3] 1920 Census of Agriculture, vol. VI, part 1, table 5, p. 19.   [4] Assumes same proportion of owner and part-owner as in 1910.   [5] 1964 Census of Agriculture, vol. II, chapter 8, p.757.   [6] The 2002 Census of Agriculture introduced new methodology to account for all farms in the United States.   All 2002 published census items were reweighted for undercoverage.   Strictly speaking, data for 2002 and subsequent years are not fully comparable with data from earlier years.
NASS, Environmental, Economics, and Demographics Branch, (202) 720-6146.

Table 9-9.—Land: Utilization, by State and United States, 2012

State	Cropland			Grassland pasture	Forest land
	Used for crops	Idle	Used only for pasture		
	1,000 acres	*1,000 acres*	*1,000 acres*	*1,000 acres*	*1,000 acres*
Alabama	2,231	415	161	2,892	22,800
Alaska	31	45	4	696	91,817
Arizona	908	142	84	43,580	13,000
Arkansas	7,466	585	184	4,127	18,544
California	8,316	780	481	26,667	16,991
Colorado	8,013	2,218	437	31,734	15,138
Connecticut	104	9	9	22	1,346
Delaware	420	11	7	18	331
Florida	2,122	452	260	5,100	15,827
Georgia	3,799	457	129	1,680	24,352
Hawaii	161	189	22	770	1,299
Idaho	4,790	789	221	18,391	16,771
Illinois	22,672	1,175	88	1,728	4,772
Indiana	12,216	414	80	1,656	4,748
Iowa	24,750	1,738	225	2,879	2,968
Kansas	25,545	2,598	449	17,781	2,402
Kentucky	5,400	641	328	4,742	11,886
Louisiana	3,497	869	218	2,275	14,645
Maine	328	55	8	159	17,191
Maryland	1,254	108	15	447	2,329
Massachusetts	130	14	5	79	2,088
Michigan	7,192	483	91	1,982	19,262
Minnesota	20,394	1,887	171	3,568	15,929
Mississippi	4,372	638	163	2,715	19,495
Missouri	13,455	1,591	580	9,792	15,085
Montana	12,522	3,181	902	47,629	18,429
Nebraska	20,442	1,090	326	23,677	1,470
Nevada	478	42	57	52,329	5,417
New Hampshire	73	18	2	116	4,341
New Jersey	403	29	16	78	1,116
New Mexico	1,183	534	231	54,344	13,278
New York	3,816	318	113	2,397	15,920
North Carolina	4,085	294	95	1,579	18,078
North Dakota	24,081	2,718	322	13,336	517
Ohio	10,190	530	109	2,144	7,864
Oklahoma	9,155	1,123	1,011	19,756	7,656
Oregon	3,522	834	308	23,863	24,116
Pennsylvania	3,952	446	119	1,287	16,242
Rhode Island	19	4	2	7	290
South Carolina	1,540	308	55	976	13,025
South Dakota	17,624	1,203	528	24,972	1,789
Tennessee	4,479	374	408	3,424	13,500
Texas	21,598	4,773	2,844	104,603	14,357
Utah	1,090	246	140	32,774	9,810
Vermont	379	19	15	305	4,476
Virginia	2,636	205	148	2,794	15,385
Washington	5,558	1,856	125	7,314	18,081
West Virginia	685	42	54	1,351	11,780
Wisconsin	9,301	607	164	2,864	16,727
Wyoming	1,523	207	256	46,086	7,002
United States [1]	339,900	39,306	12,769	655,486	631,682

[1] Distributions may not sum to totals due to rounding.

NASS, Environmental, Economics, and Demographics Branch, (202) 720–6146. See notes to Table 9-11 for definitions and data sources. Estimates developed for years coinciding with a Census of Agriculture.

Table 9-10.—Land in farms: Irrigated land, by State and United States, 1982–2012 [1]

State	1982	1987	1992	1997	2002	2007	2012
	1,000 acres	*1,000 acres*	*1,000 acres*	*1,000 acres*	*1,000 acres*	*1,000 acres*	*1,000 acres*
Alabama	66	84	82	80	109	113	113
Alaska	1	2	2	3	3	4	2
Arizona	1,098	914	956	1,075	932	876	881
Arkansas	2,022	2,406	2,702	3,785	4,150	4,461	4,804
California	8,461	7,596	7,571	8,887	8,709	8,016	7,862
Colorado	3,201	3,014	3,170	3,374	2,591	2,868	2,517
Connecticut	7	7	6	8	10	10	9
Delaware	44	61	62	75	97	105	127
Florida	1,585	1,623	1,783	1,874	1,815	1,552	1,493
Georgia	575	640	725	773	871	1,018	1,125
Hawaii	146	149	134	77	69	59	82
Idaho	3,450	3,219	3,260	3,544	3,289	3,300	3,365
Illinois	166	208	328	352	391	474	522
Indiana	132	170	241	256	313	397	437
Iowa	91	92	116	133	142	190	172
Kansas	2,675	2,463	2,680	2,696	2,678	2,763	2,881
Kentucky	23	38	28	60	37	59	74
Louisiana	694	647	898	961	939	954	1,093
Maine	6	6	10	22	20	21	31
Maryland	39	51	57	69	81	93	105
Massachusetts	17	20	20	27	24	23	23
Michigan	286	315	366	407	456	500	592
Minnesota	315	354	370	403	455	506	524
Mississippi	431	637	883	1,110	1,176	1,369	1,652
Missouri	403	535	709	921	1,033	1,200	1,181
Montana	2,023	1,997	1,978	2,102	1,976	2,013	1,903
Nebraska	6,039	5,682	6,312	7,066	7,625	8,559	8,297
Nevada	830	779	556	764	747	691	688
New Hampshire	1	3	2	3	2	2	3
New Jersey	83	91	80	94	97	95	88
New Mexico	807	718	738	852	845	830	680
New York	52	51	47	74	75	68	60
North Carolina	81	138	113	156	264	232	175
North Dakota	163	168	187	183	203	236	218
Ohio	28	32	29	35	41	38	47
Oklahoma	492	478	512	509	518	535	480
Oregon	1,808	1,648	1,622	1,963	1,908	1,845	1,630
Pennsylvania	18	30	23	40	43	38	39
Rhode Island	2	4	3	3	4	4	4
South Carolina	81	81	76	89	96	132	159
South Dakota	376	362	371	367	401	374	379
Tennessee	18	38	37	47	61	81	146
Texas	5,576	4,271	4,912	5,764	5,075	5,010	4,489
Utah	1,082	1,161	1,143	1,218	1,091	1,134	1,104
Vermont	1	2	2	3	2	2	4
Virginia	43	79	62	86	99	82	69
Washington	1,638	1,519	1,641	1,787	1,823	1,736	1,634
West Virginia	1	3	3	4	2	2	2
Wisconsin	259	285	331	358	386	377	422
Wyoming	1,565	1,518	1,465	1,750	1,542	1,551	1,436
United States	49,003	46,386	49,404	56,289	55,316	56,599	55,822
Puerto Rico	42	36	46	35	43	40	52
Virgin Islands	(3)	(3)	(3)	(3)	(2)	(2)	(3)
Total	49,002	46,386	49,404	55,058	55,360	56,639	55,874

[1] Distributions may not sum to totals due to rounding. [2] Less than 500 acres. [3] Not available.
NASS, Environmental, Economics, and Demographics Branch, (202) 720–6146. 1982-1992 data from the Census of Agriculture, U.S. Department of Commerce. Beginning in 1997 from the Census of Agriculture, U.S. Department of Agriculture. Estimates developed for years coinciding with a Census of Agriculture.

Table 9-11.—Land utilization, United States, selected years, 1987–2012

Major land uses	1987	1992	1997	2002	2007	2012
	Million acres	Million acres	Million acres	Million acres	Million acres	Million acres
Cropland used for crops [1]	331	338	349	340	335	340
Idle cropland	68	56	39	40	37	39
Cropland used for pasture [2]	65	67	68	62	36	13
Grassland pasture [3]	591	591	580	587	614	655
Forest land [4]	648	648	641	651	671	632
Special uses [5]	279	281	286	297	313	316
Urban areas [6]	57	59	66	60	61	70
Other land [7]	227	224	236	228	197	196
Total land area [8]	2,265	2,263	2,263	2,264	2,264	2,260

[1] Cropland harvested, crop failure, and cultivated summer fallow. [2] The 2007 and 2012 estimates declined due to a change in the methodology for determining cropland used for pasture. [3] Grassland and other nonforest pasture and range. [4] Excludes reserved and other forest land duplicated in parks and special uses of land. Includes forested grazing land. [5] Includes rural transportation areas, Federal and State areas used primarily for recreation and wildlife purposes, military areas, farmsteads, and farm roads and lanes. [6] The 2002 urban acreage estimate is not directly comparable to estimates in prior years due to a change in the definition of urban areas in the 2000 Census of Population and Housing. The apparent change in "urban" acreage between 1997 and 2002 reflects a definitional change, rather than a decline in acreage. [7] Miscellaneous areas such as marshes, open swamps, bare rock areas, deserts, and other uses not inventoried. [8] Remeasurement and increases in reservoirs account for changes in total land areas.

NASS, Environmental, Economics, and Demographics Branch, (202) 720–6146. Estimates developed for years coinciding with a Census of Agriculture.

Table 9-12.—Farm real estate: Value of farmland and buildings, Region, State, and United States, 2016–2019 [1]

Region and State	Total value of land and buildings			
	2016	2017	2018	2019
	Million dollars	Million dollars	Million dollars	Million dollars
Northeast:				
Connecticut	4,641	4,598	4,674	4,636
Delaware	4,311	4,373	4,457	4,744
Maine	2,873	3,081	3,081	3,133
Maryland	14,940	15,240	15,720	16,120
Massachusetts	5,350	5,292	5,450	5,550
New Hampshire	1,982	2,090	2,107	2,141
New Jersey	9,709	9,782	10,125	10,125
New York	21,770	21,804	22,287	22,425
Pennsylvania	42,486	44,019	45,625	47,231
Rhode Island	876	894	912	936
Vermont	4,080	4,164	4,248	4,356
Lake States:				
Michigan	48,020	48,412	48,608	48,608
Minnesota	122,624	124,185	123,675	123,420
Wisconsin	65,088	69,641	70,070	70,785
Corn Belt:				
Illinois	197,100	193,320	196,560	196,560
Indiana	101,767	98,700	98,700	98,042
Iowa	225,522	224,910	222,462	220,014
Missouri	89,838	86,736	93,626	93,840
Ohio	83,580	84,140	86,180	85,544
Northern Plains:				
Kansas	87,478	86,562	84,730	89,572
Nebraska	130,050	126,900	123,750	127,965
North Dakota	68,775	68,382	67,203	68,382
South Dakota	94,827	90,720	89,424	89,424
Appalachian:				
Kentucky	46,020	47,840	48,633	49,278
North Carolina	38,675	38,472	38,976	39,312
Tennessee	41,093	41,856	42,728	43,092
Virginia	35,313	35,802	36,036	36,270
West Virginia	9,432	9,768	9,540	9,380
Southeast:				
Alabama	24,252	25,026	25,330	25,730
Florida	52,896	56,842	57,230	57,715
Georgia	34,100	35,600	35,451	35,394
South Carolina	15,264	15,228	15,888	16,320
Delta States:				
Arkansas	41,700	43,229	43,924	46,480
Louisiana	22,960	23,680	24,320	24,960
Mississippi	27,195	27,664	28,496	29,120
Southern Plains:				
Oklahoma	57,967	59,850	61,560	64,328
Texas	234,600	243,840	260,350	268,180
Mountain:				
Arizona [2]	24,929	26,058	26,493	26,608
Colorado	47,550	48,972	49,608	49,926
Idaho	30,044	31,941	33,292	34,500
Montana	52,443	53,278	53,128	53,070
Nevada [2]	5,829	5,722	5,722	5,722
New Mexico [2]	20,586	20,977	21,100	20,982
Utah [2]	15,512	15,983	16,290	17,019
Wyoming	20,481	20,648	21,054	21,460
Pacific:				
California	200,384	219,765	227,205	243,000
Oregon	35,840	37,760	38,880	39,500
Washington	39,396	40,572	41,748	41,172
United States [3]	2,602,148	2,644,318	2,686,656	2,732,071

[1] Total value of land and buildings is derived by multiplying average value per acre of farm real estate by the land in farms. [2] Value of all land and buildings adjusted to include American Indian reservation land value. [3] Excludes Alaska and Hawaii.

NASS, Environmental, Economics, and Demographics Branch, (202) 720–6146.

Table 9-13.—Farm real estate: Average value per acre - Region, State, and United States, 2016–2019

Region and State	2016	2017	2018	2019
	Dollars	Dollars	Dollars	Dollars
Northeast:	5,270	5,380	5,550	5,690
Connecticut	11,900	12,100	12,300	12,200
Delaware	8,290	8,250	8,410	8,950
Maine	2,210	2,370	2,370	2,410
Maryland	7,470	7,620	7,860	8,060
Massachusetts	10,700	10,800	10,900	11,100
New Hampshire	4,610	4,860	4,900	4,980
New Jersey	13,300	13,400	13,500	13,500
New York	3,110	3,160	3,230	3,250
Pennsylvania	5,820	6,030	6,250	6,470
Rhode Island	14,600	14,900	15,200	15,600
Vermont	3,400	3,470	3,540	3,630
Lake:	4,730	4,880	4,890	4,900
Michigan	4,900	4,940	4,960	4,960
Minnesota	4,790	4,870	4,850	4,840
Wisconsin	4,520	4,870	4,900	4,950
Corn Belt:	6,100	5,990	6,110	6,100
Illinois	7,300	7,160	7,280	7,280
Indiana	6,830	6,580	6,580	6,580
Iowa	7,370	7,350	7,270	7,190
Missouri	3,220	3,120	3,380	3,400
Ohio	5,970	6,010	6,200	6,290
Northern Plains:	2,200	2,150	2,110	2,170
Kansas	1,910	1,890	1,850	1,960
Nebraska	2,890	2,820	2,750	2,850
North Dakota	1,750	1,740	1,710	1,740
South Dakota	2,190	2,100	2,070	2,070
Appalachian:	3,880	3,970	4,030	4,080
Kentucky	3,540	3,680	3,770	3,820
North Carolina	4,550	4,580	4,640	4,680
Tennessee	3,770	3,840	3,920	3,990
Virginia	4,470	4,590	4,620	4,650
West Virginia	2,620	2,640	2,650	2,680
Southeast:	3,830	3,990	4,050	4,090
Alabama	2,820	2,910	2,980	3,100
Florida	5,510	5,860	5,900	5,950
Georgia	3,410	3,560	3,510	3,470
South Carolina	3,180	3,240	3,310	3,400
Delta:	2,830	2,920	3,000	3,100
Arkansas	3,000	3,110	3,160	3,320
Louisiana	2,870	2,960	3,040	3,120
Mississippi	2,590	2,660	2,740	2,800
Southern Plains:	1,810	1,880	2,000	2,070
Oklahoma	1,690	1,750	1,800	1,870
Texas	1,840	1,920	2,050	2,120
Mountain:	1,140	1,170	1,200	1,220
Arizona [1]	3,570	3,770	3,780	3,800
Colorado	1,500	1,540	1,560	1,570
Idaho	2,590	2,730	2,870	3,000
Montana	898	917	916	915
Nevada [1]	1,040	1,020	1,020	1,020
New Mexico [1]	540	558	565	570
Utah [1]	2,160	2,230	2,310	2,420
Wyoming	699	712	726	740
Pacific:	4,960	5,440	5,610	5,900
California	8,080	8,970	9,350	10,000
Oregon	2,240	2,360	2,430	2,500
Washington	2,680	2,760	2,840	2,820
United States [2]	2,990	3,030	3,100	3,160

[1] Excludes American Indian Reservation Land. [2] Excludes Alaska and Hawaii.
NASS, Environmental, Economics, and Demographics Branch, (202) 720–6146.

Table 9-14.—Land values, cropland and pasture average value per acre: Region, State, and United States, 2016–2019

Region and State	Cropland			
	2016	2017	2018	2019
	Dollars	*Dollars*	*Dollars*	*Dollars*
Northeast:				
Delaware	5,650	5,700	5,940	6,040
Maryland	8,090	7,960	8,120	8,600
New Jersey	6,910	7,050	7,280	7,370
New York	13,500	13,600	13,700	13,700
Pennsylvania	2,690	2,740	2,800	2,810
Other States [1]	6,450	6,470	6,890	7,030
	7,290	7,630	7,650	7,900
Lake:				
Michigan	4,750	4,840	4,810	4,760
Minnesota	4,590	4,580	4,510	4,500
Wisconsin	4,840	4,920	4,950	4,810
	4,660	4,870	4,740	4,850
Corn Belt:				
Illinois	6,500	6,380	6,370	6,360
Indiana	7,350	7,210	7,280	7,300
Iowa	6,690	6,300	6,210	6,210
Missouri	7,510	7,440	7,290	7,260
Ohio	3,570	3,560	3,490	3,490
	6,070	6,150	6,320	6,400
Northern Plains:				
Kansas	2,900	2,760	2,740	2,790
Nebraska	2,080	2,010	2,060	2,160
North Dakota	4,750	4,430	4,380	4,390
South Dakota	1,910	1,890	1,870	1,920
	3,430	3,200	3,120	3,130
Appalachian:				
Kentucky	3,980	4,070	4,140	4,190
North Carolina	3,980	4,140	4,250	4,300
Tennessee	4,060	4,090	4,130	4,180
Virginia	3,670	3,730	3,830	3,910
West Virginia	4,610	4,730	4,760	4,720
	3,220	3,250	3,250	3,280
Southeast:				
Alabama	4,030	4,060	4,160	4,120
Florida	3,080	3,170	3,300	3,430
Georgia	6,860	6,940	7,040	7,190
South Carolina	3,420	3,430	3,430	3,210
	2,610	2,700	2,790	2,830
Delta:				
Arkansas	2,690	2,770	2,840	2,920
Louisiana	2,660	2,730	2,780	2,850
Mississippi	2,590	2,700	2,790	2,880
	2,810	2,900	3,000	3,080
Southern Plains:				
Oklahoma	1,700	1,780	1,820	1,860
Texas	1,530	1,590	1,630	1,670
	1,770	1,850	1,890	1,930
Mountain:				
Arizona [2]	1,820	1,860	1,910	1,980
Colorado	7,800	7,720	7,610	7,600
Idaho	2,020	2,070	2,100	2,160
Montana	3,420	3,570	3,740	3,930
Nevada [2]	1,010	1,010	1,020	1,040
New Mexico [2]	(D)	(D)	(D)	(D)
Utah [2]	1,500	1,560	1,580	1,550
Wyoming	3,530	3,690	3,830	3,970
	1,450	1,460	1,490	1,520
Pacific:				
California	6,350	6,650	6,830	7,190
Oregon	11,160	11,630	12,170	12,830
Washington	2,780	2,920	3,000	3,080
	2,590	2,660	2,630	2,630
United States [3]	4,040	4,030	4,050	4,100

See footnote(s) at end of table.

Table 9-14.—Land values, cropland and pasture average value per acre: Region, State, and United States, 2016–2019—Continued

Region, State, and land type	Irrigated and Non-Irrigated Cropland			
	2016	2017	2018	2019
	Dollars	Dollars	Dollars	Dollars
Corn Belt:				
Missouri all cropland	3,570	3,560	3,490	3,490
Irrigated	4,830	4,940	4,770	4,770
Non-irrigated	3,470	3,450	3,380	3,350
Northern Plains:				
Kansas all cropland	2,080	2,010	2,060	2,160
Irrigated	3,050	2,910	2,980	3,320
Non-irrigated	1,970	1,910	1,960	2,050
Nebraska all cropland	4,750	4,430	4,380	4,390
Irrigated	6,430	6,010	5,930	5,850
Non-irrigated	3,720	3,450	3,430	3,490
South Dakota all cropland	3,430	3,200	3,120	3,130
Irrigated	(D)	(D)	(D)	(D)
Non-irrigated	3,410	3,180	3,100	3,100
Southeast:				
Florida all cropland	6,860	6,940	7,040	7,190
Irrigated	7,750	7,860	7,980	8,160
Non-irrigated	6,020	6,070	6,160	6,280
Georgia all cropland	3,420	3,430	3,430	3,210
Irrigated	4,010	4,080	4,560	4,030
Non-irrigated	3,210	3,190	3,020	2,870
Delta:				
Arkansas all cropland	2,660	2,730	2,780	2,850
Irrigated	3,150	3,230	3,290	3,340
Non-irrigated	1,920	1,960	1,990	2,060
Louisiana all cropland	2,590	2,700	2,790	2,880
Irrigated	2,520	2,660	2,750	2,820
Non-irrigated	2,620	2,710	2,810	2,900
Mississippi all cropland	2,810	2,900	3,000	3,080
Irrigated	3,300	3,440	3,580	3,620
Non-irrigated	2,580	2,640	2,720	2,770
Southern Plains:				
Oklahoma all cropland	1,530	1,590	1,630	1,670
Irrigated	(D)	(D)	(D)	(D)
Non-irrigated	1,520	1,580	1,610	1,650
Texas all cropland	1,770	1,850	1,890	1,930
Irrigated	1,920	2,020	2,160	2,230
Non-irrigated	1,750	1,820	1,840	1,880
Mountain:				
Arizona all cropland [2]	7,800	7,720	7,610	7,600
Irrigated	7,800	7,720	7,610	7,600
Colorado all cropland	2,020	2,070	2,100	2,160
Irrigated	4,860	4,950	5,050	5,100
Non-irrigated	1,320	1,360	1,370	1,370
Idaho all cropland	3,420	3,570	3,740	3,930
Irrigated	5,180	5,410	5,690	6,020
Non-irrigated	1,470	1,530	1,590	1,650
Montana all cropland	1,010	1,010	1,020	1,040
Irrigated	2,970	2,970	2,990	3,010
Non-irrigated	818	827	836	835
Nevada all cropland [2]	(D)	(D)	(D)	(D)
Irrigated	(D)	(D)	(D)	(D)
New Mexico all cropland [2]	1,500	1,560	1,580	1,550
Irrigated	4,080	4,140	4,190	4,200
Non-irrigated	405	463	469	475
Utah all cropland [2]	3,530	3,690	3,830	3,970
Irrigated	5,660	5,930	6,160	6,360
Non-irrigated	1,240	1,270	1,320	1,400
Wyoming all cropland	1,450	1,460	1,490	1,520
Irrigated	2,330	2,340	2,390	2,430
Non-irrigated	816	820	836	840
Pacific:				
California all cropland	11,160	11,630	12,170	12,830
Irrigated	13,200	13,700	14,300	15,100
Non-irrigated	4,400	4,740	5,090	5,400
Oregon all cropland	2,780	2,920	3,000	3,080
Irrigated	4,730	4,950	5,180	5,290
Non-irrigated	2,060	2,170	2,200	2,220
Washington all cropland	2,590	2,660	2,630	2,630
Irrigated	7,760	8,000	7,930	7,690
Non-irrigated	1,250	1,270	1,260	1,260

See footnote(s) at end of table.

FARM RESOURCES, INCOME, AND EXPENSES

Table 9-14.—Land values, cropland and pasture average value per acre: Region, State, and United States, 2016–2019-Continued

Region and State	Pasture			
	2016	2017	2018	2019
	Dollars	*Dollars*	*Dollars*	*Dollars*
Northeast:				
Maryland	3,550	3,640	3,770	3,870
New Jersey	6,450	6,580	(D)	(D)
New York	13,000	13,100	13,300	13,400
Pennsylvania	1,460	1,480	1,560	1,530
Other States [1]	2,860	3,020	3,140	3,290
	6,040	6,160	6,410	6,530
Lake:				
Michigan	2,020	2,050	2,080	2,080
Minnesota	2,650	2,620	2,600	2,590
Wisconsin	1,680	1,740	1,750	1,700
	2,190	2,200	2,260	2,310
Corn Belt:				
Illinois	2,330	2,260	2,320	2,330
Indiana	3,350	3,240	3,200	3,170
Iowa	2,480	2,430	2,430	2,450
Missouri	3,190	2,850	2,790	2,720
Ohio	1,830	1,830	1,920	1,980
	3,250	3,240	3,370	3,350
Northern Plains:				
Kansas	1,000	1,020	1,040	1,090
Nebraska	1,310	1,310	1,320	1,390
North Dakota	891	904	975	1,050
South Dakota	794	804	776	820
	993	1,020	1,040	1,050
Appalachian:				
Kentucky	3,440	3,500	3,530	3,540
North Carolina	2,880	2,970	3,000	3,030
Tennessee	4,810	4,840	4,830	4,810
Virginia	3,610	3,670	3,870	3,860
West Virginia	4,090	4,150	4,050	4,020
	2,060	2,100	2,090	2,120
Southeast:				
Alabama	4,000	4,030	4,180	4,180
Florida	2,280	2,360	2,470	2,590
Georgia	5,200	5,240	5,380	5,360
South Carolina	3,540	3,570	3,660	3,730
	3,120	3,180	3,260	3,240
Delta:				
Arkansas	2,420	2,480	2,550	2,620
Louisiana	2,410	2,460	2,530	2,610
Mississippi	2,570	2,660	2,750	2,830
	2,300	2,350	2,410	2,430
Southern Plains:				
Oklahoma	1,480	1,490	1,540	1,620
Texas	1,380	1,350	1,380	1,460
	1,500	1,520	1,570	1,660
Mountain:				
Arizona [2]	636	647	667	683
Colorado	(D)	(D)	(D)	(D)
Idaho	803	818	835	845
Montana	1,350	1,420	1,490	1,560
Nevada [2]	649	658	667	680
New Mexico [2]	(D)	(D)	(D)	(D)
Utah [2]	363	379	394	417
Wyoming	1,100	1,130	1,160	1,240
	540	550	561	575
Pacific:				
California	1,660	1,680	1,680	1,750
Oregon	2,760	2,780	2,810	3,010
Washington	692	715	728	750
	790	782	766	766
United States [3]	1,320	1,330	1,370	1,400

(D) Withheld to avoid disclosing data for individual operations. [1] Includes: Connecticut, Delaware, Maine, Maryland (beginning in 2018), Massachusetts, New Hampshire, Rhode Island, and Vermont. [2] Excludes American Indian Reservation land. [3] Excludes Alaska and Hawaii.

NASS, Environmental, Economics, and Demographics Branch, (202) 720–6146.

Table 9-15.—Cash rents, cropland and pasture: By State, 2018–2019

State	2018				2019			
	Cropland	Irrigated cropland	Non-irrigated cropland	Pasture	Cropland	Irrigated cropland	Non-irrigated cropland	Pasture
	Dollars							
Alabama	61.50	111.00	59.00	22.00	63.50	125.00	60.00	22.00
Arizona	253.00	253.00	....	....	249.00	249.00	....	2.00
Arkansas	111.00	136.00	49.00	18.00	105.00	131.00	49.00	19.00
California	340.00	528.00	....	13.00	423.00	543.00	35.00	13.00
Colorado	74.50	144.00	....	....	79.50	151.00	29.00	6.10
Connecticut	....	....	....	....	....	....	60.00	....
Delaware	112.00	....	....	....	119.00	161.00	97.00	....
Florida	115.00	232.00	53.00	17.00	110.00	216.00	58.00	15.50
Georgia	116.00	190.00	65.00	27.00	126.00	208.00	67.00	30.00
Hawaii	....	....	....	....	271.00	375.00	180.00	16.00
Idaho	160.00	216.00	56.00	11.00	159.00	216.00	56.00	11.00
Illinois	223.00	240.00	223.00	39.00	224.00	241.00	224.00	41.00
Indiana	198.00	244.00	196.00	....	194.00	238.00	193.00	43.00
Iowa	231.00	....	231.00	54.00	230.00	235.00	230.00	59.00
Kansas	66.50	131.00	58.00	19.50	64.50	128.00	57.00	19.00
Kentucky	149.00	....	148.00	....	151.00	220.00	150.00	27.00
Louisiana	89.00	104.00	73.00	18.00	94.50	111.00	75.00	20.00
Maine	....	....	....	....	....	....	62.00	....
Maryland	113.00	....	106.00	....	109.00	196.00	100.00	44.00
Massachusetts	....	....	....	....	88.50	240.00	71.00	....
Michigan	123.00	232.00	115.00	....	127.00	220.00	120.00	30.00
Minnesota	167.00	192.00	166.00	31.00	164.00	205.00	163.00	28.00
Mississippi	120.00	143.00	84.00	19.00	123.00	148.00	87.00	20.00
Missouri	132.00	180.00	125.00	33.00	130.00	186.00	122.00	32.00
Montana	32.00	....	26.50	6.30	32.50	82.00	27.00	6.60
Nebraska	195.00	238.00	150.00	22.50	191.00	237.00	144.00	24.50
Nevada	....	....	....	....	164.00	164.00	....	10.00
New Hampshire	....	....	....	....	44.00	....	40.00	....
New Jersey	77.50	....	....	....	82.00	139.00	65.00	45.00
New Mexico	....	....	....	....	80.50	136.00	17.50	2.80
New York	63.00	....	62.00	....	66.00	145.00	65.00	26.00
North Carolina	87.00	110.00	86.00	28.00	90.50	105.00	90.00	26.00
North Dakota	65.00	163.00	64.00	17.00	70.00	164.00	69.00	17.50
Ohio	152.00	....	152.00	....	155.00	199.00	155.00	28.00
Oklahoma	34.00	72.00	32.00	13.50	34.50	78.00	32.00	13.50
Oregon	159.00	215.00	93.00	12.00	152.00	215.00	95.00	11.00
Pennsylvania	80.50	....	80.00	....	94.00	173.00	93.00	27.00
South Carolina	48.50	90.00	44.00	....	47.00	94.00	42.00	18.00
South Dakota	119.00	189.00	117.00	23.00	119.00	194.00	117.00	26.00
Tennessee	98.00	165.00	95.00	20.00	103.00	180.00	99.00	21.00
Texas	42.50	91.00	30.00	6.70	42.50	92.00	30.00	6.80
Utah	64.00	92.00	....	....	75.50	108.00	24.00	4.30
Vermont	....	....	....	....	51.00	....	50.00	29.00
Virginia	63.00	100.00	61.00	21.00	59.00	100.00	57.00	21.00
Washington	203.00	358.00	75.00	....	201.00	360.00	75.00	8.00
West Virginia	45.00	....	45.00	....	43.00	....	43.00	14.00
Wisconsin	140.00	238.00	134.00	40.00	142.00	237.00	137.00	40.00
Wyoming	....	....	....	....	57.50	81.00	16.00	4.40

NASS, Environmental, Economics, and Demographics Branch, (202) 720–6146.

Table 9-16.—Farm assets and claims: Comparative balance sheet of the farming sector, excluding operator households, United States, Dec. 31, 2015–2019

Item	2015	2016	2017	2018	2019
Assets	Billion dollars	Billion dollars	Billion dollars	Billion dollars	Billion dollars
Physical assets:					
Real estate	2,365.7	2,401.4	2,472.8	2,519.0	2,546.0
Non-real estate:					
Livestock and poultry [1]	118.2	109.0	107.1	97.1	99.2
Machinery and motor vehicles [2]	239.5	255.4	272.3	271.0	279.0
Crops [3]	52.5	55.7	56.8	59.7	49.6
Purchased inputs	16.4	14.9	15.8	16.1	13.9
Financial	80.2	70.8	72.9	65.4	81.2
Total	2,880.0	2,914.4	3,005.9	3,026.7	3,075.2
Debt					
Liabilities:					
Real estate	208.8	226.0	236.2	245.7	266.8
Non-real estate	148.0	148.2	154.2	156.3	151.8
Total Debt [4]	356.7	374.2	390.4	402.0	418.6
Equity	2,523.3	2,540.3	2,615.5	2,624.7	2,656.6
Ratio:	Percent	Percent	Percent	Percent	Percent
Debt/equity	14.1	14.7	14.9	15.3	15.8
Debt/assets	12.4	12.8	13.0	13.3	13.6

Note: Data as of February 5, 2021. [1] The U.S. total exceeds the sum of the states because NASS does not release state data for some minor producing states due to disclosure issues. Horses and mules are excluded. [2] Includes only farm share value for trucks and autos. [3] All non-CCC crops held on farms plus the value above loan rate for crops held under CCC. [4] Excludes debt for nonfarm purposes.
ERS, Farm Income Team@ers.usda.gov. http://www.ers.usda.gov/data-products/farm-income-and-wealth-statistics.aspx.

Table 9-17.—Farm labor: Number of workers on farms and average wage rates, United States, 2009–2018

Year	Hired workers [1]	Wage rate [2]
	Thousands	*Dollars Per Hour*
2009		
Jan	603	10.93
Apr	694	10.86
July	892	10.66
Oct	829	10.93
Annual average	754.5	10.83
2010		
Jan	612	11.08
Apr	746	10.82
July	885	10.79
Oct	827	11.13
Annual average	767.5	10.95
2011		
Jan	603	11.30
Apr	([3])	([3])
July	834	10.93
Oct	828	11.15
Annual average	748.8	11.07
2012		
Jan	575	11.52
Apr	748	11.41
July	906	11.36
Oct	876	11.75
Annual average	776.3	11.51
2013		
Jan	596	12.02
Apr	736	11.89
July	906	11.68
Oct	871	11.96
Annual average	777.3	11.87
2014		
Jan	540	12.23
Apr	690	12.01
July	838	11.96
Oct	782	12.12
Annual average	712.5	12.07
2015		
Jan	549	12.53
Apr	687	12.28
July	872	12.47
Oct	841	12.82
Annual average	737.3	12.54
2016		
Jan	582	12.83
Apr	703	12.75
July	840	13.02
Oct	798	13.25
Annual average	730.8	12.98
2017		
Jan	533	13.43
Apr	673	13.23
July	879	13.23
Oct	840	13.42
Annual average	731.3	13.32
2018		
Jan	534	14.08
Apr	648	13.72
July	843	14.28
Oct	784	14.47
Annual average	702.3	14.17

[1] Includes all workers, other than agricultural service workers, who were paid for at least one hour of agricultural work on a farm or ranch during the survey week.   [2] Applies to hired workers only (excludes pay for agricultural service workers).   [3] The Agricultural (Farm) Labor Survey was not conducted for this quarter.
NASS, Economic, Environmental and Demographics Branch, (202) 720–6146.

Table 9-18.—Farm labor: Number of hired workers on farms and average wage rates, by regions and United States, 2018 [1]

Region [2]	Workers on farms	Farm wage rates			
	Hired	Type of worker			
		Field	Livestock	Field and livestock	All hired workers [3]
	Thousands	Dollars per hour	Dollars per hour	Dollars per hour	Dollars per hour
January 7–13, 2018					
Northeast I	28	14.00	13.12	13.45	14.70
Northeast II	27	13.57	12.88	13.25	14.19
Appalachian I	19	12.49	11.57	12.15	13.30
Appalachian II	17	11.68	11.53	11.60	12.89
Southeast	20	10.74	11.33	10.95	11.86
Florida	37	10.80	10.80	10.80	11.64
Lake	35	12.18	12.35	12.30	13.06
Cornbelt I	31	13.09	13.20	13.15	14.29
Cornbelt II	16	13.37	13.08	13.20	13.85
Delta	19	12.35	10.83	11.50	12.23
Northern Plains	25	14.76	13.47	14.05	14.82
Southern Plains	40	11.68	12.48	12.05	12.65
Mountain I	17	13.18	13.14	13.15	14.54
Mountain II	13	12.16	13.93	13.40	14.57
Mountain III	17	12.04	12.33	12.15	13.31
Pacific	37	14.06	14.23	14.10	15.31
California	129	13.55	14.40	13.73	15.61
Hawaii	7	14.35	15.40	14.52	16.20
United States	534	12.84	12.89	12.86	14.08
April 8–14, 2018					
Northeast I	35	13.44	13.03	13.25	14.46
Northeast II	33	13.37	12.68	13.10	13.89
Appalachian I	24	11.87	11.80	11.85	12.69
Appalachian II	18	11.56	11.64	11.60	12.69
Southeast	30	10.35	11.03	10.55	11.23
Florida	38	11.20	12.20	11.25	11.89
Lake	43	12.28	12.41	12.35	13.02
Cornbelt I	42	12.49	13.20	12.75	13.71
Cornbelt II	21	12.74	13.43	13.05	13.64
Delta	32	11.30	10.91	11.15	11.62
Northern Plains	32	14.52	13.47	14.00	14.70
Southern Plains	44	11.40	12.13	11.75	12.26
Mountain I	26	13.16	13.02	13.10	13.84
Mountain II	15	12.08	13.59	13.05	14.13
Mountain III	16	11.77	12.09	11.90	13.13
Pacific	53	14.16	14.10	14.15	14.97
California	140	13.45	14.15	13.58	15.10
Hawaii	6	14.55	15.70	14.77	16.71
United States	648	12.72	12.78	12.74	13.72

See footnote(s) at end of table.

Table 9-18.—Farm labor: Number of hired workers on farms and average wage rates, by regions and United States, 2018 [1]—Continued

Region [2]	Workers on farms	Type of worker			
	Hired	Field	Livestock	Field and livestock	All hired workers [3]
	Thousands	Dollars per hour	Dollars per hour	Dollars per hour	Dollars per hour
July 8–14, 2018					
Northeast I	34	13.14	12.92	13.05	13.74
Northeast II	42	12.57	12.83	12.65	13.45
Appalachian I	40	12.17	12.54	12.25	12.73
Appalachian II	31	11.52	11.77	11.60	12.33
Southeast	27	11.75	10.85	11.50	12.32
Florida	30	11.40	11.40	11.40	12.49
Lake	70	13.76	14.05	13.90	14.49
Cornbelt I	45	13.20	13.36	13.25	14.29
Cornbelt II	24	13.48	12.62	13.15	13.84
Delta	31	11.33	11.67	11.40	11.85
Northern Plains	42	15.12	13.80	14.40	15.14
Southern Plains	57	12.33	12.28	12.30	13.12
Mountain I	27	13.53	14.23	13.85	14.34
Mountain II	21	13.15	13.01	13.10	13.79
Mountain III	18	11.30	12.67	11.95	12.49
Pacific	120	15.39	14.40	15.30	15.69
California	178	14.10	14.15	14.11	15.43
Hawaii	6	14.35	17.00	14.82	16.58
United States	843	13.58	13.22	13.48	14.28
October 7–13, 2018					
Northeast I	36	13.58	12.81	13.30	13.95
Northeast II	35	13.77	13.70	13.75	14.45
Appalachian I	37	12.52	12.68	12.55	13.07
Appalachian II	30	11.63	11.84	11.70	12.39
Southeast	27	11.92	10.82	11.60	12.48
Florida	31	11.60	11.60	11.60	12.63
Lake	66	14.81	14.39	14.60	15.14
Cornbelt I	45	13.93	13.47	13.80	14.76
Cornbelt II	23	13.94	13.65	13.85	14.53
Delta	28	11.32	11.46	11.35	11.83
Northern Plains	40	15.93	13.55	14.80	15.49
Southern Plains	53	12.67	12.73	12.70	13.53
Mountain I	31	13.05	14.11	13.55	13.95
Mountain II	20	12.91	13.26	13.05	13.87
Mountain III	19	11.45	12.67	12.00	12.53
Pacific	90	15.62	14.58	15.50	16.02
California	167	14.10	14.25	14.12	15.50
Hawaii	6	14.55	16.20	14.82	16.26
United States	784	13.74	13.38	13.64	14.47

[1] Includes all workers, other than agricultural service workers, who were paid for at least one hour of agricultural work on a farm or ranch during the survey week.   [2] Multi-state regions consist of the following: Northeast I: Connecticut, Maine, Massachusetts, New Hampshire, New York, Rhode Island, Vermont; Northeast II: Delaware, Maryland, New Jersey, Pennsylvania; Appalachian I: North Carolina, Virginia; Appalachian II: Kentucky, Tennessee, West Virginia; Southeast: Alabama, Georgia, South Carolina; Lake: Michigan, Minnesota, Wisconsin; Cornbelt I: Illinois, Indiana, Ohio; Cornbelt II: Iowa, Missouri; Delta: Arkansas, Louisiana, Mississippi; Northern Plains: Kansas, Nebraska, North Dakota, South Dakota; Southern Plains: Oklahoma, Texas; Mountain I: Idaho, Montana, Wyoming; Mountain II: Colorado, Nevada, Utah; Mountain III: Arizona, New Mexico; Pacific: Oregon, Washington.   [3] Includes field workers, livestock workers, supervisors, and others, excluding agricultural service workers.

NASS, Economic, Environmental and Demographics Branch, (202) 720–6146.

Table 9-19.—Hired farmworkers: Number of Workers and Median Weekly Earnings, 2017–2019

Characteristics	Workers [1]			Median Weekly Earnings [2]		
	2017	2018	2019	2017	2018	2019
	Thousands	Thousands	Thousands	Dollars	Dollars	Dollars
All workers	964	950	965	500	540	560
15–19 years old	69	78	66	300	300	175
20–24 years old	104	108	91	442	459	500
25–34 years old	216	191	215	560	576	560
35–44 years old	199	204	229	520	576	560
45–54 years old	192	169	157	550	570	576
55 years old and older	185	201	207	600	550	560
Male	776	744	744	554	577	576
Female	189	206	220	430	440	480
White [3]	456	426	426	600	597	600
Black and other races [3]	50	55	47	*	*	*
Hispanic	459	469	492	480	528	540
Schooling completed						
Less than 5th grade	51	68	70	464	460	520
5th-8th grade	175	165	157	461	492	500
9th-12th grade (no diploma)	165	183	151	450	480	480
High school diploma	318	300	346	560	600	580
Beyond high school	255	235	241	650	600	673
Full-time (35 or more hours per week) [4]	836	798	819	574	580	585
Part-time (less than 35 hours per week) [4]	126	148	142	240	220	200

* Insufficient number of reports to publish data.   [1] Represents annual average number of persons 15 years old and over in the civilian noninstitutional population who were employed as hired farm managers, supervisors, or laborers.   Employment estimates based on 12 monthly Current Population Survey microdata files.   Earnings estimates based on 12 monthly Current Population Survey Outgoing Rotation Group microdata files.   [2] "Median weekly earnings" is the earnings value that divides farmworkers into two equal-sized groups, one group having earnings above the median and the other group having earnings below the median.   "Earnings" refers to the weekly earnings the farmworker usually earns at a farmwork job, before deductions, and includes any overtime pay or commissions.   [3] Excludes persons of Hispanic origin.   [4] The sum of full-time and part-time workers will not equal the total because usual hours worked varies for some individuals.
ERS, Rural Economy Branch, (202) 694–5416.

Table 9-20.—Crops: Area, United States, 2009–2018

Year	Principal crops				Commercial vegetables, harvested area	Fruits and nuts, bearing area [4]
	Area harvested			Area planted total [3]		
	Feed grains [1]	Food grains [2]	Total [3]			
	1,000 acres	1,000 acres	1,000 acres	1,000 acres	1,000 acres	1,000 acres
2009	89,446	53,195	301.172	319,022	2,946.6	4,050.5
2010	89,984	50,768	303,619	315,414	2,827.2	4,091.5
2011	90,940	48,543	292,652	314,343	2,682.0	4,132.6
2012	96,639	51,687	306,855	324,304	2,762.0	4,113.1
2013	98,095	48,073	303,764	324,937	2,681.2	4,306.1
2014	93,079	49,576	308,368	326,673	2,669.6	4,375.9
2015	93,037	50,267	304,814	319,047	2,637.1	4,398.3
2016	96,455	47,356	305,826	318,977	2,636.2	4,770.4
2017	90,543	40,229	301,779	318,340	2,572.5	4,818.5
2018	89,648	42,800	300,566	319,579	2,498.1	4,056.1

[1] Corn for grain, oats, barley, and sorghum for grain.   [2] Wheat, rye, and rice.   [3] Crops included in area planted and area harvested are corn, sorghum, oats, barley, winter wheat, rye, durum wheat, other spring wheat, rice, soybeans, peanuts, sunflower, cotton, dry edible beans, potatoes, canola, proso millet, and sugarbeets. Harvested acreage for all hay, tobacco, and sugarcane are used in computing total area planted.   [4] Includes the following fruits and nuts: Citrus fruits—oranges, tangerines, Temples, grapefruit, lemons and tangelos; area is for the year of harvest; deciduous fruits—commercial apples, peaches, pears, grapes, cherries, plums, prunes, apricots, bananas, nectarines, figs, kiwifruit, olives, avocados, papayas, dates, berries, guavas, cranberries, pineapples (discontinued as of 2007 crop) and strawberries; nuts—almonds, hazelnuts, macadamias, pistachios, and walnuts.
NASS, Crops Branch, (202) 720–2127.

Table 9-21.—Crops: Area harvested and yield, United States, 2018–2019

Crop	Area harvested		Yield per acre		
	2018	2019	Unit	2018	2019
	1,000 acres	*1,000 acres*			
Grains and hay:					
Barley	1,982	2,221	Bushels	77.5	73.0
Corn for grain	81,740	81,337	Bushels	176.4	167.5
Corn for silage	6,113	6,615	Tons	19.9	20.2
Hay, all	52,839	52,425	Tons	2.34	2.46
Alfalfa	16,608	16,743	Tons	3.17	3.28
All other	36,231	35,682	Tons	1.96	2.07
Oats	865	828	Bushels	64.9	64.3
Proso millet	403	465	Bushels	29.7	35.7
Rice	2,915	2,477	Pounds	7,692	7,473
Rye	273	310	Bushels	30.9	34.3
Sorghum for grain	5,061	4,675	Bushels	72.1	73.0
Sorghum for silage	264	339	Tons	12.6	11.9
Wheat, all	39,612	37,394	Bushels	47.6	51.7
Winter	24,742	24,592	Bushels	47.9	53.6
Durum	1,974	1,177	Bushels	39.5	45.8
Other spring	12,896	11,625	Bushels	48.3	48.3
Oilseeds:					
Canola	1,942.5	1,909.0	Pounds	1,861	1,781
Cottonseed	....	....	Tons	....	....
Flaxseed	198.0	284.0	Bushels	22.6	19.8
Mustard Seed	97.8	90.0	Pounds	749	706
Peanuts	1,373.5	1,389.7	Pounds	4,001	3,934
Rapeseed	5.4	10.4	Pounds	1,524	2,160
Safflower	156.4	151.5	Pounds	1,512	1,273
Soybeans for beans	87,594	74,939	Bushels	50.6	47.4
Sunflower	1,217.4	1,253.5	Pounds	1,731	1,560
Cotton, tobacco and sugar crops:					
Cotton, all	9,990.8	11,612.5	Pounds	882	823
Pima	248.8	223.5	Pounds	1,545	1,472
Upland	9,742.0	11,389.0	Pounds	865	810
Sugarbeets	1,096.4	980.1	Tons	30.4	29.2
Sugarcane	899.7	913.2	Tons	38.4	35.0
Tobacco	291.4	227.1	Pounds	1,830	2,060
Dry beans, peas and lentils [1]:					
Austrian winter peas	10.9	(NA)	Cwt	1,138	(NA)
Dry edible beans [2]	2,016.0	1,174.3	Cwt	1,860	1,768
Chickpeas, all	846.5	404.5	Cwt	1,511	1,547
Large	623.9	313.2	Cwt	1,513	1,553
Small	222.6	91.3	Cwt	1,503	1,524
Lentils	718.0	425.0	Cwt	1,171	1,250
Peas, Dry edible [2]	807.9	1,046.0	Cwt	1,972	2,123
Peas, Wrinkled seed	....	....	Cwt		
Potatoes and miscellaneous:					
Hops	55.0	56.5	Pounds	1,943	1,981
Maple Syrup	....	....	Pounds	....	....
Mushrooms	....	....	Pounds		
Peppermint oil	58.5	52.4	Pounds	92	104
Potatoes, all	1,014.8	937.3	Cwt	443	453
Spring	51.8	....	Cwt	343	
Summer	56.4	....	Cwt	315	
Fall	906.6	....	Cwt	457	
Spearmint oil	20.8	18.3	Pounds	124	131
Sweet potatoes	144.4	....	Cwt	190	
Taro (Hawaii)	0.3	....	Pounds	9,630	

(NA) Not available. [1] Beginning in 2019, Austrian winter peas and wrinkled seed peas are included in dry edible peas.
[2] Yield in pounds.
NASS, Crops Branch, (202) 720–2127.

Table 9-22.—Crops: Production and value, United States, 2018–2019

Crop	Unit	Production		Value of production	
		2018	2019	2018	2019
		Thousands	*Thousands*	*1,000 dollars*	*1,000 dollars*
Grains and hay:					
Barley	Bushels	153,527	172,499	697,598	761,152
Corn for grain	Bushels	14,340	13,620	52,102	52,911
Corn for silage	Bushels	121,564	133,522	....	....
Hay, all	Tons	123,600	128,864	17,288	18,161
Alfalfa	Tons	52,634	54,875	8,583,806	9,184,257
All other	Tons	70,966	73,989	8,704,409	8,976,339
Oats	Bushels	56,130	53,258	167,640	162,711
Proso millet	Bushels	11,595	16,608	60,566	82,907
Rice	Cwt	223,833	185,104	2,903,041	2,459,035
Rye	Bushels	8,432	10,622	52,870	64,863
Sorghum for grain	Bushels	364,986	341,460	1,180,847	1,151,709
Sorghum for silage	Bushels	3,326	4,019	....	....
Wheat, all	Bushels	1,885,156	1,932,017	9,661,916	8,882,766
Winter	Bushels	1,183,939	1,316,963	5,985,308	5,999,460
Durum	Bushels	77,985	53,959	412,749	257,103
Other Spring	Bushels	623,232	561,095	3,263,859	2,626,203
Oilseeds:					
Canola	Pounds	3,615,440	3,400,865	568,622	494,295
Cottonseed	Tons	5,631	5,945	878,254	1,021,832
Flaxseed	Bushels	4,466	5,625	43,533	56,062
Mustard Seed	Pounds	73,297	63,580	20,974	16,748
Peanuts	Pounds	5,495,935	5,466,487	1,169,953	1,129,584
Rapeseed	Pounds	8,230	22,464	1,526	4,509
Safflower	Pounds	236,270	192,900	47,976	38,361
Soybeans for beans	Bushels	4,428,150	3,551,908	36,819,008	31,202,680
Sunflower	Pounds	2,107,045	1,956,035	370,446	358,408
Cotton, tobacco and sugar crops:					
Cotton, all	Bales	18,367	19,912	6,375,167	6,012,662
Upland	Bales	17,566	19,227	5,931,451	5,631,849
American Pima	Bales	801	685	443,716	380,813
Sugarbeets	Tons	33,282	28,650	1,177,992	1,099,574
Sugarcane	Tons	32,934	30,287	1,100,218	1,144,859
Tobacco	Pounds	533,241	467,956	1,093,418	946,252
Dry Beans, peas and lentils [1]:					
Austrian winter peas	Cwt	124	(NA)	1,830	(NA)
Dry edible beans [2]	Cwt	37,745	20,756	951,047	608,870
Chickpeas, all	Cwt	12,787	6,256	281,451	117,056
Large	Cwt	9,441	4,865	209,744	93,037
Small	Cwt	3,346	1,391	71,677	24,019
Lentils	Cwt	8,408	5,311	131,739	78,799
Peas, dry edible [2]	Cwt	15,929	22,210	163,963	212,328
Peas, wrinkled seed	Cwt	389	(NA)	13,564	(NA)
Potatoes and miscellaneous:					
Hops	Pounds	106,906.7	112,041.2	583,444	636,580
Maple Syrup	Gallons	4,199	4,180	141,825	129,479
Mushrooms	Pounds	917,235	....	1,131,564	....
Peppermint oil	Pounds	5,377	5,452	106,489	105,439
Potatoes, all	Cwt	450,020	424,419	4,006,340	....
Spring	Cwt	17,757	....	282,093	....
Summer	Cwt	17,764	....	207,518	....
Fall	Cwt	414,499	....	3,516,729	....
Spearmint oil	Pounds	2,571	2,400	43,178	40,765
Sweet potatoes	Cwt	27,378	31,972	634,228	588,125
Taro (Hawaii) [3]	Pounds	2,985	(NA)	1,970	....

(NA) Not available. [1] Beginning in 2019, Austrian winter peas and wrinkled seed peas are included in dry edible peas. [2] Yield in pounds. [3] Estimates discontinued in 2019.
NASS, Crops Branch, (202) 720–2127.

Table 9-23.—Fruits and nuts: Bearing acreage and yield, United States, 2017–2018

Crop	Bearing acreage		Yield per acre		
	2017	2018	Unit	2017	2018
	Acres	Acres			
Noncitrus fruits:					
Apples, Commerical	328,200	291,200	Tons	17.60	17.61
Apricots	11,300	10,600	Tons	4.04	3.73
Avocados	58,140	53,640	Tons	3.23	3.46
Bananas (Hawaii)[1][2]	950	....	Tons	3.50	....
Blackberries Cultivated (Oregon)[1][2]	6,300	....	Tons	3.19	....
Blueberries Cultivated[1]	83,900	89,200	Tons	3.06	3.15
Blueberries Wild (Maine)[1]	17,000	18,800	Tons	1.99	1.34
Boysenberries (Oregon)[1][2]	330	....	Tons	3.03	....
Cherries, Sweet	92,500	85,000	Tons	4.73	4.05
Cherries, Tart	35,300	35,200	Tons	3.68	4.24
Coffee (Hawaii)	7,200	7,100	Tons	1.77	1.92
Cranberries	39,900	39,300	Tons	10.46	11.36
Dates	13,400	13,100	Tons	3.23	3.13
Figs (California)[2]	6,700	....	Tons	4.66	....
Grapes	997,800	937,000	Tons	7.40	8.11
Kiwifruit (California)	3,600	3,900	Tons	9.33	9.70
Nectarines	17,000	14,000	Tons	8.34	8.60
Olives (California)	40,000	37,500	Tons	4.81	1.43
Papayas (Hawaii)[1]	1,100	800	Tons	11.64	6.50
Peaches	91,950	74,500	Tons	7.62	8.74
Pears	46,200	46,300	Tons	16.00	17.40
Plums (California)	15,000	14,000	Tons	7.86	7.16
Prunes (California)	45,000	44,000	Tons	7.22	6.36
Raspberries[1]	19,960	16,900	Tons	5.65	6.47
Strawberries[1]	53,200	49,220	Tons	25.57	29.03
Tree nuts:					
Almonds (California)[3]	1,030,000	1,090,000	Tons	1.79	1.69
Hazelnuts (Oregon)[3]	40,000	44,000	Tons	0.80	1.16
Macadamia (Hawaii)[3]	17,000	16,900	Tons	1.44	1.04
Pecans[3]	404,800	409,900	Tons	0.38	0.30
Pistachios (California)[3]	250,000	264,000	Tons	1.20	1.87
Walnuts (California)[3]	335,000	350,000	Tons	1.88	1.93
Citrus fruits:					
Grapefruit[4]	59,600	54,800	Boxes	285	228
Lemons[4]	54,300	54,300	Boxes	406	409
Oranges[4]	527,500	517,500	Boxes	225	176
Tangerines and Mandarins[4]	68,400	71,300	Boxes	372	280

[1] Harvested acreage. For 2017, yield based on utilized production. For 2018, yield based on total production. [2] Estimates discontinued in 2018. [3] Yield based on utilized production on an in-shell basis. [4] Crop year begins with bloom in one year and ends with completion of harvest the following year. Citrus production is for the the year of harvest.
NASS, Crops Branch, (202) 720–2127.

Table 9-24.—Fruits and nuts: Production and value, United States, 2017–2018

Crop	Total production		Value of utilized production	
	2017	2018	2017	2018
	1,000 tons [1]	*1,000 tons [1]*	*1,000 dollars*	*1,000 dollars*
Noncitrus fruits:				
Apples, Commerical	5,776.9	5,128.5	3,601,447	3,013,713
Apricots	45.7	39.6	44,556	48,465
Avocados	187.7	185.8	392,012	400,354
Bananas (Hawaii) [2]	3.3		6,028	
Blackberries Cultivated (Oregon)) [2]	20.1		31,115	
Blueberries Cultivated	259.3	281.2	815,908	797,295
Blueberries Wild (Maine)	33.9	25.2	17,561	23,155
Boysenberries (Oregon)) [2]	1.0		1,693	
Cherries, Sweet	437.6	344.4	891,652	637,700
Cherries, Tart	129.8	149.2	56,868	56,635
Coffee	12.7	13.7	43,774	50,160
Cranberries	419.7	446.3	252,088	222,440
Dates	43.3	41.1	150,959	152,175
Figs (California)) [2]	31.2		28,568	
Grapes	7,383.9	7,596.0	6,507,849	6,615,121
Kiwifruit (California)	33.6	37.8	34,860	32,886
Nectarines	141.9	120.5	128,255	104,626
Olives (California)	192.3	53.6	186,649	40,523
Papayas (Hawaii)	12.8	5.2	9,400	5,702
Peaches	700.8	651.5	599,862	511,226
Pears	737.5	805.5	519,290	428,940
Plums (California)	117.9	100.0	114,897	92,570
Prunes (California)	325.5	279.6	207,900	194,832
Raspberries	113.4	109.4	493,945	367,001
Strawberries [3]	1,360.4	1,428.9	2,895,813	2,670,523
Tree Nuts:				
Almonds, shelled (California) [4]	1,892.5	1,872.5	5,603,950	5,468,040
Hazelnuts, in-shell (Oregon) [5]	(NA)	(NA)	73,600	91,800
Macadamia, in-shell (Hawaii) [5]	(NA)	(NA)	53,900	42,007
Pecans, in-shell [5]	(NA)	(NA)	709,218	425,331
Pistachios, in-shell (California) [5]	(NA)	(NA)	1,014,507	2,615,550
Walnuts, in-shell (California) [5]	(NA)	(NA)	1,568,700	878,800
Citrus fruits [3]:				
Grapefruit	698	509	256,917	207,970
Lemons	882	888	763,446	715,761
Oranges	5,088	3,875	1,943,678	1,830,445
Tangerines and mandarins	1,029	804	568,084	575,976

(NA) Not available.   [1] Tons refers to the 2,000 lb. short Tons.   [2] Estimates discontinued in 2018.   [3] Value of production is packinghouse-door equivalent.   [4] Value is based on the edible portion of the crop only.   [5] Only utilized production estimated.

NASS, Crops Branch, (202) 720–2127.

Table 9-25.—Vegetables, commercial: Area harvested and yield, United States, 2017–2018

Crop	Total area harvested		Total yield per harvested acre		
	2017	2018	Unit	2017	2018
	Acres	*Acres*			
Artichokes	7,200	6,900	Cwt	130.0	145.0
Asparagus	26,300	21,700	Cwt	32.0	36.0
Beans, lima	24,100	23,750	Cwt	27.8	28.7
Beans, snap	212,100	221,500	Cwt	85.2	79.4
Broccoli	128,600	113,900	Cwt	158.5	151.7
Cabbage	60,600	54,200	Cwt	393.2	359.9
Cantaloupes	63,250	60,700	Cwt	243.4	240.6
Carrots	75,900	79,800	Cwt	408.4	413.8
Cauliflower	45,800	43,900	Cwt	198.1	211.5
Celery	31,800	30,200	Cwt	505.9	589.4
Corn, sweet	464,600	473,100	Cwt	162.9	154.9
Cucumbers	117,200	110,900	Cwt	161.4	139.3
Garlic	33,000	32,800	Cwt	155.0	175.0
Honeydews	11,600	14,900	Cwt	290.0	310.0
Lettuce					
Head	140,700	120,300	Cwt	351.1	337.2
Leaf	67,200	69,300	Cwt	203.5	162.7
Romaine	117,400	99,600	Cwt	309.3	293.5
Onions	151,500	130,200	Cwt	543.8	556.1
Pea, green	134,200	131,100	Cwt	44.8	38.7
Peppers, bell	42,200	39,700	Cwt	341.0	324.8
Peppers, chile	16,000	14,200	Cwt	208.5	187.7
Pumpkins	72,300	65,900	Cwt	220.2	228.5
Spinach	64,730	61,450	Cwt	125.0	138.0
Squash	45,900	44,800	Cwt	174.5	165.0
Tomatoes	310,500	321,900	Cwt	791.2	863.8
Watermelons	107,800	111,400	Cwt	378.3	350.5

NASS, Crops Branch, (202) 720–2127.

Table 9-26.—Vegetables, commercial: Production and value, United States, 2017–2018

Crop	Unit	Total production		Total value of utilized production	
		2017	2018	2017	2018
		Thousands	*Thousands*	*1,000 dollars*	*1,000 dollars*
Artichokes	Cwt	936.0	1,000.5	65,520	63,032
Asparagus	Cwt	841.1	781.8	100,672	87,584
Beans, lima	Cwt	671.0	681.7	19,493	21,622
Beans, snap	Cwt	18,076.3	17,595.2	349,445	363,506
Broccoli	Cwt	20,384.0	17,273.0	925,716	738,527
Cabbage	Cwt	23,826.0	19,507.5	431,307	409,446
Cantaloupes	Cwt	15,394.8	14,607.0	295,975	331,542
Carrots	Cwt	31,001.0	33,018.0	696,129	731,504
Cauliflower	Cwt	9,074.5	9,286.0	415,737	425,350
Celery	Cwt	16,089.0	17,799.0	322,047	444,013
Corn, sweet	Cwt	75,674.4	73,279.7	892,179	858,862
Cucumbers	Cwt	18,912.8	15,450.4	392,013	332,867
Garlic	Cwt	5,115.0	5,740.0	390,021	452,599
Honeydews	Cwt	3,364.0	4,619.0	94,192	90,532
Lettuce					
Head	Cwt	49,395.5	40,561.0	1,774,522	1,219,857
Leaf	Cwt	13,675.0	11,277.0	833,077	585,299
Romaine	Cwt	36,308.0	29,233.0	1,628,136	901,186
Onions	Cwt	82,389.0	72,409.0	1,042,090	817,496
Pea, green	Cwt	6,012.4	5,071.0	85,475	64,901
Peppers, bell	Cwt	14,390.0	12,895.0	625,577	533,307
Peppers, chile	Cwt	3,336.0	2,665.0	113,562	94,767
Pumpkins	Cwt	15,919.6	15,058.4	196,541	190,162
Spinach	Cwt	8,090.6	8,480.5	470,860	422,879
Squash	Cwt	8,009.1	7,392.5	235,613	192,922
Tomatoes	Cwt	245,654.5	278,071.0	1,677,960	1,856,280
Watermelons	Cwt	40,781.5	39,045.0	594,033	656,655

NASS, Crops Branch, (202) 720–2127.

Table 9-27.—Livestock and livestock products: Production and value, United States, 2016–2018

Product	Production [1]			Value of production		
	2016	2017	2018	2016	2017	2018
	Millions	*Millions*	*Millions*	*1,000 dollars*	*1,000 dollars*	*1,000 dollars*
Eggs	103,202	107,242	109,192	6,591,359	7,635,359	10,586,262
	1,000 pounds	*1,000 pounds*	*1,000 pounds*	*1,000 dollars*	*1,000 dollars*	*1,000 dollars*
Cattle and calves	42,694,001	44,197,461	46,318,583	48,572,501	50,398,374	49,844,530
Hogs	35,898,712	36,962,875	38,829,022	17,363,044	19,159,248	19,060,203
Broilers [2]	54,259,100	55,573,900	56,791,100	25,935,852	30,232,203	31,746,230
Mature chickens	1,060,677	1,001,386	1,019,695	87,949	46,999	49,364
Turkeys [3]	7,486,978	7,544,391	7,598,289	6,184,247	4,873,677	3,875,131
Milk	212,451,000	215,527,000	217,575,000	34,712,099	38,119,254	35,411,485
Catfish [3][4]	320,174	342,241	358,604	385,985	379,713	360,401
Trout [3][4]	60,933	55,709	49,772	113,904	120,302	110,554
Honey	162,246	148,980	152,348	343,962	334,166	333,482
Wool (shorn)	25,795	24,810	24,00	37,423	36,774	42,772
Mohair	800	740	755	3,650	3,661	3,963

[1] For cattle, sheep, and hogs, the quantity of net production is the live weight actually produced during the year, adjustments having been made for animals shipped in and changes in inventory. Estimates for broilers and eggs cover the 12-month period Dec. 1, previous year through Nov. 30. [2] Young chickens of meat–type strains raised for meat production. [3] Live weight. [4] Value of fish sold, excludes eggs.
NASS, Livestock Branch, (202) 720–3570.

Table 9-28.—Farm product prices: Marketing year average prices received by farmers; Parity prices, United States, 2017–2018

Commodity	Unit	Marketing year average price [1]		Parity price [2]	
		2017	2018	2017	2018
		Dollars	*Dollars*	*Dollars*	*Dollars*
Basic commodities:					
Cotton:					
Upland	pound	0.686	0.703	1.93	2
Extra long staple(American Pima)	pound	1.39	1.15	3.83	3.99
Wheat	bushel	4.72	5.16	17.7	17.6
Rice	cwt	12.9	12.3	39.5	39.9
Corn	bushel	3.36	3.61	13	13.2
Peanuts	pound	0.229	0.215	0.663	0.675
Tobacco:					
Flue-cured, types (class 1)	pound	2.004	1.933	5.21	5.46
Types 21	pound	(NA)	(NA)	(NA)	(NA)
Burley, type 31	pound	1.935	1.96	5.13	5.34
Maryland, type 32 [3]	pound	1.8	1.8	4.9	5.05
Dark air-cured, types 35–36	pound	(NA)	(NA)	(NA)	(NA)
Sun-cured, type 37	pound	(NA)	(NA)	(NA)	(NA)
Pa., seedleaf, type 41	pound	2.36	2.14	5.5	5.78
Cigar binder type 51	pound	(NA)	(NA)	(NA)	(NA)
Puerto Rican filler, type 46	pound	(NA)	(NA)	(NA)	(NA)
Cigar wrapper, type 61	pound	(NA)	(NA)	(NA)	(NA)
Designated nonbasic commodities:					
All milk, sold to plants	cwt	17.69	16.28	51.9	52.2
Honey, all	pound	2.200	2.166	4.72	5.14
Wool and mohair:					
Wool [4]	pound	1.48	1.75	3.63	3.87
Mohair [5]	pound	4.95	5.25	11.4	11.9
Other nonbasic commodities:					
Field crops and miscellaneous:					
Austrian winter peas	cwt	12.7	16.4	(NA)	(NA)
Barley	bushel	4.47	4.62	14.3	14.9
Beans, dry edible	cwt	26.7	25.4	93.3	96
Cottonseed	ton	142	155	591	593
Crude pine gum	barrel	(NA)	(NA)	400	408
Flaxseed	bushel	9.53	(NA)	33.1	33.8
Hay, all, baled	ton	142	166	424	431
Hops	pound	5.6	5.46	10.6	11.6
Lentils	cwt	25.9	17.7	73.5	77.8
Oats	bushel	2.59	2.66	8.41	8.57
Peas, dry edible	cwt	11.8	10.5	54.5	55.5
Peppermint oil	pounds	18.3	19.8	58.8	60.8
Popcorn, shelled basis	cwt	(NA)	(NA)	52.1	53.1
Potatoes	cwt	9.17	8.9	24.6	(NA)
Rye	bushel	4.7	6.27	18.2	18.5
Sorghum grain	cwt	5.75	5.82	22.2	22.3
Soybeans	bushel	9.33	8.48	31.4	32.6
Spearmint oil	pound	16.2	16.8	49	50.8
Sweet potatoes	cwt	18.4	23.2	59.3	60.5
Fruits:					
Citrus (equiv. on-tree): [6]					
Grapefruit	box	12.48	14.24	19.2	21.7
Lemons	box	28.5	26.03	50.4	54.9
Oranges	box	13.32	16.86	25.4	26.7
Tangerines	box	18.76	25.39	51.6	53.7
Deciduous and other:					
Apples:					
For fresh consumption [7]	pound	0.407	0.394	0.98	1.03
For processing [8]	ton	248	206	545	575
Apricots:					
For fresh consumption [9]	ton	1,400	1,540	3400	3,400
Dried, California (dried basis) [8]	ton	(D)	(D)	7630	8,750
For processing (excl dried) [8]	ton	(NA)	(NA)	1160	1,230
Avocados [9]	ton	2,110	2,190	5100	5,370

See footnote(s) at end of table.

Table 9-28.—Farm product prices: Marketing year average prices received by farmers; Parity prices, United States, 2017–2018—Continued

Commodity	Unit	Marketing year average price [1]		Parity price [2]	
		2017	2018	2017	2018
		Dollars	*Dollars*	*Dollars*	*Dollars*
Deciduous and other—Continued					
Berries for processing:					
Blackberries (Oregon)	pound	0.692	....	17.90	18.20
Boysenberries (Oregon)	pound	0.835	....	2.54	2.58
Gooseberries	pound	....	....	1.07	1.09
Loganberries (Oregon)	pound	....	....	1.73	1.76
Raspberries, black (California, Oregon & Washington)	pound	....	....	3.05	3.11
Raspberries, red (California, Oregon & Washington)	pound	....	....	2.42	2.47
Cherries:					
Sweet	ton	2,060	1,860	5,930	6,250
Tart	pound	0.224	0.196	0.922	0.939
Cranberries [10]	barrel	30.20	25.10	121	119
Dates [9]	ton	3,510	3,800	4,260	4,230
Grapes:					
For all sales	ton	881	871	....	....
Raisin varieties dried, California (dried basis) [8]	ton	1,840	....	4,090	4,110
Wine dried grapes	ton	928	....	1,860	2,010
Kiwi	ton	1,050	870	2,780	3,050
Nectarines					
For fresh consumption [17]	ton	943	(D)	1,830	1,970
For processing [18]	ton	144	(D)	121	124
Olives (California): [11]					
For all sales	ton	974	766	....	....
Crushed for oil	ton	810	566	1,690	1,800
For all sales (excl crushed)	ton	....	....	2,520	2,610
For canning	ton	1,320	1,270	2,790	2,910
Papayas	pound	0.422	0.554	1.15	1.20
Peaches:					
For all sales	ton	864	801	....	....
For fresh consumption [7]	ton	1,350	1,250	2,490	2,660
Dried, California (dried basis) [8]	ton	(NA)	....	1,320	1,280
For processing California (excl dried):					
Clingstone [11]	ton	474	480	980	1,060
Freestone [8]	ton	393	410	798	869
Pears:					
For all sales	ton	710	536	....	....
For fresh consumption [7]	ton	875	610	1,670	1,770
For processing (excl dried) [8]	ton	384	367	....	....
Plums (California):					
For all sales [9]	ton	1,000	935	....	....
For fresh consumption [17]	ton	(D)	(D)	1,840	1,910
For processing [18]	ton	(D)	(D)	....	....
Prunes, dried (California) [8]	ton	1,980	....	4,520	4,700
Prunes and plums (excl California):					
For fresh consumption [12]	ton	....	....	1,760	1,800
For processing (excl dried) [8]	ton	....	....	686	699
Strawberries:					
For fresh consumption [13]	cwt	125	106	253	282
For processing [8]	cwt	37.20	43.60	101	106
Sugar crops:					
Sugarbeets	ton	41.2	35.5	150	150
Sugarcane for sugar	ton	31	33.4	99.70	102
Tree nuts: [14]					
Almonds	pound	2.53	2.44	6.60	6.93
Hazelnuts	ton	2,300	1,800	6,250	6,840
Macadamia	pound	1.10	1.19	....	....
Pecans, all	pound	2.33	1.75	4.98	(NA)
Pistachios	pound	1.69	2.65	6.63	6.93
Walnuts	ton	2,490	1,300	6,680	6,870

See footnote(s) at end of table.

Table 9-28.—Farm product prices: Marketing year average prices received by farmers; Parity prices, United States, 2017–2018—Continued

Commodity	Unit	Marketing year average price [1]		Parity price [2]	
		2017	2018	2017	2018
		Dollars	Dollars	Dollars	Dollars
Vegetables for fresh market: [13]					
Artichokes, California	cwt	70	63	131	134
Asparagus	cwt	132	122	323	335
Beans, snap	cwt	57.1	59.8	130	132
Broccoli	cwt	46	43.1	111	115
Cabbage	cwt	19.8	22.9	39.8	40.5
Cantaloupes	cwt	19.2	22.7	61.4	62.5
Carrots [15]	cwt	30.2	27.3	78.7	81.9
Cauliflower [15]	cwt	46.8	46.1	130	135
Celery [15]	cwt	20.5	25.9	58.8	58.1
Cucumbers	cwt	29.4	28.6	65.7	66.9
Eggplant	cwt	(NA)	(NA)	69.4	70.7
Escarole/Endive	cwt	(NA)	(NA)	89.3	91
Garlic	cwt	184	190	84.4	86
Green peppers [15]	cwt	48.7	44.3	104	106
Honeydew melons	cwt	28	19.6	55.6	59.3
Lettuce	cwt	35.9	30.1	66.3	71.3
Onions [15]	cwt	14.4	13.5	39.8	41.4
Spinach	cwt	68.8	59	114	116
Sweet corn	cwt	29.2	29.3	76.3	79.8
Tomatoes	cwt	36.8	41.5	116	119
Watermelons	cwt	14.8	16.9	24.4	24.8
Vegetables for processing: [8]					
Asparagus	ton	1570	1,580	42100	4,340
Beets	ton	(NA)	(NA)	224	229
Cabbage	ton	202	123	173	176
Cucumbers	ton	352	352	(NA)	(NA)
Green peas	ton	250	251	977	989
Lima beans	ton	561	625	19300	1,970
Snap beans	ton	188	182	645	660
Spinach	ton	196	197	418	426
Sweet corn	ton	78.5	79.7	305	311
Tomatoes	ton	82.7	81.5	235	243
Livestock and livestock products:					
All beef cattle	cwt	120	115	320	335
Cows	cwt	69.1	62.6	(NA)	(NA)
Steers and heifers	cwt	122	117	(NA)	(NA)
Calves	cwt	168	170	464	484
Chickens:					
Broilers, live [18]	pound	0.545	0.567	1.44	1.5
All Eggs	dozen	0.863	1.15	2.94	2.96
Hogs	cwt	53.1	50.2	161	166
Milk cows [16]	head	1,620	1,360	(NA)	(NA)
Turkeys, live	pound	0.645	0.51	187	194

(NA) Not available. [1] Unless otherwise noted, these prices are for marketing year average or calendar year average computed by weighing State prices by quantities sold, or by production for those commodities for which the production is sold. [2] Parity prices are for January of the year shown as published in the January issue of Agricultural Prices. [3] Previous year. [4] Average local market price for wool sold excluding incentive payment. [5] Average local market price for mohair sold excluding incentive payment. [6] Crop year begins with bloom in one year and ends with completion of harvest the following year. Prices refer to the year harvest begins. [7] Equivalent packinghouse-door returns for California, Oregon (pears only), Washington, and New York (apples only), and prices as sold for other States. [8] Equivalent returns at processing plant-door. [9] Equivalent returns at packinghouse-door. [10] Weighted average of co-op and independent sales. Co-op prices represent pool proceeds excluding returns from non-cranberry products and before deductions for capital stock and other retains. [11] Equivalent per unit returns for bulk fruit at first delivery point. [12] Average price as sold. [13] FOB shipping point when available. Weighted average of prices at points of first sale. [14] Prices are in-shell basis except almonds which are shelled basis. [15] Includes some processing. [16] Simple average of States weighted by estimated Jan. 1 head for U.S. average. [17] Prices for fresh and processing breakdown no longer published to avoid disclosure of individual operations. [18] Live weight equivalent price.

NASS, Environmental, Economics, and Demographics Branch (202) 720–6146.

Table 9-29.—Producer prices: Index numbers, by groups of commodities, United States, 2011–2020

[1982=100]

Year	Total finished goods	Consumer foods	Personal consumption goods [1]	Total intermediate materials	Unprocessed Goods for intermediate demand [2]
2011	190.7	193.9	203.3	199.8	249.4
2012	194.3	199.1	207.5	200.7	241.4
2013	196.7	203.5	210.3	200.8	246.7
2014	200.4	212.5	214.7	201.9	249.3
2015	193.9	209.7	204.4	188.0	189.1
2016	191.9	204.6	201.3	182.2	173.4
2017	198.0	207.2	209.2	190.7	190.8
2018	204.1	207.4	216.8	200.9	200.1
2019	205.7	211.6	217.5	198.1	185.9
2020	203.0	214.6	212.6	192.4	167.5

ERS, Food Marketing Branch, (202) 694–5349. Compiled from reports of the U.S. Department of Labor.

Table 9-30.—Prices received by farmers: Index numbers by groups of commodities and parity ratio, United States, 2008–2018 [1]

[1910–14=100]

Year	Food grain	Feed grain	Cotton	Tobacco	Oilseed	Fruit & tree nut [2]	Vegetable & melon	Other crop
2008	820	1,010	515	1,409	1,107	1,038	1,076	604
2009	590	579	416	1,569	971	977	1,153	609
2010	560	587	601	1,557	944	1,031	1,161	622
2011	758	902	745	1,497	1,225	1,162	1,224	645
2012	779	1,010	673	1,576	1,356	1,339	1,040	649
2013 [3]	759	943	651	1,760	1,343	1,311	1,330	645

Year	Potato & dry edible bean	Crop Production	Meat animal	Dairy	Poultry & egg	Livestock Production	Agricultural Production	Parity ratio [4]
2009	761	747	1,075	790	390	857	832	35
2010	708	690	1,256	1,000	427	1,002	850	35
2011	867	872	1,540	1,239	422	1,161	1,032	38
2012	846	933	1,633	1,140	459	1,190	1,083	38
2013	901	922	1,669	1,230	515	1,260	1,104	38
2014	(3)	805	(3)	(3)	(3)	1,495	1,113	37
2015	(3)	759	(3)	(3)	(3)	1,317	1,024	34
2016	(3)	752	(3)	(3)	(3)	1,096	935	32
2017	(3)	752	(3)	(3)	(3)	1,160	963	33
2018	(3)	609	(3)	(3)	(3)	1,095	938	32

[1] These indexes are computed using the price estimates of averages for all classes and grades for individual commodities being sold in local farm markets. In computing the group indexes, prices of individual commodities have been compared with 2011 weighted average prices. The resulting ratios are seasonally weighted by average quantities sold for the most recent 5–year period. For example, 2013 indexes use quantities sold for the period 2007–11. Then, the 2011 indexes are used to adjust the 1910–14 base period. [2] Fresh market for noncitrus, and fresh market and processing for citrus. [3] Data series discontinued after 2013. [4] Ratio of Index of Prices Received to the Index of Prices Paid by Farmers for Commodities and Services, Interest, Taxes, and Farm Wage Rates.

NASS, Environmental, Economics, and Demographics Branch, (202) 720–6146.

Table 9-31.—Prices received by farmers: Index numbers by groups of commodities and ratio, United States, 2009–2018 [1]

(2011=100)

Year	Food grain	Feed grain	Cotton [2]	Tobacco [2]	Oilseed	Fruit & tree nut [3]	Vegetable & melon	Other crop
2009	78.5	65.1	55.9	99.7	83.5	83.9	102.8	94.1
2010	74.4	66.0	80.6	98.9	81.2	88.5	103.5	95.9
2011	100.0	100.0	....	....	100.0	100.0	100.0	100.0
2012	103.8	110.8	....	....	111.9	112.4	91.9	102.7
2013	101.5	102.4	....	....	111.6	119.1	103.8	100.5
2014	90.4	69.1	....	....	98.8	136.3	103.3	94.7
2015	75.5	62.7	....	....	76.0	138.6	108.8	84.3
2016	62.1	58.6	....	....	75.0	138.8	103.9	79.1
2017	65.5	56.5	....	....	75.1	133.8	113.6	81.5
2018	74.8	58.3	....	....	73.5	132.4	107.3	88.5

Year	Potato [4] & dry edible bean [5]	Crop Production	Meat animal	Dairy product	Poultry & egg	Livestock Production	Agricultural Production	Parity ratio [6]
2009	88.3	85.7	73.8	63.7	93	69.9	80.6	92
2010	82.1	87.0	85.7	80.7	101.6	81.6	86.8	96
2011	....	100.0	100	100.0	100	100	100	100
2012	....	107.0	102.5	92.1	109	103.9	105	100
2013	....	105.7	108.5	99.8	123.3	106.8	107	100
2014	....	92.3	128.7	119.2	133.1	131.1	107.9	96
2015	....	87.0	113.4	85.2	127.8	119.8	99.2	90
2016	....	86.2	94.4	81.1	100.4	97.9	90.6	85
2017	....	86.8	99.9	87.8	107.5	100.5	93.3	87
2018	....	86.8	94.3	80.9	116.3	95.8	90.9	83

[1] These indexes are computed using the price estimates of averages for all classes and grades for individual commodities being sold in local farm markets. In computing the group indexes, prices of individual commodities have been compared with 2011 weighted average prices. The resulting ratios are seasonally weighted by average quantities sold for the most recent previous 5–year period. For example, 2013 indexes use quantities sold for the period 2007–11. [2] Included in Other crop index group beginning in 2010. [3] Fresh market for noncitrus, and fresh market and processing for citrus. [4] Included in Vegetable and melon index group beginning 2010. [5] Included in Food grain index group beginning 2010. [6] Ratio of Index of Prices Received (2011=100) to Index of Prices Paid by Farmers for Commodities & Services, Interest, Taxes, and Wage Rates (2007–11=100).
NASS, Environmental, Economics, and Demographics Branch, (202) 720–6146.

Table 9-32.—Prices paid by farmers: Index numbers, by groups of commodities, United States, 2009–2018

(2011=100)

Year	Production all commodities	Feed	Livestock & Poultry	Seeds	Fertilizer	Agricultural chemicals	Fuels	Supplies & Repairs	Autos & trucks
2010	87.7	79.7	86.0	93.4	76.8	99.5	78.3	96.1	97.3
2011	100.0	100.0	100.0	100.0	100.0	100.0	100.0	100.0	100.0
2012	105.4	115.3	106.6	105.5	101.4	105.4	99.3	102.9	101.9
2013	107.4	117.5	108.3	110.2	96.7	108.5	98.4	103.8	103.4
2014	114.1	114.9	153.6	113.5	94.5	109.5	97.9	105.7	104.4
2015	112.0	106.1	147.1	124.6	87.2	106.5	63.5	105.8	105.5
2016	104.7	101.4	105.2	121.4	71.8	107.7	55.6	106.0	106.0
2017	104.5	94.8	107.0	119.9	66.2	104.0	63.2	107.9	106.0
2018	106.4	99.9	105.8	118.5	66.7	100.7	71.1	111.6	105.5
2019	84.8	82.5	74.6	90.1	83.8	102.5	63.1	94.3	94.9

Year	Farm machinery	Building materials	Farm services	Rent	Interest	Taxes	Wage rates	Production, interest, taxes, & wage rates	Family living	Commodities, interest, taxes, & wage rates [2]
Production indexes [1] - continued										
2009	91.2	95.4	95.3	89.6	94.2	91.9	97.9	86.4	95.4	87.3
2010	94.3	96.6	98.1	92.6	91.6	95.9	98.9	89.0	96.9	90.0
2011	100.0	100.0	100.0	100.0	100.0	100 0	100.0	100.0	100.0	100.0
2012	105.3	102.6	101.8	101.7	99.3	101.0	102.9	104.8	102.1	104.4
2013	108.1	104.6	105.5	105.6	93.3	103.4	106.3	106.7	103.6	106.3
2014	112.0	106.9	109.1	114.2	93.1	116.3	108.0	113.1	105.3	112.0
2015	114.6	107.4	113.7	130.3	98.4	110.9	111.9	111.6	105.4	110.7
2016	115.4	107.6	115.6	123.8	103.9	114.7	115.9	105.8	106.7	105.9
2017	117.7	110.4	112.4	123.8	111.9	116.3	119.1	106.3	109.0	106.6
2018	120.0	116.1	114.5	119.5	117.6	117.1	126.3	108.7	111.7	109.1

[1] Annual price index computed using annual weights. Base period (2011=100) are now being published to one decimal digit. [2] Family Living component included.
NASS, Environmental, Economics, and Demographics Branch, (202) 720–6146.

Table 9-33.—Prices paid by farmers: Index numbers, by groups of commodities, United States, 2009–2018 [1]

[1910–14=100]

| Year | Family living | Production indexes | | | | | | | |
		Production all commodities	Feed	Livestock & poultry	Seed	Fertilizer	Agricultural chemicals	Fuels	Supplies & repairs
2009	2,038	1,766	909	1,472	2,960	1,009	921	1,765	1,113
2010	2,071	1,825	879	1,698	3,070	925	893	2,191	1,134
2011	2,136	2,082	1,102	1,974	3,286	1,204	898	2,797	1,180
2012	2,181	2,193	1,270	2,104	3,468	1,221	946	2,779	1,214
2013	2,213	2,237	1,295	2,137	3,622	1,164	974	2,752	1,225
2014	2,249	2,376	1,266	3,032	3,729	1,138	983	2,739	1,247
2015	2,252	2,331	1,168	2,904	4,096	1,050	957	1,775	1,248
2016	2,280	2,179	1,118	2,076	3,990	864	967	1,556	1,251
2017	2,328	2,175	1,045	2,113	3,940	797	934	1,768	1,272
2018	2,385	2,214	1,100	2,089	3,893	803	904	1,988	1,316

| Year | Production indexes—Continued | | | | Interest | Taxes | Wage rates | Production, interest, taxes, & wage rates | Commodities, interest, taxes, & wage rates [2] |
	Autos & trucks	Farm machinery	Building materials	Farm services & rent					
2009	2,917	5,575	2,218	1,976	3,436	5,453	7,007	2,435	2,364
2010	2,992	5,762	2,248	2,036	3,339	5,694	7,079	2,509	2,434
2011	3,074	6,111	2,326	2,123	3,646	5,935	7,161	2,820	2,706
2012	3,131	6,432	2,387	2,162	3,620	5,993	7,366	2,954	2,824
2013	3,179	6,609	2,434	2,241	3,402	6,137	7,607	3,010	2,877
2014	3,209	6,845	2,486	2,360	3,394	6,904	7,731	3,190	3,031
2015	3,243	7,003	2,497	2,554	3,587	6,520	8,015	3,146	2,996
2016	3,259	7,051	2,504	2,524	3,789	6,808	8,295	2,983	2,866
2017	3,259	7,190	2,569	2,486	4,082	6,904	8,529	2,996	2,885
2018	3,242	7,329	2,700	2,474	4,288	6,952	9,047	3,066	2,954

[1] Based on Consumer Price Index-Urban of Bureau of Labor Statistics. [2] The index known as the Parity Index is the Index of Prices Paid by Farmers for Commodities and Services, Interest, Taxes, and Wage Rates expressed on the 1910–14=100 base.

NASS, Environmental, Economics, and Demographics Branch, (202) 720–6146.

Table 9-34.—Grazing fees: Rates for cattle by selected States and regions, 2017–2018

| State | Monthly lease rates for private non-irrigated grazing land [1] | | | | | |
| | Animal unit [2] | | Cow-calf | | Per head | |
	2017	2018	2017	2018	2017	2018
	Dollars per month	Dollars per month	Dollars per month	Dollars per month	Dollars per month	Dollars per month
Arizona	9.50	10.00	(S)	(S)	(S)	(S)
California	20.60	22.40	28.00	29.00	19.50	21.00
Colorado	19.00	19.50	23.00	23.00	18.00	18.50
Idaho	18.00	18.00	22.00	22.50	18.50	19.00
Kansas	21.00	21.00	27.00	27.00	24.50	22.00
Montana	24.50	24.50	27.00	26.00	24.00	24.50
Nebraska	39.80	46.00	45.00	52.00	39.00	35.00
Nevada	9.90	9.50	18.10	(S)	15.50	15.20
New Mexico	15.50	16.00	(S)	(S)	16.00	16.50
North Dakota	19.00	24.50	23.00	32.00	19.00	19.00
Oklahoma	12.50	12.50	(S)	(S)	11.50	13.00
Oregon	16.50	17.50	19.50	21.00	19.50	21.50
South Dakota	31.50	31.50	39.00	40.50	35.00	34.00
Texas	12.50	12.50	(S)	(S)	11.50	14.50
Utah	16.50	17.00	20.00	19.00	18.50	18.50
Washington	14.00	14.50	16.50	16.50	16.00	16.00
Wyoming	21.50	22.00	23.50	24.00	22.00	23.00
17-State [3]	20.20	21.30	23.70	25.20	20.60	21.00
16-State [4]	22.60	24.00	26.40	28.40	23.40	23.00
11-State [5]	19.30	19.70	22.80	22.80	19.80	20.50
9-State [6]	20.50	21.70	23.80	25.70	20.70	21.00

(S) Insufficient number of reports to establish an estimate. [1] The average rates are estimates (rates over $10.00 are rounded to the nearest dime) based on survey indications of monthly lease rates for private, non-irrigated grazing land from the January Cattle Survey. [2] Includes animal unit plus cow-calf rates. Cow-calf rate converted to animal unit (AUM) using (1 aum=cow-calf *0.833). [3] Seventeen Western States: All States listed. [4] Sixteen Western States: All States, except Texas. [5] Eleven Western States: Arizona, California, Colorado, Idaho, Montana, Nevada , New Mexico, Oregon, Utah, Washington and Wyoming. [6] Nine Great Plains States: Colorado, Kansas, Nebraska, New Mexico, North Dakota, Oklahoma, South Dakota, Texas and Wyoming.

NASS, Environmental, Economics, and Demographics Branch, (202) 720–6146.

Table 9-35.—Agricultural commodities: Support prices per unit, United States, 2016–2020 [1]

Commodity	Unit	2016	2017	2018	2019	2020
		Dollars	Dollars	Dollars	Dollars	Dollars
Basic commodities:						
Corn:						
Target/reference price	Bushel	3.70	3.70	3.70	3.70	3.70
Loan rate	do	1.95	1.95	1.95	2.20	2.20
Cotton:						
American upland:						
Loan rate	do	52.00	49.49	52.00	52.00	52.00
Extra-long staple:						
Loan rate	do	79.77	79.77	79.77	95.00	95.00
Peanuts:						
Target/reference price	Short tons	535.00	535.00	535.00	535.00	535.00
Loan rate	do	355.00	355.00	355.00	355.00	355.00
Rice:						
Target/reference price [2]	Cwt	14.00	14.00	14.00	14.00	14.00
Loan rate	do	6.50	6.50	6.50	7.00	7.00
Wheat:						
Target/reference price	Bushel	5.50	5.50	5.50	5.50	5.50
Loan rate	do	2.94	2.94	2.94	3.38	3.38
Barley:						
Target/reference price	Bushel	4.95	4.95	4.95	4.95	4.95
Loan rate	do	1.95	1.95	1.95	2.50	2.50
Sorghum grain:						
Target/reference price	Cwt	7.05	7.05	7.05	7.05	7.05
Loan rate	do	3.48	3.48	3.48	2.20	2.20
Oats:						
Target/reference price	Bushel	2.40	2.40	2.40	2.40	2.40
Loan rate	do	1.39	1.39	1.39	2.00	2.00
Other oilseeds: [3]						
Target/reference price	Cwt	20.15	20.15	20.15	20.15	20.15
Loan rate	do	10.09	10.09	10.09	10.09	10.09
Soybeans:						
Target/reference price	Bushel	8.40	8.40	8.40	8.40	8.40
Loan rate	do	5.00	5.00	5.00	6.20	6.20
Dry Peas:						
Target/reference price	Cwt	11.00	11.00	11.00	11.00	11.00
Loan rate	do	5.40	5.40	5.40	6.15	6.15
Small chick peas:						
Target/reference price	Cwt	19.04	19.04	19.04	19.04	19.04
Loan rate	do	7.43	7.43	7.43	10.00	10.00
Large chick peas:						
Target/reference price	Cwt	21.54	21.54	21.54	21.54	21.54
Loan rate	do	11.28	11.28	11.28	14.00	14.00
Lentils:						
Target/reference price	do	19.97	19.97	19.97	19.97	19.97
Loan rate	do	11.28	11.28	11.28	13.00	13.00
Sugar, raw cane:						
Loan rate	Pound	0.188	0.188	0.188	0.1975	0.1975
Sugar, refined beet:						
Loan rate	do	0.241	0.241	0.241	0.2538	0.2538
Honey, extracted:						
Loan rate	Pound	0.69	0.69	0.69	0.69	0.69
Mohair:						
Loan rate	do	4.20	4.20	4.20	4.20	4.20
Wool, graded:						
Loan rate	Pound	1.15	1.15	1.15	1.15	1.15
Wool, nongraded:						
Loan rate	Pound	0.40	0.40	0.40	0.40	0.40

[1] National averages during the marketing years for the individual crops. [2] Target and reference price shown is for long grain and medium (including short) grain rice. The reference price for temperate japonica rice is $16.10 per Cwt beginning with crop year 2014 and $17.30 per Cwt beginning with crop year 2019. The loan rate for temperate japonica is the same as for other types of rice, at 7.00 per Cwt. [3] Other oilseeds are flaxseed, sunflower seed (oil and other types), safflower, rapeseed, canola, mustard seed, crambe, and sesame seed.
FPAC-BC, Commodity Analysis Branch.

Table 9-36.—Farm income: Cash receipts by commodity groups and selected commodities, United States, 2015–2019 [1]

Commodity	2015	2016	2017	2018	2019
	Thousand dollars				
All commodities	377,432,066	358,481,924	370,427,294	371,424,695	369,321,157
Animals and products	189,515,589	162,730,663	175,559,718	176,330,553	175,993,463
Cattle and calves	78,252,807	63,691,327	66,936,726	67,038,059	66,239,043
Hogs	20,552,958	19,037,752	21,038,034	20,881,335	22,015,189
Sheep and lambs	(NA)	(NA)	(NA)	(NA)	(NA)
Dairy products	35,716,849	34,546,316	37,940,662	35,242,255	40,498,398
Broilers	28,716,398	25,935,852	30,232,203	31,749,919	28,313,919
Farm chickens	104,828	87,949	46,999	49,365	37,585
Chicken eggs	13,762,519	6,591,359	7,635,001	10,653,315	7,704,595
Turkeys	5,707,928	6,184,247	4,873,677	3,785,695	4,303,596
Miscellaneous animals and products	6,701,302	6,655,861	6,856,416	6,930,610	6,881,138
Crops	187,915,547	195,751,261	194,867,576	195,094,142	193,327,694
Food grains	12,296,220	11,288,344	11,201,209	12,117,509	11,516,423
Feed crops	56,930,107	55,443,315	53,920,441	57,340,254	58,923,133
Cotton	4,756,100	5,496,889	7,573,587	7,484,369	7,181,857
Tobacco	1,606,619	1,337,542	1,378,695	1,246,889	1,003,929
Oil crops	35,518,959	44,042,747	41,093,900	39,467,914	36,375,048
Vegetables	20,358,992	19,542,550	20,494,457	18,499,392	18,895,276
Fruits/nuts	28,447,492	29,698,085	30,588,949	29,204,518	28,768,747
All other crops	28,001,987	28,901,788	28,616,339	29,733,297	30,663,281

Data as of February 5, 2021. (NA) Not available   [1] USDA estimates and publishes individual cash receipt values only for major commodities and major producing States.   The U.S. receipts for individual commodities, computed as the sum of the reported States, may understate the value of sales for some commodities, with the balance included in the appropriate category labeled "other" or "miscellaneous".   The degree of underestimation in some of the minor commodities can be substantial.

ERS, Farm Income Team, (202) 694–5344. FarmIncomeTeam@ers.usda.gov. http://www.ers.usda.gov/data-products/farm-income-and-wealth-statistics.aspx.

Table 9-37.—Farm income: United States, 2015–2019

Item	2015	2016	2017	2018	2019
	Thousand dollars				
Total gross farm income	440,795,239	412,252,718	425,400,103	425,122,479	431,865,348
Value of production	429,990,753	399,273,041	413,868,492	411,453,469	409,418,148
Crops	184,330,180	189,302,159	187,915,365	186,220,191	180,543,580
Livestock and product	194,143,948	165,429,595	176,896,045	177,406,367	176,262,775
Services and forestry	51,516,625	44,541,288	49,057,081	47,826,910	52,611,793
Direct government payments	10,804,486	12,979,677	11,531,611	13,669,010	22,447,200
Total production expenses [1]	359,131,252	349,938,198	350,285,924	343,815,714	348,737,395
Net farm income	81,663,987	62,314,520	75,114,179	81,306,765	83,127,953
Gross cash income	422,613,418	399,353,213	413,165,004	414,219,231	426,494,121
Cash expenses	315,828,783	303,783,582	311,891,580	311,398,050	317,513,135
Net cash income	106,784,635	95,569,630	101,273,424	102,821,181	108,980,986

Data as of February 5, 2021. [1] Includes expenses associated with operator dwellings.
ERS, Farm Income Team, (202) 694–5344. FarmIncomeTeam@ers.usda.gov. http://www.ers.usda.gov/data-products/farm-income-and-wealth-statistics.aspx.

Table 9-38.—Expenses: Farm production expenses, United States, 2016–2019

Item	2016	2017	2018	2019
	Thousand dollars			
Total production expenses [1]	349,938,198	350,285,294	343,815,714	348,737,395
Feed purchased	55,636,890	54,538,086	53,837,596	59,441,510
Livestock and poultry purchased	22,060,469	27,413,658	29,154,722	28,657,638
Seed purchased	21,823,770	22,515,616	21,915,200	21,214,714
Fertilizer and lime	23,541,108	22,032,717	23,234,502	22,333,163
Pesticides	15,230,869	15,716,091	15,415,784	15,515,886
Fuel and oil	12,155,180	12,761,072	13,187,914	13,193,921
Electricity	5,585,083	5,805,753	6,052,989	5,745,542
Other [2]	65,592,758	67,236,565	67,274,025	67,134,568
Interest [1]	17,337,685	18,567,706	20,637,498	20,663,636
Contract and hired labor expenses	34,425,216	36,266,282	34,148,554	35,053,362
Net rent to landlords [3]	19,473,379	17,643,858	15,473,731	16,830,660
Capital consumption [1]	44,444,813	36,314,762	29,925,923	28,809,080
Property taxes [1]	12,630,978	13,473,759	13,557,276	14,143,715

[1] Includes expenses associated with operator dwellings. [2] Includes repair and maintenance, machine hire and custom work, marketing, storage and transportation, insurance premiums, and miscellaneous other expenses. [3] Data includes landlord capital consumption.
ERS, Farm Income Team, (202) 694-5344. FarmIncomeTeam@ers.usda.gov. http://www.ers.usda.gov/data-products/farm-income-and-wealth-statistics.aspx. Data as of February 5, 2021.

Table 9-39.—Principal farm operator household finances, United States, 2017–2020

Item	2017	2018	2019	2020 [1]
Number of family farms	1,989,574	1,979,368	1,967,617	1,967,617
	Income, median dollars per household			
Farm income	(1,035)	(1,735)	296	767
Off-farm income	67,500	65,841	68,750	69,784
Earned income	43,225	37,500	39,574	38,527
Unearned income	19,000	20,404	27,225	28,078
Household income	74,707	72,481	83,111	86,086
U.S. household income [2]	61,372	63,179	68,703	(NA)
	Income, average dollars per household			
Farm income	21,842	18,425	21,730	27,781
Off-farm income	89,747	93,786	101,638	101,732
Earned income	61,359	65,596	73,320	71,878
Unearned income	28,387	28,190	28,318	29,854
Household income	111,589	112,210	123,368	129,513
U.S. household income [2]	86,220	90,021	98,088	(NA)

(NA) Not available. [1] Forecast. [2] Estimates of U.S. Household Income are produced by the U.S. Census Bureau, Current Population Reports, p60-263, *Income and Poverty in the United States: 2019 (and earlier editions)*.
ERS, Farm Economy Branch, farmincometeam@usda.gov. Source: USDA, Economic Research Service and National Agricultural Statistics Service, 2017-2019 Agricultural Resource Management Survey. Data as of February 5, 2021.

CHAPTER X

INSURANCE, CREDIT, AND COOPERATIVES

The statistics in this chapter deal with insurance, agricultural credit and farm cooperatives. Some of the series were developed in connection with research activities of the Department, while others, such as data from agricultural credit agencies, are primarily records of operations.

Table 10-1.—Crop losses: Average percentage of indemnities attributed to specific hazards, by crops, 1948–2020

Crop	Year	Drought heat (excess)	Hail	Precip. (excess poor drainage)	Frost freeze (other cold damage)	Flood	Cyclone, tornado, wind, hot wind	Insects	Disease	Decline in price	Other
						Percent					
Adj. gross revenue	2004-2014	9	10	9	22	0	2	0	0	48	0
Adj. gross revenue-lite	2004-2014	8	10	10	31	1	1	0	1	39	0
Alfalfa seed	2002-2020	33	8	19	18	0	15	6	0	0	0
All other citrus trees	2001-2018	0	0	4	9	0	25	0	0	0	63
All other grapefruit	2003-2009	0	0	0	11	0	89	0	0	0	0
Almonds	1981-2020	8	3	50	35	0	4	0	0	0	0
Annual Forage	2014-2020	0	0	0	0	0	0	0	0	0	0
Apiculture	2009-2020	0	0	0	0	0	0	0	0	0	0
Apples	1963-2020	7	28	6	55	0	2	0	0	0	1
Avocado trees	1996-2018	0	0	6	1	0	94	0	0	0	0
Avocados	1998-2020	52	0	1	23	0	16	0	0	1	7
Banana	2012-2013	100	0	0	0	0	0	0	0	0	0
Barley	1956-2020	41	16	31	6	0	2	2	2	0	0
Blueberries	1995-2020	5	4	13	64	0	5	1	1	0	7
Buckwheat	2010-2020	42	26	20	11	0	2	0	0	0	0
Burley tobacco	1997-2019	36	2	48	2	6	2	0	3	0	1
Cabbage	1999-2020	21	2	40	24	1	5	3	3	0	3
Camelina	2012-2015	100	0	0	0	0	0	0	0	0	0
Canning beans	1988-1997	44	5	26	13	0	3	1	6	0	1
Canning peaches	1986-1987	4	0	92	0	0	0	0	0	0	4
Canola	1995-2020	21	9	53	11	0	3	1	1	1	0
Carambola trees	2001-2018	0	0	17	0	0	83	0	0	0	0
Cherries	1963-2020	13	3	38	35	0	2	0	0	8	0
Chile peppers	2001-2016	1	26	11	19	6	22	9	5	0	1
Cigar:											
binder tobacco	1997-2020	11	19	26	3	0	2	0	38	0	1
filler tobacco	1998-2020	9	0	83	0	0	2	0	4	0	1
wrapper tobacco	1997-2019	0	0	44	1	0	0	0	55	0	0
Citrus	1952-1997	2	1	1	94	0	2	0	0	0	0
Citrus I	1998-2012	0	0	0	6	0	94	0	0	0	0
Citrus II	2000-2013	0	0	0	25	0	74	0	0	0	0
Citrus III	2005-2013	0	0	0	12	0	88	0	0	0	0
Citrus IV	1998-2011	0	6	0	6	0	88	0	0	0	0
Citrus tree	1990-1997	0	0	0	100	0	0	0	0	0	0
Citrus trees	1984-1986	0	0	0	100	0	0	0	0	0	0
Citrus trees I	2008-2010	0	0	66	0	0	34	0	0	0	0
Citrus trees II	2008-2010	0	0	100	0	0	0	0	0	0	0
Citrus trees III	2010-2010	0	0	100	0	0	0	0	0	0	0
Citrus trees IV	2004-2010	0	0	100	0	0	0	0	0	0	0
Citrus trees V	2010-2010	0	0	100	0	0	0	0	0	0	0
Citrus V	1999-2013	0	4	0	35	0	61	0	0	0	0
Citrus VI	2005-2006	0	0	0	0	0	100	0	0	0	0
Citrus VII	1998-2013	0	3	0	14	0	83	0	0	0	0
Citrus VIII	2009-2012	0	13	0	87	0	0	0	0	0	0
Clams	2001-2020	0	0	0	26	0	8	0	2	0	64
Clary sage	2016-2020	5	1	75	4	0	16	0	0	0	0
Coffee	2009-2020	40	0	22	0	0	15	3	0	0	20
Coffee tree	2009-2020	0	0	0	15	0	0	0	0	0	85
Corn	1948-2020	45	5	31	4	2	3	0	1	9	0
Cotton	1948-2020	53	12	13	4	1	14	0	0	2	0
Cotton ex long staple	1984-2020	81	3	5	7	1	2	1	0	0	0
Crambe	1999-2003	31	8	35	10	0	11	0	5	0	0
Cranberries	1984-2020	14	16	19	40	1	1	3	0	0	4
Cucumbers	2014-2020	16	2	67	4	0	10	0	1	0	0
Cultivated wild rice	1999-2020	39	9	8	9	1	18	1	1	0	15
Dark air tobacco	1997-2020	19	1	69	0	2	3	0	5	0	1
Dry beans	1948-2020	16	19	45	15	0	2	0	2	1	0
Dry peas	1963-2020	44	23	23	4	0	1	0	1	3	0

See note(s) at end of table.

X–2   INSURANCE, CREDIT, AND COOPERATIVES

Table 10-1.—Crop losses: Average percentage of indemnities attributed to specific hazards, by crops, 1948–2020—Continued

Crop	Year	Drought heat (excess)	Hail	Precip. (excess poor drainage)	Frost freeze (other cold damage)	Flood	Cyclone, tornado, wind, hot wind	Insects	Disease	Decline in price	Other
						Percent					
Early & midseason oranges	1998-2017	0	7	23	37	0	32	0	0	0	0
Figs	1988-2020	23	0	39	35	0	2	0	0	0	0
Fire cured tobacco	1997-2020	15	5	60	1	4	5	0	4	0	6
Flax	1948-2020	38	8	42	8	0	2	1	1	0	0
Flue cured tobacco	1997-2020	29	4	31	2	0	21	0	12	0	0
Forage production	1979-2020	66	2	7	22	0	0	1	0	0	0
Forage seeding	1978-2020	24	0	22	51	1	2	0	0	0	0
Fresh:											
Apricots	1997-2020	9	11	24	53	0	3	0	0	0	0
Freestone peaches	1997-2020	12	17	20	49	0	2	0	0	0	0
Market beans	2001-2020	3	0	67	13	0	9	0	7	0	0
Market sweet corn	1985-2020	14	2	34	26	1	17	3	1	0	2
Market tomatoes	1984-2020	7	4	48	27	0	8	1	5	0	0
Nectarines	1997-2020	7	28	23	42	0	1	0	0	0	0
Plum	1990-1997	1	32	41	25	0	0	0	0	0	0
Grain sorghum	1959-2020	75	3	11	4	1	4	1	0	2	0
Grapefruit	1997-2020	5	1	5	9	0	77	2	0	0	0
Grapefruit trees	2001-2020	0	0	8	5	0	14	0	0	0	73
Grapes	1967-2020	17	3	12	40	0	2	0	0	0	25
Grass Seed	2012-2020	29	3	41	6	0	0	21	0	0	0
Green peas	1962-2020	44	4	38	10	0	2	0	1	0	0
Hemp	2020-2020	48	0	15	4	0	31	1	1	0	0
Hybrid corn seed	1983-2020	55	5	22	2	2	12	0	1	0	0
Hybrid seed rice	2016-2020	76	0	23	0	0	0	0	0	0	1
Hybrid sorghum seed	1988-2020	25	19	9	17	0	29	0	0	0	0
Hybrid sweet corn seed	2018-2020	47	0	6	42	0	5	0	0	0	0
Hybrid Vegetable seed	2020-2020	0	8	0	89	0	2	0	0	0	0
Income protection corn	1996-1996	3	0	93	3	0	0	0	0	0	0
Income protection cotton	1996-1996	96	0	4	0	0	0	0	0	0	0
Income protection wheat	1996-1996	9	0	90	0	1	0	0	0	0	0
Late oranges	1998-2017	0	11	24	24	0	41	0	0	0	0
Lemon trees	2005-2018	0	0	0	0	0	100	0	0	0	0
Lemons	1997-2020	18	2	3	72	0	4	0	0	0	1
Lime trees	1998-2005	0	0	0	0	0	0	0	0	0	100
Macadamia nuts	1996-2020	57	0	16	7	0	9	5	0	0	6
Macadamia trees	2005-2012	0	0	0	0	0	82	0	0	0	18
Mandarins	1997-2014	17	2	1	77	0	4	0	0	0	0
Mandarins/tangerines	2015-2020	53	2	9	25	0	11	0	0	0	0
Mango trees	1997-2018	0	0	8	2	0	90	0	0	0	0
Maryland tobacco	1997-2020	49	7	31	3	0	5	0	5	0	0
Millet	1996-2020	70	17	10	2	0	1	0	0	0	0
Minneola tangelos	1998-2014	11	0	5	80	0	3	0	0	0	0
Mint	2001-2020	35	4	23	30	1	2	1	3	0	0
Mustard	1999-2020	49	19	21	6	0	3	1	0	0	0
Navel oranges	1998-2014	19	2	2	76	0	1	0	0	1	0
Nursery (container)	1987-1999	9	1	18	19	11	21	8	14	0	0
Nursery (fg&c)	2001-2020	1	6	4	12	5	68	3	1	0	0
Oats	1956-2020	55	10	25	5	0	2	1	1	0	0
Olives	2012-2020	26	2	11	51	0	9	0	0	0	0
Onions	1988-2020	21	7	46	10	1	2	0	13	0	0
Orange trees	1996-2020	0	0	6	5	0	31	0	0	0	58
Oranges	1958-2020	17	2	4	17	0	59	0	0	0	0
Orlando tangelos	1998-2012	0	0	0	100	0	0	0	0	0	0
Papaya	2007-2018	0	0	16	0	0	10	4	45	0	25
Papaya tree	2014-2020	0	0	44	2	0	17	0	16	0	21

See note(s) at end of table.

Table 10-1.—Crop losses: Average percentage of indemnities attributed to specific hazards, by crops, 1948–2020—Continued

Crop	Year	Drought heat (excess)	Hail	Precip. (excess poor drainage)	Frost freeze, (other cold damage)	Flood	Cyclone, tornado, wind, hot wind	Insects	Disease	Decline in price	Other
					Percent						
Pastures/Rangeland forage	2007-2020	0	0	0	0	0	0	0	0	0	0
Peaches	1957-2020	2	12	3	79	0	0	0	0	0	4
Peanuts	1962-2020	64	0	21	3	0	6	0	5	0	4
Pears	1989-2020	14	22	16	43	0	3	0	1	0	1
Pecans	1998-2020	25	5	12	20	0	29	0	1	0	0
Peppers	1984-2020	0	4	64	19	0	11	0	2	0	0
Pistachios	2012-2020	74	1	17	6	0	2	0	0	0	0
Plums	1998-2020	14	23	20	41	0	2	0	0	0	0
Popcorn	1984-2020	37	20	27	6	2	4	0	1	3	0
Potatoes	1962-2020	25	5	43	15	1	2	0	9	0	0
Prevented planting endorse	1990-1994	31	0	11	5	53	0	0	0	0	0
Prevented planting endorse	1982-1985	0	0	97	0	3	0	0	0	0	0
Prevented planting endorse	1986-1986	0	0	24	0	76	0	0	0	0	0
Processing:											
Apricots	1997-2020	15	5	35	42	0	4	0	0	0	0
Beans	1998-2020	43	6	41	5	0	2	0	2	0	0
Cling peaches	1997-2020	20	13	32	33	0	2	0	0	0	0
Cucumbers	2001-2005	34	3	49	3	0	1	2	6	0	0
Freestone	1998-2020	24	6	31	39	0	1	0	0	0	0
Prunes	1986-2020	40	2	31	19	0	8	0	0	0	0
Pumpkins	2009-2020	10	0	56	32	0	0	0	1	1	0
Raisins	1961-2020	0	0	100	0	0	0	0	0	0	0
Rangeland	1999-2008	0	0	0	0	0	0	0	0	0	100
Raspberry and blackberry	2002-2006	10	0	0	62	0	28	0	0	0	0
Revenue coverage corn	1996-1996	5	35	47	4	7	1	0	0	0	0
Revenue coverage soybeans	1996-1996	7	22	51	5	12	0	0	2	0	0
Rice	1960-2019	20	0	62	3	3	7	0	1	2	1
Rio red & star ruby	1998-2017	0	5	31	33	0	30	0	0	0	0
Ruby red grapefruit	1998-2017	0	12	36	17	0	35	0	0	0	0
Rye	1980-2020	34	12	32	20	0	1	0	0	0	0
Safflower	1964-2020	53	5	18	13	0	7	2	2	0	0
Sesame	2011-2020	53	1	27	3	3	11	1	0	0	1
Silage sorghum	2005-2020	72	6	2	3	0	16	0	0	0	0
Soybeans	1955-2020	39	6	38	4	3	1	0	0	7	1
Special citrus	1992-1994	7	13	0	80	0	0	0	0	0	0
Stonefruit	1988-1996	3	12	59	19	0	2	0	0	0	4
Strawberries	2001-2015	22	1	33	24	0	0	3	17	0	0
Sugar beets	1965-2020	10	4	49	25	1	4	1	6	0	0
Sugarcane	1967-2020	24	0	17	37	1	8	3	7	0	3
Sunflowers	1976-2020	25	8	49	8	0	3	1	3	1	2
Sweet corn	1978-2020	47	2	28	15	0	5	0	1	0	1
Sweet oranges	1998-2014	20	0	5	72	0	4	0	0	0	0
Sweet potatoes	2011-2020	1	0	98	0	0	1	0	0	0	0
Sweet potatoes	1998-2009	36	0	45	0	0	15	3	0	0	0
Table grapes	1984-2020	42	7	27	22	0	1	0	2	0	0
Tangelos	1997-2020	31	2	9	30	0	28	0	0	0	0
Tangors	2014-2019	0	0	0	1	0	99	0	0	0	0
Tobacco	1948-1996	32	10	32	2	1	11	0	11	0	1
Tomatoes	1963-2020	35	6	38	9	1	1	3	8	0	0
Triticale	2018-2020	41	9	4	38	0	8	0	0	0	0
Tung Nuts	1965-1970	0	0	0	100	0	0	0	0	0	0
Valencia oranges	1998-2014	18	2	2	74	0	3	0	0	0	0
Walnuts	1984-2020	28	6	34	28	1	4	0	0	0	0
Watermelons	1999-1999	22	2	11	5	0	7	0	48	0	6
Wheat	1948-2020	43	12	23	13	0	3	0	2	3	0
Whole Farm Revenue Protection	2015-2020	16	7	18	19	0	4	0	1	34	0
Winter squash	1999-2005	35	4	54	1	5	0	0	0	0	2

GRP crops do not have any specific cause of loss.
RMA, Requirements, Analysis and Validation Branch, (816) 926–7910.

INSURANCE, CREDIT, AND COOPERATIVES

Table 10-2.—Crop insurance programs: Coverage, amount of premiums and indemnities, by crops, United States, 2018–2020

Commodity and year	Coverage				Amount of premium	Indemnities		
	County programs	Insured units	Area insured	Maximum insured production		Number	Area in-demnified	Amount
	Number	*Number*	*1,000 acres*	*1,000 dollars*	*1,000 dollars*		*1,000 acres*	*1,000 dollars*
Alfalfa seed:								
2018	35	659	43	54,257	3,969	273	12	8,672
2019	35	400	25	33,841	2,130	76	6	3,632
2020	32	363	20	24,092	1,765	17	1	728
All other citrus trees:								
2018	28	231	0	36,047	488	45	0	1,871
2019	28	228	0	36,777	498	0	0	0
2020	28	305	0	56,705	1,120	0	0	0
Almonds:								
2018	32	6,730	787	2,132,584	64,964	1,050	77	51,697
2019	32	7,251	836	2,146,525	61,912	991	61	35,116
2020	32	7,815	896	2,617,583	73,133	148	11	7,570
Annual Forage:								
2018	744	3,963	646	151,485	37,106	2,899	0	65,037
2019	744	4,551	678	170,911	42,496	2,340	0	29,339
2020	744	7,613	1,240	213,760	49,618	5,226	0	57,888
Apiculture:								
2018	3,069	7,669	0	165,903	35,677	4,162	0	30,481
2019	3,069	9,975	0	222,777	49,228	4,663	0	29,917
2020	3,069	10,795	0	251,392	56,416	7,372	0	77,572
Apples:								
2018	600	7,430	229	1,402,693	123,244	1,457	24	77,446
2019	612	7,580	230	1,434,274	113,822	1,669	27	88,767
2020	688	8,001	232	1,517,372	121,669	1,278	18	65,757
Avocado trees:								
2018	1	129	0	24,734	806	114	0	7,898
2019	1	118	0	29,585	1,044	0	0	0
2020	1	113	0	31,592	1,155	0	0	0
Avocados:								
2018	8	1,025	33	80,020	5,082	183	1	5,190
2019	16	977	34	87,152	5,697	431	14	25,150
2020	18	965	32	90,846	6,079	83	2	2,887
Banana:								
2018	4	4	0	1,867	41	0	0	0
2019	4	4	0	1,870	41	0	0	0
2020	8	6	0	1,826	42	0	0	0
Banana tree:								
2018	4	2	0	508	14	0	0	0
2019	4	2	0	537	15	0	0	0
2020	8	3	0	566	13	0	0	0
Barley:								
2018	5,379	12,031	1,586	295,229	36,172	2,183	240	20,375
2019	5,391	12,793	1,780	319,245	39,214	2,515	282	22,470
2020	5,595	12,045	1,740	319,210	38,984	1,905	215	19,672
Blueberries:								
2018	171	1,376	69	248,501	16,530	536	17	35,288
2019	171	1,574	70	290,140	22,270	438	10	28,311
2020	228	2,111	73	344,077	30,937	718	18	48,800
Buckwheat:								
2018	33	120	10	1,748	298	37	3	297
2019	33	121	11	1,813	317	13	1	73
2020	32	86	9	1,399	262	10	1	77
Burley tobacco:								
2018	497	4,371	51	132,537	23,144	2,652	35	54,988
2019	497	3,792	42	113,446	24,858	2,249	26	49,672
2020	511	3,542	34	108,179	24,113	1,019	17	34,343
Cabbage:								
2018	31	314	13	31,065	2,165	80	2	2,468
2019	31	343	13	33,523	2,490	86	2	3,486
2020	49	357	14	35,902	2,689	68	1	1,586
Camelina:								
2018	52	0	0	0	0	0	0	0
2019	52	0	0	0	0	0	0	0
2020	52	0	0	0	3	0	0	0
Caneberries:								
2019	4	2	1	13,067	228	0	0	0
2020	4	10	4	41,050	763	0	0	0
Canola:								
2018	1,005	12,305	1,891	421,023	84,013	2,485	320	28,476
2019	1,011	13,003	1,979	426,333	76,111	4,420	466	54,774
2020	1,020	12,049	1,857	387,183	74,177	2,590	292	31,999

See footnote(s) at end of table.

Table 10-2.—Crop insurance programs: Coverage, amount of premiums and indemnities, by crops, United States, 2018–2020—Continued

Commodity and year	Coverage				Amount of premium	Indemnities		
	County programs	Insured units	Area insured	Maximum insured production		Number	Area indemnified	Amount
	Number	Number	1,000 acres	1,000 dollars	1,000 dollars		1,000 acres	1,000 dollars
Carambola trees:								
2018	2	9	0	2,772	101	5	0	87
2019	2	10	0	3,232	113	0	0	0
2020	2	6	0	3,358	121	0	0	0
Cattle:								
2018	20	9	0	964	42	5	0	32
2019	20	17	0	1,314	42	6	0	33
2020	20	10	0	855	31	7	0	85
Cherries:								
2018	64	3,520	85	495,645	61,340	1,184	32	59,332
2019	64	3,544	87	506,363	66,456	1,608	42	96,821
2020	64	3,583	88	516,680	70,683	1,158	23	56,160
Chile Peppers:								
2018	3	11	1	457	14	0	0	0
2019	3	9	1	354	11	0	0	0
2020	3	5	1	271	7	0	0	0
Cigar binder tobacco:								
2018	21	389	3	25,294	7,162	70	0	1,923
2019	21	413	4	29,753	8,816	32	0	656
2020	26	438	4	33,443	9,561	34	1	1,848
Cigar filler tobacco:								
2018	3	11	0	331	5	1	0	4
2019	3	46	0	489	13	13	0	39
2020	5	296	2	6,255	435	143	1	2,058
Cigar wrapper tobacco:								
2018	5	13	0	1,387	175	3	0	24
2019	5	13	0	1,350	181	9	0	194
2020	10	0	0	0	0	0	0	0
Clams:								
2018	9	61	0	17,652	485	23	0	1,589
2019	9	116	0	17,936	476	6	0	231
2020	18	93	0	21,819	605	2	0	26
Clary sage:								
2018	4	154	13	8,172	883	26	1	216
2019	4	59	6	4,178	421	28	3	377
2020	8	108	8	5,518	601	24	1	59
Coffee:								
2018	4	125	4	19,699	430	40	1	1,048
2019	4	118	4	19,778	398	36	0	348
2020	8	113	4	18,743	360	3	0	213
Coffee tree:								
2018	4	79	0	23,621	98	0	0	0
2019	4	76	0	35,527	163	0	0	0
2020	8	77	0	40,570	197	2	0	89
Corn:								
2018	18,722	655,048	78,162	40,329,801	3,161,545	109,378	11,752	1,371,110
2019	18,728	718,759	86,955	43,673,088	3,746,362	218,703	22,347	4,030,901
2020	19,293	736,383	84,327	43,973,148	3,508,518	160,859	16,727	2,555,072
Cotton:								
2018	5,938	169,356	13,184	5,720,221	1,137,711	88,706	15,749	1,630,131
2019	5,938	142,755	13,109	5,483,275	958,594	69,563	11,420	1,182,594
2020	6,349	146,687	11,751	4,789,105	870,531	62,564	11,799	1,302,526
Cotton exlong staple:								
2018	58	1,048	247	208,039	15,424	209	51	22,071
2019	58	1,040	220	183,935	12,787	351	61	18,526
2020	62	1,250	233	165,588	19,581	530	123	44,025
Cranberries:								
2018	30	606	31	102,716	2,682	49	1	1,929
2019	30	597	31	133,213	3,282	82	4	4,706
2020	41	617	31	110,303	2,762	96	4	4,664
Cucumbers:								
2018	72	335	25	17,133	1,378	93	5	1,935
2019	72	410	27	20,702	1,743	79	5	1,574
2020	88	336	23	18,220	1,439	90	6	2,169
Cultivated wild rice:								
2018	22	81	22	14,196	811	9	1	175
2019	22	68	20	13,368	685	8	3	541
2020	28	71	20	12,356	652	16	4	676

See footnote(s) at end of table.

Table 10-2.—Crop insurance programs: Coverage, amount of premiums and indemnities, by crops, United States, 2018–2020—Continued

Commodity and year	Coverage				Amount of premium	Indemnities		
	County pro-grams	Insured units	Area in-sured	Maximum insured production		Number	Area in-demnified	Amount
	Number	*Number*	*1,000 acres*	*1,000 dollars*	*1,000 dollars*		*1,000 acres*	*1,000 dollars*
Dairy cattle:								
2018	48	1,370	0	319,088	6,131	609	0	5,409
2019	48	734	0	128,607	2,149	136	0	2,488
2020	48	1,000	0	277,504	4,938	206	0	4,554
Dark air tobacco:								
2018	59	1,094	9	38,573	1,861	272	4	10,932
2019	59	1,110	10	42,140	2,538	430	5	16,512
2020	60	1,134	9	39,523	2,747	369	5	16,324
Dry beans:								
2018	940	11,274	1,083	419,490	56,549	1,965	178	32,637
2019	982	11,607	1,194	436,505	64,486	4,263	413	81,357
2020	982	15,003	1,642	696,691	110,062	4,022	480	85,137
Dry Peas:								
2018	738	14,158	2,259	444,336	79,020	4,309	752	78,393
2019	878	11,597	1,843	275,585	46,631	3,190	486	42,001
2020	878	10,061	1,637	214,153	39,681	1,500	208	13,122
Fed cattle:								
2018	37	128	0	13,328	473	23	0	57
2019	37	68	0	5,917	185	39	0	211
2020	50	109	0	11,473	417	69	0	595
Feeder cattle:								
2018	38	1,385	0	110,163	4,036	599	0	2,263
2019	38	1,118	0	98,699	2,769	822	0	4,945
2020	50	857	0	84,887	3,109	445	0	4,746
Figs:								
2018	4	60	4	8,241	225	4	1	177
2019	4	68	5	10,720	289	3	0	190
2020	4	56	5	10,201	274	5	1	160
Fired cured tobacco:								
2018	63	1,519	16	88,949	5,262	232	3	8,475
2019	63	1,371	13	75,148	5,155	299	3	8,955
2020	80	1,246	12	70,023	5,349	232	2	6,233
Flax:								
2018	265	1,713	177	23,938	3,974	390	38	2,470
2019	265	2,830	320	43,279	7,960	1,442	155	15,570
2020	289	2,452	286	38,978	7,885	622	67	5,363
Flue cured tobacco:								
2016	291	11,750	210	666,273	56,540	4,465	86	131,728
2017	291	11,475	206	638,033	61,882	3,492	66	95,645
2018	291	11,686	205	657,775	69,268	5,319	119	215,500
Forage production:								
2018	1,404	14,902	2,107	260,741	25,906	2,263	205	11,286
2019	1,404	13,621	1,964	272,089	30,858	2,077	172	17,332
2020	1,434	12,311	1,800	265,287	27,953	3,011	447	22,407
Forage seeding:								
2018	590	3,560	176	31,943	3,778	1,912	91	11,156
2019	590	2,789	154	25,755	3,186	1,309	66	7,054
2020	621	4,320	233	38,946	5,230	320	19	2,133
Fresh apricots:								
2018	29	125	3	11,362	1,357	39	1	1,622
2019	29	123	3	11,358	1,229	34	0	1,224
2020	29	123	2	9,861	1,074	38	1	1,789
Fresh freestone peaches:								
2018	25	713	19	79,576	2,152	81	1	1,275
2019	25	742	20	93,911	2,734	80	1	1,496
2020	25	770	19	104,154	3,550	64	1	1,156
Fresh market beans:								
2018	15	26	6	4,117	494	10	3	440
2019	15	30	5	4,227	546	7	1	219
2020	21	40	4	3,700	625	9	1	510
Fresh market sweet corn:								
2018	230	610	47	45,405	3,234	121	5	2,627
2019	230	547	45	43,335	3,009	104	5	4,016
2020	349	545	38	38,042	2,772	119	3	2,281
Fresh market tomatoes:								
2018	57	402	29	103,267	10,452	185	4	15,518
2019	57	345	26	94,787	9,598	132	3	11,622
2020	59	375	24	92,073	10,099	146	3	13,908

See footnote(s) at end of table.

Table 10-2.—Crop insurance programs: Coverage, amount of premiums and indemnities, by crops, United States, 2018–2020—Continued

Commodity and year	Coverage				Amount of premium	Indemnities		
	County pro- grams	Insured units	Area insured	Maximum insured production		Number	Area in- demnified	Amount
	Number	Number	1,000 acres	1,000 dollars	1,000 dollars		1,000 acres	1,000 dollars
Fresh nectarines:								
2018	24	686	14	59,278	3,498	118	2	3,029
2019	24	701	14	66,420	3,802	129	1	2,703
2020	24	691	13	71,298	4,636	74	1	1,355
Grain sorghum:								
2018	7,077	54,693	4,191	714,046	151,820	14,451	1,339	87,556
2019	7,077	52,525	4,067	712,251	154,708	10,585	867	59,885
2020	7,473	56,701	4,482	764,964	156,379	14,373	1,610	116,072
Grapefruit:								
2018	56	897	45	68,091	4,798	368	0	26,333
2019	56	897	44	73,923	6,601	109	3	1,861
2020	56	858	3741	81,514	6,438	133	6	3,735
Grapefruit trees:								
2018	31	960	0	166,336	4,207	47	0	3,573
2019	31	917	0	190,333	4,829	0	0	0
2020	31	910	0	232,668	5,653	2	0	66
Grapes:								
2018	226	16,892	558	1,571,150	51,190	1,208	23	25,343
2019	226	17,419	561	1,723,694	55,973	1,687	40	58,774
2020	253	17,613	537	1,744,425	58,650	4,542	83	244,413
Grass seed:								
2018	20	96	32	8,862	628	14	4	460
2019	20	113	44	12,403	845	11	4	576
2020	20	140	59	17,585	1,281	39	16	1,881
Green peas:								
2018	321	1,570	118	55,071	6,642	729	51	10,407
2019	303	1,699	122	55,907	7,393	658	43	8,924
2020	319	1,723	128	57,222	7,602	597	44	8,577
Hemp:								
2020	1,492	247	21	27,808	3,928	88	11	11,877
Hybrid corn seed:								
2018	462	4,615	310	245,526	13,245	226	18	2,810
2019	462	5,085	334	260,275	13,842	350	20	5,630
2020	485	5,516	362	318,178	15,110	407	24	6,982
Hybrid seed rice:								
2018	50	246	19	26,058	2,335	83	10	5,591
2019	50	338	26	33,126	2,690	68	2	891
2020	71	309	19	29,956	2,420	11	0	310
Hybrid sorghum seed:								
2018	52	437	32	13,870	1,258	52	3	687
2019	52	465	36	15,356	1,391	98	6	1,718
2020	52	640	51	18,895	1,613	88	5	1,378
Hybrid sweet corn seed:								
2018	16	122	2	2,510	233	19	0	137
2019	16	127	3	4,478	377	17	0	585
2020	16	184	4	6,567	619	19	1	353
Hybrid vegetable seed:								
2020	5	83	1	7,342	521	25	0	1,180
Lamb:								
2018	28	282	0	50,139	1,430	267	0	5,582
2019	28	85	0	9,740	235	7	0	31
2020	28	96	0	22,083	714	68	0	5,397
Lemon trees:								
2018	3	8	0	1,297	29	3	0	410
2019	3	15	0	3,854	95	0	0	0
2020	14	47	1	10,484	288	0	0	0
Lemons:								
2018	34	861	43	161,178	11,541	47	0	2,225
2019	34	875	44	196,026	11,703	53	1	1,527
2020	40	900	43	208,474	11,152	20	1	1,162
Lime trees:								
2018	5	4	0	985	16	0	0	0
2019	5	5	0	1,026	14	0	0	0
2020	8	4	0	1,183	14	0	0	0
Macadamia nuts:								
2018	3	54	12	18,035	244	0	0	0
2019	3	52	11	20,733	385	29	4	1,715
2020	3	51	12	23,123	424	24	3	1,504
Macadamia trees:								
2018	3	53	12	52,808	308	0	0	0
2019	4	162	0	65,711	341	0	0	0
2020	8	167	0	74,536	389	0	0	0
Mandarins/ Tangerines:								
2018	53	1,044	50	302,843	24,517	185	0	11,100
2019	53	1,138	52	319,806	24,254	70	2	6,994
2020	53	1,222	57	366,253	24,229	115	4	11,147

See footnote(s) at end of table.

Table 10-2.—Crop insurance programs: Coverage, amount of premiums and indemnities, by crops, United States, 2018–2020—Continued

Commodity and year	Coverage				Amount of premium	Indemnities		
	County programs	Insured units	Area insured	Maximum insured production		Number	Area indemnified	Amount
	Number	Number	1,000 acres	1,000 dollars	1,000 dollars		1,000 acres	1,000 dollars
Mango trees:								
2018	1	20	0	876	32	14	0	217
2019	1	17	0	858	32	0	0	0
2020	1	19	0	1,109	46	0	0	0
Maryland tobacco:								
2018	6	0	0	0	0	0	0	0
2019	6	1	0	20	1	1	0	19
2020	6	6	0	122	10	5	0	86
Milk:								
2019	50	9,373	0	5,873,141	95,114	1,085	0	69,352
2020	50	16,884	0	13,013,717	293,215	4,812	0	414,546
Millet:								
2018	138	4,019	329	21,884	5,499	1,217	103	3,766
2019	138	4,474	394	27,481	6,021	1,060	89	3,264
2020	138	5,072	475	41,794	8,933	3,190	96	3,114
Mint:								
2018	48	246	17	15,953	747	65	3	662
2019	48	225	18	14,694	775	60	2	660
2020	52	217	16	13,694	893	44	2	659
Mustard:								
2018	75	309	48	5,704	1,529	90	10	762
2019	75	309	54	6,876	1,542	107	23	1,815
2020	76	323	52	6,418	1,614	46	9	527
Nursery (FG&C):								
2018	2,799	2,468	0	1,402,915	26,317	545	0	99,094
2019	2,799	2,568	0	1,562,484	31,642	38	0	5,659
2020	2,799	3,009	0	1,750,112	37,731	45	0	5,947
Oats:								
2018	2,805	7,764	400	39,856	6,730	1,507	70	4,304
2019	2,805	7,953	431	45,108	7,716	2,167	93	6,590
2020	3,023	9,262	517	63,994	10,419	2,261	113	7,491
Olives:								
2018	17	379	23	36,677	3,533	271	14	17,072
2019	17	369	23	45,870	4,510	29	1	935
2020	17	354	22	28,292	3,107	170	11	7,688
Onions:								
2018	178	1,935	104	237,545	44,843	856	27	41,743
2019	178	1,427	86	209,514	25,843	333	11	17,585
2020	209	1,534	86	213,446	28,484	403	14	24,327
Orange trees:								
2018	31	1,994	0	1,122,148	11,910	214	0	26,655
2019	31	2,090	0	1,271,342	13,340	0	0	0
2020	68	3,435	0	2,283,104	35,268	11	0	1,079
Oranges:								
2018	66	6,384	415	580,624	26,746	1,830	0	76,882
2019	66	6,995	442	688,851	31,620	384	11	8,606
2020	66	7,767	448	848,873	34,955	183	5	5,038
Oysters:								
2018	9	0	0	0	0	0	0	0
2019	9	0	0	0	0	0	0	0
2020	9	0	0	0	0	0	0	0
Papaya:								
2018	4	20	0	859	22	8	0	187
2019	4	7	0	352	13	0	0	0
2020	8	23	0	1,353	43	0	0	0
Papaya tree:								
2018	4	8	0	347	4	2	0	63
2019	4	4	0	265	3	1	0	76
2020	8	8	0	985	12	1	0	12
Pasture/Range-land/Forage:								
2018	3,069	159,747	98,284	2,375,261	519,517	64,871	0	498,928
2019	3,069	182,079	140,140	2,624,451	581,400	70,814	0	363,287
2020	3,069	186,537	159,824	2,992,557	676,469	100,755	0	888,172
Peaches:								
2018	383	1,411	32	82,433	24,273	426	12	18,629
2019	390	1,461	31	94,567	29,185	435	9	16,379
2020	488	1,540	30	106,682	32,091	716	13	27,603
Peanuts:								
2018	2,139	22,605	1,302	643,672	55,079	4,788	241	56,578
2019	2,139	23,059	1,330	707,414	60,315	5,994	299	78,070
2020	2,400	33,010	1,555	939,554	84,997	8,019	350	108,456
Pears:								
2018	29	1,960	33	194,705	4,299	129	4	6,408
2019	29	1,985	33	200,165	4,344	359	6	11,735
2020	31	1,951	31	206,429	4,362	165	3	5,323
Pecan trees:								
2018	233	18	0	5,204	25	0	0	0
2019	233	21	0	7,430	27	0	0	0
2020	233	141	0	46,893	214	0	0	0
Pecans:								
2018	139	1,896	166	315,116	17,251	1,086	89	78,899
2019	139	1,935	170	322,553	17,960	1,081	85	69,237

Table 10-2.—Crop insurance programs: Coverage, amount of premiums and indemnities, by crops, United States, 2018–2020—Continued—Continued

Commodity and year	Coverage				Amount of premium	Indemnities		
	County programs	Insured units	Area in-sured	Maximum insured production		Number	Area in-demnified	Amount
	Number	*Number*	*1,000 acres*	*1,000 dollars*	*1,000 dollars*		*1,000 acres*	*1,000 dollars*
2020	246	2,527	179	347,257	21,407	296	21	13,365

See footnote(s) at end of table.

Table 10-2.—Crop insurance programs: Coverage, amount of premiums and indemnities, by crops, United States, 2018–2020—Continued

Commodity and year	Coverage				Amount of premium	Indemnities		
	County programs	Insured units	Area insured	Maximum insured production		Number	Area indemnified	Amount
	Number	*Number*	*1,000 acres*	*1,000 dollars*	*1,000 dollars*		*1,000 acres*	*1,000 dollars*
Peppers:								
2018	13	123	5	19,960	2,834	50	2	6,810
2019	13	106	4	17,431	2,928	31	1	4,698
2020	58	170	5	25,063	4,239	58	1	6,129
Pistachios:								
2018	24	930	168	559,132	43,018	20	2	1,587
2019	24	969	176	549,655	45,773	192	25	30,201
2020	24	996	180	772,182	61,723	54	8	24,141
Plums:								
2018	23	623	12	40,868	3,971	97	1	1,662
2019	23	587	12	41,470	3,895	102	1	2,317
2020	23	590	11	45,300	4,173	65	1	1,350
Popcorn:								
2018	3,297	1,853	189	116,533	7,412	149	16	2,596
2019	3,300	1,835	197	121,028	8,440	494	44	12,089
2020	3,300	1,934	221	143,668	8,766	252	26	5,763
Potatoes:								
2018	531	5,072	741	1,124,843	85,543	1,037	73	72,154
2019	531	5,373	756	1,209,047	84,887	1,156	86	86,181
2020	596	5,474	727	1,187,060	83,909	887	59	59,439
Processing apricots:								
2018	13	53	3	5,895	840	25	1	1,513
2019	13	41	2	4,373	569	6	0	230
2020	13	42	1	3,252	423	25	1	1,312
Processing beans:								
2018	258	1,371	89	43,703	4,583	401	22	5,196
2019	258	1,454	90	45,519	4,861	290	18	3,979
2020	275	1,493	94	47,018	5,203	240	23	4,612
Processing cling peaches:								
2018	10	784	13	51,741	1,905	115	2	1,790
2019	10	735	11	45,878	1,756	60	1	955
2020	10	731	11	44,275	1,697	68	1	763
Processing freestone:								
2018	8	91	2	10,280	289	10	0	356
2019	8	90	2	9,040	284	2	0	156
2020	8	83	2	8,605	275	15	0	385
Prunes:								
2018	28	686	39	94,170	21,272	262	14	17,073
2019	28	640	37	85,356	20,333	156	9	10,074
2020	28	556	34	78,201	18,356	310	19	23,912
Pumpkins:								
2018	22	138	6	3,874	281	8	0	83
2019	22	165	8	5,269	449	66	3	1,009
2020	22	181	9	6,416	582	34	1	275
Raisins:								
2018	7	1,874	0	179,628	5,450	127	0	532
2019	7	1,966	0	150,256	4,363	17	0	42
2020	7	1,630	0	83,989	2,535	64	0	248
Rice:								
2018	1,089	21,320	2,549	1,664,182	87,457	3,727	475	82,775
2019	1,089	20,724	2,813	1,563,756	97,689	7,850	1,069	286,639
2020	1,156	24,289	3,056	2,151,433	1,37,018	7,459	970	249,901
Rye:								
2018	89	483	35	3,446	623	209	13	722
2019	97	668	54	6,756	1,206	234	13	1,123
2020	111	534	54	5,566	944	189	15	767
Safflower:								
2018	164	556	102	11,314	1,715	104	16	711
2019	164	583	86	7,820	1,357	206	31	1,992
2020	164	553	98	10,607	1,738	93	15	1,011

See footnote(s) at end of table.

Table 10-2.—Crop insurance programs: Coverage, amount of premiums and indemnities, by crops, United States, 2018–2020—Continued

Commodity and year	Coverage				Amount of premium	Indemnities		
	County pro-grams	Insured units	Area in-sured	Maximum insured production		Number	Area in-demnified	Amount
	Number	Number	1,000 acres	1,000 dollars	1,000 dollars		1,000 acres	1,000 dollars
Sesame:								
2018	102	710	58	6,215	1,830	345	25	2,121
2019	138	869	70	8,223	2,456	359	28	1,877
2020	162	1,568	112	13,980	4,196	1,077	73	7,454
Silage Sorghum:								
2018	194	626	58	14,577	1,741	102	11	1,403
2019	194	798	75	17,557	2,225	163	17	1,736
2020	194	809	75	11,055	2,155	252	26	4,250
Soybeans:								
2018	15,790	671,546	78,863	28,888,117	2,244,711	161,529	16,656	1,286,409
2019	15,818	647,718	71,439	24,618,764	1,882,060	206,459	18,875	1,971,899
2020	16,302	685,440	75,660	26,208,642	2,003,266	132,290	10,719	961,420
Strawberries:								
2018	7	3	0	4,345	206	0	0	0
2019	7	3	0	1,718	63	0	0	0
2020	7	1	0	812	49	0	0	0
Sugar beets:								
2018	239	13,001	983	944,577	49,221	2,126	158	47,828
2019	243	13,157	1,011	983,519	53,621	3,797	286	172,458
2020	243	13,561	1,036	999,229	55,600	2,195	159	39,285
Sugarcane:								
2018	62	4,828	789	357,455	6,717	167	9	1,678
2019	62	4,858	800	347,773	6,122	324	26	4,789
2020	62	5,096	827	414,401	18,348	380	3	6,098
Sunflowers:								
2018	1,806	5,786	1,146	216,862	42,885	1,426	249	22,159
2019	1,806	6,291	1,275	241,221	44,226	2,299	447	53,786
2020	1,810	8,157	1,634	314,662	61,377	2,403	318	29,067
Sweet corn:								
2018	332	2,347	198	85,989	4,225	412	28	5,383
2019	326	2,378	200	90,795	4,434	399	28	5,436
2020	340	2,269	195	93,557	4,699	343	28	6,750
Sweet potatoes:								
2018	9	20	7	6,334	638	5	1	1,209
2019	9	19	9	10,679	1,380	1	1	405
2020	14	43	8	8,557	1,231	3	1	337
Swine:								
2018	85	126	0	18,649	767	63	0	1,430
2019	85	85	0	16,273	920	52	0	1,311
2020	98	362	0	52,901	4,210	262	0	9,581
Table grapes:								
2018	10	1,213	77	360,558	11,352	207	6	18,002
2019	10	1,208	77	362,256	11,174	207	5	19,100
2020	10	1,231	72	361,105	11,957	157	5	14,759
Tangelos:								
2018	49	344	7	20,638	1,404	78	0	820
2019	49	336	7	21,679	1,361	21	1	654
2020	49	321	7	22,807	1,261	11	0	317
Tangerine trees:								
2018	3	13	0	381	14	0	0	0
2019	3	12	0	658	20	0	0	0
2020	6	12	0	678	19	0	0	0
Tangors:								
2018	29	138	3	7,139	357	105	3	4,919
2019	29	133	3	5,168	268	1	0	11
2020	29	126	2	4,602	243	0	0	0
Tomatoes:								
2018	148	2,694	240	512,868	10,854	102	8	4,163
2019	148	2,512	230	530,353	11,008	159	16	14,928
2020	161	2,520	227	531,076	10,794	110	9	3,788
Triticale:								
2018	116	196	23	2,702	309	49	3	157
2019	135	2850	29	3,496	355	55	5	351
2020	135	329	34	4,985	529	86	8	559
Walnuts:								
2018	52	1,884	169	303,827	6,036	113	4	3,041
2019	52	1,963	180	222,393	4,043	180	8	3,495
2020	52	2,065	190	280,693	4,749	62	4	1,210
Wheat:								
2018	15,672	337,422	38,725	6,908,398	997,875	86,847	9,161	574,097
2019	15,738	327,832	38,737	7,227,322	1,111,007	101,567	11,540	944,674
2020	16,080	305,867	36,170	5,991,858	894,772	66,242	7,416	486,937
Whole Farm Revenue Protection:								
2018	3,140	2,491	0	2,657,659	135,843	703	0	153,644
2019	3,140	2,159	0	2,338,219	130,771	674	0	170,721
2020	3,140	2,003	0	2,229,662	130,199	123	0	4,043

RMA, Requirements, Analysis and Validation Branch, (816) 926–7910.

Table 10-3.—Farm real estate debt: Amount outstanding by lender, United States, Dec. 31, 2010–2019 [1]

Year	Farm Credit System	Farm Service Agency	Farmer Mac	Commercial banks [1]
	Billion dollars	Billion dollars	Billion dollars	Billion dollars
2010	72.5	3.5	3.6	51.2
2011	75.3	3.3	3.8	52.9
2012	80.3	3.7	3.8	64.6
2013	85.3	3.7	4.5	68.9
2014	88.8	4.3	4.7	73.3
2015	96.7	4.9	4.8	79.2
2016	103.7	5.9	5.5	84.4
2017	107.2	6.0	6.2	88.4
2018	113.0	6.6	6.5	92.8
2019	125.2	8.0	7.6	97.9

Year	Individuals and others [1]	Life insurance companies	Storage facility loans	Total farm mortgage debt
	Billion dollars	Billion dollars	Billion dollars	Billion dollars
2010	10.2	12.4	0.6	154.1
2011	18.1	13.0	0.7	167.2
2012	8.7	11.5	0.7	173.4
2013	10.1	12.0	0.7	185.2
2014	12.5	12.4	0.8	196.8
2015	10.0	12.5	0.8	208.8
2016	12.5	13.2	0.7	226.0
2017	12.6	15.0	0.8	236.2
2018	9.9	15.9	0.8	245.7
2019	10.6	16.7	0.9	266.8

Data as of February 5, 2021.
[1] Beginning with 2012 estimates, farm sector debt held by savings associations is reported with the commercial bank lender group instead of the individuals and others grouping.
ERS, Farm Farm Income Team, (202) 694–5586. FarmIncomeTeam@ers.usda.gov. http://www.ers.usda.gov/data-products/farm-income-and-wealth-statistics.aspx.

Table 10-4.—Nonreal estate farm debt: Amount outstanding, by lender, United States, Dec. 31, 2010–2019

Year	Commericial banks [1]	Farm Credit System	Farm Service Agency	Individuals and others [1]	Total nonreal estate debt
	Billion dollars	Billion dollars	Billion dollars	Billion dollars	Billion dollars
2010	56.2	39.2	3.6	25.8	124.9
2011	59.2	41.1	3.5	23.5	127.3
2012	59.9	42.7	3.4	18.2	124.2
2013	63.7	44.0	2.8	19.6	130.2
2014	70.7	47.9	3.6	26.2	148.4
2015	73.2	48.3	3.7	22.8	148.0
2016	73.2	49.4	3.8	21.8	148.2
2017	73.3	51.1	4.0	25.8	154.2
2018	74.9	53.4	3.9	24.2	156.3
2019	70.3	53.0	3.8	24.7	151.8

Data as of February 5, 2021.
[1] Beginning with 2012 estimates, farm sector debt held by savings associations is reported with the commercial bank lender group instead of the individuals and others grouping.
ERS, Farm Farm Income Team, (202) 694–5586. FarmIncomeTeam@ers.usda.gov. http://www.ers.usda.gov/data-products/farm-income-and-wealth-statistics.aspx.

Table 10-5.—Farm Service Agency: Credit assistance made to individuals, entities, and associations for farming purposes, and amount outstanding, United States and Territories, 2010–2019 [1]

Year	Direct loans and loan guarantees				
	Farm ownership			Soil and water	Recreation
	Obligations (initial and subsequent)	Loans made	Outstanding Jan. 1	Outstanding Jan. 1	Outstanding Jan. 1
	Number	1,000 dollars	1,000 dollars	1,000 dollars	1,000 dollars
2010	8,837	2,313,902	10,875,039	10,364	4,632
2011	8,516	2,498,626	11,872,786	8,053	208
2012	7,088	2,029,778	12,498,221	6,585	191
2013	6,086	1,946,988	12,842,052	5,483	133
2014	10,106	3,012,450	13,768,000	4,617	102
2015	9,970	3,050,383	14,985,868	4,082	79
2016	10,712	3,489,028	16,560,650	3,579	64
2017	10,405	3,322,717	18,195,830	2,864	46
2018	10,667	3,264,634	19,753,319	2,333	45
2019	10,607	3,528,293	21,505,224	1,912	19

Year	Direct loans and loan guarantees					
	Operating			Emergency		
	Obligations (initial and subsequent)	Loans made	Outstanding Jan. 1	New borrowers	Loans made	Outstanding Jan. 1
	Number	1,000 dollars	1,000 dollars	Number	1,000 dollars	1,000 dollars
2010	27,337	2,934,097	7,047,105	340	35,598	661,950
2011	23,411	2,285,131	6,953,778	176	32,610	578,846
2012	24,667	2,103,112	6,594,239	309	31,436	537,640
2013	23,667	1,960,150	6,254,820	382	33,387	479,869
2014	26,862	2,201,420	6,214,490	177	18,106	428,304
2015	27,523	2,617,000	6,352,898	124	13,383	385,951
2016	28,562	2,832,984	6,778,399	376	42,725	379,094
2017	27,888	2,650,932	7,135,916	124	15,131	343,455
2018	23,935	2,198,126	7,119,181	96	12,713	313,088
2019	21,635	2,199,657	7,380,820	103	13,170	284,989

Year	Loans to associations			Economic opportunity individual loans	Economic emergency loans
	Indian tribe land acquisition	Grazing association	Irrigation, drainage, and soil conservation		
	Outstanding Jan. 1	Outstanding Jan. 1	Outstanding Jan. 1	Outstanding Jan. 1	Outstanding Jan. 1
	1,000 dollars				
2010	34,306	2,232	707	6	100,515
2011	29,539	1,848	605	6	85,915
2012	25,112	1,618	511	6	76,843
2013	24,246	1,014	468	6	65,040
2014	19,825	798	284	6	57,053
2015	15,590	673	227	6	49,517
2016	11,619	408	181	5	42,545
2017	10,461	365	152	4	39,216
2018	9,227	326	121	4	33,651
2019	7,450	256	91	0	29,180

[1] Includes loans made directly by FSA and those guaranteed by the Agency. Amounts of loans made represent new obligations (initial and subsequent) for the fiscal year displayed. Amounts outstanding are less principal repayments for loans made directly by the Agency.
FSA, Loan Making Division, (202) 720–3889.

Table 10-6.—Loans to farmers' cooperative organizations: Outstanding amounts held by the agricultural credit bank classified by type of loan, United States, Jan. 1, 2011-2020

Year	Operating capital loans	Facility loans
	1,000 dollars	1,000 dollars
2011	10,871,732	35,413,410
2012	32,789,008	39,191,450
2013	32,449,687	41,153,688
2014	32,171,519	48,210,977
2015	35,316,639	53,723,941
2016	39,243,137	56,015,144
2017	35,681,814	63,583,691
2018	39,317,966	65,175,889
2019	33,662,950	75,191,303
2020	37,437,647	83,418,153

FCA, Office of Information Technology, (703) 883–4260.

Table 10-7.—Farmers' marketing, farm supply, and related service cooperatives: Number, memberships, and business volume, United States, 2011–2020

Year [1]	Cooperatives [2]				Estimated memberships [4]			
	Marketing	Farm supply	Related service [3]	Total	Marketing	Farm supply	Related service [3]	Total
	Number				1,000 members			
2011	1,222	935	128	2,285	846	1,398	36	2,279
2012	1,200	916	120	2,236	652	1,426	37	2,115
2013	1,195	871	120	2,186	655	1,284	37	1,977
2014	1,114	876	116	2,106	627	1,333	35	1,996
2015	1,079	874	94	2,047	591	1,296	34	1,921
2016	1,040	827	86	1,953	584	1,280	37	1,901
2017	1,010	777	84	1,871	604	1,251	35	1,890
2018	961	760	85	1,806	594	1,262	33	1,889
2019	931	759	89	1,779	677	1,184	38	1,900
2020	915	742	87	1,744	636	1,196	37	1,869

Year [1]	Marketing volume		Farm supply volume		Service Receipts [7]	Total marketing and farm supply volume and service receipts	
	Gross [5]	Net [6]	Gross [5]	Net [6]		Gross [5]	Net [6]
	Billion dollars						
2011	128.041	121.784	80.898	57.322	4.453	213.391	187.100
2012	140.900	133.200	92.200	64.700	4.700	237.800	202.600
2013	144.615	135.810	95.933	67.175	5.572	246.120	208.557
2014	147.731	138.340	92.624	65.638	6.315	246.670	210.293
2015	124.892	115.409	81.709	59.023	5.458	212.059	179.890
2016	114.587	108.603	71.048	51.589	5.440	191.075	165.632
2017	119.807	112.754	71.754	51.516	5.579	197.141	169.849
2018	126.333	118.962	71.728	53.634	5.753	203.814	178.349
2019	124.916	119.497	71.041	53.220	7.090	203.047	179.807
2020	126.293	120.252	67.080	50.873	7.546	200.918	178.671

[1] Reports of cooperatives are included for their fiscal year ending in calendar year. [2] Includes independent local cooperatives, centralized cooperatives, federations of cooperatives, and cooperatives with mixed organizational structures. Cooperatives are classified according to their major activity. If, for example, more than 50 percent of a cooperative's business is derived from marketing activities, it is included as a marketing cooperative. [3] Includes cooperatives whose major activity is providing services related to marketing and farm supply activities. [4] Includes members (those entitled to vote for directors) but does not include nonvoting patrons. (Some duplication exists because some farmers belong to more than one cooperative.) [5] Estimated gross business includes all business reported between cooperatives, such as the wholesale business of farm supply cooperatives with other cooperatives or terminal market sales for local cooperatives. [6] Estimated net business represents the value at the first level at which cooperatives transact business for farmers, adjusted for duplication resulting from intercooperative business. [7] Services related to marketing or purchasing but not included in the volumes reported for those activities, plus other operating and non-operating income and losses and extraordinary items.

Rural Development, Cooperative Services Branch, (202) 720-7395.

Table 10-8.—Farmers' cooperatives: Business volume of marketing, farm supply, and related service cooperatives, United States, 2019–2020

Item	Gross business		Net business [1]	
	2019	2020	2019	2020
	Billion dollars			
Products marketed:				
Beans and peas (dry edible)	0.232	0.255	0.224	0.248
Cotton and cotton products	2.954	2.812	2.866	2.723
Dairy products	43.559	45.525	42.396	44.468
Fish	0.232	0.211	0.232	0.211
Fruits and vegetables	8.095	8.193	6.721	6.850
Grain and oilseeds [2]	49.704	48.501	48.444	46.670
Livestock and livestock products	3.835	3.540	3.835	3.439
Nuts	1.672	1.721	1.713	1.721
Poultry products	0.943	0.916	0.943	0.916
Rice	1.713	1.752	1.713	1.752
Sugar products	6.055	5.906	4.875	4.637
Tobacco	0.316	0.327	0.316	0.327
Wool and mohair	0.012	0.012	0.012	0.012
Other products [3]	5.594	6.620	5.247	6.277
Total farm products	124.916	126.293	119.497	120.252
Supplies purchased:				
Crop protectants	8.119	8.386	5.599	5.844
Feed	11.759	11.803	9.932	9.926
Fertilizer	13.632	12.922	10.714	10.393
Petroleum	26.885	23.578	18.905	16.721
Seed	5.576	5.335	3.443	3.363
Other supplies [4]	5.070	5.055	4.627	4.625
Total farm supplies	71.041	67.080	53.220	50.873
Receipts for services: [5]				
Trucking, cotton ginning, storage, grinding, locker plants, miscellaneous	5.440	7.546	5.440	7.546
Total business	201.397	200.918	178.157	178.671

[1] Represents value at the first level at which cooperatives transact business for farmers; adjusted for inter-cooperative business.   [2] Excludes oilseed meal and oil.   Oilseed meal is included in feed sales while oil sales are included in other products sales.   [3] Includes coffee, forest products, hay, hops, seed marketed for growers, nursery stock, other farm products not separately classified, and sales of farm products not received directly from member-patrons.   Also includes manufactured food products and resale items marketed by cooperatives.   [4] Includes automotive supplies, building material, chicks, containers, farm machinery and equipment, hardware, meats and groceries, and other supplies not separately classified.   [5] Trucking, cotton ginning, storage, grinding, locker plants, and/or miscellaneous services related to marketing or purchasing but not included in the volume reported for those activities, plus other operating and non-operating income and losses and extraordinary items.

Rural Development, Cooperative Services Branch, (202) 720–7395.

Table 10-9.—Farmers' cooperatives: Number of cooperatives, memberships, and business volume of marketing, farm supply, and related service cooperatives, by State, United States and Foreign, 2019–2020

State	Cooperatives headquartered in State		Memberships in State [1]		Net business [2]	
	2019	2020	2019	2020	2019	2020
	Number	Number	Number	Number	Million dollars	Million dollars
Alabama	46	46	25,337	25,141	1,013.75	1,013.75
Arkansas	28	27	38,245	35,245	2,274.61	2,281.82
California	101	100	34,963	37,068	13,692.10	13,895.45
Colorado	25	25	18,702	19,771	2,526.49	2,724.75
Florida	23	22	21,082	21,229	2,364.74	2,263.83
Georgia	9	9	13,784	13,229	1,155.42	1,047.59
Hawaii	9	8	488	370	17.66	20.97
Idaho	20	17	13,449	12,996	2,303.20	2,365.99
Illinois	89	85	109,333	103,970	11,129.04	11,064.73
Indiana	26	25	49,953	45,939	3,891.75	4,241.68
Iowa	73	73	99,594	102,510	18,315.75	17,211.97
Kansas	75	78	104,930	106,894	6,869.97	7,300.06
Kentucky	20	21	161,973	161,425	1,403.25	1,421.89
Louisiana	25	26	7,731	7,197	1,320.14	1,408.04
Maine	21	20	5,574	5,429	277.22	294.13
Maryland	11	11	35,614	35,691	431.34	430.08
Massachusetts	7	6	4,959	5,108	342.86	348.36
Michigan	33	34	42,817	44,223	4,645.24	5,446.39
Minnesota	160	157	125,853	134,226	16,172.06	16,874.28
Mississippi	38	39	42,886	44,512	1,351.86	1,358.83
Missouri	50	50	93,482	94,789	4,972.42	4,699.04
Montana	42	42	18,768	18,542	1,408.91	1,437.63
Nebraska	38	39	60,174	69,826	8,318.59	7,776.52
New Jersey	11	11	1,715	1,770	313.13	314.29
New York	42	41	10,284	10,450	3,930.56	4,393.65
North Carolina	11	11	21,887	21,955	778.95	778.95
North Dakota	120	119	67,092	69,755	6,732.53	6,674.53
Ohio	33	34	39,060	40,573	4,808.19	4,779.95
Oklahoma	47	45	42,154	42,155	1,993.07	1,625.07
Oregon	24	24	29,422	30,150	3,596.39	3,136.84
Pennsylvania	24	20	12,471	12,376	3,107.33	2,994.28
South Dakota	63	61	55,687	57,193	5,108.20	4,869.19
Tennessee	57	56	66,935	66,252	1,318.92	1,427.37
Texas	157	151	75,180	74,403	5,865.18	6,057.12
Utah	10	10	9,299	8,589	737.35	791.20
Virginia	42	41	116,081	111,179	1,736.94	1,698.42
Washington	50	46	25,569	27,060	7,367.93	7,495.80
West Virginia	9	9	58,231	58,537	102.15	103.33
Wisconsin	100	99	102,182	92,096	8,765.69	9,419.76
Wyoming	7	6	4,765	4,150	437.99	435.45
Other States [3]	34	34	21,172	21,884	4,251.96	4,954.91
United States	1,806	1,779	1,888,340	1,899,056	167,155.87	168,877.88
Foreign [4]	....	....	561	569	11,193.54	10,929.11
Total	1,806	1,779	1,888,901	1,899,625	178,349.40	179,807.00

[1] Actual memberships in State. [2] Represents value at the first level at which cooperatives transact business for farmers; adjusted for inter-cooperative business. Totals may not add due to rounding. [3] Dollar volume or membership is not shown to avoid disclosing operations of individual cooperatives. [4] Sales outside the United States and sales of certain products not received directly from member-patrons.

Rural Development, Cooperative Services Branch, (202) 720–7395.

CHAPTER XI

STABILIZATION AND PRICE-SUPPORT PROGRAMS

The statistics in this chapter relate to activities of the Commodity Credit Corporation (CCC), loan and inventory acquisition and disposition programs, the CCC and Farm Service Agency payment programs, and marketing agreements and order programs for fruits and vegetables. Statistics for Federal Milk Marketing Order programs are contained in chapter VIII.

Table 11-1.—Commodity Credit Corporation: Price-supported commodities owned as of September 2019[1] (Inventory quantity)

Year	Corn Meal	Sorghum and products	Milk and products	Rice and products	Peanut and products	Cotton
	Million pounds	Million bushels	Million pounds	Million cwt	Million pounds	Million pounds/bales
2010	0	([3])	7	([3])	0	0
2011	0	([3])	0	([2])	0	0
2012	0	0	0	0	0	0
2013	0	([3])	0	([3])	0	0
2014	0	0	0	([3])	4	0
2015	0	0	0	0	168	0
2016	0	0	0	0	0	0
2017	8	0	0	([3])	55	0
2018	2	([3])	0	0	133	0
2019	1	0	0	([3])	26	([2])

Year	Beans, dry edible	Dry whole peas	Wheat	Blended Foods	Vegetable Oil Products	Value of all commodities owned
	Million bushels	Million cwt	Million bushels	Million pounds	Million pounds	Million dollars
2010	([4])	0	([2])	16	5	48
2011	([2])	0	0	16	33	53
2012	0	0	0	2	12	14
2013	0	0	0	25	23	71
2014	0	0	0	18	32	40
2015	0	2	2	13	23	55
2016	0	0	0	27	10	24
2017	0	0	0	0	21	35
2018	0	0	0	12	15	45
2019	([2])	([3])	0	14	4	23

Cotton and Dry whole peas were added to the table. This table represents the total value of all commodities owned by CCC, including price-supported commodities not shown and commodities acquired under programs other than price-support programs, less reserve for losses on inventory.[1] Commodities with data consistently zero for 2010-2019 are not listed. [2] Less than 50,000 units. [3] Less than 500,000 units. [4] Less than 500 units.
FPAC, Business Center, Budget Division, Program Budget Branch, CCC Program Section, (202) 720-4697.

Table 11-2.—Commodity Credit Corporation: Loans pledged, by quantity and face amount, United States and Territories, by crop year 2018–2019[1]

Commodity[2]	Unit[3]	2018		2019	
		Quantity pledged	Face amount	Quantity pledged	Face amount
		1,000	1,000 dollars	1,000	1,000 dollars
Barley	1,000 bushels	1,711	3,196	2,001	4,709
Canola Seed	1,000 cwt	464	4,666	208	2,103
Chickpeas	1,000 cwt	109	1,183	747	8,325
Corn	1,000 bushels	78,890	152,614	66,091	130,973
Cotton, ELS & Upland	1,000 bales	260	67,888	393	105,291
Dry Whole Peas	1,000 cwt	277	1,478	578	3,413
Flaxseed	1,000 cwt	19	196	1	13
Grain sorghum	1,000 bushels	469	928	702	1,494
Honey	1,000 pounds	3,711	2,561	4,517	3,117
Lentil Dry	1,000 cwt	242	2,702	460	5,355
Mustard Seed	1,000 cwt	26	269	....	....
Oats	1,000 bushels	273	365	452	876
Peanuts	1,000 pounds	538,966	95,856	470,553	83,563
Rice	1,000 bushels	2,064	13,470	2,381	15,773
Safflower Seed	1,000 cwt	....	....	4	34
Seed cotton, ELS & Upland	1,000 pounds	6	1,892	....	....
Soybeans	1,000 bushels	7,272	36,013	16,609	81,810
Sunflower Seed	1,000 cwt	85	843	37	378
Sunflower Seed (non-oil)	1,000 cwt	18	183	2	18
Wheat	1,000 bushels	28,113	85,570	35,251	119,227

[1] Includes loans pledged directly by Commodity Credit Corporation. [2] Commodities with no pledges for 2018 and 2019 were removed. [3] Includes Upland & ELS Bales and CFLS Pounds.
FPAC, Business Center, Budget Division, Program Budget Branch, CCC Program Section, (202) 720-4697.

Table 11-3.—Commodity Credit Corporation: Loan transactions for fiscal year 2019, by commodities [1]

Commodity	Unit [5]	Loans out-standing Oct. 1, 2018 [2]	New loans made	Loan repayments	Collateral acquired in settle-ment [3]	Loans written off and trans-ferred to accounts receiv-able [4]	Loans outstanding Sept. 30, 2019 Value	Loans outstanding Sept. 30, 2019 Quantity collateral remaining pledged
				1,000 dollars				
Basic commodities:								
Corn	Bushel	152,614	1,752,104	(1,768,021)	....	(5,723)	66,091	130,973
Cotton (Upland and ELS)	Bale	69,779	2,286,948	(2,115,069)	(123,454)	(12,912)	394	105,291
Peanuts	Pound	95,856	933,790	(824,355)	(34,560)	(87,168)	470,553	83,563
Rice	Cwt	13,470	230,708	(228,228)	....	(178)	2,381	15,773
Seed cotton	Pound	....	31,611	(31,512)	....	(99)	....	....
Wheat	Bushel	85,570	220,863	(187,170)	....	(36)	35,251	119,227
Total [6]		417,289	5,456,024	(5,154,355)	(158,014)	(106,116)	574,670	454,827
Designated nonbasic commodities								
Barley	Bushel	3,196	11,599	(10,086)	....	....	2,001	4,709
Canola seed	Cwt	4,666	14,626	(17,190)	....	....	208	2,103
FlaxSeed	Cwt	196	381	(564)	....	....	1	13
Honey	Pound	2,561	5,619	(5,063)	....	....	4,517	3,117
Mustard seed	Cwt	269	340	(609)	....	....	....	....
Oats	Bushel	365	1,125	(600)	....	(14)	452	876
Raw sugar, cane	Pound	....	348,916	(348,916)	....	....	....	....
Raw sugar beet	Pound	....	233,832	(233,832)	....	....	....	....
Refined sugar beet	Pound	....	442,296	(441,347)	....	(949)	....	....
Safflower seed	Cwt	....	34	....	....	....	4	34
Sorghum	Bushel	928	4,824	(4,258)	....	....	702	1,494
Sunflower seed (oil)	Cwt	843	5,264	(5,729)	....	....	37	378
Sunflower seed, non oil	Cwt	183	687	(852)	....	....	2	18
Total [5]		13,207	1,069,543	(1,069,046)	....	(963)	7,924	12,742
Other nonbasic commodities:								
Chickpeas	Pound	1,183	14,894	(7,752)	....	....	747	8,325
Lentils	Pound	2,702	11,188	(8,534)	....	....	460	5,355
Peas, dry whole	Pound	1,478	6,303	(4,369)	....	....	578	3,413
Soybeans	Bushel	36,013	1,082,992	(1,032,718)	....	(4,477)	16,609	81,810
Total [5]		41,376	1,115,377	(1,053,373)	....	(4,477)	18,394	98,903
Grand total [5]		471,872	7,640,944	(7,276,774)	(158,014)	(111,556)	600,988	566,472

[1] Loans made directly by Commodity Credit Corporation.   [2] Book value of outstanding loans; includes face amounts and any charges paid.   [3] Includes Commodity Certificate Exchanges.   [4] Includes transfers to accounts receivable.   [5] Totals do not include allowance for losses.

Commodities with no loan activity from October 1, 2018 to September 30, 2019 were eliminated.

FPAC, Business Center, Budget Division, Program Budget Branch, CCC Program Section, (202) 720-4697.

Table 11-4.—Commodity Credit Corporation: Selected inventory transactions, programs and commodities, as of September 30, 2019

Program and commodity	Unit	Inventory Oct. 1, 2018	Purchases	Collateral acquired from loans	Other addition deduction	Sales and other dis-positions [1]	Inventory Sept. 30, 2019
				Quantity			
				Thousands			
Feed grains:							
Corn products	Pound	2,172	63,114	0	0	(64,759)	527
Grain sorghum	Bushel	396	9,797	0	0	(10,193)	0
Food grains, cotton and tobacco:							
Wheat	Bushel	5	13,319	0	0	(13,324)	0
Wheat flour	Pound	0	(4)	0	0	4	0
Rice, milled	Cwt	0	1,679	0	0	(1,525)	154
Upland cotton	Bale [2]	0	0	42,481	0	(42,462)	20
Oils and oilseeds:							
Peanut butter	Pound	0	0	0	2,649	(2,649)	0
Peanuts	Pound	132,952	0	194,167	(243,370)	(57,603)	26,146
Soybean products	Pound	0	88,183	0	0	(88,183)	0
Dry edible beans	Cwt	0	433	0	....	(400)	34
Blended foods	Pound	12,119	95,497	0	0	(94,109)	13,508
Dry whole peas and lentils	Cwt	248	2,083	0	0	(2,233)	98
Sugar cane and beet	Pound	240	0	0	0	(240)	0
Vegetable oil products	Pound	14,828	335,234	0	0	(346,515)	3,547
Other	....	0	2,337	0	0	(2,337)	0
Total inventory operations	....	162,960	611,672	236,648	(240,721)	(726,528)	44,034

Program and commodity	Unit	Inventory Oct. 1, 2018	Purchases	Collateral acquired from loans	Other addition deduction	Sales and other disposi-tions [1]	Inventory Sept. 30, 2019
				Value			
				1,000 dollars			
Feed grains:							
Corn products	Pound	542	12,049	0	(121)	(12,364)	106
Grain sorghum	Bushel	2,877	50,405	0	(899)	(52,384)	0
Food grains, cotton and tobacco:							
Wheat	Bushel	14	137,161	0	0	(137,175)	0
Wheat flour	Pound	0	(1)	0	0	1	0
Rice, milled	Cwt	0	37,191	0	0	(33,977)	3,215
Upland cotton	Bale [2]	0	0	122,065	236	(117,784)	4,517
Oils and oilseeds:							
Peanut butter	Pound	0	0	0	3,304	(3,304)	0
Peanuts	Pound	24,039	0	34,560	(43,484)	(10,401)	4,713
Soybean products	Pound	0	15,625	0	0	(15,625)	0
Dry edible beans	Cwt	0	17,072	0	0	(15,631)	1,441
Blended foods	Pound	4,166	42,613	0	679	(42,970)	4,487
Dry whole peas and lentils	Cwt	5,476	41,616	0	(637)	(44,307)	2,148
Sugar, cane and beet	Pound	0	0	0	0	0	0
Vegetable oil products	Pound	8,463	142,054	0	(426)	(147,851)	2,240
Other	....	471	801,235	0	0	(800,773)	933
Total inventory operations	....	46,048	1,297,020	156,625	(41,348)	(1,434,545)	23,800

[1] Includes sales, commodity donations, transfers to other government agencies and inventory adjustment.   [2] Includes Upland Bales and CFLS Pounds.

Selected inventory transactions, programs and commodities without activity from October 1, 2018 to September 30, 2019 were eliminated.

FPAC, Business Center, Budget Division, Program Budget Branch, CCC Program Section, (202) 720-4697.

Table 11-5.—Commodity Credit Corporation: Cost value of export and domestic commodity dispositions, by type of disposition, fiscal year 2019

(In Thousands)

Commodity [1]	Domestic				
	Dollar sales (Costs)	Transfers to other Government agencies	Donations [2]	Inventory adjustments and other recoveries (domestic)	Total domestic
Feed grains:					
Corn products	0	0	0	0	0
Grain sorghum	0	0	0	0	0
Food grains, cotton and tobacco:					
Wheat	0	0	0	0	0
Wheat flour	0	0	0	0	0
Rice, milled	0	0	0	0	0
Cotton, extra long staple & upland	0	0	0	117,784	117,784
Oils and oilseeds:					
Peanuts	0	0	0	10,401	10,401
Peanut butter	0	0	3,304	0	3,304
Soya flour	0	0	0	(2)	(2)
Soybeans & Soybean products	0	0	0	0	0
Grains and seeds:					
Lentils dry	0	0	0	0	0
Dry edible beans	0	0	0	0	0
Vegetable oil products	0	0	0	0	0
Other (miscellaneous,tallow & TMP-Food Distribution)	0	0	0	796,157	796,157
Total	0	0	3,304	924,340	927,644

Commodity [1]	Export				Total export and domestic
	Dollar sales (Costs)	Public law 480 (Costs)	Donations [1]	Total export	
Feed grains:					
Corn products	0	0	12,364	12,364	12,364
Grain sorghum	0	0	52,384	52,384	52,384
Food grains, cotton and tobacco:					
Wheat	0	15,044	122,117	137,175	137,175
Wheat flour	0	0	(1)	(1)	(1)
Rice, milled	0	19,743	14,234	33,977	33,977
Cotton, extra long staple & upland	0	0	0	0	117,784
Oils and oilseeds:					
Peanuts	0	0	0	0	10,401
Peanut butter	0	0	0	0	3,304
Soya flour	0	0	42,973	42,970	42,968
Soybeans & Soybean products	0	15,625	0	15,625	15,625
Grains and seeds:					
Lentils dry	0	0	8,069	8,069	8,069
Dry edible beans	0	0	15,631	15,631	15,631
Peas, dried whole		0	36,238	36,238	36,238
Vegetable oil products	0	47,691	100,160	147,852	147,852
Other (miscellaneous, tallow & TMP-Food Distribution)	0	1,123	3,494	4,616	800,773
Total	0	99,227	407,662	506,900	1,434,544

[1] Commodities without any activity were removed from the table. [2] Includes donations under section 202,407,416, Section 210, P.L. 85-540, miscellaneous donations under various other authorizations.
FPAC, Business Center, Budget Division, Program Budget Branch, CCC Program Section, (202) 720-4697.

Table 11-6.—Commodity Credit Corporation: Investment in price-support operations, March 31 and June 30, 2008–2019 [1]

Year Month	Inventory investment	Loan investment	Total investment
	Million dollars	*Million dollars*	*Million dollars*
2008:			
March	168	5,926	6,094
June	11	3,335	3,346
2009:			
March	174	4,647	4,821
June	209	2,215	2,424
2010:			
March	119	4,054	4,173
June	70	1,996	2,066
2011:			
March	41	3,259	3,300
June	66	1,588	1,654
2012:			
March	63	2,740	2,803
June	27	1,260	1,287
2013:			
March	28	2,981	3,009
June	43	1,664	1,707
2014:			
March	188	2,094	2,282
June	94	890	984
2015:			
March	32	2,734	2,766
June	41	1,572	1,613
2016:			
March	25	3,934	3,959
June	23	1,956	1,979
2017:			
March	11	4,142	4,153
June	24	2,095	2,119
2018:			
March	7	4,192	4,199
June	13	2,291	2,304
2019:			
March	57	4,828	4,885
June	51	2,826	2,877

[1] Reflects total CCC loans and inventories investment.
FPAC, Business Center, Budget Division, Program Budget Branch, CCC Program Section, (202) 720-4697.

Table 11-7.—Commodity Credit Corporation: Loans made in fiscal year 2019 as of September 30, by State and Territories [1]

State or Territory	Barley	Corn	Cotton-bales	Dry whole peas	Flaxseed
			1,000 dollars		
Alabama		1,573	24,143		
Alaska	6				
Arizona		1,854			
Arkansas		12,109	155,902		
California			496,048		
Colorado	160	17,958			
Connecticut					
Delaware		603			
Florida					.
Georgia		7,473	5,670		
Hawaii					
Idaho	2,823	384		620	
Illinois		136,940	76		
Indiana		147,402			
Iowa		359,405			
Kansas City Commodity					
Kansas		22,601			
Kentucky	50	40,004			
Louisiana		4,729	19,620		
Maine	327	60			
Maryland		7,425			
Massachusetts		15			
Michigan		54,438			
Minnesota	1,012	372,489		30	17
Mississippi		12,004	571,146		
Missouri		45,644	6,906		
Montana	3,742			20,387	212
Nebraska		146,310		419	
Nevada					
New Hampshire		21			
New Jersey		559			
New Mexico		1,100			
New York		30,115			
North Carolina	23	3,281	38,827		
North Dakota	3,086	50,991		7,509	152
Ohio		76,141			
Oklahoma		1,137	128		
Oregon					
Pennsylvania		10,708			
Rhode Island					
South Carolina		3,596			
South Dakota	62	90,795		239	
Tennessee		10,407	215,194		
Texas		12,327	753,236		
Utah	45	45			
Vermont					
Virginia	24	5,215	49		
Washington	61	515		3,180	
West Virginia		1,349			
Wisconsin		61,503			
Wyoming	180	880			
Total	11,601	1,752,105	2,286,945	32,384	381

See footnote(s) at end of table.

Table 11-7.—Commodity Credit Corporation: Loans made in fiscal year 2019 as of September 30, by State and Territories [1]—Continued

State or Territory	Honey	Oats	Oilseeds	Peanuts	Rice	Seed Cotton
	1,000 dollars					
Alabama				6,462		
Alaska						
Arizona						568
Arkansas	56				96,765	69
California	457				88,391	
Colorado	4		108			
Connecticut						
Delaware						
Florida	48			24,349		
Georgia				745,593		
Hawaii						
Idaho	364		602			
Illinois		29				
Indiana						
Iowa	103	6				
Kansas City Commodity						
Kansas		56				8,698
Kentucky						
Louisiana	53				5,716	
Maine		98				
Maryland						
Massachusetts						
Michigan		33				
Minnesota	713	68	1,029			
Mississippi				3,376	16,582	2,077
Missouri					10,157	3,928
Montana	758	75	1,174			
Nebraska	65	24				
Nevada						
New Hampshire						
New Jersey						
New Mexico				1,623		
New York	22	3				
North Carolina				35,395		
North Dakota	96	169	14,062			
Ohio						
Oklahoma				1,080		8,111
Oregon	88					
Pennsylvania		60				
Rhode Island						
South Carolina		18		2,217		
South Dakota	1,605	459	3,976			
Tennessee	15				896	
Texas	981	14		46,307	12,201	8,158
Utah	33					
Vermont						
Virginia				67,387		
Washington	108					
West Virginia						
Wisconsin	50	11				
Wyoming						
Total	5,619	1,123	20,951	933,789	230,708	31,609

See footnote(s) at end of table.

Table 11-7.—Commodity Credit Corporation: Loans made in fiscal year 2019 as of September 30, by State and Territories [1]—Continued

State or Territory	Sorghum	Soybeans	Sugar	Wheat
		1,000 dollars		
Alabama		689		49
Alaska				
Arizona				
Arkansas		25,952		
California				
Colorado	171	84	126,168	6,161
Connecticut				
Delaware		304		
Florida			95,002	
Georgia		232		57
Hawaii				
Idaho			310,925	6,117
Illinois		76,279		490
Indiana		116,369		114
Iowa		184,417		
Kansas City Commodity				
Kansas	1,419	14,047		7,840
Kentucky		29,953		2,765
Louisiana		3,551	253,914	
Maine				
Maryland		3,420		903
Massachusetts				
Michigan		40,002	83,279	1,476
Minnesota		190,475	138,909	30,599
Mississippi		25,634		
Missouri	376	50,721		1,115
Montana				50,930
Nebraska	199	48,227		1,630
Nevada				
New Hampshire				
New Jersey		399		32
New Mexico				676
New York		12,019		1,349
North Carolina		3,318		63
North Dakota		48,803		71,769
Ohio		88,693		195
Oklahoma	249	878		4,798
Oregon				3,962
Pennsylvania		5,788		649
Rhode Island				
South Carolina		1,197		42
South Dakota	1,044	68,246		12,113
Tennessee		10,316		62
Texas	1,367			631
Utah				795
Vermont				
Virginia		4,517		166
Washington				12,247
West Virginia		1,450		
Wisconsin		27,012		228
Wyoming			16,848	843
Total	4,825	1,082,992	1,025,045	220,866

[1] Loans made directly by Commodity Credit Corporation. As much as possible, loans have been distributed according to the location of producers receiving the loans. Direct loans to cooperative associations for the benefit of members have been distributed according to the location of the association.
FPAC, Business Center, Budget Division, Program Budget Branch, CCC Program Section, (202) 720-4697.

Table 11-8.—Farm Service Agency programs: Payments to producers, by program and commodity, United States, calendar year 2018–2019 [1]

Program and commodity	2018	2019
	1,000 dollars	*1,000 dollars*
Additional risk coverage	1,116,830	712,051
Auto conservation reserve program (CRP)-cost shares	90,391	54,708
Biomass crop assistance	392	283
Cotton ginning cost share	215,831	100
Cotton transition program	12	1
CRP annual rental	1,816,927	1,796,319
CRP incentives	44,661	21,730
CRP transition incentive	3,964	3,906
Dairy indemnity	91	4,141
Direct and counter cyclical program	164	29
Emergency Assistance program	64,889	39,211
Emergency conservation program	65,008	27,822
Emergency forest restoration	2,354	1,478
Grasslands reserve program	1,993	2,055
Geographic disadvantaged program [2]	9,755	7,829
Livestock forage program	460,377	166,362
Livestock indemnity program	38,299	63,366
Loan deficiency	23	6,729
Margin protection-Dairy	253,615	15,105
Milk income loss II	1	1
Noninsured assistance program	176,955	145,560
Pima cotton trust fund program	14,814	0
Price loss coverage	2,075,956	1,959,025
Tree assistance program	43,514	(12,277)
Trade mitigation programs	5,096,102	15,335,595
Upland cotton assistance	11,258	14,403
Wool manufacturers trust fund	27,942	(2)
Grand Total	11,632,118	20,365,530

[1] Programs with no payment activity in CY2018 and CY2019 were eliminated. [2] Geographic Disadvantaged Program, $1,870, was added to CY2018 since it was not included previously.
FPAC, Business Center, Budget Division, Program Budget Branch, CCC Program Section, (202) 720-4697.

Table 11-9.—Farm Service Agency programs: Payments received, by States, calendar year 2018–2019 [1]

State [2]	Payments	
	2018	2019
	1,000 dollars	*1,000 dollars*
Alabama	80,429	201,733
Alaska	668	806
Arizona	31,898	75,775
Arkansas	487,565	862,715
California	165,820	277,831
Colorado	184,745	229,389
Connecticut	2,157	1,420
Delaware	6,619	28,224
District of Columbia	492	32,998
Florida	61,318	71,877
Georgia	218,521	502,953
Hawaii	7,888	5,369
Idaho	136,985	137,290
Illinois	1,001,352	1,635,341
Indiana	473,037	806,481
Iowa	1,126,699	1,976,908
Kansas	725,996	1,338,962
Kentucky	138,711	300,094
Louisiana	211,632	319,776
Maine	4,946	2,915
Maryland	26,566	94,521
Massachusetts	3,144	7,700
Michigan	209,462	316,651
Minnesota	734,829	1,175,432
Mississippi	262,839	482,918
Missouri	519,580	1,001,744
Montana	288,699	268,341
Nebraska	610,895	1,027,961
Nevada	3,904	6,849
New Hampshire	1,621	974
New Jersey	5,192	15,538
New Mexico	74,241	89,466
New York	64,557	75,096
North Carolina	86,801	321,014
North Dakota	648,477	947,515
Ohio	421,416	635,538
Oklahoma	268,081	361,741
Oregon	74,157	92,057
Pennsylvania	65,184	118,353
Rhode Island	394	296
South Carolina	30,429	97,331
South Dakota	693,308	698,320
Tennessee	107,568	288,942
Texas	737,820	1,637,917
Utah	36,165	30,671
Vermont	11,189	6,045
Virginia	49,121	112,464
Washington	159,642	184,782
West Virginia	2,872	6,322
Wisconsin	252,092	373,876
Wyoming	19,136	22,758
KCCO	83,252	1,053,496
Puerto Rico	11,369	3,866
Virgin Islands	389	46
Guam	154	53
North Mariana Islands Nat	33	48
American Samoa	64	28
Total [3]	11,632,120	20,365,527

[1] Only for programs listed on Table 11-8. [2] Geographic Disadvantaged Program, $1,870, was added to CY2018 since it was not included previously. [3] Immaterial rounding differences of ($.02) and $.03 are due to presenting information by programs on Table 11-8 and by State on Table 11-9. This addition affected the totals for Alaska, Hawaii, North Dakota, KCCO, Puerto Rico, Virgin Island, Guam, North Mariana Islands and American Samoa.

FPAC, Business Center, Budget Division, Program Budget Branch, CCC Program Section, (202) 720-4697.

Table 11-10.—Value of marketing order commodities, 2019-20 season [1]

Commodity	Crop Value	Number of producers
	1,000 dollars	*Number*
Citrus fruits		
Oranges, grapefruit, tangerines,and tangelos (FL)	112,744	375
Oranges and grapefruit (TX)	89,850	170
Deciduous fruits		
Olives (CA)	130,218	800
Desert grapes (CA)	36,721	21
Kiwifruit (CA)	67,795	130
Avocados (FL)	23,332	400
Apricots (WA)	5,425	315
Cherries, sweet (WA)	363,280	1,421
Pears (OR and WA) [2]	247,446	2,320
Cherries, tart (7 States) [3]	35,533	400
Cranberries (10 States) [4]	270,213	1,100
Dried fruits		
Dates (CA)	137,499	70
Plums (CA)	159,066	800
Raisins (CA)	366,609	2,600
Vegetables [5]		
Tomatoes (FL)	424,477	65
Onions (ID-Eastern OR)	101,832	134
Onions (South TX)	36,415	70
Onions (Vidalia, GA)	103,731	65
Onions (Walla Walla, WA and OR)	2,772	15
Potatoes (CO) [6]	192,663	165
Potatoes (ID-Eastern OR)	278,374	450
Potatoes (WA)	86,218	250
Nuts and Spearmint Oil		
Almonds (CA)	6,169,100	6,800
Pecans (15 States) [7]	470,999	2,500
Pistashios (CA, AZ and NM) [8]	2,082,210	1,500
Walnuts (CA)	1,237,950	4,400
Hazelnuts (OR and WA) [9]	86,400	800
Spearmint oil(WA, ID, OR, parts of UT and NV) [10]	33,654	126
Total for marketing orders [11]	13,352,526	28,262

Additional programs under the oversight authority of AMS Specialty Crops Program	*1,000 dollars*	*Number of U.S. farms, 2017 Ag Census*
Apples (export act) [12]	2,427,909	26,408
Grapes (export act) [13]	1,178,702	28,387
Peanuts(Nationwide standards) [14]	1,129,584	6,379
Total for 3 programs [15]	4,736,195	61,174

[1] Programs under the oversight authority of the Specialty Crops Program, Agricultural Marketing Service.
[2] Includes fresh and processed pears. Producer number (2,320) is the sum 820 and 1,500 for fresh and processed pears, respectively.
[3] The marketing order regulates the handling of tart cherries in the states of Michigan, Utah, Wisconsin, Washington, New York, Pennsylvania, and Oregon. The crop value shown is for the sum of the values for 5 states, excluding Pennsylvania and Oregon, for which NASS does not publish data.
[4] The marketing order regulates the handling of cranberries in Wisconsin, Massachusetts, Oregon, New Jersey, Washington, Rhode Island, Connecticut, Michigan, Minnesota, Oregon, and Long Island in New York. The crop value shown is the sum of crop values for the first 4 states listed and excludes the other 7 states for which NASS does not publish crop value data.
[5] Sources for vegetable data: For tomatoes, Florida Tomato Committee, 2019 Annual Report. For the four onion marketing orders, NASS season average grower prices for dry onions in ID, TX, GA, and WA, respectively, were multiplied by shipment quantity data from the marketing order committees. For the three potato marketing orders, the state season average grower prices for all potatoes (fresh and processed utilization combined) were multiplied by shipment quantity data from the marketing order committees; for the Idaho-Eastern Oregon order, the Idaho price for all potatoes was used.
[6] The Colorado potato marketing area producer number (165) is the sum of Area 2 (160) and Area 3 (5).
[7] The crop value shown is the sum of values for five states for which NASS pecan crop data is published: Georgia, New Mexico, Texas, Arizona, Oklahoma.
[8] NASS publishes pistachio crop value only for California.
[9] NASS publishes hazelnut crop value only for Oregon.
[10] The spearmint crop value shown is the sum of values for Washington and Idaho. It excludes the value in Oregon, which has not been published since 2016 due to NASS confidentiality restrictions. It also excludes the minor level of production in Nevada and Utah, which is not published by NASS.
[11] The total number of producers for all marketing orders is likely overstated to a moderate extent, since some producers may grow more than one of the commodities listed in this table.
[12] Value of production of U.S. fresh market apples. Farm numbers are for all apples (fresh and processed) from 2017 Agricultural Census.
[13] Value of production of U.S. fresh market grapes. Farm numbers are for all grapes (fresh and processed) from 2017 Agricultural Census.
[14] Value of U.S. production of peanuts. Farm numbers from 2017 Agricultural Census. The Farm Security and Rural Investment Act of 2002 terminated the Peanut Administrative Committee (which locally administered Marketing Agreement No. 146). As a result, the marketing agreement was terminated and new quality standards were established for domestic and imported peanuts, administered by the Peanut Standards Board.
[15] The number of farms for the 3 programs is likely overstated to a moderate extent, since some farm operations may grow more than one of the commodities listed in this table.
AMS, Specialty Crops Programs. Compiled June 2021.

CHAPTER XII

AGRICULTURAL CONSERVATION AND FORESTRY STATISTICS

Statistics in this chapter concern conservation of various natural resources, particularly soil, water, timber, wetlands, wildlife, and improvement of water quality. Forestry statistics include area of private and public-owned forest land, timber production, imports and exports, pulpwood consumption and paper and board production, area burned over by forest fires, livestock grazing, and recreational use of national forest lands.

Conservation Practices on Active CRP Contracts, September 2019

Practice code	Practice	Acres
CP1	Introduced grasses and legumes	3,157,028
CP2	Native grasses	5,308,305
CP3	Tree planting	670,717
CP4	Wildlife habitat with woody vegetation	1,472,170
CP5	Field windbreaks	63,164
CP6	Diversions	4
CP7	Erosion control structures	8
CP8	Grass waterways	121,083
CP9	Shallow water areas for wildlife	26,467
CP10	Existing grasses and legumes[1]	2,353,928
CP11	Existing trees	170,280
CP12	Wildlife food plots	33,248
CP15	Contour grass strips	59,188
CP16	Shelterbelts	21,285
CP17	Living snow fences	4,508
CP18	Salinity reducing vegetation	181,252
CP21	Filter strips (grass)	716,815
CP22	Riparian buffers (trees)	617,179
CP23	Wetland restoration	1,244,049
CP24	Cross wind trap strips	58
CP25	Rare and declining habitat	1,185,314
CP26	Sediment retention	40
CP27	Farmable wetland pilot (wetland)	98,113
CP28	Farmable wetland pilot (upland)	217,308
CP29	Wildlife habitat buffer (marginal pasture)	92,650
CP30	Wetland buffer (marginal pasture)	35,741
CP31	Bottomland hardwood	160,049
CP32	Hardwood trees	1
CP33	Upland bird habitat buffers	221,431
CP34	Flood control structure	69
CP36	Longleaf pine	159,255
CP37	Duck nesting habitat	450,312
CP38	State acres for wildlife enhancement	1,981,161
CP39	FWP--Constucted wetlands	489
CP40	FWP--Aquaculture wetlands	16,711
CP41	FWP--Flooded praire wetlands	63,073
CP42	Pollinator Habitat[2]	505,566
CP87	Grasslands-Native grass	80,579
CP88	Grasslands-Introduced grass	836,716
	Total	22,325,377

[1] Includes both introduced grasses and legumes and native grasses.   [2] Does not include about 40,000 acres from Signup 39 before CP42 was implemented.
FSA, Conservation and Environmental Programs Division, (202) 690-1612.

CRP enrollment by sign up and initial contract year [1], as of September 2019

Sign up	Before 2011	2011	2012	2013	2014	2015	2016	2017	2018	2019	Total
26	41,999										41,999
28	75,299										75,299
29	261,405										261,405
30	232,408										232,408
31	207,346										207,346
32	1,332,375	232,765									1,565,140
33	179,678										179,678
35	221,624										221,624
36	269,913										269,913
37	437,450			69							437,518
38	211,545	376,960									588,505
39		3,625,346									3,625,346
40		169,231	304,394								473,626
41			2,460,237								2,460,237
42			114,484	481,202							595,686
43				3,408,222							3,408,222
44				22,808	497,144						519,951
45					1,523,621						1,523,621
46					3,221	515,169					518,390
47						171,859	689,463				861,322
48							511,630	812,501	7,403		1,331,534
49								384,461			384,461
50								30,833	1,297,213	1,016	1,329,062
51									11,019	281,080	292,099
52										434	434
200							464	87,908	448,580	40	536,992
201										383,558	383,558
All	3,71,041	4,404,303	2,879,115	3,912,300	2,023,986	687,028	1,201,557	1,315,704	1,764,215	666,127	22,325,377

[1] For CRP, contract year is the same as fiscal year, which begins Ocer 1.
General Signup Numbers: 1-13, 15, 16, 18, 20, 26, 29, 33, 39, 41, 43, 459. Continuous Sign-up Numbers: 14, 17, 19, 21-25, 27, 28, 30, 31, 35-38, 40, 42, 44, 46, 47, 48, 50, Grasslands Signup Number: 200.
FSA, Conservation and Environmental Programs Division, (202) 690-1612.

Table 12-1.—Conservation Reserve Program (CRP): Enrollment by practice, under contract, September 2019
(CP1 and CP2)

State	CP1 Establishment of permanent introduced grasses and legumes			CP2 Establishment of permanent native grasses		
	Total acres treated	Total cost share	Avg cost share per acre treated [1]	Total acres treated	Total cost share	Avg cost share per acre treated [1]
Alabama	13,863	727,739	67.69	2,816	146,574	88.14
Alaska	1,100	0	....	....	0	....
Arkansas	3,769	150,055	61.48	3,153	255,877	101.71
California	19,659	748,616	156.26	157	2,100	300.00
Colorado	66,712	3,065,157	64.69	838,186	47,533,518	70.39
Delaware	31	11,105	358.23	23	16,310	700.00
Florida	28	0	....	108	3,718	143.00
Georgia	803	69,876	114.21	47	10,962	812.00
Hawaii	....	0	....	....	0	....
Idaho	202,381	13,379,637	78.41	40,652	2,586,011	81.00
Illinois	182,777	8,545,423	61.92	43,202	6,281,955	198.21
Indiana	17,172	916,726	72.85	11,842	1,491,913	178.75
Iowa	230,226	7,352,062	41.65	126,002	18,013,567	218.92
Kansas	12,164	371,324	42.96	630,031	24,948,861	44.94
Kentucky	31,551	2,839,304	122.66	19,859	1,691,694	128.04
Louisiana	599	75,107	147.01	1,140	142,567	186.41
Maine	2,229	419,335	199.99	....	0	....
Maryland	6,702	584,703	164.51	1,893	223,307	226.76
Massachusetts	....	0	....	....	0	....
Michigan	14,798	1,359,871	123.78	8,278	1,264,473	195.69
Minnesota	63,508	2,100,222	45.09	41,903	1,746,665	78.32
Mississippi	21,756	169,068	89.61	2,178	43,101	109.40
Missouri	429,071	18,322,183	82.37	126,038	11,338,994	158.94
Montana	382,816	5,664,584	27.08	226,141	3,494,928	33.76
Nebraska	29,554	1,557,301	70.09	241,110	15,060,891	76.68
Nevada	130	12,810	98.39	....	0	....
New Jersey	....	0	....	40	0	....
New Mexico	52,423	4,116,452	92.59	264,440	23,440,110	115.22
New York	4,989	1,148,645	270.72	373	76,595	294.23
North Carolina	937	35,607	64.72	94	7,590	126.69
North Dakota	129,466	5,208,293	49.00	13,296	949,362	89.23
Ohio	11,412	542,495	87.71	45,456	2,884,682	113.28
Oklahoma	114,410	5,120,419	60.33	290,602	14,823,509	68.31
Oregon	200,695	13,014,823	72.89	59,392	5,043,263	94.88
Pennsylvania	69,518	6,577,229	146.14	24,633	2,622,255	181.33
South Carolina	574	18,132	145.79	182	0	....
South Dakota	47,425	1,095,566	34.86	63,650	2,886,085	71.09
Tennessee	31,612	1,264,267	96.78	20,500	1,816,199	166.71
Texas	272,022	15,181,070	88.11	1,617,861	261,887,673	201.63
Utah	70,812	2,123,996	42.51	13,760	966,379	73.69
Vermont	7	0	....	....	0	....
Virginia	2,014	283,804	242.16	726	143,654	326.54
Washington	263,084	13,389,590	63.30	502,985	33,300,930	93.15
West Virginia	160	17,778	337.15	....	0	....
Wisconsin	54,309	3,986,378	93.81	22,419	2,381,405	170.56
Wyoming	97,754	1,636,834	28.13	3,136	83,701	48.28
United States	3,157,028	143,203,583	66.13	5,308,305	489,611,379	120.42

[1] Not including acres which receive no cost share.
Total acres treated may not add due to rounding.
FSA, Conservation and Environmental Programs Division, (202) 690-1612.

Table 12-2.—Conservation Reserve Program (CRP): Enrollment by practice, under contract, September 2019
(CP3 and CP4)

State	CP3 Tree planting			CP4 Permanent wildlife habitat		
	Total acres treated	Total cost share	Avg cost share per acre treated [1]	Total acres treated	Total cost share	Avg cost share per acre treated [1]
Alabama	97,158	8,298,216	110.41	4,378	839,066	330.73
Alaska	0	0	....	0	0	....
Arkansas	28,952	2,050,423	107.74	1,663	90,233	70.97
California	14	0	....	9,651	1,028	250.12
Colorado	14	0	....	281,654	16,294,208	88.66
Delaware	2,120	643,674	335.32	554	152,488	371.22
Florida	13,708	611,605	158.68	330	0	....
Georgia	54,564	5,790,762	135.64	1,358	241,242	234.47
Hawaii	13	55,854	4,168.21	0	0	....
Idaho	5,277	435,214	90.29	58,991	2,030,200	49.10
Illinois	32,899	7,656,378	311.02	80,727	22,946,709	462.74
Indiana	12,032	2,550,320	340.19	6,185	546,839	187.92
Iowa	16,813	4,084,624	316.81	106,996	2,619,306	144.43
Kansas	312	29,133	186.93	321,479	15,524,830	57.25
Kentucky	3,016	658,153	278.07	243	23,200	105.15
Louisiana	36,352	2,377,857	101.84	32,354	2,267,511	104.88
Maine	90	84,326	938.00	38	0	....
Maryland	978	181,604	529.46	1,229	78,493	179.54
Massachusetts	0	0	....	0	0	....
Michigan	4,520	612,974	197.86	7,806	273,894	116.39
Minnesota	20,337	1,601,888	120.85	115,783	1,225,071	85.01
Mississippi	224,477	3,604,599	108.33	2,262	155,844	821.62
Missouri	12,964	1,061,813	202.82	2,185	157,100	159.67
Montana	31	0	....	11,175	554,464	293.74
Nebraska	520	30,263	185.44	36,855	1,412,498	63.07
Nevada	0	0	....	0	0	....
New Jersey	0	0	....	0	0	....
New Mexico	0	0	....	140	16,800	120.00
New York	457	380,129	962.42	439	257,229	766.68
North Carolina	20,906	3,768,847	229.08	637	347,358	700.81
North Dakota	418	33,298	179.18	200,305	12,250,080	78.30
Ohio	6,406	1,447,887	429.72	9,061	259,484	94.10
Oklahoma	37	0	....	756	30,492	99.25
Oregon	1,353	165,728	381.56	8,415	885,094	158.36
Pennsylvania	373	236,316	963.77	4,036	894,803	328.88
South Carolina	18,919	605,289	71.30	595	55,411	226.49
South Dakota	21	946	220.00	36,322	1,135,065	58.58
Tennessee	23,151	1,576,439	164.94	2,246	45,211	146.09
Texas	1,199	49,708	95.48	13,310	329,993	97.20
Utah	0	0	....	13	0	....
Vermont	0	0	....	0	0	....
Virginia	5,574	378,483	94.01	223	23,965	118.70
Washington	2,412	164,864	73.63	107,464	7,190,271	111.62
West Virginia	16	4,102	431.79	0	0	....
Wisconsin	22,310	3,627,471	328.43	3,071	206,535	190.76
Wyoming	2	0	....	1,223	41,451	81.81
United States	670,717	54,859,187	165.84	1,472,170	91,403,464	102.13

[1] Not including acres which receive no cost share.
Total acres treated may not add due to rounding.
FSA, Conservation and Environmental Programs Division, (202) 690-1612.

Table 12-3.—Conservation Reserve Program (CRP): Enrollment by practice, under contract, September 2019

(CP5, CP6, and CP7)

State	CP5 Establishment of field windbreaks			CP6 Diversions			CP7 Erosion control structures		
	Total acres treated	Total cost share	Avg cost share per acre treated [1]	Total acres treated	Total cost share	Avg cost share per acre treated [1]	Total acres treated	Total cost share	Avg cost share per acre treated [1]
Alabama	0	0	....	....	0	....	....	0	....
Alaska	0	0	....	....	0	....	....	0	....
Arkansas	0	0	....	....	0	....	....	0	....
California	0	0	....	....	0	....	....	0	....
Colorado	906	439,785	768.99	....	0	....	....	0	....
Delaware	0	0	....	....	0	....	....	0	....
Florida	0	0	....	....	0	....	....	0	....
Georgia	0	0	....	....	0	....	....	0	....
Hawaii	0	0	....	....	0	....	....	0	....
Idaho	55	81,853	2,041.73	....	0	....	....	0	....
Illinois	1,908	339,124	259.64	3	0	....	4	0	....
Indiana	1,202	178,224	235.30	....	0	....	0	0	....
Iowa	5,579	970,988	304.58	....	0	....	1	0	....
Kansas	1,054	285,102	483.06	....	0	....	....	0	....
Kentucky	0	0	....	....	0	....	....	0	....
Louisiana	0	0	....	....	0	....	....	0	....
Maine	0	0	....	....	0	....	....	0	....
Maryland	0	0	....	....	0	....	....	0	....
Massachusetts	0	0	....	....	0	....	....	0	....
Michigan	1,694	344,221	269.40	1	0	....	....	0	....
Minnesota	5,343	843,703	228.34	....	0	....	0	0	....
Mississippi	0	0	....	....	0	....	....	0	....
Missouri	31	2,327	323.19	....	0	....	1	0	....
Montana	53	10,115	511.38	....	0	....	....	0	....
Nebraska	20,592	5,299,859	634.85	....	0	....	....	0	....
Nevada	0	0	....	....	0	....	....	0	....
New Jersey	2	16,537	6,695.14	....	0	....	....	0	....
New Mexico	0	0	....	....	0	....	....	0	....
New York	0	0	....	....	0	....	....	0	....
North Carolina	8	161	84.74	....	0	....	....	0	....
North Dakota	2,706	1,314,948	717.93	....	0	....	....	0	....
Ohio	3,164	600,463	381.06	....	0	....	....	0	....
Oklahoma	31	0	....	....	0	....	....	0	....
Oregon	0	0	....	....	0	....	....	0	....
Pennsylvania	0	0	....	....	0	....	....	0	....
South Carolina	11	115	42.71	....	0	....	....	0	....
South Dakota	18,627	7,436,516	630.09	....	0	....	....	0	....
Tennessee	0	0	....	....	0	....	....	0	....
Texas	0	0	....	....	0	....	....	0	....
Utah	0	0	....	....	0	....	....	0	....
Vermont	0	0	....	....	0	....	....	0	....
Virginia	0	500	1,250.00	....	0	....	....	0	....
Washington	6	0	....	....	0	....	....	0	....
West Virginia	0	0	....	....	0	....	....	0	....
Wisconsin	88	14,400	514.84	....	0	....	1	0	....
Wyoming	104	1,986	139.98	....	0	....	....	0	....
United States	63,164	18,180,928	518.55	4	....	....	8	....	....

[1] Not including acres which receive no cost share.
Total acres treated may not add due to rounding.
FSA, Conservation and Environmental Programs Division, (202) 690-1612.

Table 12-4.—Conservation Reserve Program (CRP): Enrollment by practice, under contract, September 2019

(CP8 and CP9)

State	CP8 Grass waterways			CP9 Shallow water areas for wildlife		
	Total acres treated	Total cost share	Avg cost share per acre treated [1]	Total acres treated	Total cost share	Avg cost share per acre treated [1]
Alabama	0	0	....	107	30,233	700.00
Alaska	0	0	....	......	0	....
Arkansas	5	66	12.74	466	4,520	57.10
California	0	0	....	......	0	....
Colorado	468	6,687	189.65	12	0	....
Delaware	1	0	....	202	233,472	1,725.59
Florida	0	0	....	......	0	....
Georgia	23	4,265	947.78	13	14,424	1,109.54
Hawaii	0	0	....	......	0	....
Idaho	0	0	....	23	224	70.00
Illinois	30,961	24,028,568	1,387.41	4,102	1,539,973	821.10
Indiana	18,084	37,798,209	5,150.67	864	179,191	937.49
Iowa	35,517	12,301,680	595.93	10,146	741,722	167.08
Kansas	7,301	2,373,462	549.04	884	235,285	655.99
Kentucky	5,029	7,287,877	1,999.87	1,751	607,557	1,458.20
Louisiana	2	0	....	476	65,580	342.74
Maine	45	250,347	7,988.11	......	0	....
Maryland	220	553,355	6,450.10	1,017	971,070	2,820.58
Massachusetts	0	0	....	......	0	....
Michigan	423	547,555	3,360.68	1,195	398,098	555.81
Minnesota	3,178	530,426	444.88	159	1,799	56.95
Mississippi	52	0	....	469	62,858	2,104.39
Missouri	1,803	1,031,369	1,480.73	1,692	28,515	285.46
Montana	58	270	40.30	11	0	....
Nebraska	1,128	329,270	530.35	147	36,997	574.58
Nevada	0	0	....	......	0	....
New Jersey	162	1,651,843	11,847.96	......	0	....
New Mexico	0	0	....	......	0	....
New York	37	47,389	2,163.87	3	3,462	1,018.24
North Carolina	200	255,006	1,659.98	167	40,583	366.93
North Dakota	81	12,985	362.00	......	0	....
Ohio	11,472	23,302,687	6,301.21	473	143,879	1,111.98
Oklahoma	133	297	23.17	53	1,685	168.50
Oregon	16	54	100.00	......	0	....
Pennsylvania	200	266,442	2,529.60	31	6,200	984.13
South Carolina	15	510	1,020.00	34	41,000	2,113.40
South Dakota	1,388	261,165	324.50	41	0	....
Tennessee	164	148,667	2,119.88	57	10,660	640.24
Texas	1,160	796,914	1,202.60	83	6,806	680.60
Utah	6	0	....	......	0	....
Vermont	15	12,315	1,021.15	......	0	....
Virginia	83	340,173	4,767.00	52	119,189	3,144.83
Washington	335	1,912	47.28	50	0	....
West Virginia	0	0	....	......	0	....
Wisconsin	1,313	990,678	2,678.96	1,688	525,949	1,165.77
Wyoming	0	0	....	......	0	....
United States	121,083	115,132,444	1,847.79	26,467	6,050,932	615.71

[1] Not including acres which receive no cost share.
Total acres treated may not add due to rounding.
FSA, Conservation and Environmental Programs Division, (202) 690-1612.

Table 12-5.—Conservation Reserve Program (CRP): Enrollment by practice, under contract, September 2019
(CP10, CP11, and CP12)

State	CP10 Vegetative-cover-grass-already established			CP11 Vegetative-cover-trees-already established			CP12 Wildlife food plots		
	Total acres treated	Total cost share	Avg cost share per acre treated[1]	Total acres treated	Total cost share	Avg cost share per acre treated[1]	Total acres treated	Total cost share	Avg cost share per acre treated[1]
Alabama	9,806	566,605	80.87	26,138	2,018,213	129.57	758	0	....
Alaska	1,414	0	....	....	0	....	....	0	....
Arkansas	3,774	78,450	148.75	7,487	89,297	200.38	292	0	....
California	8,851	0	....	....	0	....	1	0	....
Colorado	450,400	4,770,261	32.65	11	0	....	110	0	....
Delaware	....	0	....	....	0	....	3	0	....
Florida	133	0	....	6,051	12,500	690.61	19	0	....
Georgia	694	24,000	568.72	12,149	383,241	146.69	102	0	....
Hawaii	....	0	....	....	0	....	....	0	....
Idaho	52,190	22,063	11.50	291	0	....	71	0	....
Illinois	26,023	15,485	55.73	3,647	3,194	48.32	3,631	0	....
Indiana	4,338	4,282	13.52	1,430	0	....	311	30	50.00
Iowa	52,144	1,364,208	112.97	1,324	99,572	549.45	4,006	0	....
Kansas	76,198	77,585	10.26	54	0	....	2,931	12	....
Kentucky	2,723	4,358	33.25	272	536	43.23	462	0	....
Louisiana	369	0	....	5,134	0	....	479	0	....
Maine	823	0	....	212	0	....	....	0	....
Maryland	336	0	....	114	0	....	28	0	....
Massachusetts	....	0	....	....	0	....	....	0	....
Michigan	4,121	9,757	92.75	1,346	21,343	67.28	578	0	....
Minnesota	38,710	21,078	52.45	4,423	113,014	388.58	3,400	263	43.75
Mississippi	9,254	0	....	67,718	445,158	389.97	1,676	0	....
Missouri	43,823	88,363	65.58	1,043	39,151	588.73	2,784	0	....
Montana	170,900	35,515	19.09	131	0	....	715	0	....
Nebraska	57,588	441,716	32.90	290	32,019	1,351.01	424	50	....
Nevada	....	0	....	....	0	....	....	0	....
New Jersey	14	0	....	....	0	....	....	0	....
New Mexico	12,240	4,382	9.68	....	0	....	196	0	....
New York	3,555	152,349	107.42	147	9,360	248.28	33	0	....
North Carolina	452	0	....	6,788	1,359,364	399.83	10	0	....
North Dakota	121,649	1,384,791	19.71	102	61	45.19	1,787	0	....
Ohio	4,085	9,222	39.66	790	0	....	331	0	....
Oklahoma	169,527	487,199	10.19	84	0	....	666	0	....
Oregon	57,599	7,740,499	327.97	281	151,417	1,202.10	99	0	....
Pennsylvania	4,597	265,094	135.20	21	0	....	736	142	106.77
South Carolina	898	0	....	10,356	96,362	48.96	85	0	....
South Dakota	67,206	16,437	16.68	60	0	....	2,263	500	100.00
Tennessee	10,928	621	17.91	5,212	3,444	59.38	252	0	....
Texas	626,801	11,262,662	112.23	1,142	0	....	2,378	1,880	100.00
Utah	74,361	5,454	3.00	....	0	....	8	0	....
Vermont	....	0	....	....	0	....	....	0	....
Virginia	568	56,629	422.26	1,615	79,937	246.11	20	0	....
Washington	96,132	114,542	23.36	423	3,923	55.01	713	80	....
West Virginia	....	0	....	....	0	....	....	0	....
Wisconsin	17,085	151,666	83.73	3,981	70,358	408.04	869	0	....
Wyoming	71,618	0	....	12	0	....	18	0	....
United States	2,353,928	29,175,270	65.00	170,280	5,031,464	186.97	33,248	2,815	88.70

[1] Not including acres which receive no cost share.
Total acres treated may not add due to rounding.
FSA, Conservation and Environmental Programs Division, (202) 690-1612.

Table 12-6.—Conservation Reserve Program (CRP): Enrollment by practice, under contract, September 2019

(CP15, CP16, and CP17)

State	CP15 Contour grass strips			CP16 Shelter belts			CP17 Living snow fences		
	Total acres treated	Total cost share	Avg cost share per acre treated[1]	Total acres treated	Total cost share	Avg cost share per acre treated[1]	Total acres treated	Total cost share	Avg cost share per acre treated[1]
Alabama	0	0	....	0	0	....	0	0	....
Alaska	0	0	....	0	0	....	0	0	....
Arkansas	0	0	....	0	0	....	0	0	....
California	0	0	....	0	0	....	0	0	....
Colorado	9	0	....	2,166	1,271,744	693.66	23	9,084	925.05
Delaware	0	0	....	0	0	....	0	0	....
Florida	0	0	....	0	0	....	0	0	....
Georgia	0	0	....	0	0	....	0	0	....
Hawaii	0	0	....	0	0	....	0	0	....
Idaho	180	1,007	10.58	18	14,551	1,549.63	0	0	....
Illinois	844	21,088	59.80	96	9,515	292.59	41	3,491	170.130
Indiana	20	170	113.33	19	3,057	285.70	0	48	266.67
Iowa	11,202	526,961	143.99	1,792	943,105	785.74	672	125,998	255.57
Kansas	2,690	88,386	69.82	492	132,585	459.73	35	12,644	630.00
Kentucky	30	0	....	0	0	....	0	0	....
Louisiana	0	0	....	0	0	....	0	0	....
Maine	0	0	....	0	0	....	0	0	....
Maryland	1	0	....	0	0	....	0	0	....
Massachusetts	0	0	....	0	0	....	0	0	....
Michigan	2	0	....	25	1,986	198.80	11	0	....
Minnesota	739	16,682	56.65	2,874	539,787	258.06	2,410	366,745	202.00
Mississippi	40	0	....	0	0	....	0	0	....
Missouri	735	9,054	83.31	48	24,328	859.65	0	0	....
Montana	0	0	....	103	16,097	825.49	188	9,022	405.30
Nebraska	277	4,763	47.44	1,033	269,121	410.49	89	3,617	291.46
Nevada	0	0	....	0	0	....	0	0	....
New Jersey	1	4,391	7,841.07	0	0	....	0	0	....
New Mexico	0	0	....	0	0	....	0	0	....
New York	0	0	....	0	0	....	0	0	....
North Carolina	0	0	....	5	0	....	0	0	....
North Dakota	1	0	....	2,917	1,780,325	765.20	472	243,695	667.20
Ohio	14	0	....	67	11,514	290.75	0	0	....
Oklahoma	0	0	....	21	0	....	0	0	....
Oregon	0	0	....	0	0	....	0	0	....
Pennsylvania	44	1,492	78.65	0	0	....	0	0	....
South Carolina	0	0	....	0	0	....	0	0	....
South Dakota	25	111	30.25	9,597	4,103,060	674.34	556	227,728	643.83
Tennessee	20	0	....	0	0	....	0	0	....
Texas	71	0	....	0	0	....	0	0	....
Utah	18	0	....	0	0	....	0	0	....
Vermont	0	0	....	0	0	....	0	0	....
Virginia	2	286	130.00	0	0	....	0	0	....
Washington	41,679	110,992	46.91	8	1,750	5,833.33	0	0	....
West Virginia	0	0	....	0	0	....	0	0	....
Wisconsin	484	7,568	205.15	3	842	701.67	10	616	150.30
Wyoming	0	0	....	2	0	....	0	0	....
United States	59,188	792,951	95.46	21,285	9,123,367	623.52	4,508	1,002,689	321.69

[1] Not including acres which receive no cost share.
Total acres treated may not add due to rounding.
FSA, Conservation and Environmental Programs Division, (202) 690-1612.

Table 12-7.—Conservation Reserve Program (CRP): Enrollment by practice, under contract, September 2019

(CP18 and CP21)

State	CP18 Salt tolerant grasses			CP21 Alternative perennials		
	Total acres treated	Total cost share	Avg cost share per acre treated [1]	Total acres treated	Total cost share	Avg cost share per acre treated [1]
Alabama	0	0	....	230	10,105	218.25
Alaska	0	0	....	0	0	....
Arkansas	0	0	....	4,540	339,518	227.64
California	0	0	....	0	0	....
Colorado	7	0	....	97	10,325	398.96
Delaware	0	0	....	497	131,930	351.21
Florida	0	0	....	0	0	....
Georgia	0	0	....	308	25	10.87
Hawaii	0	0	....	0	0	....
Idaho	0	0	....	615	49,449	90.97
Illinois	4	261	104.40	100,765	7,274,242	118.57
Indiana	0	0	....	43,721	2,144,531	126.50
Iowa	0	0	....	185,578	14,875,995	149.10
Kansas	562	0	....	19,559	972,195	88.46
Kentucky	0	0	....	16,041	738,722	101.32
Louisiana	0	0	....	307	3,984	99.01
Maine	0	0	....	57	0	....
Maryland	0	0	....	22,444	1,319,777	159.65
Massachusetts	0	0	....	20	14,274	714.77
Michigan	0	0	....	22,681	2,193,851	130.16
Minnesota	4,355	186,013	59.75	110,523	5,797,455	88.43
Mississippi	0	0	....	4,533	110,385	105.80
Missouri	0	0	....	22,647	453,491	114.75
Montana	63,854	133,644	30.16	174	2,331	23.59
Nebraska	449	3,588	42.57	13,665	693,169	72.17
Nevada	0	0	....	0	0	....
New Jersey	0	0	....	317	50,597	217.43
New Mexico	0	0	....	0	0	....
New York	0	0	....	316	110,455	415.67
North Carolina	0	0	....	785	166,919	512.18
North Dakota	93,173	1,392,640	41.48	7,055	220,936	48.45
Ohio	0	0	....	67,932	2,634,815	91.50
Oklahoma	1,514	10,961	78.01	471	38	3.52
Oregon	0	0	....	1,456	103,321	239.00
Pennsylvania	0	0	....	711	26,143	132.98
South Carolina	0	0	....	1,031	19,113	133.54
South Dakota	16,897	564,407	41.23	9,467	273,166	42.10
Tennessee	0	0	....	4,220	319,442	218.69
Texas	436	20	0.13	556	36,000	160.46
Utah	0	0	....	0	0	....
Vermont	0	0	....	123	23,956	217.31
Virginia	0	0	....	2,416	145,492	124.87
Washington	0	0	....	32,404	1,184,609	82.04
West Virginia	0	0	....	577	197,278	885.85
Wisconsin	0	0	....	17,976	1,383,955	159.31
Wyoming	0	0	....	0	0	....
United States	181,252	2,291,534	41.52	716,815	44,031,988	118.35

[1] Not including acres which receive no cost share.
Total acres treated may not add due to rounding.
FSA, Conservation and Environmental Programs Division, (202) 690-1612.

Table 12-8.—Conservation Reserve Program (CRP): Enrollment by practice, under contract, September 2019
(CP22 and CP23)

State	CP22 Riparian buffer			CP23 Wetland restoration		
	Total acres treated	Total cost share	Avg cost share per acre treated [1]	Total acres treated	Total cost share	Avg cost share per acre treated [1]
Alabama	23,095	1,641,914	185.66	5	0	....
Alaska	50	0	....	0	0	....
Arkansas	53,342	2,119,927	111.02	66,364	15,068,268	532.47
California	576	266,400	576.36	572	0	....
Colorado	429	171,836	1,008.90	1,472	68,183	86.98
Delaware	57	8,125	273.57	192	230,544	1,651.22
Florida	64	0	....	0	0	....
Georgia	566	146,111	703.78	403	0	....
Hawaii	1,248	3,820,840	4,800.05	0	0	....
Idaho	2,916	247,240	244.81	401	2,125	83.99
Illinois	95,106	14,660,211	212.01	44,690	7,726,575	210.60
Indiana	4,729	524,778	250.74	11,910	1,478,243	214.50
Iowa	40,874	7,689,384	320.62	133,104	19,979,513	194.41
Kansas	2,311	100,966	178.09	9,822	597,435	99.96
Kentucky	15,326	3,511,550	302.27	220	75,113	1,264.95
Louisiana	3,717	189,122	138.93	137,637	7,341,961	192.92
Maine	30	38,163	8,875.12	0	0	....
Maryland	10,196	2,214,231	812.85	2,153	1,158,729	1,319.36
Massachusetts	0	0	....	0	0	....
Michigan	1,399	427,775	446.16	18,327	3,201,036	223.43
Minnesota	24,337	2,076,123	151.05	345,009	28,002,708	101.87
Mississippi	156,268	2,824,887	81.58	21,350	884,848	184.90
Missouri	20,259	1,057,093	296.99	21,059	2,629,322	268.34
Montana	2,229	89,279	136.02	1,827	744	8.01
Nebraska	1,345	265,377	431.06	13,008	715,447	99.34
Nevada	0	0	....	0	0	....
New Jersey	265	231,946	963.43	0	0	....
New Mexico	1,694	485,455	454.29	0	0	....
New York	7,019	5,489,707	1,499.78	60	4,616	1,394.56
North Carolina	6,367	669,667	179.42	842	122,078	219.95
North Dakota	238	116,408	717.99	196,362	1,821,549	45.60
Ohio	6,590	878,875	400.96	12,726	5,763,135	931.69
Oklahoma	1,027	286,109	495.08	1,825	83,439	60.93
Oregon	31,186	15,552,083	825.95	268	120,166	776.42
Pennsylvania	19,075	14,181,685	1,337.05	649	368,426	981.11
South Carolina	8,821	146,305	51.60	172	0	....
South Dakota	4,277	1,146,044	566.92	187,125	3,909,643	35.095
Tennessee	4,551	528,443	431.35	673	31,976	106.26
Texas	13,390	1,604,445	258.72	8,860	95,837	52.877
Utah	26	0	....	0	0	....
Vermont	2,267	2,651,935	1,565.28	0	0	....
Virginia	17,536	14,464,214	1,658.10	141	14,895	450.00
Washington	18,776	6,562,370	965.54	62	4,636	111.44
West Virginia	4,918	4,988,056	1,179.51	0	0	....
Wisconsin	6,637	842,512	556.19	4,761	414,666	357.89
Wyoming	1,922	458,683	420.19	0	0	....
United States	617,179	115,376,273	421.58	1,244,049	101,915,855	146.64

[1] Not including acres which receive no cost share.
Total acres treated may not add due to rounding.
FSA, Conservation and Environmental Programs Division, (202) 690-1612.

Table 12-9.—Conservation Reserve Program (CRP): Enrollment by practice, under contract, September 2019
(CP25, CP26, and CP27)

State	CP25 Rare and declining habitat			CP26 Sediment retention			CP27 Farmable wetland pilot (wetland)		
	Total acres treated	Total cost share	Avg cost share per acre treated [1]	Total acres treated	Total cost share	Avg cost share per acre treated [1]	Total acres treated	Total cost share	Avg cost share per acre treated [1]
Alabama	393	17,622	142.46		0			0	
Alaska		0			0			0	
Arkansas		0			0			0	
California		0			0			0	
Colorado	1,604	28,812	65.28		0		2	0	
Delaware		0			0			0	
Florida		0			0			0	
Georgia		0			0			0	
Hawaii		0			0			0	
Idaho	79	4,120	100.00		0		4	606	173.14
Illinois	543	180,583	392.06		0		663	149,991	244.48
Indiana	1,961	347,801	183.99		0		302	378,092	1,970.67
Iowa	140,601	29,935,876	263.95		0		26,932	3,404,380	179.20
Kansas	596,427	30,049,124	61.21		0		800	8,071	78.31
Kentucky	32,089	6,276,111	210.60		0		0	0	
Louisiana		0			0		335	0	
Maine		0			0			0	
Maryland	596	145,883	252.70		0			0	
Massachusetts		0			0			0	
Michigan	35	462	65.00	40	117,708	3,372.73	22	995	199.00
Minnesota	84,060	6,859,021	98.93		0		12,955	1,107,871	118.82
Mississippi		0			0		40	5,109	129.34
Missouri	22,297	2,556,724	182.29		0		2	0	
Montana	57,886	1,868,715	51.92		0		175	240	27.59
Nebraska	147,376	9,283,939	92.51		0		1,373	45,536	87.83
Nevada		0			0			0	
New Jersey		0			0			0	
New Mexico		0			0			0	
New York		0			0			0	
North Carolina		0			0			0	
North Dakota	10,315	722,501	74.13		0		26,405	1,026,362	60.55
Ohio	4,055	1,020,575	409.76		0		88	377,774	5,261.48
Oklahoma	16,736	1,071,949	72.69		0		9	7,316	2,090.29
Oregon	41,733	1,583,892	110.24		0			0	
Pennsylvania		0			0			0	
South Carolina		0			0			0	
South Dakota	13,267	898,518	95.16		0		27,952	613,396	46.11
Tennessee		0			0			0	
Texas		0			0			0	
Utah		0			0			0	
Vermont		0			0			0	
Virginia		0			0			0	
Washington	1,162	62,911	128.02		0		2	0	
West Virginia		0			0			0	
Wisconsin	11,417	2,030,802	218.14		0		55	603	118.24
Wyoming	685	40,517	60.00		0			0	
United States	1,185,314	94,986,458	103.40	40	117,708	3,372.73	98,113	7,126,343	118.50

[1] Not including acres which receive no cost share.
Total acres treated may not add due to rounding.
FSA, Conservation and Environmental Programs Division, (202) 690-1612.

Table 12-10.—Conservation Reserve Program (CRP): Enrollment by practice, under contract, September 2019

(CP28, CP29, and CP30)

State	CP28 Farmable wetland pilot (buffer)			CP29 Wildlife habitat buffer (marginal pastureland)			CP30 Wetland buffer (marginal pastureland)		
	Total acres treated	Total cost share	Avg cost share per acre treated [1]	Total acres treated	Total cost share	Avg cost share per acre treated [1]	Total acres treated	Total cost share	Avg cost share per acre treated [1]
Alabama	0	0	....	374	1,400	250.00	....	0	....
Alaska	....	0	....	....	0	....	140	12,252	2,005.24
Arkansas	0	0	....	268	126,723	919.61	2,706	26,865	107.59
California	....	0	....	....	0	....	....	0	....
Colorado	4	0	....	58	0	....	32	0	....
Delaware	....	0	....	....	0	....	....	0	....
Florida	....	0	....	....	0	....	....	0	....
Georgia	....	0	....	26	0	....	....	0	....
Hawaii	....	0	....	....	0	....	....	0	....
Idaho	2	62	31.00	194	46,728	768.43	142	15,406	137.31
Illinois	1,128	187,737	179.26	246	36,587	307.74	33	4,143	134.12
Indiana	558	51,555	129.88	56	21,965	480.63	41	7,366	180.54
Iowa	65,063	7,251,713	158.71	6,245	1,259,714	339.09	1,537	179,455	223.91
Kansas	1,555	45,161	47.84	4	224	56.00	....	0	....
Kentucky	....	0	....	49,408	7,625,012	166.91	....	0	....
Louisiana	0	0	....	....	0	....	176	0	....
Maine	....	0	....	5	18,088	36,176.00	11	33,012	2,895.79
Maryland	....	0	....	1,054	208,240	354.66	154	5,630	499.56
Massachusetts	....	0	....	....	0	....	....	0	....
Michigan	47	3,149	185.02	4	0	....	300	280,626	1,113.90
Minnesota	26,974	2,120,552	107.24	230	11,055	98.43	5,000	240,467	116.47
Mississippi	157	20,462	130.17	40	3,266	85.01	37	746	78.53
Missouri	8	0	....	1,114	227,152	500.68	1,614	288,725	461.76
Montana	134	149	27.59	....	0	....	....	0	....
Nebraska	1,845	67,808	72.46	1,051	107,765	199.17	291	18,611	276.29
Nevada	....	0	....	....	0	....	....	0	....
New Jersey ...	....	0	....	....	0	....	....	0	....
New Mexico ...	....	0	....	....	0	....	....	0	....
New York	....	0	....	1,998	1,082,908	1,037.43	1,171	950,223	1,006.44
North Carolina	0	0	....	27	41,592	8,318.40	....	0	....
North Dakota .	60,423	2,763,118	75.52	35	0	....	....	0	....
Ohio	208	16,258	100.05	2,951	185,541	145.43	127	151,075	3,417.99
Oklahoma	21	465	62.84	....	0	....	....	0	....
Oregon	....	0	....	15,841	2,245,064	562.81	540	799,528	1,481.54
Pennsylvania .	....	0	....	1,138	296,111	523.54	417	113,085	542.89
South Carolina	....	0	....	35	19,137	694.63	61	7,189	116.99
South Dakota .	59,107	2,508,835	59.21	4,269	199,985	97.94	20,642	240,483	43.32
Tennessee	....	0	....	74	6,761	535.34	....	0	....
Texas	....	0	....	1,674	124,797	99.90	2	2,973	1,351.36
Utah	....	0	....	....	0	....	....	0	....
Vermont	....	0	....	....	0	....	1	1,612	2,302.86
Virginia	....	0	....	733	1,093,764	1,861.09	....	0	....
Washington ...	8	0	....	695	31,340	519.73	543	669,128	1,309.40
West Virginia .	....	0	....	....	0	....	....	0	....
Wisconsin	67	796	118.81	1,149	161,369	234.26	22	13,446	619.63
Wyoming	....	0	....	1,314	173,350	432.08	....	0	....
United States	217,308	15,037,820	101.53	92,650	15,355,639	242.00	35,741	4,062,046	333.84

[1] Not including acres which receive no cost share.
Total acres treated may not add due to rounding.
FSA, Conservation and Environmental Programs Division, (202) 690-1612.

Table 12-11.—Conservation Reserve Program (CRP): Enrollment by practice, under contract, September 2019

(CP31, CP32, and CP33)

State	CP31 Bottomland hardwood			CP32 Hardwood trees			CP33 Upland bird habitat buffers		
	Total acres treated	Total cost share	Avg cost share per acre treated [1]	Total acres treated	Total cost share	Avg cost share per acre treated [1]	Total acres treated	Total cost share	Avg cost share per acre treated [1]
Alabama	1,206	88,081	122.64		0		681	65,527	130.75
Alaska		0			0			0	
Arkansas	19,446	814,459	121.52		0		3,390	87,443	126.98
California		0			0			0	
Colorado		0			0		1,434	70,329	95.75
Delaware		0			0			0	
Florida		0			0			0	
Georgia		0			0		393	22,057	126.00
Hawaii		0			0			0	
Idaho		0			0			0	
Illinois	6,240	1,184,922	233.59		0		59,801	6,479,795	123.57
Indiana	9,382	1,976,975	246.67		0		9,660	651,385	107.74
Iowa	3,947	951,187	318.92		0		24,200	3,922,324	239.87
Kansas	216	31,663	223.97		0		25,592	1,143,921	76.03
Kentucky	651	173,220	281.12		9		5,605	653,030	149.75
Louisiana	51,364	2,767,813	99.06		0		134	8,478	97.56
Maine		0			0			0	
Maryland		0			0		415	38,587	140.83
Massachusetts		0			0			0	
Michigan		0			0		571	69,660	146.70
Minnesota	798	35,868	133.79		0		495	26,644	92.10
Mississippi	61,153	1,210,382	98.08		0		1,304	26,232	264.09
Missouri	2,030	112,948	184.33		0		24,385	1,563,423	109.87
Montana		0			0		404	30,974	82.00
Nebraska	9	4,794	542.92		0		9,315	418,737	94.91
Nevada		0			0			0	
New Jersey		0			0			0	
New Mexico		0			0			0	
New York	2	2,000	869.57		0			0	
North Carolina	57	1,978	139.30		0		3,311	113,691	125.50
North Dakota		0			0			0	
Ohio	109	24,427	336.00		0		10,291	648,591	131.82
Oklahoma	443	70,970	169.46		0		368	976	61.00
Oregon		0			0			0	
Pennsylvania		0			0		292	25,869	158.76
South Carolina		0			0		1,124	11,271	56.44
South Dakota		0			0		1,447	76,582	69.35
Tennessee	2,616	185,702	126.31		0		3,421	230,468	91.68
Texas	381	2,925	65.73		0		30,800	1,153,553	123.81
Utah		0			0			0	
Vermont		0			0			0	
Virginia		0			0		836	52,804	141.12
Washington		0			0		1,553	39,395	110.52
West Virginia		0			0			0	
Wisconsin		0		1	0		208	5,869	170.66
Wyoming		0			0			0	
United States	160,049	9,640,313	142.94	1			221,431	17,637,615	129.22

[1] Not including acres which receive no cost share.
Total acres treated may not add due to rounding.
FSA, Conservation and Environmental Programs Division, (202) 690-1612.

Table 12-12.—Conservation Reserve Program (CRP): Enrollment by practice, under contract, September 2019
(CP34, CP36, and CP37)

State	CP34 Flood control structure			CP36 Longleaf pine			CP37 Duck nesting habitat		
	Total acres treated	Total cost share	Avg cost share per acre treated [1]	Total acres treated	Total cost share	Avg cost share per acre treated [1]	Total acres treated	Total cost share	Avg cost share per acre treated [1]
Alabama	....	0	....	13,749	2,752,896	228.91	....	0	....
Alaska	....	0	....	....	0	....	....	0	....
Arkansas	....	0	....	....	0	....	....	0	....
California	....	0	....	....	0	....	....	0	....
Colorado	....	0	....	....	0	....	....	0	....
Delaware	....	0	....	....	0	....	....	0	....
Florida	....	0	....	2,354	766,268	349.37	....	0	....
Georgia	....	0	....	121,098	22,609,126	297.92	....	0	....
Hawaii	....	0	....	....	0	....	....	0	....
Idaho	....	0	....	....	0	....	....	0	....
Illinois	....	0	....	....	0	....	....	0	....
Indiana	....	0	....	....	0	....	....	0	....
Iowa	....	0	....	....	0	....	2,441	202,038	123.83
Kansas	....	0	....	....	0	....	....	0	....
Kentucky	....	0	....	....	0	....	....	0	....
Louisiana	....	0	....	34	3,560	105.01	....	0	....
Maine	....	0	....	....	0	....	....	0	....
Maryland	....	0	....	....	0	....	....	0	....
Massachusetts	....	0	....	....	0	....	....	0	....
Michigan	....	0	....	....	0	....	24,028	1,965,905	92.38
Minnesota	69	5,617	112.90	147	5,621	142.30	....	0	....
Mississippi	....	0	....	147	5,621	142.30	....	0	....
Missouri	....	0	....	....	0	....	3,394	20,229	16.39
Montana	....	0	....	....	0	....	....	0	....
Nebraska	....	0	....	....	0	....	....	0	....
Nevada	....	0	....	....	0	....	....	0	....
New Jersey	....	0	....	....	0	....	....	0	....
New Mexico	....	0	....	....	0	....	....	0	....
New York	....	0	....	....	0	....	....	0	....
North Carolina	....	0	....	7,325	1,226,074	270.61	....	0	....
North Dakota	....	0	....	....	0	....	188,594	6,304,196	49.68
Ohio	....	0	....	....	0	....	....	0	....
Oklahoma	....	0	....	....	0	....	....	0	....
Oregon	....	0	....	....	0	....	....	0	....
Pennsylvania	....	0	....	....	0	....	....	0	....
South Carolina	....	0	....	14,169	1,485,470	144.00	....	0	....
South Dakota	....	0	....	....	0	....	231,855	7,395,357	41.57
Tennessee	....	0	....	....	0	....	....	0	....
Texas	....	0	....	....	0	....	....	0	....
Utah	....	0	....	....	0	....	....	0	....
Vermont	....	0	....	....	0	....	....	0	....
Virginia	....	0	....	378	42,172	122.84	....	0	....
Washington	....	0	....	....	0	....	....	0	....
West Virginia	....	0	....	....	0	....	....	0	....
Wisconsin	....	0	....	....	0	....	....	0	....
Wyoming	....	0	....	....	0	....	....	0	....
United States	69	5,617	112.90	159,255	28,891,187	274.18	450,312	15,887,724	48.30

[1] Not including acres which receive no cost share.
Total acres treated may not add due to rounding.
FSA, Conservation and Environmental Programs Division, (202) 690-1612.

Table 12-13.—Conservation Reserve Program (CRP): Enrollment by practice, under contract, September 2019
(CP38, CP39, and CP40)

State	CP38 State acres for wildlife enhancement			CP39 Constructed wetlands			CP40 Aquaculture wetlands		
	Total acres treated	Total cost share	Avg cost share per acre treated [1]	Total acres treated	Total cost share	Avg cost share per acre treated [1]	Total acres treated	Total cost share	Avg cost share per acre treated [1]
Alabama	2,114	126,966	116.01	0	0	....	14	504	36.52
Alaska	....	0	....	0	0	....	0	0	....
Arkansas	18,585	1,008,913	155.26	0	0	....	2,012	517,991	293.64
California	....	0	....	0	0	....	0	0	....
Colorado	73,121	3,956,024	81.25	0	0	....	0	0	....
Delaware	....	0	....	0	0	....	0	0	....
Florida	....	0	....	0	0	....	0	0	....
Georgia	15,804	1,010,174	126.63	0	0	....	0	0	....
Hawaii	....	0	....	0	0	....	0	0	....
Idaho	145,740	10,557,754	78.18	0	0	....	0	0	....
Illinois	27,398	4,268,487	207.62	30	0	....	0	0	....
Indiana	57,476	6,337,791	132.39	0	0	....	0	0	....
Iowa	288,933	42,170,420	159.53	263	60,060	280.27	0	0	....
Kansas	204,027	8,153,305	63.59	7	830	350.21	0	0	....
Kentucky	15,355	1,365,495	177.85	0	0	....	0	0	....
Louisiana	477	33,668	92.75	1	138	156.82	3,220	559,700	173.79
Maine	2,099	368,072	417.21	0	0	....	0	0	....
Maryland	....	0	....	0	0	....	0	0	....
Massachusetts	....	0	....	0	0	....	0	0	....
Michigan	19,530	4,226,316	280.82	0	0	....	0	0	....
Minnesota	98,506	7,869,876	97.39	89	32,044	358.11	0	0	....
Mississippi	11,847	1,683,120	305.88	0	0	....	11,182	1,300,930	158.67
Missouri	56,949	5,862,955	196.51	0	0	....	222	0	....
Montana	88,093	4,829,742	97.67	0	0	....	0	0	....
Nebraska	129,155	8,396,087	80.15	0	0	....	0	0	....
Nevada	....	0	....	0	0	0	0	....	
New Jersey	979	148,196	189.13	0	0	....	0	0	....
New Mexico	2,600	0	....	0	0	....	0	0	....
New York	2,279	328,881	215.85	0	0	....	0	0	....
North Carolina	875	103,413	212.24	0	0	....	58	692	197.71
North Dakota	158,613	4,225,643	46.78	0	0	....	0	0	....
Ohio	37,202	3,129,045	155.46	84	54,829	2,383.89	0	0	....
Oklahoma	8,319	2,647,326	573.36	0	0	....	0	0	....
Oregon	5,450	304,550	63.21	0	0	....	0	0	....
Pennsylvania	....	0	....	0	0	....	0	0	....
South Carolina	1,066	176,990	227.65	0	0	....	0	0	....
South Dakota	164,544	5,090,484	46.93	14	0	....	3	0	....
Tennessee	9,968	1,204,328	144.98	0	0	....	0	0	....
Texas	178,067	14,250,046	102.32	0	0	....	0	0	....
Utah	....	0	....	0	0	....	0	0	....
Vermont	....	0	....	0	0	....	0	0	....
Virginia	510	48,548	114.23	0	0	....	0	0	....
Washington	112,365	14,582,732	165.87	0	0	....	0	0	....
West Virginia	....	0	....	0	0	....	0	0	....
Wisconsin	31,959	4,080,676	179.73	0	0	....	0	0	....
Wyoming	9,831	850,961	87.95	0	0	....	0	0	....
United States	1,979,835	163,396,986	112.31	489	147,901	448.16	16,711	2,379,817	180.28

[1] Not including acres which receive no cost share.
Total acres treated may not add due to rounding.
FSA, Conservation and Environmental Programs Division, (202) 690-1612.

Table 12-14.—Conservation Reserve Program (CRP): Enrollment by practice, under contract, September 2019

(CP41 and CP42)

State	CP41 Flooded prairie wetlands			CP42 Pollinator Habitat [1]		
	Total acres treated	Total cost share	Avg cost share per acre treated [1]	Total acres treated	Total cost share	Avg cost share per acre treated [2]
Alabama	0	0	....	85	10,259	122.73
Alaska	0	0	....	0	0	....
Arkansas	0	0	....	50	6,553	412.14
California	0	0	....	1,819	0	....
Colorado	0	0	....	19,046	2,295,663	152.02
Delaware	0	0	....	4	2,800	700.00
Florida	0	0	....	0	0	....
Georgia	0	0	....	27	3,847	167.48
Hawaii	0	0	....	0	0	....
Idaho	0	0	....	7,830	658,264	101.40
Illinois	0	0	....	105,702	45,233,686	433.40
Indiana	0	0	....	5,244	802,537	162.85
Iowa	125	21,879	196.91	219,435	112,321,932	520.62
Kansas	0	0	....	5,533	226,826	68.78
Kentucky	0	0	....	4,715	1,223,038	266.90
Louisiana	0	0	....	22	1,850	82.42
Maine	0	0	....	0	0	....
Maryland	0	0	....	32	2,889	300.00
Massachusetts	0	0	....	0	0	....
Michigan	0	0	....	5,487	874,254	163.93
Minnesota	1,052	72,521	80.59	14,495	3,935,145	279.41
Mississippi	0	0	....	0	0	....
Missouri	0	0	....	45,055	6,002,455	222.44
Montana	0	0	....	5,492	234,469	56.97
Nebraska	0	0	....	28,172	1,940,360	82.37
Nevada	0	0	....	16	2,795	173.61
New Jersey	0	0	....	14	63,891	4,656.78
New Mexico	0	0	....	857	83,328	120.00
New York	0	0	....	44	21,152	530.38
North Carolina	0	0	....	20	5,145	643.13
North Dakota	48,175	1,394,833	40.09	4,635	797,319	180.46
Ohio	0	0	....	3,305	235,721	117.86
Oklahoma	0	0	....	146	7,967	107.11
Oregon	0	0	....	353	15,304	94.87
Pennsylvania	0	0	....	8	1,371	285.03
South Carolina	0	0	....	0	0	....
South Dakota	13,720	568,939	47.07	4,438	735,424	174.61
Tennessee	0	0	....	4,988	669,949	164.48
Texas	0	0	....	11,993	946,285	130.43
Utah	0	0	....	743	62,006	83.48
Vermont	0	0	....	0	0	....
Virginia	0	0	....	196	28,764	359.64
Washington	0	0	....	3,096	300,202	117.44
West Virginia	0	0	....	0	0	....
Wisconsin	0	0	....	2,236	648,036	398.21
Wyoming	0	0	....	230	43,386	188.40
United States	63,073	2,058,172	42.98	505,566	180,444,870	394.89

[1] Not including acres which receive no cost share.
Total acres treated may not add due to rounding.
FSA, Conservation and Environmental Programs Division, (202) 690-1612.

Table 12-15.—Conservation Reserve Program (CRP): Enrollment by practice, under contract, September 2019

(CP87 and CP88)

State	CP87 Grasslands-Native Grass			CP88 Grasslands-Introduced grass		
	Total acres treated	Total cost share	Avg cost share per acre treated [2]	Total acres treated	Total cost share	Avg cost share per acre treated [1]
Alabama	2,035	0	....	166	482,528	2,904.35
Alaska	....	0	....	....	0	....
Arkansas	....	0	....	60	0	....
California	847	0	....	588	0	....
Colorado	1,401	16,368	100.00	81,153	506,386	46.81
Delaware	....	0	....	....	0	....
Florida	378	0	....	....	0	....
Georgia	1,350	2,624	17.01	....	0	....
Hawaii	....	0	....	....	0	....
Idaho	....	0	....	23,784	861,429	49.28
Illinois	450	0	....	3	0	....
Indiana	54	0	....	47	0	....
Iowa	2,256	0	....	793	0	....
Kansas	607	261	25.02	24,206	13,818	25.00
Kentucky	3,376	0	....	51	0	....
Louisiana	1,217	0	....	165	0	....
Maine	....	0	....	....	0	....
Maryland	894	11,899	46.53	35	0	....
Massachusetts	....	0	....	....	0	....
Michigan	6,360	70,255	255.56	....	0	....
Minnesota	752	0	....	1,781	0	....
Mississippi	420	0	....	156	0	....
Missouri	1,171	0	....	784	0	....
Montana	4,773	0	....	43,114	33,648	14.04
Nebraska	21,164	7,426	43.87	310,770	648,942	61.51
Nevada	....	0	....	....	0	....
New Jersey	154	0	....	....	0	....
New Mexico	1,944	0	....	93,196	804,034	70.35
New York	1,607	230,331	472.65	2	0	....
North Carolina	538	0	....	7	0	....
North Dakota	2,966	0	....	22,894	14,088	30.29
Ohio	4,069	13,627	152.55	61	0	....
Oklahoma	1,577	0	....	33,347	8,629	27.57
Oregon	1,145	0	....	15,930	0	....
Pennsylvania	425	29,178	850.17	110	301	15.00
South Carolina	101	7,708	76.26	....	0	....
South Dakota	6,440	13,555	143.11	128,732	517,821	37.62
Tennessee	2,279	5,609	67.96	1,022	0	....
Texas	1,731	27,359	88.72	27,885	564,081	124.23
Utah	85	0	....	797	0	....
Vermont	....	0	....	....	0	....
Virginia	987	20,272	111.85	80	0	....
Washington	276	0	....	4,850	0	....
West Virginia	2,140	16,682	51.07	....	0	....
Wisconsin	821	0	....	23	0	....
Wyoming	1,789	0	....	20,125	0	....
United States	80,579	473,154	173.07	836,716	4,455,705	61.46

[1] Not including acres which receive no cost share.
Total acres treated may not add due to rounding.
FSA, Conservation and Environmental Programs Division, (202) 690-1612.

Table 12-16.—Emergency Conservation Program: Assistance, fiscal years 2010–2019 [1]

Year	Emergency Conservation Program
	1,000 dollars
2010	76,735
2011	32,262
2012	56,114
2013	41,206
2014	22,548
2015	24,001
2016	26,017
2017	56,353
2018	94,038
2019	71,852

[1] Totals are from unrounded data.
FSA, Conservation and Environmental Protection Division, (202) 690-1612.

Table 12-17.—Conservation Reserve Program (CRP): Enrollment by State, September 2019

State [1]	Number of contracts	Number of farms	Acres	Annual rent ($1,000)	Avg Payments [2] ($/acre)
Alabama	4,851	3,635	199,170	9,148	45.93
Alaska	14	13	2,704	103	38.09
Arkansas	5,259	3,051	220,324	17,170	77.93
California	172	129	42,735	2,253	52.71
Colorado	9,919	5,355	1,820,532	63,068	34.64
Connecticut	*	*	*	*	*
Delaware	323	191	3,684	523	141.89
Florida	561	467	23,173	1,121	48.39
Georgia	6,356	4,403	209,729	13,443	64.10
Hawaii	27	18	1,261	61	48.59
Idaho	3,590	2,041	541,835	28,481	52.56
Illinois	76,531	42,768	853,668	167,270	195.94
Indiana	33,276	18,756	218,638	40,663	185.99
Iowa	107,327	54,040	1,744,748	387,369	222.02
Kansas	34,812	20,498	1,946,905	85,868	44.10
Kentucky	12,326	6,482	207,775	32,870	158.20
Louisiana	4,464	2,921	275,713	25,073	90.94
Maine	243	170	5,641	265	47.03
Maryland	4,834	2,773	50,493	10,895	215.77
Massachusetts	6	3	20	3	153.65
Michigan	9,381	5,508	120,929	15,827	130.88
Minnesota	55,355	29,157	1,058,276	133,995	126.62
Mississippi	14,565	9,617	598,515	44,682	74.66
Missouri	26,714	16,112	841,875	100,395	119.25
Montana	6,265	2,857	1,063,871	32,565	30.61
Nebraska	20,100	11,874	1,068,595	71,645	67.05
Nevada	*	*	*	*	*
New Hampshire	*	*	*	*	*
New Jersey	337	203	1,947	174	89.48
New Mexico	1,688	1,086	429,730	13,595	31.64
New York	1,574	1,135	24,533	2,279	92.90
North Carolina	3,459	2,477	50,417	3,659	72.58
North Dakota	20,826	10,890	1,293,082	67,215	51.98
Ohio	35,223	19,546	242,527	42,545	175.42
Oklahoma	5,475	3,826	642,121	21,265	33.12
Oregon	3,687	2,053	441,752	28,033	63.46
Pennsylvania	7,785	5,204	127,015	16,573	130.48
Puerto Rico	5	5	515	27	51.55
Rhode Island	*	*	*	*	*
South Carolina	2,734	1,592	58,251	2,362	40.55
South Dakota	29,252	13,597	1,141,377	101,455	88.89
Tennessee	5,258	3,569	127,955	12,276	95.94
Texas	18,895	13,665	2,811,809	103,526	36.82
Utah	793	514	160,627	5,483	34.13
Vermont	370	271	2,413	276	114.34
Virginia	3,744	2,898	34,691	2,353	67.84
Washington	10,901	5,052	1,191,082	71,449	59.99
West Virginia	502	414	7,811	503	64.43
Wisconsin	13,765	8,778	204,964	30,530	148.95
Wyoming	768	490	209,765	5,139	24.50
United States	604,317	340,109	22,325,377	1,815,477	81.32

*Data withheld to avoid disclosure of individual operations.   [1] State in which land is administered.   [2] Payments made October, 2019.
FSA, Conservation and Environmental Programs Division, (202) 690-1612.

Table 12-18.—Forest land: Total forest land and area and ownership of timberland, by regions, Jan. 1, 2017

Region	Total forest land [1]	Timberland [2]							
		All own-erships	Federal			State, county, and municipal	Private		
			Total	National forest	Other		Total	Private corporate	Private non-corporate [3]
	1,000 acres	1,000 acres	1,000 acres	1,000 acres	1,000 acres	1,000 acres	1,000 acres	1,000 acres	1,000 acres
Northeast	84,727	78,539	2,852	2,355	498	10,103	65,586	22,090	43,496
North Central	91,062	86,355	8,495	7,792	704	15,549	62,310	8,106	54,204
North	175,789	164,894	11,348	10,146	1,202	15,650	127,896	30,196	97,700
Southeast	89,692	85,754	7,016	5,061	1,955	5,618	73,119	27,283	45,836
South Central	155,821	122,338	9,380	7,197	2,183	3,942	109,016	36,220	72,795
South	245,513	208,092	16,397	12,258	4,138	9,561	182,135	63,504	118,632
Great Plains	6,797	6,084	1,217	1,051	166	265	4,602	202	4,400
Intermountain	123,844	63,569	45,894	43,154	2,740	2,927	14,748	4,890	9,858
Rocky Mountains	130,641	69,654	47,111	44,206	2,905	3,193	19,350	5,091	14,259
Alaska	128,735	12,996	4,874	3,848	1,025	4,810	3,313	2,827	486
Pacific Northwest	51,827	41,462	19,200	16,802	2,397	3,637	18,625	10,903	7,722
Pacific Southwest [4]	32,986	17,326	9,249	8,877	372	245	7,833	4,634	3,198
Pacific Coast	213,549	71,784	33,323	29,527	3,795	8,691	29,771	18,364	11,406
All regions	765,493	514,425	108,178	96,138	12,040	47,095	359,152	117,155	241,997

Source: Forest Resources of the United States 2017 (a periodic compilation of the USDA Forest Service's continuous forest inventory, the next edition of which is due in 2022). Data may not add to totals because of rounding. [1] Forest land is land at least 10 percent stocked by forest trees of any size, including land that formerly had such tree cover and that will be naturally or artificially regenerated. Forest land includes transition zones, such as areas between heavily forested and non-forested lands that are at least 10 percent stocked with forest trees, and forest areas. The minimum area for classification of forest land is 1 acre. Roadside, streamside, and shelterbelt strips of timber must have a crown width at least 120 feet wide to qualify as forest land. Unimproved roads and trails, streams, and clearings in forest areas are classified as forest if less than 120 feet in width. [2] Timberland is forest land that is producing or is capable of producing crops of industrial wood and that is not withdrawn from timber utilization by statute or administrative regulation. Areas qualifying as timberland have the capability of producing more than 20 cubic feet per acre per year of industrial wood. Currently inaccessible and inoperable areas are included. [3] Includes Indian lands. [4] Includes Hawaii.
Prepared by Forest Service Research and Development, Washington Office, IMAR Staff.

Table 12-19.—Timber volume: Net volume of growing stock on timberland, by softwoods and hardwoods, and regions, 2017

Region	Growing stock [1]		
	All species	Softwoods	Hardwoods
	Million cubic feet		
Northeast	152,780	37,108	115,672
North Central	117,261	23,494	93,768
North	270,041	60,601	209,440
Southeast	142,603	67,540	75,063
South Central	176,485	73,767	102,717
South	319,088	141,307	177,781
Great Plains	4,487	1,885	2,601
Intermountain	125,518	117,217	8,301
Rocky Mountains	130,005	119,102	10,903
Alaska	37,140	33,761	3,379
Pacific Northwest	159,238	146,480	12,758
Pacific Southwest [2]	69,726	59,273	10,452
Pacific Coast	266,104	239,515	26,589
All regions	985,238	560,526	424,712

Source: Forest Resources of the United States 2017 (a periodic compilation of the USDA Forest Service's continuous forest inventory, the next edition of which is due in 2022). Data may not add to totals because of rounding.   [1] Live trees of commercial species meeting specified standards of quality or vigor. Cull trees are excluded. Includes only trees 5.0-inches diameter or larger at 4½ feet above ground.   [2] Includes Hawaii.
Prepared by Forest Service Research and Development, Washington Office, IMAR Staff.

Table 12-20.—Total volume of roundwood harvested in the United States, by sources and category, 2016

Category	All sources			Growing stock [1]			Other sources [2]		
	All species	Soft-woods	Hard-woods	All species	Soft-woods	Hard-woods	All species	Soft-woods	Hard-woods
	Million cubic feet								
Roundwood products:									
Sawlogs	5,521	4,075	1,446	5,334	3,959	1,374	187	115	72
Pulpwood	5,368	3,640	1,728	4,772	3,280	1,493	596	360	235
Veneer logs	660	590	69	648	582	65	12	8	4
Other products [3]	728	575	153	563	423	141	165	153	12
Fuelwood	1,695	599	1,096	332	149	183	1,363	450	913
Total	13,972	9,480	4,493	11,650	8,393	3,257	2,323	1,086	1,236
Logging residue[4]	3,758	1,942	1,815	1,126	451	676	2,631	1,492	1,139
Other removals [5]	510	134	376	274	67	207	236	67	169
Total	4,268	2,076	2,191	1,400	518	883	2,867	1,559	1,308

Source: Forest Resources of the United States 2017 (a periodic compilation of the USDA Forest Service's continuous forest inventory, the next edition of which is due in 2022). Data may not add to totals because of rounding.   [1] Includes live trees of commercial species meeting specified standards of quality or vigor. Cull trees are excluded. Includes only trees 5.0-inches diameter or larger at 4½ feet above ground.   [2] Includes salvable dead trees, rough and rotten trees, trees of non-commercial species, trees less than 5.0-inches diameter at 4½ feet above ground, tops, and roundwood harvested from nonforest land (for example, fence rows).   [3] Includes poles, pilings, posts, and miscellaneous products.   [4] Net of wet rot or limbs.   [5] Unutilized wood volume from cut or otherwise killed growing stock, from nongrowing stock sources on timberland (for example, precommercial thinnings), or from timberland clearing. Does not include volume removed from inventory through reclassification of timberland to reserved timberland.
Prepared by Forest Service Research and Development, Washington Office, IMAR Staff.

Table 12-21.—Net annual growth, removals, and mortality of growing stock on timberland in the United States, 2016

Region	Growth [1]			Removals [2]			Mortality [3]		
	All species	Soft-woods	Hard-woods	All species	Soft-woods	Hard-woods	All species	Soft-woods	Hard-woods
	Million cubic feet								
Northeast	3,264	917	2,347	1,176	377	799	1,242	336	906
North Central	2,668	629	2,039	1,315	277	1,038	1,379	231	1,147
North	5,932	1,546	4,386	2,491	654	1,837	2,621	567	2,053
Southeast	6,393	4,285	2,108	3,527	2,736	790	1,085	528	557
South Central	7,371	4,983	2,388	4,333	2,911	1,422	1,845	630	1,215
South	13,764	9,268	4,496	7,859	5,647	2,212	2,930	1,158	1,772
Great Plains	57	(2)	59	34	29	6	82	43	39
Intermountain	242	192	50	370	367	3	2,487	2,354	133
Rocky Mountain	299	189	109	404	396	9	2,570	2,397	173
Alaska	254	133	121	39	39	-	302	275	27
Pacific Northwest	3,707	3,423	284	1,891	1,811	81	1,201	1,030	171
Pacific Southwest [4]	1,054	909	145	355	355	-	574	472	102
Pacific Coast	5,015	4,465	550	2,286	2,204	82	2,078	1,777	300
All regions	25,009	15,468	9,542	13,041	8,901	4,140	10,198	5,900	4,299

Source: Forest Resources of the United States 2017 (a periodic compilation of the USDA Forest Service's continuous forest inventory, the next edition of which is due in 2022). Data may not add to totals because of rounding.   [1] The net increase in the volume of trees during a specified year. Components include the increment in net volume of trees at the beginning of the specific year surviving to its end, plus the net volume of trees reaching the minimum size class during the year, minus the volume of trees that died during the year, and minus the net volume of trees that became cull trees during the year.   [2] The net volume of trees removed from the inventory during a specified year by harvesting, cultural operations such as timber stand improvement, or land clearing.   [3] The volume of sound wood in trees that died from natural causes during a specified year.   [4] Includes Hawaii.
Prepared by Forest Service Research and Development, Washington Office, IMAR Staff.

Table 12-22.—Net volume of growing stock on timberland in the Western United States, region and species, 2017

Species	Total West	Inter-mountain	Alaska	Pacific Northwest	Pacific Southwest [1]	Great Plains
	Million cubit feet					
Softwoods:						
Douglas-fir	128,235	30,003	0	79,650	18,582	0
Ponderosa and Jeffrey pines	42,389	17,118	0	12,389	11,143	1,739
True fir	54,703	23,272	17	16,791	14,624	0
Western hemlock	34,770	1,486	13,009	20,175	101	0
Sugar pine	3,684	0	0	675	3,009	0
Western white pine	1,057	418	0	318	321	0
Redwood	5,904	0	0	21	5,883	0
Sitka spruce	12,149	0	10,536	1,405	208	0
Engelmann and other spruces	24,408	18,601	4,302	1,505	0	0
Western larch	6,242	4,117	3	2,122	0	0
Incense cedar	4,381	0	0	873	3,508	0
Lodgepole pine	19,765	15,661	84	2,960	1,060	0
Other softwoods	20,931	6,544	5,811	2,260	834	146
Total	358,617	117,217	33,761	146,480	59,273	2,021
Hardwoods:						
Cottonwood and aspen	10,990	8,082	1,126	748	46	988
Red alder	6,711	20	140	6,220	331	0
Oak	5,175	0	0	608	4,114	453
Other	14,615	199	2,114	5,181	5,961	1,160
Total	37,492	8,301	3,379	12,758	10,452	2,601
All species	396,109	125,518	37,140	159,238	69,726	4,487

Source: Forest Resources of the United States 2017 (a periodic compilation of the USDA Forest Service's continuous forest inventory, the next edition of which is due in 2022). International ¼-inch rule. Data may not add to totals because of rounding.   [1] Includes Hawaii.
Prepared by Forest Service Research and Development, Washington Office, IMAR Staff.

Table 12-23.—Net volume of softwood growing stock on timberland in the Eastern United States, by region and species, 2017

Species	Total East	North		South	
		Northeast	North Central	Southeast	South Central
	Million cubit feet				
Softwoods:					
Longleaf and slash pines	17,820	0	0	13,320	4,500
Loblolly and shortleaf pines	105,748	882	1,093	42,253	61,520
Other yellow pines	8,585	1,784	358	4,690	1,752
White and red pines	25,508	12,945	9,620	2,350	592
Jack pine	912	6	906	0	0
Spruce and balsam fir	13,646	9,202	4,374	70	0
Eastern hemlock	11,252	9,005	1,342	413	493
Cypress	7,309	11	11	3,969	3,318
Other	11,128	3,273	5,789	474	1,592
Total	201,909	37,108	23,494	67,540	73,767
Hardwoods:					
Select white oaks	35,869	5,885	10,132	7,680	12,172
Select red oaks	28,764	12,064	7,007	3,489	6,204
Other white oaks	23,036	5,670	2,187	5,659	9,520
Other red oaks	45,323	6,047	8,109	11,746	19,421
Hickory	23,104	4,146	5,533	3,896	9,529
Yellow birch	4,585	3,778	731	72	3
Hard maple	26,937	13,899	10,049	531	2,097
Soft maple	41,951	22,095	11,229	5,266	3,360
Beech	8,570	4,921	1,059	922	1,668
Sweetgum	20,431	686	251	8,407	11,086
Tupelo and black gum	11,743	829	337	5,846	4,732
Ash	18,948	6,941	6,310	1,823	3,874
Basswood	6,349	2,012	3,527	361	449
Yellow-poplar	33,998	7,554	3,046	14,594	8,804
Cottonwood and aspen	15,539	3,756	11,125	121	537
Black walnut	3,130	479	1,859	253	540
Black cherry	10,655	6,752	2,593	509	800
Other	28,292	8,157	8,325	3,888	7,921
Total	387,221	115,672	93,768	75,063	102,717
All species	589,129	152,780	117,261	142,603	176,485

Source: Forest Resources of the United States 2017 (a periodic compilation of the USDA Forest Service's continuous forest inventory, the next edition of which is due in 2022). International ¼-inch rule. Data may not add to totals because of rounding.
Prepared by Forest Service Research and Development, Washington Office, IMAR Staff.

Table 12-24.— National Forest System: National Forest System lands and other lands in States and Territories, as of September 30, 2019

State or other area	Gross acreage	National Forest System acreage [1]	Other acreage [2]
	1,000 acres		
USA Total	234,023	192,994	41,029
Alabama	1,290	671	620
Alaska	23,932	22,139	1,793
Arizona	11,813	11,179	633
Arkansas	3,549	2,593	955
California	24,288	20,811	3,477
Colorado	15,960	14,487	1,472
Connecticut	0.02	0.02	0
Florida	1,423	1,203	220
Georgia	1,796	868	929
Idaho	21,714	20,449	1,266
Illinois	958	305	653
Indiana	647	204	443
Kansas	109	109	0
Kentucky	2,205	818	1,387
Louisiana	1,032	609	423
Maine	94	54	41
Michigan	4,887	2,876	2,011
Minnesota	5,488	2,845	2,642
Mississippi	2,374	1,191	1,183
Missouri	3,093	1,508	1,585
Montana	19,190	17,195	1,994
Nebraska	562	351	211
Nevada	6,288	5,761	528
New Hampshire	851	754	97
New Mexico	10,249	9,225	1,024
New York	17	16	0
North Carolina	3,027	1,257	1,770
North Dakota	1,103	1,103	0
Ohio	856	244	612
Oklahoma	759	400	359
Oregon	17,654	15,698	1,956
Pennsylvania	741	514	227
South Carolina	1,381	635	746
South Dakota	2,436	2,007	429
Tennessee	1,291	723	568
Texas	2,002	757	1,245
Utah	9,205	8,192	1,013
Vermont	837	411	426
Virginia	3,254	1,669	1,586
Washington	11,990	9,336	2,654
West Virginia	1,893	1,047	846
Wisconsin	2,003	1,525	478
Wyoming	9,726	9,226	500
Puerto Rico	56	29	27
Virgin Islands	0.14	0.14	0

Source: Land Areas of the National Forest System 2019 (https://www.fs.fed.us/land/staff/lar-index.shtml).

[1] *National Forest System acreage.*—A nationally significant system of Federally owned units of forest, range, and related land consisting of national forests, purchase units, national grasslands, land utilization project areas, experimental forest areas, experimental range areas, designated experimental areas, other land areas; water areas, and interests in lands that are administered by USDA Forest Service or designated for administration through the Forest Service.

National forests.—Units formally established and permanently set aside and reserved for national forest purposes.

Purchase units.—Units designated by the Secretary of Agriculture or previously approved by the National Forest Reservation Commission for purposes of Weeks Law Acquisition.

National grasslands.—Units designated by the Secretary of Agriculture and permanently held by the Department of Agriculture under Title III of the Bankhead-Jones Farm Tenant Act.

Land utilization projects.—Units designated by the Secretary of Agriculture for conservation and utilization under Title III of the Bankhead-Jones Farm Tenant Act.

Research and experimental areas.—Units reserved and dedicated by the Secretary of Agriculture for forest or range research and experimentation.

Other areas.—Units administered by the Forest Service that are not included in the above groups.

[2] *Other acreage.*—Lands within the unit boundaries in private, State, county, and municipal ownership and Federal lands over which the Forest Service has no jurisdiction. Areas of such lands which have been offered to the United States and have been approved for acquisition and subsequent Forest Service administration, but to which title had not yet been accepted by the United States.

Prepared by Forest Service Research and Development, Washington Office, IMAR Staff.

Table 12-25.—Forest products cut on National Forest System lands: Volume and value of timber cut and value of all products, United States, fiscal years 2010–2019

Year	Timber cut [1]		Value of non-covertible products [3]	Total value including free-use timber
	Volume	Value [2]		
	Million bd. ft.	1,000 dollars [4]	1,000 dollars [4, 5]	1,000 dollars [4]
2010	2,138	72,174	3,263	104,809
2011	2,440	105,869	2,603	131,904
2012	2,500	112,943	2,748	140,428
2013	2,408	114,878	2,850	143,383
2014	2,437	122,794	2,618	148,979
2015	2,543	129,186	3,346	162,651
2016	2,537	162,444	2,962	165,406
2017	2,596	175,847	2,906	178,753
2018	2,797	185,285	3,480	188,765
2019	2,556	164,208	2,547	166,755

Source: USDA Forest Service, Forest Products Cut and Sold from the National Forests. (https://www.fs.fed.us/forestmanagement/products/cut-sold/index.shtml).   [1] Commercial and cost sales and land exchanges.   [2] Includes collections for forest restoration or improvement under the Knutson-Vandenberg Act, 1930.   [3] Includes materials not measurable in board feet, such as Christmas trees, tanbark, turpentine, seedlings, Spanish moss, etc.   [4] Nominal dollars not adjusted for inflation.   [5] 2010-2015 revised in 2019.
Prepared by Forest Service Research and Development, Washington Office, IMAR Staff.

Table 12-26.—Lumber: Production, United States, 2010–2019

Year	Total	Softwoods	Hardwoods [1]
	Million bd. ft.		
2010	30,461	24,802	5,659
2011	33,304	26,754	6,550
2012	34,791	28,256	6,535
2013	37,321	29,982	7,339
2014	39,810	31,490	8,320
2015 [2]	42,085	32,028	9,538
2016 [2]	42,085	32,535	9,550
2017	43,538	33,888	9,650
2018	44,508	34,908	9,600
2019	45,423	35,919	9,504

Source: Howard, James L.; Liang, Shaobo, 2019. U.S. timber production, trade, consumption, and price statistics, 1965-2017. USDA Forest Service Research Paper FPL-RP-701. [1] In-house estimate. [2] Revised in 2019.
Prepared by Forest Service Research and Development, Washington Office, IMAR Staff.

Table 12-27.—Timber products: Production, imports, exports, and consumption, United States, 2009–2018

Year	Industrial roundwood used for—										Other industrial products, production and consumption [1]
	Lumber				Plywood and veneer				Pulpwood chip		
	Production	Imports	Exports	Consumption	Production	Imports	Exports	Consumption	Imports	Exports	
	Million cu. ft., roundwood equivalent										
2009	4,576	1,347	288	5,636	616	146	34	728	9	196	294
2010	4,569	1,422	341	5,650	655	137	55	736	9	235	294
2011	5,005	1,403	387	6,022	651	139	52	738	9	235	294
2012	5,219	1,480	374	6,324	679	139	57	761	9	235	294
2013	5,607	1,675	406	6,911	703	147	55	796	9	234	294
2014	5,995	1,869	406	7,458	693	187	46	834	9	234	294
2015	6,065	2,100	371	7,793	683	222	38	867	9	235	294
2016	6,143	2,426	527	8,042	703	263	43	923	6	262	732
2017	6,338	2,328	580	8,086	729	274	47	967	2	280	822
2018	6,467	2,953	694	8,726	716	361	44	1,033	2	290	912

Year	Industrial roundwood used for—									
	Pulpwood-based products				Logs		Total			
	Production	Imports [2]	Exports [2]	Consumption	Imports	Exports	Production	Imports	Exports	Consumption
	Million cu. ft.									
2009	4,733	902	785	4,849	17	322	10,737	2,421	1,625	11,532
2010	4,779	911	832	4,857	20	407	10,938	2,498	1,870	11,566
2011	4,748	887	899	4,736	19	485	11,418	2,457	2,058	11,817
2012	5,805	883	875	5,815	28	432	12,663	2,539	1,972	13,231
2013	5,959	942	1,073	5,827	26	463	13,260	2,799	2,231	13,862
2014	6,562	1,205	1,340	6,427	22	444	14,222	3,292	2,470	15,044
2015	6,569	1,172	1,348	6,392	22	279	14,124	3,524	2,272	15,376
2016	5,099	896	995	5,000	24	390	13,329	3,615	2,216	14,727
2017	5,081	875	1,013	4,943	32	393	13,643	3,511	2,315	14,851
2018	5,228	916	1,051	5,093	26	378	13,991	4,258	2,457	15,792

Year	Fuelwood production and consumption	Production, all products	Consumption, all products
	Million cu. ft.		
2009	1,400	12,137	12,932
2010	1,380	12,318	12,946
2011	1,366	12,784	13,183
2012	1,440	14,103	14,671
2013	1,520	14,780	15,382
2014	1,566	15,788	16,610
2015	1,566	15,690	16,942
2016	2,195	15,524	16,922
2017	2,273	15,917	17,124
2018	2,528	16,519	18,320

Source: Howard, James L.; Liang, Shaobo, 2019. U.S. timber production, trade, consumption, and price statistics, 1965-2017. [1] Includes cooperage logs, poles and piling, fence posts, hewn ties, round mine timbers, excelsior bolts, chemical wood, shingle bolts, and miscellaneous items. [2] Includes both pulpwood and the pulpwood equivalent of wood pulp, paper, and board.

Prepared by Forest Service Research and Development, Washington Office, IMAR Staff.

Table 12-28.—Timber products: Producer price indexes, selected products, United States, 2010–2019

[2009=100]

Year	Lumber	Softwood plywood	Woodpulp	Paper	Paperboard
2010	112.0	114.7	123.8	101.4	108.5
2011	111.5	108.1	129.7	106.5	111.2
2012	115.4	127.2	123.8	106.7	110.0
2013	133.0	137.7	120.3	106.2	117.6
2014	143.8	142.7	122.3	107.3	120.0
2015	133.4	136.4	120.9	105.7	117.3
2016	133.9	122.8	115.6	103.3	108.8
2017	145.4	136.6	107.5	103.8	124.3
2018	155.4	159.7	143.7	110.0	132.0
2019	140.8	129.6	115.8	111.7	129.4

Source: Federal Reserve Bank of St. Louis Economic Data Service (https://fred.stlouisfed.org/).
Prepared by Forest Service Research and Development, Washington Office, IMAR Staff.

Table 12-29.—Timber products: Pulpwood consumption, woodpulp production, and paper and board production and consumption, United States, 2010–2019

Year	Pulpwood consumption [1]	Woodpulp production [2]	Paper and board [3]		
			Production	Consumption or new supply [4]	Per capita consumption
	1,000 cords [5]	1,000 tons	1,000 tons	1,000 tons	Pounds
2010	80,307	55,343	82,968	85,331	551
2011	80,040	55,125	81,519	82,858	531
2012	81,422	55,475	80,916	82,321	524
2013	91,251	54,466	80,478	78,603	497
2014	92,186	53,367	79,488	78,046	490
2015	93,141	*52,646	79,024	77,444	481
2016	92,004	*52,701	78,342	76,002	484
2017	90,873	*52,485	78,445	76,625	470
2018	90,281	*51,840	78,114	*75,862	*465
2019	87,632	50,699	78,114	73,096	446

Source: 2009-2016--Howard, James L.; Liang, Shaobo. 2019. U.S. timber production, trade, consumption, and price statistics, 1965-2017. USDA Forest Service Research Paper FPL-RP-701. 2017-2019--In house estimate. All series compiled from U.S. Department of Commerce and American Forest and Paper Association.
*Revised in 2020.   [1] Includes changes in stocks.   [2] Excludes defibrated and exploded woodpulp used for hard pressed board, dissolving and special Alpha, and wood pulp used for construction paper & board.   [3] Excludes hardboard. Includes wet machine board and construction grades.   [4] Production plus imports and minus exports (excludes products); changes in inventories not taken into account.   [5] One cord equals 128 cubic feet.
Prepared by Forest Service Research and Development, Washington Office, IMAR Staff.

Table 12-30.—Lumber and competing engineered wood products: Production by type of product, 2010–2019

Year	Laminated veneer lumber	Wood glulam	Structural Panels		Lumber	
			Oriented strandboard	Softwood Plywood	Hardwood [1]	Softwood
	Million cubic feet	Million board feet	Million square feet (3/8-in. basis)	Million square feet (3/8-in. basis)	Billion board feet	Billion board feet
2010	37	176	10,299	9,131	5.7	24.8
2011	38	184	10,039	8,980	6.6	26.8
2012	46	204	11,038	9,181	6.5	28.3
2013	54	230	12,492	9,346	7.3	30.0
2014	60	233	13,008	8,985	8.3	31.5
2015	61	252	13,283	8,751	8.3	32.0
2016	65	257	13,922	8,809	9.6	32.5
2017	73	271	14,609	9,026	9.7	33.8
2018	71	281	15,129	8,869	9.6	34.9
2019 [2]	71	281	15,181	8,679	9.5	35.9

Sources: APA-The Engineered Wood Association; US Department of Commerce, Bureau of the Census; American Forest and Paper Association; Luppold and Dempsey. Hardwood Market Report: 2008-present.
[1] 2016 data revised in 2020.   [2] Preliminary estimates.
Prepared by Forest Service Research and Development, Washington Office, IMAR Staff.

CHAPTER XIII

CONSUMPTION AND FAMILY LIVING

The statistics in this chapter deal with the consumption of food by both rural and urban people, retail price levels, and other aspects of family living of farm people. Data presented here on quantities of food available for consumption are based on material presented in the earlier commodity chapters, but they are shown here at the retail level, a form that is more useful for an analysis of the demand situation faced by the producer. Data on quantities of farm-produced food consumed directly by farm households are presented in the commodity chapters. Its value and the rental value of the farm home are given in the section on farm income.

Table 13-1.—Population estimates for the United States, Jan. 1 and July 1, 2011-2020

Year	Jan. 1	July 1
2011	309,321,437	310,339,224
2012	311,551,431	312,590,831
2013	313,791,267	314,751,147
2014	316,003,389	317,075,077
2015	318,377,796	319,438,649
2016	320,689,908	321,738,826
2017	322,891,342	323,794,924
2018	324,741,274	325,500,580
2019	326,353,145	327,052,602
2020	327,948,163	328,690,584

Note: The monthly estimates beginning with August 1, 2019 are short-term projections.
Monthly Population Estimates for the United States: April 1, 2010 to December 1, 2020 (NA-EST2019-01). Source: U.S. Census Bureau, Population Division. Release Date: December 2019.
ERS, Rural Economy Branch (202) 694–5435.

Table 13-2.—Consumers' prices: Index number of prices paid for goods and services, United States, 2011–2020 [1]

[1982–84=100]

Year	Food	Nonfood items					All items
		Apparel and upkeep	Housing		Transportation	Medical care	
			Total	Rent			
2011	227.8	122.1	219.1	262.2	212.4	400.3	224.9
2012	233.8	126.3	222.7	267.8	217.3	414.9	229.6
2013	237.0	127.4	227.4	274.0	217.4	425.1	233.0
2014	242.7	127.5	233.2	281.8	215.9	435.3	236.7
2015	247.2	125.9	238.1	290.4	199.1	446.8	237.0
2016	247.9	126.0	244.0	300.3	194.9	463.7	240.0
2017	250.1	125.6	251.2	310.3	201.6	475.3	245.1
2018	253.6	125.7	258.5	320.7	210.7	484.7	251.1
2019	258.3	124.0	265.9	331.6	210.1	498.4	255.7
2020	267.2	118.1	271.8	339.8	201.3	518.9	258.8

[1] Reflects retail prices of goods and services usually bought by average families in urban areas of the United States. This index is the official index released monthly by the U.S. Department of Labor. Data are for all urban consumers.
ERS, Food Markets Branch, (202) 694–5349. Compiled from data of the U.S. Department of Labor.

Table 13-3.—Consumption: Per capita consumption of major food commodities, United States, 2012–2016 [1]

Commodity	2012	2013	2014	2015	2016
	Pounds	Pounds	Pounds	Pounds	Pounds
Red meats [2]	98.0	98.0	95.0	98.6	100.5
Beef	54.5	53.6	51.5	51.4	52.9
Veal	0.3	0.3	0.2	0.2	0.2
Lamb and mutton	0.6	0.7	0.7	0.7	0.8
Pork	42.6	43.5	42.6	46.3	46.6
Fish	14.3	14.5	15.5	14.9	16.1
Canned	3.7	3.3	3.7	3.3	3.7
Fresh and frozen	10.4	10.9	11.5	11.3	12.0
Cured	0.3	0.3	0.3	0.3	0.3
Poultry	69.3	70.3	71.3	75.2	76.3
Chicken	56.7	57.7	58.8	62.6	63.2
Turkey	12.6	12.6	12.5	12.6	13.1
Eggs	32.7	33.2	34.2	33.0	35.0
Dairy products [3]					
Total dairy products	615.1	607.3	616.0	630.1	645.7
Fluid milk and cream	188.6	184.6	178.6	174.7	172.0
Plain and flavored whole milk	46.5	46.2	45.9	47.6	49.8
Plain reduced fat and light milk (2%, 1%, and 0.5%)	84.7	82.6	79.8	76.8	74.2
Plain fat free milk (skim)	24.8	22.6	20.0	17.7	15.6
Flavored lower fat free milk	12.5	12.3	12.0	12.1	12.3
Buttermilk	1.5	1.6	1.5	1.6	1.6
Eggnog	0.4	0.4	0.4	0.4	0.4
Yogurt (excl. frozen)	14.0	15.0	14.9	14.4	13.8
Sour cream and dip	4.1	4.1	4.1	4.1	4.3
Cheese (excluding cottage) [4]	33.3	33.4	34.2	35.1	36.4
American	13.3	13.4	13.7	14.0	14.4
Cheddar	9.6	9.6	9.8	10.2	10.4
Italian	13.8	13.8	14.2	14.5	15.2
Mozzarella	10.7	10.7	11.2	11.3	11.7
Cottage cheese	2.3	2.1	2.1	2.1	2.1
Condensed and evaporated milk	7.3	7.2	6.8	7.7	7.4
Ice cream	13.2	13.0	12.5	12.9	12.9
Butter	5.5	5.5	5.5	5.6	5.7
Fruits and vegetables [5]	636.0	636.6	636.6	631.9	651.7
Fruits	244.6	254.6	250.1	252.7	256.4
Fresh	131.8	136.3	136.3	136.1	142.3
Citrus	23.5	23.9	23.3	22.7	24.0
Noncitrus	108.3	112.4	113.1	113.4	118.3
Processing	112.8	118.2	113.8	116.6	114.1
Citrus	52.6	55.1	52.6	52.7	51.9
Noncitrus	60.2	63.1	61.2	63.8	62.2
Vegetables	391.4	382.1	386.5	379.2	395.3
Fresh	188.7	184.6	186.4	186.4	199.5
Processing	202.7	197.5	200.1	192.9	195.8
Flour and cereal products	174.1	174.7	174.4	172.9	171.9
Wheat flour [6]	134.3	135.0	134.7	133.0	131.7
Corn products	33.9	33.9	34.0	34.0	34.2
Oat products	4.7	4.5	4.5	4.6	4.6
Barley and rye products	1.1	1.2	1.2	1.3	1.4
Caloric sweeteners (dry weight basis)	129.3	128.2	129.1	129.1	128.1
Sugar (refined)	66.6	68.0	68.4	69.1	69.7
Corn sweeteners [7]	61.0	58.4	58.5	57.8	56.5
Honey and edible syrups	1.8	1.9	2.1	2.1	1.9
Others					
Coffee (green bean equivalent)	9.7	9.9	10.0	10.2	NA
Cocoa (chocolate liquor equivalent) [8]	4.2	4.2	4.1	4.3	NA
Tea (dry leaf equivalent)	0.9	0.9	0.9	0.9	NA
Peanuts (shelled)	6.7	6.9	7.0	7.4	7.2
Tree nuts (shelled)	4.2	4.0	4.1	4.1	4.9

[1] Quantity in pounds, retail weight unless otherwise shown. Totals may not add due to rounding.   [2] Boneless, trimmed weight equivalent.   [3] Total dairy products reported on a milk-equivalent, milkfat basis. All other dairy categories reported on a product weight basis.   [4] Natural equivalent of cheese and cheese products.   [5] Farm weight.   [6] White, whole wheat, semolina, and durum flour.   [7] High fructose, glucose, and dextrose.   [8] Chocolate liquor is what remains after cocoa beans have been roasted and hulled; it is sometimes called ground or bitter chocolate.

ERS, Food Economics Division, (202) 694-5400. Historical consumption and supply-disappearance data for food may be found at https://www.ers.usda.gov/data-products/food-availability-per-capita-data-system.

Table 13-4.—USDA Food plans: Cost of food at home at four levels, U.S. average, December 2020[1]

Age-gender groups	Weekly cost[2]				Monthly cost[2]			
	Thrifty plan	Low-cost plan	Moderate-cost plan	Liberal plan	Thrifty plan	Low-cost plan	Moderate-cost plan	Liberal plan
DDollars Individuals:[3]	Dollars	Dollars	Dollars	Dollars	Dollars	Dollars	Dollars	
Child:								
1 year	22.80	30.60	34.80	42.10	99.00	132.80	150.90	182.60
2-3 years	24.90	32.10	38.50	46.90	107.90	139.20	166.80	203.10
4-5 years	26.20	32.90	41.20	49.60	113.60	142.50	178.40	215.10
6-8 years	33.30	46.50	56.10	66.00	144.30	201.40	243.20	285.90
9-11 years	37.70	49.70	65.10	75.60	163.20	215.20	282.20	327.50
Male:								
12-13 years	40.30	57.40	71.80	84.40	174.70	248.90	311.00	365.80
14-18 years	41.40	58.10	73.60	85.10	179.20	251.90	319.10	368.70
19-50 years	44.40	57.70	72.30	88.60	192.60	250.00	313.20	383.70
51-70 years	40.50	54.50	68.10	82.30	175.50	236.30	295.20	356.50
71+ years	40.80	53.50	66.70	82.30	176.60	231.70	289.10	356.70
Female:								
12-13 years	40.10	49.20	59.90	73.10	173.60	213.20	259.60	316.60
14-18 years	39.50	49.20	58.90	72.90	171.00	213.30	255.20	316.00
19-50 years	39.50	50.00	61.40	78.60	171.20	216.80	266.20	340.50
51-70 years	39.10	48.80	60.70	73.50	169.60	211.40	263.00	318.30
71+ years	38.40	48.10	60.10	72.40	166.50	208.60	260.30	313.80
Families:								
Family of 2 (Male and Female)[4]								
19-50 years	92.40	118.50	147.10	183.90	400.20	513.50	637.40	796.60
51-70 years	87.60	113.70	141.70	171.30	379.60	492.40	614.00	742.20
Family of 4:								
Couple (Male and Female), 19-50 years and children—								
2-3 and 4-5 years	135.10	172.80	213.40	263.70	585.30	748.50	924.70	1,142.40
6-8 and 9-11 years	154.90	203.90	255.00	308.70	671.30	883.40	1,104.80	1,337.60

[1] The Food Plans represent a nutritious diet at four different cost levels. The nutritional bases of the Food Plans are the 1997-2005 Dietary Reference Intakes, 2005 Dietary Guidelines for Americans, and 2005 MyPyramid food intake recommendations. In addition to cost, differences among plans are in specific foods and quantities of foods. Another basis of the Food Plans is that all meals and snacks are prepared at home. For specific foods and quantities of foods in the Food Plans, see *Thrifty Food Plan, 2006* (2007) and *The Low-Cost, Moderate-Cost, and Liberal Food Plans, 2007* (2007). All four Food Plans are based on 2001-02 data and updated to current dollars by using the Consumer Price Index for specific food items.

[2] All costs are rounded to nearost 10 cents.

[3] The costs given are for individuals in 4–person families. For individuals in other size families, the following adjustments are suggested: 1 person-add 20 percent; 2 person-add 10 percent; 3 person-add 5 percent; 4 person-no adjustment; 5- or 6-person–subtract 5 percent; 7- (or more) person-subtract 10 percent. To calculate overall household food costs, (1) adjust food costs for each person in household and then (2) sum these adjusted food costs.

[4] Ten percent added for family size adjustment.

Food and Nutrition Service, Center for Nutrition Policy and Promotion, (703) 305–7600. This file and the referenced Food Plans may be accessed at https://www.fns.usda.gov/cnpp/usda-food-plans-cost-food-reports-monthly-reports.

Table 13-5.—Food and Nutrition Service program benefits: Cash payments made under the National School Lunch, School Breakfast, Child and Adult Care, Summer Food and Special Milk Programs and the value of food benefits provided under the SNAP, WIC, Commodity Distribution and The Emergency Feeding Food Assistance Programs, fiscal year 2019 [1]

State/Territory	Child Nutrition Program (cash payments only) [2]					Special Supplemental Food (WIC)	SNAP (formerly Food Stamp Program) [4]	Emergency food assistance (TEFAP)	Commodity distribution [3]	Total [4]
	Child and Adult Care Food	Summer Food	Special Milk	National School Lunch	School Breakfast					
	1,000 dollars									
Alabama	56,169	8,534	23	214,638	79,599	65,412	1,084,563	10,381	24,822	1,544,141
Alaska	8,868	1,372	0	38,061	13,090	11,519	187,357	958	3,808	265,034
Amer. Samoa [4]	0	0	0	0	0	4,588	0	0	0	4,588
Arizona	49,479	3,154	43	275,940	94,481	68,824	1,210,430	12,600	38,091	1,753,042
Arkansas	50,411	3,108	0	136,045	55,619	37,571	480,473	6,890	17,449	787,564
California	445,135	18,903	281	1,511,917	523,067	524,633	6,332,718	65,288	199,424	9,621,366
Colorado	25,073	4,427	199	133,410	48,214	37,816	668,611	6,857	17,023	941,630
Connecticut	17,248	4,146	98	105,335	32,726	24,981	614,968	5,210	10,556	815,268
Delaware	17,213	1,994	16	36,215	13,982	7,289	196,899	2,157	7,159	282,923
District of Columbia	10,025	2,017	2	28,446	11,693	6,362	188,433	1,407	3,294	251,679
Florida	275,203	37,357	14	895,124	281,088	235,464	5,763,763	33,621	94,622	7,616,257
Georgia	111,871	13,816	29	529,911	195,953	103,556	2,336,788	16,985	52,118	3,361,028
Guam	458	0	0	8,781	3,258	6,067	106,449	337	35	125,384
Hawaii	6,302	594	0	46,003	10,849	17,507	469,434	1,314	2,481	554,485
Idaho	7,693	3,704	68	53,053	18,476	13,334	199,514	2,630	8,368	306,841
Illinois	137,943	11,834	1,843	465,650	145,542	122,293	2,777,949	23,883	51,998	3,738,935
Indiana	55,385	7,839	118	269,034	82,086	58,130	867,533	11,295	39,071	1,390,491
Iowa	25,079	3,860	61	110,968	27,599	22,738	446,260	4,459	15,679	656,703
Kansas	28,307	4,284	55	106,106	31,698	22,032	293,540	4,048	14,968	505,037
Kentucky	41,876	9,127	18	232,259	95,413	46,085	853,987	8,040	30,615	1,317,420
Louisiana	87,481	7,311	0	249,066	89,640	63,153	1,297,322	10,470	38,492	1,842,935
Maine	8,803	2,266	12	33,863	12,783	9,205	218,218	2,303	6,742	294,196
Maryland	50,419	9,015	263	178,763	69,287	60,309	910,099	6,771	24,080	1,309,004
Massachusetts	61,383	7,258	162	198,670	65,838	49,103	1,159,119	9,073	27,268	1,577,874
Michigan	66,437	10,222	189	311,190	115,102	94,028	1,894,037	17,223	53,189	2,561,618
Minnesota	61,527	9,783	706	168,385	53,671	53,687	544,420	6,455	27,849	926,485
Mississippi	45,888	7,261	4	170,248	63,861	52,239	679,723	6,338	23,749	1,049,310
Missouri	53,835	13,515	428	212,151	79,070	47,697	1,061,334	10,287	34,492	1,512,809
Montana	10,316	2,101	6	28,992	10,432	6,966	158,390	1,525	8,258	226,986
Nebraska	28,553	2,685	56	75,709	19,848	17,487	229,206	2,342	14,230	390,117
Nevada	12,153	1,760	45	103,538	40,361	26,357	614,242	5,771	13,228	817,454
New Hampshire	4,624	910	145	21,594	5,440	4,601	101,470	1,530	5,054	145,369
New Jersey	81,397	11,683	254	262,359	94,775	94,730	1,012,654	15,104	34,614	1,607,570
New Mexico	31,249	5,115	0	101,740	43,961	21,086	638,422	4,731	15,940	862,245
New York	228,288	55,304	532	780,949	253,988	265,486	4,526,971	33,888	73,864	6,219,270
North Carolina	93,476	12,384	103	376,307	134,776	112,992	1,870,952	17,474	48,333	2,666,797
North Dakota	8,725	923	22	21,861	5,986	6,707	75,391	1,029	10,248	130,892
Northern Marianas [4]	0	0	0	0	0	1,164	0	0	0	1,164
Ohio	89,366	11,939	373	365,742	126,136	77,957	2,078,237	19,519	46,181	2,815,450
Oklahoma	59,598	4,363	21	180,185	64,053	39,836	832,653	6,601	45,209	1,232,520
Oregon	32,473	5,001	83	116,417	39,990	37,084	937,799	7,455	15,246	1,191,550
Pennsylvania	118,880	12,422	269	400,460	125,440	116,512	2,592,184	20,372	65,100	3,451,639
Puerto Rico [4]	19,558	6,621	0	110,809	25,885	121,030	0	9,410	15,280	308,594
Rhode Island	8,796	1,356	37	30,642	10,072	9,979	0	1,600	4,417	66,900
South Carolina	35,138	7,833	6	210,630	81,158	49,018	943,922	8,632	20,286	1,356,625
South Dakota	7,600	1,511	17	29,497	7,763	8,666	131,113	988	10,198	197,353
Tennessee	64,484	9,154	18	284,612	113,758	60,847	1,424,891	10,515	30,967	1,999,246
Texas	398,515	27,630	12	1,518,148	597,506	238,069	5,525,177	44,055	179,761	8,528,871
Utah	26,410	545	39	101,112	22,811	22,498	258,536	3,178	16,107	451,237
Vermont	5,789	1,207	26	16,022	6,651	6,202	106,782	1,113	2,940	146,732
Virginia	48,603	9,798	101	254,641	95,123	42,115	1,051,801	10,753	25,426	1,538,363
Virgin Islands	655	280	0	2,296	300	2,473	86,936	335	600	93,875
Washington	46,069	5,377	212	199,785	57,388	69,292	1,268,735	12,112	27,942	1,686,912
West Virginia	15,523	1,617	11	81,167	42,364	16,685	440,299	4,102	10,848	612,616
Wisconsin	35,791	8,389	842	171,279	53,871	41,990	816,882	7,740	31,533	1,168,318
Wyoming	4,327	801	22	14,863	4,155	3,502	40,676	1,073	2,815	72,234
DoD [5]	0	0	0	6,146	16	0	0	0	1,997	8,160
Total [4]	3,321,867	415,410	7,885	12,586,736	4,397,694	3,386,954	60,608,261	540,227	1,644,069	86,909,103

[1] Excludes all administrative and program evaluation costs. [2] Excludes totals for Food Safety Education and Team Nutrition. [3] Includes distribution of bonus and entitlement commodities to the National School Lunch, Child and Adult Care, Summer Food Service, Charitable Institutions, Summer Camps, Food Distribution on Indian Reservations, Nutrition Services Incentive Program (NSIP, formerly Nutrition Program for the Elderly), Commodity Supplemental Food, and Disaster Feeding Programs. Also includes cash-in-lieu of commodities for the National School Lunch and the Child and Adult Care Food programs (NSIP cash grants were transferred to the Agency on Aging, DHHS, in FY 2003). [4] Excludes Nutrition Assistance grants for Puerto Rico, Northern Marianas, and American Samoa. [5] Dept. of Defense represents food service to children of armed forces personnel in overseas schools.

FNS, Budget Division/Program Reports, Analysis and Monitoring Branch (703) 305–2165.

Table 13-6.—Food and Nutrition Service Programs: Persons participating, fiscal years 2010–2019

Fiscal year	National School Lunch Program [1]	School Breakfast Program [1]	Child and Adult Care Program [2]	Summer Food Service [3]	WIC Program [4]
	Thousands	Thousands	Thousands	Thousands	Thousands
2010	31,753	11,669	3,411	2,304	9,175
2011	31,842	12,175	3,431	2,278	8,961
2012	31,653	12,868	3,571	2,348	8,908
2013	30,683	13,203	3,681	2,428	8,663
2014	30,460	13,636	3,897	2,663	8,258
2015	30,496	14,049	4,181	2,570	8,024
2016	30,361	14,564	4,407	2,569	7,696
2017	29,992	14,658	4,530	2,646	7,286
2018	29,624	14,681	4,629	2,689	6,870
2019	29,519	14,730	4,706	2,679	6,400

[1] Average monthly participation (excluding summer months). [2] Average daily attendance (data reported quarterly). [3] Average daily attendance for peak month (July). [4] Average monthly participation. WIC is an abbreviation for the Special Supplemental Food Program for Women, Infants and Children.

FNS, Budget Division/Program Reports, Analysis and Monitoring Branch, (703) 305–2165.

Table 13-7.—Food and Nutrition Service Programs: Federal costs of the National School Lunch, School Breakfast, Child Care Food, Summer Food Service, WIC, Special Milk, and Food Distribution Programs, fiscal years 2010–2019 [1]

Fiscal year [2]	Child Nutrition					WIC [6]	Special Milk	Food Distribution Programs [7]
	Cash payments				Cost of food distribution programs [5]			
	School Lunch	School Breakfast	Child & Adult Care [3]	Summer Food [4]				
	1,000 dollars	1,000 dollars	1,000 dollars	1,000 dollars	1,000 dollars	1,000 dollars	1,000 dollars	1,000 dollars
2010	9,751,742	2,859,231	2,397,545	314,794	1,223,249	6,689,911	11,926	895,761
2011	10,105,029	3,034,159	2,471,494	327,232	1,298,925	7,180,750	12,296	829,719
2012	10,414,295	3,276,989	2,589,619	350,378	1,278,804	6,801,320	12,295	755,894
2013	11,057,635	3,513,985	2,720,122	375,781	1,288,858	6,501,668	10,721	997,936
2014	11,356,023	3,685,352	2,848,901	409,418	1,437,493	6,356,356	10,495	938,923
2015	11,695,742	3,891,787	3,008,620	427,797	1,457,385	6,239,931	10,515	839,975
2016	12,258,568	4,211,848	3,216,683	417,789	1,466,849	6,020,420	9,061	977,274
2017	12,250,693	4,252,279	3,239,578	423,756	1,545,880	5,695,963	8,284	991,625
2018	12,579,977	4,396,483	3,321,813	415,949	1,401,743	5,445,183	7,888	995,869
2019	12,833,585	4,526,623	3,424,292	416,200	1,484,499	5,184,189	7,376	1,157,153

[1] See table 13-8 for Special Nutrition Assistance Program costs. [2] October 1–September 30. [3] Includes sponsor administrative, audit, and startup costs. [4] Includes sponsor administrative, State administrative and health clinic costs. [5] Includes entitlement commodities, bonus commodities, and cash-in-lieu for the National School Lunch, School Breakfast, Child and Adult Care Food, and Summer Food Service Programs. [6] Includes food costs, administrative costs, program evaluation funds, special grants, and Farmer's Market projects for the Special Supplemental Food Program for Women, Infants and Children. [7] Includes entitlement and bonus commodities, cash-in-lieu of commodities, and administrative costs of the following programs: Food Distribution to Indian Reservations, Nutrition Services Incentive Program (formerly Nutrition Program for the Elderly), Commodity Supplemental Food, Charitable Institutions, Summer Camps, Emergency Food Assistance Program (TEFAP), Disaster Feeding, Bureau of Federal Prisons, Veteran Affairs Administration, and the Food Stamp Program Elderly Pilot Project.

FNS, Budget Division/Program Reports, Analysis and Monitoring Branch, (703) 305–2165.

Table 13-8.—SNAP: Participation and federal costs, fiscal years 2010–2019

Fiscal year [1]	Average monthly participation [2]		Recipient benefits	Total cost [3]	Average monthly benefit	
	Persons	Housholds			Per person	Per household
	1,000	1,000	1,000 dollars	1,000 dollars	Dollars	Dollars
2010	40,302	18,618	64,702,165	68,283,468	133.79	289.60
2011	44,709	21,072	71,810,924	75,686,540	133.85	283.99
2012	46,609	22,330	74,619,345	78,411,096	133.41	278.48
2013	47,636	23,052	76,066,319	79,859,028	133.07	274.98
2014	46,664	22,744	69,998,836	74,060,327	125.01	256.47
2015	45,767	22,522	69,645,138	73,946,652	126.81	257.69
2016	44,220	21,778	66,539,269	70,913,549	125.40	254.61
2017	42,228	20,901	63,711,051	68,174,548	125.73	254.02
2018	39,431	19,566	58,996,500	63,524,579	124.68	251.27
2019	34,474	17,374	53,761,254	58,277,365	129.96	257.86

SNAP is the Special Nutrition Assistance Program, formerly known as the Food Stamp Program. [1] October 1 to September 30. [2] Participation data are 12-month averages. [3] Total cost includes matching funds for state administrative expenses (e.g., certification of households, quality control, anti-fraud activities; employment and training); and for other Federal costs (e.g., benefit redemption processing; computer support; electronic benefit transfer systems; retailer redemption and monitoring; certification of SSI recipients; nutrition education and program information).

FNS, Budget Division/Program Reports, Analysis and Monitoring Branch, (703) 305–2165.

CHAPTER XIV

STATISTICS OF FERTILIZERS AND PESTICIDES

This chapter contains statistics on percentages of crop acres treated by various types of fertilizers and pesticides. Nitrogen, phosphate, potash, and sulfur are the most common fertilizers; herbicides, insecticides, fungicides, and other chemicals are the main categories of pesticides. Other chemicals include soil fumigants, vine killers, and desiccants. The tables show data for field crops for 2010-2019, fruits for 2019, and vegetables for 2018. NASS collects data for field crops on an annual basis. The surveyed States are generally the major producing States for each crop shown in the tables and represent 65-95 percent of the U.S. planted acres, depending on the selected crop.

Application data for specific pesticide active ingredients and additional fertilizer data are available in the series of NASS ''Agricultural Chemical Usage'' reports and data sets.

Table 14-1.—Field crops: Fertilizer, and percent of area receiving applications, all States surveyed, 2010–2019 [1]

Crop	Nitrogen	Phosphate	Potash	Sulfur
	Percent	*Percent*	*Percent*	*Percent*
2010:				
Corn	97	78	61	15
Cotton, Upland	90	62	52	42
Potatoes, Fall	99	96	90	73
2011:				
Barley	86	68	28	30
Sorghum	81	54	9	16
2012:				
Soybeans	27	37	37	7
Wheat, Durum	98	89	12	12
Wheat, Other Spring	97	87	27	20
Wheat, Winter	85	55	13	19
2013:				
Rice	97	75	54	23
Peanuts	40	42	42	17
2014:				
Corn	97	80	65	29
Potatoes, Fall	99	97	90	79
2015:				
Cotton	78	56	42	30
Oats	76	62	40	24
Soybeans	28	39	38	8
Wheat, Spring (Excl Durum)	97	89	40	30
Wheat, Spring Durum	98	95	32	31
Wheat, Winter	88	60	16	22
2016:				
Corn	97	79	65	33
Potatoes, Fall	98	92	90	76
2017:				
Cotton	78	59	45	38
Soybeans	31	41	42	9
Wheat, Durum	98	91	28	36
Wheat, Other Spring	96	89	34	38
Wheat, Winter	83	58	15	25
2018:				
Corn	98	79	63	32
Peanuts	32	32	33	12
Soybeans	29	42	43	10
2019:				
Barley	86	72	26	48
Sorghum	89	58	10	21
Wheat, Spring (Excl Durum)	97	89	31	32
Wheat, Spring Durum	98	84	11	24
Wheat, Winter	88	63	15	27

[1] Refers to percent of planted acres receiving one or more applications of a specific fertilizer ingredient. See tables 14-2 through 14-21 for surveyed States.

Note: See planted acreage estimates in tables 1-56 for barley, 1-36 for corn, 2-2 for upland and all cotton, 1-48 for oats, 3-16 for peanuts, 1-27 for rice, 1-65 for sorghum, 3-32 for soybeans and 1-8 for wheat.

NASS, Environmental, Economics, and Demographics Branch, (202) 720–6146.

Table 14-2.—Barley: Pesticide usage, 2011 and 2019 [1]

State and Year	Percent treated and amount applied							
	Herbicide		Insecticide		Fungicide		Other Chemicals	
	Area applied	Pounds applied	Area applied	Pounds applied	Area applied	Pounds applied	Area applied	Pounds applied
	Percent	Thousands	Percent	Thousands	Percent	Thousands	Percent	Thousands
Arizona:								
2011	37	16	*	*	....	....	....	....
2019	*	*	*	*	....	....	....	....
California:								
2011	39	48	*	*	....	....	....	....
2019	21	7	*	*	....	....	....	....
Colorado:								
2011	96	36	22	1	25	2	....	....
2019	90	23	*	*	*	*	....	....
Idaho:								
2011	91	302	11	1	18	11	14	27
2019	89	326	6	2	11	7	9	6
Minnesota:								
2011	58	19	10	2	32	3	....	....
2019	89	24	34	1	68	11	....	....
Montana:								
2011	92	1,065	*	*	26	16	*	*
2019	84	949	*	*	3	5	*	*
North Dakota:								
2011	95	236	6	4	48	26	....	....
2019	94	304	*	*	63	52	*	*
Oregon:								
2011	74	21	*	*	31	1	*	*
2019	70	33	*	*	*	*	*	*
Pennsylvania:								
2011	39	7	*	*	3	**	....	....
2019	61	7	*	*	6	**	....	....
South Dakota:								
2019	*	*	....	....	....	....	....	....
Virginia:								
2011	59	29	20	**	15	1	*	*
2019	71	17	*	*	18	1	....	....
Washington:								
2011	93	111	....	....	19	2	....	....
2019	96	68	*	*	10	1	....	....
Wisconsin:								
2011	25	4	....	....	....	....	....	....
2019	17	2	*	*	....	....	*	*
Wyoming:								
2011	76	32	*	*	13	1	....	....
2019	68	30	22	**	16	1	....	....

*Insufficient number of reports to publish data.　　**Amount applied is less than 500 lbs. [1] Data not available for all States for all years.

Note: Planted acres are in table 1-56.

NASS, Environmental, Economics, and Demographics Branch, (202) 720–6146.

Table 14-3.—Barley: Fertilizer usage, 2011 and 2019[1]

State	Percent treated and amount applied							
	Nitrogen		Phosphate		Potash		Sulfur	
	Area applied	Pounds applied	Area applied	Pounds applied	Area applied	Pounds applied	Area applied	Pounds applied
	Percent	*Millions*	*Percent*	*Millions*	*Percent*	*Millions*	*Percent*	*Millions*
Arizona								
2011	97	8.2	39	1.5	*	*	21	0.3
2019	96	1.6	34	0.5	....	....	*	*
California:								
2011	41	2.6	*	*	....	....	14	0.2
2019	38	1.5	23	0.4	*	*	*	*
Colorado:								
2011	82	7.2	40	1.5	28	0.6	36	0.4
2019	89	5.0	81	3.3	*	*	*	*
Idaho:								
2011	93	44.2	66	10.0	37	4.9	65	9.6
2019	93	42.2	57	12.2	21	4.9	69	6.6
Minnesota:								
2011	60	3.3	56	1.3	44	1.0	11	0.1
2019	89	5.5	77	2.2	78	2.0	43	0.3
Montana:								
2011	90	29.1	83	16.6	37	3.6	16	1.2
2019	84	33.0	79	18.2	32	3.5	55	4.3
North Dakota:								
2011	96	28.3	92	11.1	16	1.0	4	0.1
2019	92	42.0	85	18.8	20	1.5	29	1.7
Oregon:								
2011	77	1.6	26	0.1	*	*	36	0.1
2019	100	2.7	6	0.6	*	*	60	0.2
Pennsylvania:								
2011	64	1.9	32	0.8	32	0.8	10	0.1
2019	72	1.2	16	0.3	16	0.2	28	0.1
South Dakota:								
2019	63	1.8	60	0.8	....	....	*	*
Virginia:								
2011	77	4.9	39	1.7	35	1.7	24	0.3
2019	56	1.0	19	0.2	18	0.4	15	0.1
Washington:								
2011	91	9.0	59	1.1	9	0.2	90	1.6
2019	94	6.4	81	1.2	20	0.3	82	1.2
Wisconsin:								
2011	34	0.2	*	*	34	1.0	14	0.1
2019	23	0.3	15	0.1	23	0.5	8	**
Wyoming:								
2011	73	5.2	55	1.8	30	0.8	18	0.4
2019	93	6.2	79	2.0	58	1.5	20	0.2

*Insufficient number of reports to publish data.   **Area applied is less than 0.5 percent.   [1] Data not available for all States for all years.

Note: Planted acres are in table 1-56.

NASS, Environmental, Economics, and Demographics Branch, (202) 720–6146.

Table 14-4.—Corn: Pesticide usage, 2014–2018 [1][2]

State	Percent treated and amount applied							
	Herbicide		Insecticide [2]		Fungicide [2]		Other Chemicals	
	Area applied	Pounds applied	Area applied	Pounds applied	Area applied	Pounds applied	Area applied	Pounds applied
	Percent	*Thousands*	*Percent*	*Thousands*	*Percent*	*Thousands*	*Percent*	*Thousands*
Colorado:								
2016	85	3,819	23	94	(D)	(D)	(D)	(D)
2018	93	2,978	11	69	6	46	(D)	(D)
Georgia:								
2016	98	1,417	22	38	31	30	....	....
2018	....	....	....	....	....	....	....	....
Illinois:								
2014	98	26,870	23	237	21	321	(D)	(D)
2016	99	32,524	18	146	19	256	(D)	(D)
2018	97	31,289	20	149	31	604	(D)	(D)
Indiana:								
2014	100	14,609	9	45	12	80	(D)	(D)
2016	99	14,689	17	78	16	144	(D)	(D)
2018	98	14,345	12	25	28	1,481	(D)	(D)
Iowa:								
2014	95	30,240	13	122	19	296	(D)	(D)
2016	97	35,858	10	280	22	438	(D)	(D)
2018	95	32,371	18	274	32	706	(D)	(D)
Kansas:								
2014	97	11,432	10	244	3	13	....	....
2016	98	18,892	6	500	(D)	(D)	(D)	(D)
2018	98	16,373	5	175	5	39	....	....
Kentucky:								
2014	94	4,102	29	15	11	19	(D)	(D)
2016	95	6,263	30	26	26	49	(D)	(D)
2018	97	4,787	20	22	16	82	(D)	(D)
Michigan:								
2014	98	5,710	4	5	12	36	....	....
2016	93	4,845	6	21	(D)	(D)	(D)	(D)
2018	98	4,999	8	13	5	71	4	7
Minnesota:								
2014	98	13,596	2	26	(D)	(D)	(D)	(D)
2016	97	16,461	7	43	3	32	....	....
2018	99	15,885	8	50	4	63	(D)	(D)
Missouri:								
2014	98	8,517	24	43	14	61	....	....
2016	92	10,121	12	16	(D)	(D)	....	....
2018	92	11,451	19	102	12	70	(D)	(D)
Nebraska:								
2014	95	21,320	16	213	10	118	(D)	(D)
2016	95	27,905	15	186	10	142	(D)	(D)
2018	99	30,070	16	618	20	309	(D)	(D)
New York:								
2016	98	2,370	(D)	(D)	....	....	(D)	(D)
2018	93	2,279	5	4	....	....	(D)	(D)
North Carolina:								
2016	95	3,447	5	3	(D)	(D)	(D)	(D)
2018	96	3,082	16	15	13	53	(D)	(D)
North Dakota:								
2014	97	4,489	(D)	(D)	4	16	....	....
2016	100	6,242	(D)	(D)	(D)	(D)	....	....
2018	99	5,481	(D)	(D)	(D)	(D)	(D)	(D)
Ohio:								
2014	99	9,231	13	64	9	81	(D)	(D)
2016	98	9,025	17	45	13	39	(D)	(D)
2018	100	10,650	19	32	12	124	6	336
Pennsylvania:								
2014	97	4,080	20	46	4	6	4	2
2016	96	4,446	23	12	9	17	(D)	(D)
2018	92	3,840	23	10	9	12	(D)	(D)
South Dakota:								
2014	98	10,803	(D)	(D)	9	47	....	....
2016	99	13,157	(D)	(D)	(D)	(D)	....	....
2018	99	13,471	(D)	(D)	(D)	(D)	(D)	(D)
Texas:								
2014	89	4,338	14	528	23	27	(D)	(D)
2016	84	5,992	13	364	26	40	....	....
2018	92	4,027	16	492	13	61	5	48
Wisconsin:								
2014	90	6,952	8	22	(D)	(D)	(D)	(D)
2016	98	8,572	12	24	5	6	....	....
2018	97	7,344	8	21	6	30	(D)	(D)

(D) Withheld to avoid disclosing data for individual operations.   [1] Data not available for all States for all years.   [2] Amount applied excludes Bt (bacillus thuringiensis) and other biologicals.
Note: Planted acres are in table 1-36.
NASS, Environmental, Economics, and Demographics Branch, (202) 720–6146.

Table 14-5.—Corn: Fertilizer usage, 2014–2018 [1]

State and Year	Percent treated and amount applied							
	Nitrogen		Phosphate		Potash		Sulfur	
	Area applied	Pounds applied	Area applied	Pounds applied	Area applied	Pounds applied	Area applied	Pounds applied
	Percent	*Millions*	*Percent*	*Millions*	*Percent*	*Millions*	*Percent*	*Millions*
Colorado:								
2016	96	149.8	66	31.3	13	2.9	38	8.4
2018	92	206.5	77	51.7	32	16.3	47	12.8
Georgia:								
2016	97	74.2	84	23.4	88	46.8	43	4.0
2018	....	....	....	....	....	....	....	....
Illinois:								
2014	99	1,918.3	85	938.4	81	1,066.9	8	17.5
2016	98	1,908.8	86	892.7	81	1,036.9	15	43.1
2018	98	1,851.6	87	1,042.6	77	1,139.2	20	40.0
Indiana:								
2014	96	877.7	81	351.1	79	530.5	22	16.0
2016	98	895.1	78	321.4	85	517.6	30	21.1
2018	100	842.0	91	310.9	80	455.0	43	38.2
Iowa:								
2014	96	1,842.2	64	600.5	63	705.3	18	40.2
2016	98	2,036.1	67	701.1	70	938.8	21	45.3
2018	97	1,784.3	71	698.2	70	823.4	22	51.0
Kansas:								
2014	98	549.6	87	148.5	35	60.5	29	10.1
2016	99	721.2	88	165.1	48	61.3	33	10.6
2018	100	798.2	75	246.2	39	117.5	31	21.3
Kentucky:								
2014	98	214.1	88	109.0	87	119.0	14	4.5
2016	96	249.7	82	97.0	87	121.4	23	9.6
2018	98	195.0	90	106.9	88	128.1	19	5.3
Michigan:								
2014	98	338.7	84	89.2	82	192.6	25	7.4
2016	94	276.0	80	83.9	71	141.2	35	11.6
2018	97	322.4	79	86.1	71	156.4	29	7.5
Minnesota:								
2014	94	1,091.8	86	491.4	80	570.2	51	72.5
2016	96	1,126.0	86	442.8	75	495.2	43	63.8
2018	96	1,041.9	79	462.6	72	517.2	37	56.1
Missouri:								
2014	98	603.3	81	191.1	83	228.0	32	16.2
2016	97	590.7	69	173.0	74	213.9	40	20.1
2018	98	577.9	83	208.4	82	226.8	27	16.7
Nebraska:								
2014	99	1,359.9	77	329.9	29	100.8	42	71.6
2016	100	1,400.1	79	314.6	35	65.3	41	68.6
2018	99	1,569.9	73	361.8	25	75.3	38	74.7
New York:								
2016	98	77.6	70	25.2	60	31.7	24	4.0
2018	97	103.0	79	30.9	69	46.6	16	2.2
North Carolina:								
2016	91	127.7	63	32.6	68	62.8	35	7.5
2018	94	125.7	74	39.4	76	63.2	26	10.1
North Dakota:								
2014	99	349.7	88	132.1	44	34.7	43	12.3
2016	97	446.5	92	195.4	59	63.6	56	32.4
2018	97	444.3	88	165.7	62	66.1	40	20.3
Ohio:								
2014	98	558.8	85	228.9	80	282.2	15	5.1
2016	99	585.4	87	225.6	79	302.4	31	22.9
2018	99	604.7	81	225.5	68	258.1	26	12.8
Pennsylvania:								
2014	96	137.7	67	39.7	66	40.5	35	5.6
2016	91	124.4	41	23.8	46	30.4	47	11.2
2018	94	155.6	55	30.7	48	34.6	34	7.3
South Dakota:								
2014	97	684.8	83	216.4	50	113.2	35	24.0
2016	99	715.9	87	249.9	52	136.1	44	36.2
2018	99	657.0	88	258.1	60	147.0	44	52.0
Texas:								
2014	95	310.5	77	77.9	37	19.2	43	10.7
2016	87	313.3	60	59.5	22	12.7	36	11.4
2018	97	301.8	73	68.1	40	23.0	41	10.2
Wisconsin:								
2014	98	407.6	85	127.9	88	222.2	49	31.7
2016	96	427.2	78	103.8	84	217.3	55	36.0
2018	97	426.2	80	116.6	79	232.2	38	29.9

[1] Data not available for all States for all years.
Note: Planted acres are in table 1-36.
NASS, Environmental, Economics, and Demographics Branch, (202) 720–6146.

Table 14-6.—Cotton, Upland: Pesticide usage, 2017–2019 [1]

State and Year	Herbicide Area applied	Herbicide Pounds applied	Insecticide [2] Area applied	Insecticide [2] Pounds applied	Fungicide Area applied	Fungicide Pounds applied	Other Chemicals Area applied	Other Chemicals Pounds applied
	Percent	Thousands	Percent	Thousands	Percent	Thousands	Percent	Thousands
Alabama:								
2017	99	1,422	66	120	(D)	(D)	100	919
2019	100	1,900	78	166	....	....	97	954
Arizona:								
2019	91	329	63	41	....	....	91	82
Arkansas:								
2017	86	1,681	94	786	6	7	100	1,400
2019	98	2,210	98	1,057	8	15	100	1,895
California:								
2019	99	609	96	226	(D)	(D)	85	620
Georgia:								
2017	99	4,409	71	348	1	9	99	3,185
2019	100	4,445	73	486	8	31	91	2,574
Louisiana:								
2019	99	1,297	97	496	(D)	(D)	100	592
Mississippi:								
2017	99	3,017	93	1,271	(D)	(D)	96	1,675
2019	100	3,116	89	1,321	(D)	(D)	96	1,438
Missouri:								
2017	100	1,037	92	382	18	9	100	730
2019	100	1,126	90	485	(D)	(D)	100	1,205
North Carolina:								
2017	98	1,378	81	140	(D)	(D)	91	699
2019	100	2,002	95	343	(D)	(D)	99	896
Oklahoma:								
2017	59	765	38	112	....	....	15	173
2019	90	2,501	48	247	(D)	(D)	71	767
South Carolina:								
2019	94	1,153	87	86	(D)	(D)	91	716
Tennessee:								
2017	98	1,266	96	429	(D)	(D)	100	739
2019	98	1,711	100	385	(D)	(D)	97	786
Texas:								
2017	90	14,554	23	881	....	....	58	4,366
2019	88	21,076	32	2,412	(D)	(D)	41	3,744

(D) Withheld to avoid disclosing data for individual operations. [1] Data not available for all States for all years. [2] Amount applied excludes Bt (bacillus thuringiensis) and other biologicals.

Note: Planted acres are in table 2-2.

NASS, Environmental, Economics, and Demographics Branch, (202) 720–6146.

Table 14-7.—Cotton, Upland: Fertilizer usage, 2017–2019 [1]

State and Year	Percent treated and amount applied							
	Nitrogen		Phosphate		Potash		Sulfur	
	Area applied	Pounds applied	Area applied	Pounds applied	Area applied	Pounds applied	Area applied	Pounds applied
	Percent	Millions	Percent	Millions	Percent	Millions	Percent	Millions
Alabama:								
2017	93	42.0	72	19.5	81	29.3	38	2.6
2019	98	57.0	78	23.9	96	46.2	48	5.0
Arizona:								
2019	96	23.3	28	2.3	(D)	(D)	(D)	(D)
Arkansas:								
2017	97	69.2	74	17.5	79	35.3	53	4.8
2019	99	89.9	83	28.1	94	53.3	36	5.4
California:								
2019	95	31.5	26	2.0	(D)	(D)	(D)	(D)
Georgia:								
2017	100	143.5	81	58.0	91	103.7	63	14.3
2019	98	140.0	88	71.2	93	125.1	41	10.9
Louisiana:								
2019	94	23.9	70	11.6	69	18.9	61	2.3
Mississippi:								
2017	99	72.4	47	15.2	60	34.6	37	3.7
2019	97	82.7	43	18.9	73	54.1	36	3.4
Missouri:								
2017	98	33.3	87	12.4	96	20.5	62	3.3
2019	100	41.6	91	15.8	86	26.1	41	1.8
North Carolina:								
2017	96	30.6	67	12.4	87	32.0	56	6.6
2019	97	45.3	52	13.3	89	43.7	41	7.7
Oklahoma:								
2017	54	31.8	44	11.4	19	4.8	7	0.3
2019	63	47.5	58	14.8	29	3.6	11	0.9
South Carolina:								
2019	92	28.3	59	8.5	88	30.9	45	2.6
Tennessee:								
2017	100	35.0	99	19.0	95	29.9	82	3.3
2019	100	40.7	94	21.2	100	38.4	84	4.5
Texas:								
2017	68	363.7	52	133.2	25	35.1	31	26.0
2019	79	316.8	54	113.4	22	17.7	42	27.8

(D) Withheld to avoid disclosing data for individual operations. [1] Data not available for all States for all years.
Note: Planted acres are in table 2-3.
NASS, Environmental, Economics, and Demographics Branch, (202) 720–6146.

Table 14-8.—Peanuts: Pesticide usage, 2013 and 2018 [1]

State and Year	Percent treated and amount applied							
	Herbicide		Insecticide		Fungicide		Other Chemicals	
	Area applied	Pounds applied	Area applied	Pounds applied	Area applied	Pounds applied	Area applied	Pounds applied
	Percent	Thousands	Percent	Thousands	Percent	Thousands	Percent	Thousands
Alabama:								
2013	99	219	32	33	95	632	*	*
2018	99	312	37	13	95	469	....	1
Florida:								
2013	93	237	59	28	100	670	*	*
2018	96	250	47	34	94	471	(D)	(D)
Georgia:								
2013	100	853	48	177	97	1,692	*	*
2018	98	1,187	40	78	98	2,738	5	2
North Carolina:								
2013	99	190	71	54	87	144	*	*
2018	97	299	58	38	92	173	27	18
South Carolina:								
2013	96	150	60	33	81	261	....	....
2018	95	232	34	13	80	221	(D)	(D)
Texas:								
2013	65	93	11	2	33	42	....	....
2018	73	123	4	1	38	38	(D)	(D)

* Insufficient number of reports to publish data.　(D) Withheld to avoid disclosing data for individual operations.　[1] Data not available for all States for all years.
Note: Planted acres are in table 3-16.
NASS, Environmental, Economics, and Demographics Branch, (202) 720–6146.

Table 14-9.—Peanuts: Fertilizer usage, 2013 and 2018 [1]

State and Year	Percent treated and amount applied							
	Nitrogen		Phosphate		Potash		Sulfur	
	Area applied	Pounds applied	Area applied	Pounds applied	Area applied	Pounds applied	Area applied	Pounds applied
	Percent	Millions	Percent	Millions	Percent	Millions	Percent	Millions
Alabama:								
2013	48	1.5	54	3.0	57	5.2	19	0.6
2018	41	1.5	41	3.0	41	3.9	8	0.2
Florida:								
2013	81	2.2	86	4.9	93	11.7	36	1.3
2018	40	1.6	36	2.5	40	7.0	(D)	(D)
Georgia:								
2013	27	2.1	31	6.5	26	6.5	*	*
2018	22	2.6	26	6.8	26	10.4	7	0.8
North Carolina:								
2013	21	0.5	22	0.7	51	4.1	23	0.5
2018	(D)	(D)	(D)	(D)	56	5.4	14	0.2
South Carolina:								
2013	13	0.5	14	0.4	22	1.5	*	*
2018	(D)	(D)	(D)	(D)	10	0.9	(D)	(D)
Texas:								
2013	57	5.3	47	2.4	34	1.4	37	0.7
2018	74	7.1	66	3.3	48	2.5	43	0.8

* Insufficient number of reports to publish data.　(D) Withheld to avoid disclosing data for individual operations.　[1] Data not available for all States for all years.
Note: Planted acres are in table 3-16.
NASS, Environmental, Economics, and Demographics Branch, (202) 720–6146.

Table 14-10.—Oats: Pesticide usage, 2005 and 2015[1]

State and Year	Percent treated and amount applied					
	Herbicide		Insecticide		Fungicide	
	Area applied	Pounds applied	Area applied	Pounds applied	Area applied	Pounds applied
	Percent	Thousands	Percent	Thousands	Percent	Thousands
California:						
2005	36	59	....	....	....	....
Idaho:						
2005	26	17	....	....	....	....
Illinois:						
2005	7	1	....	....	....	....
2015	(D)	(D)	....	....	(D)	(D)
Iowa:						
2005	3	2	....	....	....	....
2015	(D)	(D)	....	....	(D)	(D)
Kansas:						
2005	27	13	....	....	....	....
2015	41	28	....	....	(D)	(D)
Michigan:						
2005	61	26	....	....	....	....
2015	66	33	(D)	(D)	(D)	(D)
Minnesota:						
2005	21	26	....	....	....	....
2015	43	66	(D)	(D)	13	4
Montana:						
2005	34	18	....	....	....	....
Nebraska:						
2005	7	4	....	....	....	....
2015	35	21	....	....	(D)	(D)
New York:						
2005	51	23	....	....	....	....
2015	63	26	(D)	(D)	(D)	(D)
North Dakota:						
2005	54	167	....	....	....	....
2015	82	186	(D)	(D)	9	2
Ohio:						
2015	59	22	....	....	....	....
Pennsylvania:						
2005	58	46	....	....	....	....
2015	60	43	(D)	(D)	....	....
South Dakota:						
2005	37	52	....	....	....	....
2015	81	130	(D)	(D)	21	9
Texas:						
2005	26	80	18	35	....	....
2015	45	95	14	28	9	10
Wisconsin:						
2005	18	25	....	....	....	....
2015	30	37	(D)	(D)	6	2

(D) Withheld to avoid disclosing data for individual operations.   [1] Data not available for all States for all years.
Note: Planted acres are in table 1-48.
NASS, Environmental, Economics, and Demographics Branch, (202) 720–6146.

Table 14-11.—Oats: Fertilizer usage, 2005 and 2015[1]

State and Year	Percent treated and amount applied							
	Nitrogen		Phosphate		Potash		Sulfur	
	Area applied	Pounds applied	Area applied	Pounds applied	Area applied	Pounds applied	Area applied	Pounds applied
	Percent	Millions	Percent	Millions	Percent	Millions	Percent	Millions
California:								
2005	26	4.4	....	....	....	....	....	....
Idaho:								
2005	42	1.6	22	1.4	5	0.1	12	0.2
Illinois:								
2005	15	0.4	12	0.4	26	1.7	....	....
2015	28	0.4	20	0.5	28	0.9	(D)	(D)
Iowa:								
2005	31	1.8	30	2.5	40	6.9	....	....
2015	27	1.4	26	2.1	28	2.7	11	0.3
Kansas:								
2005	84	4.4	39	1.4	17	0.8	....	....
2015	87	4.5	33	0.9	12	0.3	(D)	(D)
Michigan:								
2005	82	2.6	72	2.8	77	3.4	....	....
2015	81	2.0	75	1.7	78	2.0	6	(Z)
Minnesota:								
2005	28	4.2	22	2.4	28	5.9	5	0.2
2015	60	8.3	50	3.6	53	6.7	21	0.7
Montana:								
2005	53	2.0	35	1.0	14	0.4	9	0.1
Nebraska:								
2005	68	4.5	24	1.3	7	0.1	5	....
2015	77	5.1	65	2.6	36	0.8	29	0.4
New York:								
2005	75	1.9	72	2.7	72	2.8	....	....
2015	66	1.3	63	1.7	62	1.8	(D)	(D)
North Dakota:								
2005	71	15.8	49	5.7	9	0.7	5	0.1
2015	88	12.1	70	7.2	27	0.9	22	0.6
Ohio:								
2015	70	1.3	69	2.2	66	2.7	(D)	(D)
Pennsylvania:								
2005	90	4.5	81	4.9	82	5.1	2	0.1
2015	81	2.2	76	2.9	75	2.7	(D)	(D)
South Dakota:								
2005	64	11.8	46	5.6	17	1.7	....	....
2015	91	22.1	74	9.2	20	1.1	17	0.7
Texas:								
2005	79	45.4	56	12.7	39	4.9	25	1.7
2015	97	27.8	82	12.1	39	3.2	51	3.0
Wisconsin:								
2005	23	2.1	24	3.9	35	15.1	8	0.4
2015	51	3.9	36	2.9	45	8.4	21	1.0

(D) Withheld to avoid disclosing data for individual operations. (Z) Less than half the rounding unit.   [1] Data not available for all States for all years.

Note: Planted acres are in table 1-48.

NASS, Environmental, Economics, and Demographics Branch, (202) 720–6146.

Table 14-12.—Potatoes, Fall: Pesticide usage, 2010–2016[1]

State and Year	Percent treated and amount applied							
	Herbicide		Insecticide[2]		Fungicide		Other Chemicals	
	Area applied	Pounds applied	Area applied	Pounds applied	Area applied	Pounds applied	Area applied	Pounds applied
	Percent	Thousands	Percent	Thousands	Percent	Thousands	Percent	Thousands
Colorado:								
2010	92	173	93	108	98	191	74	5,156
2014	78	83	50	37	96	120	74	5,696
2016	73	73	77	8	74	87	(D)	(D)
Idaho:								
2010	98	829	67	190	93	983	63	36,080
2014	89	717	89	287	95	1,618	57	36,437
2016	92	662	65	81	99	846	49	23,552
Maine:								
2010	93	36	91	8	100	373	73	30
2014	97	30	84	9	90	329	78	37
2016	90	46	93	5	99	402	22	31
Michigan:								
2010	90	70	90	18	96	298	67	46
2014	99	86	96	32	99	442	73	35
2016	99	118	100	24	99	511	....	....
Minnesota:								
2010	90	44	99	9	100	586	48	3,099
2014	91	34	93	13	91	612	52	4,067
2016	90	90	94	7	98	879	(D)	(D)
North Dakota:								
2010	89	71	85	13	96	874	60	6,872
2014	90	71	89	10	99	801	30	1,653
2016	98	103	96	33	100	1,943	(D)	(D)
Washington:								
2010	98	376	97	392	99	1,197	80	16,901
2014	92	566	98	489	99	1,109	87	16,635
2016	100	662	98	205	98	1,472	56	14,517
Wisconsin:								
2010	82	73	91	12	96	866	92	2,742
2014	95	96	99	16	100	987	96	4,913
2016	99	120	84	39	100	825	48	4,502

(D) Withheld to avoid disclosing data for individual operations. [1] Data not available for all States for all years. [2] Amount applied excludes Bt (bacillus thuringiensis) and other biologicals.
NASS, Environmental, Economics, and Demographics Branch, (202) 720–6146.

Table 14-13.—Potatoes, Fall: Fertilizer usage, 2010–2016 [1]

State and Year	Nitrogen		Phosphate		Potash		Sulfur	
	Area applied	Pounds applied	Area applied	Pounds applied	Area applied	Pounds applied	Area applied	Pounds applied
	Percent	*Millions*	*Percent*	*Millions*	*Percent*	*Millions*	*Percent*	*Millions*
Colorado:								
2010	97	10.0	92	10.4	66	3.9	93	5.2
2014	94	9.2	93	7.2	70	1.6	94	2.6
2016	93	7.8	93	9.1	86	6.3	92	2.3
Idaho:								
2010	100	75.0	96	53.2	91	35.9	81	30.0
2014	99	78.1	98	47.5	85	36.3	90	23.6
2016	100	88.3	94	62.5	94	43.3	83	29.3
Maine:								
2010	99	8.8	99	8.2	95	10.2	(D)	(D)
2014	98	8.3	98	7.1	98	8.7	12	0.1
2016	98	8.5	96	7.0	98	10.4	5	(Z)
Michigan:								
2010	100	8.6	98	3.5	100	8.6	(D)	(D)
2014	100	7.9	99	3.8	100	9.6	52	1.7
2016	100	8.8	99	2.8	99	10.0	87	2.2
Minnesota:								
2010	98	9.2	100	4.6	100	14.6	80	1.3
2014	100	6.2	88	2.8	80	5.9	66	0.9
2016	99	6.7	98	3.0	91	5.7	73	1.7
North Dakota:								
2010	100	15.1	89	7.9	84	14.3	44	1.3
2014	100	12.3	97	8.9	100	8.7	79	1.7
2016	100	16.0	99	8.8	81	14.0	52	1.3
Washington:								
2010	100	32.6	99	24.9	94	36.0	90	9.7
2014	100	29.2	100	20.1	97	18.2	82	7.2
2016	95	30.6	75	19.0	81	18.3	80	8.1
Wisconsin:								
2010	100	16.5	100	5.3	93	17.7	91	3.9
2014	100	15.0	96	5.4	99	20.8	89	4.2
2016	100	15.5	100	5.9	98	20.5	90	4.5

(D) Withheld to avoid disclosing data for individual operations.   (Z) Less than half of rounding unit for data item shown (see data item definition for rounding unit).   [1] Data not available for all States for all years.
NASS, Environmental, Economics, and Demographics Branch, (202) 720–6146.

Table 14-14.—Rice: Pesticide usage, 2006 and 2013 [1]

State and Year	Percent treated and amount applied							
	Herbicide		Insecticide		Fungicide		Other Chemicals	
	Area applied	Pounds applied	Area applied	Pounds applied	Area applied	Pounds applied	Area applied	Pounds applied
	Percent	Thousands	Percent	Thousands	Percent	Thousands	Percent	Thousands
Arkansas:								
2006	95	3,054	10	14	37	109	5	269
2013	97	2,646	30	10	45	103	5	251
California:								
2006	93	2,500	14	2	50	738	....	....
2013	96	2,986	28	6	45	553	*	*
Louisiana:								
2006	96	475	42	49	46	30	....	....
2013	99	680	17	13	73	82	*	*
Mississippi:								
2006	100	502	55	14	46	16	3	36
2013	100	364	51	2	35	9	6	37
Missouri:								
2006	100	454	....	....	25	12	....	....
2013	100	512	18	1	55	22	20	159
Texas:								
2006	97	496	77	83	55	21	....	....
2013	88	263	35	3	35	11	*	*

* Insufficient number of reports to publish data. [1] Data not available for all States for all years.
Note: Planted acres are in table 1-27.
NASS, Environmental, Economics, and Demographics Branch, (202) 720–6146.

Table 14-15.—Rice: Fertilizer usage, 2006 and 2013 [1]

State and Year	Percent treated and amount applied							
	Nitrogen		Phosphate		Potash		Sulfur	
	Area applied	Pounds applied	Area applied	Pounds applied	Area applied	Pounds applied	Area applied	Pounds applied
	Percent	Millions	Percent	Millions	Percent	Millions	Percent	Millions
Arkansas:								
2006	97	281.2	68	54.7	60	64.9	9	6.0
2013	96	195.8	76	53.2	56	51.3	14	2.1
California:								
2006	94	61.4	75	18.2	40	7.2	31	4.0
2013	98	83.9	81	21.2	38	7.2	41	4.4
Louisiana:								
2006	99	52.8	78	14.6	75	16.2	4	0.3
2013	100	63.9	87	16.0	79	23.0	14	1.3
Mississippi:								
2006	99	35.8	29	2.5	4	0.5	42	1.5
2013	100	23.3	13	0.8	*	*	50	1.2
Missouri:								
2006	100	45.2	47	5.5	42	5.7	29	0.7
2013	100	32.7	56	4.7	*	*	29	0.6
Texas:								
2006	97	29.2	92	5.8	89	6.0	30	0.6
2013	90	22.3	82	5.5	79	5.4	11	0.1

* Insufficient number of reports to publish data. [1] Data not available for all States for all years.
Note: Planted acres are in table 1-27.
NASS, Environmental, Economics, and Demographics Branch, (202) 720–6146.

Table 14-16.—Sorghum: Pesticide usage, 2011 and 2019 [1]

State and Year	Percent treated and amount applied							
	Herbicide		Insecticide		Fungicide		Other chemicals	
	Area applied	Pounds applied	Area applied	Pounds applied	Area applied	Pounds applied	Area applied	Pounds applied
	Percent	Thousands	Percent	Thousands	Percent	Thousands	Percent	Thousands
Colorado:								
2011	75	285	....	....	....	....	....	....
2019	96	1,129	....	....	....	....	....	....
Kansas:								
2011	96	9,411	4	3	....	....	....	....
2019	94	9,471	(D)	(D)	....	....	(D)	(D)
Missouri:								
2019	....	....	(D)	(D)	(D)	(D)	....	....
Nebraska:								
2011	84	362	(D)	(D)	....	....	....	....
2019	100	760	(D)	(D)	(D)	(D)	....	....
New Mexico:								
2019	....	....	(D)	(D)	....	....	....	....
Oklahoma:								
2011	74	505	(D)	(D)	....	....	....	....
2019	87	539	(D)	(D)	(D)	(D)	....	....
South Dakota:								
2011	89	289	(D)	(D)	....	....	....	....
2019	100	786	(D)	(D)	....	....	....	....
Texas:								
2011	72	1,901	10	9	(D)	(D)	....	....
2019	78	2,891	27	192	(D)	(D)	(D)	(D)

(D) Withheld to avoid disclosing data for individual operations. [1] Data not available for all States for all years.
Note: Planted acres are in table 1-65.
NASS, Environmental, Economics, and Demographics Branch, (202) 720–6146.

Table 14-17.—Sorghum: Fertilizer usage, 2011 and 2019 [1]

State	Percent treated and amount applied							
	Nitrogen		Phosphate		Potash		Sulfur	
	Area applied	Pounds applied	Area applied	Pounds applied	Area applied	Pounds applied	Area applied	Pounds applied
	Percent	Millions	Percent	Millions	Percent	Millions	Percent	Millions
Colorado:								
2011	75	7.4	41	1.5	(D)	(D)	(D)	(D)
2019	57	7.9	(D)	(D)	....	....	20	0.7
Kansas:								
2011	83	135.7	51	32.8	8	2.9	9	1.5
2019	97	198.9	65	34.4	(D)	(D)	19	1.9
Missouri:								
2019	....	....	....	....	....	....	(D)	(D)
Nebraska:								
2011	88	11.0	41	1.9	15	0.2	22	0.4
2019	94	16.2	58	5.0	191	0.2	45	0.6
New Mexico:								
2019	(D)	(D)	(D)	(D)	....	....	(D)	(D)
Oklahoma:								
2011	81	11.9	58	3.8	13	0.2	13	0.3
2019	85	14.9	67	7.3	5	0.1	(D)	(D)
South Dakota:								
2011	88	8.9	45	1.9	(D)	(D)	(D)	(D)
2019	(D)	(D)	77	5.0	(D)	(D)	(D)	(D)
Texas:								
2011	77	94.1	63	27.2	11	3.7	29	5.1
2019	83	99.0	50	23.2	22	6.2	25	3.5

(D) Withheld to avoid disclosing data for individual operations. [1] Data not available for all States for all years.
Note: Planted acres are in table 1-65.
NASS, Environmental, Economics, and Demographics Branch, (202) 720–6146.

Table 14-18.—Soybeans: Pesticide usage, 2017 and 2018 [1]

State and Year	Percent treated and amount applied							
	Herbicide		Insecticide [2]		Fungicide		Other Chemicals [2]	
	Area applied	Pounds applied	Area applied	Pounds applied	Area applied	Pounds applied	Area applied	Pounds applied
	Percent	Thousands	Percent	Thousands	Percent	Thousands	Percent	Thousands
Arkansas:								
2017	97	7,898	33	350	13	76	(D)	(D)
2018	95	9,729	26	244	17	328	....	....
Illinois:								
2017	95	20,547	19	98	22	399	5	22
2018	98	23,531	16	98	24	643	(D)	(D)
Indiana:								
2017	98	14,058	15	48	16	209	6	7
2018	97	12,624	16	28	18	172	6	1
Iowa:								
2017	95	19,887	19	221	17	280	(D)	(D)
2018	100	21,526	19	283	19	357	(D)	(D)
Kansas:								
2017	93	9,362	15	87	4	22	(D)	(D)
2018	100	12,629	19	165	11	109	(D)	(D)
Kentucky:								
2017	97	3,759	33	87	21	55	5	2
2018	95	4,826	18	11	12	32	7	1
Louisiana:								
2015	97	4,186	63	....	43	107	(D)	(D)
2018	96	4,296	59	512	46	659	3	(Z)
Michigan:								
2017	98	3,986	5	9	7	24	(D)	(D)
2018	99	4,026	6	59	(D)	(D)	3	(Z)
Minnesota:								
2017	94	12,240	38	577	13	203	(D)	(D)
2018	99	12,060	30	637	21	299	....	....
Mississippi:								
2017	100	8,596	50	493	40	135	14	498
2018	100	8,582	26	85	35	291	8	163
Missouri:								
2017	92	10,982	21	222	12	102	3	(Z)
2018	97	12,082	17	93	6	201	(D)	(D)
Nebraska:								
2017	98	11,089	6	189	9	105	(D)	(D)
2018	99	12,978	8	18	13	244	....	....
North Carolina								
2017	97	3,264	38	77	18	52	(D)	(D)
2018	97	4,726	23	27	14	33	(D)	(D)
North Dakota								
2017	94	11,454	13	241	6	82	(D)	(D)
2018	99	10,056	(D)	(D)	(D)	(D)	(D)	(D)
Ohio:								
2017	96	9,448	11	20	18	126	4	6
2018	100	9,726	8	12	11	123	(D)	(D)
South Dakota								
2017	98	11,515	(D)	(D)	3	18	(D)	(D)
2018	99	11,044	....	....	(D)	(D)	(D)	(D)
Tennessee:								
2015	100	4,427	22	14	15	40	(D)	(D)
2018	100	4,790	15	11	14	37	(D)	(D)
Virginia:								
2015	96	1,224	37	25	16	19	(D)	(D)
2018	100	1,124	27	12	24	33	(D)	(D)
Wisconsin:								
2017	96	3,058	(D)	(D)	14	47	(D)	(D)
2018	98	3,705	(D)	(D)	14	49	....	....

(D) Withheld to avoid disclosing data for individual operations.   (Z) Less than the rounding unit.   [1] Data not available for all States for all years.   [2] Amount applied excludes Bt (bacillus thuringiensis) and other biologicals.
Note: Planted acres are in table 3-32.
NASS, Environmental, Economics, and Demographics Branch, (202) 720–6146.

Table 14-19.—Soybeans: Fertilizer usage, 2017 and 2018 [1]

State and Year	Percent treated and amount applied							
	Nitrogen		Phosphate		Potash		Sulfur	
	Area applied	Pounds applied	Area applied	Pounds applied	Area applied	Pounds applied	Area applied	Pounds applied
	Percent	Millions	Percent	Millions	Percent	Millions	Percent	Millions
Arkansas:								
2017	13	18.9	51	106.7	59	205.0	2	2.6
2018	7	8.1	51	113.3	56	155.0	7	4.0
Illinois:								
2017	25	63.8	36	279.8	53	713.6	5	7.4
2018	25	60.0	43	350.6	61	733.9	5	9.7
Indiana:								
2017	31	57.3	39	144.2	62	417.2	6	8.4
2018	28	32.0	33	111.1	50	309.5	10	2.9
Iowa:								
2017	13	14.4	23	145.0	34	357.1	6	8.1
2018	13	17.2	21	125.9	32	276.3	8	16.3
Kansas:								
2017	49	40.6	54	118.0	26	65.4	14	4.7
2018	29	22.8	38	76.9	18	48.7	10	4.7
Kentucky:								
2017	28	13.7	68	94.4	70	130.2	7	2.5
2018	32	21.3	74	109.9	85	186.7	5	3.0
Louisiana:								
2015	(D)	(D)	29	22.0	29	27.9	7	1.8
2018	10	4.3	41	31.1	51	51.8	10	2.0
Michigan:								
2017	48	15.9	49	49.2	74	141.0	11	1.8
2018	50	16.9	48	45.7	77	155.6	18	8.9
Minnesota:								
2017	26	35.2	28	95.0	34	161.0	6	5.1
2018	29	32.8	35	124.9	36	191.4	11	11.5
Mississippi:								
2017	4	0.7	17	20.6	38	66.6	4	1.6
2018	6	2.6	31	43.8	44	99.9	6	1.8
Missouri:								
2017	20	32.4	46	143.9	55	272.0	11	7.4
2018	11	11.6	33	89.1	44	193.0	6	2.9
Nebraska:								
2017	43	34.4	46	128.1	16	28.1	19	14.2
2018	36	29.5	43	154.2	18	53.1	17	11.0
North Carolina								
2017	54	20.3	46	30.1	72	95.5	15	4.2
2018	46	17.5	45	28.4	70	83.8	9	3.1
North Dakota								
2017	45	48.7	50	167.4	11	19.2	12	13.4
2018	55	39.1	62	145.7	18	20.4	12	6.6
Ohio:								
2017	32	25.2	30	72.0	61	329.5	8	15.9
2018	33	22.8	37	107.5	57	295.1	4	1.4
South Dakota								
2017	40	22.4	56	124.1	26	50.3	4	5.7
2018	42	28.9	55	141.4	28	53.1	13	5.6
Tennessee:								
2015	48	22.1	66	78.1	70	116.5	17	2.9
2018	65	26.7	76	89.3	72	107.4	21	3.1
Virginia:								
2015	58	9.2	64	19.6	79	40.6	25	2.0
2018	53	6.3	56	15.4	65	34.7	27	1.1
Wisconsin:								
2017	59	24.3	56	52.5	80	156.0	31	9.1
2018	37	15.9	50	70.0	74	171.9	29	11.7

(D) Withheld to avoid disclosing data for individual operations.   [1] Data not available for all States for all years.
Note: Planted acres are in table 3-32.
NASS, Environmental, Economics, and Demographics Branch, (202) 720–6146.

Table 14-20.—Wheat: Pesticide usage, 2017 and 2019 [1]

State and Year	Herbicide		Insecticide		Fungicide [2]		Other Chemicals [2]	
	Area applied	Pounds applied	Area applied	Pounds applied	Area applied	Pounds applied	Area applied	Pounds applied
	Percent	*Thousands*	*Percent*	*Thousands*	*Percent*	*Thousands*	*Percent*	*Thousands*
Winter								
Colorado:								
2017	83	3,230	(D)	(D)	24	63	(D)	(D)
2019	79	2,910	(D)	(D)	30	65	(D)	(D)
Idaho:								
2017	95	496	15	20	60	79	(D)	(D)
2019	96	506	(D)	(D)	17	52	(D)	(D)
Illinois:								
2017	59	39	33	5	46	61	(D)	(D)
2019	54	32	46	8	65	87	11	6
Kansas:								
2017	69	4,917	(D)	(D)	21	250	....	....
2019	72	3,486	(D)	(D)	14	121	(D)	(D)
Michigan:								
2017	66	80	40	4	67	67	11	5
2019	79	123	34	4	62	88	19	9
Missouri:								
2017	62	133	33	12	44	54	(D)	(D)
2019	54	64	24	4	39	33	....	....
Montana:								
2017	96	4,105	....	....	21	47	....	....
2019	99	3,703	(D)	(D)	20	39	(D)	(D)
Nebraska:								
2017	69	1,424	(D)	(D)	31	45	....	....
2019	75	917	(D)	(D)	36	77	(D)	(D)
North Dakota:								
2017	81	53	(D)	(D)	25	2	....	....
2019	80	33	....	....	(D)	(D)	....	....
Ohio:								
2017	41	44	17	4	29	28	....	....
2019	26	34	16	2	39	32	(D)	(D)
Oklahoma:								
2017	37	1,534	(D)	(D)	6	52	....	....
2019	36	899	8	60	10	64	(D)	(D)
Oregon:								
2017	98	1,525	(D)	(D)	39	53	(D)	(D)
2019	100	1,106	(D)	(D)	55	64	(D)	(D)
South Dakota:								
2017	60	542	(D)	(D)	25	22	....	....
2019	60	409	(D)	(D)	(D)	(D)	....	....
Texas:								
2017	23	607	6	109	17	91	....	....
2019	48	1,924	13	173	8	27	....	....
Washington:								
2017	99	1,885	(D)	(D)	67	222	(D)	(D)
2019	95	1,326	(D)	(D)	48	183	....	....
Durum								
Arizona:								
2017	72	14	....	....	(D)	(D)	(D)	(D)
2019	84	5	....	....	....	....	....	....
California:								
2019	77	23	(D)	(D)	....	....	(D)	(D)
Idaho:								
2017	96	11	(D)	(D)	(D)	(D)	....	....
Montana:								
2017	87	944	....	....	11	7	(D)	(D)
2019	98	710	(D)	(D)	16	11	....	....
North Dakota:								
2017	100	1,358	(D)	(D)	55	77	(D)	(D)
2019	96	613	(D)	(D)	53	59	(D)	(D)
Other Spring								
Idaho:								
2017	93	211	16	2	45	27	(D)	(D)
2019	100	310	9	1	23	12	(D)	(D)
Minnesota:								
2017	96	538	37	16	86	199	....	....
2019	99	537	29	8	79	226	....	....
Montana:								
2017	94	3,603	....	....	7	27	....	....
2019	98	3,971	(D)	(D)	5	10	(D)	(D)
North Dakota:								
2017	99	4,467	12	48	57	416	....	....
2019	95	4,595	7	20	58	631	(D)	(D)
South Dakota:								
2017	89	613	13	3	28	22	....	....
2019	97	317	10	2	57	92	....	....
Washington:								
2019	100	441	(D)	(D)	42	29	....	....

(D) Withheld to avoid disclosing data for individual operations. [1] Data not available for all States for all years. [2] Amount applied excludes biologicals.
Note: Planted acres are in table 1-8.
NASS, Environmental, Economics, and Demographics Branch, (202) 720–6146.

Table 14-21.—Wheat: Fertilizer usage, 2017 and 2019 [1]

State and Year	Percent treated and amount applied							
	Nitrogen		Phosphate		Potash		Sulfur [2]	
	Area applied	Pounds applied	Area applied	Pounds applied	Area applied	Pounds applied	Area applied	Pounds applied
DPercent	Millions	Percent	Millions	Percent	Millions	Percent	Millions	
Winter Wheat								
Colorado:								
2017	63	50.2	39	19.6	(D)	(D)	22	2.4
2019	85	63.7	67	31.6	(D)	(D)	14	1.0
Idaho:								
2017	92	88.2	80	17.6	37	7.2	76	15.3
2019	99	71.4	19	7.4	(D)	(D)	15	5.7
Illinois:								
2017	92	52.5	86	35.0	70	40.1	14	2.3
2019	94	63.9	88	41.5	78	56.3	20	3.5
Kansas:								
2017	85	466.0	62	137.5	(D)	(D)	18	10.9
2019	99	528.9	81	152.9	6	8.7	25	17.0
Michigan:								
2017	92	47.1	62	13.4	80	23.4	46	4.5
2019	96	57.6	81	23.8	78	28.9	53	4.7
Missouri:								
2017	98	65.4	66	27.2	65	30.6	29	3.2
2019	84	49.9	75	26.2	75	33.0	29	2.9
Montana:								
2017	95	133.4	94	57.1	42	11.6	43	6.7
2019	98	128.1	96	56.0	28	7.0	35	5.1
Nebraska:								
2017	79	46.8	50	18.0	14	1.7	25	2.3
2019	88	65.0	68	23.1	12	2.5	42	4.0
North Dakota:								
2017	87	5	70	2.0	(D)	(D)	(D)	(D)
2019	94	6.4	78	2.2	60	1.2	(D)	(D)
Ohio:								
2017	97	45.6	81	21.7	82	28.2	39	3.6
2019	89	39.1	72	24.4	65	21.2	46	4.6
Oklahoma:								
2017	92	294.5	53	63.6	12	11.6	(D)	(D)
2019	93	277.0	63	75.3	13	9.6	8	1.2
Oregon:								
2017	96	39.2	39	3.8	9	0.8	36	3.2
2019	100	55.9	21	6.6	(D)	(D)	29	5.3
South Dakota:								
2017	86	51.0	76	31.3	22	3.9	15	1.6
2019	60	38.4	30	8.4	(D)	(D)	(D)	(D)
Texas:								
2017	65	166.8	42	45.5	5	5.7	22	6.0
2019	57	164.9	34	35.9	6	10.9	26	13.2
Washington:								
2017	97	138.3	59	13.1	10	1.4	66	13.5
2019	100	124.3	46	16.1	(D)	(D)	75	15.2
Durum								
Arizona:								
2017	98	21.4	(D)	(D)	(D)	(D)	(D)	(D)
2019	88	6.1	(D)	(D)	(D)	(D)	(D)	(D)
California:								
2017					(D)	(D)	(D)	(D)
2019	94	3.8			(D)	(D)	(D)	(D)
Idaho:								
2017	96	3.1	(D)	(D)	(D)	(D)	91	0.4
Montana:								
2017	97	64.0	92	23.7	31	4.0	42	3.9
2019	97	35.0	84	11.7	14	0.9	22	0.9
North Dakota:								
2017	100	108.2	95	38.3	29	3.8	33	3.4
2019	100	63.8	(D)	(D)	10	0.8	28	1.6
Other Spring								
Idaho:								
2017	94	51.5	55	11.7	21	3.4	61	8.2
2019	95	70.4	74	16.0	47	7.9	50	4.7
Minnesota:								
2017	98	134.3	96	52.3	59	25.2	31	4.0
2019	100	170.8	91	55.9	66	23.8	40	4.2
Montana:								
2017	92	145.2	90	68.9	31	8.6	43	9.4
2019	96	153.7	90	71.3	22	11.5	34	6.5
North Dakota:								
2017	99	566.5	92	201.2	32	29.2	34	18.1
2019	96	747.5	89	262.9	25	43.2	24	16.5
South Dakota:								
2017	92	87.1	81	33.6	32	7.4	46	5.7
2019	99	59.5	91	24.0	43	7.8	20	1.0

Note: Planted acres are in table 1-8.
(D) Withheld to avoid disclosing data for individual operations. [1] Data not available for all States for all years.
NASS, Environmental, Economics, and Demographics Branch, (202) 720–6146.

Table 14-22.—Fruits, Pesticides: Percent of bearing acres receiving applications, for surveyed States, 2019 [1]

Crop	Herbicide	Insecticide	Fungicide	Other
		Percent		
Apples	36	88	85	86
Apricots	35	58	67	37
Avocados	58	44	4	47
Blueberries	63	91	91	47
Cherries, Sweet	43	85	85	80
Cherries, Tart	46	94	97	80
Dates	9	(D)	(D)	(D)
Grapefruit	70	90	86	88
Grapes, All	51	55	84	46
Grapes, Juice	81	(D)	38	31
Grapes, Raisin	51	71	95	52
Grapes, Table	31	65	96	66
Grapes, Wine	54	51	80	41
Kiwifruit	53	24	36	53
Lemons	61	82	56	79
Nectarines	52	80	79	73
Olives	41	28	57	18
Oranges	69	92	81	87
Peaches	54	86	88	67
Pears	35	89	90	93
Plums	46	65	53	66
Prunes	53	56	70	39
Raspberries	51	91	86	48
Strawberries	19	92	93	53
Tangerines	54	77	55	67

(D) Withheld to avoid disclosing data for individual operations. [1] Refers to acres receiving one or more applications of a specific agricultural chemical.
NASS, Environmental, Economics, and Demographics Branch, (202) 720–6146.

Table 14-23.—Fruit, Fertilizers: Percent of acres receiving applications, for surveyed States, 2019 [1]

Crop	Nitrogen	Phosphate	Potash	Sulfur
		Percent		
Apples	62	38	56	34
Apricots	87	55	14	(D)
Avocados	77	54	67	28
Blueberries	84	79	83	37
Cherries, Sweet	81	66	68	25
Cherries, Tart	79	33	63	19
Dates	37	(D)	(D)	(D)
Grapefruit	72	46	55	31
Grapes, All	73	27	62	(D)
Grapes, Juice	48	33	46	14
Grapes, Raisin	43	10	25	(D)
Grapes, Table	42	30	50	38
Grapes, Wine	82	29	69	(D)
Kiwifruit	66	44	60	38
Lemons	80	57	66	44
Nectarines	30	49	49	(D)
Olives	71	22	57	(D)
Oranges	39	64	74	38
Peaches	59	42	54	20
Pears	63	54	48	33
Plums	30	41	42	7
Prunes	54	21	37	14
Raspberries	79	67	68	39
Strawberries	95	49	58	(D)
Tangerines	82	81	85	74

(D) Withheld to avoid disclosing data for individual operations. [1] Refers to acres receiving one or more applications of a specific agricultural chemical.
NASS, Environmental, Economics, and Demographics Branch, (202) 720–6146.

Table 14-24.—Vegetables, Pesticides: Percent of acres receiving applications, for surveyed States, 2018 [1]

Crop	Herbicide	Insecticide	Fungicide	Other
	Percent			
Asparagus	65	64	39	(D)
Beans, Snap	79	59	56	1
Broccoli	43	77	55	2
Cabbage	(D)	(D)	(D	(D)
Carrots	34	23	51	17
Cauliflower	53	77	11	(D)
Celery	50	79	69	4
Cucumbers, Fresh	39	67	83	2
Garlic	77	47	77	(D)
Lettuce, Excl head	33	63	54	(D)
Lettuce, Head	44	73	68	(D)
Melons, Cantaloupe	(D)	76	(D)	13
Melons, Honeydew	35	98	93	(D)
Melons, Watermelon	52	73	77	9
Onions, Dry	(D)	(D)	(D)	(D)
Peas, Green	88	28	(D)	....
Peppers, Bell	(D)	(D)	(D)	(D)
Pumpkins	(D)	(D)	(D)	(D)
Spinach	(D)	68	83	(D)
Squash	37	79	68	5
Sweet Corn	(D)	(D)	(D)	(D)
Tomatoes, in the open	(D)	81	82	(D)

(D) Withheld to avoid disclosing data for individual operations.   [1] Refers to acres receiving one or more applications of a specific agricultural chemical.
NASS, Environmental, Economics, and Demographics Branch, (202) 720–6146.

Table 14-25.—Vegetables, Fertilizers: Percent of acres receiving applications, for surveyed States, 2018 [1]

Crop	Nitrogen	Phosphate	Potash	Sulfur
	Percent			
Asparagus	80	30	60	22
Beans, Snap	88	82	84	57
Broccoli	88	80	22	60
Cabbage	(D)	(D)	(D)	(D)
Carrots	83	64	46	30
Cauliflower	97	80	54	18
Celery	100	70	68	74
Cucumbers	99	93	92	63
Garlic	92	46	3	(D)
Lettuce, excluding Head	98	89	(D)	(D)
Lettuce, Head	88	85	(D)	(D)
Melons, Cantaloupe	99	89	(D)	(D)
Melons, Honeydew	95	89	(D)	(D)
Melons, Watermelon	86	82	62	6
Onions, dry	(D)	(D)	(D)	(D)
Peas, Green	71	29	34	47
Peppers, Bell	(D)	(D)	(D)	(D)
Pumpkins	(D)	(D)	(D)	(D)
Spinach	94	94	(D)	(D)
Squash	89	82	85	24
Sweet Corn	(D)	(D)	(D)	(D)
Tomatoes, in the open	99	73	49	(D)

(D) Withheld to avoid disclosing data for individual operations.   [1] Refers to acres receiving one or more applications of a specific agricultural chemical.
NASS, Environmental, Economics, and Demographics Branch, (202) 720–6146.

CHAPTER XV

MISCELLANEOUS AGRICULTURAL STATISTICS

This chapter contains miscellaneous data which do not fit into the preceding chapters. Included here are summary tables on foreign trade in agricultural products; statistics on fishery products; tables on refrigerated warehouses; and statistics on crops in Alaska.

Foreign Agricultural Trade Statistics

Agricultural products, sometimes referred to as food and fiber products, cover a broad range of goods from unprocessed bulk commodities like soybeans, feed corn and wheat to highly-processed, high-value foods and beverages like sausages, bakery goods, ice cream, or beer sold in retail stores and restaurants. All of the products found in Chapters 1-24 (except for fishery products in Chapter 3) of the U.S. Harmonized Tariff Schedule are considered agricultural products. These products generally fall into the following categories: grains, animal feeds, and grain products (like bread and pasta); oilseeds and oilseed products (like canola oil); livestock, poultry and dairy products including live animals, meats, eggs, and feathers; horticultural products including all fresh and processed fruits, vegetables, tree nuts, as well as nursery products and beer and wine; unmanufactured tobacco; and tropical products like sugar, cocoa, and coffee. Certain other products are considered "agricultural," the most significant of which are essential oils (Chapter 33), protein isolates and modified starches (Chapter 35), raw rubber (Chapter 40), raw animal hides and skins (Chapter 41), and wool and cotton (Chapters 51-52). Manufactured products derived from plants or animals, but which are not considered "agricultural" by USDA's definition are cotton yarn, textiles and clothing; leather and leather articles of apparel; and cigarettes and spirits. The World Trade Organization's definition of agricultural products varies in that it includes some products like spirits and tobacco products.

U.S. foreign agricultural trade statistics are based on documents filed by exporters and importers and compiled by the Bureau of the Census. Puerto Rico is a Customs district within the U.S. Customs territory, and its trade with foreign countries is included in U.S. export and import statistics. U.S. export and import statistics include merchandise trade between the U.S. Virgin Islands and foreign countries even though the Virgin Islands of the United States are not officially a part of the U.S. Customs territory.

The export value, the value at the port of exportation, is based on the selling price and includes inland freight, insurance, and other charges to the port. The country of destination is the country of ultimate destination or where the commodities are consumed or further processed.

Agricultural products, like manufactured goods, are often transhipped from the one country to another. Shippers are asked to identify the ultimate destination of a shipment. However, transhipment points are often recorded as the ultimate destination even though the actual point of consumption may be in a neighboring state. Thus, exports to countries which act as transhipment points are generally overstated, while exports to neighboring countries are often understated. Major world transhipment points include the Netherlands, Hong Kong, and Singapore. In such cases, exports to the Netherlands are over reported, but under reported for Germany, Belgium and the United Kingdom. Exports to Hong Kong are overstated, but under reported to China, and exports to Singapore are overstated, but understated to Malaysia and Indonesia.

Imports for consumption are a combination of entries for immediate consumption and withdrawals from bonded warehouses for consumption. The import value, defined generally as the market value in the foreign country, excludes import duties, ocean freight, and marine insurance. The country of origin is defined as the country where the commodities were grown or processed. Where the country of origin is not known, the imports are credited to the country of shipment.

Table 15-1.—Foreign trade: Value of total agricultural exports and imports, United States, fiscal years 2010–2019

Fiscal year Oct. 1- Sep. 30	U.S. total domestic exports			U.S. total imports for consumption, customs value			Surplus agricultural exports over agricultural imports
	Total merchandise exports	Agricultural exports [1]	Agricultural exports share of total exports	Total merchandise imports	Agricultural imports	Agricultural imports share of total imports	
	Million dollars	Million dollars	Percent	Million dollars	Million dollars	Percent	Million dollars
2010	1,077,045	108,529	10	1,832,595	78,963	4	29,566
2011	1,268,437	137,465	11	2,128,266	94,511	4	42,955
2012	1,343,129	135,907	10	2,248,129	103,371	5	32,536
2013	1,360,350	141,139	10	2,235,764	103,871	5	37,269
2014	1,398,923	152,326	11	2,304,072	109,258	5	43,068
2015	1,327,349	139,757	11	2,267,135	113,633	5	26,124
2016	1,222,350	129,597	11	2,160,641	114,439	5	15,158
2017	1,283,329	140,215	11	2,273,403	120,964	5	19,251
2018	1,402,288	143,414	10	2,506,195	128,678	5	14,736
2019	1,396,075	135,470	10	2,538,445	130,945	5	4,525

[1] Includes food exported for relief or charity by individuals and private agencies.
ERS, Market and Trade Economics Division, (202) 694–5257.

Table 15-2.—Foreign trade: Value and quantity of bulk commodity exports, United States, fiscal years 2010–2019 [1]

Fiscal year	Wheat, unmilled	Rice, milled	Feed grains [2]	Oilseeds [3]	Tobacco unmanufactured	Cotton and linters	Bulk commodities
	Value						
	Million dollars						
2010	5,840	2,296	9,806	17,951	1,223	4,836	41,951
2011	11,504	2,117	13,969	21,571	1,116	8,982	59,260
2012	8,376	1,963	11,719	21,101	1,051	6,551	50,761
2013	10,126	2,212	6,198	22,456	1,193	5,649	47,834
2014	8,260	2,002	12,480	25,758	1,114	4,614	54,228
2015	5,914	2,036	11,057	23,175	1,250	4,146	47,578
2016	5,136	1,834	10,768	21,923	1,042	3,451	44,154
2017	6,198	1,714	10,798	25,313	1,029	5,866	50,917
2018	5,086	1,636	12,238	23,175	1,093	6,624	49,852
2019	6,233	1,826	9,484	18,515	755	6,076	42,889
	Quantity						
	1,000 metric tons						
2010	25,698	4,260	53,849	42,499	185	2,746	129,236
2011	34,583	3,920	49,170	41,365	174	3,113	132,325
2012	26,969	3,578	40,024	39,247	167	2,731	112,716
2013	31,110	3,848	20,460	35,862	165	2,921	94,366
2014	27,091	3,355	56,630	46,050	152	2,202	135,480
2015	21,398	3,971	56,316	51,212	177	2,535	135,610
2016	22,538	3,789	59,075	55,146	156	2,202	142,904
2017	28,078	3,986	61,708	60,755	150	3,298	157,976
2018	21,155	3,052	68,475	57,924	155	3,661	154,422
2019	26,567	3,599	51,651	49,120	105	3,433	134,475

[1] Fiscal years, Oct. 1–Sept. 30. [1] Corn, barley, sorghum, rye, and oats. [3] Soybeans, peanuts, rapeseed, cottonseed, sunflowerseed, safflowerseed, and others.
ERS, Market and Trade Economics Division, (202) 694–5257.

Table 15-3.—Agricultural exports: Value to top 50 countries of destination, United States, fiscal years 2017–2019 [1]

Country	2017	2018	2019
	Million dollars		
Canada	20,444.0	20,701.0	20,997.3
Mexico	18,605.9	18,869.4	18,996.7
EU27+UK	11,552.5	12,707.6	12,615.2
Japan	11,856.7	12,655.0	12,146.7
China	21,838.8	16,262.9	10,115.9
South Korea	6,851.2	7,958.9	7,819.6
Taiwan	3,399.7	3,812.2	3,611.4
Vietnam	2,559.2	3,895.2	3,596.3
Hong Kong	4,043.3	4,198.3	3,512.5
Indonesia	2,968.4	3,091.5	2,888.8
Philippines	2,627.4	2,836.1	2,868.8
Colombia	2,554.2	2,750.1	2,664.5
Thailand	1,781.7	2,143.6	1,884.6
India	1,504.3	1,579.3	1,782.3
Egypt	772.0	1,703.0	1,473.2
Australia	1,368.7	1,425.8	1,443.9
Saudi Arabia	1,588.0	1,330.0	1,318.0
Guatemala	1,081.8	1,202.5	1,307.2
Dominican Republic	1,231.6	1,272.2	1,295.4
Turkey	1,711.5	1,706.5	1,180.7
Malaysia	903.1	959.6	1,147.7
United Arab Emirates	1,071.5	1,033.2	1,115.7
Pakistan	834.0	1,433.4	1,082.1
Peru	1,187.8	1,325.4	1,021.3
Chile	912.3	942.7	1,013.1
Singapore	824.0	792.1	955.4
Bangladesh	892.4	858.6	935.8
Argentina	174.2	350.5	765.4
Costa Rica	691.4	723.3	733.2
Panama	661.7	668.1	716.9
Honduras	597.7	679.0	694.6
Israel	527.7	665.9	622.1
Brazil	725.7	584.1	582.4
El Salvador	487.1	503.5	567.7
Nigeria	500.5	326.5	551.0
New Zealand	379.7	463.3	534.6
Ecuador	271.4	343.7	460.7
Switzerland	454.1	386.2	406.5
Jamaica	376.8	393.6	397.7
Haiti	390.2	394.2	384.4
South Africa	360.6	323.8	361.7
Trinidad and Tobago	331.4	341.7	346.2
Iraq	106.8	335.2	303.4
Morocco	485.2	587.6	275.0
Cuba	266.1	230.0	270.7
The Bahamas	254.0	261.6	262.3
Nicaragua	218.5	214.1	240.2
Kuwait	222.1	237.1	238.9
Netherlands Antilles	219.7	219.9	224.7
Jordan	282.8	208.0	219.7
Other Countries	4,264.0	4,527.2	4,519.3
World Total [2]	140,215.4	143,414.3	135,469.5

[1] Fiscal years Oct. 1–Sept. 30. [2] Totals may not add due to rounding.
ERS, Market and Trade Economics Divison, (202) 694–5257.

Table 15-4.—Foreign trade in agricultural products: Value of exports by principal commodity groups, United States, fiscal years 2016–2019 [1]

Commodity	2016	2017	2018	2019
	1,000 dollars	*1,000 dollars*	*1,000 dollars*	*1,000 dollars*
Total Merchandise Exports	1,427,982,211	1,427,401,788	1,410,626,357	1,419,857,072
Nonagricultural U.S. Exports (Na)	1,298,385,211	1,287,186,788	1,267,212,357	1,284,387,072
Total Agricultural exports	129,597,000	140,215,000	143,414,000	135,470,000
Animals and animal products	24,915,038	28,269,536	29,939,818	29,561,343
Animals, live	457,572	542,795	643,031	642,476
Cattle	67,762	158,462	274,713	236,937
Horses,mules,burros-live	372,184	361,631	342,864	388,276
Swine, live	13,709	18,930	21,672	14,516
Sheep, live	2,280	2,551	2,424	1,518
Other live Animals	1,637	1,221	1,358	1,230
Red meat and products	12,265,093	14,155,005	15,328,372	15,390,245
Beef and Veal	5,196,925	6,173,070	7,342,105	7,283,838
Beef and Veal, fresh/frozen	4,966,796	5,960,005	7,128,147	7,082,067
Beef prep/pres	230,129	213,065	213,958	201,771
Horsemeat, fresh/frozen	204	806	52	25
Lamb and Goat, fr/frozen	11,525	14,851	14,401	14,398
Pork	4,737,457	5,227,433	5,440,608	5,516,852
Pork, fresh/frozen	3,992,969	4,477,735	4,681,686	4,774,617
Pork, prep/pres	744,488	749,698	758,922	742,235
Variety meats	1,660,265	1,884,164	1,731,062	1,674,419
Beef variety meats	897,749	896,036	878,777	956,960
Pork variety meats	689,246	905,847	757,189	604,853
Other variety meats	73,270	82,281	95,096	112,605
Other meats, fresh/frozen	658,718	854,681	800,144	900,714
Poultry and products	4,551,342	4,908,080	5,253,058	5,136,394
Poultry, live	165,604	196,218	216,294	281,246
Baby chicks	148,859	179,075	199,965	264,571
Other live poultry	16,745	17,143	16,329	16,675
Poultry meats	3,595,801	3,845,509	4,097,399	3,988,541
Chickens, fresh/frozen	2,587,149	2,788,146	3,006,205	2,962,248
Turkeys, fresh/frozen	437,249	429,313	411,995	477,315
Other poultry, fresh/frozen	4,944	6,246	4,160	4,597
Poultry meats, prep	566,458	621,804	675,039	544,381
Poultry, misc	235,963	313,388	342,756	283,923
Eggs	553,973	552,965	596,610	582,684
Dairy products	4,622,845	5,403,069	5,653,344	5,743,420
Evaporated/condensed milk	35,198	34,029	36,169	31,741
Nonfat dry milk	1,184,268	1,372,886	1,450,475	1,562,918
Butter and milkfat	48,924	103,698	144,731	97,360
Cheese	1,173,091	1,415,408	1,475,577	1,488,204
Whey,fluid/dried	548,497	695,162	669,284	632,879
Other dairy products	1,632,866	1,781,886	1,877,108	1,930,318
Fats, oils, and greases	489,611	606,058	585,151	633,131
Lard	55,835	97,809	89,440	55,430
Tallow, inedible	206,771	256,221	216,773	206,860
Other animal fats	227,005	252,028	278,938	370,841
Hides and skins	1,887,730	1,931,099	1,580,560	1,108,071
Bovine hides, whole	1,018,548	1,128,521	884,918	635,347
Other cattle hides	12,945	18,177	17,377	13,138
Calf skins, whole	47,385	102,640	127,187	65,453
Horse hides, whole	80,186	23,742	12,703	3,312
Sheep and lamb skins	14,100	15,106	12,977	5,944
Other hides and Skin	421,596	428,034	373,222	267,023
Furskins	292,969	214,880	152,175	117,855
Mink pelts	272,258	199,224	136,433	99,989
Other furskins	20,712	15,656	15,741	17,866
Wool and mohair	18,459	23,191	27,089	18,262
Sausage casings	245,525	277,883	397,712	413,083
Bull semen	160,576	162,648	187,376	204,169
Miscellaneous animal products	216,285	259,708	284,125	272,092
Grains and feeds	29,800,241	30,507,690	31,455,366	30,189,075
Wheat,unmilled	5,136,021	6,197,654	5,086,206	6,233,349
Wheat flour	171,611	161,392	126,867	152,450
Other wheat products	153,565	135,736	147,170	154,064
Rice-paddy, milled	1,834,482	1,714,013	1,636,179	1,826,348
Feed grains and products	11,224,817	11,284,328	12,730,294	9,980,880
Feed grain	10,767,971	10,798,005	12,238,048	9,483,652
Barley	40,168	31,233	28,462	29,944
Corn	9,124,474	9,683,360	11,267,677	8,995,926
Grain sorghum	1,590,054	1,071,130	931,433	447,888
Oats	7,248	8,817	6,703	5,453
Rye	6,027	3,465	3,772	4,441
Feed grain products	456,846	486,322	492,246	497,229

See footnote(s) at end of table.

Table 15-4.—Foreign trade in agricultural products: Value of exports by principal commodity groups, United States, fiscal years 2016–2019 [1]—Continued

Commodity	2016	2017	2018	2019
	1,000 dollars	*1,000 dollars*	*1,000 dollars*	*1,000 dollars*
Grains and feeds--Continued				
Popcorn	95,115	120,465	114,481	108,538
Blended food products	50,173	53,526	48,644	58,921
Other grain products	3,670,714	3,636,125	3,694,067	3,848,457
Feeds and fodders	7,463,743	7,204,451	7,871,458	7,826,068
Corn by-products	624,823	625,418	689,629	613,705
Alfalfa meal and cubes	73,599	65,790	51,828	41,649
Beef pulp	97,747	94,493	108,913	95,146
Citrus pulp pellets	1,056	26	171	649
Other feeds and fodders	6,666,518	6,418,724	7,020,916	7,074,919
Fruit and prep	6,138,011	6,307,658	6,394,412	5,945,527
Fruits, fresh	4,491,929	4,676,914	4,721,795	4,333,844
Citrus fruits	983,861	1,016,248	971,950	851,023
Grapefruit	106,136	94,411	61,519	69,161
Lemons and limes	180,093	187,091	179,081	166,040
Oranges and tangerines	679,606	723,164	711,014	593,263
Other citrus	18,026	11,582	20,335	22,559
Noncitrus Fruits	3,508,068	3,660,666	3,749,846	3,482,821
Apples	894,191	958,313	1,079,704	866,106
Berries	677,923	673,549	707,141	699,652
Cherries	476,419	643,770	518,453	493,936
Grapes	765,229	748,231	769,626	784,394
Melons,	153,556	159,605	160,001	136,461
Peaches	140,184	118,491	125,311	129,860
Pears	176,004	144,820	153,922	168,276
Plums	59,080	59,358	60,312	53,853
Other noncitrus	165,481	154,528	175,376	150,283
Fruits, dried	577,168	544,301	529,393	467,384
Raisin	321,685	304,912	296,012	264,451
Prunes	165,000	142,980	145,288	128,715
Other dried fruits	90,483	96,409	88,093	74,218
Fruits, canned	605,718	641,843	683,241	661,165
Fruits, frozen	135,414	122,974	128,448	134,263
Other fruits, prep	327,782	321,626	331,535	348,871
Fruits, juices	1,096,074	984,370	910,098	821,094
Apple juice	46,510	49,840	57,847	51,852
Grape juice	68,295	69,481	77,132	65,653
Grapefruit juice	36,797	36,307	39,811	30,073
Orange juice	382,748	339,569	252,361	221,844
Other fruit juices	561,724	489,173	482,947	451,672
Wine	1,528,841	1,416,818	1,459,096	1,326,576
Nuts and prep	8,235,776	8,760,134	9,431,264	9,635,246
Almonds	4,647,338	4,199,529	4,584,942	4,749,005
Filberts	74,184	94,898	85,562	90,393
Peanuts	595,969	549,844	578,167	540,757
Pistachios	775,538	1,514,356	1,532,628	2,181,500
Walnuts	1,250,986	1,371,122	1,516,684	1,152,906
Pecans	465,097	617,955	688,822	472,933
Other nuts	426,664	412,430	444,459	447,752
Vegetables and prep	7,148,372	7,328,379	7,014,224	7,160,559
Vegetables fresh	2,480,008	2,505,050	2,549,031	2,705,787
Aspargus	48,250	62,297	81,688	78,540
Broccoli	117,248	103,280	102,709	98,018
Carrots	111,240	110,804	111,203	109,581
Cabbage	48,456	59,473	76,006	84,407
Celery	96,764	87,452	79,716	119,225
Cauliflower	135,060	147,424	158,826	161,420
Corn sweet	46,765	49,819	49,762	44,149
Cucumbers	14,493	15,871	13,409	16,688
Garlic	14,949	17,064	14,526	14,018
Lettuce	488,803	499,952	480,983	518,966
Mushrooms	26,848	25,313	34,588	39,156
Onions and shallots	196,622	170,173	185,070	243,554
Peppers	79,938	77,494	76,595	84,519
Potatoes	202,462	232,420	233,197	252,740
Tomatoes	122,977	113,004	110,721	114,172
Other fresh vegetables	729,133	733,211	740,030	726,633

See footnote(s) at end of table.

Table 15-4.—Foreign trade in agricultural products: Value of exports by principal commodity groups, United States, fiscal years 2016–2019 [1]—Continued

Commodity	2016	2017	2018	2019
	1,000 dollars	*1,000 dollars*	*1,000 dollars*	*1,000 dollars*
Vegetables and prep--Continued				
Vegetables, frozen	1,482,153	1,534,695	1,515,472	1,549,597
Corn, sweet	107,487	113,027	107,473	104,392
Potatoes	1,137,484	1,165,600	1,166,940	1,218,771
Other frozen vegetables	237,182	256,068	241,059	226,433
Vegetables, canned	633,919	587,393	546,558	533,012
Pulses	776,779	869,549	620,087	615,291
Dried Beans	298,078	312,475	307,206	288,712
Dried Peas	255,952	189,915	118,899	110,925
Dried Lentils	173,308	256,208	93,798	120,351
Dried chickpeas	49,441	110,952	100,184	95,304
Other vegetables, prep/pres	1,775,513	1,831,692	1,783,076	1,756,872
Oilseeds and products	29,192,243	32,460,021	31,197,490	25,608,461
Oilcake and meal	4,225,951	3,933,033	4,998,037	4,457,068
Bran and residues	12,558	13,443	23,488	26,733
Corn oilcake and meal	3,033	928	666	726
Soybean meal	4,155,007	3,873,278	4,933,693	4,392,407
Other oilcake and meal	55,354	45,385	40,189	37,203
Oilseeds	21,922,530	25,312,750	23,174,724	18,514,702
Rapeseed	106,103	98,775	99,409	120,687
Safflower seeds	981	826	658	1,045
Soybeans	20,426,101	23,808,967	21,688,843	16,996,612
Sunflowerseeds	101,451	78,666	72,975	62,724
Peanuts, oilstock	213,436	128,468	119,082	109,766
Other oilseeds	82,948	141,310	126,429	100,589
Protein substances	991,510	1,055,738	1,067,327	1,123,280
Vegetable oils	3,043,762	3,214,238	3,024,729	2,636,691
Soybean oil	842,844	953,402	896,256	676,486
Cottonseed oil	21,495	32,402	40,470	31,614
Sunflower oil	51,519	42,165	47,232	67,164
Corn oil	430,201	469,927	289,143	212,613
Peanut oil	11,611	11,974	11,547	8,828
Rapeseed oil	94,427	110,214	96,362	83,778
Safflower oil	26,555	17,632	16,569	14,418
Other vegetable oils/waxes	1,565,109	1,576,521	1,627,149	1,541,789
Tobacco, unmfg	1,042,410	1,028,510	1,093,423	754,574
Tobacco, light air	160,616	144,913	126,818	127,995
Tobacco, flue	671,652	651,849	753,509	424,761
Other tobacco, unmfg	210,142	231,748	213,096	201,818
Cotton, excluding linters	3,443,196	5,849,567	6,609,963	6,069,606
Cotton linters	7,475	16,604	13,916	6,577
Essential oils	1,834,209	1,969,901	2,109,209	2,155,531
Seeds, field and garden	1,572,761	1,698,435	1,809,101	1,855,830
Sugar and tropical products	5,034,548	4,927,713	5,050,073	4,883,652
Sugar and related products	1,734,404	1,680,134	1,790,203	1,651,656
Sugar, cane or beet	73,142	65,737	110,215	45,109
Related sugar products	1,661,263	1,614,397	1,679,988	1,606,547
Coffee	937,513	865,479	875,950	875,092
Cocoa	235,822	208,762	188,476	182,628
Chocolate and prep	1,511,799	1,558,390	1,565,361	1,582,761
Tea, including herbal	381,918	363,421	371,115	362,107
Spices	184,499	189,334	198,006	193,393
Rubber, crude	45,130	56,934	54,740	31,379
Fibers, excluding cotton	3,463	5,259	6,222	4,636
Other hort products	6,276,107	6,389,997	6,606,411	7,263,532
Hops, including extract	243,674	275,051	339,993	378,929
Starches, not wheat/corn	135,604	132,609	138,844	144,033
Yeasts	92,762	103,112	104,468	100,937
Misc hort products	5,804,067	5,879,225	6,023,106	6,639,633
Nursery & greenhouse	401,839	417,315	439,295	438,862
Beverages, excluding juice	1,930,038	1,882,792	1,881,144	1,793,461

[1] Fiscal years, Oct. 1–Sept. 30. Totals may not add due to rounding.
ERS, Market and Trade Economics Division, (202) 694–5257.
Compiled from reports of the U.S. Department of Commerce.

Table 15-5.—Foreign trade in agricultural products: Value of imports by principal groups, United States, fiscal years 2016–2019[1]

Product	2016	2017	2018	2019
	1,000 dollars	*1,000 dollars*	*1,000 dollars*	*1,000 dollars*
Total merchandise imports	2,177,103,456	2,288,033,279	2,499,691,523	2,532,820,540
Non-agricultural U.S. imports	2,062,664,456	2,167,069,279	2,371,013,523	2,401,875,540
Total agricultural imports	114,439,000	120,964,000	128,678,000	130,945,000
Animals & prods.	16,594,053	15,778,997	16,539,892	17,105,618
Animals - live, excluding poultry	2,634,280	2,495,026	2,563,143	2,714,394
Cattle and calves	1,688,912	1,487,359	1,564,249	1,749,673
Horses, mules, burros	548,516	629,370	627,365	594,314
Swine	334,417	323,244	313,365	310,585
Sheep, Live	1,224	498	281	491
Other live animals	61,212	54,555	57,883	59,331
Red meat & products	8,239,788	8,164,540	8,697,188	8,920,077
Beef & veal	5,371,892	5,114,995	5,584,110	5,790,777
Beef & veal - fresh or frozen	4,997,263	4,741,504	5,147,596	5,309,413
Beef & veal - prep. or pres.	374,629	373,490	436,513	481,363
Pork	1,658,024	1,705,340	1,644,300	1,499,146
Pork - fr. or froz.	1,335,915	1,375,854	1,287,052	1,101,118
Pork - prep. or pres.	322,109	329,486	357,248	398,028
Mutton, goat & lamb	775,142	924,135	989,037	1,089,420
Horsemeat - fr. or froz.	1,875	1,872	2,161	2,200
Variety meats - fr. or froz.	300,613	260,150	292,845	354,887
Other meats - fr. or froz.	45,336	54,502	64,743	65,661
Other meats & prods.	86,906	103,547	119,992	117,986
Poultry and prods.	863,321	742,801	777,094	809,823
Poultry - live	50,020	49,383	43,571	42,971
Poultry meat	527,524	470,456	511,912	513,302
Eggs	169,880	83,937	65,077	79,926
Poultry, misc.	115,897	139,026	156,535	173,625
Dairy products	3,395,862	2,939,582	2,958,006	3,117,193
Milk & cream, fresh or dried	105,049	105,885	125,388	124,081
Butter & butterfat mixtures	185,582	185,665	282,931	380,630
Cheese	1,274,575	1,167,399	1,279,347	1,345,586
Casein & mixtures	529,484	513,472	437,491	424,203
Other dairy prods.	1,301,171	967,160	832,848	842,693
Fats, oils, & greases	183,266	221,047	216,482	293,755
Hides & skins	177,594	101,926	58,432	44,154
Sheep & lamb skins	357	443	554	375
Other hides & skins	41,474	31,714	26,750	15,194
Furskins	135,763	69,768	31,128	28,584
Wool - unmfg.	17,726	15,283	14,872	17,223
Apparel grade wool	8,904	6,970	8,604	10,360
Carpet grade wool	8,822	8,312	6,268	6,863
Sausage casings	182,695	193,893	205,042	91,416
Bull semen	43,400	42,404	37,287	35,446
Misc. animal prods	855,872	862,324	1,012,166	1,061,983
Silk, raw	249	171	180	154
Grains & feeds	11,075,221	11,714,644	13,360,868	13,976,050
Wheat, ex. seed	511,095	590,408	830,545	483,128
Corn, unmilled	371,116	298,698	191,980	175,477
Oats, unmilled	318,305	314,107	318,819	312,927
Barley, unmilled	100,797	53,789	39,266	31,713
Rice	666,836	638,352	857,185	970,571
Biscuits & wafers	3,823,489	4,260,520	4,752,985	5,258,279
Pasta & noodles	593,509	565,327	579,635	596,133
Other grains & preps.	3,002,326	3,262,538	3,719,637	4,038,802
Feeds & fodders, excluding oilcake	1,687,748	1,730,905	2,070,816	2,109,020
Fruits & preps.	14,870,410	16,218,914	17,049,053	17,929,435
Fruits - fr. or froz.	12,058,808	13,356,022	13,837,119	14,774,616
Apples, fresh	264,706	237,266	201,279	211,171
Avocados	1,717,897	2,605,107	2,431,484	2,693,030
Berries, excl. strawberries	1,986,251	2,065,450	2,367,284	2,841,018
Bananas & plantains - fresh or frozen	2,271,361	2,296,646	2,415,952	2,425,164
Citrus, fresh	955,802	1,060,013	1,276,777	1,253,876
Grapes, fresh	1,449,269	1,618,416	1,574,652	1,615,883
Kiwifruit, fresh	127,963	121,492	137,271	129,835
Mangoes	545,951	544,045	531,911	562,518
Melons	691,252	664,403	686,521	679,591
Peaches	76,867	69,564	72,513	67,765
Pears	111,125	116,337	131,800	117,204
Pineapples - fr. or froz.	663,304	682,451	678,408	653,966
Plums	53,915	43,707	46,530	43,066
Strawberries - fr. or froz.	725,167	800,018	800,798	1,002,682
Other fruits - fr. or froz.	417,980	431,107	483,942	477,847
Fruits - prep. or pres.	2,811,602	2,862,892	3,211,934	3,154,819
Bananas & plantains - prep. or pres.	143,414	147,902	169,265	168,765
Pineapples - canned or prep.	389,838	355,656	285,608	275,220
Other fruits - prep. or pres.	2,278,350	2,359,334	2,757,061	2,710,834

See footnote(s) at end of table.

Table 15-5.—Foreign trade in agricultural products: Value of imports by principal groups, United States, fiscal years 2016–2019 [1]—Continued

Product	2016	2017	2018	2019
	1,000 dollars	1,000 dollars	1,000 dollars	1,000 dollars
Fruit juices	1,760,525	1,937,797	2,169,101	2,192,542
Apple juice	476,474	438,970	466,608	468,591
Grape juice	73,353	64,472	74,796	82,643
Grapefruit juice	1,293	4,777	14,985	27,627
Lemon juice	114,142	122,661	123,017	113,109
Lime juice	30,173	33,404	31,678	29,038
Orange juice	556,712	774,656	932,206	786,953
Pineapple juice	118,602	110,346	65,011	59,891
Other fruit juice	389,776	388,511	460,800	624,690
Nuts & preps	2,724,812	3,328,514	3,495,030	3,279,495
Brazil nuts	72,546	72,164	52,713	42,559
Cashew nuts	1,234,762	1,688,328	1,682,998	1,344,366
Chestnuts	15,386	13,069	12,855	10,790
Coconut meat	220,925	237,845	260,888	222,111
Filberts	34,799	41,382	46,484	48,756
Macadamia nuts	140,624	146,812	183,488	258,117
Pecans	484,073	634,622	673,506	750,953
Pistachio nuts	10,803	12,490	15,385	15,167
Other nuts	510,894	481,802	566,713	586,676
Vegetables & preps.	13,159,109	13,276,028	14,310,805	14,970,887
Vegetables, fresh	8,009,144	7,697,210	8,362,234	8,909,062
Tomatoes	2,221,247	2,074,235	2,389,574	2,290,915
Asparagus	609,777	696,162	623,357	698,110
Beans	121,866	116,219	142,839	144,701
Cabbage	47,584	40,715	48,171	75,285
Carrots	94,992	85,766	119,131	111,440
Cauliflower & broccoli, fresh	267,797	294,325	286,323	342,627
Celery,	26,576	35,409	30,149	65,944
Cucumbers	704,241	657,350	740,890	815,986
Eggplant	68,154	60,366	64,131	67,282
Endive	3,978	3,843	4,073	4,976
Garlic	205,356	223,076	166,354	155,577
Lettuce	276,595	280,764	275,231	350,093
Okra	25,721	29,511	40,617	43,934
Onions	469,759	412,694	440,544	438,233
Peas	74,879	73,099	87,917	76,331
Peppers	1,451,384	1,305,923	1,460,992	1,673,748
Potatoes	186,601	214,670	229,433	198,462
Radishes	21,181	23,436	34,521	28,060
Squash	383,247	324,765	365,447	373,030
Other fresh vegetables	748,209	744,880	812,540	954,329
Vegetables - prep. or pres.	3,030,523	3,312,934	3,435,521	3,507,678
Bamboo shoots, preserved	26,263	27,520	24,890	24,697
Cucumbers, preserved	57,176	58,068	63,991	61,757
Garlic, dried	73,450	113,801	61,118	30,674
Olives - prep. or pres.	415,202	424,214	451,788	485,664
Mushrooms, canned	109,120	106,592	106,288	107,763
Mushrooms, dried	28,285	28,487	31,930	25,903
Onions, preserved	48,921	52,457	54,781	61,320
Artichokes - prep.	138,255	159,755	144,717	136,927
Asparagus- prep.	20,962	19,137	16,265	13,117
Tomatoes, incl. paste & sauce	204,822	211,682	231,258	245,933
Waterchestnuts	21,440	28,136	31,620	22,871
Peppers & pimentos, prep.	110,100	98,398	112,113	85,103
Veg Starches, excluding wheat & corn	171,854	174,291	216,435	229,452
Soups & sauces	464,535	493,133	529,448	589,076
Other vegetables - prep. or pres.	1,140,140	1,317,264	1,358,878	1,387,420
Vegetables, frozen	1,867,923	1,999,431	2,230,941	2,306,262
Tomatoes	7,109	6,680	7,919	10,363
Asparagus	16,021	14,847	16,967	14,879
Beans	69,359	75,322	75,364	70,817
Carrots	7,796	10,193	9,567	8,338
Cauliflower & broccoli	356,639	356,391	399,808	422,818
Okra	16,494	12,757	15,975	12,852
Peas	40,940	39,411	44,503	54,080
Potatoes	772,005	844,154	937,181	953,136
Other frozen vegetables	581,562	639,677	723,656	758,981
Pulses	251,519	266,453	282,109	247,885
Dried peas	44,483	44,534	63,257	46,822
Dried beans	143,998	145,849	129,266	128,430
Dried lentils	28,149	33,538	36,037	35,019
Dried chickpeas	34,889	42,531	53,550	37,614
Sugar & related prods.	4,469,243	4,612,790	4,743,534	4,529,220
Sugar - cane & beet	1,652,713	1,692,323	1,703,807	1,469,245
Molasses	161,512	118,625	140,918	146,024
Confectionery prods.	1,727,605	1,764,973	1,891,008	1,918,303
Other sugar & related prods.	927,413	1,036,869	1,007,801	995,648

See footnote(s) at end of table.

Table 15-5.—Foreign trade in agricultural products: Value of imports by principal groups, United States, fiscal years 2016–2019 [1]—Continued

Product	2016	2017	2018	2019
	1,000 dollars	*1,000 dollars*	*1,000 dollars*	*1,000 dollars*
Cocoa & products	4,939,220	5,243,686	4,630,500	4,934,897
Coffee & products	5,934,064	6,617,179	6,086,250	6,163,421
Tea	750,078	718,611	703,749	727,971
Spices & herbs	1,859,806	1,979,025	2,044,202	1,981,417
Pepper	991,728	788,970	639,041	607,083
Other spices & herbs	868,078	1,190,055	1,405,161	1,374,334
Drugs, crude & natural	1,792,016	1,826,458	1,993,616	1,968,408
Essential oils	2,627,381	3,056,600	3,176,003	2,997,727
Fibers, excl. cotton	127,817	126,249	122,501	136,156
Rubber & gums	1,306,736	1,700,050	1,583,821	1,513,865
Tobacco - unmfg.	793,605	673,127	661,243	672,243
Tobacco - filler	763,423	650,975	643,234	640,239
Tobacco - scrap	10,770	8,104	7,543	10,701
Other tobacco	19,412	14,048	10,466	21,303
Beverages, ex. fruit juice	13,958,618 5	14,386,991	15,816,195	16,371,913
Wine	5,526,951	5,965,998	6,312,581	6,430,661
Malt beverages	4,831,814	4,988,000	5,368,737	5,548,108
Other beverages	3,599,853	3,432,993	4,134,877	4,393,144
Oilseeds & products	826,295	823,299	860,675	738,299
Oilseeds & oilnuts	826,295	823,298	860,675	738,300
Flaxseed	68,941	64,319	80,859	86,685
Rapeseed	186,040	239,698	262,597	201,357
Soybeans	361,252	331,919	325,567	224,338
Sunflower seeds	45,170	47,145	58,645	71,056
Other oilseeds & oilnuts	164,892	140,217	133,007	154,864
Oils & waxes - vegetable	6,154,477	7,072,533	7,213,267	6,411,556
Castor oil	69,675	80,424	94,989	93,986
Coconut oil	774,366	880,867	753,511	588,115
Cottonseed oil	2,508	30	40	35
Olive oil	1,323,409	1,387,740	1,491,105	1,362,684
Palm oil	828,848	1,024,315	1,103,296	930,837
Palm kernel oil	351,795	477,117	447,027	284,145
Peanut oil	29,633	37,847	33,114	21,397
Rapeseed oil	1,516,558	1,795,063	1,690,628	1,574,250
Soybean oil	99,425	118,829	120,632	136,497
Sesame oil	76,695	83,187	91,067	95,435
Other vegetable oils	1,081,566	1,187,113	1,387,858	1,324,176
Oilcake & meal	1,252,360	1,153,467	1,314,220	1,397,552
Cotton, excl. linters	11,226	3,422	2,803	1,158
Cotton, linters	1,868	4	1,105	269
Seeds - field & garden	1,003,105	1,020,561	1,074,994	979,217
Cut flowers	1,103,005	1,170,801	1,228,519	1,306,724
Nursery stock, bulbs, etc.	719,339	761,010	821,155	897,890
Other hort products	3,202,738	3,878,187	6,507,369	7,660,967
Hops, including extract	58,478	60,811	71,692	72,973
Starches, ex wheat/corn	127,563	133,901	141,229	140,937
Yeasts	300,568	307,041	339,760	346,186
Misc horticultural products	2,716,129	3,376,434	5,954,688	7,100,871

[1] Fiscal years, Oct. 1–Sept. 30.
ERS, Market and Trade Economics Division, (202) 694–5257. Compiled from reports of the U.S. Department of Commerce.

Table 15-6.—Agricultural exports: Value of U.S. exports to the top market, Canada, by commodity, fiscal years 2017–2019 [1]

Commodity	Value		
	2017	2018	2019
	1,000 dollars	*1,000 dollars*	*1,000 dollars*
Total agricultural exports	20,444,018	20,701,022	20,997,341
Animals and animal products	3,521,050	3,556,417	3,396,708
Animals Live, ex. Poultry	118,319	219,700	222,476
Cattle, live	75,336	171,803	175,721
Horses, live	40,717	46,012	43,886
Swine, live	1,676	1,262	2,443
Sheep, live	29	34	13
Other live animals	562	589	414
Red meat and products	1,853,003	1,798,750	1,705,840
Beef and veal	772,534	748,139	649,459
Beef and Veal, fresh or frozen	604,536	574,381	497,476
Beef, prep or pres	167,998	173,759	151,983
Lamb, goat, fresh or frozen	2,009	924	823
Pork	774,217	741,233	762,367
Pork-fresh or frozen	385,612	343,782	369,272
Pork-prep or pres	388,604	397,451	393,094
Variety meats, Ed Offals	36,415	37,284	35,908
Beef variety meats	15,788	19,477	14,380
Pork variety meats	18,149	16,034	18,980
Other variety meats	2,478	1,773	2,548
Other meats-fr or froz	267,829	271,169	257,284
Poultry and poultry products	619,161	612,590	538,925
Poultry-Live	58,019	63,556	63,471
Baby chicks	48,178	55,716	55,278
Other live poultry	9,841	7,839	8,193
Poultry meats	469,024	427,453	366,489
Chickens, fresh or frozen	301,494	278,670	238,547
Turkeys, fresh or frozen	13,936	7,942	7,884
Other poultry, fresh or frozen	2,141	1,159	747
Poultry meats, prep or pres.	151,453	139,681	119,310
Poultry misc.	580	1,791	4,862
Eggs	91,538	119,790	104,103
Dairy prods	735,613	690,724	721,965
Evap and condensed milk	973	952	1,242
Nonfat dry milk	13,852	14,583	12,200
Butter and Milkfat	64,164	62,642	46,126
Cheese	67,460	54,993	54,115
Whey, fluid or dried	77,200	50,387	50,726
Other dairy products	511,964	507,166	557,556
Fats, oils and greases	58,478	65,580	53,157
Lard	963	436	342
Tallow, inedible	16,372	19,386	22,877
Other animal fats	41,143	45,758	29,938
Hides and skins include furs	72,425	94,748	69,937
Bovine hides, whole	916	-	-
Calf skins, whole	89	-	
Horse hides whole	200	126	31
Sheep and lamb skins	118	117	133
Other hides and skins, ex. furs	4,531	2,042	1,372
Furskins	66,572	92,463	68,400
Mink pelts	59,275	85,112	60,916
Other furskins	7,297	7,352	7,484
Wool and Mohair	180	136	142
Sausage casings	7,826	9,028	16,689
Bull semen	8,747	9,642	8,476
Misc animal products-other	47,298	55,519	59,101
Grains and feeds	3,706,872	3,947,684	4,250,047
Wheat, unmilled	18,898	19,755	28,622
Wheat flour	54,658	35,620	33,520
Other wheat products	66,394	80,034	85,346
Rice-paddy,milled parb	147,904	164,642	191,046
Feed grains and products	235,837	362,021	484,961
Feed grains	128,366	275,578	406,106
	16,886	9,917	6,288
Corn	106,920	262,669	397,288
Grain sorghums	1,122	1,118	905
Oats	3,297	1,754	1,518
Rye	140	120	107
Feed grain products	107,471	86,443	78,855
Other grain prods	2,039,040	2,085,880	2,170,594
Feeds and fodders, ex. oilcakes	1,036,670	1,113,289	1,177,103
Corn by-products	39,164	49,952	36,336
Alfalfa meal and cubes	716	721	231
Beet pulp	6,099	5,998	6,906
Other feeds and fodder	990,691	1,056,617	1,133,629

See footnote(s) at end of table.

Table 15-6.—Agricultural exports: Value of U.S. exports to the top market, Canada, by commodity, fiscal years 2017–2019 [1]—Continued

Commodity	Value		
	2017	2018	2019
	1,000 dollars	*1,000 dollars*	*1,000 dollars*
Fruits and prep. excluding juice	2,061,354	2,048,514	1,984,441
Fruits, fresh	1,577,670	1,542,893	1,468,075
Citrus fruits	231,301	228,024	198,053
Grapefruit	19,812	16,379	15,492
Lemons and limes	54,745	52,180	45,270
Oranges and tangerines	156,474	159,062	136,834
Other citrus fruits	270	402	457
Noncitrus fruits	1,346,369	1,314,869	1,270,022
Apple	168,027	163,733	157,992
Berries	506,409	518,982	513,635
Cherries	136,890	118,502	120,774
Grapes	213,514	205,789	190,014
Melons	131,858	124,946	110,903
Peaches	65,315	60,767	61,028
Pears	46,811	45,781	44,446
Plums	21,672	20,570	19,116
Other noncitrus	55,872	55,800	52,113
Fruits, dried	65,457	66,832	67,319
Raisins	33,856	30,478	30,675
Prunes	12,479	12,997	11,513
Other dried fruits	19,122	23,357	25,131
Fruits-canned, excluding juice	226,846	238,548	224,372
Fruits-frozen, excluding juice	53,818	51,224	62,933
Other fruits, prep. or pres	137,563	149,017	161,742
Fruit juices, including frozen	386,070	374,536	339,086
Apple juice	18,105	19,267	17,930
Grape juice	26,045	28,387	25,092
Grapefruit juice	6,837	8,063	9,576
Orange juice	193,390	173,817	155,499
Other fruit juices	141,693	145,002	130,989
Wine	395,769	427,823	405,505
Nuts and prep	860,085	894,622	926,053
Almonds	257,811	266,920	282,858
Filberts	21,590	11,201	44,831
Peanuts, shelled or prep	170,668	168,724	169,863
Pistachios	77,738	92,091	103,109
Walnuts	72,491	98,696	74,352
Pecans	81,695	71,404	63,192
Other nuts	178,092	185,586	187,848
Vegetables and prep	3,158,525	3,064,511	3,198,944
Vegetables, fresh	1,852,596	1,843,346	2,017,741
Asparagus	9,232	10,782	10,268
Broccoli	67,791	74,152	78,284
Carrots	97,198	97,799	97,934
Cabbage	56,802	70,706	81,148
Celery	67,483	61,038	103,699
Cauliflower	123,159	131,332	140,130
Corn, sweet	46,476	44,291	41,881
Cucumbers	15,698	13,337	16,630
Garlic	11,231	9,693	10,219
Lettuce	428,991	412,552	448,759
Mushrooms	19,510	29,374	33,841
Onion and Shallots	103,944	109,519	136,943
Peppers	74,233	73,214	80,404
Potatoes	102,399	96,419	114,053
Tomatoes	103,030	103,317	107,775
Other fresh vegetables	525,417	505,820	515,775
Vegetables, frozen	191,681	192,001	195,550
Corn, sweet	14,534	10,044	7,975
Potatoes	76,050	72,486	75,979
Other frozen vegetables	101,097	109,471	111,596
Vegetables, canned	172,755	164,340	160,671
Pulses	138,886	79,824	104,829
Dried beans	52,725	38,120	38,414
Dried peas	7,659	3,383	21,930
Dried lentils	56,979	14,587	26,222
Dried chick peas	21,524	23,734	18,262
Other vegetables, prep or pres	781,083	761,266	701,891

See footnote(s) at end of table.

Table 15-6.—Agricultural exports: Value of U.S. exports to the top market, Canada, by commodity, fiscal years 2017–2019 [1]—Continued

Commodity	Value		
	2017	2018	2019
	1,000 dollars	*1,000 dollars*	*1,000 dollars*
Oilseeds and products	1,286,945	1,327,118	1,437,675
Oilcake and meal	306,201	360,766	339,350
Bran and residues	4,683	4,482	2,863
Soybean meal	294,600	350,413	331,131
Other oilcake and meal	6,918	5,870	5,356
Oilseeds	434,487	443,826	610,404
Rapeseed	86,245	85,257	105,761
Safflower seeds	694	577	876
Soybeans	133,680	162,911	304,724
Sunflowerseeds	16,205	16,031	17,704
Peanuts, including oilstock	7,069	7,558	8,621
Other oilseeds	14,323	11,549	11,555
Protein substances	176,271	159,943	161,163
Vegetable oils	546,257	522,526	487,921
Soybean oil	25,193	23,756	24,551
Cottonseed oil	5,832	6,845	5,863
Sunflower oil	26,747	27,329	27,845
Corn oil	14,596	12,971	11,414
Peanut oil	4,313	5,168	4,103
Rapeseed oil	38,758	19,124	21,122
Safflower oil	2,558	2,209	1,982
Other Vegetable oils and Waxes	428,258	425,125	391,041
Tobacco-unmanufactured	7,256	15,920	6,522
Cotton, excluding linters	635	683	619
Cotton linters	33	29	26
Essential oils	434,192	446,512	437,528
Seeds-field and garden	329,534	335,894	355,579
Sugar and tropical products	2,020,813	1,987,685	1,888,585
Sugar and related products	546,820	541,957	506,078
Sugar, cane or beet	6,706	7,211	9,546
Related sugar product	540,114	534,746	496,531
Coffee	529,885	540,086	498,730
Cocoa	131,133	121,892	116,108
Chocolate and prep	619,875	598,634	580,902
Tea, including herbal	124,209	124,874	127,831
Spices	62,803	53,625	55,834
Rubber, crude	6,088	6,617	3,102
Fibers, excluding cotton	906	1,113	727
Other hort products	1,360,181	1,387,525	1,492,875
Hops, including extract	24,270	31,794	38,638
Starches, not wheat/corn	80,045	80,061	82,103
Yeasts	38,790	39,487	37,719
Misc hort products	1,217,076	1,236,183	1,334,415
Nursery and greenhouse	204,844	218,892	221,379
Beverages, excluding juice	837,950	775,718	752,164

[1] Fiscal years Oct. 1–Sept. 30.
ERS, Market and Trade Economics Division, (202) 694–5257.

Table 15-7.—Agricultural imports for consumption: Value of Top 50 countries of origin, United States, fiscal years 2017–2019 [1]

Country	2017	2018	2019
	1,000 dollars		
Mexico	24,070,256	25,657,093	27,869,944
EU27+UK	21,359,059	23,699,510	24,678,802
Canada	21,958,461	22,961,211	23,390,158
China	4,472,800	4,770,143	4,054,120
Australia	3,093,993	3,264,828	3,419,887
Brazil	3,320,430	3,380,010	3,325,414
Singapore	81,690	2,182,709	3,126,375
Indonesia	3,586,724	3,472,153	2,983,532
Chile	2,989,725	3,039,228	2,874,354
Thailand	2,387,364	2,636,682	2,826,619
Colombia	2,590,605	2,565,535	2,699,872
India	2,526,629	2,660,230	2,680,949
Peru	1,976,529	2,168,652	2,438,736
New Zealand	2,585,348	2,586,537	2,368,045
Guatemala	2,096,941	2,132,753	2,129,079
Vietnam	2,400,214	2,382,429	2,030,625
Costa Rica	1,606,185	1,638,421	1,516,039
Switzerland	1,269,705	1,318,617	1,363,222
Argentina	1,366,579	1,415,104	1,356,260
Ecuador	1,055,404	1,034,472	1,116,640
Malaysia	964,687	997,937	1,026,316
Turkey	887,777	983,489	974,822
Philippines	1,260,625	1,164,344	958,695
Honduras	817,919	737,655	814,612
Japan	650,136	696,358	764,064
Cote d'Ivoire	1,185,412	852,707	751,703
South Korea	542,453	606,149	680,557
Nicaragua	630,915	661,630	672,043
Madagascar	384,417	524,349	477,475
Dominican Republic	405,283	514,750	467,272
Taiwan	360,331	390,637	441,630
South Africa	283,631	341,398	402,431
Israel	370,139	383,441	400,688
Uruguay	339,510	302,034	338,387
Ghana	290,304	201,474	279,892
El Salvador	225,381	218,729	228,130
Morocco	156,091	192,482	210,526
Sri Lanka	190,158	198,549	189,093
Ukraine	104,397	93,634	156,736
Ethiopia	161,470	175,469	155,223
Kenya	162,929	151,624	136,561
Egypt	112,226	132,616	133,582
Jamaica	120,588	132,573	129,385
Pakistan	105,239	123,591	128,438
Tunisia	86,298	204,381	125,592
Paraguay	97,494	70,926	108,350
Norway	91,141	100,368	105,741
Bolivia	111,017	91,753	98,287
Hong Kong	96,243	98,278	92,744
Malawi	88,690	47,638	71,909
Other countries	1,001,399	1,153,189	1,075,340
Total U.S. Agricultural Imports [2]	119,078,941	127,510,469	130,844,896

[1] Fiscal years Oct. 1–Sept. 30.   [2] Totals may not add due to rounding.
ERS, Market and Trade Economics Division, (202) 694–5257. Compiled from reports of the U.S. Department of Commerce.

Table 15-8.—European Union: Value of agricultural imports by origin, 2010–2019

Year [1]	United States	EU countries	Other countries	Total
	Million dollars			
2010	10,822	329,477	113,650	453,950
2011	12,760	389,811	138,954	541,525
2012	12,049	374,067	131,836	517,952
2013	14,768	406,306	133,729	554,802
2014	15,361	405,760	136,580	557,700
2015	14,456	353,918	122,328	490,702
2016	13,672	360,318	121,664	495,654
2017	13,757	400,005	129,610	543,372
2018	16,044	420,372	133,274	569,689
2019	10,311	427,510	84,888	522,709

[1] Data on calendar year basis. Users should use cautious interpretation on reports that include summarized reporter groupings. These groupings will only include the members that have reported data for any particular year.
ERS, Market and Trade Economics Division, (202) 694–5257. Data Source: United National Commodity Trade Statistics, United Nations Statistics Division.

Table 15-9.—Fisheries: U.S. Commercial landings and value of principal species: 2017 and 2018 [1]

Species	Landings	
	2017	2018
	Thousand pounds	Thousand pounds
Fish:		
Cod, Atlantic	1,857	2,152
Flounder	544,866	525,070
Haddock	12,101	14,455
Halibut	26,466	21,929
Herring, sea	179,920	145,792
Jack mackerel	1,043	239
Menhaden	1,413,104	1,581,578
Ocean perch, Atlantic	11,387	9,902
Walleye (Alaska) Pollock	3,388,620	3,363,901
Salmon, Pacific	1,008,198	575,972
Tuna	54,904	51,684
Whiting (silver hake)	11,800	11,393
Shellfish:		
Clams (meats)	84,883	85,670
Crabs	274,578	289,021
Lobsters, American	132,973	146,176
Oysters (meats)	31,805	30,304
Scallops (meats)	51,733	58,382
Shrimp	283,272	289,178
	Value	
	Thousand dollars	Thousand dollars
Fish:		
Cod, Atlantic	4,444	4,777
Flounder	141,228	153,235
Haddock	11,947	13,354
Halibut	125,785	89,318
Herring, sea	36,396	32,605
Jack mackerel	49	27
Menhaden	125,495	161,088
Ocean perch, Atlantic	6,307	5,036
Walleye (Alaska) Pollock	419,425	456,510
Salmon, Pacific	687,770	598,067
Tuna	154,392	149,053
Whiting (silver hake)	9,009	9,630
Shellfish:		
Clams (meats)	210,755	244,107
Crabs	610,3377	644,912
Lobsters, American	552,057	624,228
Oysters (meats)	236,418	258,748
Scallops (meats)	511,945	540,583
Shrimp	530,977	496,114

[1] Landings are reported in round (live) weight for all items except univalve and bivalve mollusks such as clams, oysters, and scallops, which are reported in weight of meats (excluding the shell). Landings for Mississippi River drainage are not available.
Totals may not add due to rounding. Data do not include landings by U.S.-flag vessels at Puerto Rico or other ports outside the 50 States. Data do not include aquaculture products, except oysters and clams.
U.S. Department of Commerce, NOAA, NMFS, Fisheries Statistics Division, (301) 427–8103.

Table 15-10.—Fresh and frozen fishery products: Production and value, 2017 and 2018

Product	Production	
	2017	2018
	Thousand pounds	*Thousand pounds*
Fish fillets	795,146	745,394
Cod	72,488	62,365
Flounder	11,888	9,792
Haddock	11,233	8,068
Ocean perch, Atlantic	1,166	1,847
Rockfish	2,874	3,198
Pollock, Atlantic	9,931	789
Pollock, Alaska	455,341	441,590
Other	241,458	217,745
	Value	
	Thousand dollars	*Thousand dollars*
Fish fillets	2,146,555	2,157,359
Cod	318,348	332,436
Flounder	49,941	43,785
Haddock	52,912	42,255
Ocean perch, Atlantic	3,526	7,851
Rockfish	8,587	9,187
Pollock, Atlantic	15,898	2,759
Pollock, Alaska	582,604	608,493
Other	1,114,739	1,110,593

U.S. Department of Commerce, NOAA, NMFS, Fisheries Statistics Division, (301) 427–8103.

Table 15-11.—Canned fishery products: Production and value, 2017 and 2018

Product	Production	
	2017 [1]	2018
	Thousand pounds	*Thousand pounds*
Tuna [2]	333,913	346,407
Salmon	133,878	65,585
Clam products [3]	63,191	64,293
Crab meat and specialties	153	81
Other Shellfish	28,826	20,372
Total [4]	855,551	665,148
	Value	
	Thousand dollars	*Thousand dollars*
Tuna [2]	677,721	775,900
Salmon	309,593	185,676
Clam products [3]	106,075	107,054
Crab meat and specialties	607	314
Other Shellfish	20,480	19,992
Total [4]	1,341,712	1,219,000

[1] Revised based on additional data.　[2] Flakes included with chunk.　[3] "Cut out" or "drained" weight of can contents are given for whole or minced clams, and net contents for other clam products.　[4] Includes Sardines (Maine), Shrimp, Oysters, and other products not shown separately.
U.S. Dept. of Commerce, NOAA, NMFS, Fisheries Statistics Division, (301) 427–8103.

Table 15-12.—Fisheries: Fishermen and craft, 1977, and catch, 2017–2018 by area

Area	1977 [1]			2017 [3]		2018 [3]	
	Fishermen	Fishing vessels	Fishing boats [2]	Total catch	Value	Total catch	Value
	1,000	*Number*	*1,000*	*Million pounds*	*Million dollars*	*Million pounds*	*Million dollars*
New England States	31.7	929	15.4	556	1,266	572	1,394
Middle Atlantic States	17.3	573	11.3	620	508	628	473
South Atlantic States	11.6	1,463	6.7	122	223	109	179
Gulf States	29.3	5,328	11.0	1,386	856	1,541	887
Pacific Coast States	54.0	7,643	15.4	7,182	2,435	6,487	2,500
Great Lakes States	1.2	217	0.5	13	17	13	18
Hawaii	2.7	101	1.3	37	116	35	119
United States	182.1	17,545	89.2	9,916	5,421	9,385	5,571

[1] Exclusive of duplication among regions. Computation of area amounts will not equal U.S. total. Mississippi River data included with total.   [2] Refers to craft having capacity of less than 5 net tons.   [3] Great Lakes data are one year behind the heading years.   Note: Table may not add due to rounding.
U.S. Department of Commerce, NOAA, NMFS, Fisheries Statistics Division, (301) 427–8103.

Table 15-13.—Fisheries: U.S. Commercial landings of fish and shellfish, 2009–2018

Year	For human food		For industrial purposes [2]		Total	
	Quantity	Value	Quantity	Value	Quantity	Value
	Million pounds	*Million dollars*	*Million pounds*	*Million dollars*	*Million pounds*	*Million dollars*
2009	6,198	3,733	1,833	158	8,031	3,891
2010	6,526	4,356	1,705	164	8,231	4,520
2011	7,909	5,108	1,949	181	9,858	5,289
2012	7,477	4,923	2,157	180	9,634	5,103
2013	8,043	5,268	1,827	198	9,870	5,466
2014	7,828	5,256	1,658	192	9,486	5,448
2015	7,750	4,972	1,968	231	9,718	5,203
2016	7,484	5,007	2,088	305	9,572	5,312
2017	8,228	5,187	1,688	234	9,916	5,421
2018	7,500	5,322	1,885	249	9,385	5,571

[1] Live weight.   [2] Meals, oil, fish solubles, homogenized condensed fish, shell products, bait, and animal food.
U.S. Department of Commerce, NOAA, NMFS Fisheries Statistics Division, (301) 427–8103.

Table 15-14.—Fisheries: Disposition of domestic catch, 2017–2018 [1]

Disposition	2017	2018
	Million pounds	*Million pounds*
Fresh and frozen	8,091	7,443
Canned	289	180
Cured	136	139
Reduced to meal, oil, etc	1,400	1,623
Total	9,916	9,385

[1] Live weight catch. In addition to whole fish, a large portion of waste derived from canning, filleting, and dressing fish and shellfish is utilized in production of fish meal and oil in each year shown.
U.S. Department of Commerce, NOAA, NMFS, Fisheries Statistics Division, (301) 427–8103.

Table 15-15.—Fishery products: Supply,[1] 2017–2018[2]

Item	2017	2018
	Million pounds	
For human food	19,805	19,478
Finfish	14,422	13,941
Shellfish[3]	5,383	5,538
For industrial use	2,461	2,625
Domestic catch	9,916	9,385
Percent of total	45	42
For human food	8,228	7,500
Finfish	7,121	6,409
Shellfish[3]	1,107	1,091
For industrial use	1,688	1,886
Imports[4]	12,350	12,718
Percent of total	55	58
For human food	11,577	11,979
Finfish	8,074	8,271
Shellfish[3]	4,276	4,447
For industrial use[5]	773	739
Total	22,266	22,103

[1] Supply totals are the domestic catch and imports without accounting for exports taken out. [2] Live weight, except percent. May not add due to rounding. [3] For univalve and bivalve mollusks (conchs, clams, oysters, scallops, etc.), the weight of meats, excluding the shell is reported. [4] Excluding imports of edible fishery products consumed in Puerto Rico; includes landings of tuna caught by foreign vessels in American Samoa. [5] Fish meal and sea herring.
U.S. Department of Commerce, NOAA, NMFS, Fisheries Statistics Division, (301) 427–8103.

Table 15-16.—Processed fishery products: Production and value, 2017–2018[1]

Item	Production		Value	
	2017	2018	2017	2018
	Thousand pounds	Thousand pounds	Thousand dollars	Thousand dollars
Fresh and frozen:.				
Fillets	795,146	745,394	2,146,555	2,157,359
Steaks	5,269	5,344	30,909	32,042
Fish sticks	55,245	55,087	85,085	93,248
Fish portions	100,135	73,620	177,179	139,313
Breaded shrimp	84,235	84,391	344,274	338,958
Canned products[2]	855,551	665,148	1,341,712	1,219,000
Fish and shellfish	560,321	497,056	1,116,793	1,090,983
Animal feed	295,230	168,092	224,919	128,017
Industrial products	(X)	(X)	679,740	753,578
Meal and scrap	568,882	630,256	379,806	418,073
Marine animal oil	112,253	154,777	108,175	114,771
Other	(X)	(X)	191,759	220,734

(X) Not applicable. [1] Includes cured fish. [2] Includes salmon eggs for baits.
U.S. Department of Commerce, NOAA, NMFS, Fisheries Statistics Division, (301) 427–8103.

Table 15-17.—Selected fishery products: Imports and exports, 2017–2018 [1]

Product	Quantity	
	2017	2018
	Thousand pounds	Thousand pounds
Imports		
Edible	5,919,333	6,086,590
Fresh and frozen	5,001,948	5,125,531
Salmon [2]	299,253	306,437
Tuna [2]	257,944	188,924
Groundfish fillets, blocks [3]	298,908	300,639
Other fillets and steaks	1,315,789	1,413,517
Scallops (meats)	39,438	44,775
Lobster, American and spiny	111,471	108,690
Shrimp and prawn	1,460,711	1,528,745
Canned	723,205	778,726
Sardines, in oil	42,577	34,786
Sardines and herring, not in oil	43,695	43,761
Tuna	311,414	345,326
Oysters	12,164	15,250
Pickled or salted	63,082	61,538
Cod, haddock, hake, pollock, cusk	12,758	12,877
Nonedible meal and scrap	138,056	131,983
Exports		
Canned salmon	63,380	55,150
Fish oil, nonedible	139,036	140,597

Product	Value	
	2017	2018
	Thousand dollars	Thousand dollars
Imports		
Edible	21,519,015	22,438,476
Fresh and frozen	18,959,483	19,502,541
Salmon [2]	1,072,424	1,173,173
Tuna	653,261	618,903
Groundfish fillets, blocks [3]	720,659	808,018
Other fillets and steaks	4,747,576	5,262,319
Scallops (meats)	258,427	237,208
Lobster, American and spiny	1,039,585	1,162,162
Shrimp and prawn	6,511,108	6,197,363
Canned	1,961,002	2,349,728
Sardines, in oil	79,040	84,788
Sardines and herring, not in oil	61,283	63,318
Tuna	631,774	765,982
Oysters	34,211	43,447
Pickled or salted	110,103	110,047
Cod, haddock, hake, pollock, cusk	33,590	35,460
Nonedible meal and scrap	111,918	106,220
Exports		
Canned salmon	159,750	166,556
Fish oil, nonedible	146,279	154,218

[1] Includes Puerto Rico.   [2] Excludes fillets.   [3] Includes cod, cusk, haddock, hake, pollock, ocean perch, and whiting.
U.S. Dept. of Commerce, NOAA, NMFS, Fisheries Statistics Division (301) 427–8103.

Table 15-18.—Fishery products: Imports and exports, 2009–2018 [1]

Year	Imports [2]				Exports			
	Total value	Edible products		Non-edible, value	Total value	Edible products		Non-edible, value
		Quantity	Value			Quantity	Value	
	Million dollars	*Million pounds*	*Million dollars*	*Million dollars*	*Million dollars*	*Million pounds*	*Million dollars*	*Million dollars*
2009	23,554	5,161	13,124	10,430	19,636	2,546	3,980	15,656
2010	27,352	5,447	14,811	12,542	22,386	2,733	4,389	17,997
2011	30,943	5,349	16,618	14,326	26,218	3,267	5,447	20,771
2012	31,107	5,384	16,690	14,417	27,384	3,254	5,470	21,914
2013	33,156	5,415	18,006	15,150	29,113	3,324	5,584	23,529
2014	35,915	5,567	20,264	15,650	29,978	3,402	5,754	24,225
2015	34,400	5,736	18,791	15,609	28,396	3,141	5,567	22,829
2016	35,875	5,827	19,486	16,389	27,989	2,931	5,384	22,605
2017	38,372	5,920	21,520	16,853	28,973	3,200	5,730	23,243
2018	40,304	6,087	22,438	17,865	28,755	2,938	5,590	23,165

[1] Includes Puerto Rico.   [2] Includes landings of tuna by foreign vessels in American Samoa.
U.S. Department of Commerce, NOAA, NMFS, Fisheries Statistics Division, (301) 427–8103.

Table 15-19.—Fish trips: Estimated number of fishing trips taken by marine recreational fishermen by subregion and year, Atlantic, Gulf, and Pacific Coasts, 2017–2018

Subregion	2017	2018
	Thousands	*Thousands*
Atlantic and Gulf:		
North Atlantic	16,751	15,103
Mid-Atlantic	46,004	39,029
South Atlantic [1]	76,870	75,100
Gulf	58,633	55,755
Total	198,258	184,987
Pacific: [2]		
Southern California	2,350	1,411
Northern California	1,054	615
Oregon	187	210
Washington	146	127
Hawaii	1,280	3,420
Alaska	545	539
Total	5,562	6,322

[1] Does not include trips from headboats (party boats) in the South Atlantic or Gulf of Mexico.   [2] Pacific state estimates do not include salmon data collected by recreational surveys.
Note: Recreational estimates have been revised back through 1981 (as of November 2019). Any data previously provided (for past reports) are no longer appropriate or valid.
U.S. Department of Commerce, NOAA, NMFS, Fisheries Statistics Division, (301) 427–8103.

Table 15-20.—Fish harvested [1] by marine recreational anglers by subregion, area, and mode, Atlantic, Gulf Coasts, and Pacific Coasts, 2017–2018

Subregion	2017	2018
	Thousands	*Thousands*
Atlantic and Gulf [2]:		
North Atlantic	33,338	27,101
Mid-Atlantic	76,606	45,848
South Atlantic [2]	114,242	104,252
Gulf	167,340	145,541
Total	391,526	322,742
Pacific: [3]		
Southern California	4,426	3,905
Northern California	3,175	2,234
Oregon	646	539
Washington	421	398
Hawaii	3,012	10,360
Alaska	1,395	1,208
Total	13,075	18,644

Area	2017	2018
	Thousands	*Thousands*
Atlantic and Gulf: [2][4]		
Inland	204,628	181,527
State Territorial Sea [5]	141,141	106,204
Federal Exclusive Economic Zone [6]	37,152	28,948
Total	391,526	322,742
Pacific: [3]		
Inland	1,851	2,727
State Territorial Sea [5]	8,399	12,653
Federal Exclusive Economic Zone [6]	1,430	2,056
Total	11,680	17,436

Mode	2017	2018
	Thousands	*Thousands*
Atlantic and Gulf: [2]		
Shore	188,523	160,879
Party/charter	12,604	10,378
Private/rental	190,399	151,485
Total	391,526	322,742
Pacific: [3]		
Shore	5,678	9,740
Party/charter	3,412	3,578
Private/rental	2,590	4,118
Total	11,680	17,436

[1] "Harvested" includes dead discards and fish used for bait but does not include fish released alive; totals may not match due to rounding. [2] Does not include trips from headboats (party boats) in the South Atlantic or Gulf of Mexico. [3] Does not include recreational catch from Alaska. Pacific state estimates do not include salmon data collected by recreational surveys. [4] Includes fish harvested from an undetermined area. [5] Open Ocean extending 0 to 3 miles from shore, except West Florida (10 miles). [5] Open ocean extending to 200 miles offshore from the outer edge of the State Territorial Seas.
Note: Recreational estimates have been revised back through 1981 (as of November 2019). Any data previously provided (for past reports) are no longer appropriate or valid.
U.S. Department of Commerce, NOAA, NMFS, Fisheries Statistics Division, (301) 427–8103.

Table 15-21.—U.S. Recreational Harvest [1] by species group and year, 2017–2018 [2]

Species group	2017	2018
	Thousands	*Thousands*
Atlantic Cod	229	28
Atlantic Croaker	14,308	11,997
Atlantic Mackerel	17,745	9,495
Black Drum	2,433	2,001
Black Sea Bass	7,467	4,826
Blue Runner	15,787	7,837
Conger Eels	5	3
Crevalle Jack	2,438	1,711
Cunner	116	130
Epinephelus Groupers	317	362
Florida Pompano	2,404	1,506
Freshwater Catfishes	1,968	2,220
Gray Snapper	6,590	5,771
Greater Amberjack	122	116
Gulf Flounder	452	381
King Mackerel	1,201	1,204
Kingfishes	22,626	18,472
Lane Snapper	1,524	1,289
Little Tunny/Atlantic Bonito	849	803
Moray Eels	-	-
Mycteroperca Groupers	391	397
Pigfish	1,525	1,455
Pinfishes	12,345	13,143
Pollock	606	386
Red Drum	4,350	3,909
Red Hake	158	191
Red Porgy	492	436
Red Snapper	3,107	2,864
Saltwater Catfishes	908	1,655
Sand Seatrout	10,105	5,567
Scup	13,823	14,544
Sheepshead	6,130	4,942
Silver Perch	2,355	480
Skates/Rays	204	388
Southern Flounder	1,169	1,291
Spanish Mackerel	8,147	7,211
Spot	23,637	12,831
Spotted Seatrout	11,041	9,427
Striped Bass	3,008	2,455
Striped Mullet	6,026	7,069
Summer Flounder	3,233	2,428
Tautog	2,073	1,072
Vermilion Snapper	2,314	2,702
Weakfish	296	132
White Grunt	3,634	3,551
White Perch	6,818	3,794
Winter Flounder	327	158
Yellowtail Snapper	1,548	1,695
Other Barracudas	272	325
Other Bluefish	14,166	10,436
Other Cods/Hakes	1,828	1,005
Other Dolphins	2,491	2,935
Other Drum	909	488
Other Eels	74	151
Other Flounders	840	310
Other Grunts	2,065	3,918
Other Herrings	85,085	66,612
Other Jacks	3,438	8,606
Other Mullets	23,253	21,883
Other Porgies	574	501
Other Puffers	876	897
Other Sculpins	2	8
Other Sea Basses	388	863
Other Searobins	926	759
Other Sharks	383	357
Other Snappers	435	285
Other Temperate Basses	-	1
Other Toadfishes	133	18
Other Triggerfishes/Filefishes	875	624
Other Tunas/Mackerels	1,249	1,018
Other Wrasses	231	89
Other fishes	22,682	24,328
Total [3]	391,526	322,742

- Represents zero. [1] "Harvested" includes dead discards and fish used for bait but does not include fish released alive. [2] Data do not include headboats (party boats) in the South Atlantic and the Gulf of Mexico. [3] Totals may not add due to rounding.
Note: Recreational estimates have been revised back through 1981 (as of November 2019). Any data previously provided (for past reports) are no longer appropriate or valid.
U.S. Department of Commerce, NOAA, NMFS, Fisheries Statistics Division (301) 427–8103.

Table 15-22.—Fish harvested [1] by marine recreational anglers by species group and year, Pacific coast, 2017–2018 [2]

Species group	2017	2018
	Thousands	*Thousands*
Albacore	1	6
Barred Sand Bass	41	50
Barred Surfperch	451	10
Bigeye Scad	1,064	3,639
Bigeye Trevally		1
Bigscale Soldierfish	74	481
Black Perch	21	2
Black Rockfish	698	579
Blackspot Sergeant	11	89
Blacktail Snapper	9	57
Blue Rockfish	482	471
Bluefin Trevally	77	117
Bluestripe Snapper	79	94
Bocaccio	137	158
Brown Rockfish	123	150
Cabezon	26	22
California Corbina	16	7
California Halibut	36	46
California Sheephead	39	34
Canary Rockfish	146	125
Chilipepper Rockfish	13	9
Chub Mackerel	1,419	1,188
Conger Eels	1	
Convict Tang	58	273
Copper Rockfish	237	195
Giant Trevally	11	39
Goldring Surgeonfish	78	230
Gopher Rockfish	114	95
Greater Amberjack	4	12
Green Jobfish	19	38
Greenspotted Rockfish	38	33
Halfmoon	13	14
Hawaiian Flagtail	94	206
Hawaiian Hogfish	8	2
Highfin Rudderfish	2	7
Island Jack	19	26
Jacksmelt	512	186
Kawakawa	8	33
Kelp Bass	99	93
Kelp Greenling	23	11
Lingcod	312	276
Mackerel Scad	108	404
Manybar Goatfish	14	57
Moray Eels	5	10
Northern Anchovy	215	212
Olive Rockfish	61	75
Opaleye	43	16
Pacific Barracuda	10	19
Pacific Bonito	96	86
Pacific Cod	20	15
Pacific Hake	-	-
Pacific Herring	67	56
Pacific Tomcod	-	-
Pile Perch	10	1
Pink Snapper	10	56
Queenfish	17	17
Quillback Rockfish	18	22
Razorfishes	44	115
Redtail Surfperch	148	-
Rock Sole	-	2
Sanddabs	259	252
Shiner Perch	15	24
Silver Surfperch	57	7
Skates/Rays	9	1
Skipjack Tuna	114	213
Smallmouth Bonefish	19	45

See footnote(s) at end of table.

Table 15-22.—Fish harvested [1] by marine recreational anglers by species group and year, Pacific coast, 2017–2018 [2]—Continued

Species group	2017	2018
	Thousands	*Thousands*
Spiny Dogfish	-	-
Spotted Sand Bass	3	1
Squirrel Fishes		2
Starry Flounder	1	-
Striped Bass	27	30
Striped Mullet	14	72
Striped Seaperch	36	3
Surf Smelt	-	-
Unicornfishes	3	16
Wahoo	32	127
Walleye Surfperch	56	24
White Croaker	59	47
White Seaperch	6	3
Whitemouth Trevally	-	-
Whitesaddle Goatfish	2	12
Whitetip Soldierfish		
Widow Rockfish	15	46
Yellowfin Tuna	82	216
Yellowstripe Goatfish	380	1,651
Yellowtail	61	15
Yellowtail Rockfish	176	180
Other Anchovies		
Other Barracudas	2	14
Other Cods/Hakes	-	-
Other Damselfishes	10	28
Other Dolphins	47	216
Other Drum	59	25
Other Flounders	385	386
Other Goatfishes	25	317
Other Greenlings	-	-
Other Groupers	3	18
Other Herrings	156	108
Other Jacks	45	66
Other Mullets	21	163
Other Rockfishes	1,429	1,424
Other Sablefishes	23	26
Other Scorpionfishes	180	220
Other Sculpins	2	1
Other Sea Basses	-	-
Other Sea Chubs	26	96
Other Sharks	8	7
Other Silversides	69	82
Other Smelts	9	10
Other Snappers	9	91
Other Soldierfishes	3	279
Other Sturgeons	-	-
Other Surfperches	68	10
Other Surgeonfishes	27	201
Other Tunas/Mackerels	47 58	
Other Wrasses	26	56
Other fishes	1,471	1,488
Total [3]	13,075	18,644

- Represents zero. [1] "Harvested" includes dead discards and fish used for bait but does not include fish released alive. [2] Pacific estimates do not include salmon data collected by state recreational surveys. [3] Totals may not add exactly due to rounding.

Note: Recreational estimates have been revised back through 1981 (as of November 2019). Any data previously provided (for past reports) are no longer appropriate or valid.

U.S. Department of Commerce, NOAA, NMFS, Fisheries Statistics Division, (301) 427–8103.

Table 15-23.—Catfish water surface acres used for production and total sales - States and United States: 2018–2020

State	Acres intended for utilization during January 1-June 30					Acres taken out of production during Jul 1-Dec 31 prev. year
	Foodsize	Fingerlings	Broodfish	Currently under or scheduled for:		
				Renovation	New construction	
	Acres	*Acres*	*Acres*	*Acres*	*Acres*	*Acres*
2019						
Alabama	16,500	110	(D)	300	(D)	350
Arkansas	3,000	910	235	440	(D)	550
California	910	(D)	35	90	-	(D)
Mississippi	27,100	4,900	1,300	(D)	660	540
North Carolina	1,200	(D)	(D)	(D)	-	(D)
Texas	1,700	55	50	80	(D)	195
Other States [1]	1,220	1,010	210	4,575	120	255
United States	51,630	6,985	1,830	5,485	780	1,890
2020						
Alabama	15,600	250	25	25	115	690
Arkansas	2,700	770	(D)	(D)	-	230
California	(D)	(D)	35	35	(D)	(D)
Mississippi	26,700	4,200	1,400	1,400	(D)	700
North Carolina	(D)	(D)	(D)	(D)	(D)	(D)
Texas	1,700	(D)	35	35	-	(D)
Other States [1]	2,650	1,200	285	285	265	880
United States	49,350	6,420	1,780	1,780	380	2,500

- Represents zero.   (D) Withheld to avoid disclosing data for individual operations.   [1] Other States include State estimates not shown and States suppressed due to disclosure.
NASS, Livestock Branch, (202) 720–3570.

Table 15-24.—Catfish water surface acres used for production total sales - States and United States: 2018–2020

State	Water surface acres used for production during Jan 1 - July 30		Total sales	
	2019	2020	2018	2019
	Acres	*Acres*	*1,000 dollars*	*1,000 dollars*
Alabama	16,800	15,900	91,128	97,714
Arkansas	4,300	4,000	21,624	21,671
California	1,100	(D)	9,109	(D)
Mississippi	35,700	35,300	207,543	226,194
North Carolina	1,300	(D)	2,932	(D)
Texas	1,900	1,800	20,889	17,969
Other States [1]	2,220	4,245	7,176	15,600
United States	63,320	61,245	360,401	379,148

(D) Withheld to avoid disclosing data for individual operations.   [1] Other States include State estimates not shown and States suppressed due to disclosure.
NASS, Livestock Branch, (202) 720–3570.

Table 15-25.—Catfish: Sales by size category, by State and United States, 2018–2019

Size category and State	Number of fish		Live weight		Sales			
					Total		Average price per pound	
	2018	2019	2018	2019	2018	2019	2018	2019
	1,000	*1,000*	*1,000 pounds*	*1,000 pounds*	*1,000 dollars*	*1,000 dollars*	*Dollars*	*Dollars*
Foodsize:								
Alabama	63,600	60,300	104,600	102,500	91,002	97,375	0.87	0.95
Arkansas	10,900	10,700	18,300	18,600	18,666	19,716	1.02	1.06
California	1,600	1,210	2,850	2,400	9,063	7,632	3.18	3.18
Mississippi	121,000	113,000	192,000	203,500	188,160	213,675	0.98	1.05
North Carolina	1,400	(D)	2,500	(D)	2,900	(D)	1.16	(D)
Texas	8,520	(D)	20,200	(D)	20,806	(D)	1.03	(D)
Other States [1]	1,780	11,235	3,151	20,990	4,409	23,650	1.40	1.13
United States	208,800	196,445	343,601	347,990	335,006	362,048	0.97	1.04
Stockers:								
Alabama	(D)	(D)	(D)	(D)	(D)	(D)	(D)	(D)
Arkansas	(D)	(D)	(D)	(D)	(D)	(D)	(D)	(D)
California	(D)	(D)	(D)	(D)	(D)	(D)	(D)	(D)
Mississippi	(D)	(D)	(D)	(D)	(D)	(D)	(D)	(D)
North Carolina	(D)	-	(D)	-	(D)	-	(D)	-
Texas	(D)	(D)	(D)	(D)	(D)	(D)	(D)	(D)
Other States [1]	65,465	22,450	6,553	2,819	7,727	5,181	1.18	1.84
United States	65,465	22,450	6,553	2,819	7,727	5,181	1.18	1.84
Fingerlings and fry:								
Alabama	(D)	310	(D)	9	(D)	68	(D)	7.60
Arkansas	12,400	(D)	472	(D)	939	(D)	1.99	(D)
California	190	5	5	(D)	42	(D)	8.30	(D)
Mississippi	168,000	146,000	5,950	3,850	14,340	8,971	2.41	2.33
North Carolina	(D)	(D)	(D)	(D)	(D)	(D)	(D)	(D)
Texas	(D)	(D)	(D)	(D)	(D)	(D)	(D)	(D)
Other States [1]	9,865	23,240	315	794	956	2,464	3.03	3.10
United States	190,455	169,550	6,742	4,653	16,277	11,503	2.41	2.47
Broodfish:								
Alabama	(D)	(D)	(D)	(D)	(D)	(D)	(D)	(D)
Arkansas	(D)	-	(D)	-	(D)	-	(D)	(D)
California	(D)		(D)		(D)		(D)	
Mississippi	(D)	(D)	(D)	(D)	(D)	(D)	(D)	(D)
North Carolina	(D)	(D)	(D)	(D)	(D)	(D)	(D)	(D)
Texas		(D)		(D)		(D)		
Other States [1]	410	75	1,708	296	1,391	416	0.81	1.41
United States	410	75	1,708	296	1,391	416	0.81	1.41

- Represents zero.　(D) Withheld to avoid disclosing data for individual operations.　[1] Other States include State estimates not shown and States suppressed due to disclosure.
NASS, Livestock Branch, (202) 720–0585.

Table 15-26.—Trout: Value of fish sold and distributed, by State (excluding eggs), and United States (including and excluding eggs), 2018–2019

State	Total value of fish sold		Total value of distributed fish	
	2018	2019	2018	2019
	1,000 dollars	*1,000 dollars*	*1,000 dollars*	*1,000 dollars*
Arkansas	-	-	3,479	2,550
California	(D)	(D)	8,278	9,434
Colorado	2,978	2,085	6,427	6,452
Georgia	(D)	(D)	1,213	(D)
Idaho	40,290	37,416	(D)	(D)
Michigan	1,558	1,636	2,565	3,658
Missouri	(D)	(D)	4,252	3,738
New York	736	714	5,553	4,760
North Carolina	8,790	7,627	1,973	1,940
Oregon	(D)	(D)	(D)	(D)
Pennsylvania	6,685	6,457	14,823	14,588
Utah	997	1,629	7,961	7,857
Virginia	1,733	1,483	1,983	2,266
Washington	(D)	(D)	(D)	19,269
West Virginia	1,005	1,116	2,663	2,916
Wisconsin	1,493	1,525	1,514	(D)
Other States [1]	35,029	33,884	65,939	56,878
United States				
Value excluding eggs	101,294	95,572	128,623	136,306
Value including eggs ..	111,879	105,631	(NA)	(NA)

- Represents zero.   (D) Withheld to avoid disclosing data for individual operations.   (NA) Not available.   [1] Other States include State estimates not listed and States supressed due to disclosure.
NASS, Livestock Branch, (202) 720–3570.

Table 15-27.—Trout: Egg Sales, United States, 2014–2019

Year	Number of Eggs	Average Price per 1,000 Eggs	Total Sales [1]
	1,000	*Dollars*	*1,000 dollars*
2014	427,125	20.50	8,774
2015	431,475	20.20	8,706
2016	422,904	21.10	8,921
2017	442,145	21.00	8,844
2018	461,947	22.90	10,585
2019	441,404	22.80	10,059

[1] Due to rounding, total number of eggs multiplied by average price per 1,000 eggs may not exactly equal total sales.
NASS, Livestock Branch, (202) 720-3570.

Table 15-28.—Trout: Sales by size category, States and United States, 2018 and 2019

Size category and State	Number of fish		Live weight		Sales			
	2018	2019	Total [1]		Total [2]		Average price per pound	
			2018	2019	2018	2019	2018	2019
	1,000		1,000 pounds		1,000 dollars		Dollars	
12 inch or longer:								
Arkansas	-	-	-	-	-	-	-	-
California	(D)	(D)	(D)	(D)	(D)	(D)	(D)	(D)
Colorado	430	(D)	591	(D)	2,695	(D)	4.56	(D)
Georgia	(D)	(D)	(D)	(D)	(D)	(D)	(D)	(D)
Idaho	22,200	19,900	27,000	25,000	39,960	37,250	1.48	1.49
Michigan	(D)	(D)	(D)	(D)	(D)	(D)	(D)	(D)
Missouri	(D)	(D)	(D)	(D)	(D)	(D)	(D)	(D)
New York	(D)	(D)	(D)	(D)	(D)	(D)	(D)	(D)
North Carolina	3,640	(D)	4,000	(D)	7,600	(D)	1.90	(D)
Oregon	(D)	(D)	(D)	(D)	(D)	(D)	(D)	(D)
Pennsylvania	1,210	1,090	1,200	1,200	5,136	5,280	4.28	4.40
Utah	200	260	192	288	939	1,336	4.89	4.64
Virginia	460	440	512	540	1,577	1,453	3.08	2.69
Washington	(D)	(D)	(D)	(D)	(D)	(D)	(D)	(D)
West Virginia	450	400	435	410	1,005	1,074	2.31	2.62
Wisconsin	370	340	357	314	1,339	1,410	3.75	4.49
Other States [3]	6,975	9,960	13,261	16,006	31,508	38,039	2.38	2.38
United States	35,935	32,390	47,548	43,758	91,759	85,842	1.93	1.96
6 inch-12 inch:								
Arkansas	-	-	-	-	-	-	-	-
California	(D)	(D)	(D)	(D)	(D)	(D)	(D)	(D)
Colorado	(D)	(D)	(D)	(D)	(D)	(D)	(D)	(D)
Georgia	60	(D)	22	(D)	45	(D)	2.05	(D)
Idaho	(D)	(D)	(D)	(D)	(D)	(D)	(D)	(D)
Michigan	50	80	30	40	156	252	5.20	6.30
Missouri	(D)	(D)	(D)	(D)	(D)	(D)	(D)	(D)
New York	75	65	34	27	214	154	6.30	5.70
North Carolina	(D)	(D)	(D)	(D)	(D)	(D)	(D)	(D)
Oregon	(D)	(D)	(D)	(D)	(D)	(D)	(D)	(D)
Pennsylvania	580	420	339	206	1,454	1,092	4.29	5.30
Utah	(D)	(D)	(D)	(D)	(D)	(D)	(D)	(D)
Virginia	(D)	20	(D)	12	(D)	30	(D)	2.53
Washington	(D)	3,800	(D)	600	(D)	2,226	(D)	3.71
West Virginia	(D)	(D)	(D)	(D)	(D)	(D)	(D)	(D)
Wisconsin	(D)	95	(D)	26	(D)	111	(D)	4.28
Other States [3]	7,285	4,615	1,765	1,268	6,283	4,554	3.56	3.59
United States	8,050	9,095	2,190	2,179	8,152	8,419	3.72	3.86

Size category and State	Number of fish		Live weight		Sales			
	2018	2019	Total [1]		Total [2]		Average price per 1,000 fish	
			2018	2019	2018	2019	2018	2019
	1,000		1,000 pounds		1,000 dollars		Dollars	
1 inch-6 inch:								
Arkansas	-	-	-	-	-	-	-	-
California	(D)	(D)	(D)	(D)	(D)	(D)	(D)	(D)
Colorado	(D)	(D)	(D)	(D)	(D)	(D)	(D)	(D)
Georgia	(D)	-	(D)	-	(D)	-	(D)	-
Idaho	(D)	(D)	(D)	(D)	(D)	(D)	(D)	(D)
Michigan	(D)	(D)	(D)	(D)	(D)	(D)	(D)	(D)
Missouri	(D)	(D)	(D)	(D)	(D)	(D)	(D)	(D)
New York	(D)	(D)	(D)	(D)	(D)	(D)	(D)	(D)
North Carolina	(D)	(D)	(D)	(D)	(D)	(D)	(D)	(D)
Oregon	(D)	(D)	(D)	(D)	(D)	(D)	(D)	(D)
Pennsylvania	210	280	5	7	95	85	452	304
Utah	(D)	(D)	(D)	(D)	(D)	(D)	(D)	(D)
Virginia	(D)	-	(D)	-	(D)	-	(D)	-
Washington	(D)	(D)	(D)	(D)	(D)	(D)	(D)	(D)
West Virginia	(D)	(D)	(D)	(D)	(D)	(D)	(D)	(D)
Wisconsin	(D)	40	(D)	1	(D)	4	(D)	111
Other States [3]	6,505	5,421	149	159	1,288	1,222	198	225
United States	6,715	5,741	154	167	1,383	1,311	206	228

- Represents zero. (D) Withheld to avoid disclosing data for individual operations. [1] Due to rounding, total number of fish multiplied by the average pounds per unit may not exactly equal total live weight. [2] Due to rounding, total number or live weight multiplied by average value per unit may not exactly equal total sales. [3] Other States include State estimates not listed and States supressed due to disclosure.
NASS, Livestock Branch, (202) 720-3570.

Table 15-29.—General storages: Gross and usable cooler and freezer space, by State and United States, October 1, 2019 [1]

State	Cooler		Freezer		Total	
	Gross	Usable	Gross	Usable	Gross	Usable
	1,000 Cubic Feet					
Alabama	613	551	32,808	28,340	33,421	28,892
Alaska	(D)	(D)	(D)	(D)	(D)	(D)
Arizona	(D)	(D)	(D)	(D)	4,103	3,487
Arkansas	4,374	3,780	77,216	69,879	81,590	73,659
California	70,357	53,929	318,953	265,346	389,310	319,275
Colorado	(D)	(D)	(D)	(D)	(D)	(D)
Connecticut	(D)	(D)	(D)	(D)	(D)	(D)
Delaware	(D)	3,241	(D)	15,151	25,033	18,392
Florida	104,771	80,282	147,105	124,800	251,876	205,081
Georgia	33,301	26,860	155,753	132,150	189,054	159,010
Hawaii	-	-	-	-	-	-
Idaho	7,006	5,830	58,358	48,570	65,365	54,400
Illinois	32,521	26,740	158,329	126,798	190,849	153,538
Indiana	(D)	(D)	(D)	(D)	93,964	74,824
Iowa	12,146	9,504	58,526	49,986	70,673	59,490
Kansas	(D)	(D)	(D)	(D)	41,639	33,042
Kentucky	1,529	(D)	22,512	(D)	24,041	22,127
Louisiana	(D)	(D)	(D)	(D)	(D)	(D)
Maine	(D)	(D)	(D)	(D)	7,211	5,638
Maryland	(D)	(D)	(D)	(D)	(D)	(D)
Massachusetts	9,494	7,201	49,977	41,296	59,471	48,497
Michigan	6,912	5,632	82,258	67,135	89,170	72,767
Minnesota	22,219	14,657	73,827	59,231	96,047	73,888
Mississippi	(D)	(D)	(D)	(D)	13,556	11,386
Missouri	27,330	22,249	63,978	55,135	91,308	77,385
Montana	(D)	(D)	(D)	(D)	(D)	(D)
Nebraska	4,325	2,770	43,595	35,195	47,920	37,966
Nevada	(D)	(D)	(D)	(D)	(D)	(D)
New Hampshire	-	-	-	-	-	-
New Jersey	49,632	38,109	87,698	72,773	137,331	110,882
New Mexico	(D)	(D)	(D)	(D)	11,873	8,730
New York	19,074	16,041	42,099	37,939	61,173	53,980
North Carolina	4,453	3,376	58,511	46,693	62,964	50,069
North Dakota	(D)	(D)	(D)	(D)	10,325	7,800
Ohio	6,700	6,179	47,264	39,003	53,963	45,182
Oklahoma	716	(D)	8,824	(D)	9,540	7,330
Oregon	6,102	3,968	134,530	107,026	140,633	110,994
Pennsylvania	48,955	36,683	184,744	158,816	233,699	195,499
Rhode Island	-	-	-	-	-	-
South Carolina	(D)	(D)	(D)	(D)	26,362	17,990
South Dakota	(D)	(D)	(D)	(D)	11,627	6,279
Tennessee	(D)	(D)	(D)	(D)	60,742	52,432
Texas	65,021	52,975	177,175	144,807	242,196	197,782
Utah	12,126	10,636	32,590	26,121	44,715	36,757
Vermont	(D)	(D)	(D)	(D)	4,818	3,219
Virginia	13,079	11,442	64,545	53,597	77,624	65,039
Washington	13,085	10,914	268,557	210,979	281,642	221,893
West Virginia	(D)	(D)	(D)	(D)	(D)	(D)
Wisconsin	113,286	83,501	133,879	115,974	247,166	199,475
Wyoming	-	-	-	-	-	-
United States	758,826	583,333	2,886,664	2,384,326	3,645,495	2,967,658

- Represents zero. (D) Withheld to avoid disclosing data for individual operations.   [1] Totals may not add due to rounding.
NASS, Livestock Branch, (202) 720–4751.

Table 15-30.—Refrigerated warehouses: Gross refrigerated space by type of warehouse, United States, biennially, October 2011–2019 [1] [2]

Type	2011	2013	2015	2017	2019
	1,000 Cubic Feet				
General:					
Public	3,028,243	3,076,959	3,138,463	2,834,824	2,683,640
Private and Semiprivate	931,117	978,426	1,030,460	767,331	961,851
Total	3,959,354	4,055,385	4,168,921	3,602,154	3,645,495

[1] Warehouse space is defined as all space artificially cooled to temperatures of 50 degrees F. or less, in which food commodities are normally held for 30 days or longer.   [2] Totals may not add due to rounding.
NASS, Livestock Branch, (202) 720–4751.

Table 15-31.—Alaska crops: Acreage harvested, volume harvested, and value of production, 2010–2019

Year	Oats for grain [1]	Barley for grain	All hay	Potatoes [2]
	Acreage harvested			
	Acres	Acres	Acres	Acres
2010	800	4,200	20,000	750
2011	1,000	4,800	19,000	720
2012	900	4,300	22,000	650
2013	400	3,300	20,000	620
2014	1,000	5,100	18,000	620
2015	1,000	4,300	18,000	540
2016	1,200	4,700	22,000	530
2017	900	5,200	21,000	540
2018	(NA)	4,000	'22,000	500
2019	(NA)	5,000	22,000	(NA)
	Volume harvested			
	Bushels	Bushels	Tons	Cwt.
2010	48,000	185,000	24,000	150,000
2011	80,000	175,000	22,000	134,000
2012	59,000	207,000	27,000	140,000
2013	15,000	110,000	15,000	130,000
2014	57,000	217,000	25,000	155,000
2015	47,000	146,000	20,000	140,000
2016	74,000	230,000	30,000	147,000
2017	66,000	239,000	25,000	120,000
2018	(NA)	172,000	29,000	140,000
2019	(NA)	190,000	29,000	(NA)
	Value of production			
	Dollars	Dollars	Dollars	Dollars
2010	161,000	814,000	7,320,000	3,570,000
2011	276,000	788,000	6,600,000	3,176,000
2012	212,000	1,107,000	8,505,000	3,864,000
2013	56,000	594,000	5,925,000	3,055,000
2014	211,000	1,183,000	9,625,000	3,395,000
2015	179,000	796,000	7,400,000	2,884,000
2016	274,000	1,208,000	10,200,000	3,308,000
2017	241,000	1,255,000	9,000,000	3,446,000
2018	(NA)	894,000	10,295,000	3,276,000
2019	(NA)	988,000	10,150,000	(NA)

(NA) Not available.   [1] Alaska removed from the National Oats Program in 2018.   [2] Alaska removed from the National Potato Program in 2019.
NASS, Crops Branch, (202) 720–2127.

Table 15-32.—Crop ranking: Major field crops, rank by production, major States, 2020

Rank	State	Corn, grain	State	Soybeans	State	All wheat
		1,000 bushels		*1,000 bushels*		*1,000 bushels*
1	IA	2,296,200	IL	604,750	ND	312,782
2	IL	2,131,200	IA	493,960	KS	281,250
3	NE	1,790,090	MN	359,170	MT	227,345
4	MN	1,441,920	IN	329,440	WA	165,635
5	IN	981,750	NE	294,120	ID	112,506
6	KS	766,480	MO	290,500	OK	104,000
7	SD	729,000	OH	262,980	MN	72,080
8	OH	564,300	SD	223,860	SD	70,520
9	MO	560,880	ND	190,950	TX	61,500
10	WI	516,780	KS	190,350	OR	46,400
	US	14,182,479	US	4,135,477	US	1,825,820

Rank	State	Winter wheat	State	Durum wheat	State	Other spring wheat
		1,000 bushels		*1,000 bushels*		*1,000 bushels*
1	KS	281,250	ND	35,295	ND	275,870
2	WA	133,000	MT	26,715	MT	124,640
3	OK	104,000	AZ	4,257	MN	72,080
4	MT	75,990	CA	1,740	ID	45,045
5	ID	66,660	ID	801	SD	35,720
6	TX	61,500			WA	32,635
7	OR	46,400				
8	CO	41,040				
9	IL	35,360				
10	SD	34,800				
	US	1,171,022	US	68,808	US	585,990

Rank	State	Sorghum, grain	State	Barley	State	Oats
		1,000 bushels		*1,000 bushels*		*1,000 bushels*
1	KS	238,000	ID	55,000	SD	10,780
2	TX	94,500	MT	45,675	MN	10,560
3	NE	13,650	ND	28,980	WI	8,253
4	SD	11,360	CO	6,525	ND	8,190
5	OK	10,350	WA	6,390	IA	5,694
6	CO	5,100	WY	5,952	PA	2,750
7			MN	2,350	TX	2,700
8			PA	2,280	NE	1,827
9			OR	1,800	MT	1,710
10			MD	1,533	NY	1,696
	US	372,960	US	165,324	US	65,355

Rank	State	All cotton	State	Peanuts	State	Rice
		1,000 bales		*1,000 pounds*		*1,000 cwt.*
1	TX	4,613	GA	3,280,000	AR	108,107
2	GA	2,180	AL	637,000	CA	44,810
3	AR	1,277	FL	561,000	LA	32,306
4	MS	1,180	TX	490,000	MO	15,522
5	MO	720	NC	424,000	TX	14,597
6	OK	636	SC	278,800	MS	12,241
7	OK	640	AR	182,400		
8	CA	615	VA	110,700		
9	TN	611	MS	96,800		
10	NC	522	OK	58,800		
	US	14,608	US	6,133,900	US	227,583

Rank	State	All hay, baled	State	Alfalfa hay, baled	State	Other hay, baled
		1,000 tons		*1,000 tons*		*1,000 tons*
1	TX	9,604	ID	4,545	TX	9,065
2	MO	6,437	MT	4,180	MO	5,843
3	NE	6,370	CA	3,420	KY	4,920
4	MT	5,908	NE	3,268	OK	4,680
5	KS	5,893	SD	3,240	TN	4,066
6	KY	5,428	IA	2,905	KS	3,895
7	SD	5,365	WI	2,688	NE	3,102
8	OK	5,364	MN	2,664	AR	2,667
9	ID	5,270	CO	2,380	VA	2,585
10	CA	4,610	AZ	2,210	AL	2,325
	US	126,812	US	53,067	US	73,745

Rank	State	All tobacco	State	Dry edible beans	State	Potatoes
		1,000 pounds		*1,000 cwt.*		*1,000 cwt.*
1	NC	184,127	ND	12,794	ID	134,775
2	KY	107,235	MI	6,033	WA	98,560
3	TN	29,380	MN	5,525	WI	27,800
4	VA	27,555	NE	3,607	OR	27,000
5	GA	19,276	ID	1,592	MI	23,134
6	PA	13,440	WA	1,120	CO	22,913
7	SC	8,400	CO	1,069	ND	17,860
8			CA	695	MN	17,638
9			WY	528	CA	12,878
10					ME	12,560
	US	389,413	US	32,963	US	414,248

NASS, Crops Branch, (202) 720–2127.

Table 15-33.—U.S. crop progress: 2019 crop and 5-year average
[In percent]

Winter wheat

Week-ending date	Planted 2018	Planted Avg	Emerged 2018	Emerged Avg	Headed 2019	Headed Avg	Harvested 2019	Harvested Avg
2018:								
Sep 9	5	5						
Sep 16	13	14						
Sep 23	28	26						
Sep 30	43	40	14	14				
Oct 7	57	54	30	28				
Oct 14	65	67	44	41				
Oct 21	72	77	53	55				
Oct 28	78	85	63	67				
Nov 4	84	90	70	77				
Nov 11	89	94	77	83				
Nov 18	93	97	81	88				
Nov 25	95	99	86	92				
2019:								
Apr 7					3	4		
Apr 14					6	9		
Apr 21					9	18		
Apr 28					19	29		
May 5					29	41		
May 12					42	54		
May 19					54	66		
May 26					66	76		
Jun 2					76	84		
Jun 9					83	91	4	10
Jun 16					89	95	8	20
Jun 23					94	99	15	34
Jun 30					97	100	30	48
Jul 7							47	61
Jul 14							57	71
Jul 21							69	79
Jul 28							75	86
Aug 4							82	92
Aug 11							89	96
Aug 18							93	98
Aug 25							96	99

Spring wheat

Week-ending date	Planted 2019	Planted Avg	Emerged 2019	Emerged Avg	Headed 2019	Headed Avg	Harvested 2019	Harvested Avg
2019:								
Apr 7	1	5						
Apr 14	2	13						
Apr 21	5	22						
Apr 28	13	33						
May 5	22	49	4	19				
May 12	45	67	10	34				
May 19	70	80	26	51				
May 26	84	91	47	69				
Jun 2	93	96	69	84				
Jun 9	97	99	85	93				
Jun 16			95	97	2	12		
Jun 23					7	29		
Jun 30					25	52		
Jul 7					56	73		
Jul 14					78	87		
Jul 21					92	94		
Jul 28					97	98		
Aug 4							2	14
Aug 11							8	30
Aug 18							16	49
Aug 25							38	65
Sep 1							55	78
Sep 8							71	87
Sep 15							76	93
Sep 22							87	97
Sep 29							90	99
Oct 6							91	99
Oct 13							94	100
Oct 20							96	100

See footnote(s) at end of table.

Table 15-33.—U.S. crop progress: 2019 crop and 5-year average—Continued

[In percent]

Rice

Week-ending date	Planted 2019	Planted Avg	Emerged 2019	Emerged Avg	Headed 2019	Headed Avg	Harvested 2019	Harvested Avg
2019:								
Mar 31	12	12	2	3				
Apr 7	19	21	7	8				
Apr 14	26	35	13	15				
Apr 21	31	47	18	25				
Apr 28	38	57	27	37				
May 5	48	69	35	50				
May 12	55	82	42	63				
May 19	73	90	52	75				
May 26	84	96	63	83				
Jun 2	91	98	76	91				
Jun 9	96	99	87	96				
Jun 16	....	....	94	99				
Jun 23	....	....	97	100	5	8		
Jun 30					10	15		
Jul 7					16	22		
Jul 14					24	31		
Jul 21					31	43		
Jul 28					42	57		
Aug 4					60	73		
Aug 11					76	85	7	9
Aug 18					88	93	10	13
Aug 25					96	97	15	18
Sep 1							21	27
Sep 8							30	37
Sep 15							46	48
Sep 22							58	61
Sep 29							68	71
Oct 6							76	80
Oct 13							87	88
Oct 20							93	94
Oct 27							97	98

Corn

Week-ending date	Planted 2019	Planted Avg	Emerged 2019	Emerged Avg	Silking 2019	Silking Avg	Dough 2019	Dough Avg	Dented 2019	Dented Avg	Mature 2019	Mature Avg	Harvested 2019	Harvested Avg
2019:														
Apr 7	2	2												
Apr 14	3	5												
Apr 21	6	12												
Apr 28	15	27	3	5										
May 5	23	46	6	13										
May 12	30	66	10	29										
May 19	49	80	19	49										
May 26	58	90	32	69										
Jun 2	67	96	46	84										
Jun 9	83	99	62	93										
Jun 16	92	100	79	97										
Jun 23	96	100	89	99										
Jun 30	....	....	94	100										
Jul 7	....	....	98	100	8	22								
Jul 14			....	....	17	42								
Jul 21			....	....	35	66	5	10						
Jul 28					58	83	13	23						
Aug 4					78	93	23	42						
Aug 11					90	97	39	61	7	16				
Aug 18					95	99	55	76	15	30				
Aug 25					....	....	71	87	27	46				
Sep 1							81	93	41	63	6	13		
Sep 8							89	97	55	77	11	24		
Sep 15							93	98	68	87	18	39	4	7
Sep 22							96	100	79	94	29	57	7	11
Sep 29							....	....	88	98	43	73	11	19
Oct 6									93	99	58	85	15	27
Oct 13									96	100	73	92	22	36
Oct 20									....	....	86	97	30	47
Oct 27											93	99	41	61
Nov 3											96	100	52	75
Nov 10											....	....	66	85
Nov 17													76	92
Nov 24													84	96
Dec 1													89	98
Dec 8													92	100

See footnote(s) at end of table.

Table 15-33.—U.S. crop progress: 2019 crop and 5-year average—Continued

[In percent]

Week-ending date	Sorghum									
	Planted		Headed		Coloring		Mature		Harvested	
	2019	Avg	2019	Avg	2019	Avg	2019	Avg	2019	Avg
2019:										
Mar 31	13	9								
Apr 7	14	14								
Apr 14	16	19								
Apr 21	17	22								
Apr 28	20	25								
May 5	22	29								
May 12	24	33								
May 19	26	38								
May 26	28	44								
Jun 2	35	53								
Jun 9	49	68	14	12						
Jun 16	69	81	15	16						
Jun 23	84	91	17	20						
Jun 30	94	96	20	23						
Jul 7	97	99	22	26	13	16				
Jul 14	....	....	24	31	14	19				
Jul 21			27	40	16	22				
Jul 28			33	50	21	25				
Aug 4			45	62	23	30				
Aug 11			61	74	26	35	19	23		
Aug 18			75	83	31	43	21	26		
Aug 25			86	90	41	52	22	30	20	20
Sep 1			92	95	52	64	24	33	21	22
Sep 8			97	98	65	74	27	37	22	24
Sep 15			....	....	79	84	34	44	24	27
Sep 22					90	90	42	53	26	31
Sep 29					95	95	54	63	30	35
Oct 6					....	....	65	73	33	40
Oct 13							81	82	40	46
Oct 20							92	89	49	53
Oct 27							96	94	65	62
Nov 3							....	....	78	72
Nov 10									88	80
Nov 17									93	87
Nov 24									97	92

Week-ending date	Soybeans											
	Planted		Emerged		Blooming		Setting Pods		Dropping Leaves		Harvested	
	2019	Avg	2019	Avg	2019	Avg	2019	Avg	2019	Avg	2019	Avg
2019:												
Apr 21	1	2										
Apr 28	3	6										
May 5	6	14										
May 12	9	29										
May 19	19	47	5	17								
May 26	29	66	11	35								
Jun 2	39	79	19	56								
Jun 9	60	88	34	73								
Jun 16	77	93	55	84								
Jun 23	85	97	71	91								
Jun 30	92	99	83	95								
Jul 7	96	99	90	98	10	32						
Jul 14	....	....	95	99	22	49						
Jul 21			....	....	40	66	7	28				
Jul 28					57	79	21	45				
Aug 4					72	87	37	63				
Aug 11					82	93	54	76				
Aug 18					90	96	68	85				
Aug 25					94	99	79	91				
Sep 1					96	100	86	96				
Sep 8					....	....	92	99				
Sep 15							95	100	15	38		
Sep 22							....	....	34	59		
Sep 29									55	76	7	20
Oct 6									72	87	14	34
Oct 13									85	93	26	49
Oct 20									94	97	46	64
Oct 27									97	99	62	78
Nov 3									....	....	75	87
Nov 10											85	92
Nov 17											91	95
Nov 24											94	97
Dec 1											96	99

See footnote(s) at end of table.

Table 15-33.—U.S. crop progress: 2019 crop and 5-year average—Continued

[In percent]

Week-ending date	Cotton, Upland									
	Planted		Squaring		Setting Bolls		Bolls Opening		Harvested	
	2019	Avg	2019	Avg	2019	Avg	2019	Avg	2019	Avg
2019:										
Mar 31	4	3								
Apr 7	6	5								
Apr 14	7	7								
Apr 21	9	9								
Apr 28	11	13								
May 5	18	19								
May 12	26	32								
May 19	44	45								
May 26	57	58								
Jun 2	71	72	8	7						
Jun 9	75	87	11	11						
Jun 16	89	94	19	18						
Jun 23	96	98	30	28	3	5				
Jun 30			37	39	7	9				
Jul 7			47	54	13	16				
Jul 14			60	69	20	25				
Jul 21			78	80	33	37				
Jul 28			86	87	45	48				
Aug 4			95	93	59	61				
Aug 11					77	76	20	10		
Aug 18					85	85	24	13		
Aug 25					90	91	28	19		
Sep 1					97	96	36	27		
Sep 8							43	37	7	6
Sep 15							54	47	9	8
Sep 22							64	57	11	11
Sep 29							77	67	16	14
Oct 6							83	75	25	20
Oct 13							87	83	32	27
Oct 20							93	89	40	35
Oct 27							95	93	46	43
Nov 3									53	51
Nov 10									62	59
Nov 17									68	66
Nov 24									78	74
Dec 1									83	81
Dec 8									89	

Week-ending date	Barley								Oats							
	Planted		Emerged		Headed		Harvested		Planted		Emerged		Headed		Harvested	
	2019	Avg	2019	Avg	2019	Avg	2019	Avg	2019	Avg	2019	Avg	2019	Avg	2019	Avg
2019:																
Mar 31									25	25	25	23				
Apr 7	2	9							27	32	25	26				
Apr 14	8	19							30	40	26	28				
Apr 21	17	29	2	7					36	51	27	33				
Apr 28	28	41	6	15					43	61	31	41				
May 5	37	56	12	27					50	72	36	51				
May 12	59	72	25	42					62	83	43	64				
May 19	76	84	39	57					77	90	53	76				
May 26	87	93	54	74					85	96	65	86				
Jun 2	94	97	73	85					91	98	77	93	23	33		
Jun 9	97	99	86	92					96	99	87	97	28	41		
Jun 16			92	96	2	12					94	99	33	54		
Jun 23			97	99	9	30					97	100	43	68		
Jun 30					31	52							58	81		
Jul 7					55	75							74	90		
Jul 14					75	89							87	95		
Jul 21					90	95							94	98	12	22
Jul 28					96	98							97	100	21	35
Aug 4							3	18							32	49
Aug 11							15	39							48	64
Aug 18							31	59							60	78
Aug 25							54	74							75	86
Sep 1							72	83							84	91
Sep 8							82	92							89	95
Sep 15							87	96							92	97
Sep 22							92	99							96	99
Sep 29							96	100								

See footnote(s) at end of table.

Table 15-33.—U.S. crop progress: 2019 crop and 5-year average—Continued

[In percent]

Week-ending date	Sugarbeets				Sunflower			
	Planted		Harvested		Planted		Harvested	
	2019	Avg	2019	Avg	2019	Avg	2019	Avg
2019:								
Apr 7	3	3						
Apr 14	8	16						
Apr 21	14	34						
Apr 28	25	48						
May 5	31	67						
May 12	63	80						
May 19	90	89			3	12		
May 26	94	97			9	27		
Jun 2	97	100			19	44		
Jun 9					42	65		
Jun 16					68	80		
Jun 23					85	89		
Jun 30					95	95		
Sep 15			8	9				
Sep 22			11	13				
Sep 29			16	20				
Oct 6			19	40			1	5
Oct 13			30	60			5	13
Oct 20			42	73			9	27
Oct 27			58	84			17	45
Nov 3			70	91			31	62
Nov 10			96	96			44	75
Nov 17							47	83
Nov 24							56	89
Dec 1							65	94
Dec 8							73	

Week-ending date	Peanuts					
	Planted		Pegging		Harvested	
	2019	Avg	2019	Avg	2019	Avg
2019:						
Apr 21	2	3				
Apr 28	8	8				
May 5	22	19				
May 12	40	36				
May 19	63	55				
May 26	79	72				
Jun 2	86	85				
Jun 9	91	93				
Jun 16	94	97	16	10		
Jun 23	97	99	34	24		
Jun 30			47	38		
Jul 7			58	53		
Jul 14			67	66		
Jul 21			78	77		
Jul 28			84	85		
Aug 4			92	91		
Aug 11			96	95		
Sep 15					5	5
Sep 22					14	10
Sep 29					26	19
Oct 6					41	30
Oct 13					55	42
Oct 20					67	55
Oct 27					77	67
Nov 3					84	78
Nov 10					89	85
Nov 17					93	90
Nov 24					96	94

NASS, Crops Branch, (202) 720–2127.

Appendix I

Telephone Contact List

Appreciation is expressed to the following agencies for their help in this publication. The information offices are listed to provide help to those users who require additional information about specific tables in this publication.

Agricultural Marketing Service:
USDA/AMS
Room 2619 South Bldg.
Washington, DC 20250
202–720–8998

Agricultural Research Service:
USDA/ARS
5601 Sunnyside Ave
Bldg 1, Rm 2251
Beltsville, MD 20705–5128
301–504–1636

Animal and Plant Health Inspection Service:
USDA/APHIS
4700 River Rd
Riverdale, MD 20737
301–851–4100

Center for Nutrition Policy and Promotion:
USDA/CNPP
3101 Park Center Drive
Alexandria, VA 22302
703–305–7600

Economic Research Service:
USDA/ERS
355 E Street, S.W.
Washington, DC 20024-3221
202–694–5050

Farm Credit Administration:
FCA
1501 Farm Credit Dr.
McLean, VA 22102
703–883–4056

Farm Service Agency:
USDA/FSA
Room 4078 South Bldg.
Washington, DC 20250
202–720–7163

Food and Nutrition Service:
USDA/FNS
3101 Park Center Drive, Room 914
Alexandria, VA 22302
703–305–2062

Foreign Agricultural Service:
USDA/FAS
Room 5076 South Bldg.
Washington, DC 20250
202–720–7115

Forest Service:
USDA/FS
2nd Floor Central Wing, Yates Bldg.
Washington, DC 20250
202–205–8333

National Agricultural Statistics Service:
USDA/NASS
Room 5038 South Bldg.
Washington, DC 20250
202–720–3878

National Marine Fisheries Service:
USDC/NOAA/NMFS
1315 East/West Highway,
SSMC III - Room 12405
Silver Spring, MD 20910–3282
301–427–8103

Natural Resources Conservation Service:
USDA/NRCS
Room 6121 South Bldg.
Washington, DC 20250
202–720–2182

Risk Management Agency:
USDA/RMA
Room 403
Kansas City, MO 64133-4675
816–926–1805

Rural Business-Cooperatives Service:
USDA/RECD/RBS
Room 4801 South Bldg.
Washington, DC 20250
202–720–1019

Rural Utilities Service:
USDA/RD/RUS
Stop 1510, Room 5135
1400 Independence Avenue, SW
Washington, DC 20250
202–720–9540

INDEX

INDEX

INDEX

INDEX